<u>Helvetica</u>/ <u>Objectified</u>/ <u>Urbanized</u>:

The Complete Interviews —Edited by Gary Hustwit (GH)

–Edited by Gary Hustwit / hustwit.com
–Editing assistance by Katie Herman
–Additional editing by Mariam Aldhahi & Anne Quito
–Design by Build / wearebuild.com
–Typeface: Maison Neue / milieugrotesque.com
–Cover photo: the microphone used to record
  most of the interviews in the book
–Printed in Canada by the Prolific Group

Helvetica/ Objectified/ Urbanized: The Complete Interviews —Edited by Gary Hustwit (GH)

Foreword

Helvetica

Objectified

Urbanized

Thanks

Foreword/
Gary
Hustwit
(GH)/
December
16, 2014
New York

I actually never wanted to be a filmmaker. I really just wanted to watch a documentary about fonts, but in 2005 I looked around and couldn't find one. And as I sit here writing a foreword to a book of interviews from the three films I've made since then, I'm struck by the thought that if a good font documentary had existed back then, say, *Times New Roman: The Movie*, I probably never would've started making films. And then I never would've had the privilege of talking with so many incredible people for those films.

I also never intended for to make a trilogy of design documentaries. But after *Helvetica* was released, I started thinking about other ways design affects our lives. Exploring how manufactured objects are designed seemed like an interesting project, and like my desire to watch a font film that didn't exist, I hadn't yet seen a compelling documentary about industrial design. *Objectified* felt like an natural extension of the questions and ideas we'd looked at in *Helvetica*. And I think that somehow all the travel I was doing during the production of exhibition of those two films got me thinking more about cities and how they're designed.

Before I started production on each film, I spent around six months just researching the subject matter, trying to get a feel for the various issues involved, talking to people in the field and asking them, "If you were going to make a film about this, who would you want to be in it?" I spoke with writers, curators, educators, and designers and started compiling lists of potential interviewees whom I thought might be interesting. Then at some point, I sent out the first email and started scheduling the interviews.

Many times during one of these conversations, the person I'm interviewing would say, "Are you going to talk to so-and-so?" I'm always the first to admit that I'm not an expert in these areas, and I was more than willing to ask for help or ideas from those who are. So with each conversation, I learned a little bit more, and the network of people participating in the film expanded.

I never started out with a thesis or any preconceived idea of what the content of the films would be. I'm just interested in what these people had to say and what they thought were the important issues in their field. It was only after we'd finished the conversations that the themes and "story" for the film would become apparent. But I've always been fascinated by the creative process, and when it comes down to it, I just really wanted to know how and why these people do what they do. I generally didn't prepare questions before each conversation; I sometimes scribbled down a few topics I wanted to discuss. I wanted these talks to be as casual and fluid as possible. But as you'll see, there are a few questions I asked almost everyone I interviewed.

Once the films were finished, the sad part was that there was so much that we'd talked about that didn't make it into them. I couldn't stand the idea of all those conversations just sitting on a hard drive some-where—hence the idea for this book.

A few notes on the book's contents: we've arranged the interviews into three sections, one for each film. The individual conversations for each film are presented chronologically by the dates we filmed them. We've edited the conversations for readability and left out some of what we called "show and tells," which were sections of the interviews where someone is walking us through a specific piece of work and which maybe didn't make sense once transcribed since you couldn't see what the speaker was referring to. In some cases these parts of the interviews were intended as "b-roll" footage that would be on screen during the conversation in the film, but they weren't intended to stand on their own. We've also taken out sections where the subject restated an answer or idea.

There's no way that I can express the gratitude I feel to all the people in this book who've taken the time to share their knowledge, stories, and creativity with me for these films. Some were my design heroes before I started making films; others I discovered along the way. It's truly been a privilege and an honor to be able to talk with all of them.

In the years since we conducted these interviews, several of the films' stars have passed away. I'd like to dedicate this book to memory and genius of Massimo Vignelli, Mike Parker, Bill Moggridge, and Oscar Niemeyer.

Thanks to everyone who's been part of these conversations and everyone who's helped me to document them. And thanks to you for your interest and support of these films.
—

Helvetica:
The Complete Interviews

20 Interviews/207 Pages/
108,503 Words

Massimo Vignelli (MV)/ March 29, 2006 New York

Massimo Vignelli was the first interview I did for *Helvetica*. I emailed Massimo first because, well, he was the easiest to contact; his email was right on his website: massimo@vignelli.com.

When our crew arrived at Massimo's home studio for the interview, he brought us into his kitchen and made us all espressos served in cups he'd designed. Anyone who met him instantly felt his love for life and for design. We had a long conversation that day—though it was admittedly one-sided; it's tough to get a word in when Massimo starts talking about type—and many more conversations in the years after.

Massimo passed away on May 27, 2014, as we were editing this book. The design world lost one of its most passionate practitioners and a true gentleman, and I lost a good friend. Ciao, Massimo.
—

Gary Hustwit — I wanted to initially talk about your beginnings. You told me you were studying to be an architect. How did you end up being exposed to graphic design?

Massimo Vignelli — Well, I started to be interested in architecture very early. When I was 16 years old, I was lucky enough to go to work as a freelance draftsman in the office of the Castiglioni brothers. The Castiglioni brothers were very, very good Italian architects in Milan, where I come from. Now, they were designing everything really—radios and furniture and exhibitions and buildings and houses. And I was mesmerized by the fact that an architect could do everything, and eventually I discovered that an architect was supposed to, really, design everything from a spoon to a city, as they say. So that was my beginning.

At the same time, I was exposed to some posters by Max Huber. Max Huber was a fantastic graphic designer from Switzerland who came to Milan. In 1946 he did a fabulous poster for a dance club; then in 1948 he did the poster for the Monza car races. You know, beautiful poster. You've probably seen it, with the arrows coming like cars, *swoosh,* passing each other. Eventually I met him, and he was looking for a place to live, and I had space in my house, so I said, "I can rent you some space. Why don't you move in?" And that's how I got exposed to graphic design, really, on an everyday basis, and I learned a lot from him. I learned about grids; I learned about colors; I learned about type; I learned about approach and so on.

In the meantime, I was working in the architectural offices. But I began to be more interested in graphic design and started to do some graphic-design work. Then I started to do some product-design work, like glass for Venini. I was doing graphics and glass and books and things like that, and then furniture, and then exhibits. And so it all came at the same time because of my interest in all these things, you know. I was fascinated by all these fields, and I wanted to do everything.

GH — Do you remember when you first encountered Helvetica?

MV — Since I was, I would say, an admirer of the work of Max Huber and the Swiss school, I eventually became familiar with the sans-serif typefaces that the Swiss were using, and at that time the most popular was Akzidenz-Grotesk. I worked with Akzidenz-Grotesk. You might know that type, in the old times, was made in lead. And so each letter had shoulders that determined the kerning, the letterspacing between one letter and another.

Now, we always liked type to be kerned tighter, so we were cutting the letters, cutting the spaces between, and destroying letters very often. The cutting was a tremendous amount of work. Eventually the Swiss developed a typeface that is now called Helvetica that had very, very tight shoulders on each individual letter, in the lead. So we could finally get the tight letterspacing that we liked, and then there was an explosion right away, because we were all ready for it. There was nothing else available besides Akzidenz-Grotesk in Europe and Standard over in the United States. At that time there weren't as many weights as there are today. It was just Regular and Light in the beginning. Then, of course, Bold came about and then Extra Bold, blah, blah, blah, blah, blah, and Extra Thin. And now the range is very, very wide and even more appealing than ever from that point of view. But at the time when Helvetica came out, it was a sensation, because of the possibility of having very tight letterspacing.

The impact, the sense of modernity, that was a given. Of course in the thirties there was Futura—that was used by the Bauhaus very much—and also Akzidenz-Grotesk. But Helvetica had all the right connotations that we were looking for in a typeface, for anything that had to spell out, loud and clear, *modern*. If it had to be classic, then we would use Garamond or Bodoni. We always had the tendency to use very few typefaces. It's not that we don't believe in type; we believe that there are not that many good typefaces, you know. If I want to be really generous, there's a dozen. Basically, I use no more than three, I guess. Yeah, in my life, most of the time, I'm very happy with Helvetica and Garamond and Bodoni, basically. Then, of course, I use Century Expanded, and I can use Univers; I can use Futura, Gill—it depends on the job.

But if I had to name one typeface by default it would be certainly Helvetica. And as a matter of fact, I can say that I'm probably the one responsible for bringing Helvetica to this country, because when I came, in 1965, there was no Helvetica. So I told the typesetter, "Get it," and they got it. You know, right in '65, '66, before that, everybody was using Akzidenz-Grotesk, or Standard, as it was called. I got Helvetica. I had Knoll, the furniture company, as a client, so I could use a lot of it in the proper context because it's modern furniture. And that is what we did, you know.

I was predicting back in 1966, '67, I would say, "Oh, just be patient, and two or three years from now there will be no other typefaces. There will be only Helvetica." Little did I know that I was so right. It almost, indeed, became the universal type in a sense. Well, we used it a lot. We used it very well, because we knew how to use contrast of size and proper spacing, all these details, which are the ABCs of typography. And therefore, since we were using it well, a lot of people started to imitate us and be fascinated by Helvetica. A lot of people, they just used it because it was a sans-serif type, and they didn't know good from bad—they were just using it. And that's it. And then the computer came around and made it even more popular.

GH — I know you've done hundreds, or thousands, of different commissions. Was there ever a time where you proposed Helvetica to a client and they didn't want it—they had a negative reaction to it?

MV — No, because we cook it very well! If you know how to cook, you can eat eggs for life, so to speak, or chicken for life, or pasta for life. It's like pasta. You can cook spaghetti so many different ways, you can hardly ever be tired of it. And the same is true with Helvetica. It's spaghetti. It's the slow food of typography.

GH — Can we talk about the New York subway system signage, how you got involved, and what the challenges were?

MV — Yeah, back in 1966 the Transit Authority realized that the signage they had was kind of poor for the job it had to do. So they went to MoMA, and asked them if they could suggest who would be the best designer to do that. And I had just arrived over here, so they told them, "Oh, you're lucky because Vignelli can do these things very well, and he's in New York." They got in touch with us. At that time we had a company that was called Unimark International. They came to Unimark, and we got the assignment.

They first asked us to study four stations, as a test, you know. Times Square was one of them; Grand Central, I think, was another one, and then another station in Queens, and then Broadway-Nassau, if I recall. We did the studies on these four stations, the traffic flow and all the analysis needed to determine where the points of decision were—because the whole thing in signage, the number one rule, is to give information at the point of decision. Never before and never after. When you drive, you find out most of the time that this rule is not followed—you're getting information too early, so by the time you get to the fork, you miss it. Or it's given too late, even after the fork, so you miss it. It's very typical to make this kind of mistake in terms of signage. So to determine where the signs had to be was the first part of the study. Then, of course, it was, for us, obvious to use Helvetica. It was the perfect type, and legible, and so on, and so forth. I must say that at the time it was not even around here, so we used Standard at the time of the study. Then eventually it turned into Helvetica.

The second thing was to standardize the supports for the signs. Prior to this the signs were made according to the amount of space that they had available in each instance—they were all done custom. In order to extend the signage throughout the whole system of 485 stations, we devised a system of supports and sings that were standardized. There were three categories of signage, and each one had its own appropriate size, which happened to be twice the size of the previous one. Everything had a relationship. This is not "one time like this, one time like that," you know?

The approach was consistent throughout, because consistency is extremely important in design. This is forgotten most of the time by people designing books, magazines, signs, packaging, whatever it is. The least number of typefaces you use, the better, and the least number of type sizes is even better. It all stems, naturally, from that good Swiss approach. The Swiss, maybe because they make watches, they are so precise. It's interesting that all these theories were developed there, but they're really universal; they have nothing to do with a specific country. It just has a lot to do with logic, and, of course, logic is not something that is really a currency over here in the USA. It is a different kind of culture, a different kind of sensitivity. This is the country for emotions, it's the country for novelty, the country for being different. It's not the country for consistency, logic, and that systematic approach.

GH — Sure, sure.

MV — Now, talking about Helvetica, for instance, Helvetica is a sans-serif typeface. You know, the serif typefaces, those are the typefaces that have feet, basically—they go back to the time of the chisel, and that's why they have those terminals. And there are, of course, older typefaces that go back to Roman times, the Renaissance. Throughout history until 1800, you know, really, serif type was the only kind of typeface available. Then with the advent of industrialization, mechanization, and foundries, it was much easier to cast something without serifs than something with serifs.

All of a sudden the sans-serif typeface was born and became increasingly more popular. And of course, both typefaces, they had their own fans, so to speak. There were people who said you cannot read sans serif, you can only read it if it has the serifs, the feet. And there were people like the modernists saying, "It's not true. You can read modern typefaces. They're easier on the eye, dah, dah, dah, dah, dah." And this went on for many, many years. I mean, 40 years ago, 50 years ago, they were still fighting about these things. I remember when I was still fighting about these things.

There was a great graphic designer in New York—unfortunately, he's not alive anymore—Rudolph de Harak. I remember we stayed up one night all night—we were helped by booze, I must admit—but we stayed up all night talking about the difference between Standard, which was Akzidenz-Grotesk, and Helvetica. I was defending Helvetica, Rudy was defending Standard, and we were throwing one example over the other, one reference over the other. How is one better than the other?

Now, the reason I'm saying this is that, in the families of sans-serif typefaces, there are a lot of different typefaces. For instance, you have Helvetica—which you are familiar with by now—and you have Akzidenz-Grotesk. Then you have Futura, which was designed in Germany in the thirties and is a terrific typeface. It's very, very modern in a sense. And then, of course, you had many other sans-serif type-faces. Oh! There is an endless number. And then each one of these typefaces has different weights, or condensed or extended versions. Like, for instance, Microgramma or Eurostyle, typefaces I don't like that were really very extended.

So there are many things within a family that could be done and could give you plenty of options to find the most appropriate type for certain things. Another great thing about Helvetica is that it has an incredibly wide range of applications. It's great for instructions on medicine packaging in 6-point type, for instance, and it's great for signage with 1-foot-tall type. I've done it 13 feet high for a gallery in Houston or on the ferryboat in New York, where it was huge. I've done Helvetica in many kinds of sizes, as well as Bodoni. Great typefaces, both of them. Anyhow, that is why Helvetica became so popular, because you could use it in so many different contexts, which you cannot really do with Garamond, for instance. Garamond, you can go up to a certain point, then it becomes too thin.

Now, Helvetica was designed by a Swiss designer, Max Miedinger. And another great type designer, Adrian Frutiger, designed Univers. Now, Univers, from a certain standpoint, is the most advanced typeface. It did what Helvetica missed out on at the time it was first designed. With Univers, Frutiger designed one typeface with 54 different variations in terms of weight, in roman and italic. Ultra Thin, Regular, Medium, Bold, Extra Bold, and so forth. Condensed, Extended, blah, blah, blah, blah. That is the right way to design a typeface. Most people think they have to design a new typeface. It's not new typefaces that we need—actually we don't need them at all; we have plenty. But what we need, still, is refinement of some of the good ones and then to develop them into a family.

GH — We talked before about computer technology, how since the nine-ties there's been an explosion of new typefaces. Could you talk about your opinion of the impact of the computer on typography?

MV — I was telling you before that in the sixties we were taking Stan-dard and cutting the sides of the letters in order to get the type tighter. A good typographer always has sensitivity about the distance between letters. It makes a tremendous amount of difference. We think typog-raphy is black and white. Typography's really white, you know. It's not even black, in a sense. It is the space between the blacks that really makes it. In a sense, it's like music—it's not the notes; it's the space you put between the notes that makes the music. It's very much the same situation.

The spacing between letters is important, and the spacing between the lines is important too. And what typographers do, what we do all the time, is continuously work with those two elements, kerning and leading. Now, in the old times we were all doing this with a blade and cutting type and cutting our fingers all the time. But eventually, thank God, the Apple computer came about. Apple made the right kind of computer for the communication field. IBM made the PC, and the PC was no good for communication. The PC was great for numbers, and they probably made studies that there were more people involved with numbers— banks, insurance companies, businesses of all kinds. But they made a tremendous mistake at the same time by not considering the size of the communications world. That community is enormous, you know—news-papers, television, anything that is printed. It's enormous. Advertising, design, you name it.

Anyhow, Apple, thank God, got the intuition of going after that market, and so in 1990 they came out with a computer that we designers could use. Now, let's face it: the computer is a great thing, but it's just a tool, just like a pencil is a tool. The computer has much more memory, the pencil has no memory whatsoever, and I have even less. But it is a fan-tastic tool which allowed the best typography ever done in the history of typography, because you can do the kerning perfectly for the situa-tion. You can do the leading perfectly for whatever you're encountering. It's the best—there is nothing that can be compared. Not only that, but you see it right away; you can print it right away. It brings immediacy to your thoughts, and that is something that never happened before in the history of mankind. It allows you to do the best typography ever, but it also allows you to do the worst ever.

So we have seen, particularly at the beginning when the computer came about, people taking type and doing all kinds of things. Everybody became a designer. They were taking type and squeezing it in, stretch-ing it. It was unbelievable what they were doing. All of a sudden we were facing the greatest amount of vulgarity, or what I call visual pollution, that had ever been done before. But at the same time, we also had some of the best work ever done. Of course, the best work you never see, but vulgarity is very ubiquitous, so it's everywhere.

But this is another incentive for us. It gives us another reason to fight. The life of a designer is a life of fight, to fight against the ugliness. Just like a doctor fights against disease. For us, visual disease is what we have all around, and what we try to do is to cure it somehow with design, by eliminating, as much as possible, the people who make it. Not phys-ically, but at least limiting their possibility of polluting the world. It's a mission. Is it arrogant? Perhaps. Is it pretension? Perhaps. But so is every other field. You find the same attitude in music; you find the same attitude in literature; you find it in any kind of art, and in architecture. There's a continuous fight against ugliness, a continuous fight against noise instead of music. It doesn't surprise me that a great tool like the computer can allow this explosion of visual pollution. But in good hands, it's the best thing that ever came about.

GH — Do you feel now, 15 years later, that the situation has changed?

MV — Yeah, maybe. I'm basically an optimist, you know. I think that people who originally started to use the computer, to do their own news-letter, for instance, eventually, they learn how to use it. The computer is a very seductive kind of machinery; it offers you a lot of alternatives. And if you don't have the discipline of choosing between what it offers, you might take a lot of its suggestions. Some of the suggestions are even interesting, exciting—it's certainly more stimulating than what people without imagination could do. Therefore, there has been, definitely, an improvement. There is less visual pollution than there was 10, 15 years ago. People are beginning to find out that you don't have to squeeze Helvetica, because there is already a version of Helvetica that is con-densed. They can use the proper type for the proper use. People are much more accustomed to working with a computer now, and they know more about what the computer can do.

GH — What are your thoughts about people's awareness of type? Do you think the average person in New York notices the differences, con-sciously or unconsciously?

MV — One of the interesting questions is, do people really care about type? Do they care about typography? Do they know anything? They don't know about Helvetica, Bodoni, and Garamond, and Cooper Black, or things like that, you know. It's funny, but you'd be surprised how much people respond to typefaces, and even if they don't know the names, they say, "I like something like that." So they have some kind of desire to be satisfied by a certain kind of type rather than another.

I was just watching the other day a funny mini-documentary, whatever they call them, on TV. And they were saying that ABC, the television channel, has done all kinds of programs over the last 25 years. They have done documentaries about everything that you can imagine, but they've never once done something on graphic design, which is unbe-lievable. Their logo was designed by Paul Rand, who was the greatest American graphic designer of the century, and nobody knows him! Everybody knows about singers, they know about architects, they know about painters, they know about writers, they know about good doctors, but very few people know about graphic designers. So maybe graphic design doesn't have the right kind of exposure.

They know sometimes, maybe, about somebody doing posters; I think more people are aware, for instance, of Milton Glaser, because he's a terrific designer, an artist, and he does fabulous posters. People were aware of Peter Max back 30 years ago. But generally speaking, there is very little awareness of graphic design and graphic designers. Even with clients. Do they care about type, what kind of typeface we use, and so on and so forth? Sometimes they do, sometimes they don't, and maybe it's better that way.

GH — What's the future of typography and graphic design?

MV — You know, we know everything about the past of typography. We know something about the present of typography. What about the future? It's hard to say. I don't think that there are going to be drastic changes until the printed word is no longer around—it has to be done with typefaces. And the sensibilities come and go; newer technology comes and goes; the computer brings the use of certain type that is more appropriate for the computer, et cetera. So there might be new technology that changes it. There are people working on typefaces all the time, continuously. There are as many type designers, probably even more, than there are people making wallpaper. There's no need for one or the other in my mind, but still, they are occupations for people to work on.

There are people who think that the type should be expressive—they have a different point of view from mine. I don't think type should be expressive at all. I can write the word "dog" with any typeface, and it doesn't have to look like a dog. But there are people who, when they write "dog" think it should bark, you know? So there are all kinds of people, and therefore, there will always people who will find work designing funky type, and it could be that all of a sudden a funky typeface takes the world by storm, but I doubt it. I'm a strong believer in intellect and intelligence, and I'm a strong believer in intellectual elegance, so that, I think, will prevent vulgarity from really taking over the world more than it has already.

Some defenses need to be put up, and I think, actually, that the more culture spreads out and the more refined education becomes, the more refined the sensibility about type becomes too. The more uneducated the person is who you talk to, the more he likes horrible typefaces. Look at comics like *The Hulk*, things like that. It's not even type. Look at anything which is elegant and refined; you find elegant and refined typefaces. The more culture is refined in the future—this might take a long time, but eventually education might prevail over ignorance—the more you'll find good typography. I'm convinced of that.

GH — If you had to describe Helvetica to someone who had never seen it before, how would you describe it?

MV — What is Helvetica? Okay. It's a typeface that, number one, was generated by a desire to have better legibility. So it's a very legible type; it is a modern type; it is a very clear type. It has a pretty good family of weights, so it can be very expressive if you want to have different tones. It's good for everything, pretty much. I've done wine labels in Helvetica. I've done pharmaceutical packages in Helvetica. I've done timetables for airlines and trains and boats in Helvetica. I've done all kinds of books in Helvetica. So it has a tremendous range. It's a very, very flexible, very, very usable typeface. I'm trying to think of drawbacks of Helvetica . . . I hardly know one.

Now, you can say, "I love you," in Helvetica, and you can say it with Helvetica Extra Light if you want to be really fancy, or you can say it with Extra Bold if it's really intense and passionate, and it might work!

You don't have to use Clarendon, or Jenson, or a gentle typeface like Garamond or Sabon to say something as clear as "I love you." You can also say, "I hate you." I certainly can write a few letters in Helvetica saying that . . . to Washington DC, in particular, if I can put it that way. So I think it's a very, very flexible type.

GH — Can you talk about the map you designed for the New York subway system in the seventies?

MV — Such a controversial thing. It's funny, but I realized the other day the mistake I made. So this is really the clearest kind of map I have ever seen in terms of information for the subway. It's very simple. Every subway line on the map has a color, and in reality they already have one. And every station has a dot, you know. Every stop is a dot—no dot, no stop. It couldn't be easier than that. There is nothing to fragment the legibility of this. Instead, if you look at today's map, it's a total disaster, with fragmentation all over the place. I can show it to you. And this is what we tried to avoid.

Now, 75 years ago, in London, they did the first map with a 90- and 45-degree grid like this one here, and it's been working fine in London for all this time. But New York is a different kind of a city. And now I just realized that maybe, possibly, I made a mistake by indicating, even in a deformed way, the areas—Manhattan, Queens, the Bronx, et cetera. I probably should have done what they've done in London—not have any indication of the geography. It's a completely blank, white background so that there is no suggestion of geography whatsoever.

One of the problems they had in New York is that the people, they couldn't relate the geography with the station, with the lines, and they were confused by that. But it's just because they shouldn't. There were neighborhood maps in the subway stations, so really there's no reason why this map had to be literal—it could be completely abstract. But I think that it would've been even better if I had pushed the envelope even further and not had anything, just the lines and the stops. Maybe that would have been better. Otherwise, it's perfect—I think it's the most beautiful spaghetti work ever done. It's terrific. And it's so clear, it's unbelievable.

Now, the reality is that 50 percent of humanity is visually oriented, and 50 percent of humanity is verbally oriented. The visually oriented people have no problem reading any kind of map, and the verbal people, they can never read a map. But the verbal people have one great advantage over the visual people: they can be heard. And that's why they changed this map! They started to complain, these people, opening their mouths, until this beautiful map was substituted with the junky one that you can see now by going into the subway station. It is a map that is so loaded with information, which is so difficult to retrieve, that it makes the whole point of the map useless. If I made a mistake, it was not making the geography abstract—making the water beige and the parks gray instead of green— it was just the fact that we indicated these things when we shouldn't have. We should have just made it blank. It would have been better.

GH — And this is the graphics manual for the subway signage?

MV — Yes. It starts by telling you where to put signs in the station, which are at the decision points. Then it shows you the alphabet, which in this case, as I said, was Standard. The different heights—this is for information, this is for the directional signs, and this is for identification signs. This is the name of the station, this is the direction the train goes, and this is what time the train is running. These are the three levels of information that you have in the signage. Then there are other mechanicals—this was done before the computer, long before the computer. Therefore, all these things were done as a hard copy, including the colors for each line. And then, of course, the sample showing the different kinds of sign supports. There was 1 foot, 2 feet, 4 feet, 10 feet, et cetera. It covers the construction details for the signs, the entire thing. This is, again, a mega job, in a sense, but well done for a huge system of transportation like the New York subway.

GH — And it's still in use, right?

MV — And it's still in use. This was 1966, so it's over 40 years. I mean, the background changed from white to black when they had the graffiti explosion, and somebody had the idea of doing the signs in black with white type. That's okay; it's fine. Not a big difference. I like the white background better, but that's okay. I'm glad the signage was not changed. The map is an easy thing to change—it's fast and inexpensive. The signage is a very expensive thing to change, so it's going to be there for a long time.

GH — Do you want to show us some things in the *Design Is One* book?

MV — Yeah. It's basically highlights of our work, our career. You know, here you have American Airlines, for instance—this was done in 1966 as well. It's the corporate identity for American Airlines, and the novelty at the time was the fact of making it one word instead of two—we made it AmericanAirlines, all one word, half red and half blue, just divided by the color. What could be more American than red and blue? So it's perfect. When it came to the planes, we decided not to put any paint on the plane so it would be lighter, less expensive, and less maintenance. What is interesting is, it's the only airline in the last 40 years that has not changed their identity. It's amazing. United has changed theirs several times, and Continental changed a couple of times. Delta changed again. All the airlines come and go, and they're changing. American Airlines is still the same. There is no need to change it. And how could they improve it? They've got the best already, you know—American Airlines in Helvetica. How about that for irony?

I'll show you some other uses of Helvetica. Well, of course, we did everything for Knoll from 1966 to the eighties. But this is a fun one—this package was designed for the Heller dishes and the Heller bakeware that we designed. The box was white with big orange type saying "Heller." And the name of the company and the size of the type was kept consistent regardless of the size of the box. So sometimes you get the whole word "Heller"; sometimes you just get "Hell," which is kind of fun, you know. Or just "H." We were having fun. It shows that you can even have fun with the typefaces.

Dot Zero was another magazine we were designing, and it was completely done in Helvetica as well, and that was the time when I was saying, "In a couple years, Helvetica will be the only typeface left." That was back in '67, '68. I would say the sixties and seventies were a time of heavy use of Helvetica for us. Then in the eighties we started to use more Bodoni and Century. But we kept using Helvetica; we never really dropped it completely. And now, for instance, we're using it a lot, and I've seen a great resurgence of the use of Helvetica in the last 10 years. It's amazing, and it's the young generation indeed. It's funny because in the sixties and seventies, the young generation was after psychedelic type and all the junk that you could find. And also, in the eighties, with their minds completely confused by that disease called postmodernism, people were just going around like chickens without their heads by using all kinds of typefaces that would say "not modern."

They didn't know what they were caring for, they only knew about what they were against, you know? And what they were against was Helvetica, because the connotation of Helvetica in the seventies became the typeface of the industrial army of conglomerates. Most of the corporate identities were done in Helvetica, and therefore the young people looked at these things; they put everything in one bag and just rejected Helvetica as the wrong kind of typeface. And there are people who hated it, and they really hated it because they thought it was the type that represented evil. For me it was never that kind of a thing. I've always been of the opinion that all postmodernism was just a fad. Leave it alone, give it time to fade out, and it will. And as a matter of fact, it did. But instead, modernism, which was never a fad—it was a philosophy; it was an attitude; it was based on logic rather than emotions—it kept going on.

And what you see today is that after the terrible things that were built during the postmodernist time, those funky buildings that they were doing, now you see terrific modern buildings, buildings which really go back to the great tradition of modern architecture. They keep developing it and updating it, but plenty of great architects still work with a modernist philosophy. And now what is interesting to see is that a lot of the young generation in graphic design and design in general are again modernists, and they like Helvetica. They use it with a great sense of space—sometimes they exaggerate, but that's okay. I'd rather see that than those horrible concoctions put together by the flower children.

GH — Great.

    MV — [Laughing.] I did it. I managed to get it out.

GH — Damn hippies!

    MV — Well, damn hippies. You know, good for nothing. They only knew what they hated; they never knew what they loved. And they never constructed anything, they would only go about destroying. Terrorism? That was the real terrorist act. A generation wasted. Bang! Boom! Gone! The wasted generation—that's what it was. You know in the thirties when they were talking about the lost generation going to Paris—Hemingway, and so on? Those were kids. They were nothing in comparison to the wasted generation of the hippies.

GH — Great . . .

MV — I'm glad that you're doing this film. I think that this should really come out loud and clear—that if there is a carrier of logic, it has really been Helvetica. It's been a carrier of clarity, a carrier of reason. Not the funny typefaces that we saw in the seventies. So I'm really glad it exists. I love it.

[Later, we attempt to film a "still" portrait of Massimo, but characteristically he continues talking.]

MV — Now do you want me to talk or not talk? Say something; say nothing?

Nara Garber (sound mixer) — Tell us what you *really* think about the flower children.

MV — Oh my God, you don't want to hear that. That certainly was a bad moment, you know, a wasted generation. Completely wasted. Unbelievable. I'm glad that you were born after that. You know, it's amazing: there was nothing, nothing. They were becoming bums. The whole idea was that, if you were with it, if you were cool, you were a bum. You just, say, lay on the sidewalk there, that kind of thing. You did all the things that were against anything that makes sense. So if it made sense, you had to do the opposite.

You know, I was talking the other night with a guy who was doing a magazine called *Punk*, and he said a thing that was absolutely correct. He said, "We were not for anything. We were against everything." And that sums up the entire generation of that time. I mean, I understand it was troubled times with the war, and so it felt just like today to a certain extent. That was the first time that America was doing something completely wrong. Now we're getting used to it. It's a big difference. I guess that's why the protests are much more mild today than it used to be in '69 and '70, you know, with the Vietnam War. It's amazing.

GH — Okay, one more. Just a still portrait . . .

MV — You really wonder how long it's going to take before people will really go down in the square, in the streets, and say, "Enough is enough! Go home!" you know? "Go back to Texas where you belong!" I mean, how long are they going to wait? I don't know. I'm ready. Just tell me to go and I'll go in the square, in the plazas, anyplace. In Central Park. Anywhere, you know, where millions can congregate and say, "Enough is enough." You can pass that on to the CIA, and I will be extradited immediately back to my home country!
—

Michael Bierut (MB)/ April 17, 2006 New York City

Michael Bierut is a designer and partner at Pentagram, one of the most prolific and respected design firms in the world. He's also a natural comedian, I think, who definitely got his share of punch lines in the film. I interviewed Michael in Pentagram's New York City office.

—

Gary Hustwit — Do you remember your first encounter with Helvetica?

Michael Bierut — I decided at a really early age that I wanted to be a graphic designer. I was a 14- or 15-year-old in suburban Cleveland. I didn't know any real working graphic designers, but I found out that graphic design was what they called the art of making things like album covers and movie posters—things that I thought were really cool. That was what I wanted to do. So I started doing it in an amateur sort of way myself.

The hardest part, of course, is lettering. To do the lettering, what I basically did when I was a kid was I would find models of letters that I thought looked cool. Then I would sort of copy them, usually with a black Bic ballpoint pen on a plastic ruler and a little dime-store protractor. For instance, I would copy the cover of an album called *Golden Bisquits* by Three Dog Night that had really beautiful kind of quasi-Victorian lettering on it that I thought was really cool. What I noticed was that none of these things that I did looked real. They all looked amateurish and kind of fake, like some 14-year-old kid in Ohio trying to pretend to do design.

Then my dad, who sold printing presses for a living, came home from a trade show. He had with him a single thing in a little envelope and he said, "You might get a kick out of this." It turned out to be a single sheet of what's now a bygone technology, dry-transfer lettering. This is rub-down lettering. You'd rub down letters off of this thing and they'd stick to the paper you were rubbing them down onto. The sheet was 36-point Helvetica Medium. I just remember probably the first thing I might have done is my own name, M-i-c-h-a-e-l, capital *M* and then lowercase the rest of it. It was the first time I had set type, and there was no typeface you could possibly use that had more authority, more professionalism, more sophistication, actually, than Helvetica Medium.

It was just like doing magic compared with scratching away, hacking away at something with a Bic ballpoint pen. In just one fell swoop, just in seconds, you could have something that looked as real as anything you'd see in a magazine, as anything you'd see in a movie, as anything you'd see in a record store. To me, that's always what Helvetica has been. It's the one thing that immediately conferred automatic unassailable authority on any message you wanted to have. That was my first encounter with Helvetica. Oddly enough, one of the charms of dry-transfer lettering was you had a single sheet with a finite number of letters. So the whole thing had, built within it, an expiration date.

You'd use up the common letters like *A*s and *E*s and *T*s pretty quickly, and then you'd have a lot of leftover *Q*s and *G*s and *X*s and things. But sooner or later you also mastered the ability to kind of convert *C*s into *E*s by rubbing down the crossbar of the *E* and everything else. I got a lot of mileage out of that single sheet before I could work up the nerve to go acquire another one.

GH — When you went on to art school and decided you wanted to be a designer, who were the designers you were influenced by at the time? When you moved to New York, what was your experience coming here and being a young graphic designer?
    MB — Should I refer to Helvetica in this discussion?

GH — Not necessarily, this is just talking about you a little more.
    MB — Okay. But did you know I was born the same year that Helvetica was designed? In 1957?

GH — That's a good sound-bite.
    MB — I was born in 1957. In 1975, I went off to design school—University of Cincinnati, which can be classified a number of different ways—but the design program, I would say, was sort of what was then referred to as a Swiss design program. It emphasized sort of a rigorous structure; kind of this objective Helvetica-friendly view of graphic design. Although Helvetica wasn't quite as popular as Univers was, for some reason. I think a lot of the history of that kind of typography is trying to discover alternatives or superior versions of Helvetica. Mostly in vain, by the way. That began when I was in school, I would say.

    Although my enthusiasms for design were very broad then, and continue to be very broad today, I like and admire the kind of Swiss-based, International Style graphic design that was in vogue at Cincinnati then. But I also liked the more eclectic sorts of work that Milton Glaser and Seymour Chwast and Push Pin did. I also liked the kind of more idea-driven design that Chermayeff & Geismar and Pentagram did. So I liked all sorts of graphic design. But the guy who offered me a job when I graduated was one of my heroes, Massimo Vignelli, who some people credit with the introduction and propagation of Helvetica into North America—which he did when he was a principal at Unimark in the sixties. Where should I go now?

GH — I'm interested in a couple things. Obviously, from the Helvetica standpoint, the popularization of it, the reason behind it, why it's on everyone's computer, why you see it every time you walk out on the street. That's one kind of overreaching question. We can also talk about technology and its impact on typography—and obviously the Macintosh and the kind of ramifications the computer has now on the type that we see and graphic design that we see. Those are two tracks that I'd love to talk about. I don't know. Wherever you feel like.

MB — I was actually going to say something about what I call the social history, in America at least, of the typeface.

GH — Sure.

MB — When I think back about it, actually, my mixed feelings about Helvetica have something to do with the time that I came of age as a designer. I was studying design in the late seventies, and I started my professional life here in New York, in 1980. The high tide of Helvetica might have been 10 years before that in terms of its having an absolutely clear, ideological, self-ratifying, single-minded assurance behind it.

I think that, actually, it was kind of associated with modernity, with authority. When Nixon ran for reelection, I think, all of his posters were in Helvetica. So not just a designy typeface, but a typeface that kind of came to be associated with the corporate establishment, particularly in the United States. By the time I started as a designer, it sort of seemed there was only one trick in town—which was like, what could you use instead of Helvetica? ABH: Anything But Helvetica. You do need lots of sans-serif typefaces, but it seemed like Helvetica had just been used so much, and overused so much, and associated with so many big faceless things, that it had lost all its capacity even—to my eyes at least—to look nice.

So I just went on a font binge. It could be old typefaces like Futura or Trade Gothic or Franklin Gothic. Then into the eighties and nineties a succession of new sans-serif fonts was introduced, each one of which was seen as being the new Helvetica—whether it was Meta, or DIN, or Letter Gothic, or Gotham, or Interstate—all typefaces that we graphic designers seized upon with a vengeance. Oddly enough, Helvetica never seems to be extinguished. It sort of prevails and gets more and more and more and more ubiquitous to the point where normal, civilian, nonprofessional people might know it by one of its aliases; Arial, or something like that. But one way or another, every time they do a PowerPoint presentation, every time they print out a lost-dog poster, every time one of my children prints out a report for school, half the time it's in something that looks, pretty much, for all intents and purposes, like Helvetica.

GH — Do you think that's because of that sense of bringing authority to the work, or is it the other way around? I'm trying to get to the chicken-and-egg thing.

MB — Yeah.

GH — Like, did Helvetica cause this feeling in us, or is there something about it that we suddenly think "Oh, it's authoritative"? Or is just because it was used by so many people?

MB — Well, aesthetics is a tricky subject. Why does something look right to us, or sound right to us? My tendency as a person is to just think that most things are subjective. You were exposed to something under pleasant circumstances at a formative point in your life, and then you associate it with nice things now. So you think "Oh, that's pretty," or "That's beautiful," or "That looks right to me."

I remember having that theory about music too. A lot of people know that you hear certain songs and they take you back to some time in your life, or there are certain chord structures that seem to be central to Western music, whether it's Bach or 12-bar blues or whatever it is. Then I remember discovering very late in life the principles of harmonic theory that Pythagoras actually helped work out, where it's not just that we keep hearing one-four-five chord structures and they sort of start to sound right. Pythagoras's idea was that because of the way the vibrations of the harmonics worked, they were somehow related to each other mathematically, right? So it wasn't just that they sounded right because we were used to them. There was something inherently perfect about them that made them sound right.

So I'm not sure that you can make the same statements when it comes to art or design. However, there's just something about Helvetica, something about the fact that people keep repeatedly saying, "I've come up with an improvement of Helvetica," or "I've done a version of Helvetica where it's as good as Helvetica, except it combines Helvetica with superior qualities of whatchamacallit," and it never is really good. You can sort of modify it. You can do a parody of it. You can kind of do a hybridization of it, but it just stands there like some ginormous magnetic north or something, where you can't change it. It's like the axis upon which all this other stuff revolves, whether you like it or you don't like it, whether you're trying to avoid it or you believe it 100 percent with your heart and soul. It just is there.

I wonder whether there's some whole undiscovered science of typography that would say that it's not just because we're used to seeing it. It's not just because it was associated with all these things that we consider authoritative. But it somehow has this kind of inherent rightness. You know, the rightness of the way the lowercase *a* meets the curve, the rightness of the way the *G* has a thing that comes down, the rightness of the way the *C* strokes are like that instead of like that. I wouldn't have believed that those things actually could be right or wrong as opposed to someone's taste, yet you have 50 years of history of the thing just sitting there daring people to fix it. It seems to be unfixable.

GH — I wanted to talk about what you were alluding to with the rebellion against Helvetica and that type of face, and the 1980s technology like Fontographer and how that explosion of typefaces affected graphic design. That whole technological move and the kind of rebellion against the corporate-looking faces. And maybe how it's come full circle now, like to just use Helvetica is more rebellious today?

MB — When I first started out in the eighties as a designer, setting type was something only professionals could do. It was a fairly high-risk operation. Not because it was physically dangerous, but because it was costly to make a mistake. What you would do is you'd take a typewritten manuscript that had come off someone's IBM Selectric. You'd write on the top of it the typeface you wanted it set in, and the only way you'd really know what it would look like is you'd have to call up a typesetter, have the typesetter pick it up, take it away, usually overnight. Then the next morning they'd return it to you, set in the font you specified. If you made a mistake, it would cost a lot of dollars. It would cost tens of dollars, maybe hundreds of dollars. Maybe if you really were bold or indecisive, say, you could piss away thousands of dollars sort of saying, "Let's see how this looks in 24-point, in 28-point, in 27-point, flush left, flush right, in Helvetica, in Futura, in Garamond, in Janson, in Bembo, and in Franklin Gothic." The kind of thing that now people do on a computer in 10 minutes used to cost thousands of dollars, would take 24 hours, and would somehow still maybe not give you the answer you were looking for.

It turned out that no matter how many choices you sampled, you couldn't quite get the right one. That made people, my age at least, tend toward going with what they knew. If they knew what 36-point Helvetica Medium looked like and they were picturing a design, they would just riff through the things that they could already picture clearly. And if Helvetica Medium was one of those things, by God, Helvetica Medium was one of the few options that you could go with. Scribble it down on the top of that manuscript. Send it off. Get up the next morning. It would look exactly the way you were picturing. I think that's one of the reasons why typefaces like Helvetica and a few other ones managed to maintain their hegemony so long, going into the late eighties and early nineties.

What happened then, of course, was the rise of desktop publishing and computer-assisted design, and that permitted you to have a big suitcase full of as many different fonts as you could afford or in some cases illegally steal. Or programs like Fontographer would allow you to design typefaces in minutes or at least in hours, whereas old-style type designers would have to spend weeks or months designing a font. All those things kind of conspired to chip away at these ageless carved-in-stone monuments that had existed through most of my youth and into my young adulthood.

Then they sort of served to back up the rebellion against all that stuff you saw happening particularly in the nineties with the rise of what's referred to as grunge typography, variously attributed to David Carson, the famous and some may say notorious designer of surfing and skateboard magazines, and Kyle Cooper, the guy who designed the titles to the movie Seven—both of whom took all the tools of sophisticated precision that the Macintosh and the associated design software programs provided and used those to undermine perfection in design completely, so that you have things that look beat up, chipped, messed up, hybridized, overlapped, done wrong, done wrong on purpose.

That became an all-consuming aesthetic for about two, three, four, five years as that trend worked its way down from the masters who originated it to anyone who already had a tendency to make mistakes and all of a sudden found that they looked good now instead of incompetent, which was the way they looked the day before. Just like any fad, it runs its course.

I think we're looking now at the tail end, perhaps, of a backlash against that, where everything has gone through a phase of being clean again, back to Helvetica and other kinds of clean understated sans-serif fonts. What makes these fads cycle so quickly now is that it's all just so easy and fast to do. Things that used to take overnight you can do in a minute. Things that used to take months can take days. Fads that used to have a nice long gestation period of months and years and have a nice arc that would start at the beginning of a decade and end at the turn of the following decade, now they can be done from winter through the following spring. I think that just means that there is this hunger, at least among graphic designers, for what the next thing is.

Somehow, on some screwy level—just like couture designers deciding for the spring show all of the lapels or shoulders will be this big; a few months later in Penney's or Sears all the shoulders get that much bigger—I think the same thing happens in graphic design, where if somehow a bunch of influential designers decide that everything's going to look really grungy, everyone's PowerPoint presentations nine months later start to look a little bit grungier. Thus it always is with things filtering themselves down, all enabled now by technology which makes it just faster and faster and faster. What was the question?

GH — That was good. Doesn't matter. Just kind of taking off from that, what's next? Any thoughts on what the next phase of design is going to be?

MB — I'm not particularly good at predicting what the next thing will be. I've tried. Every time I try, I tend to get it wrong or else get it right but a day later. My big idea about what the next thing will be will still be on my drawing board when I see it getting launched by other people who actually do have this instinct in a more deeply rooted way than I seem to.

But I would say that there's a couple of factors at work nowadays. I mean, people really are getting a lot of information onscreen. The much-hyped Internet revolution of nearly 10 years ago is finally bearing fruit. So people don't even think about it anymore. They just get lots of their news and lots of their gossip and lots of their ways of whiling away their time by looking at things onscreen.

Because of the vagaries of the way that screens are built, there's a couple of fonts that are easy to show onscreen and other ones that are much harder. One of the easier ones to do is this font that's called Arial, which experts can distinguish from Helvetica and dare each other to do at certain quasi-design sporting events. But most normal people can't and probably shouldn't be able to tell Arial apart from Helvetica.

But it's become, if anything, all the more ubiquitous because of that. You sort of have all the motion that onscreen graphics seems to be able to provide both in a sophisticated way, when it's some big advertiser pitching something to you, and in a more primitive way, when it's just some kid with Final Cut Pro or something jazzing up their biology report in the 7th grade in the same way that I used to do a really elaborate drawing of a frog using a black Bic pen. They'd make some elaborate onscreen animation to sort of accomplish the same thing, or disguise the same lack of actual research they've done, which was my motivation.

I think all these things are continuing to get more ubiquitous. It may very well be that when it comes to trends, at least in graphic design, we've reached sort of the end of history, and the pendulum that swings back and forth doesn't have any more directions it can swing in. The final trend may simply be the completely democratic distribution of the means of production to anyone who wants it or anyone who can afford it, meaning that we'll soon reach a point where anyone can be a designer. Anyone is a designer. Anyone who communicates right now using words or pictures will be able to have the same tools available to them and perhaps nearly the same skills as professionals once did, which will mean that the only thing to debate is whether that's a good thing or a bad thing.

GH — Let's back up a bit. Can we talk more about Vignelli? How long did you work with him?

MB — I worked for Massimo Vignelli for 10 years, and one of the things that Massimo is famous for in my profession is his claim that he uses only five typefaces. I don't know if he admits this, but he actually uses more than five typefaces. But there's just something nice and satisfying about ideologically committing yourself to five typefaces.

The implication, I think, has always been that he picked those five type-faces. They were the best typefaces, and all the other ones were various degrees of inferior typefaces. Some of them were just so awful in theory, or they amounted to being mortal sins or apocalyptically disastrous typefaces. So if you just stuck with those top five, you'd be assured that everything you did would be good, or at least as good as something Massimo Vignelli designed.

I actually bought into this whole theory, not because I really think that those five typefaces are the best in the world, but I came to discover that most normal people can't distinguish between more than five type-faces. Graphic designers spend a lot of time brooding about, "Should it be Garamond or Bembo or Sabon or Dante?" But to most people, my mom being the person I think of when I think of most people, they all look exactly the same. The difference between them is so negligible that it's almost insane to talk about. If you just decide, "I'm just going to use Garamond," which is on Massimo's list of typefaces, think about all the time you'd save, time you would have spent brooding about whether it should be Garamond or Bembo. Instead, you just decide early on you're going to use Garamond #3, and that's that. If you need a Garamond kind of typeface, just use Garamond. You know?

I think Helvetica was always on that list, but oddly, it was actually used pretty rarely during the 10 years that I worked for Massimo in the eighties. Massimo associated Helvetica mostly with Knoll, a real signature program for the most high-design furniture company of its time. It sort of seemed like Helvetica was associated with Knoll to the degree that it excluded a lot of other possibilities for it. And that's sort of the ultimate thing—if an institution or a company can seem to have primary claim on a single typeface, that's the ultimate power. In a way, anyone is allowed to use that typeface, but if you rig it so that if someone writes something in that font, it looks like it came from that company, that's pretty diabolical.

Volkswagen achieved that with Futura to a certain degree. Apple used to have that with ITC Garamond condensed to 85 percent, which was what everything was before the launch of the iPod. Now I think it's Myriad, but it's been modified in some way. It's this urge that companies have to get us to establish that sort of association.

I think by the time I was starting my career, Helvetica already had so many associations, it didn't seem to be able to bear any more in a useful way for projects I was working on. So we would use Univers or Futura. Occasionally, although it wasn't allowed, I would sneak in Franklin Gothic or News Gothic.

GH — It seems like there were quite a few companies trying to corner the market on Helvetica in the sixties.

MB — I imagine there was a time when it just felt so good to take something that was goofy and old and dusty and homemade and crappy-looking and replace it with Helvetica. It just must have felt like you were scraping the crud off of filthy old things and kind of restoring them to shining beauty. And in fact, with corporate identity in the '60s, that's what it sort of consisted of.

Clients would come in, and they'd have piles of goofy old brochures from the fifties that had shapes on them and goofy bad photographs. They'd have some letterhead that would say "Amalgamated Widget" on the top in some goofy, maybe a script, typeface. Above "Amalgamated Widget" it would have an engraving showing their headquarters in Paducah, Ohio, with smokestacks belching smoke. You know?

Then you go to a corporate-identity consultant circa 1965, 1966, and they would take that and lay it here and say, "Here's your current stationery, and all it implies, and this is what we're proposing." And next to that, next to the belching smokestacks and the nuptial script and the ivory paper, they'd have a bright-white piece of paper. Instead of "Amalgamated Widget, founded 1857," it just would say "WIDGCO" in Helvetica Medium.

Can you imagine how bracing and thrilling that was? That must have seemed like you'd crawled through a desert with your mouth just caked with filthy dust, and then someone's offering you a clear, refreshing, distilled icy glass of water to kind of clear away all this horrible burden of history. It must have just been fantastic. You know it must have been fantastic, because it was done over and over and over again.

A signature moment was when the original insignia for NASA—which was designed, supposedly, by an engineer at one of their technical centers, consisting of, if you can picture it, a globe with things going around it, with "NASA" in some kind of horrible kind of weird serif-y typeface underneath—was changed. Danne and Blackburn, a great corporate-identity firm, replaced it with these hand drawn letters N-A-S-A. No crossbars in the As, so it just felt like one single line of progress. All the subordinate text was in Helvetica. So the space shuttles were all just that new NASA font with "The United States of America" next to it in Helvetica. It just seemed so beautiful and futuristic.

Then when NASA fell on hard times following the first space shuttle disaster, the new administration came in, and in order to restore the glory of the Gemini and Apollo days, the first thing they did was get rid of that curvy logo, which was called internally "the worm." They restored the original logo, the disavowed horrible, musty and dusty, goofy-looking, drawn-by-some-engineer-probably-with-a-Bic-pen logo with the sphere and the things, which is called internally "the meatball."

They said, "To bring us back to glory, here it is. You know it. You love it. The meatball." Graphic designers viewed that with real alarm. It was sort of like people were rebelling. You know, "We gave you Helvetica. We showed you Helvetica. It's perfect. Then all of a sudden these witless fools want this meatball thing again, thinking it has some magical qualities. It has no magical qualities. The only thing that has magical qualities is Helvetica. Use Helvetica." I think that that was sort of like the dream of modernism in a way, that somehow there was some objective truth in this and that it represented progress. If the past could be obliterated and replaced with things like Helvetica, that would signify endless progress.

Its corollary in urban planning was the leveling of neighborhoods of row houses that were associated with crime and dirt. Then giant beautiful towers and a park were established in their place, which soon were covered with dirt and associated with crime because they forgot to help change the people, as it was with NASA, as it is always. Progress remains illusory even when you have a formidable tool like Helvetica at your disposal.

GH — So is this idea of modernism still a factor in your design?

MB — Personally, as a designer, it's taken me a long time to figure out what I believe in, in terms of design. I'm not ideological in terms of imposing some sort of aesthetic on things. I think when I look at my own work, it seems sometimes, at its worst moments, to be all over the place. But I do still favor things that are clean rather than messy, that are organized rather than disorganized, that are communicative rather than oblique or baffling.

I think that there are certain things that should be that way, that you can defend as being that way by necessity, whether it's airport signs or safety instructions or words on pill bottles. There are other things that don't have to be that way at all. In fact, they can be enigmatic and hard to figure out, depending on whether you are communicating with a small target audience that you can invent a secret code for. I think that most of us, whether we want to admit it or not, have a kind of handwriting that you can't figure out where it came from. People that analyze handwriting actually can impute all kinds of personality traits onto the way you loop your Ls or finish your Ys, and whether or not your design choices have the same sort of tells about your personality, I wouldn't presume to say.

All I know is, at the end of the day I've tried doing complicated, messy design, and I don't seem to be good at it. That's all. I'm not against it. When it's done well by people who are good at it, I salute them and I'm kind of in awe of it. There are certain projects that really need that, but for the kind of stuff I do, one idea is more then enough for me, and usually one typeface is where I start. That ends up looking like modernism to people, but I have to admit I probably lack the ideological conviction behind it to actually say that it's modernism or that I'm a modernist. I simply do what I think works for me and for the situation, and it ends up looking a certain way.

[At this point we starting looking through old magazines.]

MB — Here we go. This is what I'm talking about. This is *Life* magazine, 1953. One ad after another in here showing every single visual bad habit that was endemic in those days. You've got zany hand lettering everywhere. This cartoon superimposed on top of retouched photographs. Lots of swash typography to signify elegance.

Here's Betty Crocker speaking in a speech bubble. A microscopic view of how flaky the crust is. Exclamation points, exclamation points, exclamation points. There's a big Buick ad, kind of this bizarre hand-lettered typography. Four little inserts of Studebakers and Roadmasters and zany things from those days. A guy waving a baton up above the whole thing. Just a complete mess.

Now cut to 1970. Here's *Life* magazine again. Look how great this Helvetica looks. This is an RCA ad talking about "the age of AccuColor." It's beautiful, reasonable. One big target here signifying the singularity of their vision. Just so clean, so sharp, so completely nice. AT&T. Completely elegant profile here. All Helvetica typography up here. Helvetica logo down there. Just beautiful. Here's an actual ad from ARCO announcing triumphantly, taking a full two-page ad in *Life* magazine, that they've abandoned the dusty, weird, cumbersome past of the Atlantic Richfield Company. It sounds like grimy oil wells in the Atlantic, and who's Richfield and all that? But now they're just going to the abstract, beautiful future represented by four letters, ARCO, in, of course, Helvetica.

Here another magazine from the fifties. This shows you what I'm talking about. This is from the summer of 1955. Helvetica has almost been invented—certainly unimagined on the shores of the United States of America. This is how we were sold Coca-Cola in those days. A corny picture of this perfect family wearing their summer whites, each one of them enjoying a frosty Coke. Wedding invitation typography: "Almost everyone appreciates the best . . ." A picture of a Coke bottle. A lot of kind of corny typography here. Lots of ellipses. Lots of exclamation points. Lots of barely controlled hysteria about the flavor of Coke. This was everywhere in the fifties. This is how everything looked in the fifties. It looks a little charming now through the haze of nostalgia, but believe me, when you were surrounded by this stuff, it must have felt oppressive.

Now, 1970, same product. Here's how we sold Coke at Christmastime. A little holiday sprig there. No people. No smiling fakery. Just a beautiful big glass of ice-cold Coke with a beautiful iceberg-sized ice cube floating on the top. The slogan underneath, "It's the real thing," period. Coke, period. In Helvetica, period. Any questions? Of course not. Drink Coke, period. Simple.

GH — Great, perfect.
MB — So who else are you speaking to for this film?

GH — We're talking with Matthew Carter tomorrow. Hoefler and Frere-Jones, Spiekermann, lots of people. Rick Poynor . . .
MB — Oh, good. Certainly a movie I'd like to watch. But I don't know if anyone else, if normal people, will want to see it. You never can tell, though. What's funny is that when I was president of the American Institute of Graphic Arts (AIGA), our professional organization, we were always trying to get normal people, or at least the business community, interested in graphic design. We're always saying, "Oh, *New York Times*, you should run a story about annual reports or run a story about this. Run a story about that." It's actually really hard—they don't care about that stuff that much, as it turns out. If it's design, they think that it's fashion design or industrial design, things that conveniently you can go to a store and buy. You can't go buy graphic design. You can go buy a book, but then it's about the author and the subject matter. It's not about the font that it's in.

But the one thing that you can actually get writers, mainstream writers, interested in is typefaces. Probably because their words are set in type-faces, so it cuts close to the bone for them. That's why *the New Yorker* had a profile of a type designer, Matthew Carter, in it, where what he does seems to be part of everyone's life, but it's this mysterious thing that works below the surface. That's why Tobias Frere-Jones and Jonathan Hoefler were both profiled in *Esquire* magazine. They knew this mysterious thing that everyone sees but no one knows about. It seems kind of cool in a way. You know?

The mystery of typefaces, I think, even as they become more and more ubiquitous, is somehow the fact that they're made by people, that people have to make decisions about every single aspect of them and that somehow those minute decisions kind of accrue one after another after another in this almost overwhelming complexity, then just become this thing you see when you open a magazine or when you turn on the TV or when you go to the movies or when you walk down a 7-Eleven aisle. There it is, and it just seems to come from nowhere. It seems like air. It seems like gravity, but there are people somewhere that kind of decided all of that.

GH — But everybody now feels like they're a graphic designer. If you've got a Macintosh and Microsoft Word . . . you've got a favorite font. Everybody's got a favorite.

       MB — Yeah, yeah. Well, you look at . . . wait, is this wasting film time?

GH — It's all digital. Go for it.

       MB — If you look at the *McSweeney's* phenomenon, I think a lot of it is attributable to the fact that Dave Eggers writes in Quark or was famous for writing in Quark and did everything in Garamond #3. All those journals, all the book covers, everything was Garamond #3, which created this amazing brand around these things he made in this sort of quiet, insidious sort of way. People who couldn't figure out how it all went together started to be able to spot something that looked like it was a *McSweeney's* associated thing, all because of the relentless dedication to a single font. That's happened through the years all the time, usually through the agency of an art director.

       In music, for instance, Cheap Trick always used distressed typewriter type. Barbra Streisand always used Century Schoolbook Italic. It's sort of a way to build a brand for anything you want. Just pick a font and use it over and over again. I think every person on earth can do the same thing, and it would probably be nearly as effective. If you have an interest for whatever perverse reason in becoming a brand yourself, the first thing you can do is pick a font, nearly any font. Not Comic Sans probably, but nearly any other font. Just use that one over and over and over again on everything you do. Then of course you might want to decide what your color is and dress entirely in that color. Then come up with a couple of characteristic catchphrases, like taglines that you would incorporate into your normal speech. Then you could be sort of like the IBM or the Coca-Cola or the Nike or the Target or the Apple of your block.

—

Matthew Carter (MC)/ April 18, 2006 Cambridge, Massachusetts

Matthew Carter is undoubtedly one of the greatest living type designers. His work spans hundreds of typefaces, and almost every technological change the type industry has seen. I talked with Matthew at his home near Boston.

For me, one of the most enlightening parts of these conversations usually comes when we start talking about who else is going to be in the film. When I spoke with Matthew, I wasn't familiar with Mike Parker or his role in Helvetica's story, but Matthew insisted that I speak with him. This has been the case so often with these films: one conversation leads to another, and so on . . .

—

Gary Hustwit — I guess we can begin by talking about your beginnings and how you got involved in this crazy type world.

Matthew Carter — My dad was a typographer, and although he didn't push me to follow in his footsteps, when I left high school in the UK, I had a year to fill before going to university. I got sent as an unpaid trainee to a type foundry in the Netherlands, where I spent a year learning what turned out to be a completely obsolete trade of making type by hand.

When I came back, I'd gotten interested in this and I really couldn't face going back into academic life, so I started trying to make a living as, first of all, an engraver. But there was no business really in that line. So I gradually started doing lettering, and then eventually that became type over a period of time. Then I got involved in London with one of the phototypesetting businesses, Photon. I was there for a couple of years, and then in '65 I moved to New York, to Brooklyn, to work for Mergenthaler Linotype, the parent company of the Linotype Group, where I spent six years. Then I went back to London for about 10 years. But I still continued to work for the Linotype companies during that time.

Then in '81, four of us with Linotype backgrounds started a new company here in Cambridge, Massachusetts, called Bitstream, which was one of the first digital type companies, and I worked there for another decade or so and then left along with one of the other cofounders, Cherie Cone. At the end of '91 we formed our own company, which we still have, Carter & Cone—and that's still going on. That's what we do now.

GH — Can you talk a little bit about the technology in terms of type design in the fifties when you were still doing metal type? I can imagine the kind of work that went into making a single letter, let alone designing a whole typeface.

MC — This very anachronistic trade that I learned in the mid-fifties was the same way of making type that as far we know goes all the way back to Gutenberg, essentially. It was a matter of cutting letters in steel— punches, they're called. Engraving them at actual size, making copper matrices out of those by hammering the punch, driving the punch into the copper, and the copper matrix then serves as the mold in which multiple pieces of type are cast. This is the real basis of typographic technology. I learned to do that. You can't become fully proficient in the course of just a year doing that, but I had some sort of journeyman ability in doing it. As I say, there was really no commercial opportunity to do this to speak of, and that led me into designing type, and my getting into contact with a bunch of graphic designers in London at that time.

I'm talking about the very early sixties now, and we wanted to work in what you would call an International Style. But we found it very difficult to get typesetting work in the British type-founding trade, which at that time was very conservative. I spent a couple of years drawing lettering and alphabets for very good, discriminating designers in London, and that gradually moved me into working at first one and then two different photocomposing companies.

At that time the way type was made was, I made drawings—proper, well-made drawings—and those were the image source of the photographic font. I had to be able to draw them fairly well and to scale and in register and all that stuff. I continued for many years drawing in that way, ink on paper, or ink on drafting film.

In the mid-to-late seventies I was making digital type and Linotype by very painstaking means: drawing letters on graph paper with little pixel edges and encoding them on a keyboard. Then gradually when the technology moved toward desktop type and the coming of the Mac and PostScript, we moved into the present situation where all design-ers work on computers. Some of them still like to draw first. They like to make sketches and scan them and put them into the background of the computer and work in them.

I don't do that. I work directly on the screen, but then I never could draw very well in the first place and I'm not a calligrapher. I don't have very good control of the pen or pencil. So I'm just as happy with the new technology working directly on the screen. The wonderful thing about what we have now, the digital medium, is that alongside the Mac sits a laser printer. This is a very hard point to make to students who think I'm an idiot when I say this. But I had to wait 536 years as a type designer before I could see in real time what it is I'm actually doing. In other words, I digitize a letter on the screen, and then within seconds I can print that out from the laser printer at actual size. I can combine two, three, four letters and immediately I've done them, and this was really a great novelty when it came about in the late eighties, around 1990.

And so font formats became open, and this whole field opened up. So that really made a huge difference, this ability to see what I was doing. Because in the days of punch cutting, I could hold a punch in the flame of a candle and dab it on a bit of paper, but it was very difficult to get the letters to line up. And then in my Linotype days, if we wanted trial matrices from the factory for a Linotype face, trial work competed with production work, so sometimes I had to wait for weeks for mats to come back.

Even in the days of photocomp it was still a sort of industrial process and so I would take my drawings down to the factory. I mean, the least I would have to wait would be a week or so before I got the results back. So there's always been historically this sort of suspension between doing something and actually seeing what it is that he or she had done, and it was the computer and the laser printer which short-circuited that and closed the loop. Which made a very big difference to the way I work and also to teaching, and which brings a level of reality and immediacy into it. So I could say that really I've made type by practically all the means that it's ever been made in the 51 years that I've been working. But if I had to choose, if I was able to choose a period in which I could have worked, I think I would really have chosen the one that I lucked into. Because I'm glad to have seen how it was done in the past and to have practiced that, but I'm also endlessly grateful to have survived into the day of digital technology. There are gains and losses, but for me the balance is clear. There have been more gains than losses. So I'm delighted to be able to work with the current technology.

GH — Obviously, there are huge advantages to it. But I'd like to talk about the disadvantages of some of the digital technology, in terms of the number of typefaces that get designed and produced, and I guess the mentality of the people who only know digital as the tool to create it.

MC — I'm very open-minded about those questions. I had traditional training because it was really the only thing that was around when I left school in '55, and it was almost the only way I could have gotten into it. I suppose there may have been others. I could have gone to work for Linotype or Monotype at that time, but I chose to do it in this rather old-fashioned manner. And of course, it's true that type design in the past used to be a very inaccessible thing to get involved in. I had the advantage of having a father in the business and this introduction to one of the last type foundries that made type by hand. But it was a pretty difficult business to get into. Nowadays, of course, that's changed dramatically. Anyone with a Macintosh and FontLab or the right software can make type, make fonts of type. I myself am in favor of that.

I'm old enough to be considered a designosaur where these things are concerned, but I don't really feel that way. It's true that a good deal of the type that's produced nowadays is probably not going to get assimilated into the mainstream of the typographic repertoire. But for me that's fine, because the economics of things have changed. In the Linotype days, to bring out a new hot metal face, as was done with say, Helvetica, as one obvious example—it was architectural in scale. The amount of time and money involved in bringing out a new family of type in all its sizes and weights was an absolutely colossal investment. That got cheaper by orders of magnitude when we went, first of all to photocomposition and then to digital type.

So I don't really have this feeling that the barbarians have come through the gates and typography got trashed in the early nineties when everyone started experimenting with type. A lot of the people who experimented at that time have gone on to things which are trendier now, web design or multimedia design or whatever. But I think it stimulated a lot of experimental work and a lot of very good work, some less good for obvious reasons. But I don't myself have this feeling that everything went to hell at a certain point and all the good traditions got junked and everything we have now is better. I just don't feel that way about it. I'd actually go further and say I get asked very often a question which I find completely impossible to answer. Which is, what will be the next big thing in typography? What fashion is coming up? What typefaces are going to be popular?

I haven't a clue. But the way I answer the question is to say that there are more good, young type designers—and by young I mean probably late 20s, early 30s—now than at any time in history. Who knows what typefaces they will design in terms of style? But they'll be good, and to my way of thinking, that is a huge gain, a huge benefit that comes with this more democratic, more accessible technology.

GH — Can you talk about when you set out to design a typeface, the process that you go through?

MC — Well, obviously it varies a good deal with the typeface and what it's intended for. What's the reason you're doing it? Who's the client? Is there no client? Is it speculative? I think it's actually hard to generalize about type designs. There isn't a generality about it, but I think that most type designers, if they were sitting in this chair, would essentially start in much the same way. For me, if a typeface has both capitals and lowercase, as most do, I would start with the lowercase. And I would start with a small group of letters that embody the maximum amount of information about the typeface, in order to nail that down first.

I would probably start with a lowercase h. It tells me first of all whether this is a sans serif or a serif typeface. If it has serifs, are they heavy? Are they light? Are they bracketed? Are they unbracketed? What is the nature of the serif? Is there a lot of thick/thin contrast in the letterform? Does the weight modulate as the direction of the gesture changes? What are the proportions of the overall height, the ascender, so called, of the h and the x-height part of it, the lower part of it? Then maybe because an h is a straight-sided letter more or less, I would then do an round letter like an o alongside it, in order that I can see how the thick/thin works. I can get a sense of how the weight of the curved part of the o relates to the weight of the straight part of the h. I can then put them together, output them from the laser printer and look at them in combination.

Already there is a huge amount of DNA in just a couple of letterforms like that from which one can extrapolate. I'd then probably do something like a lowercase p, because it's half straight and half round, and also it has a descending stroke, which is another vertical dimension that I would be interested in establishing. So having done that and probably redone them many times in order to be comfortable with the way they looked and worked together, I would then build on that.

If you've got an h, you've got an awful lot of information about m, n, and u in the lowercase. If you've got a p, you've got q and b and d. So to the extent that there are systematic relationships within the lowercase alphabet or the capital alphabet too, when you get to that, I would follow those out. When you're learning to identify type, most people look for slightly capricious letters, like lowercase g or cap Q or something or other. But those are really the last letters that I would look at, because they don't really give me much information about other letters that are related to them. So this rather painstaking business goes on of refining these forms until I'm fairly comfortable with them. Then building on that, and then just as soon as possible, I would get them into words or something that looked like words.

I have a whole lot of text files on the Mac in Quark, some of them not even requiring the complete alphabet. Because for me, the experience of reading something is so critical in judging it as a typeface. Obviously I start without looking at any context or meaning or anything. I'm just looking at forms, but fairly soon I am setting words and phrases and reading. Because I find that that is the acid test, really, of how a typeface performs.

The design process then becomes one of going between, in my case, Fontographer, the software I use where we're actually digitizing the characters, making the font, and Quark, where I'm able to look at text files, different diagnostic files that I have that put letters in awkward combinations, and different things that I need to be aware of. It builds from a very small beginning, like an acorn or a seed, and you just build on that all the time, being conscious of the fact that perhaps you'll have to go back and change the foundation again.

This process is more or less the same with any typeface that I'm involved in. I always make the same mistakes over and over again. The first time I see something output off the laser printer, I often feel very disappointed. You get seduced by working on these big forms on the screen. Then when you see them at actual size, you realize you've been kidding yourself in some way. You then have to back up and revisit them. So this iterative and this rather long-winded process of producing pages and pages and pages of proofs is essentially the way I work.

GH — Are there type designs you did 20 or 30 years ago that you look back at now and say, "What the hell was I thinking then?"

MC — I do, and I don't have to go back 20 or 30 years to look at something and say, "What was I doing?" I often have that reaction. But I find, maybe because I've been doing this for a certain amount of time, that I don't get too hung up. I try to learn from what I've done in the past, and type designers are dependent on the feedback we get from seeing our work in newspapers, magazines, books, on CD covers, wherever they go.

That's the only way we can learn, by seeing how the typeface works well and less well in different circumstances. I'm always alert to that kind of feedback. But I guess I don't often pick up a book at the bookstore and start tearing my hair out because I screwed up something 30 years ago. That happens actually more with the thing that I'm currently working on.

GH — What was the first typeface you designed? Did you design original typefaces when you were in the Netherlands?

MC — Well, in the Netherlands I was learning the technique of cutting punches, which is a very arduous thing. You're working in actual size, in steel, which is beautiful material but pretty resistant. You're working through a loupe the whole time, because you're working at actual size. I doubt if I ever got up quite to one letter a day at that time, and we know from history that many punch cutters cut at least two a day when they were very skilled and proficient.

I was a very raw trainee during the time I was making type by hand. It wasn't until later when I started working with photocomposition that I was able to get some stuff done in the course of the day and feel a sense that things were moving along in a typeface in a more rapid way, which is satisfying. Again, one of these questions that comes up, particularly with students now, is that when I started out making type by hand there was very big penalty for making a mistake. If I'd worked all day on a punch and then at 5 o'clock in the afternoon I made a mistake, I had to start over the following day. It's very difficult to undo a mistake in steel. Nowadays on a computer you have 8 to 10 levels of "undo," or whatever it is. So I get in these interesting conversations with students about what is the best way to learn about metal forms and how to make them.

I was in a situation where I had to think really long and hard before I committed myself to making a letter, because as I say, if I screwed up, there was a big penalty. Nowadays there's essentially zero penalty for making a mistake, and so I would say that I learned the judgment that you need in order to be a designer by having to put a lot of forethought into something. Like someone who's carving an inscription in marble, if you cut the wrong letter you've lost a lot of work and you've got to go out and buy a new piece of marble. So you take a lot of care before you whack the chisel with the mallet. But now a student would say, "Well, big deal—at the end of the day you've done one letter. In the course of a day working on a computer I can make a dozen or maybe more. That's how I learned the judgment. I lay out all these different forms at the end of the day, and I choose one."

I think that's an absolutely valid argument. I don't think the way I did it is inherently any better. It happens to be the way I did it because there wasn't any alternative at that time. But I would never tell a student now that they had to go and learn to make type by very painstaking hand methods and that they would thereby be a better designer. I actually don't believe that. I think there's a lot to be said for the present ability to change your mind without a very big penalty.

GH — The anthropomorphizing of letterforms, how people see them as having a perceived emotion, like a typeface is happy-looking or it's serious—when you're designing a typeface, do those things come into play?

MC — Only very exceptionally. The whole topic of the emotional content of type is a very interesting one. I've often thought about it. But I think in some ways I'm a little bit too close to it to have objective reactions to typefaces in the same way. But yes, I've done some typefaces which perhaps are a little bit more lighthearted than others. Generally speaking, typefaces which are used for display purposes can afford to be a little bit more eccentric than text types.

Most of my types, for one reason or another, have been text types which are fairly sobersided things. They don't have much imagination in them. But I'm not greatly influenced by that when I'm working on a face. What is important, of course, if you have a client, if I'm working for a particular magazine, the people at the magazine—not only the art directors and designers but the editors and writers—will have an image of what this magazine is and how it should appear in the world or should appear to its readers.

That's something I have to be sensitive to, obviously, and that's generally arrived at really by trial and error, by looking at faces that they like or dislike. I'm trying to find a way into their view of the thing typographically, which maybe they can't articulate in typographic terms but I have to try to pick up. So there is an aspect of appropriateness in type design which I am conscious of more than a sort of "Hello, this is a funny typeface. This is a bouncy typeface. This is a deliberately very boring typeface." I don't have that kind of reaction very much myself.

GH — Do you have any examples of magazines you've done this for?

MC — Yeah, it happens that I've been responsible for text type for a number of newsmagazines. There's been *Time, Newsweek, US News and World Report*, also *Sports Illustrated* and some others. Although the types are very different, I think that those are all examples where plainly I couldn't cut loose and do crazy things, because there's a pact between the people who produce magazines like that and the readers. They expect legibility. They expect a pleasing sensation as they read the thing without perhaps being conscious of typographic refinements. On the other hand, I did some work for the wonderful Walker Art Center in Minneapolis, a very avant-garde cultural institution where the typeface I designed for them was distinctly experimental. There were a lot of crazy ways the people in the design department at the Walker could modify this face. So that had a great deal more imagination in it than perhaps something done for a daily newspaper.

I did a lot of type for the local paper here, the *Boston Globe,* and I'm very happy with the way it appears. But if I walk into the offices of the *Globe* for the first time, I can't tell them how the type should appear in their newspaper. It's their newspaper. They are highly sensitized to it. All I can do is try to pick up the right vibes and then put things in front of them where they can then say, "Yeah, this is going in the right direction," or, "No, that's not us at all." You learn that by the experience of working with the resident design staffs of publications.

GH — Great. I'm wondering if we can talk a little bit about Miedinger and Haas, as a sort of introduction to Helvetica. And the reasons why Haas wanted to make a new sans serif.

MC — Well, one way to get into that, Gary, is for me to talk about my joining Linotype in '65, and what was involved in that. That will lead us to cover some of this. I was hired by Mergenthaler Linotype, the American Linotype company, in 1965. The reason for my being invited to do that was that they had a photocomposing machine which was gradually displacing the old Linotype hot metal machine. By '65 the bulk of the work of transferring the library of typefaces that had existed in metal to two-dimensional type had been done and there was an opportunity for us—us being Mike Parker, Director of Typographic Development at Mergenthaler, and me, his new hire—to look at whether photocomposition gave opportunities to do any categories of type that for technical reasons had been impossible in metal. And we did indeed do some typefaces that exploited certain freedoms that came with photocomposition.

But one of the first jobs I got—in fact it was finished the year after I got there in 1966—was to design three very narrow versions of Helvetica. They were called Helvetica Condensed, Extra Condensed, and Ultra Condensed, I think. The relationship between these faces and Helvetica was a little tenuous, perhaps, but there was a great fashion in the sixties for very condensed sans serifs, and Linotype didn't have such a thing. I got the job of designing this trio of condensed faces, which was my first experience in working with Helvetica, but at a considerable remove.

There were three Linotype companies in those days. There was the American company, Mergenthaler, which had its name derived from the inventor of the machine. Then there were two other Linotype companies, one in Britain and one in Germany, more or less controlled, I think, by the American parent company. Then within Germany the German Linotype Company was at least part-owner of Stempel, which was an old, established German type foundry making hand type. Then Stempel, in turn, had a controlling interest in the Haas Type Foundry which was near Basel in Switzerland. So in my early days there in the late sixties and early seventies, working with Mike at Linotype, we went two or three times to visit Stempel and Linotype in Frankfurt and then to went on to Basel to visit Haas.

So I knew some of the people involved in those days with those companies. Miedinger, of course, had left Haas by then. He was still living—I think he lived until about 1980 or so. And Eduard Hoffmann, who had been the boss at Haas when Helvetica, originally called the Neue Haas Grotesk, was designed, had retired. I knew his son Alfred well, who was then running the Haas business. Miedinger I met a few times—he used to come to the meetings of a group called AtypI, an international typographic association which met in different places in Europe—but I didn't speak any German, so we couldn't communicate very much. But Max was well-disposed toward the American company, because when the Mergenthaler Company decided to manufacture Helvetica in this country, it did a lot of good to Max's royalty stream. So he liked Mike Parker and anyone from the American company.

The whole story of how Helvetica came into being is not entirely clear to me. It is said, and I think it's true, that Hoffmann wished to make a modernized version of Akzidenz-Grotesk—or Standard, as it was known in this country—which was essentially a traditional 19th century German sans serif. And his method of doing that was to clean it up, and it was, of course, Max Miedinger who made the drawings for Helvetica. But the curious thing is that when Miedinger worked for Haas, he did not work as a designer. He was actually a salesman. His job was to travel around Switzerland taking orders for fonts of type. And I remember being told, obviously not by Max but by some scuttlebutt at the time, that his boss discovered and noticed that he was only making sales in the large towns in Switzerland. It turned out that Max had lost his driver's license and was having to go around the country by train to get his orders.

So I think he left Haas before Helvetica was designed. He had some art school training, and I believe he had a brother who was also a quite well-known graphic designer in Switzerland. But the puzzling thing, I think, is that Max's name of course is on Helvetica, quite rightly. He received royalties and so on, but most people I knew who were in the know at that time, around Haas and Stempel and Linotype, really thought that the boss, Eduard Hoffmann, had played a very, very important part in the creation of this typeface. Much more important than just saying to Max, "Hey, clean up Akzidenz-Grotesk."

Now, how much of the resulting type design was Hoffmann's brain and how much was Max's eyes and hands is really hard to establish. And by the way, this is not the only case in the history of typography where it's rather hard to disentangle the individual contributions of a pair of people. Usually in this kind of relationship someone, a type founder, or a printer like the Didots in the 1780s, did not, in fact, make their own type. Instead, they employed a skillful person to do that job, like Baskerville in England in the 1750s. He employed a punch cutter. I mean both Baskerville and Didot's names are on those typefaces, but they did not themselves cut them, in the hands-on sense. So as I say, I received the impression from people I knew back in the sixties and seventies that Hoffmann's part in this was a very much more significant one than you might just assume by reading in a textbook that Max Miedinger was the designer of Helvetica.

So that's an interesting situation. As you know, the face was initially called the Neue Haas Grotesk, and then when its beauty and its potential were seen by the German Linotype company, they decided to put it on the Linotype machine. I guess they considered that the name was a little cumbersome, and I guess it was Walter Cunz, the president of Stempel, who came up with the name Helvetica, which is of course what it's been known by ever since.

Looking at it from an American point of view, or perhaps I should say from the point of view of this hemisphere, one very, very important moment in the history of all of this is a decision that Mike Parker took in 1966, soon after I arrived in Brooklyn, to actually make Helvetica as American standard matrices. You could of course import matrices from Europe for a Linotype machine, but they were more expensive, and I think you may have had to have some sort of special mold in order to cast them on the machine. But anyway, Mike's decision to provide Helvetica for the domestic market was hugely important and has been largely forgotten or at least underrated.

By the way, this was not a popular decision internally at Mergenthaler at the time. The factory fought against it because they were still making Trade Gothic, an American-style sans serif that Mike's predecessor Jackson Burke had initiated sometime before. They were still working on that, and they did not at all initially want to do Helvetica. But Mike's a tough guy, and he ramrodded it through. As the factory made each new size and weight of Helvetica, a proof would go up to Mike's office for approval, and I have one of those. I think it's for 7-point Helvetica in Bold, which is dated April of '67, so 7-point wouldn't have been the first size to be made. So they must have been well at work on the series by the spring of 1967.

But as I say, I think when you look at the enormous success that Helvetica had in this country, Mike deserves a huge amount of credit for that just by his business decision of saying, "We're going to make it. We're going to make it here. We're going to make it now and as fast as possible and get it into the market." I don't know if you'll be talking to Mike in the course of this exercise, but it might well be worthwhile. Mike went through the Graduate Graphic Design School at Yale, where in Mike's day Armin Hofmann, the very eminent, wonderful Swiss designer, was one of the professors. I think that Mike was very influenced by Armin and liked Armin very much, as an instructor and as an influence. And so I think Mike came out of his Yale training with perhaps more of an appreciation for Swiss graphic design than might have been the case if he'd been to a different school in this country, which perhaps didn't have the strong links that Yale has had historically with the school in Basel where Armin was based. I think Mike was very open to Swiss graphic design at the time, and that helped enormously in his appreciation when he started to see the Helvetica fonts coming from Germany and saw all the type when we went to Haas. I think he was very receptive to it and very quick to see its virtues in a way that affected the history of the whole thing as it played out.

GH — At that point, what was the atmosphere like? Were people demanding Helvetica, or was there a larger trend toward sans serifs? Was that all that people wanted at the time?

    MC — I was not in a position at Linotype to know about things like sales figures, but my impression is that once Helvetica got manufactured as

American matrices, it took off like wildfire. I think that the ground was prepared for it, in a way—in the sense that typographers were working in a style at that time that allowed Helvetica to come onto a stage which was very much ready for it. And it did take off and was used perhaps more than it should have been, strictly speaking, at the time. But it was a fashion which then solidified into a hugely important part of our typographic repertoire. Times and Helvetica are still the bedrocks of Latin typography.

GH — Are there typefaces, past or present, that you wish you would've designed?

MC — I really don't have favorite and un-favorite typefaces, either of my own or anyone else's, historical or contemporary. The reason is that type design is the raw material end of this. We're the bottom of the food chain. What we do goes into the hands of typographers, graphic designers, art directors, and they have a huge amount of influence, of leverage, on how typefaces appear out there in the world.

So while I don't really have strong feelings like, "This is my very favorite," or, "I hate this typeface," or something, what I tend to say is, "Oh, I like this use of a typeface," or, "I really hate this use of a typeface," whatever the typeface is. Because sometimes you see a designer using a face in a way that has to fail and that makes the typeface look bad, whereas maybe inherently it's not a bad typeface at all.

There are situations in which you find faces which are perhaps not at first glance very promising but that can be splendid in the way they're used, and by the same token, typefaces you would think would be very solid and good ones can be put into situations where they look pretty terrible. For me it's not an objective good/bad thing where typefaces are concerned. It has very much more to do with how well or how badly they are used. That I do react to, much more than I react to typefaces, and of course again, if you work in this business for some time, you get a form of professional deformation, I suppose. I can see a typeface that perhaps my initial reaction to is not tremendously warm, but then I probably know the designer and I probably like the designer very much, so that colors my reaction to the typeface. So my reactions to the extent they happen at all are very subjective ones, generally.

GH — I'm wondering, when you look at Helvetica's letterforms, what do you think? What are your thoughts?

MC — Well, I find them extremely beautiful. I think they've been beautifully formed. There are, by the way, some subtle differences between Neue Haas Grotesk and Helvetica. That's something a little too detailed to get into, but it did change in some ways. And the original cutting of Neue Haas Grotesk is something which I slightly prefer to Helvetica as it was manufactured more broadly.

But when you look at this and you compare it to Akzidenz-Grotesk, on which it's acknowledged to have been based, it is cleaner. The terminals are all horizontal in Helvetica, whereas in Akzidenz they're sheared off on an angle. I just think the whole balance of the face is beautifully constructed. It has sort of an elemental quality. It's very hard for a designer to look at these characters and say, "How would I improve them? How would I make them any different?" They just seem to be, at a fundamental level of being, just exactly right. And as I say, I'm glad I never had to second-guess Helvetica because I wouldn't know what to do.

The only time I found myself at all critical of the design, and this is a little unfair to Helvetica, was in the seventies and I was working with Linotype, and we were commissioned by AT&T to develop a new face for the American telephone books, eventually called Bell Centennial. Since Saul Bass had used Helvetica for AT&T's house style, the initial thought was to base the new phone book typeface on Helvetica. A phone book face, of course, has to exist in tiny size, 6-point, microscopic, and it's going to be printed on newsprint at very high speed. And when we did tests of Helvetica at these miniature sizes at which it was never intended to be super-legible, we found that these in-curling terminals are sheared off on the horizontal in letters like lowercase e and s, and a and c, and many of the figures did not reproduce well at very small sizes. So in Bell Centennial there was a different structure. The letters are much more open, but that is a function of putting a typeface in the very inhospitable typographic environment of the phone book. At the larger sizes, you can't beat Helvetica for its elegance and this ultimate perfection of the forms, I think.

In an obvious sense, type designers make black marks on a white ground, but really type designers think in terms of white ground interrupted by black marks. And Helvetica is a particularly beautiful case where really you are, to a very large extent, looking at the counters, the enclosed spaces in the inside of the letters, which have a beauty of their own. They are almost designed from the inside out—these lovely forms trapped inside the positive part of the letterform. On the other hand, the relationship between the letters in the line is of course, very basic to the design and its legibility, and it's something which is done triumphantly in the design for Helvetica, never better really. There's a lot of foreground/background switching when you're thinking about type design.

GH — Who are some younger type designers whose work you like?
    MC — I said I felt there were an outstanding number of young designers working with type at the moment. You're asking me for some names, which I'm happy to do. I think two of them you'll probably speak to in New York are Tobias Frere-Jones and Jonathan Hoefler, who I've known for a long time and whose work I enormously admire. Cyrus Highsmith works with the Font Bureau here in Boston. Christian Schwartz down in New York—all of these are terribly young designers and of course there are lots in Europe as well, and in Britain.

GH — I read in the profile that the *New Yorker* did of you about how people you meet usually react when you tell them you're a type designer. What do people think of it as a profession?
    MC — I have to say that for a lot of my life I rather dreaded the moment of having to explain that to someone. You find yourself sitting next to some nice person on a plane or a train or something, and you get into a conversation and sooner or later they ask what you do. And if you

say type designer, they generally look completely blank. Occasionally someone will actually know the term but then will say, "I thought they were all dead."

But more recently, since the coming of the personal computer, pretty much everyone knows what a font is. The word "font" is more used than "typeface," of course. You can have a perfectly sensible conversation about fonts with a nine-year-old. They all know how to handle a computer. They may not know all the names, but it's a very different world I live in now. People are aware of fonts. They don't necessarily realize that there's any human agency involved in making the things, designing the things in the first place. They probably think they just sort of fall out of some software ether, that they've just sort of materialized in some way. So when I get into conversations with people about it, it's very interesting to see their reactions.

They're rather incredulous that someone would do something like this as a way of making a living. Then you meet people also who've had the experience of perhaps buying a PC and being given a lot of free fonts with it by a dealer who's trying to make a sale and he's tempting someone by saying, "Look, I have this CD full of fonts." So a lot of people have the impression that fonts don't have a great deal of inherent value in the market, and therefore how can I possibly make a living out of something like that? The economics of it puzzle people very much.

I did some work for Microsoft in the mid-nineties on screen fonts, particularly Verdana and Georgia. Something Microsoft sells gets pretty good distribution, but if they give it away, it goes everywhere, as they did with these screen fonts. So a lot of people know the name Verdana, and I've had quite comical encounters with people who'll say, "Oh, you work with fonts. We just got this memo around the office. We've all got to start using something called Verdana. Have you ever heard of it?" Funny conversations that never would have happened to me 30, 40 years ago.

GH — You've designed typefaces that millions of people read every day. Do you ever think about the way that people may be influenced by the typeface that you created and the words they read in it?

MC — I think my main feeling where that's concerned is that I rather hope they're not aware of my presence. If someone who's reading a daily newspaper or a magazine becomes conscious of the type, it's generally because there's a problem, and I would hope that they didn't have that reaction. So my part in this tends to be fairly anonymous. My type is used in the local paper, the *Boston Globe*. But if I went on the subway in the morning during rush hour and held up an 8 1/2 X 11" piece of paper with the lowercase e in Miller, which happens to be the typeface the *Globe* uses for its text—held it up in front of someone who's reading the *Globe* and said, "Do you recognize this e?" They would not. They'd think I was a lunatic probably. But if they'd been reading the *Globe* for 10 minutes—the "e" is the most frequent letter in the English language, so they've probably consumed thousands of these e's in the course of reading half a page of the *Globe*.

So why don't they recognize the *e*? Again, I'm glad they don't because there would be a problem with the e, probably, if it jumped out of the page and they said, "Oh, God, that's the e that's been tripping me up 10 times every line." But the analogy that I've arrived at is a bit like if I were to hold up a piece of thread in front of someone on the train and say, "Is this thread out of your suit?" "I have no idea." Then I'd say, "You bought this suit. You chose to put in on this morning. Why don't recognize this thread?" Well, the thread is the concern of the person who wove the cloth, the tailor maybe. It's sort of at the atomic level, and it would be very unusual for someone to be able to recognize their suit thread by thread, the same way that people don't recognize typefaces letter by letter on the page. They are consuming something. They're consuming a text. They're reading. They are immersed in the reading. They are getting the sense out of it. It may be easier to read, it may be hard to read. It may be obscure or less obscure. It may be interesting. It may be boring. The typeface can really in those kinds of circumstances only hope to mediate between the writer and the reader in a way that is not too obvious.

If you start talking about posters or the use of display type in other ways, it's a very different situation. There you get the possibilities of other forms of mediation. You start thinking about the psychedelic posters of the sixties, other forms of typography which are perhaps deliberately obscure. Because you are asking people who are, perhaps, almost members of a cult to figure out what it is you're saying. They are prepared to do that. They're prepared to look at a poster for some rock band and say, "Where is this concert and when is it," because they have an interest in that particular form of music, and the labor of deciphering the poster is something which gives them pleasure in itself. But that's a rather unusual reaction. It's an interesting one, but it's an unusual one.

You could not have that relationship with the *Boston Globe* or *Time* magazine or *Newsweek.* That's inconceivable, and most of my work, I would say, has been with text typefaces and other typefaces which are self-effacing for the most part. You hope they have interesting visual qualities because they sometimes get used at larger sizes, but their job is a functional one.

GH — You just said they don't notice the lowercase e, because if they did notice it then there's a problem with it. That concept is fluid from decade to decade or century to century, right? What people thought was legible and clear 200 years ago would be unreadable today.

MC — Absolutely. If you look at Blackletter text or at the typefaces of Gutenberg, even in the German-speaking world they are very difficult to read for anyone who's been brought up on conventional roman and italic. But if you've been brought up on Blackletter, you read that with equal ease and familiarity, and archivists who have to read ancient documents get extremely fluent with scripts that you and I would find totally baffling because we're so un-used to them.

So there's a huge amount of conditioning involved in that. It would be very unusual to go into a book shop in New York or Boston, pick up the latest Elmore Leonard paperback, and find it set in Helvetica. That would be really bizarre. You would normally expect to find it set in some serif typeface. If you cracked the book and it was Helvetica, you'd think, "What is this?"

But then again, in Europe it's much more common to find sans serif used in magazines in a way that it isn't used very much in America. So you do find differences in reading habits and familiarity with the different typefaces in different cultures. In the 18th century when Baskerville's types first came out, people contrasted them with Caslon's types of a few years earlier and they found Baskerville's so shocking that they thought they would blind people, that people would really suffer. Their eyesight would suffer from reading it.

Nowadays it's hard for even typographers sometimes to tell the difference between Baskerville and Caslon. To us they look pretty similar. The idea that one of them would be considered detrimental to your health seems quite absurd to us nowadays. Of course, we're conditioned to such a plurality of different styles of type now. But at one time this was an issue, and introducing new styles of type required people to read something that was pretty unfamiliar to them.
—

Stefan Sagmeister (SS)/ April 19, 2006 New York

Stefan Sagmeister was one of the designers I knew I wanted to have in the film from the start of the project. His graphic design work, with its emphasis on organic, hand-lettered typography, seemed like the antithesis of Helvetica. I spoke with Stefan at his studio.

—

Gary Hustwit — How did you get started in graphic design?

Stefan Sagmeister — In my case, I truly wanted to become a graphic designer. I might have been one of the few students in my class who really wanted to become that rather than a fine artist. Then your parents tell you, "No, no, no, become a graphic designer. At least you won't be a starving artist." I really wanted to be one mostly because when I was 15, 16, 17, I used to be in very bad rock bands, and through that I became interested in the album cover. By the time I actually went to art school, I discovered there was much more to it than that. For a period of at least 10 years after art school, I did many other things before I opened the studio. And at that point, I really concentrated on designing for the music industry, and of course by then the album was gone and we did CD covers.

GH — Did you go to art school in Austria or in Germany?

SS — I attended an art school in Vienna, the University for Applied Arts. Then I came here to the US with a scholarship to study at Pratt in Brooklyn, where I did a master's program in media. I loved art school, every aspect of it. If it would be up to me, I would still be in art school right now. It was just that they forced me out to get a proper job. But in some ways I still am, because I do teach at the School of Visual Arts here in New York and at Cooper Union. I also do plenty of workshops around the world—in Lebanon, Alaska, Venezuela, Paris. It is a good job. I've been doing it probably for 20 years now, and I still like it.

GH — When you first attended art school in Vienna, what was the curriculum like? What was the style that was prevalent in design at that time?

SS — They have a master class system there, so you basically stay with the same professor for the entire four years you are at university. We wound up learning mostly from each other, which I think is the same case in many good art schools—you learn more from your fellow students than you actually do from the faculty. We had a very old professor. His favorite designer was Cassandre, and so we learned about composition quite extensively, which is definitely something that helped. But with anything else that was happening at that time—in the eighties or so—we basically had to figure it out ourselves.

GH — When you were in school, who were some of the designers who influenced you?

SS — I think that in the eighties, the biggest influence on me would have definitely been a company in London called Hipgnosis. As you know, they were the kings of the album cover. They did most of the work for Pink Floyd and all of the work for Led Zeppelin. So they had big bands, big budgets, and big ideas. At one time, I actually visited them in London and wanted to work for them but they had just closed.

GH — What was the first album cover that you actually designed?

SS — The very first album cover that I designed was for friends of mine, in Switzerland—a jazz orchestra. They were very good; it was an excellent CD, but self-published. So it went nowhere as far as sales were concerned. We had done the cover in Hong Kong, designed it in Hong Kong, because I was working there at the time, and it worked out well. It definitely was an experience that I felt I should do more of.

At that time, there were so many advantages to doing a CD cover. It did not get thrown away, so it was one of those very few packages that really was kept and treasured. It was small so you could put a lot of work in there and then wind up with something very portable. It was definitely international, so you would see the results everywhere in the world. It was printed in large quantities. Maybe best of all, it allowed you to visualize something that is nonvisual. So you could just listen to music and have that inspire the visuals, which is something that I actually miss now that we do not do them anymore. That is a beautiful process.

So much good art came out from the album covers and CD covers. In contrast, relatively few good pieces came out of the movie poster. In the movie poster, you start with some sort of visual and translate that from one medium to another, which is successful in only very few cases. The movie still that's often used in the design rarely works well on the poster. While in the music world, there is a complete transformation of the content, which I think is responsible for the fact that a lot of good work came out of that.

GH — I want to talk about typography. When you started out and when you were designing record covers, were you using Letraset? Were you hand-drawing things? What was your creative process like when you first started using type?

SS — My first design job—I call it a job because it resulted in doing something that was printed—was at a youth magazine in Western Austria. I actually joined the team as a writer but found out fairly quickly that I enjoyed doing the layout for the magazine much more than writing the articles. And of course, there was no money whatsoever, so we did not really have money to buy Letraset sheets. We got them donated from design companies, and of course they were all missing the As and the Es, so we always had to come up with some sort of trick of making an upside-down 9 into something else, or in many cases, when there were too many letters missing, you redrew it by hand altogether. Definitely, it was an important experience for me to get to see what a different layout can do to the meaning of text and content in general.

GH — Were you in art school right around the time of the Macintosh and early layout software?

SS — It probably would have been in California at that time, but for sure not in Vienna. I probably was part of the last generation that was taught doing everything by hand. I think it literally changed a year or two after me. We used to draw 10-point type with a brush, but I do not have my students do that now. I don't think that there was an exceptionally fruitful learning experience in that. But I could do it when called upon. By the time I opened this studio, the computer had completely transformed the field, and we were set up in that way from the very beginning.

GH — I'm wondering if you can talk about your approach to designing with words, both on a computer using fonts and the more hand-drawn work. It seems like you do more organic-looking, not just straight-out-of-the-computer type, or use photographs of three-dimensional objects?

SS — I think, in general, I was always fairly bored looking at type books and deciding over and over again which type to pick for a certain project. It just did not seem like a very interesting task to do. So here and there, on records and on CD covers, we started to do our own type. There was one instance, the cover of Lou Reed's album *Set the Twilight Reeling,* where the feedback was wonderful, both from the artist as well as from the audience.

I think it has a lot to do with timing, as these things often have. This must have been in the mid-to-late nineties, when modernism got hip again and you had a lot of people, even younger people, doing International Style. I think there was also a web influence that is thankfully long forgotten by now, the time when everybody working in print mimicked what was going on onscreen. I think because of that—not so much by design but by accident—this hand-drawn typography that we first did for Lou Reed resonated. And at the same time, I also got tired of our "Style Equals Fart" manifesto . . . you know, saying that style means nothing and that it was just hot air. I really learned that stylistic questions *can* actually help transport the content quite efficiently.

In the studio, I also allowed us to stay with that method after we had done one handwriting project. I let us explore that for a while, and numerous projects came out that way—in all sorts of directions. They came in more funny directions, like for an AIGA cover that had a headless chicken on it, and in a more serious direction when our intern carved a hand type onto my skin for a lecture poster. That kind of typography strangely became so well known in the design community that some people thought that it was all we did. Thankfully that is not the case.

I still love that aspect of the job. I still appreciate the fact that type can tell the story of its making in an instant, with a single image. It tells you about its process in a very elegant way, in a very fast way. And I think that is probably the reason why it got well known. Of course, there was a shock effect as well, which I do not mind either, shock being another element of surprise.

GH — And then that approach evolved into the three-dimensional, sculptural typographic pieces? Can you talk about this?

SS — Yeah, I think this idea came almost directly from the handwriting projects, even though I am absolutely, 100 percent sure that it's not our idea to develop type into a more sculptural form, you know, like make it in 3-D, photograph it, make it out of something, have it grow in many ways and develop it. At that time, we had a series that called for typographic pieces, and I just did not want them to be visually boring, so I thought that there was a way to make a stronger visual out of it. I feel that as powerful and constructive as the computer is in our lives, it made the job much more boring on a daily basis. If we look at pictures of a design studio in the sixties and seventies, you see 20 different tools, from an inkwell to sanders to paints. People moved all around. This was all replaced with a single seat in front of a screen.

By building it, by being much more hands-on, I think it made the process of making more interesting. Because of the coldness of many pieces of communication, vast parts of the audience do not even recognize that there is a human being behind it, making these things. I am sure if we go down to 14th Street and ask people, "Who do you think makes the *New York Times*? How does that come out?" People would probably know that there are writers, obviously, but as far as the design is concerned, they think that it is made by a machine. Part of that is because it is made to *look* like it is being done by a machine. They would not really recognize that there is actually a person behind it, making very clear decisions about form and about beauty, even to design a functional front page.

So I thought that a more personal approach would be able to beat that. In addition, I myself got fairly disappointed with modernism in general, from numerous angles. I think that the whole revival of modernism—just taking the style and leaving everything else alone—was fairly lame to start with. I think many people criticized that—even the original version of modernism, be it in Vienna 1900 or be it in the Bauhaus—and how it disagrees with so many of these statements. I mean, I was in Dessau at the Bauhaus last year, and I couldn't believe how much inherent fakeness there was. For one thing, all this talk about being on the worker's side and being against the bourgeoisie, and then a week later, I go over to Brno in the Czech Republic, and there is a gigantic villa built by Mies van der Rohe at exactly the same time for this industrial tycoon—the very pinnacle of a bourgeois building done in radical modernist style. But if you go to the Bauhaus and read Mies's quotes on the wall at the exhibit, it's all very anti-bourgeois.

In architecture, for sure, but also in communications, the International Style has been the dominant way of expression for such a long time—definitely since the sixties—that it simply became boring. If I see a brochure now with lots of white space that has six lines of Helvetica on top and a little abstract logo on the bottom, and a picture of a business-man walking somewhere, the overall communication that it conveys to me is, "Do not read me, because I will bore the shit out of you." Not just visually but also in content, because the content would likely say the same as it says to me visually. This aspect was totally different in the twenties, when this was all fresh and new and had bite.

GH — So this modernist revival approach of only using three or four fonts and that it's all about clear communication, are you at odds with this kind of philosophy and process now?

SS — Well, I've always thought that this entire idea of using three or four typefaces was very suspect. I think this could be interesting to do for a single project as an exercise to put up additional limitations in order to focus yourself. But as a strategy over a lifetime, I think it's akin to a writer saying, "I am only going to write in three or four words." Yes, you probably could do it, but for one, why would you, and secondly, would it really yield an interesting body of work over a lifetime? I just always thought that was a strange long-term limitation.

And in my own case, I am interested in doing very, very different kinds of jobs. We'll do an annual report for a lighting company; we might do an exhibit for a museum; we might do a cover for a speedmetal band. Now, if I would use the same approach to these projects, I would be an idiot. If I would use the same typefaces and the same approach to these projects, it would be like me having only three pieces of clothing that I would wear, if I jump into a public swimming pool or if I go to a black-tie dinner. It just makes no sense to me. That is unless I have a very limited client base that calls for the same approach over and over again.

GH — What are your thoughts about Helvetica? Obviously, it is so linked to that International Style, sixties advertising, logos. Fifty years later, it's still here. What are your thoughts about it?

SS — I think Helvetica is a fine typeface. It has all the aspects that you would want from a multi-usable typeface. I think what most people love about it is its readability, even though there was a fairly good argument by Zuzana Licko, who says that readability is directly connected to how much you are used to seeing any typeface. So considering that Helvetica is probably one of the top five most-used typefaces in the world, by default its readability becomes very high.

To my eye, it is fine. But in the sans-serif families, it was never my favorite. To me Frutiger or News Gothic are just as fine. And I remember that when Lars Müller did his book on Helvetica, he wrote to us to send in samples. And it was then that I discovered that we had never used it. It was not because I hated it or anything it was just that we had never used it. Perhaps I thought there were enough other designers out there who could make good use of it. And you'll have them as part of the movie, Experimental Jetset, I would assume? They will be part of the movie?

GH — Yes, and also people who think that it's the worst thing ever and it's the bane of visual culture. What are your thoughts about the effect of technology and the explosion of typefaces linked with computer design in the nineties. Did it seem like that was a good thing for design?

SS — I think that we all had very big hopes with the democratization of the tools, that it would spawn an incredible revolution—not just in design but also throughout the arts. Now that you can have a music studio for $3,000 or $4,000 in your home that is comparable in quality to a $200,000 music studio in the eighties, or you could make a film with ten grand, you are very much in the picture. And I would have thought and hoped that it would create incredible pieces of work. I believe it did some here and there, but it really did not.

I think that just like in film, just like in music, there is much, much more of it, because the tools are accessible and fairly easy to use. Everybody looks much slicker than they used to. I think it has definitely created a much wider awareness of design. Helvetica being one of those cases where it is now a word that's widely understood among the general public. I am sure it was not 20 years ago. That has something to do with so many more people dealing with it on their own computers and being somehow engaged in the business of design. I think that this is another reason why you see a design topic on the cover of *Time* or *Newsweek*, or that you have a little design show on TV. It is now part of people's everyday life.

GH — This is sort of off-topic, but what do you think about graffiti? Are you inspired by it at all?

SS — I have several but not necessarily matching views on graffiti. Tagging, in general, I find fairly boring. I mean, to leave your name on the corner of a street seems like such an act of self-promotion, such a boring expression of "I have been here," that there is no attractiveness, no inherent attractiveness to me at all, outside of—of course, yes I suppose there are some letterforms. What falls under the term "street art"—people doing interesting things on the street—I find much more interesting. I also think that there is a true expression going on. There is graffiti that has the beautification of the city in mind, and there, I've seen many interesting things. Here in New York there are several artists who do fantastic work. I saw Swoon talk about it recently; she's a lovely woman. I lived for a number of months last year in Berlin, where there is much of that direction also going on. For a city to bring art to the street, I think is a very, very interesting thing. And you know, stickers and stencils probably live somewhere in between. There are those that are truly interesting and there are those that are truly boring.

GH — I suppose, the same could be said about signage, commercial signage and advertising?

SS — Absolutely. I mean, if you now happen to walk down to Times Square at 11:30 at night, I think it is pretty exciting, it's more exciting than it was 10 years ago. Truly I think that the more that is going on there the better—more layers, more blinking. And at the same time, I find those LED screens above the subway stations in the Village unbelievably annoying. For one thing, they do not fit with anything else that is going on in that neighborhood. For somebody like me who does not watch a lot of TV at all, if I see something that is moving, I tend to have to watch it, so it becomes very annoying. In airports, I cannot stand those CNN screens hanging everywhere, so I literally have to find a seat where I am not facing one, because otherwise I have to look at that thing, and I do not want to look at that thing. I have other things to do.

GH — Have you done any environmental signage or that type of environment information architecture, or whatever they call it? Is it something that you would want to do?

SS — Not extensively, no. We have done 3-D-ish things, we've done charts that blow up, or we've designed cars that go around and have a message. But we wouldn't be known as a studio that does signage for a museum or an airport.

GH — But it is something you would be interested in trying?

SS — You know, I'm not interested enough to jump through the learning curve. If you were doing an airport project, you would want some very extensive knowledge about people's behavior, and all that stuff. I mean, I know Paul Mijksenaar, the guy who did Amsterdam Schiphol, and he's also working on the New York airports that they've just started implementing. Of course, they're implementing it so crappily that whatever he does has only limited power. So I think I would have to turn down an airport job, because I would have to immerse myself for a year or two into this to do it properly.

GH — Earlier you talked about how most people, when they see the *New York Times,* or pretty much any printed piece, they just assume that it popped out of a computer and that there was no human involvement. Can you talk a little bit more about that? Or the flip side, how much do you think about the viewer and their relationship to your design?

SS — We think quite a bit about the viewer on every project. Every project is custom-made for that audience. And I would think that the audience is my deciding factor if I, in the end, wind up liking my design or not. If I design a cover for the Stones that I love, but their audience hates, I would think that it is a bad cover. No matter if I loved it at the time I designed it, or when I gave it to the Stones. If I learn that the audience really thinks that this is a bad cover, it is a bad cover. Period. It's totally different in the art world, but in the design world, I think that these things have to work. And in the case of a CD cover, working means being accepted by the fan base of the band.

Of course, if we are talking about airport signage, the function is a completely different one. Nobody has to like it, but it has to get you there in a very, very efficient way. But I am a big believer in the fact that design has to work. I do think that—in a fairly simplistic way—modernism led to everything being on a grid. It led to everything looking similar, being designed in a similar way. When you present these things to the client— yes, of course it works, because it says all the things that you were briefed on and what it was supposed to say. It has all the elements in place, but because everybody is so bored by it and nobody looks at it, it actually does not work anyway. The six pieces of junk mail that I got from various banks yesterday, probably all of them were designed under a heavy modernist influence and all of them went unread and went straight into the garbage bin. It did not work, at least in my case.

GH — Maybe you should start designing some junk mail.

SS — For banks? Maybe later.

GH — Have you ever designed a typeface?

SS — No, we have never designed a typeface. We designed numerous custom faces for projects and numerous custom-designed headlines. But I just never felt the need to make a typeface out of it. There was one instance when a talented intern worked here—she did an experimental face for a typographic magazine, but it was more of an experimental project rather than an actual usable face. With the thousands and thousands of faces out there and thousands that we have on our systems, I've just never felt the need to add to that.

GH — So there's not going to be a Sagmeister Bold Italic?

SS — No, I have no desire to have Sagmeister Bold Italic be part of the FontShop catalog. It is not one of my goals in life. I think I will happily die without it.

—

Jonathan Hoefler (JH) & Tobias Frere–Jones (TFJ)/ May 4, 2006 New York City

Few young type designers have reached the level of success and respect that Jonathan and Tobias have, through their partnership in the Hoefler & Frere-Jones type foundry. But in 2014, at the time of this book's publication, Jonathan and Tobias were probably better known for the fact that they were no longer working together. "The Beatles of Typography Split Up" and similar headlines have reached beyond the design world and into mainstream media. But at the time of my interview with them in their studio, they were still (seemingly) working well together.

—

Gary Hustwit — How did each of you get involved in this?

Jonathan Hoefler — It's the one question I'm always unprepared for, it seems. I've always wanted to be involved in typography. I came to graphic design through an interest in type. I worked as a designer for a few years and found that when I was doing that, I was focusing just on the typography of a project to the exclusion of everything else. I would get a job as a book cover designer and focus on the lettering of the title and ignore the author photograph and the illustration and the color palette, the paper, the format, all the important things. Through doing design for a few years, I realized that there's actually business to be had in designing typefaces themselves as opposed to merely working with fonts, and I gradually began the business to create fonts on a custom basis for clients.

Tobias Frere-Jones — I never actually had much of an interest in general graphic design by itself. For me, the interest was always drawing the letters and making the typefaces. I had many years ago planned to be a writer but found it just too hard, actually. I had also wanted to be a painter, but I had a terrible sense of color and perspective and so on. I found this was actually sort of a nice middle ground between the two, between painting and working with forms and working with the language, but still not doing all the hard work of being a writer. I came to it through a compromise of the fields that I wanted to be working in. I went to the Rhode Island School of Design with a specific intent of going into its design program and learning how to draw typefaces and coming out the other end and being a professional typeface designer. Then I found out that no one actually teaches anyone how to do this. All type designers, historically, have just learned on the job through apprenticeships or just experimenting on their own. That's what I ended up doing myself.

JH — I think it's a common thing for type designers to have an interest in many things that are all peripheral to typography. I mean, Tobias and I certainly share an interest in language and computer science and design—

TFJ — And music.

JH — And music. It's sort of more peripheral, but there are a lot of things that inform the nature of the process of typeface design. The more of those things you tend to engage yourself in, the more interesting the work can be.

TFJ — I think typeface design, more than other kinds of design, is the intersection of lots of other disciplines. Especially these days, it's as much engineering as it is artistry. You could say the same thing about architecture, I suppose. Certainly within the specialties of graphic design, it's the one that's most frequently tied up with other kinds of disciplines, whether it's language and orthography or engineering and computer science and so on.

GH — When you guys are at dinner parties and you tell people that you're type designers, what's the reaction people have?

TFJ — Well, for a long time it just used to be a blank stare. Then a long explanation of what we do. "There are these things called typefaces. You use them. You see them. Trust me, you've seen them. We make those for these people and these other people." But now I tell someone that I'm a typeface designer, and they say, "Oh, you mean fonts? Oh, yeah. That's cool."

JH — Or worse. They say, "I've done a little of that too. My brother does that." You find people have actually been engaged in typography more and more on a nonprofessional level than ever in the past. I mean, it's sort of a standing joke in the industry that for years the worst thing you could do on an airline flight is not have headphones on, because somebody would say, "What do you do?" Then suddenly you're spending eight hours describing the history of printing and typography and the nature of graphic design, what advertising is. Now people are beginning to get it. I think with the font menu on their computers it's easier to appreciate and understand.

TFJ — I think one of the best experiences I had—or one of the more memorable experiences—in trying to explain what it is I do was just as I was leaving college. I was in a bar in Providence, Rhode Island, unwinding after a class or something. I was drawing, just doodling a couple of letters on the back of a bar napkin, and some Providence local saw this and was trying to figure out what I was doing.

He couldn't figure it out, so he had to come over and ask me what I was doing. So I explained, "I'm a typeface designer. I make these things called typefaces." He had absolutely no idea what I was talking about. So I explained it again using some kind of metaphor, I forget what, and he still didn't understand. So I explained it a third time, using some other kind of metaphor I just made up on the spot, and he finally got it. A lightbulb went off. He said, "Okay, wait. Let me see if I understand this. Your job is, you make new letters and new alphabets. Is that it?" I said, "Yeah, that's it. That's what I do." He thought about that for a minute, and he looked kind of worried. So he leaned over to me and said, "Is that illegal?" I was never quite sure why he would think that. Like, I'm breaking the law or rearranging the laws of gravity or something by messing with the alphabet.

GH — That's hilarious. When you both started working, were you hand-drawing type?

TFJ — Oh, the very first things I drew were done in high school with a rapidograph on a drawing board when I was 16 years old. I didn't have those tools available to me right at that time. I got my hands on them relatively soon after that.

GH — Obviously, technology has changed the worlds of graphic design and type design. Can you explain your process? When clients come to you, how do you work with them?

JH — We really do two different kinds of work for clients. Half of them are things where we have a very specific visual brief to address, and the other half are ones where we have a very specific technical brief. A visual brief might be from a client like *GQ* magazine that says, "We want a sans-serif typeface that looks modern that can also look racy and have a kind of credibility to it."

TFJ — "It should be masculine."

JH — "Masculine, but not clichéd." Or a brief from *Harper's Bazaar* that says, "We want a typeface that is elegant and has a sort of high-waisted fashion quality to it that other fonts lack." Those are challenging things to do. To turn adjectives into form is kind of the thrust of what we do. It can be a very frustrating process. It can be a very satisfying one also. To try to turn these interpretations into things that are not merely visual but are recognizable to others and are interpreted the same way is really the big challenge.

The other projects are ones that have a much more material brief. These are times like when the *Wall Street Journal* came to us saying, "We're redesigning our stock section, and we need to fit six pages of stock listings into a smaller-sized page, but remain equally legible." That was the brief we got for the Retina typeface that Tobias designed. In that case there was no visual brief. No one said, "The typeface has to look quirky or elegant," or anything like that. It just had to work in some purely functional way. In some ways that's a much more challenging brief, to not have anything to push against. To not have any kind of starting point visually can be difficult. At the same time, to have a very material construct for a project makes it easy to evaluate. We can say, "Did this indeed satisfy the brief? Have we fit as much copy in as before? When focus groups read the new newspaper, are they aware the typeface has changed? If so, is that a good thing or a bad thing?"

The best jobs have equal aspects of both. We have a visual criterion that has to do with the flavor of the design and a much more measurable mechanical one having to do with how it works. That's sort of the intersection where I think most of the work that we do really lives.

TFJ — It's rare that we have a project that's entirely one and none of the other; there's usually some aspect of both. We did a number of typefaces for *Martha Stewart Living* magazine, and they had a very precise aesthetic agenda to them. We had to fit into a style that's already very well established. But there are also very elaborate technical considerations with how the magazine is printed and how the designers will use the typeface at large sizes and at small sizes and for captions and photos and so on. We had to absorb that into our strategy, and also create one seamless solution for them.

JH — It's really fun when a typeface comes to us from one of those two orientations and we have a chance to solve the other one as well. *Martha Stewart Living* is a great example. They came to us with an editorial brief about their plan to reorganize the magazine, and a visual one in terms of the things they wanted the typeface to do, and then gave us a chance to solve some production problems for them as well that they really hadn't thought about in the past. Doing a little of each is always the most fun and most gratifying, I think.

GH — Are there other case studies of past work you'd like to talk about?
    JH — I think Lever House is probably a good one. One of the great challenges in typeface design is working as a team. It has historically been seen, whether it is or not, as a one-person activity. It's very difficult for two designers with two very distinct styles to collaborate on a project, especially since you can always tell who drew what.

When Tobias and I began working together seven years ago, one of the first commissions we got was from Pentagram, the design studio, to do a typeface based on the existing signage of Lever House, the Gordon Bunshaft skyscraper on Park Avenue. In the case of that project, we had to take the existing lettering as it was rendered in a variety of media—metal letters applied to the Park Avenue facade, an engraved cornerstone, cast metal letters on the window—a bunch of things that were all kind of a comparable style but not quite the same.

TFJ — Not quite exact.

JH — Right. We had to distill those down to one master plan or typeface and deliver it to the client so it could be the Lever House typeface. They had digital compilations of at least three different technologies being used to make the original lettering. The material came to us and we collaborated on making the actual characters together. I think if the job works, you really can't tell that the old and new are different or that Tobias's characters and mine are different. We're actually not really sure who drew what in that typeface. We'll see that capital G, and I remember discussing it, but I don't actually remember whose hand it came from. We do a lot of work in architecture; a lot of it satisfies those two different criteria of having a visual brief and a functional one. It's a lot of fun to do.

TFJ — We have a kind of fascination with things that are difficult in some way. The briefs that are very straightforward, where you can immediately see what the answer is, aren't really that exciting. It's figuring out how to capture this historical style and sort of fill in the blanks of something, of a design that's missing, and make it work in cast aluminum, or engraved in stone. That's a much higher hurdle to jump. It's the same as making something legible at 6-point on newsprint in columns of data. That's a tough nut to crack. So we find that proportionally more interesting.

JH — But the good news for us is that clients are more aware of that than ever. We have clients working on signage for railway platforms or LED signs for airplanes or things like that, and they suddenly realize that typography is an integral part of the experience and that there's no font that exists that satisfies that specific situation. That creates these opportunities for us to come in and think about what we can do with the material available.

TFJ — Right. There are many situations where you can't just use any old font. There are only a small number of designs that will work in a newspaper because of its particular pressures and constraints versus text on screens, or text on signs, or in wayfinding and so on. You can't just use any old thing that happens to look nice. There has to be a strategy behind it that anticipates what's going to happen.

JH — There are also more restrictions than you would think. We have a client who last year redesigned a newspaper in Croatia. The universe of typefaces that work in newsprint is already pretty small; you combine that with the fonts that can work on a newspaper that's getting smaller in its format, where the type has to be much more economical, and that's fewer fonts still. Combine those with the number of fonts that exist in the Croatian language, and you're looking at a very small number of fonts that turned out to be zero. The project for us was to come in, figure out what the newspaper actually needed in terms of its linguistic and technical and aesthetic demands, and create a font that satisfied all three of these things at once.

GH — Walk us through a little bit of the mechanics of actually designing a typeface. When we talked to Matthew Carter, he was like, "Oh, I start with the lowercase h. Then I go to the lowercase o."
  JH — I'm afraid we do the exact same thing.

TFJ — Yeah, the process he was describing hasn't changed much for 200 years or so. It establishes these controls against which other later drawings can be judged. But even in just drawing the capital H, the capital O, capital D, lowercase n, o, and p, there are already dozens of decisions you have to make about weight and width and proportion and curvature. If there are serifs going on, there's a whole other realm of things to contend with. Drawing those first six characters can actually take quite a while.

JH — It's certainly the case that there's kind of a logarithmic curve for the amount of work that goes into a typeface. There's tons and tons of work to the first three characters, and then half as much work in the next three characters. By the time you get to doing the bullet and the vertical bar, there are fewer decisions to make, and it's a little bit easier. But the ratio of time in to characters out is daunting on a project. I think the only thing that's really changed about typeface design in the last 100 years in terms of the process is that the medium in which designers are designing letterforms, and the medium in which they record it for reproduction, are the same.

Going back a century, you have a draftsman doing drawings on paper, somebody else converting this into templates that somebody else might trace with a pentagraph to make an engraved matrix, and so on down the line. Now when we design a typeface, the actual data that we use as our medium is the data users experience when they set the font. That certainly made it easier to think about type from a technological perspective and an aesthetic one at the same time, but it also means the designers are now making more of the decisions than ever before. I don't think a designer like Dwiggins in the 1930s and 1940s thought much about kerning the way we do. That's sort of the bête noir of typography for a lot of designers.

GH — Can we talk about Gotham and what went into the making of that typeface? The inspiration, the process of designing it, and then the end?

TFJ — Yeah. Gotham was the face that came out of the commission for GQ. Their initial brief to us was almost entirely aesthetic, where they wanted a sans serif with a geometric structure that would look masculine and new and fresh and be versatile in the various parts of the magazine, their editorial settings.

JH — There was a second part of that, as well. Arem Duplessis and Paul Martinez, who were designing the magazine, gave us a collection of things they had been looking at as possible candidates. Half of them were incredibly slick, sort of techno CD, band poster, rave things, very up to the moment. The other half was very traditional, typefaces like Futura, which is now 80 or 90 years old.

TFJ — Lots of Bauhaus stuff.

JH — A lot of things from the Bauhaus, a lot of things from early modernism. It was clear they had this sort of dual agenda of something that was going to be very, very fresh and yet very established, to have a credible voice to it. That's where we began our process.

TFJ — One of the first things that occurred to us is that there were already quite a lot of typefaces that were taxonomically similar, Futura being one of them. We wanted to be sure that what we gave them was actually something new and something original or a new contribution to the palette of what's out there. As we were thinking about this, we both remembered a piece of lettering here in New York City.

We both grew up in Manhattan. Independently, we've walked around the streets and earmarked pieces of lettering or signage that we thought would be a good seed or starting point for a project somewhere down the line. We had both, on our own, noticed the lettering on the Port Authority Bus Terminal up on 42nd Street and 8th Avenue. The lettering over the front door is this very plain, geometric letter, but it's not the kind of letter that a type designer would make. It's a kind of letter that an engineer would make. It was born outside of type design in some other world and has a very distinct flavor from that.

JH — I'd say it's also representative of a style of lettering we'd both noticed for years. It even began before the Gotham project. We'd been discussing this kind of lettering that we've seen, and I don't know whether there's a name for it in literature; we sort of describe it as this, like, American vernacular, mid-century thing. You see it painted. You see it engraved. You see it made of aluminum. The Port Authority example just seemed like an especially exemplary one. Some of the difficult letters have been handled really well. It had the kind of evenness and spacing that recommended it to a typeface. So we took that as the seed for the Gotham project.

TFJ — It also just had the personality that seemed to fit the magazine really well. It was very strong and emphatic in a way that seemed to suit their content.

JH — But it wasn't self-aware. There's something very unmannered about it, that I felt—we both felt, well, actually, all four of us felt—was useful to the magazine. It's very plainspoken. I think "nonnegotiable" was one of the words we used earlier on to describe it, and they thought that was a good fit for the editorial content in the magazine.

GH — So then you took those starting letters in-house and . . .
TFJ — Well, that was the primary source, but we noticed, as Jonathan was saying, that this style exists elsewhere in the city, just in smaller pieces and scattered more widely. I began looking at other sources around the city, getting out a camera and walking the streets, taking pictures of the fronts of office buildings with the building number above the door, and signs over liquor stores, and so on. I was seeing this unrecognized thread of common style that has existed in these structures for years and hadn't really been identified and named. That was one of the more exciting parts of this, doing the literal legwork in finding the style and sort of capturing that in a typeface.

JH — When Gotham began, the source material that we had to work with was one inscription in one weight and one size, capitals only. To make a typeface from that, the first step is to expand that source into a full character set, which means inventing a lowercase, numbers, punctuation, things that are really morphologically quite alien to the letters we had to work with.

Step two is adapting a set of weights from that; taking the font that became a bold and making that into a medium, book, light, extra light, black, ultra, and then doing italics for all those things, and then doing it condensed for all those weights. It's really this one seed crystal that grew into this vast universe of things.

GH — What has the response been to Gotham? How does it feel to see it out there being used?

JH — I think part of the ways that Gotham has been used—it's been either satisfying or surprising or both in the year since it was released—is seeing the way the most distant parts of the family are used for unexpected things, and the ways in which that core member, the Gotham Bold typeface, is still used in ways that are very, I think, sympathetic with the Port Authority sign. When you think about things like the Tribeca Film Festival logo that's all set in Gotham Bold, it almost literally quotes the arrangement of lettering in the Port Authority. Clearly, some have recognized that it has this New York quality to it that's very recognizable.

TFJ — Right. It was really satisfying for us to see it used for the inscription at the Ground Zero Memorial cornerstone, which is still, what, that was laid two years ago now?

JH — Yeah.

TFJ — And still 100 percent of what's been built there is that one stone. But the designer at Pentagram, Michael Gericke, was quoted as saying it was not only the formal qualities of Gotham that brought him to choose it for that design, but also its history of being made of the local stuff of the streets of Manhattan. It seemed appropriate to put it in that position.

GH — On the topic of usage of your typefaces, and this is just across the board, not just Gotham, what are some of the best uses you've seen? We just talked about a couple of them. But also, what are some of just the worst and the strangest usages that you've run into?

JH — That's getting harder to say.

TFJ — Yeah. I think some of the things that we would find irritating are because we put so much work into anticipating how a typeface might be used and how it can best accommodate its content, and it's frustrating to see someone needing that but not knowing that it's there and not knowing how to use it. In many cases we have specific variations meant for very large sizes or very small sizes, because the eye needs different proportions and different renditions to see things most clearly at those sizes. So when someone is using the version we made for very small sizes up at a headline size and everything looks kind of weird, or they're using the headline version cut down to a text size and everything looks kind of starved and crowded together, that's frustrating.

JH — I think a good art director can pull those things off, though. I mean, we worked with Scott Dadich, from *Texas Monthly* magazine, who used the Retina typeface that Tobias designed for *The Wall Street Journal*. This is a font designed for type between 4- and 5-point. And he uses it in the size of a full page. I think an art director who is sensitive and witty can pull those things off well.

TFJ — But that's rare.

JH — Yes, it's rare. I think it's more that people don't know what's inside. It's like, invariably, when I travel, I hear somebody at a hotel desk screaming about something. It's always, "My room is too hot. Why is the room so damn hot?" and the concierge says, "Did you turn the thermostat down?" The guest says, "I didn't find a thermostat in the room." But of course, there is one.

Typography has that sort of same analogy. I mean, there are all kinds of things in a typeface that people don't know about. If they don't know about them, they're going to complain that they're absent. I think the big frustration is finding that the work we put into things isn't always recognized as being inside. I think that's ultimately our fault as well. It's kind of a public education issue we need to get more involved in.

GH — It's like you're designing a jet aircraft, and people are just taxiing it around the runway, never taking off?
　　JH — Exactly.

　　TFJ — Yeah.

GH — But are there any specific really bizarre uses you've encountered, like you walked into a store and saw one of your fonts on a toilet paper package or something?
　　JH — I do have one experience that still is hands above the rest of them. Years ago I was at a resort in Belize and there was this condominium development going up down the road. I drove down to see what was happening. They had this big billboard up saying, "The future home of," whatever it was, "Palm Village Condominiums." The pool was in place and some of the first buildings were being done.

But the billboard was in a hand-painted rendering of a typeface that Tobias had designed for an experimental type magazine produced by an editor in London and a font company in Berlin. This typeface was designed to degrade itself as you used it, to have this kind of industrial pollution quality to it, and here it was being used for this Shangri-La getaway in the tropics. Somebody had painted it by hand. They had chosen this typeface that was so culturally diametrically opposed to the environment it was being used in, and rendered it so lovingly. I was amazed.

TFJ — Also it's one of the most difficult things you could ever hope to render by hand. There are a thousand other things that would have been easier to make, never mind the visual mismatch between this kind of aggressive industrial disaster look, and the tropics. You can see the individual brushstrokes making all these sort of crinkly edges and sort of degraded bits. That was pretty startling.

GH — That's great. You talked a little bit about inspirations and some of them being non-typographic inspirations. Do you want to talk about how those things can relate to type design somehow—music or painting, et cetera?

JH — Well, the most immediate thing outside of typography is other kinds of lettering. Typography is specifically the history and science of printing types, but lettering is expressed in every other possible media. There's calligraphy, inscription lettering, signage. One thing that we often try to do is look outside of just printing types for visual inspiration for things. Typefaces based upon engraved maps or Renaissance calligraphy and things that aren't just fonts for book reading. In terms of things that are further afield, I'm not sure how those translate.

TFJ — Yeah, I think it's difficult to draw a straight line from this piece of music we heard to this thing we drew or something like that. I think there are some parallels certainly with music and architecture, if nothing else, for the kind of mind-set that they require of looking at the very microscopic details and the grand overall picture at exactly the same time. That's one of the things we have to do in every typeface as we're drawing it. I think it's one of the things that make it difficult to hand this work off to someone else, because to do it properly, you have to get completely inside it and know all of its details from not only inside and out, but back and front simultaneously. We've both done bits of music composition; I think that kind of mind-set is pretty similar.

JH — I will say that we describe almost everything by analogy. Typography has this real poverty of terms to describe things beyond x-height and cap height and weight and so on. I find when Tobias and I are working on projects together, we tend to use a lot of qualitative terms that are entirely subjective. Working on the typeface for *Esquire* years ago, I remember my saying, "No, this has that, like, Saturn Five rocket, early NASA quality. It needs to have that orange plastic Olivetti typewriter, *Roman Holiday,* espresso feeling." I know you got exactly what I was saying.

TFJ — I did!

JH — But there's really no way to describe the qualitative parts of a typeface without resorting to things that are fully outside it. We're constantly saying, "It feels kind of Erik Satie. It needs to be Debussy," or, "This has a kind of belt-and-suspenders look. It needs to be much more elegant . . . hand-lasted shoe." There are tons of things that could be used to describe type.

TFJ — I think it's just the nature of what a typeface is. I mean, it's a vessel to carry something else. As we're working on it, we don't know what kind of content this is going to set, and it's going to change from one day to the next in a magazine or a newspaper. The conversation, I think, has to be in kind of evocative terms, like things that have a similar flavor, or a kind of memory that we might have that would suit this kind of image or this kind of personality.

GH — Can we talk about your thoughts about Helvetica?

JH — I think it's hard to—even though Tobias and I are in the business—I think it's very hard to divorce any kind of formal analysis of the typeface from our experience with it. We've grown up in a world that is filled with Helvetica. I remember Helvetica being on the Kroy lettering machine that my friend's father, who was an architect, had when I was growing up. I had the vinyl Helvetica letters and the press type. It's simply been everywhere, forever. Occasionally somebody will talk to us in a professional context about it; a client wants to do a magazine in Helvetica, wants to know what our thoughts are, which is the best version to buy, what its strengths and weaknesses are. But I still find it's hard to evaluate. It's like being asked what you think about off-white paint; it's just there. It's hard to get your head around something that's that big.

TFJ — True, but pretty early on I was clear on the fact that I was pretty sick of off-white paint. I still associate Helvetica with the 1970s and advertising typography and public spaces. A lot of urban-renewal projects in New York seemed to include Helvetica on their signage. When I was in school at RISD, I was taught by a generation of designers who came out of the sixties and seventies. They had a great fondness for Helvetica; it was part of the ascendant style of that period and they were really enthusiastic about it. I could not figure out what they were going on about, what was so great about this typeface. I would look at Helvetica coming out of the laser printer, and it was kind of dull. It would just sort of sit there and stare at you. It didn't have any kind of life to it or any kind of elegance to it.

But later I found specimens of the original Helvetica and the original Neue Haas Grotesk that came before it, as it existed in its very first state as a hand-set letterpress type, and it's a terrific piece of work. It's so far away from today's version. It's almost like they're entirely different designs. I remember this moment of getting an old specimen book and seeing the original state of Helvetica and suddenly getting it. It's like, "This is what everyone was getting so excited about." It's a shame that it doesn't exist anymore. You can't get Helvetica anywhere in digital form that looks as good as that did, for any number of reasons.

It's not that I like Helvetica any better now, but at least I understand how it got the kind of reputation that it has. Unfortunately, what we have now is a digital copy of the photoset version of the Linotype refitting of the original drawings. So it's not surprising that it's lost some of its very subtle character after being copied and copied and copied.

JH — It's interesting, though, that you talk about the 1970s housing projects, or civic works projects, as being one of the places Helvetica was used. I think one of the things that I'm noticing about the two of us talking about the typeface is that we're speaking of it solely in associative ways. I mean I've never had a conversation with Tobias about the fit or the color or the curvature or the shape or the function of Helvetica. It's merely what it evokes. It really evokes so many things at this point. Just looking back at its ironic uses in the last decade, all those techno albums that look like pill packages before that, and then the actual pill packages they were based on, and some of the amazing work that designers like Massimo Vignelli did in the seventies with the typeface—they gave it a kind of warmth, which I didn't expect of a sans serif like that.

TFJ — It was probably the last time it looked really good.

JH — I think it can still be made to look really good, but it is simply so universal. Part of that certainly is the personal computer. There's practically nobody who isn't familiar with what Helvetica is. At the beginning of our career—certainly before everybody had a PC or a Mac—no one knew what fonts were. I think even then people might have known what Helvetica was.

The fact that it's been so heavily licensed and made available through these very popular technologies has kind of furthered the mythology that it's the ultimate typeface in some way. I think that it's hard to escape from, even for us professionals. I sort of find myself buying into the idea that, "Oh, the sans serif evolved for 100 years, and the ultimate expression of it was Helvetica." That's not quite true historically or aesthetically or culturally or politically, but there's something about it that does have the feeling of finality to it. The conclusion of one line of reasoning was this typeface, and perhaps everything after it is secondary in some way.

GH — Is so much of it the context in which you see it or how you've grown up with it? This is expanding on what Experimental Jetset from Amsterdam said. To them, this is the font they grew up with. It was on their textbooks, on everything. So it has a warm, homey feeling to them. But someone else might just see it as clean and cold. It's subjective. When you say a typeface is high-waisted and elegant, and it's used in the context of *Martha Stewart Living,* I get it. But is there something intrinsic in the design that communicates those qualities? Or is it just people's repeated viewing in these contexts that makes them link those feelings to typefaces?

JH — Certainly when Tobias and I design a custom typeface for a client, it's a font that's never existed before. So any associative powers that it has are partially to do with the tradition it comes from, whether it's from the French Neoclassical period or from the Renaissance or whatever, and partially the way in which it's used. A typeface used by *Harper's Bazaar* is going to be filled with the essence of *Harper's Bazaar.*

I think with Helvetica, there's the belief that it's always been around. Designers, and I think even readers, invest so much of the surrounding in the typeface. American Apparel uses Helvetica and it looks cheeky, and American Airlines uses it and it looks sober. It's not just a matter of the weight they choose and the letterspacing and the colors. There's something about the typeface that I think really invites this open interpretation. I suppose you can say that typefaces are either fully open to interpretation or merely have one association attached to them. You know, a typeface made of icicles or candy canes or something just says one thing, and Helvetica maybe says everything, and that's perhaps part of its appeal.

TFJ — Well, I think Helvetica's popularity was based on a kind of viral quality. It became popular through not only the qualities of the typeface itself but also its association with the Swiss International Style that was all the rage in Europe for years. Just as that was reaching its peak in Europe, it was discovered over here and had a whole second act of popularity, again riding on this larger style which was concerned with more than just typography—it was also about architecture and interior design and so on. That was certainly fostered by the marketing for it. That's why it's called Helvetica. It was called Neue Haas Grotesk, which is sort of a mouthful for anyone outside Germany. The association with Switzerland was very deliberate, because at the time the Swiss style was the new thing.

JH — Technology has certainly accelerated that, though. If you saw Helvetica and liked it in 1960, you would have had the challenge of finding a type house that had the equipment with which they could set the typeface and had it in the size you wanted. Of course, now if you find a typeface you like, you enter your credit card number and buy it online and have it instantly. The curve, the time between somebody debuting a typeface and somebody else using it, has just simply gotten much smaller. To some extent, that's a business reality for the nature of what we do. When we sell a typeface to somebody for $129, we need to sell a lot more copies than Haas sold of Helvetica when it was a film master that cost thousands of dollars years ago. Those two things are different aspects of the same situation, I think.

GH — In terms of the person on the street and their relationship to type, do you think people care? Do you think about it? Is it one of these situations where they only think about it when it's not working? Is it invisible to people?

TFJ — Well, I think the sort of classical modernist line about how much awareness a reader should have of a typeface is that they shouldn't be aware of it at all. It should be this crystal goblet, there to hold, display, and organize the information. But I don't think it's really quite as simple as that. I think even if they're not consciously aware of the typeface they're reading, they'll certainly be affected by it the same way that an actor that's miscast in a role will affect someone's experience of a movie or play they're watching. They'll still follow the plot, but be less—

JH — Convinced.

TFJ — Taken with it or convinced or excited or affected or whatever. I think typography is similar to that, where a designer choosing typefaces is essentially a casting director. If they know the strengths and weaknesses of all the typefaces they have to choose from, they can choose wisely for the role at hand. The reader, while not being consciously aware of this typeface and its history and why it was chosen for this, they should just feel that it fits in some way.

It's like going to a restaurant and having a sommelier recommend this wine with this dish. I have no idea why, but I know that it fits. I might ask why that is, and I'll understand part of the answer, but there's a subtle relationship there that you don't have to understand every last piece of to gain the benefit of.

JH — I agree. An analogy that I use often for typography is film scores. When somebody writes a soundtrack for something, it is designed to enhance the experience in some way. It can be fully subliminal. You're not paying attention to the fact that, oh, the composer is using the Phrygian mode and it's all wind instruments. It's more a sort of shared heritage that a composer can understand and bring to something to more fully evoke what's happening onscreen.

But there are also soundtracks that are much more designed to be things that are recognized by a viewer. Films quote other films. If you have a scene of somebody driving and there's a Simon and Garfunkel song in the background, it's a little nod to *The Graduate*. You recognize that as well. I think people get type the same way; they are in some ways familiar with it in a subliminal way. If you use the *New Yorker* typeface on something, people will know it as the *New Yorker* typeface, or they'll know it's somehow *New Yorker*-ish but not quite know why. I think there is definitely an awareness, a perception issue with readers and type. It really makes it the important part of design that it is.

GH — What do you think is the biggest trend in typography now? Is it stylistic, or has the trend just been the democratization of the technology?

JH — As a trend, I think it's safe to say that type has been getting better. I mean, despite all the harping about amateurs ruining the business or whatever, the average printed thing today is as good as the best-printed thing 50 years ago. That you can find a newspaper with a circulation of 15,000 that's designed by three people every day and looks the way the *New York Sun* did at its high point is incredibly impressive. The tools of typography and design, of pagination, are much more sophisticated than they were before. It also means the chance to screw things up is greater than it ever was as well. But I think we're working against a baseline of real competence that was never there before. It's definitely putting more of the burden upon us as type designers to make raw materials that are dependable. The notion that we're making fonts not merely for English speakers in America, but for speakers who use the Latin alphabet throughout the world, means that a font today is three times the size of a font 10 years ago. That trend is only going to continue, I think.

TFJ — The trend that I've noticed is for there to be more and more directions all at once rather than history being seen as a straight-line continuum where one thing builds directly on the thing before it. We now have history in a pile in front of us, and you can grab any part of that you want.

If it hasn't happened already, soon you can just pick any kind of style, whether it's a historical revival of this period or that period or a hybrid of this thing and that other thing. Someone somewhere is probably doing that. I'm not sure what that means sort of going forward, if that's a kind of entropy where there are no schools and there are no movements stylistically, but I think that's where I'm seeing things going.

JH — One of the challenges, I think, for us, is that we're becoming somewhat inured to the technology. In the late eighties, early nineties when suddenly you could make a font and set something you've written in a font of your own design—

TFJ — That was big news.

JH — It was huge news. It was an aphrodisiac. You could actually make this thing and set this thing and work on the font and then the output comes out all in your own home. It was incredible. It certainly spawned this revolution of independent people being involved in typography now that it was divorced from this big manufacturing business.

But I think as technology continues to advance, we're anticipating its possible uses as things are happening. I think about things like the fax machine that came into my office. The distance between getting this thing, in which I could put a piece of paper and have it arrive at a friend's desk in The Hague at the same time, the novelty of that wore off in about a day. Suddenly it became, "Well, of course you have a fax machine. Why isn't my fax working? Where's that fax? I'm waiting for the fax from that guy." It became integrated into expectation really rapidly. I feel that technology and type is doing the same thing. In the last couple years, it became possible to make fonts that have 65,000 characters, and typefaces that deform themselves as you type in certain ways, and letters that insert themselves based upon various contexts. It's all very exciting, but what I wonder about is how future developments of technology are going to actually foster creativity. What are we going to do with these? What we're going to want to do with these things doesn't seem obvious from the way in which the tools are made. I suppose that's been an ongoing challenge with type forever, but it feels especially acute right now, for some reason.

GH — I wanted to talk about what you guys are working on right now. Can you talk about the current projects? Do you have, like, 10 different typefaces that are all at different stages of development?

TFJ — I'm working on a new newspaper text face. We were talking about newspapers before. Again, because it's difficult, we like that sort of thing. We had thought of a new angle to take to address the problem, not only of printing with cheap ink on thin paper, but also of space being at a premium because so many newspapers are going to smaller pages. We've been working on that idea for some time.

JH — We're also working on a sans-serif typeface for a corporate client that is suddenly aware of the size of its market, and the font it licensed from us for use in the US and the UK suddenly now needs to spread to Catalonia and Malta and Croatia and Greece and Russia. We've had a language project in the works for the last year and a half to figure out exactly which languages they need, exactly which characters are necessary, how best to draw those characters. This has also come to a boil right now. We have three designers working on the product and two outside consultants helping us with the linguistic aspects. That's been in the works for a while now.

TFJ — Right. That includes not only the actual design work and the research of exactly which languages need which characters, but also collecting examples of this language that we can test in as real a context as possible and not just, "Here are the letters we need for Polish, and do they look nice or not?" But here's an entire paragraph in Polish in upper- and lowercase and caps and small caps and so on, so we can put each language through all of its paces and anticipate everything that's going to happen.

JH — About 10 years ago I did a family of fonts for the Guggenheim Museum as their signature typeface. We've been slowly expanding that out from a family of 6 to a family of 30. That's just about done this week. That's been in the works for quite some time. What we're really doing there is taking the original requirements of a past project—a font for signage and print publications—and revisiting it with the idea of making the font useful in magazines and newspapers and brochures and annual reports, all the things that our clients do outside the museum.

GH — Okay: What's your favorite letter of the alphabet and why?
　　JH — Should we say it in unison?

TFJ — Sure.

JH — One, two three.

Both — Capital *R*.

JH — It's a very handy letter.

TFJ — Because a type designer doesn't see the alphabet as a linear sequence beginning with *A* and ending with *Z*. We see it more as camps of like-minded shapes sort of overlapping and intersecting with each other. They'll be the group of round shapes, like the capital *C* and *G* and *O* and *Q*. They'll be the square capitals, like the *H* and the *E* and the *F* and the *T* and so on. These shapes, the square things, round things, diagonal things, these are like the primary colors to us instead of red, yellow, and blue.

In the middle of all of this is the capital *R*. It's got one of everything. It's got the vertical. It has a bulb. It has the tail that's diagonal. If you can reconcile all of these different structures, then you have a major part of your design figured out. So it's often one of the first letters we would draw after doing those first control characters of the capital *H*, *O*, *D*, lowercase *n*, *o*, *p*.

JH — It's sort of like a sampler pack. It has everything in the entire alphabet organized into that one character. When looking at typefaces, I find that we use the capital *R* as kind of a placeholder or a representative of an entire font, because you can really see, you can get a good sense of what's going to be going on elsewhere in the font family from this one character.

TFJ — That makes it pretty hard to draw, to negotiate a peace between all these different kinds of shapes, but that also just makes it very telling and distinctive. When it turns out in a really memorable kind of way, we try to include a capital *R* in the name of the typeface. That will be part of its calling card.

GH — I find that if I'm staring at something all day, say at a film I'm editing, when I dream, I still see that footage. Do you dream type?

JH — I don't think I dream about typography. There's very little type in my world outside of work. Like everybody else, I'm aware of the fonts being used in my environment, and the standing joke that graphic designers can't see historical movies because the fonts are always wrong is certainly true. I find myself actually disliking things like all the stuff you can buy at Pottery Barn that says "bread" or "messages" and the hot and cold water taps with the *H* and *C*, or the *C* and *F* if you're French. Actually, I kind of don't like type in my environment outside of places I expect to see it, which is kind of a strange thought.

TFJ — It definitely makes the world outside the office very different. My fiancée and I were trying to remember the location of a restaurant in our neighborhood. She remembered it as "that new place that's just a couple blocks down from the dry cleaner." I remembered it as "that new place just a couple blocks down from the place with the bad letter-spacing out front." I didn't remember what this place offered, whether it was a dry cleaner or an auto body shop or what. I glazed over that part of it. But really specific dreams about typography, I don't think I've had those. I think I had an anxiety dream about serifs once, but that was a really long time ago.

JH — I will certainly say that I'm aware of type in the world more than other things. I know people who can identify any make of car at a distance or know who designed a certain dress, but I still think of things in terms of typography. That's an ingredient. I'm always looking for books at home, and I'll say to my wife, "Where is that book that your friend gave you?" She'll say, "Which book?" I'll say, "I can't remember, but it's brown and the title's running down the side all caps in Monotype Albertus." Of course that means nothing to her as a non-designer, but that's my memory of the book. That's certainly a curse, I think.

TFJ — For a long time when I'd go out to restaurants with my parents, I would drive them bananas because I could not bring myself to order anything off the menu until I'd identified the typeface. So they would be ordering their hamburgers and Cokes and whatever, and I'd be like this, trying to figure out, "What is this? This *G* looks familiar." They would be like, "What do you want to eat?" "Hang on. Hang on." Thankfully, I've gotten over that and I can actually order something off a menu without knowing what it's set in, but that kind of impulse is still there.

One of the things that I thought was kind of strange or ironic about Helvetica's popularity in America is that it comes from a very distinctly European tradition, and there's a whole American or sort of American English tradition of sans-serif types that's an entirely different thing.

You'll see Franklin Gothic and News Gothic and these kinds of types that were falling out of favor because of their contrast with this trendy new Swiss style that was coming in. We've been collecting these antique specimen books for, I don't know, something like 15, 16 years?

JH — It's 18 or 19, yeah.

TFJ — Yeah. I'm losing track, apparently. Obviously, they're prime reference sources for our own design work, but they're also just beautiful things to have. These were catalogs that would be replaced on a regular basis, but the foundries would invest so much time and effort into producing a beautiful book that's well designed and well printed and beautifully bound. It's not quite the equivalent of a Pottery Barn catalog, except in terms of being conceived of as something disposable. This is why many of these are very hard to find—because they were disposed of and replaced with the next edition a few years later.

JH — This is the first specimen book I ever bought. It's the 1923 *American Type Founders Specimen*. It's a beautiful book. Beyond just showcasing the fonts, it's been designed so attentively that there are paper changes over a few pages, and color changes, and all that good stuff. I learned a few years ago that this book was produced at a cost of $300,000 in 1923 for 60,000 copies. So this is a $50 book in 1923 dollars. Just imagine a phone book today produced at the same cost or a Pottery Barn catalog, like Tobias said. This is a piece of marketing material, a piece of ephemera, that's been just so lavishly designed and produced. It does a kindness to the type designers whose work is showcased inside.

Regarding your comment earlier about the quality of typography and design going forward, I think the average printed thing today is better than it's ever been in the past, but the ways in which typefaces are shown is somewhat disappointing. They take more work to make than ever, and they're often rendered as an alphabet in 12-point and that's it. One of the things we try to do here is to fully display the contents—the work.

TFJ — It's one of the effects of there being so many typefaces in the world now, that there's proportionally less and less space to show them. If you're a vendor that's selling 20,000 typefaces at a time, you can't spend a whole lot of real estate demonstrating each one of them. That's one of the reasons we do our own specimens, so we can show off all the work that we put in instead of leaving that to someone else.

JH — We can grab one of our specimens to have out here on the table.

GH — Yeah, that would be awesome.

JH — It's funny. Looking through these old specimen books at some of the things that came before Helvetica, we can look at them as having a kind of really lovely color and flavor to them, which Helvetica lacks. You can see how revolutionary a design like Helvetica was at the time, how dramatically new it was, and perhaps why it's endured all these years.

TFJ — In some ways, I think of it like the urban-renewal projects that were going on at the same time. In a way, Helvetica paved over all these old 19th century tenement buildings, these strange, toothy sans serifs that were cut by all these different people at all these different times and sort of tumbled together into the palette that was used in America for years and years and years. They had their strengths and weaknesses, but they were all badly out of fashion by the time Helvetica effectively demolished all of them and came through with its highway.

JH — But as with a cityscape, where blocks have old buildings and new ones that work together, the joy in it is that you can actually have Helvetica and this font that we designed that's sort of meant to evoke the same spirit as the 19th century type. You really can have the slick version and the toothy version together in the same environment, and certainly on your computer at the same time, which is a useful thing.

TFJ — Yeah. I think with a certain distance, that kind of juxtaposition is possible. But at that time, it would have been bizarre to think of those two together.
—

Michael C. Place (MCP)/ May 26, 2006 London

Michael C. Place, head of the London design studio Build, was part of what our film team referred to as the "young designers" section of the movie. A lot of the film had been devoted to the history of Helvetica, and now we wanted to speak with the next generation of designers who were using it. I spoke with Michael at his home studio in East London, which he'd recently moved into along with his lovely wife, Nicola, and their two hairless Sphynx cats, Betty and Brockmann. I've had the pleasure of continuing to work with Michael since *Helvetica*, as Build has done the identity design for *Objectified, Urbanized,* and they also designed the book you're now reading.

—

Gary Hustwit — Okay, I guess we can get started. Just the basics, like how you got involved in graphic design?

Michael C. Place — Right.

GH — Oh, wait a second. What's that sound?

MCP — That's the cats and their litter. Can you hear that at the moment? They won't be in there that long.

Luke Geissbühler (cinemtogarapher) — Do you want the cats to be running through the shot?

GH — Sure.

MCP — We could shut this door.

GH — No, no. I think it'd be great if they were just hanging out at certain points.

MCP — Cool. Okay.

GH — We'll have to get some nice cat portraits.

MCP — Yeah, definitely. Especially the one called Brockmann.

GH — Okay. So yeah, beginnings. How did you get started in design?

MCP — I was always really interested in drawing from an early age. I grew up on a farm. My dad's a pig farmer, or was a pig farmer. He's retired now; he's a gardener. Mum's a nurse. I've got three older sisters, and so I was always just, you know, the boy by himself. I just used to draw a lot—really silly stuff, like spaceships, anything, detailed stuff. Then at school, my art teacher saw my style of drawing and said, "Have you ever heard of graphic design?" That was just a magic thing. I was like, "No, never." And he said, "All right," and showed me a few books, and I sort of read up on it. He lent me his Rotring pen, and I used to just really enjoy doing technical drawing at school. I guess it's that sort of marriage of the two for me, the technical aspect as well as the arty side.

I then did a foundation course in Scarborough, just for a year, to figure out what I wanted to do. So the foundations were like graphic design, fashion, we'd do a bit of illustration, that kind of thing. And I just really, really enjoyed graphic design. I did two years at York doing OND graphic design, two years at Newcastle doing HND graphic design.

I got a job straight after college with Trevor Jackson working at Bite It! down in London. I really enjoyed that; it was really fascinating doing record sleeves. That's all I wanted to do was record sleeves when I was at college. The Newcastle College was just this horrible course. I thought it was supposed to be one of the best courses in the country to get into, but I soon realized that it's just this horrific sort of commercial-art focus. So we were doing hand-lettering, art history, stuff like that, which to me was just . . . I just didn't want to do that kind of thing. I just thought, "I'm never going to use this. I'll never have to perfectly hand-render some Times at 2-point or 12-point," or whatever.

Because I just wanted to do record sleeves, and really, music's such a huge thing for me, I just used to do my own record sleeves, you know? I'd do my own briefs while I was at college, because the briefs that we were getting were, like, the usual wine labels, fucking nappy packaging, that kind of thing. To me it was just pointless, I just didn't want to do that side of things. So I just used to do my own stuff.

When I left college and got a job straightaway with Trevor, at Bite It!, it was just insane. Just this huge learning curve, going in—I was this kid who was just, shit, you know, suddenly working with one of the best graphic designers in the city. Trevor's just incredible, a real character. When I was at Newcastle, I did a work placement at Designers Republic. I got on really well with Ian Anderson and everybody there. Then later when I was working with Trevor, I got a call from Ian, saying, "Do you want a job?" I went up there, and I did 10 years at DR. So yeah, it's just been that journey, essentially, from there.

GH — That was great. Brockmann was just all over the frickin' shot. At one point he was behind you, on the box behind your head, but the way the perspective looked, it looked like he was a little miniature cat looking into your ear. It was bizarre. So, do you remember the first proper record sleeve you did?

MCP — I was thinking about this the other day. When I was at college, one of my big heroes at the time was Vaughan Oliver—you know, that very illustrative style, completely opposite to what I do now. So I used to do a lot of really messy collages, quite gritty sort of stuff. And then I started messing around with PMT cameras. See, this was pre-computer days. Then I started chopping up type, really going to town on that. And I think that's when type started to be a big thing for me.

I did a piece of chopped-up type at college that Trevor really liked when I went to see him for the interview, and that's one of the first things I did at Bite It! I think it was on Champion Records. We got this horrible picture; it was like a female singer. So I did this real nice chopped-up type; really heavily, brutally messed-up type. I think it was Helvetica, but I'm not quite sure. That was the first one, and then we were doing stuff like Stereo MCs when they were on G Street. A lot of the stuff Trevor did then, which obviously I started doing, was more hip-hop stuff. So we were doing G Street, some Tribe Called Quest stuff, that kind of thing.

Record sleeves just always held a real fascination for me. I used to really enjoy buying a record, putting it on the turntable, and then sitting and looking at the sleeve, just poring over every little detail. Back then, record sleeve design really was at the forefront of everything. I think it's changing now, but it used to be that record sleeves were at the forefront of graphic design, and then two or three years later advertising would get hold of that style and appropriate it for the mass market. Now I think there's a lot of advertising and mainstream work that is really pushing the boundaries.

So yeah, it was just record sleeves for me. That was the thing that I really wanted to do, and it was a complete dream to get to do it. To suddenly be working on sleeves for acts that I used to buy. I just used to sit there thinking, "I'm doing this cover for Pop Will Eat Itself." It's absolutely insane to do things for people that you really respect. I did some stuff for Juan Atkins's Model 500, you know, the godfather of techno. Just going from being a kid in this little market town to doing this incredible stuff that you'd never even dreamed of—it was brilliant.

Are you trying to knock Brockmann off, then?

GH — No, right now he's out of the frame, but he looks like he might pounce on you at any moment. Maybe you can just talk about the process when you're designing, in terms of using type?

MCP — It's just completely free-form, really, I've never been into the whole design trend thing. During college and after, I quite purposely shut myself off from looking at design magazines. I'm not one of those people who will reach for a magazine first of all and think, "Oh, what's going on?" So I tried to just do my own thing. I'm more interested in looking at everyday objects for inspiration. I love instruction manuals, and all the little things that I just pick up from the street, or the graphics on the back of that power cable down there. I love all that sort of stuff.

I sketch a lot, but I also just write ideas down. So like, "Remember the thing on the back of the power cable." I make mental notes that get deployed every now and again. I'm trying to do more stuff with photography, but I generally just enjoy creating typefaces. Even if it's not a full character set, it'll just be small little bits, a few characters. It's a brilliant way of putting a personal stamp on a piece of work if you can design characters yourself. It sets this thing straight apart rather than just using a normal typeface. A lot of people say that I put a lot of myself into the designs, so it's this whole sort of personal journey. I'll try something else that might go off in a different direction. It's just this constant journey in terms of design, and it's something I'm just obsessed by. If you look at some of my work, you can see the sort of detail that goes into a lot of it. I guess for me, it's either full-on or it's just completely off, you know? The title of the exhibition we're about to do in New York, for instance, is "On or Off." And that's it, there's no middle ground for me. It's either really super full-on, or it's minimal, just absolutely, insanely minimal. But there's never any gray area at all.

It is a personal thing for me; I'm not really interested in what somebody else is doing, you know? Hence working from here, I'm not in the center of London in some Clerkenwell studio. I've never really been in that crowd, that sort of "cliqueyness" of design. In London, it is quite cliquey, but I always try to put myself outside of it, so I can just be. I just concentrate on what I'm doing and want I want to do. I've been very lucky that people also appreciate and want what I do, so it's great. I often think, "If this all quit tomorrow, what would I do?" I have absolutely no idea what I would do. It's insane.

GH — The clouds are coming in—does it seem a little dark?

LG — It is. I've been waiting for a moment to change the camera settings.

GH — We're definitely in England doing these interviews—with this light, we could not be anywhere else. It's like, the color has just been washed from the frame. There is none.

> **MCP** — That's great, isn't it? In the film it must be, like, you've got an American interview, and then you go to an English one, and it just goes completely to gray. "What's wrong with my TV?"

All — [Laughter]

> **MCP** — I have this theory of why Europe and England in particular have got a really strong heritage of good design, it's that our weather's so crap that we're all inside designing, and we're not out on the beach, you know? Surfing or whatever. Honestly, sometimes I think about it, and it's, "All right, I think I'll stay in today and design."

GH — That applies to bands and music, too. Same thing.
> **MCP** — Yeah. Yeah. Definitely.

GH — Let's talk about Helvetica. You use it quite a bit. Can you talk about some of your feelings about it and why you use it?

> **MCP** — I think I fell into step with Helvetica when I was at DR. Like I said, I'm not one of those people who is a real typographer. I don't know all the fancy words for letters, and all the ligatures and ascenders and descenders and all those kind of things. I just react to certain things and do what I feel is right with them, so I've never been a real classical type guy. I think, for me, Helvetica has a real grace to it, and I think it's just one of those fonts that works with almost anything you put with it.

> I had this really nice conversation with a friend who works in London, another designer. I'd recently done a thing for *Grafik* magazine where

you pick a character and talk about that character. And I chose Baby Teeth, the Milton Glaser font, which is like a Pac Man-type thing. That's just what I was interested in at the time. And my friend said, "Why didn't you choose Helvetica?" And part of me thought, would that have been too obvious, since I have an association with the font? And I was just like, no, Baby Teeth was what I wanted to talk about in the magazine. We got talking about Helvetica, and there's so many people who say, "People who use Helvetica, it's just the easy option, isn't it? It's just, stick it on there and everything's going to look good." But I just think that it's this timeless font for me, that it carries itself really well.

Some people say they'll use a different typeface for a certain project because it gives a different feeling. Helvetica is a neutral-looking font, but it's a really beautiful font, and I enjoy the challenge of making Helvetica speak in different ways. So it can be cool and clinical-looking, but it can have real warmth as well, and I think that's a challenge that I enjoy doing. Rather than just saying, "Okay, right. It needs to be more friendly, this thing, so we'll use a round font." You know, that's the usual solution. We'll choose a different font for this, to give this kind of meaning. But I think you can make Helvetica speak, and it can, in different ways, just by the use of scale, size, proportion, layout. I think it's a real challenge, and I think that's a way to show somebody that you can deal with it, rather than just using a different font for this, a different font for that. But yeah, I think it's just an incredibly lovely font, that's been around 50 years coming up. It's just as fresh as it ever was. Obviously it wasn't intended to be this cool thing, but it's just a beautiful font.

GH — We were talking a little bit before we started about your wedding invitation. I think that's a good story.

MCP — I don't know, really, if I should get into this or not. But I got married about three years ago, and I did the wedding invites, which, believe me, is just the worst job you could ever do as a graphic designer. I've done other people's wedding invites, and I'll never do one again. It's the most stressful job I've ever had. Dealing with mothers-in-law is just horrific. But I did ours, and on the order of service, I did a little credit to give thanks to Max Miedinger for Helvetica. But my wife vetoed that, and I had to take it off the invite. But yeah, it was funny.

GH — If you think about the general public, what do you think their sense of typography is? Do people know the difference between fonts, can they even tell the difference between Helvetica and Univers or Arial, or is it all just . . .

MCP — I think it's all just all one big mishmash. I think it's definitely better now; I think people are a lot more design-savvy for sure. You can really sense that. But it's like talking to my mum sometimes. I show stuff to my mum and dad, and it's always like "That's nice." You know, "I'm doing this exhibition in New York." "Oh, right, yeah, that's nice, dear." I think there's probably a certain sector of people out there who could go, "Yeah, I could spot that as Helvetica, or that as something else," but I think the perception of type for the general public is just, like, this blur.

GH — How do you think the message gets through via the type? You were saying before, you can make it talk in different voices. So somehow the voice that you're trying to get across gets through to the viewer.

MCP — Maybe it does.

GH — I mean, it seems like with some designs it's about you, the designer. You're doing what you want to see, and it's not about the audience, per se. It's really about your approach to the project, versus trying to design it for a specific audience?

MCP — Yeah, I'm sure it is. I generally design for the target audience, but not always. I think in terms of record sleeves or more left-field design, I think it's about feeling. But I think the biggest thing, for me, in terms of design, is to get an emotional response from a piece. That's some of the best design, I think. I see stuff, and if it makes me go, "I wish I'd done that," that, to me, is the biggest thing. "Oooh, that's nice." It's all about the emotional response that you can get from this piece of print, or the thing you're looking at.

And with print, which is the big thing that I really enjoy and do best, the experience is the thing. On one level it's just seeing the information; it's the emotional response you get from just looking at the thing, or holding it. Then there's the actual touch, feeling it, so it's a complete package. I always try to think of all those things when I'm designing a piece. And I think what you're saying about the "public" perception of stuff, sometimes there can just be absolutely no response whatsoever, you know? They could look at your T-shirt and go, "Yeah, that looks cold." And then look at the cat thing over there and go, "Oh, that's nice." As we said before, type says different things, and different typefaces speak differently to different people, and that's great.

So I don't think the general public could really be that knowledgeable, because there's so many typefaces—it's a fairly specialist thing. And I don't expect my mum and dad to know or read up about Helvetica, or any typeface. So I think type's real value is the response that somebody's going to get from it, and I think that's the beauty of typography, the feeling that somebody can get from just looking at this thing.

You were talking before about how people think that fonts just come out of thin air. I think probably type is one of the most underrated or undervalued things, you know? What do people think, there's a font fairy out there? You know, new fonts just appear one morning? I think they don't really realize that somebody actually does this.

I think it would be quite an interesting thing to do for the film, you know, to go up to somebody on the street and say, "Can you tell me what this font is, madam?" and show a granny, like, "Oh, yes, that's Helvetica, that's Univers. Yes, that's Times New Roman, that's Caslon." I don't think you'll ever get that, but it really would be nice. As designers, to a certain degree, we're in this bubble. You expect your immediate friends and other designers to know this stuff, but I think the public is this sort of outsider. I always try to treat people who buy the stuff that I do with some brains, and I never try to make it that easy for people. I guess I try to design for the way that I would like to see something.

For instance, for me, things like bar code numbers are important. I like to try to scale that up, so that's more important than the actual title of the album. That's the kind of thing that I find really interesting and fascinating—the layers of, not code, but just to make somebody spend 10 or 20 minutes staring at something and still see new things. Rather than just picking it up and being like, "All right, yeah. That's it. Done." And it's just gone. I don't know where I'm going with this, but . . .

GH — No, that was great. That's interesting, too, about the technical aspect. Like you were saying before, you were really fascinated by technical drawings and schematics. It's interesting that you ended up doing a lot of design work for techno music, and now you use computers to do the actual work. What are some of your thoughts on that whole confluence?

MCP — I think I was very lucky. I was definitely the last generation of designers that designed pre-computer. We were doing everything on PMT cameras with overlays and marking up color and specifying type, writing down how you want it set, and then the typesetter would set it and you'd paste the thing down. I don't remember who said it, but somebody said something like, "People should think, computers should work." For me, computers are just a tool. I'm not the most technical person, even though I enjoy looking at technical things. It's all about what you do with the technology and how you use it.

For me it's a progression. That's why I always try to go forward. We used to design for independent music, more guitar-y stuff, which I hate now; I just can't listen to anything like that anymore. A lot of people would really disagree, but I think electronic music is far more interesting; there's only so much you can do with a guitar and somebody singing. I'm sure I'm going to get hate mail for that, but that's how I feel.

So I think designing for electronic music, which is something we get asked to do a lot, is just the whole package, isn't it? I think technology and design, for instance, for electronic music, encompasses all things that I naturally take reference from. I don't know where I'm going with that either.

GH — What are some of the other things you're obsessed with? Things that find their way into your design, or just in general?

MCP — I don't know . . . one thing that I got slightly obsessed with a while ago was—if you look at the back of any food packages, you get this little black strip, just a small black rectangle in the corner. The bottoms of milk cartons, or the things that you pull apart to recycle—I'm really fascinated with the construction of cardboard boxes and things like that. I just find construction really fascinating, just the way things are made, and taking things to bits.

I did that *Formats* project, where I'd take something like a videotape apart and document all the bits in it. Videotape is another thing that got me—I find that whole molded-plastic thing really fascinating. The shapes, the injection-molded stuff; it's beautiful. The stuff that a lot of people would look at and go, "Oh, it's just a videotape," I find all that stuff really lovely. I just love instruction manuals, any kind of technical detail. And then marrying that with something that's more organic—I'm doing a lot more organic-y stuff at the moment, which is quite weird. Going from a very hard edge to doing stuff with very curvy line work. I always try to keep myself entertained.

I collect things. It can be anything. I've got so many bits and scraps of paper, things that you find on the street, wrappers. I've found some sandpaper that's got really beautiful graphics on the backside. It's repeat type for 3M—I really love that logo as well—and maybe that will influence a poster design or something. And boxes, type on boxes. It looks really quite generic, but somebody sat down and designed it. It isn't something that just appears. It's that invisible stuff that most people gloss over that I really enjoy picking up and adapting. That's the thing—it's like "eyes to the ground," almost. Where everybody else is looking at design magazines or whatever, I'll just be looking at instruction manuals or bits of paper on the street.

I did a poster called "Print with Love," where I took bits of videotapes and cassettes and I arranged them into the shape of our logo, which is a little bird. I quite like it, because sometimes my graphics can be cold and hard, but it's got this little bird, which is quite a cute thing. We made the bird out of these bits of tape and computer parts, and it's just about making something beautiful out of something very ordinary. And that's what I really enjoy; the ordinary things that most people would just gloss over, I find really beautiful.

Logos are some of my favorite things too. Sony's my favorite logo. 3M; I love that logo. That's Helvetica. I guess it's this corporate thing I find really fascinating. Coca-Cola's one. I'm mad on Coca-Cola, I love that logo. I collect any kind of foreign Coca-Cola stuff I can. Didn't UPS just recently do a redesign, where essentially they've just 3-D'ed the fucking logo? That's just horrible. I don't think people, these corporations or certain companies, understand what a beautiful thing they've got, and then they fuck it up by making it 3-D. I think it's the Apple thing, the way the interface has gone from OS 9 to 10, I think people are trying to amplify everything. It's all nice bubbles, trying to make themselves look more friendly by putting bubbles and shadows on everything.

So, as I'm walking around, the things that are more straightforward are the things that stand out for me, because everything's getting a drop shadow put on it, or everything's getting some kind of 3-D effect put on it. For instance, the Walkman logo. God, what an incredible logo that was, and then they do that horrible little bubbly thing on it, just to make everything friendly. I do apologize; I've got a little bit of a soapbox thing with logos. I just think, "You don't understand what a beautiful logo you've got there, but then you sod it up by putting this thing on it." And I know logos evolve; you see Coca-Cola go from what it was to what it is now; it's gone through huge changes. I'm not averse to change, of course. But

I do find these things that are purely typographic and are such lovely, timeless things. The Panasonic logo. It's just a gorgeous, really beautiful bit of type, and that's it.

But then, the marketing department—they're usually the stumbling block for me. Anytime marketing gets involved, it just gets horrible—it's dumbed down, you know. They'll go for the lowest common denominator and just make it so stupid and simple that everybody gets it, because they're shit-scared that they'll lose their job if they don't sell a million units or whatever.

GH — We interviewed Massimo Vignelli, and of course, he did the logos for American Airlines and Knoll in Helvetica. Things that the companies have stuck with for 40 or 50 years, and hopefully don't have any plans on changing.

MCP — Definitely. For me, I just think certain things shouldn't be messed with, you know? Like Helvetica is this beautiful, timeless thing that stood the test of time. It is fascinating that when you look at that Helvetica book, just the street photos in that book, it is incredible the amount of stuff that is Helvetica in there. It's just there; everybody just lives with it. And it's almost like, "Has it become invisible because it's used so much?" It's just this constant—there's no kind of hype with it. There's no nothing. It just seems to be there.

GH — What's the strangest stuff you've been asked to design? Has there been anything that you shook your head at when someone asked you to design something?

MCP — Probably not. The fun thing recently is doing this stuff for this Hong Kong shop. I've just been doing everyday objects that most people gloss over. Like, we've done beach towels. It's a challenge to me, just asking, "What would I really like to see?" Certain things, like a tea towel; I like a really well-designed tea towel. And I like a really well-designed beach towel. Silly things like that. Generally, I don't get asked to do stuff that's—I mean, there was McDonald's, but we just said no to them.

GH — Do you find that things that you'd like to see exist end up being an inspiration? Like, "I wish I had a great-looking tea mug," or . . .

MCP — Yeah, definitely. I think that's that thing. I think Vignelli said, "Everybody deserves good design." And why not have a really nicely designed mug? Some of the stuff we're doing is silly. Why not a really well-designed ruler? Or we're doing pencils. I'm quite anal about certain things, and stationery I really like. Doing a calendar that isn't puppy dogs and fluffy things. Like Massimo Vignelli's perpetual calendars, this gorgeous—actually, I think it's Helvetica—this beautiful type and this timeless calendar that keeps going and keeps going, and nobody gets bored of it. That's the value of good design.

GH — When Vignelli talks about the logos he designed, his chest is swelling with pride, like, "I did this, and of course it's great. You don't need to redesign it. It's the best logo. It fits everything."

MCP — Excellent.

GH — What other designers' work has influenced you?

MCP — Like I said, when I was at college, it was people like Vaughan Oliver and Malcolm Garrett. I guess that was more from the music that I listened to, so that work naturally fed in. But then I really did make a conscious decision not to look at other stuff, to try to find a way of doing something that hadn't been done before. Now I start to see things. I got one of the Massimo Vignelli books the other day. When you look at it now, it's just absolutely incredible stuff.

[Cat meows.] Sorry. Oy, you. Stop it. He's terrible. He just wants to sit where she sits. He's really bad.

But yeah, influences. Like I say, I'm just one of those people that isn't really about—there's so many people doing stuff that looks like other people's stuff, and I just try not to. Like look at Wim Crouwel's work. I definitely think that he's some kind of space alien who's managed to teleport from the future. Honestly, you look at his stuff now and you think, "Crikey, that could have been done yesterday," you know? But he did it 30, 40 years ago. It's absolutely insane. So you just kind of think to yourself, "Imagine what that would have looked like back then." To the general public, it must've looked like the spaceships had landed, in terms of design. It's just absolutely insane. Absolutely incredible. So I can probably identify more with people like Crouwel. I'm sure he's quite a purist to a certain degree, but I look at his work, and he sort of goes away from that approach sometimes, like with his use of color. Certain things he's done are very colorful, but with his grids applied, so I guess he's almost this hybrid. He did break the boundaries and really push things in a different way.

I guess that's what I try to do, in some way. There are certain rules that I quite like to apply in terms of grids. But sometimes I find them a bit constricting as well, so if something isn't right, then I'm not just going to impose a grid on something that I don't think is working.

GH — We're going to talk to Crouwel next week. Those early alphabets were just fucking—

MCP — Insane.

GH — And they still are.

MCP — Yeah. I've got that book, that *Alphabets* type specimen book. Gorgeous, absolutely gorgeous. I went to see him talk a couple years ago in London. Really inspirational.

For me there are certain rules that you could probably say are quite classical typography, but then if I want to chuck some Frankfurt in next to Helvetica, then I'll do it. It's not about being really anal about it. I'm anal in terms of design, but not, like, "The grid has to be applied and it has to function like this. Headline there, this there . . ." I always try to mix and match and go with whatever is in my head. My style is just trying to bend it a little bit into a different direction or a different way of looking at it. I think that's what's great about Helvetica—it's almost like this little anchor. And through generations of design, it's a point of reference, while everything else just goes off on a tangent. It would be really interesting to see some kind of "tree" diagram, to see how design peeled off into these different things.

GH — Is there anything you'd like to design that you haven't gotten to do yet?

MCP — One of the things I've always really wanted to design is an identity for an airline. I'm fascinated by airports, and one of the best ones is the Bangkok airport. It's absolutely insane. It's beautiful. Everything's Helvetica, and the color system is really gorgeous.

So I'd love to do an airline. I just think to have something on the side of a plane—I guess it's the scale, I'd just really like to try to do stuff really big. The thing for me that I really find fascinating is trying to create a whole world for something, for this company, or whatever. I'd love to do, like, uniforms, or seats, you know, the whole thing. Trucks, that kind of thing, I just think would really be brilliant. I've done these little 12-inch record sleeves; I want to go a bit bigger-scale now! And again, it's that idea that something's designed to stand the test of time. I think that's a really interesting part of design.

Hopefully some of the things that I've designed will still be used in 20 or 30 years. I'd love to think that. I'd really like to try and take this graphic-design thing into producing things, like tables or furniture, and apply the same ideas, like Vignelli did with his plates and chairs. I'm so used to doing work that generally just goes on the surface of something. To actually create an object in three dimensions would be really fascinating to get into.

We're doing this show in New York, collaborating with Commonwealth Architects. We're doing 10 prints that each have a custom frame made out of Corian. The graphics bleed out into the frames, they're CNC routed into the frames, so it's something that's really tangible. I think we all are very visual people, but to try to think in 3-D is another thing that I'd like to try to get my head 'round and do. I think it'd be a good way to keep going, to keep applying myself. I'm a workaholic, so I'm just trying to do everything. Another thing I really want to do is a dinner service. Really traditional, really lovely—just imagine this beautiful bone china, with really modern, crisp graphics. Stuff like that.

GH — I'm still trying to imagine what "Build Airlines" would look like.

MCP — I'd love it. I just think to do something on that scale would be really lovely. I'd love to design everything, from the plane graphics down to the salt packets. I think it would just be so incredible to do.

People say, you know, "This whole consumerism thing, they're conning us into buying this, this, and this." I'm just one of those people who quite likes being suckered. I like collecting all this stuff. I remember Pop Will Eat Itself used to release—I know I'm sort of going backwards and forwards—but Pop Will Eat Itself used to release stuff like five 12-inches and six CDs and whatever. I love all that kind of stuff; it's that whole collecting thing. I just find it really brilliant.

The fact that I can do all these things; I think that I've got the best job in the world. Imagine—I was thinking about this the other day— you get paid to do something you really love. Somebody else pays you for doing it, and you get to keep what you do. It's absolutely insane. It's brilliant. It's really, really good.

—

Experimental Jetset — Danny van den Dungen (DVD)/ May 29, 2006 Amsterdam

If you combine punk rock, modernism, and art criticism, you'll end up with something close to Experimental Jetset, the Dutch design team of Marieke Stolk, Erwin Brinkers, and Danny van den Dungen. I spoke with Danny at the group's studio. Marieke and Erwin thought their English wasn't good enough to speak on camera, so they made Danny the group's spokesperson. But once I got to know them better, their English was perfect, of course.

—

Gary Hustwit — Let's talk about how you met, how you got into graphic design, and the beginnings of the Jetset.

> **Danny van den Dungen** — Actually, we met before we started working together, officially, in 1997. We all met at Rietveld Academie in Amsterdam, when Marieke and I were working on our graduation project, which was the redesign of a magazine called *Blvd*. Erwin was a year below us, and we asked him to do the illustrations for the magazine, then we asked him to join us on the project. Since then we've worked together. We had a lot of different names, actually, until we settled on Experimental Jetset.

GH — What were the earlier names?

> **DVD** — One of the first names we worked under was International Jetset, because that was the name of—I think it was the name of an LP by the Beat. Or was it the Special AKA? I don't remember anymore. We used the name International Designers Jetset or International Jetset, until we got a letter from a guy, also in the Netherlands, who worked under the name Jetset International or something. So we chose Experimental Jetset to make it more specific. And of course it's the title of a record by Sonic Youth, *Experimental Jet Set, Trash and No Star*. It's not our favorite record, but a lot of people always think it is. We just thought it was an interesting name; it has a certain tension, between "experimental" and "jetset"—almost like two opposite words. We liked that. It's a terrible, complicated name to use here in the Netherlands, when you're asking for a receipt or you need to spell out the name over the telephone. It's terribly complicated. But we just stick to it because we like it.
>
> This is the issue of *Blvd*. I think here we're still called International Jetset. It's a cheesy name. This is one the issues of the magazine that we

designed. It's actually one of the first times we used Helvetica, or perhaps it was the first time we became really aware of the practical side of it. It has quite a large family of different weights and different formats—condensed, extended. So we thought it would be quite nice to use that typeface for a magazine. You could use a lot of different weights, but it still had some kind of uniform look. So that was the first time we actually used it in a conscious way.

But it's terrible designing for a magazine. We never did it again after that. We analyzed why we aren't really good at designing magazines, and we think it really comes down to the fact that we always need to have some distance to design, to analyze it and look at it. For a magazine, you have to be really engaged. To make a good magazine, you almost have to be a member of the editing team or something, and the best magazines are designed by people who are prepared to engage in such a way with the editorial staff. I think the best example is Jop van Bennekom, who does *Re-Magazine*, *BUTT* magazine, and *Fantastic Man*. I think that he's a good example of somebody who does this editorial design thing very well.

For us, we just couldn't combine it. The distance that we have to take just to come to a good design solution, and the commitment of being really engaged with the editorial teams constantly conflicted with us. A lot of people think that to design you have to be completely engaged with the subject, but we always find that it's good to have some kind of distance from it. For example, Reid Miles, who made the iconic Blue Note record sleeves, actually hated jazz. He traded in all his jazz records for classical records. I always think of that—that you don't have to particularly like the subject of what you're designing for. Some distance is good, because in a way you are the outsider looking in. Clients come to you for that, to look at something from the outside.

When you get the call for an assignment, it's always really hard to judge whether it will be an interesting assignment or not. Sometimes you say, "Okay, we will do it," because the people on the phone are really persuasive, and you say yes, and you expect nothing, and then suddenly it becomes the best assignment ever. It's always quite hard to judge that the moment you get the call. Although it is one of the nicest moments of the whole assignment—the moment you get the assignment, and then the moment it is printed. Between those two moments, it is hell, an uphill battle to get everything done. Those two moments are actually the two nicest moments, and the stuff in between is always kind of bad.

GH — Can you talk about your musical influences and your design influences?

    DVD — When we were young teenagers, all three of us were very inspired and fascinated by all these music subcultures that existed. We were all interested in stuff like psychobilly, New Wave, American hardcore music, and it formed us. These were all very consistent subcultures with a very outspoken aesthetic sensibility, in a way.

I think we were really inspired by the record sleeves, the T-shirts, the posters, the badges, that kind of stuff. I think that really shaped us. I think when people now look at our work now, they cannot see that influence anymore. But for us it's still there. It's sometimes hidden—the idea of this consistent, aesthetic, almost hermetic world that you're shaping. For us it has a lot to do with the idea of subculture—almost like a bubble, or something existing against everything else. That has a lot to do with it.

For me, personally, I was really influenced by American comics. For example, I was really influenced by *Raw* magazine. When I left the house this morning, I was thinking about what to say here and I saw this issue lying around. This is from 1984, so I was 12 or 13. I was really influenced by this, and I was really influenced by people like Savage Pencil, who did the cover of this compilation record on Blast First, *Nothing Short of Total War*.

So I came from this background, and then suddenly I was confronted with this advertisement in a magazine. This really had a big impact on me. It is a record sleeve from Foetus by Jim Thirlwell. This was in 1985 or something. It was written up in a lot of magazines that Thirlwell designed his own record sleeves. I never really gave the idea of design-ing a lot of thought, because for me, you were either drawing or writing, and I never really realized that you could make something that looked completely without a personal signature, but still had a lot of impact—a kind of aggressiveness.

Before that, I'd always thought that aggressiveness was displayed in handwriting—in the signature—then I was confronted with this stuff. I suddenly thought, "Wow, this is something else, and this is even more threatening, in a way." A lot of people always have the feeling that printed matter just comes out of nothing, you know? People don't realize that somebody is putting it together. This was really the moment when I suddenly realized it. I'm speaking for myself but I think all three of us came from this background—psychobilly, garage rock, American hardcore, that kind of stuff. So I do think that the idea of an overall aes-thetic sensibility still plays a large role in our work.

GH — So that's your collective influence as a practice. How do you explain punk ideology from a design perspective? How does it fit with modernism?

DVD — When you think about it, punk is actually an interesting system. You have these two poles, these two opposite sides. There's the "no future," nihilism side, and there is this do-it-yourself, constructive side. In the whole punk movement, these two sides are constantly coming together in different combinations, and it's like a struggle between these two opposite forces.

I think, in a way, it's very much a smaller model of what is happening in modernism. You also have these different forces, this more destructive, nihilistic side, which can be found in Dadaism, in Surrealism, and this more constructive side, from the Bauhaus. I think that this idea of relating two opposites with each other in different combinations is really similar in punk and modernism. I wouldn't mind calling punk a modernist movement, like Futurism, or Surrealism. I wouldn't be afraid to call punk one of the late, great modernist movements. I also think that a lot of things that we learned about modernism are coming, in a way, through punk.

Of course, one of the more logical movements connected with punk is Situationism, because of Greil Marcus's *Lipstick Traces*. He points out the connections between those movements very well. For example, the sleeve I just showed you, *Nothing Short of Total War*, is a compilation album from the record label Blast First. It's an English label that references the famous Blast Manifesto by Wyndham Lewis from 1914. It was part of a movement called Vorticism, an English form of Futurism. He has these two lists: blast this and bless that—like pros and cons. This record label is called Blast First, and they also show part of the actual manifesto on the inner sleeve. I think all these little references drew us into modernism.

But then again, we have a pretty exotic view of modernism. I think a lot of the things that we call modern, other people call postmodern. For us, modernism does have a more subversive side. I think that whole vision of modernism as something that is primarily concerned with functionalism, utilitarianism, is something that emerged much later. That is more like a late modernist thing. I think the early modernism movements, like Dadaism, Futurism, Surrealism, all had their more subversive sides, and their more dialectical sides, so it went against something. It wasn't only about this idea of the pure functionalism.

When I was younger, I used to design for punk bands, even for death-metal bands, and stuff like that. I used to make T-shirts and record covers, even before I went to the Rietveld, actually. But after a while, I became more and more tired of the aesthetics as some kind of formula—the idea that punk has to look like this, and metal has to look like this, you know? There's a great anecdote about that, something that I tell students quite often. Right after I made a lot of stuff for punk bands, when we started Experimental Jetset, we made a series of flyers for BaseLine, a monthly hip-hop night in a rock venue called Paradiso. In the beginning, I was talking with the guy who organized it and I had this idea of presenting these flyers in the form of Filofax pages, with holes punched. It's quite a simple idea. People must save these flyers, so you put them in your diary and you can keep them with you.

So we made these flyers, and the guy who put on these hip-hop events told us they had to look more like hip-hop. You have to put more graffiti in it, and stuff like that. We persuaded him that the look that we had, the clean look totally focused on that Filofax idea, was the best way to go. For a year we made these flyers, and we always thought that they didn't belong to the hip-hop aesthetic. And then after a year we received calls from people who said, "We want you to design these record sleeves in a typical hip-hop style, like you used for your BaseLine flyers."

That was the moment that we realized how makeable, how flexible, these styles are, and that you can dictate it. I think that the core of modernist belief is that you can make the rules as a designer. It's quite an old-fashioned idea, and a lot of people don't really believe in it anymore, but we still have the idea of the makeable world. We realized that the aesthetic style for a specific musical subculture, for example, is decided by very few people, and you can really be active in that. That was the first time that we realized that.

GH — Let's talk about Helvetica. Maybe your thoughts about it, the ideology behind it and your reasons for using it?

DVD — It's funny, that's one question we always fail to answer well. It's not because we don't have an answer but because we have so many answers, in a way. Over years of working with a typeface, you constantly see new reasons. Right now, I think there is a beauty in the idea of using something that is seen as quite standard to express something that is quite personal and unique. The tension between the two opposites — something that is widely available and that everybody uses, but then to use it in a way that nobody else would — the tension that comes from that is quite beautiful. I always compare it to electric guitar in a way, you know? I like the idea that some bands have a completely classic setup, like just electric guitar, a bass guitar, drums, and someone singing. It's a formula, but it still works in a different way every time. There's a lot you can do with it. I think it's quite beautiful.

In the beginning, our reason for using Helvetica was purely practical. It has a large family of different sizes, different weights: condensed, extended, even rounded. Not that we ever used them all, but there are a lot of different sizes you can use, and we thought that was really practical. At the same time, it also has this almost nostalgic quality. I think that a lot of people think that young designers use typefaces like Helvetica in a more superficial way — as an appropriation of a style, or as a superficial use of something that is purely formal — but I think we would very much disagree with that.

All three of us grew up in the visual landscape of the Netherlands in the 1970s. It was a time that was dominated by the last moments of late modernism. I grew up in Rotterdam, and the logotype for our city was designed by Wim Crouwel. The city where Erwin grew up, that logotype was designed by Total Design. And yesterday when we were walking around the city, you saw the logotype for de Bijenkorf, which was designed by Josef Müller-Brockmann. The de Bijenkorf has always had a very big visual impact in the cities where we grew up. The stamps were designed by Crouwel, the telephone book was designed by Crouwel, the atlas that we used in school was designed by Crouwel. So for us it's almost like a natural mother tongue. It's something really natural. A lot of people think you study it from books, and then copy it, or something, but I would really say that it's almost in our blood.

I can also see why there was a generation that was really against it, because it was quite dominant, of course, in the 1970s. But for us, we learned to deal with it in a natural way, or at least that is what we hope.

We hope to use the language, because I think it's more a language than a style, in a way. A style only refers to a superficial layer that you put over something. I think that the way we grew up with it and are using it also affects the content very much. The way the parts relate to each other, the whole and the parts. I think we learned to love this language and to use it in a more personal way. That's why we don't have a problem with it, as maybe the generation of designers did who were working in the 1970s and were rebelling against this late-modernist style.

I want to come back to opposites; a lot of our ideas have this concept of opposites that synthesize into something else. I do think that the way we use it is a sort of synthesis, a mixture of these two different viewpoints. You were talking about the flower children that Vignelli hated so much. I do think that we are some synthesis of this late-modernist style and the style that came right after it. That is how I see it, and how we're using it. A lot of critics see it more as a cynical or ironic postmodernist trick, but I don't think they realize how much it has been a part of the world we grew up in, and that it's quite honest. I do think we use it in an honest and respectful way.

GH — What are your thoughts on the general public's understanding or awareness of typography now? Do you think people care? Do you think they know they're influenced by it, but don't really understand why?

DVD — Generally speaking, I think that people have a different relationship with type than they have with images. Of course, type is also an image, and images can be also used as type, but you can see this as an underestimation of type. It's too bad that people aren't more aware of type, but in a way, I also think that's the strength of it. An image immediately pulls somebody into an atmosphere in a fairly aggressive way. People are drawn into this space suggested by the image. For example, the full-color photographic image represents reality, it's a gateway or window into another world. On the other hand, type is more of an indirect window, because it is not the type itself but what is written with the type that pulls people in.

The reason why we prefer using type rather than an image has a lot to do with the influences we had when we were just coming out of school. We were quite interested in *The Society of the Spectacle* by Guy Debord. I don't think we are so influenced by it now, but it had a large influence on us back then. Our interpretation of that manifesto had a lot to do with how Debord described a world that is dominated by images. He described a material base and a superstructure of images, projections, representations, and the disconnection between those two layers that brought forth a certain kind of alienation, and this alienation, he believed, was at the core of a lot of problems.

Even though it was written about 40 years ago, it had an impact on us because we were very aware of what is now called visual culture—this world of brands or images. So we were fairly aware of this problem and thought about how we could be graphic designers without adding to the hegemony of the image. Our simple and most naive solution was to use type instead of image. Of course, like I said, it is a false distinction between type and image, but we do think that by using type on a poster, and not a photographic image, you're not giving people the illusion that they're looking at a representation of life, for example. You give people the awareness that they're only looking at a printed piece of paper.

This also explains why we're quite interested in white space and empty space on a poster. We constantly want to make people aware that what they're looking at is not some kind of alternative reality or some kind of illusion that they have to be a part of, or some kind of projection, but just a printed piece of paper. And that plays a really large part in our thinking, and even though we're not really convinced that it automatically helps to lessen alienation, for us, it's still a very big part. We don't want to show slices of life; instead, we want to show sheets of paper, because we think that is more honest.

Helvetica plays a big part in this, because Helvetica is a type that doesn't suggest that it is handwritten, because then you have the illusion again. It doesn't suggest that it is carved into wood or stone, with the serifs, you know? Then you have the illusion of something that's not real. Since Helvetica is specifically designed for printed matter, it references only the history of graphic design, in a way. To use a typeface is a clue, or cue for people to realize that it's only a printed piece of paper they're looking at and not something else—that idea of the poster as an object plays a big part in our work. I think we're more interested in making objects—at least that's what we're trying to do. We want the viewer to see a poster as an object that you can put holes in. Even though it is only a few millimeters thick, it still is a thing more than an image. I'm not saying we always achieve this, but we're constantly trying to make people aware of this material base by puncturing through this superstructure of images.

It's funny that in the United States people tend to see Helvetica as this corporate monster, this kind of neutral, sterile typeface. It always surprises me that the people who are advocates of Helvetica and the people who are against it always agree that Helvetica is a neutral typeface. One group finds it a great typeface because it is neutral, and then the other group dislikes it because it is neutral. For us, we don't see it as neutral at all; of course it is not a neutral typeface. It has certain values. It has ideological baggage, so it isn't neutral at all, and that makes it even better, we think.

I find Helvetica self-referential. Because we grew up with it, we also think it has a certain friendliness to it. I can understand that people in the States don't have this same relationship with it at all, but for us, it speaks in a very friendly way. I also find it typically Dutch, which is strange, because, of course, it's a Swiss typeface. But because we learned it from people like Crouwel in this Dutch visual landscape of the 1970s, I always see it as typically Dutch.

It's also funny because a lot of people connect Helvetica with the dangers of globalization and standardization. Well, because I see Helvetica as typically Dutch, I'm not afraid of that quality at all, because I know that anyone can put their own twist on it. I think you can put as much nationality in the spacing of a typeface as in the typeface itself. I think that the way Crouwel uses Helvetica is typically Dutch. That's why I'm never really impressed with the argument that Helvetica is this global monster.

GH — Let's talk about the effect of technology on design. When you were at the Rietveld, was there computer design? The Macintosh was probably just starting to really catch on then.

DVD — Yes, absolutely. I remember when we were at the Rietveld, there were these fonts, the FUSE fonts. I think Neville Brody was the editor of that series. These fonts were great, because they pushed the boundaries and showed what a font can be. In a way, those FUSE fonts showed that everything that can be programmed behind a button on a keyboard was, in fact, a font. It played with that definition. Any group of characters on a floppy disk, organized in a certain way, suddenly became a typeface. It's not that we were against the experimentation that people like David Carson and Emigre, and FUSE, that Neville Brody did. Those old issues of *Ray Gun*—I love them. I think what those people did was certainly really important. We think what we do is an extension of that, in a way.

All that time spent hunting for the next typeface; it took a lot of energy. I remember students who were really disappointed because they wanted to use a certain typeface but saw that somebody else had already used it, then they felt that they couldn't use it because they wanted to be original. With Helvetica, this whole point is nonexistent, because everybody is using Helvetica. So there's never this constant drive to the next new, hip typeface. By keeping this one thing consistent, you can concentrate on so many other things—the overall concept, the paper, the binding. Just by keeping this one little element consistent, it just opens up a lot of other possibilities.

GH — Yeah, the next new, hip typeface . . . and with the Internet, that starts to spread even faster, that viral quality of people passing stuff around and getting used in different places.

DVD — It's difficult to relate Helvetica directly to stuff like the web, because it existed before that and it's not really a typeface that was shaped through the Macintosh or through web design, which you do have with other typefaces. For example, now you see a lot of bitmapped faces that are clearly inspired by how they're displayed on the web. For us personally, we think that Helvetica is very much tied in with printed matter. When you look at our website, the body text of our website is not necessarily in Helvetica, though you could do your own settings so that it is Helvetica. But Helvetica definitely has a closer relationship with printed matter than it does to websites.

What is interesting is always hearing these arguments against the readability or legibility of Helvetica, because it doesn't have serifs. In general, sans-serif type for body text is traditionally seen as being less readable than serif type. There's a kind of urban myth that German printers didn't want to get rid of their sans-serif type—the metal type—so they invented this story that sans-serif type was less readable than serif type.

But it's interesting how everything goes in cycles. For web design, it is pretty much accepted these days that sans-serif type is now more readable than serif type because of the screen resolution. It's interesting that this whole argument turned completely the other way around. So the renaissance of sans-serif type is partly because of the web.

I think it was Zuzana Licko who said, "You read best what you read most." I do believe in this dictum, in the same way that people in medieval times could read those manuscripts that we now cannot read anymore. I think that a text set in Helvetica is just as readable as a serif type. How do we measure readability anyway? Is it only about how fast you can read? It's not necessarily always true that the faster you read, the better you understand it. It's ridiculous to think that. I mean, there are people who can read hundreds of books in weeks, but it doesn't say anything about the way their memory processes everything that they've read. Sometimes you read one sentence, and you keep walking around all day trying to chew on that sentence.

People are reading stuff constantly in different ways. I think to let readability dictate your way of designing is to let a certain style control you. Like the project to design a hip-hop flyer in that hip-hop style. I don't believe in that whole idea that there exists a natural order and that you cannot go against it. Again, that's pretty much a modernist idea. But I do believe that we can let the concern for readability define us.

Maybe it's best put like this: I do think that you can look at a typeface in a scientific way, and that you can measure the speed of readability, but it doesn't really make choosing a typeface itself a science. It isn't mathematics. You can look at it in a scientific way, but in the end there are other arguments and other intentions that are as important or maybe even more important than readability.

—

Wim Crouwel (WC)/ May 30, 2006 Amsterdam

The first thing a visitor notices upon entering Dutch design legend Wim Crouwel's apartment is the abundance of chairs. They seem to be everywhere, one example each of every important modernist chair; a Le Corbusier here, a Rietveld there, an Eames tucked into a corner. Wim and I sat down on two of them (I can't remember which ones) and started our conversation.

—

Gary Hustwit — I guess we'll start with the basics. How did you originally get into design?

Wim Crouwel — Well, I was trained in an old-fashioned art school. It was a real arts-and-crafts school, the latest in Holland. It did not turn into the system of the Bauhaus. So I learned painting and sculpture and etching and lithography. In the beginning, I didn't know what to do. I thought I should be a fashion designer or an interior decorator or a painter. I painted until 1954.

Then I went to the academy here in Amsterdam, the Rietveld Academy. There I got my first exposure to typography. From that moment on, from 1953 to 1954, I became interested in typography. My first job was in an exhibition company; for a few years I had a job there. Ever since that, I've been on my own. But for two years in this company, I was doing 50 percent three-dimensional work and 50 percent graphic design. Working in that exhibition company, I met Swiss designers. They came from Paris, from the United States Information Service, and we made exhibitions for the Marshall Plan for Europe. So ever since I met those designers, I was interested in Swiss typography. I traveled to Switzerland and made many more friends. I became interested in that very specific kind of typography.

GH — I guess that's right about the time you said you were originally using Akzidenz-Grotesk and other sans-serif typefaces.

WC — Yeah. Well, the thing is that in Holland, we had one large company who distributed office equipment and printing machines and also type. It was the Amsterdam Type Foundry. They had their own typefaces. As a sans serif, they had Nobel. That was, in my view, an ugly typeface.

I tried to use Akzidenz-Grotesk like the Swiss did, but you couldn't get it in Holland. So in the beginning, it was all cutting and gluing and clipping these things together on paper to use for your posters and so on. Then we found a typesetter who had Akzidenz-Grotesk. But mainly we had to make do with similar type, like Grotesk from Monotype; I used that for catalogs. And Gill—Gill was available in Holland. Fortunately, at the end of the fifties, Helvetica came. In the beginning, we couldn't get it here in Holland. But through our channels, it was made available for designers. So let's say in 1958, I started to use Helvetica.

We were, in that period, thinking that one typeface was enough for everything. We used only one typeface. When I started my office, Total Design, in 1963, we used only one typeface throughout the company. It was mainly Univers at that time; Univers came a few years after Helvetica. It was more a system of type. Helvetica, in my practice, was more or less swept away by Univers. But throughout the sixties and seventies, I still thought you could do everything with one typeface.

I remember in that period I designed books for Abrams in New York—books about painters like Rembrandt and Dürer and so on. I remember having fights with the publisher. I wanted to do a book on Rembrandt in Univers. He said, "You can't do that. That's impossible. We won't sell the book." I said, "If you want to use typefaces specific to a certain period, you won't have enough typefaces. It's crazy. You should use only one typeface." Well, sometimes I lost the battle. Very often, I won.

GH — Do you still feel that way?

WC — Well, I'm much more generous today, although I still use sans-serif typefaces. I love them. In that respect, I'm an old-fashioned designer. I still stick to one typeface—maybe it's Helvetica sometimes, or Univers. Sometimes it's Frutiger, which I think is a beautiful new re-creation of Univers. That's what I use today. Even Gill—I rediscovered—because it's a fantastic typeface. It has a kind of human touch. It's less rigid than the Swiss typefaces. Although every time I see Helvetica, for instance, or Akzidenz-Grotesk, I feel the beauty of it and the evenness and the human atmosphere around it. I love to use these types of typefaces.

In the sixties, I became very interested in grid systems and digital systems. It was the early time of computers. When I went to a large printing exhibition in Germany in 1965, I saw the first digital typesetters from Hell in Kiel. It was the first company that came with such a machine. The results were horrible—absolutely horrible. I thought, if this is the future of digital typesetting, it's a horror. So I studied this system. The problem is that the letter shapes, especially round shapes, are changing all the time. The larger the typeface, the nicer that typeface becomes. But if it's a small typeface of 6- or 8-points, it looks horrible.

I had an idea to make another system of alphabets. It was a kind of theoretical exercise to make a typeface consisting only of 45- and 90-degree angles. They're only straight lines that would never change whether the type was at a small or a large size. I designed a whole alphabet; I called it the New Alphabet. I published it in a little book. I said, "Well, you can't use this alphabet, because it's unreadable. This is a theory. This is a way of thinking." My goal was that typeface designers should design along these lines of thinking. I got a lot of response to this New Alphabet in that period. I traveled all around the world to give lectures on it. It was a nice time for a few years. I made posters and all sorts of things that were more or less in the direction of that thinking, until the beginning of the seventies. For five or six years, I was only thinking in that direction. And then you lose interest and you go on with your work.

Suddenly, in the nineties, I discovered that they used this typeface in pop music magazines. But they made it a little more readable; they changed the type until it became readable. I said, "Well, how is it possible?" After 30 years—especially in England. It was all in England. Then, I think it was in 1997 or 1998, I was invited to England to give, again, lectures on this typeface. I said, "Christ, this is old stuff for me." But there was new interest in it. And then the Foundry in London asked if they could digitize it, so that people could use it. I said, "Well, yes, you can do it. No problem. But nobody is going to use it, because you can't read it!" The strange thing is that it sold very well. I don't understand why people want it, but anyhow. Maybe they're all just collectors or something like that.

GH — So you thought it wasn't readable either?
> WC — No. It wasn't readable. The spacing of the type is quite narrow. It is exactly the width of the stroke of the type. So the interior of the type is always open, so that the interior of the type looks like the spacing. It's very strange. If you see a page set in this type, it's a problem to read it. It was a theoretical exercise. I never expected that anyone would use it. I thought it was a nice project to do. I was working on it for a few years and published the book and then forgot about it.

GH — Do you have an opinion on whether sans serifs are more legible for body copy?
> WC — I was never that much interested in that debate. If you went to graphic-design gatherings like AGI, there was always a lecture from someone on legibility. There were a few of these connoisseurs who did a lot of research on it. The results were always a few percent more legibility for a serif typeface versus a sans-serif typeface. I was never impressed by that. I said, "It's just whatever you put in front of people. If they're interested in reading it, they read it." Today, when people read copies of copies of copies and faxes and things that are almost unreadable, they can still read everything. Sometimes I say if you redid that legibility research from the fifties now, you would have completely different results. And nobody is interested in readability and legibility research anymore. You never, at any of these conferences, see these people anymore.

It proves, more or less, what I've always thought—that it makes no sense, these things. A sans-serif type today is as readable as a serif type. It's just a question of atmosphere. I like the atmosphere around the sans-serif typefaces—the modernistic feeling. I'm a modernist, you know. I was trained in that period, I lived in that period. I love modernism. I'm going next week to London to see the exhibition on modernism. I want it, you know. But that's my life; I'm surrounded with furniture from that period, and I can't change myself anymore. But if I see designers today using all different typefaces—one day one typeface, the other day the other typeface, all in favor of a certain atmosphere—I don't like that.

GH — You talked a little bit about the beginnings of digital technology and how it affected typography. What are your feelings about it now?

WC — Well, the whole technique of digital typesetting is much better now than in the beginning. If I was a young designer using the technology now, I would never have done this experiment of doing a typeface along straight lines, because the dots are much smaller now. They can do perfect type today digitally. It's no longer an issue. But anyhow, I love technique; I'm very interested in these modern techniques.

I started late with the computer; I think it was in 1993 that I bought my first computer, and I learned it myself. I can handle it quite well now, but not like young people. I'm slow with it. I can do it. But I'm very interested. I would have liked to have the computer in the sixties, because we could have sped up our work. We could have done it so much better, especially all the layers you can bring into your work now. We had the greatest problem, for instance, in the fifties and sixties bringing two or three layers into our work. You needed to do it by photograph; you used all kinds of crazy techniques. It was very complicated. Working on a poster took us days—three, four days before you'd finish it. Now within half an hour, you have your ideas and you can make variations and make a good choice. You can't do better design with a computer, but you can speed up your work enormously. Our output is enormous today. I'm very interested in that. I hope to keep in touch with the modern techniques. I try to keep up with the new systems that come out and new programs. From that respect, I would like to be a little younger today.

GH — What are the downsides to the new technologies?

WC — What I do not understand, but young designers do, is how they design with a mouse and not with a pencil. I can't. I always do my sketching by pencil first and bring it to a certain level where I think, "This is the idea. This is what I want." And then I go to the computer and try to realize it. I see young designers starting on the computer with the mouse, without sketching. I hardly understand how people can think without a pencil—without their fingers. Now it's straight from the eyes through the head to the machine. Maybe the mouse is a replacement of the pencil, or something like that. It's difficult for me to understand.

The downside is that you have so many possibilities already prepared in software that it blocks you from thinking of original ideas, because the computer delivers you a program of doing certain things along certain lines. That cuts you off from unidentified fields where, in my opinion, the designer should be. Although, I do see work from young designers that I love very much. They are the creative ones, and that's how it should be. But I think the larger group of designers today stick to their machines, and if you look at the work, you can see that it comes from the machine.

That's a disadvantage, in my opinion. You should try to get away from that, so that people can't see how you came to your results. They shouldn't see—just as when you're making a film, the audience shouldn't notice what type of camera it comes from, whether it comes from an old-fashioned 35mm camera or from a digital camera; the results should be the main thing. That's what I think of the modern techniques in graphic design too. Maybe for young people it's not a disadvantage, but I think it stands in the way sometimes.

GH — Have the new technologies increased the amount of good design that's out there, or has the public's awareness of good design and typography changed?

WC — Well, not that much changes in the world, I think. The percentage of, from my point of view, good design, against the total output, doesn't change at all. Much more is produced now—there are many more designers, maybe 100 times more designers than there were in the fifties—but the percentage of good design always stays the same. You see a lot of rubbish around, but in the fifties we saw a lot of rubbish around too.

In terms of people's perception of design, that also hasn't changed that much, in my opinion. There is always a group of people that love good design, that have an understanding of good design. But there is a larger group that doesn't understand anything; they're not interested at all. I've thought the same way during the fifties, the sixties, the seventies, right up till now, that you work for a rather small group of people, people who are culturally interested. These are the only people that interest me. I'm not interested in all the other people, the same way they are not interested in me. We should accept it, I think. I don't give a damn.

GH — Can you talk a little bit about your approach from a philosophical standpoint, how you approach a project? What kinds of concerns do you have?

WC — Well, the thing is that I'm always interested in clarity. It should be clear. It should be readable. It should be straightforward. That's why after the first early experiments of Müller-Brockmann with grids, I became very interested in them. In 1957, when Müller-Brockmann published his first ideas on grids for graphic design, I met him for the first time. I was highly influenced by Müller-Brockmann; he was one of my great heroes.

So I started gradually using grids for my design, for my catalogs for museums. I invented a grid, and within the grid I played my game, but always along the lines of the grid, so that there was a certain order in it. Because clarity and order are very important for typography. Whatever typeface you use, it should be within a certain framework and it should, from the first page to the last page, have more or less the same line that runs through it, in order to make it easy for people to read.

Readability interests me, not in respect to the typeface, but in the order, the composition of the page, so that in one look you can see what it's all about. That's why I use grids; that's why they called me Gridnik. We overdid it in our Total Design period. We had piles of grid systems and we always, for a certain job, took a grid that was most suitable for the job, and we made our work. That's how we generated typography at Total Design. I still believe in that. When I design a book, I read the content, I decide that the structure of the page should be such and such, I develop a grid along that line of thinking, and I start to fill it in. That's how I work; I can't do it in a different way. It always starts with the content, which brings me to a certain order on the page, which brings me to a grid, and that gives me my typography.

I think that it's the same with corporate-identity programs. At Total Design we did a lot of corporate-identity programs. The idea was that it should tell what a company is about; you should differentiate the company from other companies. That was the main goal. It was always for the clarity of the people; the people who look at companies in the world should know what company this is, what company that is. That's why corporate identity was a very important thing. Today, corporate identity is often much more like publicity. In our view, corporate identity was never publicity, it was always a way for people to differentiate companies from each other. Publicity came some steps behind that. I never wanted to be involved in publicity design. Never. Advertising—I've never done advertising or things like that, because that was not my field. I couldn't do it. You have specialists for that, and I appreciate them highly. They are clever in that respect, but it was not my field.

That's how I look at type. We did a lot of signage systems, for instance, with always the same idea: it should be clear. My company did the signage system for Schiphol Airport. We used Akzidenz-Grotesk. We went back to Akzidenz-Grotesk because it was the most readable sans-serif type. Now they've changed it—they changed it to Univers or to Frutiger. Well, those are better typefaces possibly, a little step further. But in my opinion, Akzidenz-Grotesk, with all its disadvantages, is still a very readable and very good typeface for general signage. That's why I loved Switzerland so much; you saw it all around. It's the atmosphere. It's a modernistic atmosphere.

GH — Earlier you were saying that young people now just look to the computer, and the programs give them a certain way of doing things, and they don't think outside of that. But doesn't the grid sometimes have the same effect?

WC — Oh, well, of course. It's a framework that keeps me within certain limits. It works like eye blinders. You're right. I sometimes, especially, put those blinders on. I don't want to see left, and I don't want to see right, because I feel fine going down this path. It's restricting, but since I developed it in the fifties and have been so involved with it, and have learned more and more about how grid systems work, for me it's no longer a restriction. But if you bring young students, for instance, and say they have to use a grid, maybe for them it's absolutely a restriction, since they know the freedom of the computer. For me it's a tool of creating order, and creating order is typography. It's nothing but creating order.

GH — We were talking about how when you see sans-serif typefaces like Helvetica, there's a certain feeling around them that you like. You mentioned some of those adjectives that you associated with that feeling. Can you talk a little bit more about that?

WC — Well, in the beginning there was Akzidenz-Grotesk. It had slight differences in the width of the strokes. It went from a little bigger to a little smaller and the ends were cut off at 90 degrees of the direction of the stroke. That made it very readable. Then Helvetica came from

Miedinger and he made it even more straight. He cut all the strokes in the horizontal direction, so there is a little bit more horizontalism in it. That means that the lines of text, the words, become a little more quiet and even. That was an advantage; it was creating a little more quietness. Akzidenz-Grotesk, in all its different grades and heights, was always different. There was too much of a human hand in it. Helvetica was a little more machined; it was doing away with these manual details in it. We were impressed by that because it was more neutral, and neutralism was a word that we loved. It should be neutral; it shouldn't have a meaning in itself. The meaning is in the content of the text and not in the typeface. That's why we loved Helvetica very much.

After Helvetica came Univers. Univers went one step further. They created the same x-height in the Italic and the Bold and the Medium and the Light. You could use, in one line, all the various grades of the typeface. You could never do that before, even with the Helvetica. So it went a step further. At the same time, Univers had some strange things in it, like the *a*, where the rounding of the *a* came straight in the standing stroke. Helvetica always had a nice, very aesthetic touch. Univers was harsher, I would say. It was more systematic; it was system thinking. We embraced it, but something got lost that was still there in Helvetica. I can understand why today people long for Helvetica, and you see it coming up again. Meanwhile, Univers is disappearing.

So today there are many more sans-serif typefaces created, all going back to Helvetica but having their differences. We have a whole wide range of very good sans-serif typefaces now. But Helvetica was a real step from the 19th century Akzidenz-Grotesk, and suddenly, for the first time, there was a new typeface with a whole new atmosphere. That's why we embraced Helvetica.

GH — Do you think 50 years later it's still neutral? Do you think it now has taken on . . .

WC — You can say it's neutral in the sense that we saw it as neutral in that period. But it always depends on the specific time frame. In that period—having Akzidenz-Grotesk, having Futura, having Gill—Helvetica was very neutral if you compared it with those other typefaces. They all had very human touches; Helvetica was much more of a machined typeface. Today, compared with other typefaces, I think Helvetica has its own beauty, it has its own human touch. But it's still one of the most neutral typefaces. I can't think of a more neutral typeface than Helvetica, although people regard it differently now than during that period. We thought for a very long time that Futura was a neutral typeface, but it's not at all. It's constructed, and you can read the construction in it. So it's not neutral at all. It's a constructivist typeface.

I still think Helvetica is a very neutral typeface, although it has a different meaning than in the fifties. It's always changing; time is changing; the appreciation of typefaces is changing very much. Why you grab a certain typeface for a certain job has a different meaning than when we grabbed a typeface in the fifties for a certain job. You're always a child of your time, and you cannot step out of that. So young designers today, even I as an old designer—I cannot remove myself from the time frame I'm working in. I see new typefaces coming, and I compare them; I try them sometimes. I say, "Well, can I use it? Am I happy with it?"

I designed my own typeface, called Gridnik. It was a commission from Olivetti for an electric typewriter. Müller-Brockmann, and I, and another designer were invited to do typefaces for that electric typewriter. But it's a typeface that fits much better today than it ever fit in the seventies when I developed it. It's very strange. In the beginning after this experiment for Olivetti, I designed a postage stamp for the Dutch post office with that typeface on it. The word "Netherlands" was done in that typeface, and the numbers. Then afterwards, I developed the whole typeface again for the Foundry. I think it's a typeface that fits much better with today, and maybe that's why I can hardly use it myself. I can handle Helvetica much better than I can handle my own typeface. I see young designers use it perfectly. I see magazines done with it, and so on, and I think, "Well, Christ, I would have liked to use my own typeface in that way." It's very strange. That, again, has to do with the time frame.

GH — I noticed the address numbers on your building are set in . . .
WC — Well, the thing is that the facade of our apartment block was renovated last year. They repainted the whole building. We had, in the top of our entryways, little light boxes with a lamp behind and a number on it. They all were gone; the lights were broken. For many years, we didn't have a lit house number. And then after the renovation, the board of our block asked me, "Would you do the type for us, because we want to reinstall the lights."

I thought, "Should I use a typeface from 1930? This housing block is from 1930. Maybe I should use Futura, which was designed in 1928." I tried it, but against this very romantic architecture of the Amsterdam School, which was very expressionistic, I thought I should use a much more neutral typeface that stands out better against this block. You should not try to use a typeface from the same period, as I've discovered. I never liked to use typefaces that matched the kind of atmosphere of the subject. So I used Helvetica. People are very happy with it; I'm happy with it. You should include these numbers in your film. You should film them.

GH — Yeah, we're going to. We'll go outside.
WC — The facade of our apartment building last week was filmed by about 10 film crews. It was crazy because one of the largest criminals in Holland owned the garages on our block. We didn't know he was a criminal. He was killed two years ago, and we found out that he was the owner of the garages. They discovered last week from a witness that there are two bodies between the walls in two of the garages—dead bodies. So the police came, and they broke open the walls to see if there were bodies in them. All the television networks came and filmed the facade of our building. I think our Helvetica got a lot of television coverage. Unfortunately, they didn't find the bodies.

GH — Wow. Do you have any thoughts on the next step in typography and type design, like where you see it going in the next 50 years?

WC — Well, it's very difficult to predict where it's going, because there have never been so many typefaces. Every day new typefaces come, because the programs to design them are so easy and so simple today that everyone who has an idea for a typeface can very easily create it. In the fifties, we were still working with lead type. It took years to bring a new typeface to market. Today, within two days you can bring a new typeface to the market. It's a simple affair. Compared with the fifties, it's a hundredth of the time, and it's all due to the computer.

It's very hard to predict where it's going because for every subject, for every corporate identity, for every World Cup, you can design a new typeface, and use it instantly. I think this will go on for quite a long time. Maybe a counter-movement will come that says, "Let's do away with all this, because you can do it all with one typeface," which is what I've always thought. But I don't think so. I think we will see in the coming years many, many more typefaces coming into the market and as many falling off. But it adds to the whole history of typography. There are so many typefaces, every day new ones come. I can hardly say where it's going. I can't predict anything like this.

[We start looking through several books of Crouwel's work.]

WC — Shall I begin? Well, in the fifties, I used Akzidenz-Grotesk or my posters, as you see here. I worked for a museum in Eindhoven, the Van Abbe Museum. I made a whole series of posters—a lot of them with Akzidenz-Grotesk. And then around 1960, Helvetica starts to come in, like in this one where I made a poster just with type, and only Helvetica.

These are my first experiments around 1966, 1967, when the New Alphabet enters. That is for me, more or less, the end of the Helvetica period. Ever since, I've used Univers and other typefaces, and hardly Helvetica anymore, except for some specific jobs. Here, later on in the seventies, I used Helvetica again because this had to do with a dance company. The type of dance they did—it was a very advanced dance company. In my opinion, it should be Helvetica. That fit exactly the aesthetics and the way the dances were created. So that's why I went back to Helvetica, maybe as a kind of exception.

And then in the beginning of the seventies, I made Gridnik, and I used it for the Dutch postage stamps. These stamps were in use for almost 25 years until the Euro came a few years ago. But as you see here from exactly the same period, the beginning of the seventies, I made a poster with Futura. That was because this architect was a modernist architect and it was about his work. I grabbed Futura, thinking that it fit the man. So maybe I'm not consistent here. This was something I was always against, using typefaces for a certain atmosphere. But I must say that every now and then I couldn't resist doing it. I love the Univers. It's a beautiful typeface, but very much a Bauhaus typeface—very much the end of the twenties.

Later on in the eighties, I made these postage stamps on the Stijl Movement. In the beginning, if you see the sketches, I tried to use typefaces from Van Doesburg, one of the artists of the Stijl Movement. But I decided for the final designs not to use this typeface, because the illustration is already from the period. I used the most neutral typeface, Helvetica, for the lettering. I decided that there is a contrast between the subject and the neutral typeface that explains it. So that was the end of the eighties, when I still used it. Every now and then I use Helvetica again.

This is the book I made for the New Alphabet. It's all introduction. Here you see the columns of text in one typeface, and the same introduction in my typeface. It's very hard to read it. As I said, it was a very theoretical exercise. Here it's explaining why I did it. This is 6-point Garamond from the digitized period. You see the dots here, especially the curves, are changing all the time. If you have it twice as big, you have twice as many dots available. The whole shape changes. The basic idea is still there, but it changes all the time. This is what I couldn't stand. I said, "Let me do a typeface with only 90- and 45-degree angles, so that whether it's big or small, it's always the same even direction of dots." With this system, you could, with the computer, widen the type, narrow it, make it thin, make it bold. Here I show the variations. Then I used a photograph of the interior of an IBM computer, just to give the atmosphere of that period of the sixties—these very large mainframe computers. I showed the typeface with only one single dot per stroke and then the different variations—the light one, the regular one, the bold one, the stretched one—all these variations were possible. Then finally it was during this period that we went to the moon for the first time and the space walks, so I thought, "Well, this is exactly where it fits." By putting a line screen in this astronaut photograph, I put my typeface exactly within the line frame to express what I wanted to say with this typeface. It should fit this period.

One of my colleagues, Gerard Unger, who worked in my office in that period, said, "I'm going to give you an idea how, along your way of thinking, we could do a proper typeface." He published this pamphlet in response. You see here, again, 45- and 90-degree angles. He created a beautiful *a*, 40 lines per centimeter, and the numerals. He did it by handwriting; it was a quick response to my idea. And I thought, "This is exactly what I was waiting for." Unfortunately, nobody went on with it. Even Gerard Unger didn't go on with it, because he became a very well-known typeface designer, but never went further along this line of thinking. Anyhow, it was a very nice experiment. I loved that period.

[At this point the topic turns to Crouwel's collection of chairs.]

GH — We used to have an Eames chair like this in college. One of my roommates—this is before I knew anything about design or furniture— had an Aluminum Group chair. We didn't know what it was. We had it outside in the backyard—it got all rusted. We took the arms off it, we ended up just throwing it away.

WC — They're part of daily life in America.

GH — Well, there were a lot of them in offices in the '70s and '80s.

WC — There was a guy here in Holland who imported old motorcycles from America, these army cycles. What do you call them? Those large ones?

GH — Harley Davidson?

WC — Harley Davidson. He imported Harley Davidsons. He got large containers and shipped them full of Harley Davidsons to Europe. And he always filled them up with furniture—old furniture from Eames. He went out to the country and saw old chairs and bought them from people and sold them for a lot of money here.

GH — Is this an original Rietveld chair?

WC — Yeah, sure. I bought it from Rietveld.

GH — Really?

WC — Nineteen fifty-four. It has a nice poem underneath. A poem from Morgenstern—a German poem about sitting. He liked this poem very much. It's about the idea of sitting. That's what Rietveld glued underneath his chairs.

—

Erik Spiekermann (ES)/
May 31, 2006 Berlin

Of all the interviews I did for *Helvetica*, Erik Spiekermann was the only person I was scared of when I met him. On the morning we'd scheduled the interview, he was late; it was his birthday the night before and he'd been in Vienna. So while we waited, we tried to prepare a location to film the interview, so that we could start right when he got in. Luke, my cinematographer, didn't like the reflection that was coming off of a framed print on the wall, so we took the print down. When Erik showed up, the first thing out of his mouth was, "Who moved my fucking picture?" As we started to explain why we'd moved it, he said sternly, "Put it back." Of course, once we started our conversation, Erik was effusive and hilarious.

—

Gary Hustwit — First can we talk a little bit about your background, how you got involved in design and why you design typefaces?

Erik Spiekermann — You want me to start from the beginning? I mean, I turned 59 yesterday, so it's going to take two hours. I'll give you the quick *shcoop*, as we say in German. I was given a printing press by some neighbors when I was growing up, in a little town near Hanover. We call it *Hangover*. It's the most boring place in Germany. Our neighbors were printers, and I was always playing there, so they gave me little cutouts of paper. My father was a truck driver, so I didn't come from an artistic background; it was very ordinary, working-class. But the neighbors gave me this little platen press, which was this thing that you put on the table and pulled the handle down, and it would print. I guess that was desktop publishing, as we'd call it today.

So they gave me bits of type, and I'd play with them and put them together—it was almost like Legos for me. Then my father got me a book—I think I was 14 at the time—about how to set type and stuff. So I've always done this. In school when I would submit reports, I would print the covers of the reports. The type was crap. It was all stuff that I found, or that I would "liberate"—I used to work for printers and bring type back in my pockets. So I taught myself, but I had no real background.

And suddenly over time, when I started university, I had all these printing presses, because this was the late sixties when everyone was throwing away the metal type. So suddenly I had this press and that press and this type and that type, and I had a large printing office, essentially. It just kept growing, because I became known as the guy who collected this old crap. People would call me and they'd have two hundred typefaces in metal and would just want to get rid of them. I never paid for anything; it was all being thrown away. So I ended up with a printing company, and I made a living at it while I was at university.

I continued to learn more about printing after I graduated, just by doing it. My wife at the time was English, and in '73 we decided to move to London, so I put all the printing stuff into storage. And in '77 we decided to bring my press to Ladbroke Grove. We brought a massive truck over from Germany that was full of printing presses. We put all the stuff into a railway arch and went away for a holiday in Italy. When we came back, the place had burned down. Some lads next door were working on old cars and had accidentally set the place on fire. Everything burned, the ink, thinners, all my papers. So that was the end of my printing days, and I was stuck being a designer. I'd learned to be a designer out of necessity; many times I didn't have enough type, so I would have to strategize, think of how I could design a piece so that I'd be able to print it. Then I started working at a phototypesetting company in Waterloo, and I guess that was the beginning of my being a typesetter/designer, because my means of production, as my Marxist friends would call it, had disappeared.

So I was stuck being a designer, but I'd never learned design properly. I was a good typesetter. I'm a pretty good printer, or at least I was. I could do repros, all that shit, and I could spec type; I could spec type to the letter. I was very good at that stuff. In those days you had to spec type for the typesetter, and if you got it wrong, and they had to reset it, it could take two or three hours. So my role was to tell them whether it was going to be 19-point or 20-point, and how big the leading should be to fit in the given space. The advertising agencies in London would send us a sketch, and it would say "Space A," and then "Copy A," and the instructions were "FF," which meant "Fuck to Fit." In other words, get that text in there or else. And my role would be to say, "Okay, let's make it 21-point, and this or that typeface." So that's how I learned to look at type very closely, and if you do this for a while, it gets so familiar that you can do it in your sleep.

GH — So what was the first original typeface that you designed?
ES — Well, it wasn't actually original. What happened was that when my place burned down, there were a lot of typefaces that I'd brought over that were old German jobbing typefaces, very practical everyday faces that I liked, and that I used a lot, that didn't exist in phototypesetting. So I approached the Berthold foundry in Berlin, and I said, "I really think you should publish these, they're really cool, and why don't I do this for you." And they said, "Sure, go ahead." And looking back, they paid me ridiculously little money, like nothing. But I drew the letters—Berthold didn't have original specimens, or had very few, and I didn't have any complete specimens either. I basically had to cut it together from

different sizes of metal type, and my first job was to find as many letters as I could, and I found about 50 or 60. I remember I never found a *Y*, for example, and certain figures, so I had to make up a lot of stuff and also guess the weights.

It was a really good exercise. I didn't have to invent any new shapes— they were there. I just had to try to think, if I was the original designer a hundred years ago, how would I do it today? So I actually drew it in pen and ink; I still have the drawings somewhere. When I sent it in to Berthold, the artistic director there made corrections and corrections, because I was crap. I had a good eye, but I didn't know what to look for. So he just kept writing me back with corrections.

That first one was called Berliner Grotesk. It belongs to this large family of crooked-outline, heavy-duty German everyday type. Then I did a second one, Lo-Schrift, which was originally designed by Louis Oppenheim, and with that one I had to add a few weights. So I moved away from just doing artwork, essentially, to adding things, inventing new weights, and trying to think about how the old guys worked. I learned a lot just by looking at that stuff—measuring, and thinking how heavy is heavy, and how thin is thin. I learned from the old guys over the years. The first typeface I designed from scratch was the one I did for the German Post Office, in 1985.

GH — That's the typeface that would eventually become Meta?
    ES — Yes.

GH — Can you talk about that a little?
    ES — Yes, well I guess that one established the way I've worked since. I've never sort of woken up with a typeface coming out, you know, like some people, "Aha!" and they go to their easel, or whatever, and make these amazing brushstrokes. I don't have that urge. I wake up, and I usually just want to go back to sleep. For me, there's always been a problem that has to be solved by a typeface. In this case, the German Post Office, who we were doing corporate design for, they were using Helvetica, of course, but they were using hundreds of different versions; legitimate copies, illegitimate copies that didn't work properly. They would squash them to make the telephone books. It just didn't read right—it wasn't appropriate, and they knew it.

So I said, "Let's find a typeface for you." And I went through 20 type-faces. It had to be sans serif; it had to be versatile and work with bad print on bad paper. Large amounts of stuff would be printed, like the telephone book was millions and millions of copies, so to make some space savings there would save millions of trees. I could be a good boy at the same time. So I analyzed all these typefaces—I measured how much space they took, what was their vertical stem thickness compared to the horizontals, how big were the openings, how were the terminals. I put together all the details and analyzed them, and I ended up with this model skeleton of the ideal typeface. It would have to be as bold as this but as light as this, as wide as this but as narrow as this ... all this data that established what the real typeface should look like.

And of course, it didn't exist. So then I thought, "Oh, shit. I'm going to have to do it myself." I really didn't look forward to it, but I realized that it would be a good thing for them. We could do it properly; we had the right technology. The first version was digitized at Stempel in '85, from pretty rough drawings. By the time we were finished, we'd created two fonts, and printed up some forms as samples. But the German Post Office, somehow they didn't trust this. They thought it would be too costly. In those days—we're talking about phototypesetting—they were worried about how they would get the fonts out to their printers, which would cost around two thousand marks each, which in those days was a lot of money. So they suddenly lost faith in the whole operation and said, "Naaah, we're going to stay with Helvetica." It actually took them another 20 years, until just a few years ago, to switch to Frutiger.

So I had this typeface; I'd done two weights; it was in digital form, and nothing happened to it. But later, in 1991, when I reopened my company, MetaDesign, I had these typefaces sitting around and thought, "Why don't we release these." I'd started FontShop at that point, which is a company that distributes typefaces. And we had Fontographer then, so we could re-digitize it on a Macintosh from my old outlines, and use it internally. That's why it's called Meta. It was the house font at MetaDesign.

Then my ex-wife, who was running FontShop, and the other people there, thought it was pretty cool and that they should publish it. So we added a few more weights, and it came out early in the digital font era. It was the first "alternative" sans serif; it had a little more character; it was a little dirty; it was anti-authoritarian; so it was very much what people were looking for at the time. It was a little more playful, a little not straight, a little not Swiss. It's very legible; it was made for small sizes and crappy conditions, and if something is made for crappy conditions, it'll work in good conditions as well. And it became FontShop's most popular typeface; it still is. I could probably retire on the sales, if I could rely on them, but I always think, "What if tomorrow people stopped buying it?" But look at how people still buy Futura and Univers after 50 bloody years. So I probably could retire on it. But we keep making new versions, new weights.

GH — Why is Helvetica, 50 years later, still one of the best sellers?

ES — I don't know—why is bad taste ubiquitous? No, actually Helvetica was a good typeface at the time; it really answered a demand. But now it's become one of those defaults, partly because of the proliferation of the personal computer, which is now 20 years old. It was the default on the Macintosh, then it became the default on Windows, which copied everything Apple did, as you know. Then they did the clone version, Arial, which is worse than Helvetica, but fills the same purpose. Now it's never going to go away, because it is ubiquitous; it is the default. It's like air— it's just there. There's no choice. You have to breathe, so you have to use Helvetica.

Every now and then, people will make an ideology out of it by saying, "This is so totally neutral that it makes my work beyond suspicion. I'm not a designer, I'm not vain, I'm only using Helvetica." Then there are people like me, who criticize it from a functional point of view. It's actually not a very good typeface for a lot of purposes. We redid a lot of the literature for the German Railway four years ago. And you find that when you design with Helvetica, you need to . . . well, it brings a style with it, every typeface does. It's like a person—if you're slightly heavy around the middle, you're not going to walk around wearing a tight T-shirt; you'd look like an idiot. And Helvetica is heavy in the middle. It needs a certain space around it, it needs a lot of white space, you need to look at the weight gradations. It needs a lot of space sideways also, then it's very legible. But when it's very small, and very tightly done, and very lightly done, it's a nightmare, a total nightmare.

There's some stuff out there, done mostly by graphic designers, that has a nice, even, gray look to it. It's this mythical thing that designers think it's easy to read, because they don't read. Most graphic designers don't read, by and large. Graphic designers want everything to look nice and even—it's like that saying about children, that they should be seen and not heard. And that type is to be looked at, not to be read. It's indecipherable.

A real typeface needs rhythm; it needs contrast. It comes from handwriting, you know—that's why I can read your handwriting and you can read mine, and I'm sure our handwriting is miles away from Helvetica or anything that would be considered legible, but we can read it because there's a rhythm to it, there's a contrast to it. Helvetica hasn't got any of that. So the absence of anything that makes it legible, to me, makes it a total nuisance. To make it look and read well is a nightmare; it requires a lot of work. I'd much rather use another typeface that's more legible.

But every five or six years, every college generation, you get a new group of people who think the sun shines out of it, because they don't read. And you tell them to look at what makes a typeface legible, what makes it pleasing to the eye. You talk about certain physical properties, and Helvetica hasn't got any of them. And I tell them it's a bad typeface for most purposes.

GH — Umm . . .

    ES — And I've used it! I did the marketing for Neue Helvetica in 1983, so I wouldn't say this if I hadn't tried it. Because all the letters . . . it's this whole Swiss ideology. The guy who designed it tried to make all the letters look the same. Hellooo? That's called an army, that's not people. That's people having the same fucking helmet on; it doesn't further individualism. And the aim with type design is always to make it individual enough, so that it's interesting, but of course 95 percent of any alphabet has to look like the other alphabets or else you wouldn't be able to read it. But that 5 percent is where you bring your art into it, or your talent.

GH — But do you think it's a case where because Helvetica has been used so much over the past 50 years, now it's become the most legible because people are used to it?

    ES — Yes, of course, familiarity is very important. That goes for food, and music, and all sorts of stuff. Certain things that are annoying to you or me might be great music to other people. The same goes for food too. There are certain things I wouldn't touch simply because I've never touched them before. But that makes it edible; it doesn't necessarily make it pleasant. Helvetica has this ubiquity, so people are used to it. But if you ever had to test it against a decent typeface ... Unfortunately the people who test stuff, usually online, onscreen, test crap against crap. They'll test Helvetica against Times New Roman, which is a stupid, stupid competition. It's like testing an Aston Martin against a Mini—you know who's going to be the winner depending on what you're looking at, if you're looking at fuel consumption, or if you're looking at speed. So most of the tests I've seen recently have been comparing rubbish to rubbish, and then rubbish always wins.

If you look at Helvetica physically, it's a bad typeface for most continuous reading purposes. The fact that it's ubiquitous, and that we like it because it's there, has nothing to do with it. Yes, it's become the benchmark, but it doesn't make it any better. There are various theories out there, but most people who teach type design will tell you that it's totally linear, no contrast; all the shapes are trying to close in on each other; there's nowhere for the eye to go; nowhere for the eye to rest and differentiate. It's a really, really bad idea. It's an ideology, not a typeface.

GH — Can we talk a little bit about technology and its effect on type and design in general? Since most people who have a Macintosh now think they're graphic designers, does it increase the possibility for experimentation, or does it just mean more bad design out there?

ES — Oh, I'm not worried about this. The more people start designing stuff, the more they realize that the real design is difficult, so people actually appreciate it more. You know, if you always eat at McDonald's, you never know what good food tastes like. But if someone gives you a couple good ingredients, and a good knife, and a good stove, then you realize how difficult it is to make good food.

If all these people have the tools to make good design, they'll realize it ain't that easy. It's not just opening a template in Corel Draw or PowerPoint. They learn. And the pyramid gets wider, and when it gets wider, the top still stays the same. We professional designers are the top of the pyramid, the food chain, whatever you want to call it. So I'm happy. Anyone who wants to try their hand at design has my full support, because it makes my work much more special. I mean, the world is 95 percent full of crap anyway, so what's new? That goes for everything. It's like when people try to install a new washing machine and a few weeks later it's leaking everywhere, they realize what skills a plumber has. If you can find one, that is!

GH — [Laughing.] Can you talk about what you love about what you do, and about design?

ES — Well, apart from the fact that I'm obviously a typomaniac, which is an incurable if not mortal disease ... I can't explain it. I just like looking at type, I just get a total kick out of it. They are my friends, you know? Other people look at bottles of wine, or girls' bottoms or whatever, and I get my kicks out of looking at type. It's a little worrying, I must admit.

It's a very nerdish thing to do, and there are not that many of us who go that deep into it. But it's a harmless pleasure, it doesn't hurt anyone, it's not pornography. So I'm quite happy doing it.

Other than that, these days, being as old as I am, I prefer the process over the results. I don't really enjoy hanging out with clients anymore. Because I've seen it all before; I've solved the same problems 100 times over, and they're very tedious. It just doesn't mean that much to me anymore. But I do like being in an office, being with other people, having young people who come in not having heard of any of my rules and then breaking them or making stuff that I think is so very cool. Because I'm not that good of a graphic designer; I'm a mediocre graphic designer. I'm a pretty good type designer, I'm a pretty good typographer, and I'm a good information designer. I can solve really complex problems, but I'm bad visually.

I enjoy seeing talent, I enjoy the interaction. I go to work whenever I like. Okay, I'm always here first, and I go home last, but if I don't want to, I don't have to. I was just away for two and a half days. I can travel wherever I want, I can say no to clients, I can hire people, I can throw them out, I can buy the tools, I can do whatever I like. Of course I have to work for clients, and I have to make money, but I'm very, very privileged. My dad drove a truck for most of his life, and my mother worked in offices most of her life; they didn't have any choices at all. I have all these choices, and that is the best thing about being a designer.

Not that I say "no" to clients, hardly ever. But I can. Also being the age that I am, most clients are half my age. So I can tell them, "Look, just let me do it, I've done this before. Why don't you go home and watch TV or whatever, come back in the morning, and it'll all be done." And more often than not, they say, "Okay, if you say so." Because I've done this before, and it may sound arrogant, but most of this stuff is routine. If you've seen one, you've seen them all, and you apply the same methods to it.

I like cracking serious problems. Like right now, we're redesigning all the timetables for the German Railway. Yeah, it's very nerdy, but that stuff gets printed millions of times every day, at every station. I can make that work a little better, so people don't make mistakes and go to the wrong platform, because I've designed a typeface for them that's more legible. But I can also make it a little more pleasant to look at. And that's the stuff that makes a nation's culture—good architecture, good food, and good timetables and signage on the walls of stations. I think it's a very important cultural contribution. I think it's much more important than writing poems—not that that's not important; you know what I mean. But I can reach a huge audience with that. The money is crap, and I'm fighting against the system because no one wants me to interfere. But I get a kick out of that, out of solving a really tough problem, and you don't win medals for that. Most people won't even know the timetables have been changed, but that isn't the point—nobody's supposed to know they're changed. They just got better. I like that challenge, I like being the unknown designer of this stuff.

I designed the signage for the transport system here in Berlin 12 years ago, and you wouldn't know, and you're not supposed to know. It just has to work. You should've seen the stations 20 years ago. They were crap. There were no maps, they were badly lit, the whole place was rubbish. And now they're ... well, at least they work; it's not an unpleasant environment. And I think that's my contribution, but it doesn't say, "Designed by Spiekermann"—that would be horrible. People don't know. But I know, and I love the fact that nobody else does. Not because I'm modest; I'm as vain as the next guy. But I still get a kick out of being the unknown author of all this stuff.

GH — Do you have any bizarre, obsessive behavior regarding type?

ES — Yeah. I will not read anything unless I've identified the typeface. That's just an occupational hazard, but usually it's pretty easy since I know most of the stuff. But I go out and buy weird magazines, like trainspotting stuff, just to see what fonts people are using. It's interesting, and I may learn something new. The only problem is that my eyes aren't getting any better, and sometimes I have to get a magnifying glass out to identify some 7-point type. And I may not know it, so I have to run home and look it up. I hate not knowing what something it. So that's one thing. And I do read big-font specimen books in bed, which is sort of scary. A page full of ABCs, and then the next page full of ABCs, and . . . luckily my girlfriend is also a designer, so she can appreciate the differences.

GH — What's you favorite letter of the alphabet?

ES — My favorite letter of the alphabet is the lower case *a*. It's the friendliest letter, it's the most significant, it's the first. It's the most complex to design because it crosses the plane three time: the top, the middle, and the bottom. You can do a lot with it. It's the letter I use to identify any typeface, because the *a* has the most latitude. And I just like the look of it—it looks like a little guy with a fat tummy. I just totally love it.

My second favorite letter is the capital *R*, by the way. I have no idea why, because it's so ugly. And the lowercase *g* is third. I know that's more than you asked for.

GH — No, that's great. So what do you think is the worst designed typeface ever?

ES — Oh, that's unfair, because there is soooo much out there ...

GH — [Laughing.]

ES — There are certain typefaces I hate with a vengeance, but that's because of the attitude with which people use them. This is really difficult—I really don't want to insult anyone. There is one typeface that I will never use and I really hate it, and that is Optima, by Hermann Zapf. It's actually a very good typeface, but the way that it's used, especially in America, is so patronizing. It's all cosmetics or hospital signage. "This is good, it's wonderful, it's cute." Blehhh. It's so tepid, and it's tired. I hate it with a vengeance and I will never use it.

But the typeface that I most hate, maybe because it's used really badly, is Avant Garde Gothic. It's totally geometric. It's very much back in fashion these days—can you believe it? They use it really tightly, so all the shapes look alike; it looks like ornaments. There is no way anyone can read it; you have to decipher it. It's horrible, it really is horrible.

GH — What about Arial? You know, so many people have it, especially with PCs, and they can't really tell the difference . . .

ES — Yeah, it's just a benchmark now. It's a crap typeface, but for some people and some companies we design for, it's just the benchmark. It can't be a good typeface, because Helvetica in itself is totally perfect. For what it is, it's perfect. It has been improved a few times; the Helvetica we see today is not the same as it was in '57. A lot of people have invested a lot of skills in it over the years.

Then somebody like Microsoft comes along, the company without any taste, as Steve Jobs once said. And they say, "Okay, Helvetica has been very successful." For some reason, Steve Jobs put it on the first Macintosh and the first PostScript printer. For whatever reason—maybe he had an old Linotype specimen there; we don't know. It was generic. So Microsoft says, "We need this. It's a standard; we can't not have it. But we're not going to pay Linotype any money for it, because we're Microsoft." So they asked somebody, in this case Monotype, to design it for them but not design it for them. In other words, take the width, the space that every character takes up, from Helvetica, and slightly change the characters. And of course if you have a perfect typeface and you change it, you can't do better. You can only get worse.

The poor people at Monotype, Robin Nicholas and Patricia Saunders, I feel sorry for them, because you can't win. If somebody gave me Helvetica to redesign, I would refuse. If I was employed at Monotype, I probably couldn't refuse. So they didn't refuse, and they made it worse. They changed things deliberately, and they had to fit it into that corset of Helvetica's width. Because what happens is that if you move a document set in Helvetica from a Mac to a PC, it moves from Helvetica to Arial. So the character width will be identical and the line height will be the same; it'll just look a little worse.

We do something similar now when we make typefaces for companies like Bosch or the German Railway. We make a version that we put on Helvetica/Arial width. So when they do their internal stuff, it looks good—it's their own typeface. But when they send their documents outside the company, and they don't want to give people their exclusive typefaces, it defaults back to Arial, and the document's structure will remain. So even I have to bow to the pressure of this Arial benchmark now. And Microsoft did it again, recently, with Frutiger. For the new Windows Vista, they didn't want to pay royalties to Linotype for Frutiger, which is a much better typeface than Helvetica, really. So they designed their own version of Frutiger, called Segoe. It looks a little different, but the brief was redesign this so we won't have to pay a license fee.

Microsoft are just really, really bad people when it comes to that stuff. They are big bullies. That's one reason I won't go near a Microsoft product. They really are despicable, people who don't respect intellectual property. And they have to save pennies? Microsoft? Those poor people? Thirty-five billion dollars in the bank, cash, and they can't pay license fees? Christ, it just makes you sick. Mean bastards. Even though Matthew Carter did some cool stuff for them. And if they walked in here with a few thousand dollars, I wonder what I'd say? I might be corrupted, so I'm not saying I'm a hero. But they haven't asked me yet, and they won't because I'm on record calling them what I just called them.

GH — Speaking of Matthew, what other 20th century type designers do you respect or do you think have been the most influential?

    ES — That's very difficult; I respect quite a few people. It's very much a generational thing. I wouldn't be a good type designer if I didn't have all these kids working for me. These days, I have ideas, and I sketch them. It's almost like writing a script or just a treatment, to use your terms. Then I get other people to make the movie for me, and I keep an eye on it. Maybe I'm the director, to an extent, and maybe I even write some of the dialogue. But there are people I've had working for me forever; I've trained a lot of type designers. At MetaDesign we always had two or three resident type designers. Luc de Groote, he worked for me. One guy, Christian Schwartz, who's now in New York, he worked for me when he was barely out of school, like 21 or something. He does all my digital work now, and we understand each other so well that I can send him, like, five or six characters sketched on the back of a napkin, and he'll come back one day later with the full lowercase in digital form. He's fast, he's prolific—I'm only worried that he's going to burn out.

He hangs out with Tobias Frere-Jones and Jonathan Hoefler. It's sort of this group of kids in New York who at the moment are my favorite type designers, because they have the historical knowledge, they really know the old shit, but they also have an edge. They look around; they're good with the vernacular. They're technically prolific—they can write code. So they're totally ambidextrous between the digital and the analog. And they're also nice kids; they like music and they like to hang out, so it's a pleasure working with them. I have sort of a father/son relationship with them, because they are very much my kids, and most of them have worked for me at one time or another, or they published their fonts with me.

And then there's the large group in Holland, which is where the best type-design education happens in the world. There are good programs at Reading and Yale and RISD. But the most prolific type designers are this new mix of programmer/designer, because to produce a typeface today you really need to be a programmer. You can design it, like I do, but then to turn it into an OpenType font with 700 characters and 45 weights and Cyrillic and Greek and whatever is . . . science. It's tedious; it's boring; it requires a lot of knowledge because there are all these different platforms, and hinting, and different characters maps. It's really complex. I mean, if we design a typeface that has six weights, say, for a company like Bosch, that's 400 files that have to be made. Because there's Mac and PC and TrueType and PostScript Type One and OpenType and Romanian and Latvian and these weird character maps that you Americans didn't even know existed. Because people do speak other languages besides English, which has no diacritics; it's the only language without diacritics.

It's almost like being a graphic designer; 30 years ago, you had your Stanley knife and your pencil, and you could pretty much be a graphic designer. Of course you delegated all the other stuff—you had the typesetters and printers and the repro house people and so on, and they did all the negatives and positives and shit. But type designers these days, like graphic designers, have to do it all. They come up with concepts, they make sketches, they know the historical stuff, they even have to have a feel for the market, and they also have to be programmers. They have to make sure the files work on all the platforms, to make the IT people happy. It's almost too much for one person. And the Dutch learn all those skills. And they all have a great sense of humor—they do wacky, funny stuff. The guys who worked for me in the late eighties, Just van Rossum and Erik van Blokland, they made the first random type. I mean, they killed two of my PostScript printers with that—they fucking blew them up—because the guys were feeding this random data into them, and computers don't like random.

So I love these kids, because they know all the rules really well and then they break them. I love rule breaking, but only by people who know the rules. If you break the rules without knowing them, it's like children who poo in their pants because they don't know any better. These are adults, but they still have fun. With Trixie, this typeface that Erik did, he found a typewriter in his attic, typed it out, scanned it in, and the same afternoon he had a great typeface. And it's still a great typeface, because he left it alone—it just looks like a typewriter. It's random enough and bad enough. That's a talent to know when to just leave it alone and not try to make it beautiful. They're lazy and want to go do other things, like play in a band; there's a band of type designers in the Hague. They have other interests, they have families, they have a life.

If you're so nerdish that you can't let go, that's bad. Things get so perfect that they become cold. Which brings us back to Helvetica. It's so perfect that it's cold. I'm also lazy and have other stuff going on, so sometimes I think, "Ah, this is good enough." I could spend an extra four hours making this perfect; nobody will ever know except me. Or I could just fucking leave it and go and cook asparagus or something, which is much more fun. So I think laziness is a good motivator, actually.

GH — What about historically? What designers of the past do you think are—

    ES — Oh, I love all the dead guys.

GH — [Laughs.]

    ES — No, I like some people because I like them personally. I loved Aldo Novarese, the Italian. He was this tiny man, and he wore these English tweed jackets with a little brown sweater and checked shirt and a cravat. He could've been an Italian waiter. We always had to speak French, because he didn't speak English and my Italian was so bad. He designed Eurostyle and this cool stuff—most of it was stuff that I wouldn't use in a million years, but it was so Italian. Every typeface he designed looked like it could be on the side of an espresso machine. That guy had so much style. He was this sweet old man and unfortunately he died about

20 years ago. I only met him four or five times, but I loved him because he had style.

Another guy who had similar style was Roger Excoffon, the French guy who also died 20-odd years ago, who designed Antique Olive and all these weird French typefaces that are so ... French. The stuff you'll find on the side of a truck of the local plumber in the south of France somewhere. It took me a long time to appreciate his typefaces. When I was a kid, I thought they were ugly and almost too indigenous, too French for my liking. I've never been much of a Francophile. But actually it was the Dutch designer Gerard Unger who taught me to appreciate him. Excoffon did this typeface, Mistral, which was cut in metal, and even if it's set in metal it just looks like someone wrote it out quickly. Again it's that talent to just whack something down, as if you just peed it into the snow. Of course it probably took thousands of hours of work, but it looks like he just dashed it off on the way to get a coffee. He always wore a white shirt and cravat too. I'm sure he was a womanizer; he was a good-looking, tall man. He lived in the south of France and looked like a French film star. He drove a convertible, of course. And his type is just divine. I don't think I've ever used much of it, because it wouldn't work for what I design. But that stuff is totally ingenious, and to do that in metal, to bring that freshness and looseness to it, takes way more talent than I'll ever have, I'll tell you. I'm so in awe of those people.

I had a similar experience with Bodoni when I used to set type at typesetters. I hated using Bodoni—with those fine lines, it would break easily. The cuts we had were probably bad, but it read really bad, and it was always used for poncey ads or whatever. So I hated Bodoni until Günter Gerhard Lange at Berthold got me into it. He was designing a new Bodoni, and he had me look at some of the original books. I realized that Bodoni had designed hundreds of typefaces, all completely different from each other. All I'd seen was that crappy version we had at the typesetters. So I was way into my thirties before I appreciated Bodoni. It's too beautiful for me to use—again, I don't do that sort of thing. If I was designing cosmetics or expensive architectural books, I might use it, but I get this timetable crap, so I use the hard-core stuff more than the fine stuff.

But of course my teacher, and for a while my father figure, was Günter Gerhard Lange, who did all my corrections when I worked for Berthold. I did all the Berthold specimens during the eighties, and their identity. I designed those typefaces for them; I did their brochures. And I was supposed to be his successor when he finally left when he was in his late sixties, but I turned that job down because it wasn't for me. I wouldn't have been good at it. He took that very seriously, because I was like his surrogate son, and I turned down being his successor, and he had no successor. In other words, his work all went to waste. So our relationship hasn't been very good since, after I disappointed him.

But I adored him, and he had an incredible eye. He would say, "Oh, it needs a hair off here," and we'd be talking about 8-point type. And I'd go back to the drawing board, and he was right—it did need a bit taken off. He'd use words like "hair" as a measurement, but his favorite, his smallest measurement, was a *mäusedarm,* which means a mouse gut. That was thinner than a cat's hair. And he was always right. That was the worst part—he just knew that stuff. Amazing. He's 85 now, so he knows even more.

GH — Okay maybe we can take a look through your book *Stop Stealing Sheep & Find Out How Type Works,* or maybe bring some type up on the computer and talk about it?

ES — You're the director. Why should I decide? I don't bloody care. I'm easy.

GH — Let's talk about *Stop Stealing Sheep* . . .

ES — Let me find a copy. I know there was one on this shelf. Someone must've stolen it. This isn't where I keep my books; I've got an another apartment with six thousand books, a guest apartment. One day I'll read them all.

GH — How did the book come to be?

ES — Well, Adobe came to me in '92 and said, "We need a book for"—in their words—"the average housewife," who these days knows what a font is. They wanted her to appreciate that A) there's a choice, there's more out there than Arial, and B) there are things she can do with these fonts. There were certain things to do with type on certain occasions, and reasons for these choices. So this was the housewife primer for someone who has no idea about type. That was the idea. The book ended up being read not by these famous housewives, but apparently it was read by every design student in America; it sold 150,000 copies. It was read by a lot of people who should know what's in there already, but they realize, "Well, you know what, maybe there's something in there I haven't seen." Or they've forgotten it, or it's not all in one place. So this is very basic knowledge, and there's a lot of it, but it's in little chunks so you can always go back to it. You don't have to read it cover to cover.

The idea at the time was that I'd make these little margins here and put all the nerdy stuff in there and make it small, so people wouldn't read it. But of course everyone reads the small stuff first; that's the weird thing. You're hiding it, and that makes it way more interesting. We had great fun making the book. I still like it. The only problem is that it's pushed me into that corner where if anyone needs a two-sentence quote about something type—related, or a two-hundred-word description of something really complex, they come to me. Because any asshole can write long, but writing short is much more difficult, as you know. To edit a film down is much more difficult than recording it in the first place, right? You'd have five thousand hours of footage and think, "My God, what am I going to chop here?"

GH — Yep.

ES — This book is 164 pages, but I could've easily done 500. Some of the pages are too full now; they weren't supposed to be that full. And there's more in it now than the first edition, because things have changed; this was before the web. The world has changed a lot since '92.

GH — But do you think those "housewives" need to know more about type, as long as they can communicate their message?

ES — Well, yes, because they get better. If you want to communicate, if you use type on your PC at home for your Boy Scout troop or your bridge circle, then you may as well learn some of the skills. It's like, anyone can boil an egg, or make tea or coffee. But when you start to get into it, you realize that A) I can do way more, and B) it works better, it tastes better, it communicates better. It's interesting that there's a hell of a market for these books about any program on the PC—this for dummies or that for dummies. Even though there are manuals, nobody reads the manuals. They read the books because they realize that there are a hundred features in that program, but there are only two that are useful to them, so how do you pick out those two? Typography has 50,000 rules, and nobody knows them all, so you've got to pick out the stuff that is useful for someone who doesn't do it for a living.

GH — You mentioned before that millions of people see your typefaces every day. They're getting information through your typefaces. Do you think some of your, I don't know, your personality is rubbing off on people, because the typeface is affecting how they receive that information?

ES — Well, certainly the designer's personality rubs off on the typeface. I just mentioned two of my heroes, Novarese and Excoffon, because their personality was in their fonts and vice versa, which is what I like about them. And I certainly know that when I draw something . . . I mean, I'm fast; I'm loud; I'm chaotic. I'm not very rule-based even though I'm German and I love rules. But I'm a Gemini—it was my birthday yesterday—so I'm all over the place, essentially. I'm always on time but a year late, you know what I mean? But then I'm on the second, you know, so I have this horrible thing, which comes out in my typefaces. They are never perfect; they always have a little edge, in the sense that I leave them alone when I get bored of them. They always serve a purpose.

I know that some people appreciate my typefaces because they have a certain personality. Whether that rubs off on people, I strongly wonder. Certainly there wouldn't be different typefaces if it didn't make a difference to the message. The clothing that the words wear, as I put it in that BBC movie, does make a difference. People always ask, "Why are there so many typefaces?" If people didn't want so many, they wouldn't exist! I own maybe a dozen ties, even though I never wear them, but would I walk into a tie shop that had only a choice of six ties? Of course I wouldn't. I'd go to the one that has five thousand even if I'm only looking for one. It's the same with type.

I certainly know that when a lot of graphic designers choose a typeface, they're misled or influenced by the name, because the name has a certain promise. You know, using a typeface because it has a Dutch name because you want the Dutch culture to echo through it. And yes, the person who designed it is a factor. If you're a graphic designer and you're using someone else's tool, you feel that somehow it's rubbing off on you. If it wasn't for that, we wouldn't have any brands. You know, why do people buy certain things? The brand rubs off on them, and typefaces are a brand, certainly for the trade, for the designers. I know there are people who hate me, who would never use one of my typefaces in a million years. And vice versa. There are people who'll use any typeface I design, not because it's good for them or it fills the purpose, but just because I did it. I think we all do that—I mean, there are certain bands that I buy every new CD from, even though some of them are crap, because I've always bought their music.

It's the same with typefaces, and I'm not talking about the pop part of it. Though there is a pop part too, there are certain publishers like Emigre in Berkeley. There are a lot of kids out there who will always use an Emigre typeface, because for them it's the ultimate cool thing. The typeface might be totally inappropriate more often than not, but it's cool to use it. It's like being faithful to your newspaper. I always read the *The New York Times* when I'm in America; I cannot survive a day without it. I don't agree with everything in there, I don't like everything in there, but for me it's part of my American life. That's one thing about Starbucks, by the way: Where there's a Starbucks, there's the *New York Times*. You can be in Omaha, Nebraska, or weird places in between, and find a Starbucks and get your *New York Times*. That's the best thing about Starbucks. And that they serve coffee in a proper china cup. I will not drink coffee from a paper cup. I will never be that American. Halle-fucking-lujah.

GH — [Laughing.] Umm, we touched on this earlier—
ES — I won't mention the Iraq war.

GH — There's a need for new typefaces and that people want them. But there are some designers, several who are in this film, who say that we don't need any more typefaces—there are only three or four that are worth using. And that using only a few typefaces means there's one less decision, and they can focus on the design?
ES — I know Massimo is one of them. And I totally appreciate that position; it's like going to your favorite restaurant and ordering the same meal every time because you don't want to look at a menu. I totally appreciate it, but that's up to them. I think that type adds that little bit of extra to it. There are three issues there. There's the technical aspect: Does the typeface fit the technology? Onscreen is different from print. Bad paper is different from good paper. Large format is different from small format. Newspaper is different from magazine. There are technical restraints: Narrow columns need a different type than wide columns. That's the technical part. Then there's the cultural part: Certain cultures, certain audiences, expect different things, for whatever reason. You're telling an audience, "This is for you," by using a certain typographic voice. And that's also what brands do. I mean, you'd recognize a Marlboro brand from two miles away, because they use a typeface that only they use. You can buy it, I have it, anyone can buy it—it's called Neo Contact. Anyone can use it, but Marlboro have made that typeface theirs. You can recognize any Marlboro ad from miles away because of that stupid typeface. And if they'd used Helvetica, hello? It wouldn't quite work.

More and more companies are using their own typeface, partly because it saves them a shitload of money since they don't pay licenses. If you have to pay for a hundred thousand font licenses. We're talking about a lot of money here. So that's part of it too. If brands recognize that a typeface can distinguish them from the next brand, it's a pretty serious thing.

So we have three things: We have technology, we have cultural or brand exclusivity, and we have choice. If all you do is design corporate brochures, then maybe you can use just one or two typefaces, or whatever the client gives you. If you're designing for Herman Miller, you use Meta because they chose it as their house face. If you work for Knoll, as Massimo did, then you use Bodoni because he gave them that 30 years ago. But I wouldn't want to work without choices. I know some people say it's a pain in the neck, because you've got to look through all these books of fonts and sometimes it doesn't really matter, and sometimes it's our vanity. But even it it's just for vanity, it doesn't do any harm to the client or the client's customer. You know, every chef has a little spice that they like, and you and I might not know it or even have heard of it, but it's in there.

So I don't know why some of these people—not Massimo; he just says he doesn't need more than five typefaces, he doesn't say that other people shouldn't use more—but there's a lot of people in our business who say you shouldn't, and it's rubbish. Why the hell? Next thing they're going to tell me is there are only 12 pieces of music I should listen to? Four Beethoven symphonies, four Mozart concertos, and four Beatles hits? Hello? Why can't I have a choice, why can't I have a typographic choice? It's like painting—why do people still paint? Don't we have millions of paintings? Haven't all the great paintings been painted? But people go on painting because it's human expression, and type is a human expression.

GH — Any final thoughts on Helvetica?

    ES — Well, there are occasions when Helvetica might be the appropriate typeface. Every typeface has at least one purpose in life; there's one moment when this thing works. There are things that Helvetica is suited for, in large sizes or very light and ornamental, because it's so whole; it's so totally finished and perfect. It's very quiet and almost noble, in its own way. I do not like it, and this would go for any other typeface, when people only use it because it's there. It's like going to McDonald's instead of thinking about food. Because it's there, it's on every street corner, so let's eat crap because it's on the corner. Most people who use Helvetica use it because it's ubiquitous, and that to me is a really bad reason. Most people can't tell the difference between it and Arial, for example. I can tell it from Arial from miles away. That annoys me. I basically don't like people making decisions on hearsay. It's like voting on whatever president is in office because you've heard their name before. I want graphic designers to use their own judgment, but judgment means knowledge; you have to learn about this stuff.

But I'm not a graphic designer, I'm a typographic designer; there's a difference. If you want my definition—and I'm going to give it to you anyway—a graphic designer generally has a picture in their head of what the page is going to look like and then builds the page layout from that image down. They use illustration, photography, and type to build that picture. Type is just one element in that image. But as a typographic designer, I would analyze the copy. How much is there, who is going to read it? In what environment? On the train, at home? What is the client trying to say with it? I don't have any image in my head of what the page will look like. I have a structure. Then I pick a typeface and the column structure that works with that typeface. The layout isn't a painting; it's a construction drawing. I would take all the elements, I would deduct them, and then I would assemble them on a page. A typographic designer builds a layout from the word up.

There's no quality difference between the two approaches; they're just different ways of thinking. We all work differently. I'm very much a word person—that's why typography for me is the obvious extension. It makes my words visible. I'm a designer by practice, but I don't feel like a designer in that sense. That's why I have all these cool people around who are really good at it.

GH — What's the thing you don't like about what you do?

ES — Well, I'm running a business, and I'm not really interested in running a business. But I've been running a business for the past 35 years, by definition, because I've always been self-employed, and at one time I had two hundred people working for me. MetaDesign is now one of Europe's foremost design agencies, and I helped start it, but now I'm no longer part of it. And that's because I wasn't interested in the business part. I let other people take advantage, and before I knew it they'd taken the company away from me. Because I don't read contracts; I just sign shit. So that part I still don't like, and now I have hopefully trustworthy people who do all that for me, because you have to. But I hate dealing with the whole money thing—I mean, how much is my work worth? If I like doing something, I hate attaching money to it. It embarrasses me, and the clients sense that. And I hate dealing with all these MBAs, the suits.

This guy from the German Railway sat down with me recently when I did the final presentation to the boss there, who I knew from previous projects. He sat down and started drawing little squares for me, showing me how to do a PowerPoint presentation for his boss. I thought, any minute now it's going to be *Candid Camera* or something. This guy can't be serious. I'm 58, and he's 32, and he's telling me how to do a PowerPoint presentation to his boss, who I knew when this guy was still in diapers? After a few minutes he realized that I was looking at him incredulously, and he says, "Oh, I guess you know how to do this." And I said, "Yes, I've been doing PowerPoint presentations for 20 fucking years, and your boss is a friend of mine. The reason I'm here is that I can tell him this in three minutes. I don't need a PowerPoint presentation. He'll ask, 'Spiekermann, is this a good typeface for us?' and I'll say, 'Yes, it is.' And he'll say, 'Great, you're the expert.' And he's right!"

So that irks me, those fresh kids out of business school who know it all. My God, I have to be nice to these people? Aaaah! You know, the Blackberry brigade, those guys. They communicate in PowerPoint! They send PowerPoints instead of picking up the phone and calling someone. They make lunchtime arrangements in fucking PowerPoint! And then they copy everyone and their mothers on it. Just in case they can use it against you later. They leave this incredible email/paper/Blackberry trail. You get this avalanche of corporate shit that's all about covering their ass, and not making any noise, and pursuing their career. And these guys are my clients. Some of them. And that is horrible. They don't want to change anything, and by definition design is changing things. They want everything the same as always—otherwise things might move and their career will be in danger. Ugh. Really, at my age I shouldn't have to deal with that anymore.

—

Bruno Steinert (BS) & Otmar Hoefer (OH) / June 2, 2006 Bad Homburg

Linotype is the owner of the rights to the Helvetica typeface, and it was always my intention to visit their German headquarters to see what they had in their archives and interview their key people. Bruno Steinert and Otmar Hoefer spent the day with us and graciously opened the company vaults. Bruno has since left Linotype, and Otmar has taken over his position of Managing Director.

Otmar also arranged a visit for us to a letterpress printing club in Frankfurt, where Manfred Schulz, a retired typesetter, gave us a demonstration of setting and printing old metal type Helvetica. We filmed Manfred in action, and that footage ended up being the opening title sequence of the film.

—

Gary Hustwit — Could you both introduce yourselves?

Bruno Steinert — I'm Bruno Steinert, and I'm Managing Director of Linotype GmbH. I've been with Linotype for 34 years now.

Otmar Hoefer — My name is Otmar Hoefer. I'm Director of Font Marketing at Linotype. I started my career as a hot metal typesetter and worked for D. Stempel AG. I then moved over to Linotype and I've been here 28 years. I was responsible for introducing Neue Helvetica.

GH — If I had never heard of Helvetica before, how would you describe its history to me?

BS — If you think about the history of Helvetica, you have to realize that there is no such thing as one Helvetica. Helvetica today is a huge family of different weights and designs, and over time it has evolved into a variety of different interpretations. So there is no single Helvetica.

But the original weights of Helvetica go back to the Haas Type Foundry in Switzerland, where Max Miedinger was a sales rep for Haas. At that point in time he designed a few of the characters—I'm not sure if he even created the full alphabet. I spoke to Alfred Hoffmann, who is the son of Eduard Hoffmann, who used to be the Managing Director of Haas at that time. And he told me that his father asked Max to design certain characters with ideas that Eduard had. That was how it all began.

Originally they had a typeface called Haas Grotesk, but it was not very successful, and that is why they wanted to revise it. Neue Haas Grotesk became a success because it was quite different and it looked good. But with hot metal type, there were craftspeople involved in the integration of typeface punch cutters. And for each size there were different designs, and the various characters were created by various people. If you look at the first versions or the original hot metal versions of Neue Haas Grotesk, they are not very consistent design-wise.

Stempel was the parent company of Haas, and they became interested in this typeface. The Marketing Director at Stempel had the idea to give it a better name, because Neue Haas Grotesk didn't sound very good for a typeface that was intended to be sold in the United States. Linotype was an American company, and they had subsidiaries in Europe. And for the American market, Neue Haas Grotesk was nearly impossible. So someone at Stempel had the idea . . . What was his name?

OH — Heinz Eul.

BS — No, no, no.

OH — Heinz Eul, he had the idea.

BS — It was Cunz.

OH — Edward Cunz?

BS — I was told Edward Cunz had that idea to call it Helvetia. But Helvetia turned out to be a problem because that is the Latin name for Switzerland. They put the c into it and called it Helvetica. They started a very active sales and marketing campaign. And there was Heinz Eul. He was a salesperson at Stempel, and he was fully dedicated to the promotion and sale of Helvetica. And he told me personally, many years ago when I worked with him, that his greatest success was the sale of Helvetica to the German company BASF, because they were the first corporate user of it, and that was the breakthrough for Helvetica. And since it became such a great success, many additions were made, new weights were created and modifications were made to the existing designs, and Heinz made improvements. And the Helvetica family grew to what it is today.

And if you look at Helvetica now, it is the result of a team effort. Not just one team—multiple teams worked on it over many decades, and it has just evolved to what it is now and we continue improving it. We are currently working on a Helvetica world version. We've already added many international characters to it to make it usable globally, over the Internet, et cetera. And we are about to create even non-Latin interpretations of Helvetica. One major change to the Helvetica family happened in 1983. Neue Helvetica, that's your part.

OH — Yes, because we had seen at Stempel that the Helvetica family was, in many cases, very inconsistent. If you compared the weights, the strokes, thicknesses and everything, we found it did not fit together. The Helvetica Condensed series, for instance, was formerly called Stein Grotesk, from the Haas type foundry. Because there was a demand for condensed weights, but no one there was able to draw them at the speed that was necessary. So Haas took existing matrices and sold them under a new name. They revised some of the characters and made it into Helvetica Condensed.

BS — If you think about that, you realize that Helvetica really is a group of design principals, a few design elements, some core elements that are obviously strong enough to allow for a large range of extreme variations that are still considered to be Helvetica. So it is not one particular design; it's a few elements that make it, and, of course, a very strong brand name.

GH — You just mentioned the initial marketing effort, and that seems to be one of the big reasons. Do you want to tell that story?

OH — The marketing report from Heinz Eul was that he was going to the printers, to the print shops, and explained to the printers that this is an exciting new typeface. And that large corporations, like what Bruno just said, BASF and so on, had changed their corporate identity and wanted to use Helvetica. So if you want to get some work for BASF, it is a good idea to buy Helvetica as metal type, then you will get orders from BASF. And just in reverse, he went to the ad agencies and told the agencies, this is an exciting new typeface. If you choose it, many of the printers have Helvetica, so it is not a question of which printer you are going to; they'll all have it.

BS — However, it was not only this direct acquisition of clients; it was the marketing materials and the huge investments into the worldwide publication of this new design. Many people get that wrong as well. I've read comments like "Helvetica is not a good design, but it is the result of a very powerful marketing campaign." And I think that's wrong. It's the result of both. If the product were bad, even the best marketing would not help. But it is the combination of the two.

It's a design that is still considered to be fresh and in fashion and trendy and cool after more than 50 years. So there must be something in it. But on the other hand, we have other good designs around that might be as good as Helvetica or even better. I don't want to make any judgments, but those designs never became known to the public. So I think it's not sufficient to only have a good product; you have to have good marketing as well. And the combination of the two makes it a success.

GH — Can you talk about the personal computer and its role in the success of Helvetica?

BS — Helvetica was already a worldwide success, and when Steve Jobs designed the Macintosh, he had the idea of having good typography on a personal computer. And there were discussions at the time where people talked about the question whether it is really necessary, or really made sense, to have up to eight different typefaces on one computer in the beginning.

One thing was clear: Jobs wanted to have the famous Mergenthaler Linotype fonts in it, because Mergenthaler had a great reputation in the '80s for their phototypesetting font library. Steve Jobs is a man who has an appreciation for design and quality. He also likes European designs, European products, and he wanted to have Helvetica and some other Linotype fonts on the original Mac.

He contacted Linotype, and Helvetica was clearly at the top of his shopping list. At Linotype, we had discussions about whether it would make sense to license such a font for a computer that nobody really had an idea what it was good for, you know? The first Macintosh that I saw was able to talk; it had MacinTalk so it could read text and spell it. We said, "Okay, it talks, but what is it good for?"

So we licensed some bitmap fonts to Apple, and then later on Adobe found us. They had contacted Apple with the idea of a postscript controller; I think it was on a Canon print engine. They wanted to make a printer that was able to print real typefaces. Since Linotype fonts were already in the Mac, Adobe had to negotiate a license with Linotype as well, and that is how we all got together. That is how it all began, and how real typefaces came into computers.

GH — And how do you think that has affected the average person, now that they have access to this typography? Is it a good thing, is it a bad thing? Has it made for bad design, good design, or does it matter? What are your thoughts?

BS — Prior to 1984 or '85, when it really became public, one needed a huge investment in proprietary or specialized equipment, phototypesetting machines, keyboards, et cetera, and a very good professional education just to be able to produce a single typographic character on paper or film. So it was a profession to output typography, and a whole range of businesses were based on this, like typesetters and graphic arts companies, or repro companies, et cetera. All of this is gone, because everybody is able to do it now, and everybody has access to that on their computer.

But when the first Mac typography came out in the 1980s, there was a lot of discussion about the results, because unskilled and inexperienced people were able to typeset. I heard things like typography in the hands of an unskilled or untrained person is like a bomb in the hands of terrorists, you know. And there was a lot of dispute. It should be prohibited to let people play with type if they don't know the basic rules, and so on, and so on. And today there are still a lot of mistakes being made and bad typography around, because the average user doesn't have the skills. But if you really compare old, so-called desktop publishing products with what we have today, you'll see that the average design produced now by an uneducated and unskilled person is much, much, much better than what we had 20 years ago.

GH — What would you say is the biggest challenge now for Linotype? Is marketing or piracy the big issue, or inferior copies and things like that?

BS — The biggest challenge for us is to educate the world about a very simple fact, and that is that type is not growing on trees. People believe that fonts are just there, they are free, and so they copy them illegally or forward them to other people, or do all kinds of things with them. They are not considered to be intellectual property. I think that is the biggest challenge.

I personally believe that if people understand that there are human beings behind these fonts, they'll think about legal issues and see that they need to compensate those people for their work. That is one thing. The other thing I believe is that innovation is the best weapon against piracy. There are a lot of opportunities to improve our product—for instance, extending the character sets for international global communications, or hinted fonts that look much better on screen than unhinted ones, et cetera. There is a constant need for improvement, and if we can continue to further develop and enhance the product, we will always have something new for people, and it is just like in the movie industry, you know. If there is a new film out, people go and watch and stand in long queues in front of the movie theaters. Two months later everyone has a pirated copy on DVD, and Hollywood has to come up with a new film. It is basically the same concept for us.

But it is still a small business. There are no more than three to four hundred professionals in the worldwide type business, versus, I don't know exactly, something between three and four billion readers. Three to four hundred people supply the world with the type that is the fundamental ingredient for reading and typography. I think that is an incredible proportion, which is on one hand sad and on the other hand not. It is still a big market for a small group of people. We have huge potential, and my personal belief is that the rate of pirated versus purchased font is at least a thousand to one. But that's good enough for us. It would of course help if there were no piracy, we could sell our fonts for much, much cheaper, but we're doing pretty well with the current situation. We can't complain. We are a very healthy and a very successful company.

GH — I'm going to switch tracks here. I'd like to get your thoughts on the concept of legibility and how that changes from generation to generation. Some people say it's harder to read sans-serif type in body copy, that it should be used only for headlines, and serif typefaces for the text.

BS — In the sixties and seventies, there were reading courses. I still have one that was called Dynamic Reading. Remember that? They taught you how to read a whole paragraph or even a whole page at once. One man told me that he spent seven hundred marks on the course, and it worked. So I did it, and I'm still using this technique. Not as intensely as I did before, but I can still read very fast—just look at a large element and have it, because the brain works different, you know?

We don't really know how the brain works, so what do we really know about legibility? It is information, and nobody really knows how we process that in our brain and understand it. I believe it has a lot to do with our individual experience. For example, if I watch MTV and see, I don't know how many, 20 images per second, or with computer games, you know, the shooting games. I have difficulty following them, but young people, the younger generation sitting in front of the TV and computer all the time, they can easily absorb that information. I don't know why their brain works differently.

Another example is Blackletter in Germany. The generation before me, they read text in Blackletter fluently. I can read it, but it takes me at least two or three times longer to read the same amount of text. So what is really legible? I believe it is what you are used to, and I am very much used to sans-serif typefaces, so I personally read sans serif faster than serif typefaces, which is against all the theories of legibility. But everybody has their own opinion, and I believe nobody really knows the truth and why.

You can take an individual and analyze their behavior and reactions, but it has to do with age, provenance—I mean, Europeans, Americans or Asian people, or African people, or Latin American, they all have different behaviors and different ways of processing information. So some people think that Helvetica is a very legible typeface and others think it is totally illegible, and maybe they are both right.

GH — Is it self-fulfilling in a way? The increased use of Helvetica makes it more legible, and therefore more people use it?
OH — Yeah.

BS — Have you ever seen, in Adrian Frutiger's book, his analysis of the essentials of type? Have you ever seen that?

GH — Yes, I have a copy.
BS — Can we look at that book for just one second? I have it here. He used graded overlays of different typefaces. He did that in the fifties, and not on a computer; he just used different shades for the different typefaces and overlaid them. He took the different character designs and put them on top of each other just to find the essence of it.

So the idea is what is the common prototype of a character? What is the prototype of an *a* or a *b* or whatever that is memorized in our minds? That is what he was looking for. And his idea was, the closer we come to that prototype—like here, the prototype of a good-looking face, you know, the Mona Lisa portrait—the closer we are to the prototype, the easier we process it. There is less distortion, and if there is no distortion, we can easily process it.

That is how Frutiger created Univers, by the way, and most of his type-faces were based on this idea. If that is true, if we have a kind of a prototype image in our brain, and then compare more images to this, the prototype may change, you know. If the prototype evolves and changes to something else, the process, the comparison process, will be differ-ent. So that supports my idea of how, depending on where you come from and what your background is, you learn to read a specific way. That defines whether something is legible for you or not.

OH — In one case, Helvetica was used as a schoolbook typeface. But for Helvetica Textbook we had to modify specific letters like the lowercase *a*, the lowercase *i*, *q*, and some other letters, so that it would be easier to read for children, and so children could be taught with it. So it was a modified Helvetica.

BS — I don't know. I'm not a scientist, it is just my personal experience, but if there is some truth in what I said, then Helvetica must be a very legible typeface, because it is so widely used. Since everybody is constantly looking at Helvetica, it becomes part of the memorized prototype and it should be legible for everyone.

GH — I've talked to many European designers who also say that, and it is probably shaped by them seeing it used for decades. When they set something in Helvetica, there is a feeling that it brings to the word, and that is what they like about it. It is sort of an intangible concept, but there is a certain feel to words set in Helvetica. But then you've got people who say it is neutral and doesn't impart any feeling to the words.

OH — That was one of the reasons why they wanted to make Helvetica, or why it was designed to be a very unique, universal, usable typeface. If you see Univers, for instance, or you see Futura, then you see a totally different design philosophy behind it. Helvetica has an equal stroke thickness, or it seems to be equal in stroke thickness, and that makes it look a little more usable for all occasions, you know.

BS — As Adrian Frutiger says, and he doesn't like Helvetica in particular, "Helvetica is the blue jeans of typefaces. You can wear it for every occasion, but it is nothing special. It is never wrong, but it is nothing special." That is his opinion. On the other hand, there are many applications where Helvetica is being used in a very elegant way, like for cosmetics, for example. The German airline Lufthansa is using Helvetica for all their publications and glossy brochures, and it looks exclusive and elegant. So I think Helvetica is not really blue jeans; it depends on how you use it. People use it for bands and techno CD covers as well as for expensive products. BMW uses Helvetica, and that is not a cheap product, you know.

GH — There seems to be a lot of confusion over the term "typeface" versus the term "font." Can you give me a simple definition? Some people probably don't know.

BS — I think it's important to distinguish between two things: the design and the technical implementation of the design. So the typeface, in my definition, is the design. You draw it on a chalkboard or on paper or wherever—that's a design. You create that, and in some jurisdictions and some territories this is copyrightable. In the US, it is not. But with that typeface design, you need some technical implementation of it. In the past, those letters were cast in metal—there were punch cutters, and then they cast letters from those punches and sold those letters.

Today we have to digitize that work and create a piece of software that renders those shapes on the computer screen or on a sheet of paper or wherever—on an output device. So I call the technical implementation of a typeface a font. So what we really do is we are licensing fonts, and designers create the typefaces.

And the reason why that is important is that there is no original Helvetica around anymore. Nobody today is using the original design. What we have today is the result of technical evolution, and we create new versions of all our fonts in developmental cycles of no more than three years. In other words, none of the fonts that we are licensing today is older than three years in its current implementation. And that is how things get kind of reinvented all of the time. So the Helvetica that we are selling and shipping today and that you are using on your computer is not an old product. The original designer, say Max Miedinger, or the punch cutters, or other people involved in the process, they are no longer around. There are other people who left their traces in the current product; they made small improvements, enhancements, et cetera. So if you compare a version of Helvetica from 1970, let's say, and the current version, they are extremely different. And it's going to be different in the future as well. It is not a static design or a static product. It lives.

GH — Why, 50 years later, is Helvetica still among the best-selling typefaces? To paraphrase something that Bruno said earlier, why are people buying something they already have? Will they continue to buy it?

OH — Because not everyone has it. There are always young people getting into the profession of design, and they need Helvetica. So you cannot say everyone already has Helvetica. And people not only want the roman, italic, and bold italic, which you get with the computer, they also want the other weights like the light ones, the condensed ones, the black ones. That is how I see the success of Helvetica and especially Neue Helvetica, which we made in 1983. It has a better shape and is more consistent, and therefore there's more demand for it.

GH — Do you want to talk more about the development of Neue Helvetica?

OH — At Stempel we started thinking about Neue Helvetica in roughly 1980. We had seen that it needed some improvements, and so we created the complete type family with our equal system. We had a CAD system that was able to design an ultra-light design and a black design and the various instances in between. But we made intermediate steps, because the roman and the bold looked different. You can see that with the lowercase a. And so therefore, we made an intermediate step in the design stage.

All the characters, even when they were made by the CAD system, were redesigned individually. Sometimes we did not completely think that the computer was doing the right work. But it was made as a consistent family, with these 51 different weights. We have the complete condensed series and the complete upright and italic series. And these from ultra-light, which we thought would be used in fashion—it's very thin—to the extra black, where you have really expressive power.

And we made a bold italic, and a bold outline, which was especially for advertising. At that time, you didn't have a computer that could make an outline, and therefore these versions were part of the family.

BS — Should we go through these old brochures and materials and say something about them?

GH — Sure.

OH — What I found is this issue of a Swiss magazine from 1957, and here you can see a picture of how the original drawings for Helvetica were made. This is actually the only example of the original drawings that I know of, because we do not have any of the real Max Miedinger drawings. We basically have a set drawings at a larger scale, but they are an interpretation for use on the hot metal matrices where we had the limitation that the roman and bold had to be the same width, and therefore the characters in the bold version had to be distorted. That is something we eliminated with the Neue Helvetica.

And here is a very old brochure, from Stempel, showing the 505 machine. This is a machine that had film negatives in it, and by scanning these images, they were converted by a computer into scan lines and then reversed by a CRT onto photo paper. So it was a very unique machine, the 505 for Linotype.

BS — That is how I started at Linotype, as a trainer and expert on the 505. I trained users on the 505 CRT phototypesetter.

GH — How big was that machine?

BS — It would not fit into this room. But that technology was actually a breakthrough that had a significant impact on the world of design. You may not believe it, but that was the first typesetting machine that was able to condense and expand typefaces, and to electronically slant them. It was a very simple trick; the number of scan lines was variable. So you could scan at higher or lower resolutions. If you scanned at a higher number of scan lines but did not increase the wide sweep of the output tube, you got an expanded typeface. And if you reduced the number of scan lines, you got a condensed version. If you just tilted the output stroke electronically, you got an italic. That was the beginning of the disaster and the end of good typography! But everybody loved it at the time, and it was a strong selling point for the 505.

GH — And now?

OH — Today it is so easy just to modify a character, because you have such powerful programs that just work on the outlines. With Helvetica, we had to educate people about why they needed Neue Helvetica, and so we showed the history of the design, how the old hot metal version of the roman and the bold had the same widths, and how we had redesigned the weights to work better. All the numbers had been widened and opened and made more readable. To promote Neue Helvetica, Erik Spiekermann designed the brochure for it, and he came up with the idea to use the four different colors of CMYK. We used a number system, similar to Univers, to specify the different stroke thicknesses.

BS — Here's something from 1983. It's a special offer for a font package comprising eight digital fonts for the incredibly low price of 2,750 marks, which is about $3,000 for eight fonts. So things have changed.

GH — A bargain!

BS — And there is also the text from a presentation given by the Technical Director of Stempel about Neue Helvetica. He said, "Let me take this opportunity to remind you of our bestseller's history. Some 25 years ago Haas commissioned Max Miedinger to create a contemporary sans serif based on Schelter Grotesk." Not on Haas Grotesk but Schelter Grotesk, I didn't know that. "This new typeface was initially named Neue Haas Grotesk and later renamed Helvetica. This face soon became available both as foundry type and on Linotype machines. The name echoed the typeface's origins and put it in line with Swiss typography, which was just becoming the trend among designers the world over. The name Helvetica had a big share in the successful marketing campaign which Stempel developed in the sixties, and has become the typeface par excellence since then." That's sort of what we said earlier, but this was from 1983.

OH — We only had 1,300 different fonts then, and today we have 6,900. Things have changed.

BS — Yeah, and here is some correspondence with Erik Spiekermann about Neue Helvetica where he's criticizing it.

OH — Yeah, but he did design the brochure.

GH — Yeah, that's what he said too. He said, "I have a part in it."

BS — This is a letter from the director of Haas, Alfred Hoffmann, to Stempel, and it's pretty negative about the development of Neue Helvetica, because Neue Helvetica was Stempel's work and Haas did not get any compensation or only very low compensation as I can see. Stempel's people had said, and they were right, that this is our work. We redesigned it, so we're going to pay you a much lower royalty on Neue Helvetica than we did for the original one. The tone of the letter is quite sad, like "Okay, but we are not happy with it."

GH — So Haas still existed as a company in the eighties?

BS — Haas as a company existed until four years ago. I was the director of the supervisory board, and then we closed the company. There was no activity anymore; it was just an umbrella.

And also what many people don't know is that a lot of the work on Helvetica was done in the United States, at Mergenthaler Linotype—we call it ML Co. I'm just reading here—this letter is about an exchange of artwork and digital data between ML Co. and Stempel. Matthew Carter worked at ML Co., and so much of the detailed work that makes up Helvetica now was done in the US, not in Switzerland, so it is to a large extent also an American typeface.

GH — That goes along with what you were saying, that it's been touched by so many different people.

BS — Yeah, I mean, this is all evidence for that—the things we have here, the correspondence as well as the drawings and the work. There is a very popular version of the Helvetica story that is pretty short, like "The most important typeface of the last century is Helvetica. It was designed by a genius designer, Max Miedinger, who died a poor man. He never became famous during his lifetime, and Linotype made millions and didn't compensate him." That is simply a little bit too short; it is not true.

Many, many people, hundreds of people, were really involved in Helvetica's success story and made it what it is today, and many investments were made along the way. We are still making many investments, and the registration and protection of the Helvetica trademark alone costs a fortune every year. We have invested a lot into that, and for further development, of course.

GH — You mean people trying to make copies or use the name?

BS — There are many copies of Helvetica around and different digital implementations, since the designs of the original weights are no longer protectable, so everybody can create their own version of Helvetica. But the name Helvetica is a trademark that is registered worldwide, and we defend that trademark quite—I hate to say aggressively, but we do the best that we can.

GH — I want to know from both of you, why type? When you come in in the morning and do this, what are the things that drive you?

OH — Type is, I think, one of the most important things in my life, because my father was a calligrapher. And Helvetica was actually there at the start of my profession, because I was at the printer with my parents and the guy at the Linotype machine said, "What's your name?" And I said, "Otmar Hoefer." He keyed it into the machine and it cast the lines and he printed it. So I had my first business card, and I looked at it and it was in Helvetica, and I said this is the profession I want to go into. And since then it's been like an infection. I cannot get rid of it. The first I thing I do every morning, I open the newspaper, I look at the ads and see what typefaces they are using. I don't read it; I just identify the type. I am type-minded, and that is the way I do my work here.

GH — Bruno?

BS — My story was different, it had to do with soccer, with football. My dad was a soccer player, and we had a huge family, five children. He was also a craftsman; he had his own small company. And when I was 14, he became ill—he had problems with his knees as a result of his soccer playing—and his health problems became very, very serious. He had a heart attack, and the doctor said he was going to die soon.

My mother was desperate and said, "Okay, boy, finish school right now," and she sent me to an apprenticeship at a printer. And I became a type-setter at the age of 15. My father lived for another 45 years, but that is how my career started, and I've never done anything else besides typesetting. I worked in Switzerland for several years, I was a pioneer in photocomposition in the very early sixties and computerized typesetting intrigued me a lot; I used my first computer in 1964. I became an expert on these things, and Linotype hired me as an expert on photo-typesetting and computers, et cetera.

So I've never done anything else, and to me type is a challenge. It is kind of like sports, because friends ask me, or people that I meet ask me, "What do you do?" "Well, I do type." "Type? What kind of type things?" "Fonts, you know." "Oh. Okay. Is anybody buying them? Because there are lots of them in the computer." Yeah, okay, there are tiny little amounts, but we try to get them many, many times, and that is the challenge. So we have piracy, we have a total underappreciation of the value of fonts, and everybody asks me, "Uh, is that a business?" Yes it is. And that motivates me, you know? And also to be able to work with designers of all kinds, people like Hermann Zapf, but also very young people with new ideas. That is a lot of fun.

GH — Do you have a favorite letter of the alphabet? And if so why is it your favorite?

BS — Yeah, my favorite letter is the lowercase *a*. Because, I think it's the most characteristic letter in the alphabet. Versus the lowercase *l*, for instance—in a sans-serif typeface it is just a rectangle; there is not much variation in it. But the lower case *a* is the character with the strongest individual expression.

OH — For me it's the Q, the uppercase Q, because of its tails and its versatile form, which you can see over and over again. It's just a circle and a stroke, but it's interesting what the type designers have all made with it.

BS — It's the type designers' favorite, you know?

OH — Yeah, yeah.

BS — Because that's where they can really distinguish themselves from others.

OH — Yes, it is a very unique letter.

—

Hermann Zapf (HZ)/ June 2, 2006 Bad Homburg

When we arrived at Linotype's offices in Germany to interview Bruno Steinert and Otmar Hoefer, the first thing they said was, "Hermann Zapf happens to be here today. Would you like to speak with him as well?" I said yes, of course. Zapf is one of the greatest living legends of type design, still working at 95 years old. Otmar spoke to Zapf and came back saying, "Well, he said he doesn't have much to say about Helvetica, but he will speak with you."

—

Gary Hustwit — Can you first maybe talk a little bit about how you became involved with type design?

Hermann Zapf — Originally I was a calligrapher, and I started more than 60 years ago with my first type design. It was in the forties. And now, through all the years, I've done quite a lot of typefaces. Mostly for the Linotype company. Very few for others. And I feel I have done enough, and now the next generation should also do them. Better designs and maybe more sans-serif faces. There are lots of sans serifs around besides Helvetica, of course.

I must confess, I've never used Helvetica, I'm a fan of Frutiger's Univers. And for me, my feelings about Helvetica . . . It's a little too 19th century for me, in the forms. It's a good design, no question. But a typeface also represents a style, and in my case, Helvetica is always a touch of the 19th century. Therefore, I like Univers much more. It is a 20th-century design and is not so much connected with the past. Frutiger really did a design for our time. So I'm sorry, but I cannot tell you too many positive things about Helvetica.

Of course, many people like Helvetica, and it's good, I think, that not everybody has only one typeface to use. There are lots of typefaces today which you can get and which you can use for all kinds of different typography. And I hope there's more and more understanding about typography these days. The computer helps to bring people to typography who had never touched typography in their whole lives.

GH — I wanted to talk a little bit about your personal creative process when you are designing a typeface. Is it a case where it's just in your head and then you draw it out, or are you using influences from other faces? Generally, how do you go about designing a new typeface?

HZ — Most of my type designs were commissions by companies. So you get specific technical information about what is needed, what you can do, and what the limits are—for example, the problems they had with casting metal type in the old days. And later with photocomposition, there were also a lot of specifications which you had to follow. So you are not really a free designer. You have to put all your designs into this structure, whether you like it or not.

And in the old days—let's say, if I say "old days," I mean the metal typeface era in the fifties or sixties—the typefaces which I did at that time, if I see them today I see all of the compromises. Therefore I have redesigned some of my typefaces, like Optima and Palatino, to update them with all the new technical possibilities, which are immense compared to the old days. So I'm very happy that I can do this at my age. I still have a very steady hand. I don't drink coffee, and therefore my hands don't shake. So I have redesigned most of my metal typefaces for digital, and I'm very happy about that.

As I told you, I mostly had commissions; only a few typefaces were my own idea. There was Palatino—it was based on my calligraphy and transferred to a typeface. And the other one was Optima, which I started in 1950 during a visit to Italy. I thought, maybe those forms that I saw in Rome and in Florence could be used for a typeface? I needed eight years to get that idea finished. And these days, companies don't have the patience to wait eight years for you to finish a typeface. In the old days, we had to do every character by hand, and every correction had to be done by hand. So for just a little change—if the test was not coming out the way you wanted it—then you had to redraw the whole character, or the whole alphabet sometimes.

But what you see today is all these badly done redesigns or copies. Sometimes people are not critical enough to know the difference. And there's such a huge selection of sans-serif faces today, so I hope people use more sans serifs, not only Helvetica and Univers and Frutiger but also some designs from young designers. You see, the market is filled with all these great names like Helvetica, and it's hard for young designers to find a little space to put their design out. And why not? One of these days, somebody will find a new solution for a sans serif which is much better than Helvetica, perhaps. And there are a lot of young designers around now. In the old days, you could count them on two hands. Today there are hundreds, in universities, putting letters together and making typefaces, and why not? It's always a game. Which time is it successful? Which time isn't the right time? Sometimes a typeface is far ahead of the time, like Futura, for instance.

GH — Do you have a favorite typeface, either one of yours or one by another designer?

HZ — If you ask a father which of his daughters is the most beautiful, you will never get an answer, for all his daughters are beautiful. I think it's a question that is hard for me to answer. But if we are talking about

Helvetica, maybe we should not talk too much about my typefaces. It's just a coincidence that I am here, and you had the possibility to talk to me. So we should not talk about my typefaces. Let's talk about Helvetica.

GH — Okay. You mentioned that when you look at Helvetica, you see a 19th-century face. Do you see Akzidenz-Grotesk?

HZ — Yes, Akzidenz-Grotesk. That is ... let's say it's the base for Helvetica. Helvetica is very close to Akzidenz-Grotesk, but some characters are especially different in design.

GH — So why do you think Helvetica was associated with being "modern" in the sixties?

HZ — I think in the sixties it was a fashion, let's say. Helvetica was used by the big advertising companies in New York, and by people like Herb Lubalin, as you know. And other people followed these big companies, and I think the success of Helvetica maybe was based on this. I mentioned Herb Lubalin, who I knew very well. One day he said he was tired of Helvetica, so he made his own sans serif. Herb Lubalin was one of the pastors, and all the young people followed him.

[An airplane flies overhead.]

GH — That's Helvetica flying over us. It's a Lufthansa plane, so there's Helvetica on it.

HZ — Yes. Lufthansa uses Helvetica.

GH — But you think that was the biggest reason for its popularity?

HZ — I think so. It was a trend in that direction, you see, toward sans serifs, and not so much the roman typefaces of the fifties. And Optima, by the way, also came out in the fifties, in 1958. So there was a trend to have a very cool and simplified form, to get away from these fancy, bad-looking, old styles they had from the thirties and early forties in Germany.

Helvetica was offered, also, in all kinds of variations. Other faces normally had only two or three variations, roman, italic, and bold. With Helvetica, you had, at that time, at least 20. Today you have maybe 50 or more. So that also helps to put a typeface into practical use. Today you can do this digitally—you can condense or expand the typeface, stretch it like rubber—but in the fifties and sixties, you had to use what was offered by the type companies. Today, you need maybe six or eight variations of a typeface, and you can stretch it in all directions as you like. In the thirties, you could not do anything with the typeface. It was impossible. You even had a contract when you purchased the typeface that said you could not change any character. Today people change characters as needed.

GH — Did you know Max Miedinger?

HZ — Oh, yes. He was an employee of Haas, as you know. But then he had problems with Haas. Haas did some other versions of Helvetica at that time, in the sixties, which he didn't like. I think Miedinger was still alive, but they didn't ask him. I hoped he could find a solution with the company in the last moment. But last time I talked to him, he was very unhappy about the extra designs that Haas did with Helvetica, and he said, "This is not my design." But Haas owned Helvetica, and therefore they thought they had the right to do it. I don't know all the details, but this was his problem with Haas.

But he had been commissioned by Haas to redesign a typeface, Haas-Grotesk as it was then called. And then I think it was Stempel's idea to name it Helvetica. And I think Helvetica was the perfect name. Swiss typography was known worldwide at the time, so it was the best solution for Helvetica to get into the market.

GH — Do you have any comments on the relationship between the type designer and the type foundry?

HZ — I think I've had very good relationships, while others have not. Of course the type foundries were very powerful, and they spent a lot of money to cut a typeface. Therefore, they were very careful, and they did not take too many new commissions. Today there's hardly any expense. If you have a good idea, and you make it on your computer, and you send it to a type company digitally, it's done; there is no further expense. This is a big difference between the old days and now. And therefore, it's better to make a design that maybe is not successful but is good. Not all successful typefaces are good typefaces.

GH — Last question: Do you have any advice for young type designers who are just starting out?

HZ — Advice? Yes. You should always learn the basics, and the best way is to draw letters, or to write letters. Calligraphy. Then you know the structure and the relationships between the characters. But some people today, they have no idea where the basic characters come from. And sans serifs have many, many variations, besides the letters like *I*. With a capital letter *I*, you cannot make a difference, it's the same in hundreds of sans serifs. But there are a lot of other characters, like *f* and *g*, through which you can show your talent.

—

Dimitri Bruni (DB) & Manuel Krebs (MK) / June 6, 2006 Zurich

Dimitri and Manuel formed their studio NORM after meeting as design students in Biel, Switzerland. I thought it would be interesting to speak with some younger Swiss designers to get their views on Helvetica. I spoke with them at their studio.
—

Gary Hustwit — Can each of you talk about how you got started in design? And then we can talk about how the two of you ended up working together.

Manuel Krebs — I've always wanted to be a graphic designer. Since I was young, I've always been very interested in posters and stuff I saw on the street, and I thought it must be a really interesting thing to do. Then after high school, I went to art school. When you're first there, you don't really know what it is; you don't know what your education as a designer will be. Being in art school allowed me to discover what is possible. That's also where I met Dimitri.

Dimitri Bruni — It was the same for me. The first year is quite a special year, because you're making everything like an artist; you're trying everything. I didn't know exactly what graphic design was, but I was determined to do it. I started school the same year as Manuel. I think I got a better sense of exactly what graphic design *isn't* after one or two years. After that, I was really motivated. It was a really small school in a province. It's not like a high school where you see a lot of students. For each class there were just eight people; the classes were really small, very concentrated.

GH — What years were you were in school?

MK — We were in school from 1991 to 1996. After that, we worked in design agencies for two years, because we needed money. It's good to have some experience in larger companies so you know what you do and don't want to do. In January 1999, we rented this space. In the beginning, it was like the joke where you stare at the phone and wait for somebody to call you.

GH — When you were studying design, what were your influences? What was the prevailing graphic style in Switzerland?

DB — Well, the main influence was the school itself and the teachers there. When we were about to graduate, it was the period when David Carson was really on top, and everybody was talking about him and his new visual language. Neville Brody was another designer who was interesting, because he was developing his own typefaces.

MK — Our education didn't focus on type very much. It was much more about drawing and painting. Like Dimitri mentioned, the influences in graphic design were really Brody and Carson. When we got to school, Brody was already very established. He had published his second book, I think. By the time we finished school, Carson wasn't fresh anymore. And when we started our own office, we rejected the way Carson approached his work, it was something that we were not at all interested in. We wanted to go back to a more structured design, not "anything goes."

DB — It's too easy.

GH — How do you think traditional Swiss design and the International Style influence you now? Or did it influence you when you were in school?
 MK — When we started school, there was one computer in the entire school. When we finished school five years later, there were like 30 computers—everybody was on a computer. This changed what you could do and how you could work. The school was very skeptical about how you should use the computer. Our teachers were from an older generation. They were very influenced by the sixties, by classic Swiss typography and how they'd learned it should be done, but they didn't succeed in bringing that closer to us. It was only after we graduated that we really looked at Josef Müller-Brockmann's work. It was when we came to Zürich that we appreciated that work.

GH — Is that still an influence on your work now? Do you still feel it?
 DB — Very much, I think.

MK — Yes, of course. Swiss design is a very strange mix, because there is a very rational aspect to it, but there's also an almost esoteric part of it. That's how it was taught. For us it was not rational enough. There was a concept of how you should structure everything with hierarchies, but then there were also moments when it was very much about beauty. There were not really arguments or discussions. It was just, "Okay, it must be like that." Our teachers judged our work not with rational arguments but with something like the golden ratio. For example, they would say, "It must be a little bit more to the left." It was about moving things around, not about having a concept.

DB — They would say, "That's right; that's wrong," but we never understood exactly why.

MK — That's something we really try to avoid in our work. "Does it look better in blue or red?" We really try not to think about things like that. But before we start the project, we make a list of requirements. "Okay, it must be like this and like that." We have big arguments to decide on these things.

GH — What about type? How would you describe your approach to typography?

DB — Back when we opened the office, we made original typefaces for every job we got. That's not the normal way to do things, but we did it for every project. We'd develop a typeface first, and after we could design the project.

MK — It was like dogma, you know? "Okay, for this new job, we'll develop a typeface, and then we use it for the job." We never used the same typeface twice. But it was the time when the computer program Fontographer was very popular, and there were many matrices and grids and dot forms, things you could do very fast. Everybody did this.

DB — And they forgot it very fast as well. It was interesting. At that time, we made a font just for one project, and after that we'd forget about it and make another one.

MK — But now those times are over. It was a period when that was interesting—these simple typefaces that were roughly done with a very basic construction. There were so many of them, you know? We started using other typefaces when we got into more complex projects. If you do flyers and posters, it's very simple. But as soon as you work on a book or a more complex communication, you realize that you need better typefaces. We started designing a serious typeface called Normetica, but it was taking us too much time. So we started using other typefaces. We're not that radical anymore. You asked how we would describe our approach to type. I think, for us, it's very important to reduce the elements that we use. When it comes to type, we will use only one or two cuts and one size, if possible. We try to have as few elements as possible and use them in a way that gives us the best solution.

DB — We like restrictions; we can't operate without restrictions. The more restrictions we have, the happier we are. And if there are no restrictions for the job, we set them for ourselves. I think if you are totally free to do things, you can do nothing, because you don't know where to start. And maybe it's a little bit like how we use typography. It's quite simple, in a way. We're interested in doing the maximum with the minimum.

MK — It's much easier to do something very complex than to do something very simple. We are a little bit torn between these two things, but actually we try to be simple. This also applies to the choice of the typefaces we use. We don't like humanistic typefaces, for example. They must be more rational, because otherwise they have too much expression. We don't like typefaces that are expressive, unless we created them. If it's not a typeface we designed, it will influence our work too much. If we choose another designer's typeface, it must be very silent. Otherwise, everybody will just look at the typeface. Also, people on the street are not aware that it's like a subliminal message. It's just there. For instance, the font DIN is an extremely popular typeface at the moment. And maybe people don't realize it, but everything looks the same. The typeface we use for a project is always the most delicate choice.

DB — This is the one decision we make before designing anything. We have to decide on the typeface, and after that, the typeface will define how the graphics and the visuals look. It's a strategy we like to use, and it's how we're working at the moment. I don't know; maybe in five years, it will be different.

GH — It's interesting because it seems like it's either one way or the other. Some designers like to have as many restrictions as possible, because then they don't have to think about all those things. They concentrate on the message or the structure, and they know they're only going to use very simple fonts, and they don't have to look through a thousand typefaces to figure it out. Some people are just completely the opposite. They're like, "I would never give myself restrictions. I look at five hundred different typefaces."

MK — Okay, we look at many typefaces. New typefaces come out daily, and we look at them a lot.

DB — It's a part of our daily job, you know?

MK — But once we've decided, it's not open anymore.

DB — There's no going back.

GH — So you pick the typeface first, and then that determines the tone of the whole job?

DB — Well, after that you know what you want to do.

MK — The consequences of the choice become clear.

GH — Maybe we should talk about Helvetica now. Since I started making the film, of course, I'm always interested in how people feel about Helvetica. How do you feel about it?

MK — We are less obsessed with Helvetica than we used to be.

DB — Yeah, we were really obsessed with Helvetica for a while, but not so much anymore.

MK — We came to a point where we accepted that it's just there. We hardly ever use Helvetica now.

DB — Almost never.

MK — But when we design a typeface, we'll often double-check it against Helvetica, because it's like a standard. We'll check how a certain issue is solved in Helvetica or we'll look at different letter combinations. I don't mind Helvetica, really. I can work with Helvetica, but I'm not obsessed with it anymore.

GH — Were you when you were in school?

MK — No, we actually were not that aware of typefaces when we were in school. The education of a typographer and the sensibility to type is something that really takes a lot of time. There are still many things that we don't know and new things we're still discovering. It's a very long process.

DB — Yeah. We came into school one day, and one of the oldest professors came in and said, "Today, we're going to design the letter *A* in Univers and the *N* in Univers. And after that, the *A* in Univers Italic and the *N* in Univers Italic." We just copied it; it was just an exercise.

MK — We didn't have any instruction on type design. You get to know it by doing it. I think it's very difficult for people who don't normally work with type. They are often really helpless. Somebody will ask me, "What is a good typeface to use on my computer?" There's no way to answer that, since almost every typeface can be interesting if it's used in a certain way, you know?

DB — But the chance of making mistakes with Helvetica is smaller than when working with a font like Serpentine or something.

MK — Yes, if you are not a good designer or if you are not a designer, just use Helvetica Bold in one size, like for a flyer—it looks good.

DB — It looks correct, you know? Half the job is done. After that, you can design really poorly, but at least the type problem is solved.

MK — We think that Helvetica contains a design program somehow. It will lead you to a certain language. This is also one of the secrets of the success of Helvetica. In itself, it contains a certain aesthetic that you will inevitably use because the typeface wants it like that. You will do what the typeface wants you to do.

DB — For example, in the mid-sixties in Germany, the logotype of many companies involved displaying the name of the company in Helvetica. Condense the letters to the maximum, and that's it.

GH — Do you think it still has that same effect today? A lot of people, especially designers who were working back then, will say that the way we look at it now is totally different from the way they looked at it then. That concept of a typeface being really about its own time. What are your thoughts on that?

MK — Well, technological development is very important for everything in this field. And in the sixties, there were very few typefaces that were available. But the choice of Helvetica is not that radical, because everybody uses it. And I think now the number of typefaces that are available in the market is, I don't know, maybe a hundred times more than in the sixties. You can easily access them, and you can also manipulate them in FontLab—you can do so many things. These days, you can manipulate elements so that sometimes it doesn't look like the original font anymore. Back then you could only choose among the fonts your printer had. We are now in a situation where so much is available. If you use Helvetica now, it's like it's quoting something. For example, if you really want to display statements using Helvetica—which can look really right sometimes—it means something.

GH — So if you went to a printer and they had only three fonts, you think that would be a better scenario?

> **DB** — Yes, I would like that.

> **MK** — I would like that too, but we cannot simulate that. There are still designers who restrict themselves to, I don't know, Akzidenz-Grotesk, that's it. That's the language of their studio. I think this is a good concept.

> **DB** — I think Experimental Jetset uses only Univers or Helvetica.

GH — Massimo Vignelli too—he only uses Helvetica, Bodoni, and a couple others. He's like, "You don't need all those other ones."

> **MK** — We're in a little bit of a different position also because we design typefaces ourselves. We are not just users; we are somewhere in-between. But we are not typographers. The typographer will design a typeface that, in itself, is perfect, but he will not use it himself. And then there's the designer who will take a typeface and use it in his work. It's always different if we work with typefaces we've made ourselves. The creation of each letter is in the same spirit as the person creating the design. A typeface is like the molecule of the design. It can be very, very inspiring. It's why we are not interested in restricting ourselves to just two typefaces.

> **DB** — The visual language implied by a typeface is incredibly important and strong. And of course, that's what companies with corporate type-faces are trying to accomplish. For us, when we are doing a typeface for a book or something, it's somehow the same thing, because you want to have that uniqueness. If you see the typeface, you automatically rec-ognize, "Okay, this is for that project." So when we design a typeface, we're always looking to have something special and really customized for that project.

> **MK** — For corporations, we would advise them that it's not just about having a logo. It's much more important to have a corporate typeface because then you can write whatever you want; you don't even have to include the name of the company. The spirit of the company is embed-ded in the shape of the letters. It's so strong.

> **DB** — It's something you can just feel. It's not something you can show, maybe it's more subliminal.

> **MK** — But the spirit is in it. On the other hand, if you do a corporate iden-tity with Helvetica, there are so many others who have used it already. It's BMW; it's Lufthansa—there are so many, and it would be just like another version of that.

GH — Talking to a lot of different designers, it's interesting to hear where they get their inspiration. For instance, we talked to Michael C. Place from Build, and he's obsessed with bar codes and little technical draw-ings. He's really into any kind of electronics or schematics. Or for some people, it's hand-painted signs. Are there things in your daily lives that you pull into your design work?

DB — I think every profession has a professional obsession. It's like, if you do graphic design, you really look at the design of things closely. But I don't know. There are so many other things that have nothing to do with graphic design that influence me.

GH — Like what?

MK — You look at old books, or you look at manuals, stuff like that. But also, the cornflakes package can be interesting.

DB — Yes. It's so badly designed that it's incredible.

MK — But it's not by coincidence. These products sold to the masses are always done by consultants, it seems. You see these products when a lot of people are involved in the process.

DB — Music is a big influence as well; we actually have a lot of friends in Zürich who work as DJs or are involved in making music. We are just consuming the music.

MK — I can only work with music on if I know it really well, because, otherwise, I have to listen to it. If we listen to a record, we will listen to the same record all day long. We never listen to the radio. We don't even have a radio. We don't want to be surprised by music or be taken by music. But it's really not that important to me. Even if we listen to a record all day long, I will not be able to sing the songs afterwards, even after playing it 10 times.

DB — It's really not easy sharing an office with Manuel, because he's the one who plays the same song and presses repeat all day long. I'll say, "Haven't you heard that song 2 or 3 times?" He'll reply, "No, 10 or 12 times." I like to listen to other kinds of music.

MK — You are more open.

DB — Ninety percent of the music we listen to is hip-hop. I think this is really influenced by Manuel. But when he's not in the office, I'll listen to other stuff too. Can I say that?

MK — Well, when I'm not in the office, I don't know what you listen to.

GH — Do you have a favorite letter of the alphabet? And if so why?

DB — *M* is your favorite.

MK — Because I'm *M*. Okay, if you're designing them, you will like letters like *H, I, L, F, E* because they can be done very fast. I'm talking about uppercase. As soon as you have a curve, it's more work, more difficult, more questions. For example, *S* is a very complex and difficult letter. A really nice letter is the uppercase *R* because it's the only one to contain the round, diagonal, and straight lines at the same time.

DB — I don't have a favorite letter. There are combinations that look nice and combinations that look really sad. But I don't have a favorite letter.

MK — There are letters or symbols in which you can express yourself more, like an ampersand—there's more freedom. You have more opportunity in letters that are not so important in the overall image of the text. Do you have a favorite letter?

GH — Umm, I don't know! I haven't really thought about it. It's funny, because I like Helvetica, but it's not my favorite typeface in the world. I do use it more since I've been making this film. It's easy; it gets the job done. I just like that feeling around it, you know? Whatever it is.

    MK — It feels right. It's like, if you set something in a certain face, it suddenly feels right, no?

GH — Can you talk about the Swiss money design?

    MK — We won a competition for the redesign of Swiss paper currency. At the moment, we're developing the whole series of bills, which should start coming out in 2010. There are many interesting aspects to the project. For example, the typeface that's used to display the written information on the bills is Officina. Of course, this will be a subject of discussion. This was a rule for the competition—everybody had to use the same typeface. We are now really thinking about what the typeface should be on Swiss money. Should it be Helvetica Condensed? No, I'm joking. But it should be in line with a certain attitude. It should be something very straight, very clear.

GH — Didn't Erik Spiekermann design Officina? Was that why you went to see him?

    MK — No. Why did I go there? It was because of another typeface called Theinhardt. It's the model for Akzidenz-Grotesk. The head of the department in the school where we teach designed a digital version of Theinhardt, and Spiekermann had seen it and he wanted to talk to us about this typeface. He's always wanted a digital version of it; either to design it himself or to find a very complete specimen. In type design, there's a practice of digitizing existing fonts that you find in specimen books that are not yet digitized. The other thing, of course, is inventing completely new typefaces.

GH — Do you guys want to discuss some other projects?

    MK — The airport would be interesting, maybe.

GH — Yes, because that was one you designed a typeface for.

    MK — This job was important for us because it was the first time we really got a job as type designers. Before this, making typefaces was always on the side. It was an extra thing that we did, but usually it wasn't paid work.

    For our second book, we designed a typeface called Simple. It was mono-spaced and had some very eccentric letters; the lowercase r was almost like a c. When Ruedi Baur won the competition for the Cologne Airport graphics using this typeface, they decided it wouldn't really work. They commissioned us to redesign a proportional typeface that would be more legible for the airport and asked us to make certain corrections to it. So we redrew the entire set. We were very skeptical when they decided to use Simple, because we would've never developed a typeface like that for an airport. But their idea was right because, since it was a unique typeface, one would recognize the information easily just by the typeface. Our goal was to keep the characteristics of the original typeface, but make it more legible. It involved a lot of experimentation and also testing to see how readable it would be from a distance. For example, when they develop a typeface for highway signage, they test at which driving speeds it's most readable. The speed in an airport is walking speed, so it's not that fast. You have more time to read through these things.

MK — They used the typeface really well; they used it in very big sizes at the gates where the airplanes parked. So you had huge letters on the ground and on the planes. It's nice to see your typeface on a plane.

GH — That's funny because Michael C. Place told me, "I've always wanted to design an identity for an airline." Are there projects like that that you guys wish you could design?

MK — If there's a project we wish we could work on, it's our next book, actually. It's taken us a very long time. You can get very busy doing projects for clients, so we really enjoy taking the time to think about our own things—to work on content, to design for ourselves.

—

Neville Brody (NB)/
August 24, 2006
London

Neville Brody's graphic design work has been heavily informed by music. He broke new ground as creative director of the *Face* magazine in the 1980s, and in 1990 he cofounded the FontShop with Erik Spiekermann. I spoke with Neville in his London studio.

—

Gary Hustwit — Let's talk about how you started designing typefaces.

Neville Brody — Wait, are you being interviewed in the film?

GH — No. I'm not.

NB — You should be.

GH — Why?

NB — Are we rolling yet? Seriously, are you being interviewed for this?

GH — No.

NB — Surely you should be. Surely one of the most important points of this whole movie is, "Why do a movie on Helvetica?"

GH — Yeah. But I guess I'm trying to show it rather than having me say it. I like films where you come to a conclusion from what's there and from the conversations and the profiles.

NB — But what's your experience?

GH — I've been involved in record labels, and book publishing, and filmmaking, so I've always used graphic design and type in the different things that I've done. I've just been kind of a type freak for the past 20 years.

NB — Yeah. But so for you, why the film on Helvetica?

GH — It seemed like a good structure for the film, a way to talk about type and how it affects all of us, and the meaning of type.

NB — But why Helvetica specifically and not Blackletter, for example?

GH — Well, because it's a typeface that's everywhere. It's on that chocolate package there. It's just so ubiquitous and people don't realize it, but also it's one of the typefaces that most people know the name of just because it's on almost every personal computer.

NB — So it's like the "Hoover" of fonts?

GH — Sure, or "Jell-O." It's like everyone knows the name, but they have no idea what it means. They have no idea that a guy drew the font.

NB — So this film could be called "Cornflakes."

GH — It could be called "Typographica" or something like that.

NB — So you picked Helvetica because it's the most ubiquitous? I mean, do you have any facts or figures? Is it the most-used font?

GH — I don't think there are any hard numbers, but it's definitely one of the most used fonts. Or Arial—

NB — I was going to say that it's probably Arial.

GH — It's on more systems, because it's bundled with Windows, but in terms of typefaces that people actually buy, I think Helvetica is the world's bestselling typeface.

NB — So there's an interesting point there about how Windows has affected the world of typography. So Microsoft is indeed the world's biggest distributor of fonts. One of your questions was about the meaning of fonts, of type. There might be an easy way of answering that. What is the role of typography? What is a typeface? And fundamentally that could be understood as, in fact, every message is of democratic value. Normally you can judge a message by its content. If you're listening to a message, you know if something's rhetoric by the way it's delivered. But with type it's quite different; in the written word it's quite different. The way something is presented will define the way you react to it. So you can take the same message and present it in three different typefaces. The response to that—the immediate emotional response—will be different. It works on the level of the brain and recognition factors.

This week, for instance, they've said—they being science—that we assess a person completely in terms of our reactions to them—who they are, what their characteristics are, and whether we're going to speak to that person—in the first 100 microseconds. So during the first tenth of a second, we've decided who that person is and what our relationship to them will be. It's the same with type. A message will be perceived long before we've actually read it, and the choice of typeface is the prime weapon in that communication. And I say weapon largely because these days with commercial marketing and advertising, the way the message is dressed is going to define our reaction to that message in the advertisement.

So a message that's put in some grungy typeface will instantly suggest some sort of cultural response. Whereas a message put in Helvetica will sit with all of the assumptions we have about a kind of clean, well-proportioned space. There's something reassuring, it's informative, and all of that. And now our response to the message will be completely different even if it's saying exactly the same thing. So if it says, "Buy these jeans," and it's a grunge font, you would expect it to be some kind of ripped jeans or to be sold in some kind of underground clothing store. But if you see that same message in Helvetica, it's probably outside of a Gap store. It's going to be clean, you're going to fit in, you're not going to stand out and be radical.

Another way of understanding how type works in that sense, if you imagine a book—say, take a book by Shakespeare—and that book is set in a large-sized letter which has got chunky serifs and a big drop-shadow, your response to the words of Shakespeare will be entirely different than if they were set in a small, light, delicate serif typeface, which is how we're used to seeing it. We wouldn't notice if it was set in Garamond. We'd notice if it was set in Cooper Black. So the choice of typeface is a hidden tool of manipulation within society. I've always upheld my opinion that all schools should be teaching typography. We should be fundamentally aware of how typographic language is forming our thoughts.

GH — As a designer, both as a type designer but also a graphic designer, how do you approach that subtle art of influence?

NB — My attitude toward type—in fact, my attitude toward design—has always been the process of trying to reveal, not conceal. In contrast, advertising's modus operandi is to largely conceal its manipulative side, so it doesn't give clues unless it's English advertising, which is double clever. So it's saying you're part of the joke here—buy our product. Advertising tends to use typography to hide or cover its prime intent, which has to do with mood setting before the message is delivered. So I had the idea of experimenting with that as the basis of my work. That might involve choosing an inappropriate typeface in order to reveal the role of typography and the role of a font choice.

As I said, it's like doing something in a font that you wouldn't expect as a way of revealing that process. For example, taking a street sign, like a motorway sign, but doing it with sparkly letters would reveal something in the role of the choice of font. So I've always upheld the idea that convention should be challenged, and that we should be thinking about this stuff all the time—otherwise it's a hypnotic state that can be used by people in power, be it politics, government, ideologists, as well as advertising.

GH — That's interesting. One of the first times that I really noticed when the media was using typography to spin something was during a story I was watching on CNN about welfare in the US. They put the word "welfare" in this distressed, scary-looking typeface. It looked really evil. And I was thinking, what's wrong with trying to help out our fellow human beings? Who made the decision to use the scary font? If you set that word in a clean, optimistic typeface, suddenly everyone might be more optimistic toward certain concepts.

NB — That's absolutely right. You're talking about "welfare" being in a distressed typeface. By the same token, you wouldn't go into a hospital and expect hospital signs to be in a distressed font, so there are a number of other things going on, and one is appropriateness. A font choice is deemed to be appropriate, and that's usually determined by consensus. So we've all agreed that Helvetica is the best way to describe the hospital and the Gap. It's interesting that they both seem to be saying the same thing, about the need for a sanitized culture. Not that we're all going to end up sick, but in fact they are both ways of healing an abnormality.

In a way, Helvetica is a club. It's a mark of membership. It's a badge that says we're part of modern society; we share the same ideals. It's well rounded; it's not going to be damaging or dangerous. It's collusion. We've all signed up to the same kind of rounded-off ideals. Nothing's going to jump out and be different or interesting, otherwise we'd all be using Franklin Gothic.

GH — Do you use Helvetica?

NB — I use Helvetica a lot, but I originally hated Helvetica. I've always hated Helvetica. The badges you're giving out ["I Love Helvetica" and "I Hate Helvetica"], I think you should have one that says, "I Love Hating Helvetica," which I think would be more appropriate. We may have to meld them.

GH — I was going to do a red one that said, "I'm Neutral About Helvetica."

NB — No, you can't be. Well, actually, Helvetica is neutral, supposedly. But I first used Helvetica when I worked at the *Face* magazine for a number of years and there was always this expectation that we would deliver something new and radical every single month. People were disappointed when it wasn't radical or new. So in the end, the "newness" was the culture that people clamored for. It got out of hand. It became a ridiculous expectation, which was impossible to fulfill. How many months a year can you reinvent yourself totally?

So when it came to doing *Arena* magazine, which was kind of a different cultural space, it was more about consumer culture. It wasn't so much about thinking good; it was more about looking good. I felt that at that time, culture—youth culture or urban culture—needed a place where it could sit down on a park bench and breathe for a while. Helvetica was the perfect choice for that. It was unassuming. It was nonthreatening. And interestingly, its character comes from its lack of character. It's quite interesting, again, most people use Helvetica as opposed to Univers. You know, the history of the font Univers is an exercise in averaging—you take a number of outlines of sans-serif fonts, you put them on top of each other, which is what Frutiger did, and you trace the average. Then that's it. That's the universal font. But in doing so he missed the most important point—that as soon as you round off or get rid of any extraneous elements, you lose the humanity. Univers became the world's first mechanical font.

Whereas Helvetica still retains a little bit of impurity. It's not a true humanist font in the traditional sense, but it's a human font. So we used Helvetica and shifted from hand-drawn fonts. We shifted from experimenting with stressing typefaces to using Helvetica, and I chose it because it was non-emotive and signifies a non-emotive place. But what we did was, we started to experiment with it to see if we could force it to be emotive. We tried typesetting it so that things became much more fluid and poetic. We tried bunching words together and forming these more painterly uses of Helvetica so that we were turning it on its head. We were taking its use out of context. As opposed to using a typeface which would be unexpected, we were using a typeface in an unexpected way. That was really important, and I think it opened a lot of doorways about how people thought about the use of type. That it might not be the choice of font but the way you use the font that was important. That period of experimentation has informed a lot of my work since then, especially in using type in a very painterly way. At the end of the day, Helvetica is just a choice of color on the page.

GH — It's interesting because that change happened even with Helvetica itself. When I talked to people who were working at Haas when they made the original Helvetica, they look at it now and they say that it's a completely different typeface. Every technological change in typesetting over the sixties and seventies—photocomp and everything else—has subtly, but really, changed it. Looking back at the original, it's got a much more human touch to it.

NB — Yes, the original one did. It's like the original Futura, which was a very, very funky human font, but it has evolved to be this kind of geometric, cold typeface. You're right. The original Helvetica was full of character. It was almost like a crafted font. We use Neue Helvetica as it seems to have covered all the rubbish and purified the font right down to something that is faceless, hence its appeal.

But there are a number of typefaces which have come and gone and are still hanging around which had professed to be—or others have claimed then to be—the new Helvetica. Meta was the new Helvetica and was claimed as such. And then Interstate became the new Meta. Now Gotham is the new Interstate, and now DIN is the new Gotham. Of course, all of these fluctuate between Erik Spiekermann and Tobias Frere-Jones. It's an interesting tennis match. I mean, honestly, I still think Helvetica is the new Helvetica.

GH — Can you expand on the role of digital technology and the personal computer in the democratization of typefaces?

NB — That's interesting. Back in the day, type design and type use was a monastic industry. You had to study for years, practice for years; you went through apprenticeships. Only then were you deemed worthy of having your typeface cut. This was not for everyone, of course. But the advent of the computer has really taken that away. These days, anyone can design their own font. You can even turn your own handwriting into a typeface. Why not?

The tools have been taken away from that self-elected elite and given to everyone else. The parallel is, I think, between painting and the camera. Prior to the camera, everyone could paint, but you had masters. The camera democratized that and forced painters into a different kind of space where they would be focused on the role of painting and an abstract look at the state of man, because the camera gave the tools of accurate recording to the everyday person.

Most people can read and write, but you still need great writers. I remember in the early days of desktop publishing, even some of the people in your film were quite opposed to the democratization of publishing tools, thinking that it was going to flood the world with bad shit. The reality is, like with the camera, anyone can go and use a digital camera, but we still need great painters and photographers, just as with typography. We still need great typographers. The difference is, of course, as I said before, I don't think people are sufficiently educated about typography.

GH — In the same way painters had to readjust because of the rise of photography, do you think professional designers had to change?

NB — Well, when the personal computer came along and democratized publishing, typography was then liberated from its role of guardian of written language, the look of it. Then we had this whole period of experimentation including Fuse, which we published. Those Emigre fonts, T-26, Shmelvetica—there was a lot experimental typography going on, and this was quite a very liberating period.

I think now we're in a state where font choice is seen like a big supermarket. You can fancy a bit of this and a bit of that. In a way, it's lost its value a little bit. In the early days of FontFont, we felt that it was more like the music industry. You'd have a few number one hits, which would stay in the charts for a few weeks and then fall out, and then there would be another big hit. Thing is, there are so many now it's quite difficult. I suspect in the confusion of all that, people are returning to Helvetica as a kind of easy statement of modernism.

GH — Do you ascribe to the Vignelli philosophy of only needing five typefaces, and the rest are unnecessary?

NB — Yeah, I would agree with it, except I think you need five typefaces every hour. I think it should be eternal, changing, flowing. Language is a flowing space. Societies change. What society demands of its communication changes constantly. I think that digital typography has brought to the table this ability for that flow to happen. When it was all hot metal type and it was physically hammered by a press into handmade paper, it was a fixed space. Today, I think, typography is part of a more fluid state of communications.

—

Rick Poynor (RP)/
August 25, 2006
London

Rick Poynor is one of the most prolific and insightful writers on the subject of design and how it affects our lives. I spoke with Rick at the London offices of Wieden & Kennedy.

—

Gary Hustwit — Do you want to discuss a little bit of design history, about the late modernist period and what came after?

Rick Poynor — Okay. The 1950s are an interesting period in the development of graphic design as a profession. It's the point where designers really start to define themselves as professional beings offering a service to business, all kinds of organizations, and society.

In that postwar period, after the horror and the cataclysm of the Second World War, there's a real feeling of idealism among some designers —many perhaps, across the world, certainly in Europe—that design is part of that need to rebuild, to reconstruct, to make things more open, make them run more smoothly and be more democratic. There was this real sense of social responsibility among designers. This is the period when the early experiments of the high modernist period, from the 1920s in particular, in typography and design, start to be broken down, rationalized, codified. You get the emergence of this so-called International Typographic Style, or Swiss style. It's Swiss designers in the 1950s who are really driving that along, and there's still enormous interest in that period. It's almost romanticized by contemporary designers. They look back to the great days of the fifties, through to the sixties—the work coming out of Switzerland in particular. It seems to some contemporary designers to represent a kind of high point of graphic design, one of the great moments.

So the designers are thinking, in those days, the fifties through to the sixties, in a very rational way. They're prizing the idea of objectivity. They're even, maybe, at times, talking about neutrality, this idea that the designer exists as a mediator, as an interpreter, whose job it is to order visual reality, or at least the printed and typographic expression of everyday modern reality, for the viewer. To make the world more legible, in other words.

This is where Helvetica comes in. Helvetica emerges in that period, in 1957, where there's felt to be a need for rational typefaces which can be applied to all kinds of contemporary information, whether it's sign systems or corporate identity, and present those visual expressions of the modern world to the public in an intelligible, legible way. It's underpinned, is what I'm saying, by this great feeling, shared by many designers, of idealism.

GH — And then going into what is thought of as the postmodern period, what happens?

RP — Well, of course, the way these typographic styles, graphic-design styles, evolve is often quite complicated and convoluted, since we're talking about world graphic design. It's happening in different places at different speeds. You can't oversimplify it. But broadly speaking, the Swiss style that I mentioned became increasingly dominant around the world in the 1960s. People saw what was happening in Switzerland right here in Britain, looking across. They looked at Swiss typography in magazines and books. They started to think here in London about how they could use and apply this thinking: a heavy dependence on the idea of white space; typefaces almost invariably sans serif; asymmetrical compositions on the page; a very dynamic approach to layout; a heavy emphasis on photography. Illustration, in the Swiss work, was really just pushed to the side. It was felt to be subjective, impressionistic, old-fashioned. It wasn't fully contemporary. Whereas the photograph, as this supposedly objective record of reality, was modern. It was contemporary. It was the appropriate way of communicating.

The Swiss had been brilliant at bringing together this new typography based on the sans serif, based on typefaces like Helvetica with a very dynamic, bold, hard-hitting use of usually black-and-white photography. All of that inspired designers here in London. In fact, they changed things. You'd expect that. You would expect a local design population to import ideas, but also to twist and turn them and recraft them for their own ends. In fact, British design is the product of those European influences, but also American influences. A more muscular, hard-hitting, commercial approach to advertising design in particular. What you see here is a kind of fusion. But still, in the mid-sixties, if you wanted a fashionable typographic statement or if you were committed to the idea of informing and educating the public, either way, you would probably pick that Swiss design look.

So things trend along very nicely for a while, but as is always the case with any style, there's a law of diminishing returns. The more you see it, the more the public sees it, the more the designer uses those typographic and graphic solutions, the more familiar, predictable, and ultimately dull they become. If we fast-forward into the seventies, this typographic movement has been going for a long time at that stage. It's 20 years old. It's become the lingua franca of international corporations, in particular American corporations. They've all got these corporate identities that use either Helvetica or typefaces very like Helvetica.

It's getting dull as hell. We've seen it. The designers and public of the day had seen it. By the seventies, especially in America, you start to get a reaction against what it seems to those designers is the conformity, the kind of dull blanket of sameness that this way of design is imposing on the world. Something that had come out of idealism has by this time become merely routine, and there's a need for a change. The postmodern period, the height of which I guess was the 1980s, although these things started way earlier, was a reaction against that type of corporate typography. That way of designing was seen as the enemy, something to be resisted. Suddenly, designers were breaking things up. They wanted to get away from the orderly, clean, smooth surface of design—the horrible slickness of it all, as they saw it—and produce something that had vitality, that referred to ordinary, everyday design by amateurs, the so-called vernacular that you would see in the American landscape.

They wanted to express their subjectivity, their own feelings about the world, their sense that they had something to say through design, through the design choices they made. At that point the whole Helvetica look, this International Style, seems to be the very mark of a kind of dead conformity, and something to be rejected and reacted against. Of course, this caused controversy. If you take a figure like Massimo Vignelli, who had been one of the sixties high priests with his company, Unimark—it's right there in the name, Unimark: the idea of a uniform kind of expression. When he looked at this new work, this expressive, subjective, wayward—to his way of thinking—irrational new way of designing, it seemed like the barbarians were not only at the gate, but they'd stormed through and they'd taken over.

There is this interesting moment, around about 1990, as postmodernism in design really takes hold, where the old guard is worried, and they're making comments about this civilization-endangering typographic garbage which is going to bring the whole thing down. Everything they've worked through and for, everything that they thought was important, is suddenly being challenged. There was this long period from the late eighties into the nineties where no forward-looking, progressively minded, switched-on contemporary designer was going to be using Helvetica. Or maybe they still were in Switzerland. I'm not saying it completely went away, but certainly here in Britain and America.

But what actually happened is that the whole thing, the International Style, came back again in the 1990s. And the story by which that happens—again, it happens over time. It's quite complicated, but there were holdouts in the eighties. People like 8vo here in London, who published a magazine called *Octavo*, in which they declared their allegiance to Swiss modernism, and the magazine itself expressed that. I'm not saying it was an allegiance to Helvetica in particular, but some designers who had never really liked the kind of crazy, broken-up, grungy work of the early nineties had always been aware of 8vo and what they stood for, what they represented, and that started to look like the fashionable, new thing, to actually return to modernism.

Before you know it, by the mid-nineties through to the end of the nineties, modernism had returned, in the postmodern guise of neomodernism. Because it wasn't the real thing. It was a fake. It was an imitation. It was the look of modernism applied to new commercial uses. That became the fashionable new look. An outfit like Designer's Republic, again here in Britain, had actually, in the early nineties, anticipated that. They took the look of corporate graphics, information design, international corporate identities, and they scrambled the whole thing up to produce these dense visual fields of logos and bits of technical information and bursts of graphic noise, all churning together in this kind of turbulent, dense kind of new, postmodern design.

Basically, they were having fun with the corporate language. They were replaying it. They were saying, "This is part of our everyday culture, the corporate messages that bombard us all the time. Okay, we'll accept that as a given, but we're going to speed it up, scramble it, and replay it just because we can, because it's fun to do that, and because we want to show we're on top of this, we're not suckers here. We're not just mindlessly consuming it. But we're in the system, so we'll play with it. We'll have some fun."

So they had done that in the early nineties. That was published in the US, in a magazine called *Emigre*, that Designers Republic work, and it was hugely influential. Other people saw it. Germany, Japan. Suddenly this postmodern take on modernism looked immensely cool. Cooler, actually, than grunge and just messing everything up and breaking it and creating a huge mess on the page and telling the reader to sort it out.

It was almost like the best of both worlds. Neomodern design, which may or may not involve Helvetica but often did, was a way of having it both ways. It had the structure of earlier late-modern design. It was pleasing to the designer's eye. It was controlled. Elements were well placed. Nicely balanced. All those traditional design virtues. But at the same time, it was new. It was cool. It was highly contemporary. It commented on the world around the designer. It was plugged into that. It was youthful. And it just felt so right for a while. So that's fine. That's a response.

As things developed, though, this new neomodern style was so successful and so appealing to so many people that in turn, it became a cliché. And I would say that's where we still are, even now. You've got young design teams formed in the late nineties in London, still plugging away at neo-modernism. At this point, to still be stuck on that, not to be reacting against it again in favor of something a bit more varied and imaginative and creative, and even life-affirming, just looks like, to my eye, a very arid designer-ism. It's anally retentive design. It's really so hung up on itself. It exults in the conventions, the codes, the established international language of a certain kind of typography. It can't seem to think beyond that. Maybe it messes it up a little bit with some fashionable, modern-looking illustration, just to show it's not all about the type. But it's still locked into that way of thinking.

Design needs to refresh and renew itself. It's action and reaction. We seem to bounce, actually, between the same poles all the time. I would imagine the time is fast approaching where something more disorderly will look cool to people again, because we've had just too much of this cool International Style. It's like every café, every restaurant, every company packaging some luxury products for the youth market, every new hotel chain putting together its menus, seems to think in this neo-modernist way. This is why, I think, there has been a reaction.

There's a guy down in Melbourne, Australia named Stephen Banham who five years ago launched his own "Death to Helvetica" campaign. He produced these T-shirts with the phrase "Death to Helvetica" on the front or "Helvetica Thin, just say no." He spoke to journalists about it. He wrote an essay called "The Rise and Rise of Helvetica World." He argued that what we need is, in his words, typo-diversity. We want to reflect the difference and the diversity of our culture with a broad range of typographic choices. Why on earth is everyone feeling that this one way of designing, this sans serif, Helvetica, or Helvetica-like way, is the appropriate way of doing things? He made quite a lot of noise down there, and he got noticed and was in the papers for it, and those T-shirts sold out.

GH — A style becomes dominant, then gets rebelled against until the rebelling style is dominant and gets rebelled against again. So it's this cyclical thing. But communication technology changed in these decades we're talking about. The way we processed all these messages changed from print to television to the web and beyond. We're assaulted by so much media now. Is it possible that the clean, organized approach is better suited now than ever, as a way to minimize the media onslaught? Is that a reason for its resurgence?

RP — I think different designers have different motivations for using Helvetica. Of course, there is always a need to present information clearly. As was understood right from the start, Helvetica is perfect for sign systems. You can't find a better typeface for a subway system or airport signage. It has that clarity; it's got a kind of bland strength to it; it's a reassuring face; it's a straight-talking face. It lacks peculiarities, idiosyncrasies, anything that might distract you from direct reception of the message. There will always be a need for that. It's perfectly suited. I, for one, wouldn't criticize that for even a moment.

I think it's much less successful as a typeface when applied to the setting of long pieces of text. I can't imagine a typeface I would less like as a writer to have my words set in. I would almost see it as a strip-ping out of the voice of the prose, making it look bland and ordinary and official looking, without typographic color, and therefore, as I say, with very little voice.

But in those situations of signage, the kind of place that someone like Massimo Vignelli has applied Helvetica, it's pretty much unbeatable. The liking for it in the corporate realm is more problematic. If we go back to the seventies, I imagine, there was a lot of me-too-ism going on. One big, major multinational had used it, and the next one being a bit slow-moving and not visually imaginative just fell into line, and before you knew it, they'd all fallen into line, and they all looked horribly the same. Hence the postmodern revolution against that way of designing. But now it's something different. It has persisted as a kind of corporate typeface, but it's acquired the patina of cool. That's what I'm question-ing, even objecting to. I just think it's dull and boring.

Designers are paid a lot of money, and they can do much better than make an utterly familiar choice. If they can't do better than that, then you'd almost say, "Why do we need designers?" We need designers to produce something we didn't expect to see. If they merely default to the most familiar of all modern typefaces, you're not getting much value for your money, I'd suggest.

GH — Can we talk a little more about the "voice" of typefaces? Do you think people realize that when they're looking at typefaces? Do you think they consciously think, "Oh, that looks depressing and distressed"? Or is it mostly a subliminal impact? I guess I'm interested in, one, do people realize it? And two, how does it affect the message?

RP — Designers have always told us that their choice of typeface is important, that typefaces express a mood, an atmosphere. They give the words a certain coloring. They make associations with, perhaps, typefaces from the past, which, again, are identified with particular uses. So the choice of a typeface is really loaded. It sends a very powerful signal. No one, even design experts, has the time to keep stepping back from the message to think purely about the typographic signal that conveys that message. But all of us, I would suggest, are prompted in subliminal ways. Maybe the feeling you have when you see a particular typographic choice used on a piece of packaging is just "I like the look of that. That feels good. That's my kind of product." But that's the type casting its secret spell.

The whole point of design is to get us to feel about what we're looking at in a particular way. It may be to reassure us that something is much as we expected, familiar. It may be to excite us because it conveys the message that something looks new and we have to know about this now because it's happening right now. But type is saying things to us all the time. As a writer, I take this extremely seriously. I don't need any persuasion at all. I'm utterly convinced that when something I write is put into a typeface, that typeface itself conveys a signal. It gives the writing a certain tone of voice. I've had some interesting moments with designers, because it's almost like they forget that you have that knowledge and that you do see it in the same way, and that you take what they say utterly seriously. You might actually have a preference. You might feel the typeface the designer is proposing is not your tone of voice. You are not a Helvetica kind of person. This is not the way you see the world, and it's not the association you want to make through your writing. And that actually, if your writing is put into this inappropriate typeface, the typeface is working against the writing rather than working with it.

I am so tuned in now to the typographic signal. I feel quite obsessive about that issue of whether this is exactly the tone of voice I want to be speaking in. I even had an interesting moment with an earlier book where a designer did want to put my words into Helvetica, and we argued over that. He told me later he nearly walked from the project. It was such a problem, the author resisting this typographic decision. But I felt it wasn't me, and furthermore it was inappropriate to the content of the book. In the end, we settled on Univers, which is a gentler, warmer, richer sans-serif typeface that I personally prefer. But even so that wasn't quite the typographic signal that I had in mind for the book. It's a hot potato, actually.

GH — What are your thoughts on the typographic knowledge of the public? You already said you think it's gotten much deeper because of the use of personal computers. What's next? What should they be learning about now? Do they need to learn more about type?

RP — Well, for years now computer systems have presented users with a menu of typographic choices. Inevitably, people have decided whether they want to speak in Arial or Times or Verdana or something more unexpected. I think we've reached a point now where many people, especially younger people who have grown up with computers—that's really all they've ever known—are utterly familiar with the idea of a font.

I saw this for myself in a startling way a few years ago when my daughter was at primary school in Britain. The first change from when I was in school is that the work they produce is much more visual than it was then. It's often graphic work. The projects are graphically constructed, using the computer. You've got an eight-year-old doing her project on the computer, and when she needs to put a headline or a title on the front page, she has to make a typographic choice. So there was my kid, and she was doing that. I realized, without any discussion of this issue at all, that she was beginning to acquire a feeling for the particular mood and atmosphere and the associations of different pieces of type. This was incredible to me. I'd barely noticed type in the pre-desktop-computer period, until the age of about 20. Then my move toward design as a non-designer was an unusual thing to happen. It really only happened because I had studied art, and I was visually aware, and I just started thinking about type. But that was the stage or phase when most people didn't notice the type in the book they were reading. It was transparent to them. It was meant to be. It was something the printer did. It wasn't something you could decide for yourself. So it went on for years, but in this computer period people make those choices. They develop typographic preferences. They know what they want their emails to look like, even whether they want to color the type as well as choose a different font.

It does seem that typographic awareness is proceeding at quite a rapid pace now. It's taken for granted, and someone who's grown up from the age of five, six, seven years with computers, never knowing anything different, is bound to have a level of design awareness as an adult, making choices, perhaps in business, or in any kind of communications situation. I think the future will be very different from how it was 30 years ago, when the public really didn't know a thing about design. I think already people are thinking in design terms. Now, from a designer's point of view, a highly educated professional, a lot of this will seem very basic, very amateurish, very unprofessional, and a bit of a threat, because why does a designer want to be replaced by someone making these crude, uneducated choices for themselves on their own computer?

But I think that designers shouldn't worry, they shouldn't despair about this, because what we have is a climate now in which the very idea of visual communication and graphic design, if we still want to call it that, is accepted by many more people. They get it. They understand it. They're starting to see graphic communication as an expression of their own identity. The classic case of this is the social networking programs, such as MySpace or Bebo, where the user is provided with a set of tools, which, again, I know designers consider, especially in the case of MySpace, to be rather crude and inadequate. But the fact is, you can customize your MySpace profile. There are many programs and facilities to allow you to do this. You can change the background. You can change colors, put pictures in. You can change the typeface to anything you want. You can take the boxes out. You can have thicker rules around your boxes, double rules. You can do what you like.

When you make a myriad of choices like that, you create something, as a non-designer designer, that's very different from what the next person might do. Those choices, those decisions you make, become expressions of who you are. You start to care about it in the way that you care about the clothing you're wearing as an expression of who you are, or your haircut, or whatever, or how you decorate your apartment, all of those things. We accept the idea of identity being expressed in that way, through these consumer choices. Well, now it's happening in the sphere of visual communication. There's no reason, as the tools become ever more sophisticated, and the templates, and the ability to adapt those templates, why this won't just go on developing, and developing, and developing.

In that sense, graphic design has become a much more public issue than it was even 15 years ago. We're leaping over time. If you cover 10 years of design time, so much happened. It's very hard not to end up oversimplifying.

GH — Sure, sure.
RP — There are so many people involved, contrary arguments, different tendencies in different countries.

GH — I know. Again, it's more about opening people's eyes a little bit. Most "MySpace designers" have not heard of Vignelli, or Wim Crouwel, or any of the people in this film. So they'll hear them talking and expressing their ideas, and see their work, and see what they do.
RP — Yeah.

GH — Part of it is kind of demystifying the process. But I also think everyone in the film deserves a whole documentary just about them. So the concept of the neomodernists . . . there's designers like Experimental Jetset who firmly believe in the tenets of late modernism, or even the early modernists, the subversiveness of it. They kind of gravitated toward that and bring it in to their designs.
RP — Yes. I think Experimental Jetset are extremely interesting. For one thing, they're thinkers and they're writers. They write these texts and little manifesto-like statements of what they're about. They are culturally very well informed. They make sharp historical references. They're quite good with the language of critical theory, even. So when you hear the talk that explains what they're doing in the visual work, it sounds

very convincing. But then I look at the work, and all I see is the same old Helvetica. If I, as someone who is fairly tuned-in to design, don't find it very exciting, or can't draw the ideas out of it, then how is the ordinary person in the street without all this historical design knowledge going to decode their work along the lines that they suggest?

This is perhaps one of the problems, the conundrums, for design. Design desperately wants to be taken seriously. There are some very smart people in design, and they have some very sharp things to say about it. Sometimes, for that reason, designers become very self-conscious about the issue of style in their work. The last thing they want to be thought of as is decorators or hairdressers, as someone once put it, merely styling up the client's thing in a pretty and attractive but ulti-mately superficial and disposable way. So designers will often react against the idea of style.

All this love of severe Helvetica—a very manly kind of typographic choice—is actually about saying, "Our work is not about surface. It's not about style. It's not superficial. It's about the underlying idea, the content, or the sense of structure which we've brought to organizing all this material in our communication. We don't want to take the chance of you mistaking what we do as a stylistic exercise. So we'll default to this quite rigid typographic position."

I would say in the contemporary climate that maybe what you see there is a loss of nerve. Because we went through that postmodern period, in which there was a huge amount of stylistic experimentation. Often, it was underpinned by theoretical ideas. But it tended to be inter-preted, once again, as pure style. It was absorbed into advertising by the mid-nineties. This supposedly impossibly difficult new typographic experimentation was actually cheerfully taken on board, by advertising, as a great, new look and a wonderful way of talking to the kids. It's the same old process of co-option that we see over and over again with all subcultural styles, and now it was happening to rebellious typogra-phy. So the designers who came after that period—let's call it the David Carson period, or the Reagan period, the grunge typography period—they looked at all that in a slightly despairing way, and they didn't know what to do next.

There was a pressure on those young designers to keep producing innovative style. Innovative style is a way of getting yourself noticed as a designer, of building a reputation. Traditionally it's functioned that way. They didn't want to do that. It just looked bankrupt. Typog-raphy was so broken by the end of the grunge period—just lying there in a twisted heap, all rules cast aside, no apparent way forward—that all those designers could perhaps do by the late nineties, the deep-thinking, progressive designers, was to go back, to return to an earlier way of designing, but with a new set of theories to support it. I'm talking about a particular kind of slightly angst-ridden, thoughtful, highly edu-cated—probably MA-, MFA-level—young designer.

They weren't going to do what David Carson had done, not in a million years. But after you've taken everything apart and left it lying there, seemingly without any hope of putting it back together, what are you supposed to do? Where do you go? That was the problem they faced, and at the end of the nineties, you'd meet graphic designers doing master's degrees who didn't even want to design. They would rather create an installation or shoot a video. They said they were graphic designers, but you saw them doing hardly any graphic design at all.

At that time—I happened to be teaching at the Royal College of Art—you'd see people who wanted to produce printed design which had just the bare minimum of typographic content or gesture. There was almost nothing there. It was just an empty space with a small dab of type in the corner. It was really fastidious, almost Puritan, as though they were saying, "We have to strip all of that excess out—that's in the way, that's a kind of visual corruption—and we need the most stringent treatment now, a cure to get over that." And the cure is minimalism. The cure is almost nothing to look at, at all. The cure is denying the possibility of visual pleasure. Because visual pleasure may be false. It may be leading the viewer in the wrong direction. It may be lying about the true nature of the content. This is another route back to Helvetica. Because you look at Helvetica, and you say, "It's basic. It's functional. It's almost generic. Anyone can pick it up and use it. It's not identified with any particular designer, certainly not in the public mind. So that's fine. That's the basic building block I need to produce an authentic and pure visual communication."

The relationship of graphic design and advertising is another complicated one. Designers often used to talk about these two activities as though they were different things. And in certain countries—certainly America would be a case in point, certainly Britain—there was a separation, certainly from the 1960s, between designers who were involved in graphic design and designers, who in many respects might have seemed to be doing the same thing, who were involved in advertising. Ads have typography; an ad is a graphic communication; it is a piece of graphic design. Nevertheless, at various times, in various places, in the development of these two fields they've been seen as separate, with different personnel, different cultures, different aspirations, different beliefs about what communication was for.

The designers of the postwar period, the Swiss designers, were actually involved in advertising. They created some stunning ads, but they brought to these ads this high-minded commitment to the notion of a clear, objective non-manipulative communication. Now, you might argue that that was a pipe dream; it simply isn't possible. If you're involved in advertising, and you're trying to sell the product, you are aiming to convince the consumer, the viewer of the ad, that they should buy this thing. And that, ultimately, has got to be manipulative.

But still, if you look at that Swiss advertising, it was about as severe and unemotional in the way it presented information as it could possibly be. Nevertheless, these cultures were separate. But in the nineties, in Britain, for instance, you see advertising suddenly waking up to the amazing energy and the creativity of what was going on in graphic design—with the so-called new, digital typography, the grungy stuff—and actually wanting to use that kind of typography as a way of talking to what I'll call younger audiences. It was fashionable, in other words. That happens for a while, but of course in the end it's exhausted; it runs out of steam. It's old, and it's boring. What happens subsequently in the mid-to-late nineties is that advertising, too, seemed to rediscover modernism.

All this fits together, of course, with corporate identities. There were some very influential ones here such as Orange, the mobile-phone company, or First Direct Banking, which had made use in their corporate identities of this very Swiss-like, sans-serif typography. A little swatch of typography in the corner of a dynamic, big image. It looked in many ways exactly like earlier Swiss modernism. But whereas that work had this sense of idealistic social responsibility, the new work, this advertising work of the late nineties, was much more about positioning the product, the service, as a cool, contemporary thing you've just got to have. There's no social idealism there. It's just, you could say, extremely functional. It's perceived to be a fashionable look. And this is the way to reach people. But the same thing happened in advertising. It's still going on. It seemed like every would-be trendy, contemporary ad for a multinational had the same kind of minimalistic sans-serif typography.

You could say history had repeated itself. In the seventies, corporate identities based on sans-serif typefaces such as Helvetica became the sign of a kind of unimaginative conformity. Peculiarly, that's what seems to have happened in some advertising now, that we can't seem to get beyond this idea that if you put a bit of Helvetica down in the corner, very clean, very simple, with the bare minimum of design to it, that looks immensely cool and everyone's just got to fall in line.

GH — What do you think is next?

RP — I actually think it's a fool's game trying to predict what comes next. I can tell you what I hope comes next, but that's not necessarily what will come next. I'm always hopeful that people will break out of the trance, that they will become much more critical of the way communication works, of the stories it tells, maybe the illusions it confects. Perhaps sometimes the lies it spins. And that they will vote with their feet by turning away from it and finding something of their own. The problem, of course, with all these romantic ideas about the kids at street level creating their own culture, a culture of resistance, is that nowadays those ad agencies, those marketing companies, have their cool hunters out there logging what the kids are doing—recording it, interviewing them, infiltrating them—and incorporating those ideas into mass-market, global communication within months, sometimes, of their flaring into life on the street.

I think if you do want to resist all this, if you want to find a way of insulating yourself against this manipulation through communication, which ultimately is just out to get the money out of your wallet, then you've got a really tough problem. Actually, in the end, a kind of refusal, saying no to it or really just trying to ignore it, is the only way to go. There's nothing else you can do. Maybe you have to worry less about being a kind of cool, fashionable person who is just like all the other cool, fashionable people, sharing the same kind of dreams, aspirations, tastes in trendy new products.

It's really difficult because the whole system, it seems to me—in particular the kind of technology we're using and the way we're using it—actually disposes us to look toward the corporate realm for guidance. We need the stuff they're selling to us. It's all part of being a modern person, and there's no escape from it. You know, once upon a time you could be a starving artist in a garret or a poet with your notebook just writing those poems and getting loaded on absinthe in the evenings. It was actually an amazingly simple life, more about just survival than consumer indulgence. But now it seems like every aspect of our pleasure, every aspect of our identity, what we think makes us a contemporary person, is tied up in brands, products, services which we must consume at a considerable price. And because we're now so accepting of that, this is the new reality, and you sound like some kind of old curmudgeon if you mention any other possibility at all.

People are very primed to accept what advertising has to say. They need to know about it. So the resistance that you might have found if you go back 20 or 30 years to the advertiser as someone who's trying to get in your head and make you think the way they want you to think, this resistance seems to have almost disappeared. But you know, of course there's *Adbusters* and there are the anti-globalization protesters. I'm not saying there isn't any resistance, but this is not the everyday way of thinking. Those people are exceptional, and maybe they're still marginalized as kind of crazy oddballs who failed to adjust to the modern world.

So this brings us back to design, because it means that design bears this enormous responsibility. Design is the communication framework through which these corporate messages, these brand messages about what the world is now and what we should aspire to in this world, it's the way they reach us. The designer, whether he or she is prepared to acknowledge it or not, has an enormous responsibility. Those are the people putting their wires into our heads, moving our limbs, making us want things.

GH — So in a way, Helvetica is a conspirator in all this?

RP — You could see Helvetica, in some of its uses—not all the uses, but in some of its uses—as being part of this whole problem. But I don't want to lay all the fault at Helvetica's door. It's just a typeface. But it was recognized way back in the 1970s, in an article written by the *Village Voice*'s advertising critic, a woman named Leslie Savan, who went out and researched the whole subject of Helvetica and how ubiquitous it was even then, asking, "Why? What's going on here?"

Savan quotes the architect James Wines in her piece, where he says, "Actually it is part of the control system." I'm paraphrasing there. But he specifically talks about the psychology of enslavement. He says that this typeface is a voice of authority. And when you fall in with it and go along with it, you are being propelled by that whole sign system along a particular path. Now, sometimes that's pretty useful. It is useful to know how to get to Gate 5 in an airport. We all need that, and I think it would be foolish, really, to question those kinds of uses. Although there's no doubt that as a social entity in an airport your movements are being controlled, but controlled with good reason, and you benefit from it. But when the same kind of typographic signal is applied in this conformist way in advertising, to do nothing more, actually, than to get you to buy stuff, then maybe James Wines, 30 years ago, talking about the psychology of enslavement, had a point.

—

Lars Müller (LM)/
August 26, 2006 London

Graphic designer and publisher Lars Müller loves Helvetica. His 2002 book, *Helvetica: Homage to a Typeface*, definitely influenced me when I decided to make the movie. So there was no way he was not going to be in the film. I spoke with Lars at my company's London studio and out in the streets of the city, looking for Helvetica.
—

Gary Hustwit — Maybe we can just talk about the Helvetica book you did and the reasons behind it?

Lars Müller — Okay, that should be easy. I was asked a few weeks ago if I regret that I did the Helvetica book. I started thinking about it, and I definitely don't regret it. But I'll try to remember how it started.

There were two moments that might be the initial moments of the Helvetica book. One in Offenbach in 1996, 10 years ago, I guess. A student at the university there showed up one morning at a seminar and showed me his design for a poster. I don't remember what the poster was for, but he was so happy that morning. He said, "I found a new typeface." And he showed me his design, and I thought, "What's new about this?" And then he said, "This new typeface is so amazing, because it's so fresh and so timely." And then I said, "Why do you think this typeface is new?" and he said, "Well, it's Neue Helvetica."

I started laughing, and I told him the story of Helvetica. He was kind of disappointed, but to me, it was this turning point where I realized that something old can become new. And from then on, wherever I looked, even in London or in New York, I discovered Helvetica everywhere on party flyers and posters and record sleeves. Everything was full of Helvetica. So the idea grew to make this a book. But it took so much time, as all projects do which are self-initiated and where you have no pressure from the outside. You postpone; you always have something more urgent to do.

But there's another reason too, which is more personal. I think I had to give something back to my teachers, to my mentors, in a good way or in a critical way, as I think they have stolen several years of my youth or have taken my innocence in a way, by teaching me these very heavy and straightforward rules of Swiss typography. And it was mainly a lesson of don'ts—"Don't do that" and "Don't do this"—and being limited to primary colors, and Akzidenz-Grotesk, and grid-based design and so on. That was Müller-Brockmann and Richard Paul Lohse, who was an artist and an even more rigid designer than Müller-Brockmann was. They didn't say anything bad about Helvetica. Müller-Brockmann never said anything. He was a very sophisticated man. He never said anything bad about people or things; by not saying anything, he told you his opinion, in a way. But he was very precise about pointing out the quality of his favorite typeface, Akzidenz-Grotesk, which he considered his main tool. So his critique was communicated by not commenting. When he liked things, he was very generous in describing them. It was obvious that Akzidenz-Grotesk was what you needed to create the real Swiss typography at that time.

The only thing I could do to defend myself was to start loving the roughness, in a way, the crudeness of Helvetica—just to challenge my mentors. But by the time I had the idea for the book, I had outgrown that. It became more of an ironic second reason to make this homage to this typeface. I made the book over four or five years, together with the interns in my studio. We traveled, photographed, and collected material. We asked designers everywhere for quotes, which are included in the books, some pretty nice, charming quotes about Helvetica. And then one day a Swedish intern told me, "I want to finish this book." Because, of course, all these interns left after six months or a year, so we'd just continue the project with the next group of interns. And she said, "Look, I don't want leave this studio before the book is finished." So in 2002, we finally did it.

GH — Do you think Müller-Brockmann felt Helvetica was just a knockoff of Akzidenz-Grotesk?

> **LM** — No, definitely not. I believe that he had no objections against Helvetica, because when he worked on the design program for the Swiss Railways, he chose Helvetica. They did a slight correction because of the legibility, like a slight correction to the inner space of the e and the a and some other letters. I don't know all the details. So Helvetica was certainly one option, but in his poster designs he certainly preferred Akzidenz-Grotesk because of the size of the letter in relation to the format. And I agree; in terms of beauty, the single letters of Akzidenz-Grotesk are more beautiful. But beauty is not the main aim of Helvetica.

GH — What is the main aim?

> **LM** — To express an A or an E or an S. It's the main aim of Helvetica. And that's how things go. It's the pasta that goes with the sauce.

GH — What do you say to the people who dislike Helvetica and think that it's too widespread and that it's homogenizing our visual culture just because it's everywhere? What do you say to those critics?

> **LM** — As I said, Helvetica, in itself, is like pasta. I think it's a bit bizarre to dislike Helvetica; it's as if you disliked pasta. To me, pasta is the basic element of Italian cooking, as Helvetica is a good, basic element of typography. You might dislike the typography made using Helvetica,

as you might dislike some specific type of pasta dish, like puttanesca or something. I think it has become a polemic because it's a bit fashionable to be for or against it. When, in fact, I think it's more interesting to see Helvetica as representing a certain attitude in design or in culture, as Italian cuisine represents a certain attitude in food and nutrition. So I can't participate in the discussion about liking or disliking Helvetica. I think it's also a bit artificial when people get exhausted by the formal qualities of Helvetica and forget about the designer's role in creating good or bad typography with this typeface.

GH — What kind of reaction did you get when the book was released?

LM — For me, the book was a kind of release. It allowed me to show that something is not necessarily good or bad. Maybe good can be bad, and bad can be good at the same time. Judging from the first reactions, I think many people agreed or kind of felt released too, as I did. In the book, you see the good side and bad side together. Also, the bad side is not necessarily bad; the bad side is the most charming side. It's actually the soul of the book, I would say—the work of the dilettantes and amateurs. And the professionals might benefit from seeing that. Actually, the normality of Helvetica makes the professional designers' work look extraordinary, because it uses the ingredients of everyday aesthetics. It's like the excellent pasta beside the everyday dish, right?

GH — What are some of your favorite uses of it, like specific logos or signage or things? You've collected quite a bit. What do you like?

LM — I was asked what I would do with this enormous collection of images we've gathered for the book, and I just realized that I lost it during the flood last year. I was so happy it was gone, because I'm not a collector. To me the book is actually the collection. I'm also glad if I'm not asked about my favorite image in the book, because you wouldn't collect eight hundred pictures if you could single out a favorite. So it's hard to say that I like this more than that. What I like are those examples when Helvetica is used to give silly advice in the streets. This very serious typeface tells you the dos and don'ts of street life, and if you look around, they're so serious really. For example, signs that say, "Don't Park Here," in a space where you couldn't even fit a bicycle.

I've actually collected logotypes using Helvetica over several years and I've put them together in an A-to-Z collection, from American Airlines and so on. It became so obvious that Tupperware must be Helvetica and 3M must be Helvetica. It also became apparent that airlines all over the world especially like using Helvetica because Helvetica represents safety and security and punctuality and all these positive characteristics of airlines. I think it's the best typeface for a logotype ever.

As a designer, I was also taught that, if you have an idea, Helvetica will carry it further, because it will not compete with the idea. Very few other typefaces have this capacity. Amongst Antiqua typefaces, it would certainly be Times, which you would believe would also carry your idea further without giving too much formal pressure. Univers has a very strong visual attitude and presence. Let's say that if you take the dots off of the *i* and *j*, you might be better off doing it with Helvetica, because if you do it with Univers, it's already missing something. It will look wrong. That's kind of a funny thing.

GH — Do you believe in the concept that it's a neutral typeface?

LM — I wouldn't say Helvetica is neutral. That's an important point, actually. Helvetica is not about neutrality; it's about normality. Helvetica is normal; it's not neutral. Also, it is Swiss. Maybe we should just be happy to define normality in a way that allows the idea to be highlighted. Again, it's not the pasta that makes the dish, but it's the basic transporter of your idea. That's why I say Helvetica itself is an ingredient of good typography, and I don't understand why type designers are forced to create a new typeface every day when it's not proven yet if good typography can be achieved with their typeface. Whilst Helvetica has proven that it's a good assistant, a good friend, actually, of graphic designers.

GH — What are your thoughts on the period of the mid-eighties to mid-nineties when grunge typography represented the rebellion against Helvetica and everything it stood for? Were you involved in design at that time?

LM — In the eighties, I was really still a hard-core Swiss Constructivist under the influence of Müller-Brockmann, who insisted, week by week, that design has to be constructive, grid based, and rational. And there was no escaping that. But at the age of 30, I was already teaching in Zürich. It was a pretty turbulent time in Zürich, as well as in design.

GH — There's talk throughout the film about the philosophy of modernism or late modernism. Can a typeface and graphic design change the world by making information clearer? Do you ascribe to that philosophy?

LM — I believe that communication design—graphic design—is a tool to express information and truth. But again, graphic design itself is not content; it's the vehicle for something. So it really depends on what you have in mind, actually—what you want to tell. It's about typography rather than type design. What good graphic design does is give an image to content and also represent certain philosophies and maybe the attitude of the sender. And there, of course, Helvetica stands for something. It might stand for clarity, objectivity, truth, effectiveness, modernity. But since it has such a strong image, it can also be misused. For example, I think it has been heavily misused in corporate design. Multinational businesses were giving us modern, objective, rational, and informative images while they were not behaving the same way. So I would not relate Helvetica to a specific content. With Helvetica, you can design a birth announcement as well as a death announcement.

GH — But do you think that through all of the corporate use, Helvetica picked up that baggage along the way? Do you think people see that?

LM — I think very few people relate Helvetica to history—even in design. The history we might think of is of the past 10 years, definitely not of the past 50 years. But it's interesting to see the original intention of creating Helvetica in the late fifties, when it was an expression of the modern belief in changing the world in some way or the other. And I think the success of Helvetica definitely was its use in corporate design. It was not poster designers' favorite at that time at all. The history or the image of Helvetica as the corporate typeface made it, the so-called "typeface of capitalism," which I would actually reject and say it's the typeface of socialism because it is available all over, and it's inviting dilettantes and amateurs and everybody to do typography, to create their own type design. And I think that's a good thing.

GH — What about the connection between a typeface and the political message behind it? Because it is a choice; it's a strategic choice. The typeface choice can end up being propaganda, in a way, depending on where you're sitting.

LM — You know, in Switzerland, you are not necessarily considered a socialist when you use the color red, because the Swiss cross is red. And it's about the same with Helvetica. I would consider myself a socialist using Helvetica, but I wouldn't expect you to understand that that's the reason why I use it. I am not dogmatic about typefaces. It might be hard to recognize Helvetica amongst other grotesque typefaces if some letters are missing. But I don't even mind if you mistake Franklin Gothic or Univers for Helvetica. This is like the difference between Trotskyism and Leninism in socialism, if you want to see Helvetica as the most socialistic typeface ever. Of course, graphic designers might see the differences more clearly. When you get closer, you realize the difference in typefaces, and you learn which letters actually separate one from the other.

I also think it's not due to a single person's effort that Helvetica has survived and gotten this rather anonymous image. Max Miedinger just happened to be the employed type designer at that time. Of course, he should have deserved much more attention, but as he didn't get it, Helvetica remained this kind of independent, neutral typeface while Univers is always related to its designer, Adrian Frutiger, who is a great type designer, and he kind of absorbs the light from his typeface. Frutiger also designed more than just Univers, so there's competition even within his own oeuvre.

GH — So you can't see a documentary being done about Univers?

LM — I could definitely not imagine Univers being made into a movive or even a book.

GH — Do you ever use Univers?

LM — I have to confess that I was forced to use Univers when I was assisting Wim Crouwel for one year back in the early eighties. It was amazing that the designs turned out to be much more rational than they originally were when you redo them using Helvetica afterwards. I think Helvetica is still kind of a soft, rolling, humble, and gentle-formed typeface, while Univers is pretty technical. It's not my typeface.

GH — Now that I'm making this film, whenever I look at a sign, I've got to check the typeface first. Does that happen to you?

LM — It drove me crazy for quite a long time. I was obsessed with this typeface. I was more preoccupied with looking for Helvetica than for good-looking people, for example. It became a disease. But it was amazing to realize how much Helvetica is around us. And it's not about your obsession; it's reality and it's the truth. There is no other typeface that appears so frequently in the streets. It inspired me to think of Helvetica as the "perfume of the city" or maybe the "sound of the city." It is just something we don't usually notice but we would miss very much if it was not there. I think it's quite amazing that a typeface can advance to such a status in our lives, and I couldn't imagine any other typeface than Helvetica doing that. It's also interesting to see that Helvetica might be the only typeface that still looks good even when it's affected by other forms or kind of destructed. It has integrity in its form, or solidity. Helvetica also ages well—in signage as well as in printed matter. It even looks good if it's aged and kind of affected by weather and wind and storm.

GH — The "Post No Bills" signs in every country seem to be always done in Helvetica. It's in Zürich, here in London, everywhere. It's interesting.

LM — The naive approach is to stereotype the use of Helvetica. And of course, in the professional field, we know that it's a corporate typeface and that it was also heavily used in educational publications and in manuals, et cetera. But it was the everyday use—let's call it the less-professional use, the warning signs and the dos and don'ts signs—that became the main domain of Helvetica. That's something you see everywhere, from Tokyo to Helsinki to New York. It's got to be Helvetica Bold. It's just a given.

GH — Why is this the case? Obviously, it's clear and readable, but is there something more to it?

LM — I believe it's because there is just one main message, and the message is not related to any aesthetic content. And Helvetica expresses exactly that. It says, "I'm just a message." If you want to rebel against that, then you destroy the typeface, which is all right. That's what happened in the eighties. Helvetica was the symbolic enemy for everything you wanted to fight against in society, and people started to destroy this typeface. That, I think, actually led to some wonderful examples of design. We should say, "Thanks, Helvetica."

GH — Do you have a favorite letter of the alphabet?

LM — I got a gift from my friend Wolfgang Weingart that was my first name done in Helvetica lead type. And "Lars" actually contains two of the most beautiful lowercase Helvetica letters, which are the *a* and the *s*. You can look at them for hours, and they become an image. It's more than just a letterform. The *a* would probably be my favorite.

—

Alfred Hoffmann (AH)/ August 27, 2006 Zürich

Alfred Hoffmann, son of Helvetica cocreator Eduard Hoffmann, was someone I really wanted to interview for the film, but I couldn't locate him. But a few months after we launched the website for *Helvetica*, I got an email from Swiss designer Erich Alb, saying, "I can't believe you're not including Alfred Hoffmann in your film! I know him. He lives near me." I quickly replied and set up the interview, which had to be that same week since Hoffmann was leaving for an extended holiday.

I flew to Zürich from London right after my interview with Lars Müller, and I arrived late that night. This was toward the end of our filming process, and, frankly, I'd run out of money to fund the film. When I tried to check into the hotel, I didn't have room on any credit card, and I had no cash. So I sat there in the hotel lobby and tried to figure out what to do. Back then we were using PayPal to do the sales of the posters and T-shirts on our website, and the PayPal account was connected to a debit card I had. So I used the Internet in the hotel lobby to send an email blast to our *Helvetica* mailing list, something to the effect of "Poster Sale!" Then I waited. Sure enough, within an hour enough people had bought posters that I was able to check into the hotel. It's another example of how important the supporters of this film were to its creation. If you bought a poster that night, thank you!

—

Gary Hustwit — What are we looking at here?

> **Alfred Hoffmann** — This is a photo of the Haas Type Foundry booth at the Graphic '57 trade show, in Lausanne, Switzerland. At the exhibition, Haas showed Neue Haas Grotesk—the new Haas sans serif, which later on we called Helvetica—for the first time. In this picture, you see the gentleman with the tie? That's my father, Eduard Hoffmann. That's me opposite him.

GH — You said that this was the first time that Helvetica had ever been shown?

> **AH** — Oh, yes. This is also the first time Helvetica had been used for display purposes. These letters are cut out by jigsaw and fixed to the wall. If you look at it right now, you might think it's just a bread-and-butter typeface. But at the time, it was not. And at Graphic '57, this was the very first specimen that had ever been seen. Here it says, "After examination of all possible sans-serif types existing, we have created, in collaboration with graphic artists and typographers, Neue Haas Grotesk."

GH — Did Max Miedinger design the brochure?

    AH — Yes, it was Max Miedinger, the designer of Helvetica, who also designed this flyer. He liked to have many colors. Red, blue, yellow. He liked colorful perspectives. Shall I start with that?

GH — Sure.

    AH — It was around the year 1950 when my father, the director of the Haas type foundry, realized that we had a lot of competition from Akzidenz-Grotesk, which was called Standard in the United States. My father thought, "We have to have something similar, maybe a little bit better, but we have to have something. It's important that we have a typeface that all the Swiss customers will want." It was not his idea to make an international typeface, but just to compete in the Swiss market.

    So my father commissioned Max Miedinger, from Zürich, who was an experienced graphic designer, to make some designs for a new typeface. And Miedinger said, "We should call this new typeface Neue Haas Grotesk," and my father thought that was okay. First of all, he made some drawings on graph paper and used China ink. And these designs were used by our engraving department for making matrices, for casting the type. At this stage, many corrections were made in lead. And from then on, we continued with the trials and with casting this face.

GH — What are these pages that we're looking at now?

    AH — These are the first trials of Neue Haas Grotesk. In particular, I would like to draw your attention to these two lines. The first line is made from Berthold Akzidenz-Grotesk, and the second line is Neue Haas Grotesk. Here again you see the difference between Akzidenz-Grotesk and Neue Haas Grotesk. Here are a few proofs where you see the marks for correcting the typefaces and observations.

    A very important point was the distance between the letters, because in foundry type, the distance was set. You could not change the kerning as you can now. So you will see, we had to make trials with various distances between the letters. This is one of the most important things: Helvetica was absolutely the first typeface from any type foundry which had closer distances between the letters than any other. Here you have a proof of an alphabet, with observations by Max Miedinger. This is Max Miedinger's handwriting. If you notice, our proofs are not as professional as those of other type foundries.

GH — Why is that?

    AH — Because we didn't know how everyone else did it! Here again you have Akzidenz-Grotesk and Helvetica.

GH — I didn't realize you were really trying specifically to beat Akzidenz with this typeface.

    AH — Not to beat it, but we had to have something in order to compete with Akzidenz-Grotesk. There were articles coming out in design magazines in the mid-fifties saying, "The major Swiss graphic designers, they recommend Akzidenz- Grotesk." Later, we produced this specimen sheet, and young man, this says, "Designed by Hans Neuburg, photos by Josef Müller-Brockmann." These were the top designers in Switzerland, and they had been against Helvetica. But they made that brochure for Helvetica. They did not refuse to take the job. My father was pretty proud to see the "enemies" of Helvetica making this nice brochure for him.

But you cannot imagine how difficult it was in Switzerland in those days to introduce Helvetica to the market. Of course, the printers couldn't decide. That was the time the graphic artists said, "You have to have this typeface, nothing else." Adrian Frutiger, who designed Univers, was a good friend of Emil Ruder in Basel. And Ruder was the head of the Gewerbeschule, the professional school in Basel, which was quite renowned. Ruder never even mentioned the name Helvetica. He was very much in favor of Akzidenz-Grotesk and Univers, but not Helvetica. In other words, all these students were taught that Helvetica was bad. You had to use either Akzidenz-Grotesk or Univers. So it was a really big fight. On the other hand, in Germany, it was less difficult. We were so overwhelmed to hear how successful it was in Germany—also in the Scandinavian countries, and gradually also in France.

GH — How did your family originally get involved with Haas?
AH — Well, Haas Type Foundry has a long history, dating back to 1580. In 1917, my father's uncle, who was managing Haas at the time, asked my father to join him because he was looking for an assistant. Then in 1939, World War II started. This was the moment when Switzerland had no way to import type from abroad. The largest competitors were, of course, Germany, but also France and Italy. But during the war, Switzerland had no damage from bombs, so we could continue to produce typefaces.

My father became director of Haas in 1944. He had a humanist education, but he was also interested in technique. For him, it wasn't difficult to manage all the technical details of a type foundry. He also had a very good eye for aesthetics. He realized what kind of new typefaces had to be created. And after the war, most German type foundries were either bombed out or very much damaged. So this was, in a way, a possibility to expand the business.

Then gradually, in the fifties, Haas was able to sell abroad. Everything was very difficult: the prices abroad were very low, and the wages in Switzerland were very high. It was not so easy for the company, and it was a good thing that Haas released Neue Haas Grotesk in 1957; otherwise, we may not have been able to continue. You have to know that Haas had been controlled since 1954 by the German type foundry Stempel, by 51 percent. And in turn, Stempel was controlled by Linotype in Frankfurt. So in other words, our hands were more or less tied.

GH — Stempel and Linotype had an exclusive license to sell Haas type outside of Switzerland?
AH — With regard to Neue Haas Grotesk, Haas had the intention mainly to supply the Swiss market. But since Stempel had control of Haas, they were interested to see what we were doing. My father would have loved

to be able to sell Helvetica, or Neue Haas Grotesk, abroad. But Stempel, in 1960, decided to sell Neue Haas Grotesk, on the condition that the name needed to be changed. It was renamed Helvetica, and they started to sell our product. But a few months afterwards, we all realized that the demand was so huge that we had to make new matrices so that they could manufacture it in Germany as well. And Stempel paid us a small license for what they produced.

GH — When Stempel told you they wanted to call it Helvetica, what was the reaction at Haas?

AH — To be explicit, Stempel suggested the name *Helvetia*. This is very important: Helvetia is the Latin name for Switzerland. And my father said, "This is impossible. You cannot call a typeface the name of our country." He said, "Why don't we call it Helvetica?" So in other words this would be *the* Swiss typeface. And they agreed.

GH — Do you think the name had a lot to do with the popularity of the typeface?

AH — The most important reason why Helvetia was proposed was of course that everybody looked at the Swiss typography, and they said, "Oh, this is a Swiss typeface," and so on. So of course it had a good influence. And Neue Haas Grotesk was all right in Switzerland because we had so many sans-serif typefaces. We wanted to show the customers, "Look here, we have a real new typeface. This is not just an improved typeface but something really new."

GH — Can you talk a little bit about Miedinger and his role in the design of Helvetica? How did he work with your father on the design?

AH — Max Miedinger had been a traveling salesman for Haas for eastern Switzerland for 10 years. And after that period, he left the type foundry. But my father said, "If I ever have an idea for a new typeface, I am sure that you could design it." By profession, he was a graphic artist, but he realized that he could make more money selling foundry type. But after 10 years, he left and continued on as a graphic designer, and he was quite willing to cooperate with my father to create a new typeface.

My father had clear ideas about how the typeface should look. He and Miedinger sat together, and Miedinger started drawing. They kept working on the drawings and received input from other graphic artists and people who knew something about type. It is perhaps interesting to know that we did not have any type designers at the foundry. We always worked with freelance graphic designers, in contrast to the situation in Germany, where all the famous type foundries had their own specialists in type design. You can easily say that this is a joint product of both Miedinger and my father. Miedinger could not produce a typeface alone; neither could my father. But when both were working hard together, something good resulted.

GH — What was the daily routine like at the Haas factory?

AH — In the mid-fifties, we had many orders, so we were kept quite busy. In Switzerland, we had 1,500 printers who bought typefaces from us in smaller or larger quantities.

GH — But was it an interesting place to work? Did you enjoy working there?

AH — Of course, it was very, very interesting. We were taking the orders by telephone and coordinating all that with production. And then we had many correspondences with customers overseas and agents in Europe.

GH — So overall, it was enjoyable, the atmosphere there? I'm trying to imagine—was it more like a metal manufacturing facility, or were there lots of graphic designers coming in and hanging around?

AH — You want to know what was happening? We had the type foundry department, where each worker operated two machines. It was very noisy, with many machines operating. And besides the foundry itself, we had a department for brass rules and also for embossing type, which was quite successful. We had a lot of contact with our local and national customers, especially the local ones. They showed up to pick up their type orders. And then I had to check all the bills, to make sure they were correct. Sometimes I went out to see the customers myself. But most of my job was to keep in contact with the Stempel type foundry in Germany. We went there three or four times a year to discuss problems or to see new ways of producing things.

One of the main problems was always, "How can we meet the high demand?" Our facilities were restricted by the number of type founders and machines we had, because it was very difficult to find type founders. So we had quite a number of employees from Germany and some from Italy, Austria, Norway, and Holland. At that time we were quite international. When I entered the firm, we had about 80 people working there, and in the busiest season we had about 120 employees. What else? How was the atmosphere? We were all shouting at each other!

GH — Was there a sense of pride and accomplishment at Haas after the popularity of Helvetica, after it spread worldwide?

AH — Yes, we all had a sense of pride, especially when we realized that Stempel and Linotype were interested in producing and selling it.

GH — But did you realize at the time the extent to which it had spread globally?

AH — I think maybe I realized it to some extent, but the ordinary workers in the factory, they did not realize that. They would notice when they got quite a nice bonus three times a year. But otherwise, they did not quite know what had happened. And of course, we had no idea how many thousands of kilos had been sold in the United States, for example. Because most of the Helvetica which was sold was not made by us; it was copies. We could estimate about how much was out there when we got the license fees from the various manufacturers.

GH — If I had a small printing shop in the sixties and I wanted to buy Helvetica in a normal range of weights, how much would it have cost me?

AH — If you started from nothing, and you had to have, say, 6-, 7-, 8-, 9-, 10-point up to, let's say, 48-point and the spacing materials and so on, this easily ended up being $7,000. But year after year, we had to increase the prices.

GH — It's so different now. Nothing is manufactured; it's all digital.

> **AH** — Yes, true. But it was even more expensive buying a font of Linotype matrices. From 6- to 12-point, let's say, that's 1,500 or 2,200 mats. The price of one mat was about 2 francs. That was $1.20 or so. And you had to replace it once every two or three years. If you looked at a newspaper, they had 20 Linotype machines in one line. So you can imagine how much money they spent on type in addition to the machine. The most sophisticated Linotype machines cost several hundred thousand dollars. If you compare that with the new technology, what you invest now is peanuts.

GH — I wonder if you could talk about what you mentioned to me before, about visiting New York after not being there for many years?

> **AH** — Aha. Yes, I had been working in New York for 2 years, between '49 and '51, at a printing company there. And after that, I went back to Switzerland to work for Haas. It was 33 years before I went back to the United States. When I came back, I was amazed at how much Helvetica was used; I was overwhelmed. I said, "This is pretty much misused." I was surprised that people didn't get bored of it.

GH — What moments stand out in your memory during the time you worked at Haas? What were some of the high points and the low points?

> **AH** — This is the kind of question that I'm often asked, and I must say, I did not have any particular highlights or lowlights. For me it was normal to work on a Saturday. We kept busy with our jobs. We were all pretty stressed. Life just went on.
>
> —

Leslie Savan (LS)/ September 6, 2006 New York

When I started researching Helvetica in preparation for making the film, I found many references to an article written by journalist Leslie Savan in 1976 for the *Village Voice*. "This Typeface Is Changing Your Life" was the first media story that recognized Helvetica's ubiquity, and it serves as sort of a precursor to my film, 30 years earlier. I interviewed Leslie at a friend's photo studio in New York City.

—

Gary Hustwit — When did you first become aware of Helvetica?

Leslie Savan — I believe it was in the mid-seventies that I first noticed Helvetica as a typeface, not just as something in the surrounding area of my life, but distinctly as a typeface or style. I didn't know much about typefaces or anything back then, but I really became aware of it when I was in college and I was visiting friends in Cambridge, Massachusetts. Cambridge was one Helvetica town. It was just everywhere, on signs over cafés, over restaurants, over clothing stores. And each time I passed these places, I wanted to go in, especially with the clothing stores. I thought there'd be something good in there, kind of, just, perfect. So I noticed Helvetica because it was so prevalent in this one town in the space of the weekend that I was up there. I noticed it because I saw it so many times in such a condensed amount of time.

And then I think I started thinking of it in terms of, "Oh, yes, I've seen this before, and it's giving me the same feeling as before." My strongest experience of Helvetica was, I recall, when I was in an airport. The sign for the women's bathroom said "Women" in Helvetica. It made me think unconsciously, "That's probably a clean bathroom. I can use it." Usually, you see public restrooms and, especially back then, you thought, "Uh-uh." But no, this one just said, "It's going to be clean. It's going to be a good experience."

At the time, I was taking a few journalism classes—I was a psychology major, though. I wrote a piece about Helvetica in my magazine-writing class. Then I tried to, and did, give it to my favorite paper back then, *the Village Voice*. And that's how the story came out.

GH — Did you get a reaction from people?

LS — The reaction was not explosive or anything. I think I got more notice from designers, type designers, who said, "Somebody's actually noticing this and writing about it?" Somebody out there within the world and not in the trade. That was the main reaction that I recall. I think there were a bunch of letters to the editor, but they were mostly from designers.

GH — And the designers you interviewed for the story, what was their reaction?

LS — Their reaction to the fact that I was doing the story was that they were very eager to talk. It wasn't often that a type designer or graphic designer was interviewed at all, or quoted at all, outside of the trade magazines. I think a lot of them were very flattered and went on and on. I don't mean they went on and on in a bad way. They were just really cooperative and really helpful. I think there were a lot of pent-up pros and cons concerning Helvetica, because they worked with it daily. So they were really willing to talk about why they liked it or detested it.

It was so much fun to do the story, because I met Massimo Vignelli and other designers who were in the middle of distributing this typeface throughout the world, in the subway system in New York, on the sanitation trucks in New York. The fact that it was on sanitation trucks, that was a new thing. They were all-white trucks with one word in black Helvetica Medium, I believe it was, that said "Sanitation." Instead of garbage, you read "sanitized." You read, "Hey, this is a garbage truck? Not anymore." And so much of my story spun on that fascinating detail. I really wanted to write about the subtle if not semi-conscious psychological reaction, an almost sensory reaction that Helvetica created in people who saw it all the time.

GH — Did you start noticing it everywhere?

LS — Oh, yeah. I started noticing it, and as a budding reporter, I was thrilled. Whenever I could find it, it felt great because it was evidence for my thesis, so to speak. But I enjoyed reporting on it so much. It's the first piece I ever did that—I don't know if you're going to want to use this, but throughout my writing career I've looked at things that are everywhere but that most of us don't notice. I looked at advertising and its effects that we don't notice in a real conscious, deliberately analytical way. I wrote about advertising for ages, and now I'm looking at language, what I call "pop language." The words and phrases we say all the time that are persuasive, like Helvetica is persuasive. I'm interested, I think, in persuasive sensory and intellectual experiences that are not very conscious.

For instance, if I say, "I don't think so" or "Hello?" those are pop language phrases that we all use. But because they're so commercialized, because they've been through that sort of media approval process and then we use them with another little sense of power ourselves, they have that same smooth Teflon coating that makes them go down easier. Just like Helvetica does.

Helvetica has almost like a perfect balance of push and pull in its letters. There's an energy—you can almost feel the energy in those black lines against white especially. And that perfect balance of push and pull is saying to us, "Don't worry. Any of the problems you're having, or the problems in the world, or the problems getting through the subway, or finding a bathroom—all those problems aren't going to spill over. They'll be contained, and in fact maybe they don't even exist."

I wrote that piece in 1976, and now it's 30 years later, and Helvetica's just as popular if not more so. I think that the same truth is there, that it promises that the world's problems can be contained or don't exist. And I can't help but relate this to the war in Iraq and everything. To say something doesn't exist, like "We're not really creating more terrorists when we're in Iraq. That doesn't exist." Or to say something you imagine, like a weapon of mass destruction does exist. In other words, to tell yourself lies. Nice lies to make you feel better. That is part of a historical process. It's part of willfully forgetting, willfully wanting to forget things, and to just make it go down nicely. Which is what I think the Helvetica characters do.

Also I just was thinking too about 30 years ago. Who was in office back then, in those earlier years of Helvetica? It was Nixon. Wondering if he used it on his signage for his campaigns. It's very interesting. And who was working for Nixon back then? Rumsfeld and Dick Cheney. Of course, they've ascended in power, just as Helvetica has. I'm not trying to say Helvetica is like Dick Cheney or Rumsfeld; surely, it's not. But these things that seemed so old-looking are back now, in 2006.

GH — The role of Helvetica in advertising—can we talk about that? What are the advertisers trying to project, or a corporation trying to project, by using it?

LS — Well, there are a few things. The most obvious—Vignelli, the name of his firm was Unimark; all the corporations are in this together. They're saying, "We can all look like each other." And that gives us permission, or an eagerness, to conform. "Well, if they can all look like each other, we can all look like each other. It's okay." We like the things that those corporations make, Coca-Cola, cosmetics. So it's okay to look like each other and to be like each other.

I mean, conformity has been around for centuries and centuries. It's nothing new. But these corporations are also saying with Helvetica that they're very friendly. Not too friendly—they're not going to get in your face over anything, because Helvetica doesn't do that, but they're friendly. They really know what they're talking about. They have the situation in control. They've done all the thinking for you. Whatever the product is that they're selling, they've done it all. This is the most perfect product that has resulted from all their hard work and thinking and research. Here it is—this is officially the best, or this is the most authoritative version of this or that. And yet Helvetica's edges are smooth, and it goes down so easily because it's so familiar by now. But even when it wasn't familiar, even when Helvetica was newer, it had this feeling of cleanliness and pleasantness, and yet a little bit of chic as well. And they're still saying that about themselves. "We're a little hip, but not too hip. We're the final authority on this, and you can trust us."

GH — That's interesting, because I always thought advertising was about the opposite, about differentiating yourself from the other guy. Not conforming. I guess a lot of it was a kind of "me-too-ism." We want our company to look like our bigger, smarter, competitors, so we'd better use Helvetica to be part of the club.

LS — Helvetica works that way, where yes, a smaller company could associate itself with bigger companies. But the whole idea of conformity versus nonconformity and rebellion versus acceptance throughout the last 30 to 40 years of corporate America is pretty fascinating. To stereotype the fifties: conformity. To stereotype the sixties and seventies: rebellion. Then, from the eighties and nineties, and still today, I believe, we have a strange blending of rebellion and acceptance, of conformity and nonconformity, and being an individual versus being part of the corporate group, the collective.

We want to be individuals and accepted by the larger group at the same time. Many companies use this in their advertising. They flatter you, the viewer, that you are different. You are a rebel, and you can kick ass. You're just too kooky for words. Sprite did this—Sprite was a big one on this. There was recently an ad for IBM about "You are not like anyone else. You are different. You are different." This is on TV now. "You are different. I am different." This is from IBM, the epitome of corporate conformity. But the idea is that when companies, especially in advertising, try to tell you that you are different—and everybody wants to be different—then you're actually all more alike.

It's like in the movie *Life of Brian* by Monty Python. The mistaken messiah gets up on a balcony, and he has thousands of his devotees looking up to him to hear the latest word. Quite unexpectedly, he says, "You shouldn't follow me. You shouldn't follow anyone. You are all individuals." And then they all reply, in unison, "Yes, we are all individuals!" And that sort of sums up the idea of advertising—one of their big, big angles for the last 20 to 30 years. "You are all different. You are all individuals. By buying this product, we can help you express that difference and that individuality. If you all buy the same product, then you can better express your difference." It's a fascinating paradox that we live with and accept.

You can look at the different time periods of Helvetica's ascendance— the rise and fall and rise. The first rise was more tilted toward conformity. The backlash against Helvetica in the, say, mid-seventies and the eighties especially was "No, we're all going to be different." Designers did it, advertisers—it started to really come out in the advertising especially. They all had to show their difference and their edginess with different typefaces. Edginess was, and still is, the goal of what a lot of designers want to do. Then it's as if we synthesized that. We synthesized the paradox that we can all be individuals by doing the same exact thing, by looking alike and thinking alike. Because we've synthesized it with irony. "Oh, yeah, we could do that. We're in on this strange phenomenon." And yet the power of conforming or not conforming, and wanting to be popular and liked in any field—those powers and those forces still exist, of course, as they have for millennia.

Now I think it's past the irony point, even. It's just done. And people aren't winking at it at all. It's just there. But it doesn't seem as oppressively conformist as it might have in the beginning, because you choose it. You know all about it, you know the pros and the cons and the history a little bit, and you still choose it. Because you feel like you've synthesized it and processed it all, mentally, graphically, and artistically. And that applies, I think, both in advertising and in type design, and in other forms of design, too.

GH — Do you think this applies to governments too?

LS — Okay, this goes back to the seventies, but I think it's still true today. Governments and corporations love Helvetica because, on one hand it makes it them seem neutral and efficient, but also the smoothness of the letters make them seem almost human. I've also thought that Helvetica, especially Helvetica Medium, where I think its balance of push and pull is most evident—it almost seems like flesh. Very nice, vital, healthy flesh on a 25-year-old, for instance. You almost want to touch it or squeeze it. It's not just tactile; it's a sensation beyond tactile. You want to get into it and hold it, almost. People might think I'm reading a lot into this, but I don't think so.

When I say that corporations and governments love it because its smoothness makes it seem almost human, that is a quality they all want to convey. Of course, they have the image they're always fighting—they're authoritarian, they're bureaucratic, you lose yourself in them, they're oppressive. Instead, by using Helvetica, with that nice, human, smooth quality of the letters, they can come off seeming more accessible, transparent, and accountable, which are all the buzzwords for what corporations and governments are supposed to be today. They don't have to *be* accessible or accountable or transparent, but the important thing, especially in this day of "image rules all," is that they can look that way. Our tax forms from the IRS are in Helvetica. The EPA uses it—now there's someone that wants to look official and efficient. You can almost have a sensation, a physical sensation, that they are that way, because of these letters. That's what I wanted to say.

I also wanted to read one other thing for you that James Wines said, that I ended the *Village Voice* piece with. I'll read what Vignelli said first. He said, "What you see is different from what you perceive. You see Helvetica, and you perceive order. With more unusual lettering, you perceive fantasy." Then I wrote, "Fantasy and a well-ordered society have always been at odds, and as James Wines says, 'By designing fantasy out of our society, we are headed in a dangerous direction.'" I'm quoting him here. He said, "Our world is a designed extension of service. Other worlds are an aesthetic extension of spirit."

GH — What do you think his point is?

LS — That we're discouraging and, in the end, wiping out a lot of the urge to be different, to try new things, to think for yourself, and to speak out loud. There's a lot of fear in society now about speaking out against the government. It's finally starting to happen as more people are protesting the war in Iraq, but there was a really interesting period right after 9/11 for about two years when journalists held back—well, a lot of journalists are still holding back. It is scary to speak out. And Helvetica tells you, "It's okay to not speak out." Because there's a safety about it and there's a modernism about it. It's okay. I don't want to use the word "liberalism," but Helvetica is telling you that there's an enlightened quality to holding back: "It's okay. It's something you've got to do sometimes, and we understand it. It's okay. It's what people have to do." I don't know if I'm saying it that well, but in any case, when James Wines said, "Our world is a designed extension of service," I think you know what he means. He's just saying, you're getting your McDonald's, you're getting your Burger King, you know, mass-produced. And you're getting your typeface and your feelings about corporations mass-produced, too.

On the consumer end, it's because we are becoming more of a service economy. For the corporations, it's easier for them to put this out. James Wines also says, "Other worlds are an aesthetic extension of spirit." They don't go through all that bureaucratic, smooth-it-over, assembly- line food and products and cars and relationships to the IRS, even. You know? They are more about haphazardness or serendipity or folk art. Other societies all have their conformities, of course. But Helvetica leaves less room for serendipity and for a haphazard, surprising quality to life.

Something else I wanted to say: I've been working on an article about Teflon and all the toxic blowback it's having. There are going to be new rules about its use and everything. Helvetica has a lot in common with Teflon. Helvetica is the visual expression of this smoothness and this promise of protection from dirty things or bad things, while Teflon is the tactile, physical promise to protect you from all sorts of extra work that you have to do in cleanup. And it's used in piping and all sorts of industrial parts too, to protect the manufacturer from friction that it doesn't want. Teflon's smoothness is like Helvetica's smoothness in the way that it all seems very trustworthy. But just as Teflon is coming into a lot of trouble with the chemicals in it that have been found to be highly toxic, to a much lesser extent, Helvetica also has an underside to its smoothness.
—

Mike Parker (MP)/ September 15, 2006 Boston

Mike Parker is often referred to as "the Godfather of Helvetica" for his role in helping popularize the typeface in the United States. I spoke with Mike in the offices of the Font Bureau in Boston.

At a screening event for *Helvetica* after the film had been released, Mike pulled me aside and told me, "I've got an idea for you. You need to make a film about Times New Roman." I think I may have rolled my eyes a bit, and replied, "I don't know, Mike, I just finished a film about a font, I'm not sure I'm going to do another one right now." Then his voice got low and serious. "But there's a murder involved," he said, with his British accent drawing out the word *murrrrder*. It was a classic Mike Parker moment. But maybe enough time has passed now, and I should start working on that movie?

Mike passed away February 23, 2014. He was a true gentleman and one of modern typography's giants, and he will be missed.

—

Gary Hustwit — I guess I'd like to start with when you started at Linotype, basically your role at Linotype.

Mike Parker — Okay. In 1953, I came back from the war in Korea, where I'd been executive officer of an engineer combat company. I had left Yale to go to Korea, and when I came back I got in touch with the Yale architecture school, where I hadn't done very well, and they said they would take me back. I asked, "When?" This was in February. They said, "September." I said, "September? Well what should I do till then? Will I learn more working for a construction company or a wrecking company?" And they said, "Get out of here."

So I went upstairs to the graphic design department, where Alvin Eisenman was. I knew him from the days before, and I told him I was interested in graphic design. We chatted for a while, it was pleasant conversation, then he said, "You know, I think you'll do." I said, "I'll do?" He said, "Yes, but I'll have to check with the architecture school." I said, "Well, all right. But what should I do till September?" He said, "Who said September? One of our students is pregnant, she's leaving tomorrow, so how about Monday? But I've got to check and call you, you see?" So he called me and said, "Come ahead," and I was a graphic designer.

Years later I was having lunch with him—there was something he wanted from Mergenthaler for some project, we were having lunch in downtown New York. And at the end of the lunch I said, "You know, there's only one thing that really surprised me back then: that the architecture school recommended me." He said, "You know what? They didn't."

GH — What happened?

MP — Well, he'd taken me anyway. And you owe the world for something like that. You never get to pay back the person who does something like that for you, but you owe it to the world in those situations to behave yourself properly.

GH — And then how did you get involved at Linotype?

MP — Okay, I did my thesis at Yale on Garamond's types and while doing so came upon a whole set of new discoveries that had been headed up by Stanley Morison at Monotype, the great name. And I suddenly realized that my thesis was completely out of date. So I got hold of Alvin, and the way you did that was to stand outside the Yale press where he was the designer, and, when he came out at noon to head for lunch, you got into step. You had enough time for about five sentences.

So I told him, "It's all out of date. What the hell do I do?" I can still remember standing on a couple of stone steps down into the restaurant. He said, "Well, I suggest you finish the thesis, 'To be continued,' and you address a letter, 'Dear Mr. Morison.'" Which led me to the Plantin-Moretus Museum, to a fellowship in the Plantin-Moretus Museum for a couple of years, putting all that stuff in order. And when I got back, I got a phone call from Jackson Burke, who seemed to think that this might suit me for running the program at Mergenthaler, or assisting him in doing it.

So I signed on as his assistant one day in 1959—I didn't know he had phlebitis and diabetes. He was looking for a successor. Two days later, in my thirties, I had the most powerful job in the industry, because I'd got away and played at what I wanted to do. That's a profound lesson if you've got good taste in what you want to do.

GH — And what was the relationship between the various Linotype companies?

MP — Mergenthaler Linotype was the American company and it owned various parts of the overseas companies. And the German company, Linotype GmbH—in Germany there's a rule that protects minority stockholders. The majority can't give orders. There was a family that held the minority and I happened to have gone to school with one of them, so one of my jobs was to keep the German company sweet by making sure that the family were on-board before we tried to give orders to the German company. You'd never believe the way the things linked up.

GH — What was the industry like then? What sort of typefaces were the designers looking for?

MP — The big thing for all of us at the time was that figure-ground relationship that the Swiss did so well. And Trade Gothic just didn't have it—it was News Gothic under another name; it was an Intertype name, so we couldn't use it. It was a good job, but it was a 1900s design that had been popular ever since. It was clear that whoever got in there first with a really good figure-ground Swiss sans serif, that it would be the big hit. But Jackson just thought of it as European, not for us.

So one day he called me in and he said, "I'm going to retire shortly, in six months, maybe nine, and I will recommend you for the job. Is there anything you'd like me to do?" And I thought, "Oh, hell." So I said, "I think the single most important thing is for us to cut a Swiss sans serif, and Helvetica would be the logical choice." And he looked at me like I had just shot him. Then he thought about it, said nothing, and I left.

And about four months later I met him in the corridor and he said, "Oh, by the way, Mike, you'll be pleased to hear, I think, that the German drawings for Helvetica will be at the drawing department upstairs next week, and perhaps you'd like to go look at them, and maybe there's something you'd like to do with them." And you cannot ask more than that from anyone you work for. He was funny, to the point, and he was a delightful person to work for.

When you talk about the design of the Haas Neue Grotesk, or Helvetica, what it's all about is the interrelationship of the negative shape, the shapes between characters and within characters, with the black, if you like—with the inked surface. And the Swiss pay more attention to the background, so that the counters and the space between characters just hold the letters. You can't imagine anything moving—it is so firm. It's not a letter that's bent to shape, it's a letter that lives in a powerful matrix of surrounding space. Oh, it's brilliant when it's done well.

GH — Was it still called Neue Haas Grotesk at that point? Who was involved in the decision to change the name?

    MP — Walter Cunz was the head of Stempel at that time. And I talked to Walter about it, and there was a decision taken to change the name, and Walter called it Helvetica. He called up Haas and they said in horror, "You can't call it that, that's the name of our country." And Walter said, "Well, we're going to." And three or four months later came the call the other way—Haas called Stempel and asked, "Do you mind if we call it Helvetica too?" So Neue Haas Grotesk disappeared.

GH — What was the reaction when you introduced it here in the States?

    MP — Well, it had already been introduced. The first to cut it in Linotype matrices was Linotype GmbH and they exported those to the US. They were starting to press us, and we didn't really want them taking over the market—we just didn't. So we caught it just in time; we could get the same character sizes and fit them into American alignment. So we just took it away from them, underpricing them and doing the usual things, and away it went, followed up by the photocomposition versions, the digital versions, and the rest. And then one day I was riding up in an elevator and I looked at this smudgy piece of paper, the license or whatever that all elevators have, and realized it was Helvetica. And we had really won when you see it there. So it had gone all the way from the top to the bottom of the market and was everywhere.

GH — Was the marketing any different than with other typefaces Linotype released? Obviously, like you said, there was a demand for the Swiss style.

MP — The start of everything was always the trade typesetters—they don't exist now, since we all have our Macs. But in those days you went to a trade typesetter to have your work done, and they would do it overnight and you'd have it in the morning and you'd mark it up, and so forth. And the trade typesetters went for it in a big way to please their customers, the real designers, and the moment that started to happen it trickled down through the market, because people followed them knowing they were the trendsetters.

Once we'd introduced Helvetica, it really ran away. It was exactly what the designers were looking for. I don't think there's been such a hot thing since as the figure-ground relationship properly executed, and it was just a landslide waiting to go down the mountain, and away it went. So we didn't have to do much; once you'd got the head of the market, it just sort of naturally flowed down into the body and then the feet, and then there it was on the elevator certificate.

GH — Did you meet Miedinger at any point?

MP — I never met him, no. Well, probably you'll cut this out, but it seemed to me he always—just from listening—he always overplayed it. I knew the way things worked at Haas, and I gradually had picked up the importance of Eduard Hoffmann and his almost pathological shyness, and the way that he would use other people's hands. But, boy, could you see his mind at work on the faces where he was deeply involved, like the great ones, of course: Haas Clarendon and Helvetica. What a mind.

GH — We know why Helvetica got so popular initially, but why do you think it kept going?

MP — Oh, Folio, Univers, Helvetica; I would say that, just from the point of view of the design, they're as equal as any players you will ever run into. The question, then, is who controls the channels of distribution, and the Linotype machine was the key to the market in those days. So Helvetica—which maybe by some small amount is the best of the lot but not, let's say, overwhelmingly better—might have had a bit of an edge.

GH — There's something to the ubiquity of it now—when you go down to the train station here in Boston, it's everywhere; it's on all the platforms and it's on the trains. And it's not Univers; it's not Folio; it's Helvetica.

MP — I know. Well, it's good enough to stand up to that. What's that little book I've got back there, *Types* ...?

GH — The *Best Remembered/Best Forgotten* book?

MP — Yeah, *Types Best Remembered/Types Best Forgotten*. It was a joy to put Helvetica in both categories, because one was sick to death of it in one sense, and yet what a job it had done in another. So I couldn't resist including it for both.

GH — Could we back up for a minute and talk about the Linotype machine? I don't think most people understand how it worked, why it was so revolutionary. Could you describe it in layman's terms?

MP — Let's look at the giant machine of all giant machines, that for a century was the center of the industry. It's a couple of tons of machinery but it's actually relatively simple. The matrices are in a magazine—

GH — Okay, wait. Stop, stop, stop, because even the word "matrices," most people won't even understand how that applies. Can you explain it to a non-designer?

MP — It was actually a fairly simple concept. You typed words on a mechanical keyboard that put in a row the molds for each of the letters, called matrices, until you had a group of words that was the length of a line. The machine then poured hot metal into the mold, and you cast that "line o' type." The famous story behind the naming of the machine was when somebody looked at it and said to the inventor, "Why, Ottmar, you have cast a line o' type."

Anyway, you cast it one line at a time, and then the matrices were lifted back up to the top of the machine and one by one the E's would all fall back down together in a row and the A's and the O's and so forth. And there they were ready to be used again each time you hit the key. The Linotype offered a couple of great advantages. One was the fact that after you used the type you melted it down, so you didn't end up with fonts of type that were ever more worn—you were always casting fresh, new stuff, so the aging problem disappeared.

GH — And the speed?

MP — Oh, yes, the productivity was way quicker. You could hit the keys faster than you could ever reach and assemble characters one by one in a composing stick. And then you didn't have to distribute it back into the case either; you just melted it down and cast again. So it offered really substantial advantages, and very quickly newspapers could not afford to be without it.

It is said to have been the single most complex piece of mechanical gear ever built, and I believe it. I had one to play with at Mergenthaler. It's now at the Mark Twain Museum in Hartford, in the basement. They were going to put it upstairs and then discovered there was no part of the building that would support it—it's that heavy.

GH — At the time when you made the Helvetica matrices, how many typefaces were available for the Linotype?

MP — Oh, it was about 500, but a lot of those were obsolete. So probably 150 faces of any popularity. We were making 15 new ones on average per year. Given the problems of manufacture and the expense of man-ufacture—I actually have a wonderful picture, and it's right over there, of the group sitting around the table when we first put together the big production schedule. They all look like a sewer has just opened in the middle of the table. It's wonderful. I had just said, "We are going to be making this large number of faces, and it's not going to be that many Helveticas; it's going to be smaller designs that sell in a much smaller way, but now we can afford to make all the little specialties that before we had to ignore. So this is going to be our future." And in walked the photographer and took the picture and they're all sitting there. It was just interesting to see how appalled they were, the Germans, the Brits, everyone from the company—it must have been 20 people. And they were the people who would run the program and make all the money from it, and they were just to a person appalled. Oh, I know what I had said. I said, "I want you to repeat after me. We're not going to make our money on what we've always called fads. And I want you to repeat after me: Ephemeral typefaces."

GH — And then that picture was taken.

MP — Yep. The one who's most disgusted is Matthew Carter; he was sitting over there. You've spoken to him.

GH — Yes. How did you first meet Matthew?

MP — He was plinking rabbits with an air gun at his dad's house, at Harry Carter's house. I was working with his dad. Matthew was about 19. I came down for the weekend and we walked out back and plinked rabbits. So I've known him a long time.

GH — What are your thoughts on his type-design work?

MP — I put together a design team at Linotype that centered on Adrian Frutiger and Matthew. Adrian is the ultimate mystic, if you like. He has that feel for shape that a true sculptor or artist has, and he has it more strongly than anyone I know. You don't hand him a defined program, you let him run free, and the results are typefaces like Frutiger.

Matthew, on the other hand, is the ultimate technician; what he really enjoys is a spec. AT&T came to us and asked us if we could do a better typeface than Bell Gothic for the White Pages. I gave the job to Matthew and he worked on it for two years. In the end we saved 20 lines per page, and people's calls to information dropped by something like 40 percent. It was more readable, and it was smaller, but it looked bigger. Matthew stills says to this day that it's the most important thing he's ever done. He says, "Because of that typeface, there are innumerable forests that still stand."

That is, I think, where Matthew is at his best, and that's the way we used to split the work. One of the pictures I'd love to show you, if we can find it, is of the three of us in London—we really ran the program as a triumvirate. We were all equals, but the three of us were just a bit more equal than the others.

GH — What other designers' work do you truly like?

MP — Oh, I'm spoiled by those two, because with them you can do anything. I remember when Adrian had done a design for us, and I had to kill it—we were too overloaded to handle a new typeface. I think it was the first contract I had with Adrian. I called him and said, "We're giving this typeface back to you because we can't continue production." And he said, "But you paid for it." I said, "I know, but we're not going to make it. I don't want to kill a typeface this way, particularly one of this quality.

At the moment we just can't handle it; we're too busy. But I'll just ask you one thing, which is the right of refusal to purchase the face again for typesetting. By the way, do you have a project in mind for it?" He said, "Yes." I asked, "What is it?" He said, "I'd rather not tell you, if you don't mind."

Three or four years later, I walked into the airport at Roissy in Paris. We had bought a little matrix factory in Paris, because the last Linotype machines ran faster than anything ever had before and were mostly used for newspapers and telephone books, so they only used a few faces. The matrices slammed together more often and at high speeds, and the machines just ate those matrices for breakfast, lunch, and dinner. So we had to make more and more and more matrices, and we bought a little French company for that purpose.

So I'm in the airport at Roissy and there it was, Adrian's typeface. It was everywhere, gorgeous. I called him right away and said, "We want it." We ended up manufacturing it in Germany; the German Linotype company had it. I wanted to call it Roissy, but Mathew said no. I said, "Matt, what's wrong with it?" He said, "In England, it will be called Rosie." So we called it Frutiger instead.

GH — What did Adrian think of that?

MP — One never knows, but I think he was pleased. He's such a sweet man. There is something I used for my TypeCon talk—were you at my talk?

GH — Yes.

MP — I showed that poem he wrote about leaves blowing off the trees. I think he was more pleased by that than anything, and that's his quality, just sensitivity all the way through, and gentleness. That can sound weak, but in a way it's just his essence. But anyway, the three of us had a really good time together.

GH — So what kind of architect would you have been if you had stuck with architecture?

MP — Who knows? You may or may not want to use this, but my dad was murdered when I was studying architecture at Yale. A Quebec jeweler killed his wife by putting a bomb on a DC-3 and it wiped out the management at Kennecott Copper, where my dad was a vice president. So I suddenly had that hit me, and I had just about got free of my mother and worked very hard at it when I inherited her back again. I was the oldest son; I had a brother and sister. And so it was a hard time making all that work, and when I tried to complete that year at Yale, I realized I was going to flunk. I'd had it. This was during the war in Korea, and if I flunked out, the draft was going to get me, so I volunteered. I went through infantry basic training and then volunteered for officer-candidate school. They flunked three out of four candidates; I think 65 of us started and 17 of us graduated.

GH — And then how long until you came back to Yale?

MP — I was over there in Korea for about a year. And actually, I'm probably prouder of this than anything in my life: I ended up as executive officer of an engineer combat company. And then if you had two years' service, you could apply for early release. We had too many junior-grade officers in Korea, so I applied. And we had a West Point colonel who was terrific but a son of a bitch in his way—he was tough. And so I put in for early release and I got a call from battalion.

I took a Jeep and drove over. "Lieutenant Parker reporting as ordered, sir." And he looked at me and said, "I have here your request for early release." I said, "Yes." He said, "I'd rather not sign it. We need a company commander for Charlie Company—the job is yours if you serve out your term." That's the equivalent of getting a ship in the navy, and the usual grade is a captain with four or five years' service, and I was a second lieutenant with nine months' service. So I thought, "Well, I've got to be a bit better off than when I came in." But then I heard my voice say, "I'm dreadfully sorry, sir, but you're looking at a design student in disguise." He said, "Then, with regret . . ." signed it, and I came home.

GH — If you had to say who influenced you the most or who you learned the most from in this business, who would it be?

MP — That's a tough question, but I'm incredibly grateful to Jackson Burke and Chauncey Griffith for the way they set up the company. I was handed a piece of cake; it was so beautifully organized by astoundingly good people. So I got the credit, but it was really the setup and the way the company ran and the respect, that real respect for people, deep respect. And rascality too. Jackson married Ms. General Mills, so he was an incredibly wealthy man. So if we were taking competitors out to lunch, we'd take them to the New York Yacht Club and then see what they made of that. It was fun.

GH — What are your thoughts on the role of technology, the changes in typographic technology over the past 50 years since the birth of Helvetica?

MP — Well, the big thing is the advent of the machines. From Gutenberg to 1880 it was a cottage industry, a lot of little type foundries, usually several to every major city competing with each other, and there was no huge fortune ever made on type. But then along came the big machines, and the price of being in typesetting jumped more than tenfold and it became a completely different thing, a century of giant machines to get newspapers out quickly and effectively and so forth. And that ended in 1980, just about, with the advent of the digital machines, and with that anyone could play again. We were right back, happily, to our little sand pile in the corner, our little typographic cottage industry again. That meeting in Boston, TypeCon, where you and I met a few weeks ago, I doubt there were 500 people there, and that was the whole industry; you were looking at it.

GH — That was it.

MP — Yeah. One of the things I love about it is we're such gentle sweeties, mostly, the people that you meet in this industry. I've gove to these big industry meetings of several other industries, and all you see is knives, they're all out for each other and they're all competing, and it just isn't true of us. There are one or two sharks out there, but we all know who they are, and by and large they're not part of things. Have you noticed this?

GH — Well, I think everyone that I've interviewed for the film has been incredibly generous.

MP — Just gentle folk, to do what we do. But working on the intricacies of a typeface design requires a mind for this sort of thing. Typically when the phones go quiet, I'll start work about 10 p.m. and I'll be woken out of sort of a trancelike state by the sun coming up, and I honestly don't know for a moment where I am. You get completely lost in the complexities of the thing and you never get it right. There are conflicts in there that are never completely resolvable, but you find the distant corner of the carpet where you can sweep the dust under and you're done.

—

David Carson (DC)/ November 27, 2006 Portland

I knew who David Carson was before I was really even interested in graphic design. Since my background was in the independent music scene of the 1980s, I'd been exposed to David's groundbreaking work in *Ray Gun* magazine. I spoke with David at North in Portland, Oregon, where he was visiting for a project.

—

Gary Hustwit — To start out, I want to talk a little bit about the basics of how you got involved in art and design and some of the early *Transworld Magazine* stuff. Did you go to art school?

David Carson — I have a degree in sociology, and I taught high school sociology for five years. I really wasn't looking for something different; teaching just worked for me. I didn't love it. I didn't hate it. It was there. I think the hours were good. But then one summer I got a postcard in the mail announcing this two-week summer workshop in graphic design, and they wanted me to post it for the high school seniors for where they could go and study. I read this thing and I thought, "Wow, that's a profession? You can make a living doing that? You can have fun. You can be creative. That's really interesting."

So I was 26 the first time I'd heard or seen the term "graphic design." I read that postcard from the University of Arizona and I called them and I said, "Well, I'm actually a teacher, but could I come to this thing?" They said, "Sure, come on down." So I went to that workshop for two weeks in the summer at the University of Arizona, and that was it. I had a great instructor, Jackson Boelts, who's still there. I think if I'd had a different instructor maybe I wouldn't have gone into it, but at the end of that two weeks it was, "Wow, that's what I want to do." I quit teaching, enrolled in a little, tiny art school in Ashland, Oregon. It turned out to be not what I expected. They had us water-coloring ducks, and it just wasn't quite right.

So I ended up getting an internship, because I had kept in contact with friends in Southern California, at a magazine called *Action Now* that was put out by Surfer Publications, and *Action Now* was at the tail end of the first skateboard revolution. *Skateboarder Magazine* was finally ending, and they didn't know what to do with their subscription base and this magazine. So they started one called *Action Now* that lasted two or three issues, and I was an unpaid intern on that, doing little quarter-page ads, pasting them up in the corner. Ironically, that magazine turned out to be about 20 years too early, because everybody laughed it off as trying to cover all these sports and people only wanted a magazine about their own sport. So it failed miserably, and now, of course, it's all about multi-sports and everything, extreme games and this and that. But that really got me into it, and when the magazine folded, I went back to substitute teaching to make a living.

I was teaching in Del Mar, California, in San Diego, and I remember getting a call during lunch break in the teachers' room from Stacey Peralta, of numerous movies and skateboard fame, asking me if I'd be interested in art-directing this new skateboard magazine. I'm in the lunchroom, and I say, "Yeah, yeah. I would love to, yeah." That was *Transworld Skateboarding,* and basically that's what really started the whole thing. So I would teach during the day, then do *Transworld Skateboarding* in the afternoon and weekends. Then we started *Transworld Snowboarding,* and I've been in it ever since.

I have no formal training in the field, and I often say that I never learned all the things I wasn't supposed to do. I just did what made sense to me. I had to figure out how to reverse type out of a photo, for example. I hate to talk about the old days, but you still had to spec the type and write the instructions on tissue paper, and I had no training in any of that. I look at the three years at *Transworld Skateboarding* as being my schooling, in a sense, because they had 200 pages, it was very successful, and I was just experimenting, really.

GH — Did you have design influences at that point? Were you just completely subjectively looking at things and saying, "I like the way this looks," or were there things that influenced you from a style standpoint?
DC — I usually don't do well with questions about influences, because I wasn't studying those people or those movements. But I'd be naive to say that I was not influenced by things. All I can really think of is that growing up I did a lot of surfing, and from when I was 12 to 22, maybe longer, I could probably pick up any surf magazine and tell you the caption of any picture from memory. To this day, I could probably still do that. If I look at those magazines now, for the most part they weren't what I would call well-designed. There was the occasional ad. Somehow reading those magazines had to have had some effect on me, but I'd be hard-pressed to say what exactly it was.

GH — What music were you listening to back then?
DC — Music is a huge part of what I do. I literally can't work without it. But which era are we talking about? Really, my first influence would have been the Beatles, and I think largely because of that I've followed a lot of guitar bands and good singer/songwriter kinds of bands. And now I'm really enjoying alternative music, because in a way it's back to a simpler kind of vocal, heavy-guitar kind of thing. I like to think I'm pretty open to a lot of different music and it's a huge part of what I do. Early on, the Beatles, probably a little more than the Rolling Stones, but it was a little early to like the Rolling Stones.

GH — From an outside perspective, it's easy to look at the early work that you were doing and say that it was a reaction against the clean, corporate, slick-looking design. Was it?

DC — It absolutely was not. I was doing what made sense to me, and I was doing a skateboard magazine that had a certain attitude—the sport, the audience, the graphics on the boards, the articles—and I was reading that and trying to interpret it. To this day, this is the way I work, but especially then. There was never this thing of "Oh, let's break the rules" or "Oh, this has been too clean for too long. It's time to muck it up." So when people started getting really upset, I didn't really understand why.

It was many years later that somebody explained to me, probably better than I can explain it now, that it's that basically there was this group that spent a lot of time trying to organize things and get some kind of system going, and they saw me as coming in and throwing that out the window. I think I might have indeed done that, but it wasn't the starting point and it wasn't the plan. Only much later did I learn what the term "modernism" meant. It was only after *Ray Gun* that I became more aware that I was doing something that might piss them off. And then I would put type down the gutter or just something to muck with some of the critics. For the most part—even until today—I'm doing what makes sense to me. It's only later when somebody tells me or I read that you're not supposed to do that, it breaks the rules. So I think that that's a bit of a misnomer—that just moving things around implies this era or this look or this way of working.

It's like, "No, it's very hard to do the more subjective, interpretive stuff well." People are always bringing me things and saying, "Look, somebody ripped you off." I look at it and I think, "Well, no, I wouldn't have done it like that. It's not quite working." I can teach anybody off the street how to design a reasonable business card or newsletter, but if I bring in the same group off the street and play a CD and say, "Okay, now let's interpret that music for a cover," 9 out of 10 people are going to be lost. They're going to do something really corny and expected, but one person is going to do something amazing because that music spoke to them and it sent them in some direction that nobody else could go. That's the area to me where it gets more interesting and exciting and more emotional. That's where the best work comes from.

GH — During that span when you went from *Transworld* to *Beach Culture* to *Ray Gun*, what were some of the reactions? What were people saying about your work?

DC — You know, the strangest thing is that I was always hearing more about it second hand than I was actually hearing it myself. I'm busy. I'm working. I'm talking to the editor. We're looking at the new issue. We're getting ready and we're doing it, and then somewhere I might get an email or phone call or something. "Boy, did you hear about all that they're saying about you on such-and-such?" or "This so and so said," I'm thinking, "Huh, what?" Meanwhile, I'm giving lectures and they're sold out pretty much around the world, but the people who don't like my stuff aren't coming to those. So they're not there heckling me.

I remember giving a talk in England early in the whole deal. It probably was early *Ray Gun* era, and it was for the Typographic Circle in London, which I was told was an older, conservative group and this was quite a step for them to have me speak. It was the first one where I thought, "Oh boy, this could be trouble." I thought that I was finally going to get all these questions or comments I've heard about but wasn't getting directly. It was always like two separate worlds.

But the Typographic Circle went very well. It was standing room only, and they had a lot of great questions. What struck me was reading a review in London afterwards, and the reporter said that he went to hear me talk expecting the same thing I was expecting—a lot of angry questions, a lot of "What the heck are you doing?" But he wrote that there wasn't any of that. He said that basically the crowd had been disarmed. Because by that time, there had been so much press, and if you don't know the guy, you figure he's got to be a jerk. I mean, look at all this press he's getting. Some think he's the most wonderful thing in the world, or others came expecting to hate this guy. I thought he summed it up really well. It was like, "I'm not trying to say this is the only way to do something. This is what works for me. I try to have some fun with it. I try to have some fun with the lectures, and I try to work seriously and maybe not take myself so seriously." So that doesn't really answer your question. But a lot of people got really upset, and then it snowballed, because then, as you start getting more press, people dislike you even more.

While I was still in California, they had an article about me on the front page of the *New York Times*. It was a section they no longer have; maybe there's a correlation there. Being in California, I didn't realize that an article in the *New York Times* was a pretty big deal. I remember getting a fax—we still used fax machines in those days—from some anonymous person and they said, "Congratulations on the article in the *New York Times*. No doubt your phone will start ringing off the hook, and you're going to be really, really busy. May I make one suggestion? I hope you're saving some of your money. Once they build you up, they love to tear you down." So I thought, that's interesting, and he was pretty much dead on.

GH — Who was it from?

DC — It was anonymous. I don't know to this day, but it was from New York and I've saved it.

GH — Could you talk about legibility versus communication? Do you think that just because something is clear and readable means that it's communicating?

DC — This is a big mantra of mine, but it's really true: Don't confuse legibility with communication. Just because something's legible doesn't mean it communicates and, more importantly, doesn't mean it communicates the right thing. Something that may be difficult to read initially may be sending a completely different message that is valid for where it's being used and may require a little more time or the involvement of the reader. But it almost seems stronger the other way. If something is a very important message and it's said in a boring, nondescript way, then the message can be lost. Maybe it doesn't have any urgency to it.

It doesn't look intriguing. It doesn't make somebody walk across the street to read that poster. There's so much communication that goes into something before somebody starts reading, and that's really the area that interests me the most.

There's another saying, that you cannot *not* communicate, and I believe it completely. It's impossible to not communicate. For example, if I don't respond to your email, that sends a message. If I don't return your cell phone call, that sends a message. You cannot *not* communicate. If I spend two seconds on a design and throw it out the door, it will communicate something, maybe not what it should have or in the best way, and that might be the same amount of time that the reader will spend with it also. So legibility and communication are not so separate. They're really intertwined, and you can make something very legible and very boring that nobody will read and that's a disservice to the writer and the reader.

There could be something really important, really interesting, that doesn't get read because a designer didn't do their job. It's been said obviously a lot before, but you're really competing for people's attention with a lot of different media and a lot of different things. It becomes even more important that a designer become subjective in their approach and use who they are in their work to arrive at something unique, and something that maybe does get somebody's attention. Nobody else can pull from that. Everybody can take the same courses and get the same assignment to mimic a famous designer—I've never understood why they do that assignment—but nobody can pull from your background, your parents, your upbringing, your whole thing. If you can somehow utilize that and put it into the work, then you're going to arrive at something that is potentially more powerful and more intriguing, and you're going to have more fun doing it.

There are some really good messages that are lost because people think that the most important thing is that it is simple and clean and readable. It's a very thin line between simple and clean and powerful, and simple and clean and boring. That's another area where it takes whatever a good designer is to be able to do that. It's a big subject, and I think it was always extremely overstated or oversimplified in terms of the legibility and the illegibility. There were maybe one or two pages *in Ray Gun* that I would say you could not read, and they were that way for a good reason, but we're talking 30 issues. Every issue we'd try a lot of things, and a lot of them worked and a lot of them didn't work. Then there'd be a whole other issue. Then it takes on its own life of people examining and dissecting it. I never saw proofs, so a lot of times there were just mistakes, flat out mistakes that people would write long essays on, about why I did this black type on a black boot or something. But I didn't see a proof! I was like, "What are you talking about?"

When I redesigned *Surfer* magazine, they got hundreds of hate letters, and look what happened to the magazine. Within months, all the ads looked like the editorial and it became no big deal. So there's something about the shock of the new. There's something about it, and you'll read what you're interested in reading. There was writer who took a copy of the redesigned *Surfer* to Milton Glaser and asked him, "What do you think of the redesign?" Well, surprise—he hated it. It's like, no, take it to an 18-year-old kid walking out of the water from surfing and ask, "Hey, what do you think about what they did with your magazine?" That's going to be a much more valid critique.

The last thing I'm trying to say is, just do whatever you want if you think it's cool. No, you've got an audience and you have a subject matter. I've been lucky to have ones who have given me a certain amount of freedom appropriate to the subject matter. How can you do a boring *Skateboard* magazine all in Helvetica, you know? They've tried, but it doesn't capture people like the more expressive stuff does. It doesn't hit the same nerve. You can say, "Oh, that's professionally done," and "Oh, they know how to use type," but it doesn't hit the gut and the nerve the way that we did with some of the more emotional stuff, which is why you see so much hand lettering coming back. Maybe by the time this film comes out, it'll be out of fashion again. It's about time. It's wearing out its welcome a tiny bit. But nobody's come up with what's next. Well, somebody has. We just haven't heard about them yet.

GH — Obviously the computer has had a huge impact not only on professional design but in the vernacular, because anybody can do it now. I know when I bought mine back in '85, that was my entry point. I was never interested in design until I got the computer; after that I started making band flyers. What are your thoughts on the democratization of design technology?

DC — Well, the early effects of the computer were more rapid experimentation. You could try more things quickly, and you didn't have to wait till the next day. Before, you had to go home and wait for the type to come back and this sort of thing. With the computer, which everybody initially thought was going to let us work less hours, but now it's 24/7 and you never have to stop—it did just the opposite. For me it allowed more experimentation at a quicker pace. Early on there were so many unexpected things or accidents or just screw-ups, whether it was the printer or the font, and some of them were wonderful.

That seems to have gone away lately or in the last few years. But I still work at a very basic level in terms of programs. It's not about having the latest version of whatever program. If you don't have the eye, if you don't have a sense of design, the program's not going to give it to you. There are a million people out there who are proficient at any number of the latest programs and only a handful who actually have design sense or, for lack of a better word, the eye. They get it. They know that that looks better than that. I'm not sure it can be taught. So you have technicians, and you have graphic designers. I really think the better ones are graphic artists, but that's a term that we used to try to stay away from. But I think the best work comes from graphic artists doing design. If you can't design at all, then you call yourself an information architect.

GH — Really? I've heard a few people call themselves that.

DC — Yeah, if you have no good, subjective, intuitive design sense, then you can call yourself an information architect and do train timetables and plane schedules and that sort of thing, and that's fine—if you enjoy doing that sort of thing. I would say a lot of the information architects probably fall back to using Helvetica because it's safe and no one's going to get mad at them, and it seems to be pretty readable.

You know, you could take clothing that was made 100 to 200 years ago and bring it out today, and it would still basically work. It would probably keep you warm, it might keep the snow off you or the rain. It would basically work, clothing from 100 years ago, 200 years ago, 50 years ago—but you might get a few stares. It might not feel quite right on the streets. I think we could say the same thing with a lot of these typefaces that were made in a different era. Today, they'll basically work. You can read them, but they don't quite fit with these times. It was one of the great reasons John Lennon always gave for why the Beatles did not get back together. He said the whole mix has changed. You can't bring that back. The audience has changed. The world has changed. You can't re-create that, and so something made for a different era, while it still may suffice, it may not be the strongest way to communicate.

GH — So what typefaces are of this era?
    DC — I don't know. All the ones I use.

GH — But Helvetica is definitely from a different era. Why are we still using it? Are we just lazy? Are readers lazy?
    DC — Well, the bulk of the stuff readers are seeing is not coming from designers, or what I might call good designers, necessarily. It's an easy fix—to go with Times, go with Helvetica—no one's going to yell at you, and they're not going to get really excited either. There are some people who can do spectacular things with boring typefaces like Helvetica, but they're few and far between. For the rest of the people, they can't go wrong with it. To take a handwritten or a special, very unique font and do something well with it is a lot harder. And your mom's best friend can't use it quite as well as she can Helvetica. Maybe that makes the point why Helvetica's good—because anybody can use it. But if you ever go to church and you look at the thing they give you for that day's service, it's really boring. It's really horrible. Maybe if they did use Times and Helvetica, they might get more people in, I don't know. But those things are deadly, and a secretary did them because she can now.

During my first days at *Ray Gun,* they rented a computer for me and it came with five fonts, and one of them was Helvetica and one was Chicago, and it's where I first learned that fonts named after cities are usually a little scary. New York was on there, and I forget, I think that's four. But Helvetica was in there, and so I think it's fine. I don't have a real strong feeling for or against Helvetica. I've always tried to stay away from it. I think it's too easy of a fallback.

GH — I want to ask about your thoughts on what's next. I know you get asked this all the time, but there have been trends in the past 15 years and this cyclical thing between the more subjective approach like your early work, then it comes back to clean and simple, grid-based design. What are your thoughts on that?

DC — Well, that's the magic question I'm always asked. When I started doing magazines, I never used a grid, and for the most part I still don't, largely because I never learned to use one or learned what one was. By the time I did, I didn't see any good reason for it. I don't know that I've ever used a grid to this day. But that wasn't the question. Yeah, I did some early work in *Surfer* magazine in 1980 and it was all hand-done. I'm sure many other designers have done things by hand through the years. For me, it was really refreshing that after the initial *Ray Gun* crazy, looser, subjective stuff, the natural cycle would be for things to get cleaner, and it did as predicted. Then they got looser again, which was less predicted actually. Because it's harder to do it well, and the people who couldn't understand *Ray Gun* and that whole era could do the clean stuff reasonably okay when it came back. So there was this big relief: "Okay, good, it's clean again. I can do my stuff."

Now it gets to where it started with hand lettering coming back in a big way, and now it's kept going to illustration being so prevalent and so important and websites from CNN to ESPN. They just permeate it, and it's gone everywhere. That's been really exciting, I think, to see that kind of human element, almost as a backlash, maybe. I doubt that was the reason, but that has resulted somehow. I remember getting an email from a student in England 10 years ago saying, "We're revolting against Photoshop and we're going to go back to doing things by hand." I kind of brushed it off as one student. But it actually turned out to be pretty true, and so I was elated to see this hand drawn thing come back. Now it's been totally taken over by the advertising world, which basically means it's dead.

And then you started much earlier seeing all the hand fonts were being done on the computer, which kills it completely. I mean all the *E*s are identical, like, "Hello, there's another way to do that." But it's branched out to illustration, which is really nice, and that's why there's so much great stuff right now. But that still doesn't answer the question of what's next, and that's a tricky one. It's hard to believe we're going to go back to clean and simple grids and Helvetica. I just don't see that happening. Maybe it heads back in that direction, but it has now crossed over a line or something and it can never completely go back. Yeah, I wish I knew. I've been happy that the obvious thing hasn't shown itself. It's given me a little longer shelf life, because there hasn't been the obvious next big thing yet, basically.

I think a big reason for that is the web. As the web went big, it took a lot of designers with it, and unfortunately that look was already set by a lot of technicians and program writers. Designers spend a lot of time to make the Internet and websites look better, and they've done a great job with that. But it also took away a lot of the energy from print. It just dispersed it, in a way. There's a ton of good magazines out there right now, for instance, but there are very few that will blow you away or that you can't wait to see what they're doing next.

The level has risen to where there are probably hundreds of solid B/B+ magazines, professionally done, good photography, slick, nice, cool cover, but in terms of the one or two where you just go, "Where did that come from?" They may be out there, but I haven't seen it or heard it being talked about. I think some of that is because the energy's been spread out, and everybody's doing their own websites or doing videos or adding music to their own stuff. That's a great thing, but the result has kept one big, new, obvious movement from coming in.

I don't doubt for a minute that it will come in, and it's probably some kid in some little bedroom on his computer that's doing it as we speak, but I haven't seen it yet. But I like the direction now, and I have to think that somehow that's going to continue and maybe morph into more things that are a reaction to the mechanism or the technology. The very thing that's allowing everybody's parents and grandparents to do design is maybe what's driving the few really good designers to go somewhere else, and that's what will be exciting and what will be interesting—not that everybody can make okay design with Helvetica. It's like "Well, do we want that? Is that a good thing?" You know you can judge a book by its cover—that's another topic—but if the designer has done their job, you should be able to know that a book is worth reading. Same thing with CD covers: You should be able to say, "I need to listen to that. There's something about the way that cover's designed."

GH — How old are your children? Do they use computers?
DC — I have a seven-year-old daughter, Luci, and my son Luke is eight. They're starting to use computers, but more for video games and stuff. They send me emails, but I'm very suspicious that their mom actually helps write them.

GH — They haven't been experimenting with design?
DC — Not too much, but they have to appreciate that any art they do goes up somewhere in Daddy's house, office, car, website, book. I try to encourage that end of it.

[Randomly, in the conference room where we filmed David's interview, there were various words set in Helvetica taped to the walls. Apparently they were from a brainstorming session from another group of designers.]

GH — What are all these words doing here? They're in Helvetica.
DC — I have no idea. But this is exactly what I was talking about. I mean, that doesn't say "caffeinated." It's like, hello?

GH — Why not?
DC — It's just sitting there. There's nothing caffeinated about it. There's nothing "extramarital" about that. There's no "sunshine" here. That's not a fun "sand lot." Where's the "explosion"? This could be the first date. There's nothing "funny" here. No "magic." I don't want that "Christmas." There's no "wind." This might be close—these "Greyhound" buses are kind of boring. And how often do you travel on Greyhound?

GH — Let's look at some of your work. Where do you want to start?
DC — Here's a page in *Ray Gun*, an example of when everything was still being done by hand. I had this publicity photo of a singer and I

didn't really care for it, so I had taped off where I wanted it cropped and I thought, "Well, that's kind of interesting." Then I played around with some acetate and finally ended up using that, the whole image, when I never intended to. Now, that's maybe not tied in heavily to the copy, but I think a big part of my work is being open to unexpected things and accidents in a sense. Because it's an accident doesn't make it good, but if you can be open to that, sometimes that's your best result.

Here's an article on snowboarding, talking about altitude, and I wanted the type to get higher. But the article was short and I didn't have enough type to do it, so I repeated the article twice and that allowed me to get the shape I wanted, and to me, that defined the title then: "Altitude and Attitude." So I've got the altitude, and the attitude probably comes in repeating the article twice to try to get a shape I wanted, and a lot of white space, because it's a snow article.

Here's a story on another singer, John Wesley Harding, and this was a contact sheet where I had X'ed the one I wanted enlarged, outlined it, started to give it to the photo lab, then realized that I liked the look of this X and the blue and brought it back and just blew that up to use as the opener. I think if I had started out saying, "Well, I want to use a blue X on this one," it never would have worked. Again, it's just being open to things you're sometimes not expecting.

GH — A lot of your work seems to be about showing the process.

DC — I think that came from starting out at magazines where there was no budget—literally no budget, no outside photographers, nothing. So I was forced to deal with things like a skater bringing in his handwritten article or maybe mailing it in with a couple of snapshots and nothing else. I was like, "I've got to fill six pages with this?" Then I began looking at the envelope that it came in. "Well, there's a cool stamp with a mark on it. Oh, look at the guy's hand lettering. Hmm, maybe we'll use that. What about this section of this photo? I could just blow this up." And it got much more interesting. I was kind of forced to work that way and to make things more interesting. That way of working has stuck with me. So I still—when I get something, I'm looking in the corners. I'm looking at the package it arrived in. I'm looking at any possible thing that might be used to help send the message or the emotion of the piece.

Here's another issue of *Ray Gun*, again, just experimenting. It's a pretty plain cover featuring the lead signer of Pavement. But at the end of the article inside the magazine, I jumped it back to the front cover. It says, "Continued on front cover." So rather than jump to the back of the magazine for the rest of the article, we jumped to the cover to continue it. This also doesn't seem to have really caught on very well. It was an interesting experiment, I thought.

Here's an article about America's most famous unknown writer. So I thought it was appropriate not to have a title or put his name on it. The article just starts and then it talks about how he's the most famous unknown writer in America. And then some pictures of weird stuff.

GH — Are these all your photos?

DC — Yeah, these are all of stuff I'd seen in my travels and just caught my eye. I take photos all the time, zillions of them. It's a huge part of the process. It really was sometimes just for fun. I mean, here's a band called Nick Normal, so I decided what could be more normal than just copying a page out of *Rolling Stone* magazine. An identical copy of a page out of *Rolling Stone* as the layout for this group calling themselves Normal. That'll get the Pentagram mafia upset. And here, for a band called Extra Large, I simply have a big circle, and the type is like in 3-point type—as small as it could possibly be—for this band calling itself Extra Large.

This is the one article in *Ray Gun* magazine that I'd say you could not read this first paragraph. And that's because when I listened to the tape of these guys in the interview, they're all talking at once, so you really couldn't make it out. And so I thought it made sense to just do the opening like that. You can't read it.

GH — What about the one that you set in Zapf Dingbats?

DC — That was an article on the singer Bryan Ferry, and it was supposed to be a new—well, it was a new writer that we had gotten from one of the bigger magazines, and we were all excited to finally get this writer. When I read the article, it was very much like so many of these others I had read, where the writer was given 10 minutes before the guy went onstage to do his whole interview. So what do we get? We get what the hotel room looks like. He looks for signs of drugs or alcohol and talks about what the guy's wearing, and then the interview's over. And it was like, "Oh, man, how disappointing and how boring."

I went through all my fonts—which would have been hundreds and hundreds at the time, and still is—and didn't find one that seemed to fit my disgust and boredom with this article, and I finally came to the bottom and there was Zapf Dingbats. So it was literally the last one. And I'm sure I came to it and kind of chuckled, and if I have an overriding philosophy it's probably, "Why not?" That kicked in and I was like, "Well, it's boring. It's not worth reading. Why not do it in Zapf Dingbats? It's a font." So it was all set in Dingbats; it is the actual font. You could highlight it and make it Helvetica or something and you'd be able to read it. But it really wouldn't be worthwhile; it's not very well written.

GH — What was their reaction? What did the writer say?

DC — You know, I never actually heard from the writer. But you've to keep it in the scope of things too. Thirty issues of a magazine, one page on one singer—particularly Bryan Ferry, who, for this audience, wasn't even of that much interest, probably—it's not that big a deal. That's how I looked at it. Then for the readers of this magazine it might have even made it a little hipper or cooler, for lack of better words. You know, because they did an article in Dingbats. I just thought it was funny and no big deal, and on to the next article. But it gets referenced a lot; it gets shown a lot. It's like, "No, it's one article. It's not that big a deal." It's kind of funny. I don't know where else you could do it. But I'm happy I did. No reason not to.

Sometimes we've been accused of being kind of disrespectful to the writers, and I really think it's just the opposite, because I have to read the article to know where to begin. I have no other starting point. I don't have a grid. I don't have a system. I don't have an already-big drop cap to start with. It's like I've got to read the article; I've got to listen to the music; I have to have somewhere to start. So I think my work is very respectful to the writing. If something's presented in a boring way, people aren't going to read it, and so it's very important that the designer brings something to it. But with *Ray Gun* it was interesting that in the early issues, some of the writers were very upset. But what was more interesting is that later, maybe a year or two down the line, these same writers would submit something again—they'd come around to realizing this was a good place to be seen.

There were a couple times when an article came in late. The issue was shipping, so the text was just literally flowed in and sent out the door. Nothing was done to it. Well, those same writers called and complained, saying, "What happened? You didn't like my article? You didn't do anything with it? It's too easy to read. What's going on?" So it had gone through this complete shift where it signaled that this is something worthwhile for you to read because we took some time in getting the layout together and put some effort into the opener and the photography. So the very writers who were so upset in the beginning were equally upset later when they got no special treatment. It came full circle.

GH — That's amazing.

DC — Again, it's about being open to things and not being so rigid and having that system and a grid. That's where the emotion and passion and the love goes out of the work, and that's where the viewer reaction to it goes out of the work as well, because it's too simple, and it's boring.

In my lectures to students, I have this saying that I think is really true, and you've probably heard some version of it: What is the definition of a good job? The best one I've heard is that if you could afford to, if money wasn't an issue, would you do that same work? And if you would, then you've got a great job. And if you wouldn't, then what the heck are you doing? In design, we're in a field that allows us to have fun, to be creative, to actually get paid, and set our own hours. You can look forward to going to work. You don't start out with the best job in the world, but if money were not an issue, would you be doing that same thing? If it's not design, that's fine. Find out what it is. Maybe it's washing cars, I don't know. But find that thing. I think I've found it.

GH — Do you see the influence of the things you designed repeated in magazines today?

DC — I think I almost see it more now, because early on anything that was jumbled up, people would say, "Look, they're ripping you off." Now I see it more in subtle ways that I think it would be impossible to trace back. But like a conservative magazine having two lines of copy touch on a title or subtitle or something. You could never do it, but I believe if you could do a graph of the progression, somehow back there would be *Ray Gun* or *Beach Culture* leading to the fact that this conservative magazine now feels comfortable having no space between two lines of type. So I see it more in little things like that.

GH — So in a way, does it feel like you "won"?

DC — If you say we won, it's like we were *trying* to win or something, and that was never the case. You're just, like, fascinated by the whole process, but the result is that everything did change. I had a professor one time tell me he saved all these early layouts of mine to give a lecture on how to confuse a reader. Then he said he forgotten about it for a few years and came back to this lecture and pulled out all these layouts. He was looking at them, and he couldn't figure out why he had saved them. They weren't confusing three years later. It's that kind of thing.

GH — Thanks for hanging out with us, David.

DC — It sounds like a fun film. Unless you turn it around and spear me.

GH — Yeah, you're dead meat. This film's actually called *David Carson Sucks*.

DC — Yeah, well that seems to come with the territory.

GH — In your section of the film, we're going to overlap all the images and scratch the film and invert the colors.

DC — Funny, people have done that for posters for my lectures, or they'll use Dingbats. Eh, I'll get over it.

—

Paula Scher (PS)/
November 29, 2006
New York

Paula Scher is one of graphic design's most acclaimed practitioners and a partner at Pentagram. In a career spanning more than 40 years, there's not much she hasn't designed. We spoke at Pentagram's New York offices.

—

Gary Hustwit — Let's start with how you got involved in design. Can you talk about the beginnings?

Paula Scher — You come into design at the point that you start out in history without knowing you're starting out in history. And very often you don't have a sense of what came before you and how it got there, and you certainly don't know what's going to come after. When I walked into design as a student at Tyler School of Art, what struck me was that there were sort of two separate cultures of design. One was the corporate culture, and the corporate culture was the visual language of big corporations. And at that time, they were pervasively Helvetica, and they looked alike. They looked a little fascistic to me. They were clean; they reminded me of cleaning up your room. It was about order in a very restrictive sense, and I was a child of the sixties and very rebellious, so I had to rebel against that.

What looked cool to me at that point were record album covers, Zig Zag rolling papers, sort of the accoutrements of dope life and counterculture, underground newspapers and magazines, and Push Pin Studios. And all of those things borrowed from Victorian, Art Deco, discarded styles of typography. A lot of them were coupled with other images or illustration; it was a very illustrative time, and that's what was influential to me.

But I also was morally opposed to Helvetica because I viewed the big corporations that were slathered in Helvetica as sponsors of the Vietnam War. So therefore, if you used Helvetica, it meant that you were in favor of the Vietnam War, so how could you use it? That was my own meaning that I attached to it. So there was a whole political rebellion against it. If I tell this to somebody who is starting out now, I just seem idiotic. But that was the way I perceived it at that time. One can become as inspired to design through rebellion as anything else, to overthrow what existed.

GH — Do you think that was a pervasive idea? Do you think a lot of people were feeling that at the time?

PS — A broad percentage of designers my age were inspired by Push Pin. We were inspired by the terrific record covers from the Beatles and the Rolling Stones and those big, luscious concept-album covers, the work of Hipgnosis in London. And all of that was anti-corporate. Later I remember in the mid-eighties, when Helvetica started its resurgence, it was a rebellion against everything I had done. It was sort of a complete rebellion against postmodernism to go back to that form of cleanness. And I think that each generation is a reaction to the previous one, but it never comes back quite the same way.

GH — It's interesting—like half the designers we've talked to for the film got into design through album covers. They were into music or they were in bands, and the album cover was what got them interested in graphic design.

PS — That's very common that music graphics, in general, motivated a lot of the young designers to become designers. It's because that's what you saw in your culture, and that was what was designed for you. You felt you were part of some form of movement that was changing the world; the lyrics had meaning.

I remember holding album covers in my hand and sitting with an album the first time I played it. I loved those big 12-inch surfaces, and turning them over and being able to read the liner notes and finding some insider joke, as if it was all designed in a shorthand that was just for me. I think how that's changed is that technology does that for young people today. I think they're responding to things like text messaging that are sort of semiotics and little symbols, and that becomes their graphic language, as opposed to these big, pictorial surfaces. It's all electronic, but it's still the same shorthand for their own culture. And that will have its own visual effect.

GH — Can you talk about Push Pin a little bit more?

PS — At the time I was in college, everybody's ambition was to work there, to do work that was as inspiring as their work. Because it seemed fresh and alive and witty and content laden and historically influenced and loaded with all kinds of information. Aside from the fact that Seymour Chwast and Milton Glaser could really draw, and they coupled this sort of broad, eclectic view of typography with this kind of drawing.

At the same time, their counterpart was Pentagram in London, who actually were of the same period and also did incredibly eclectic work. This was counter to corporate design, which was very ordered, very gridded, and used systems in an, I think, very anal matter. Largely because the goal of corporate design at that time was to create a kind of consistency and order at the expense of, say, individuality. Whereas the work of Push Pin seemed to be highly individualistic.

GH — Are there specific works of Seymour's or Milton's that, at the time, just blew you away?

> **PS** — Well, Seymour had done a couple of posters that I loved. And I'm married to Seymour now, so I know the work intimately. "Protest Against the Rising Tide of Conformity," which was actually an ad—which also seemed like an important political statement—but the poster was all typographic. It was made out of Victorian-influenced typography, some of which he redrew, coupled with illustration. I loved the way it looked— it looked very fresh at its time. And then, of course, "End Bad Breath," which was an antiwar poster, was just iconic. I wanted to make work that looked like that.
>
> Milton's work I loved too. It was much more illustrative to me than Seymour's. I always thought Seymour, in many ways, was a more powerful designer and Milton drew in a more classical sense. But I loved his "Big Nudes" poster and, of course, the Dylan poster that was inside the *Blonde on Blonde* album. And you love that poster without even knowing about that it was influenced by Marcel Duchamp. It became its own living, breathing organism, because it was so interconnected with that particular album, and you saw it at that particular moment in time and you can't erase that experience.

GH — We could fill a whole documentary, I'm sure, about your time at CBS and Atlantic Records and all the record industry work you did. Can you talk a little bit about that time?

> **PS** — I was extraordinarily lucky; I didn't know how lucky I was. I didn't know I was having an experience that would never be duplicated. I worked in the record industry from 1972 to 1982 at CBS Records, at a time when the music industry made more money every year. Each year was economically better than the last. It was a period of time when the record cover was everybody's favorite form to work on. Every illustrator and photographer would want to work with me. I could work with Richard Avedon or Irving Penn or just the greatest, most famous artists. There was no problem in getting anybody. All we really had to do in those days was please the recording artists. The recording artists had cover approval, and some of them were quite insane.
>
> Bob James had a jazz label called Tappan Zee Records, and I did all his covers. There were 16 in that series; they were all large objects blown out of scale. It's still one of the best projects I ever worked on, and largely because he was a wonderful client and really appreciated the work. I still enjoy looking at those covers today, even though those things are 20, 25 years old. I think my first record cover was for John Prine, an album called *Common Sense* that I designed in 1973 and I'm still proud to show it. To me it's amazing. I'm told that graphic design is ephemeral, that it disappears. But these things are still in the record stores.
>
> There are two covers I did for Charles Mingus, *Changes One* and *Changes Two*, that exist in the record stores in CDs and they're folded up from the 12-inch form. They were totally typographic. They were designed, actually, in Push Pin style, with very Victorian letterforms drawn with drop shadows that I spent hours doing, emulating my heroes. And they

exist in their original form, folded up and put into the CDs. I love that that still can happen, that they're still there. I guess those were also in 1973 or 1974, so it makes them 32 years old.

In 1979 I did a series of jazz albums on brown-paper-bag paper, called *The Best of Jazz*, and I took 15 or 20 of these record covers and designed a poster for them. The poster was put together with the typography from the cover at tangents to each other. We didn't have a Xerox machine or a stat cam. The way I designed it was by taking these album covers and cutting them up and putting the type together at these funny tangents. And they created this poster that was called *The Best of Jazz*, and it became sort of emblematic, I guess, of postmodernism and Constructivist revivalism. But it really wasn't Constructivist typography, it was actually American Wood type, which was Victorian. It was put together in the style of the Constructivists. So it was this crazy hybrid, but it became a very popular style and something I was connected to for a long time and then wanted to get rid of, because everybody assumed I was going to do that over and over again.

GH — It's great. All the angles and everything.
PS — What people don't realize is they came out that way because I didn't have a stat camera. We used to do things on the Luci (Lucigraph) machine in those days. I actually was cutting up these record covers, and that's how the things were positioned, off the record covers. There was no blowing them up or shrinking them down, because there was no technology to do that.

GH — Now, the record cover's gone from 12 inches to 5 inches to—
PS — To zero.

GH — Just downloading songs, and maybe you get a little JPEG of the front cover on your iPod or something.
PS — You know, it's funny. I actually love seeing the little stamp-sized record cover on my iPod. I can't tell what it looks like, really, but I like this iteration of it, in a funny way, more than CDs. I was so disappointed when record covers shrunk in size that I never mastered the design of a CD. And I walked away from the industry when that really began happening in the eighties. I really didn't have any interest in designing for it anymore. I think that you have to be young in the business to do that work well, and I thought, as far as CD packaging, the person who mastered that was Stefan Sagmeister, because he actually did more with the form. Mostly, CDs looked to me like shrunken record covers that wanted to be bigger.

When I worked at CBS Records, when we made ads for the records, there was something called a mini, which was taking a record cover and making the type bigger in proportion to the image so it would show up in newspaper ads. That's what CDs look like to me—they look like minis. So I never really warmed up to them.

GH — And now they're gone.
PS — They're gone too.

GH — How aware were you of design before you got involved?

PS — When I went to Tyler School of Art in 1966, I did not know what graphic design was. I didn't even know what design was. I took something in my second year called "Basic Design," which was taught on the Basel system. I made white-on-white constructions, they were completely sloppy and had fingerprints all over them. We had to use rubber cement to glue them down, and I'd have these little "boogers." I can't think of the word to describe those little blobs of rubber cement that sort of congealed in the corners. And my teachers would sort of tut-tut at my terribly sloppy work. We moved a black square around a white page. Later, when I was beginning to learn typography, we were setting Helvetica flush left on a very rigid grid. And as I said, I found this very much like cleaning up my room. I felt like this was some conspiracy of my mother's to make me keep the house clean, that all of my messy-room adolescent rebellion was coming back at me in this form of Helvetica, and I had to overthrow it.

GH — So how did you do that typographically?

PS — When I was at Tyler, I wanted to be an illustrator, because the typographic experience seemed so rigid to me. I had a Polish illustration teacher named Stanisław Zagorski. He actually was a hero at school. He had designed Cream's silver album, and of course, we all wanted to be designing record covers. I never knew quite what to do with the typography on my designs. We would make book covers or record covers for a school project, and I would go to the local art store and I'd buy Helvetica as press type and I'd rub it down in the corner of the album the way I thought it was supposed to be, kind of flush left. And of course, it would never line up properly; the type would crackle and break and really be terrible.

Zagorski told me to let go of the press type. And I said, "All I can get is this Helvetica," or maybe they had Venus or Univers. I think those were the faces you could buy at Sam Flax at that point. Zagorski said, "Illustrate the type." And it hadn't dawned on me that typography could have personality the way drawing did. I mean, I began to look at forms in a different way when he gave me that simple piece of advice. I realized that type had spirit and could convey mood, that it could be your own medium. It was its own palette, a broad palette to express all kinds of things, and this was a huge breakthrough.

At first, I learned to do this by copying typography I saw in other forms. Usually on things like old Victorian tin cans or labels or things I would find in antique stores. As a matter of fact, I did an album cover that's actually now a classic. It was called *Friday Night in San Francisco* with Al Di Meola, John McLaughlin, and Paco de Lucía. It was designed off of a Buckingham pipe tobacco can. That's where the typography came from, and it was not untypical of ways I began to work. I began to make associations first through period, because it was the easiest thing to connect with a subject matter. So if I was doing an album by Bartok and the music came from the twenties, then I would couple it. I would find a face, a Cassandre design like Bifur. I would use that and make the period connection between the music and the typography.

Now, the modernists wouldn't do that because it would be too obvious. And to a degree, I agree with them now. On the other hand, I always thought they were very ungiving. I thought all that withholding was sort of just . . . withholding. Why be so mean? And I don't know if "less is more." Less is more unless it's less. And sometimes more is more. And I think that "Less is more" is a conditional statement, though I do love a certain form of minimalism right now.

GH — Really?

PS — But not with Helvetica. I became an Akzidenz-Grotesk person. That was the face before Helvetica.

GH — Do you think people are aware of the type in their environment? What are your thoughts on the average person's awareness of fonts?

PS — Recently, what's kind of amazing is that people even know what the word "font" means. I mean, technology forced them to do that— they buy their computers and they pick out different typefaces. They know that script-y faces are kind of sweet things that you want to make invitations out of, and they know that if they want to write a grown-up proposal, they need to use grown-up letterforms and it can't look goofy. I'm amazed at how much better young people in general, and society as a whole, recognize and understand typography than they did, say, 30 years ago. I don't know if people know quite why they recognize something, but they know they recognize it. They know there's a distinctive difference.

And I found with the signage work I've done on buildings that people know what the logos mean when they see them on the building, and they recognize it. Somebody who was here who was not a designer found out I had designed the signage for Jazz at Lincoln Center, and they said, "Oh, the horn." They were talking about the type that came out of a Z, and the idea that they read that as a horn, which was part of the intent of the design, is terrific. That's somebody absolutely getting it. That's visual literacy. Almost everybody I know, when I say I designed the Citibank logo, can draw the arc on a piece of paper. People remember that stuff and that's fantastic, because that's what's supposed to happen.

GH — What about technology and your design process? How has it changed? Do you still do a lot by drawing?

PS — I do paintings that are very, very laborious. I paint these very complicated maps. They're done with a little teeny brush, and there might be a painting of the United States with every single city on it, and the painting is 9 feet high by 12 feet wide. It's completely slathered with information. It's the opposite of what I do all day, because during the daytime my work is instantaneous, because everything can be done on the computer in a minute. So the painting helps me balance my need to use my hands and feel like I have a craft.

But for me, technology has always changed since I started working. When I learned how to set type, first it was hand set, then it was Linotype, then it was PhotoTypositor, then we worked on a Luci machine, then we got a stat camera, then we did things on the Xerox machine, then there was a computer, then the computer software changed, then it changed again, then the screens got bigger, then the thing got smaller— you could carry it around, it was portable. Now I'm doing my email on my little Treo wherever I am and that's the way life is. But I'm not that interested in it, to be quite honest. It's something that I expect to change, and that's been the condition of my working life. I expect it's going to change next year and the year after that and the year after that. And I'm going to find out what it does and I'll use it. And if I don't want to use it, it's because I don't like what it does.

When the computer was first being adopted by early users, the software was bad. The typefaces were cut terribly; the leading was horrible. You couldn't put type on its side, because the computer couldn't do that yet with software. When it got better, I used it. When it was impractical, I didn't use it. I don't think that technology for the sake of technology is necessarily right. Some things are broken and aren't fixed yet. But when they're fixed, I like them. I'm the kind of person who would never buy an experimental car. I would buy a car that works really well and drive it and be very happy to have it and not have much of a conversation about it and get on with it. But I'd get where I needed to go.

GH — And that's how you feel about it?
    PS — That's pretty much how I feel about computers. I like them like I like my car. They're fine. I don't like the way they smell. They don't smell like art supplies; they smell like cars. I've always been quasi-known as a technophobe, but in fact, I think all these things can be designed and controlled. I don't have any qualms about that at all.

GH — As long as it works.
    PS — As long as it works.
    —

Objectified:
The Complete Interviews

18 Interviews/200 Pages/
105,860 Words

Bill Moggridge (BM)/ April 8, 2008 Palo Alto

British industrial designer Bill Moggridge arrived in Palo Alto in the late 1970s, and quickly became one of the most influential figures in the nascent Silicon Valley design world. He designed the first laptop computer, the GRiD Compass, in 1979, and in 1983 was a cofounder of the design consultancy IDEO.

I saw Bill speak at the Industrial Designers Society of America national conference in 2007 when I was doing preliminary research for *Objectified*, and after further discussions with Bill and IDEO's CEO Tim Brown, I headed to California and spent a week filming at IDEO. Bill was the first interview we did for the film.

A few years after our conversation, Bill left IDEO and headed to New York City to become the director of the Smithsonian Cooper-Hewitt National Design Museum, a post he held until his death in September 2012.
—

Gary Hustwit — What started you on the path of being a designer?

> **Bill Moggridge** — It's a pretty boring story. I actually started wanting to be a designer when I was about 14, I think. My brother was a lot older than me, an architect. I think I hankered after something that was like what he was doing but different, and I was told about industrial design, and that was it; I just followed the path and did stuff in high school and went to college and then started designing.

GH — When you were a kid, were you just taking things apart and putting them together, or were you doing art?

> **BM** — Well, my mom was an artist. I think that had a lot of influence. So there were always sort of artistic things around the house. Painting and drawing was a normal thing. And I was always interested in problem solving, so rather than just doing pure fine art, I was interested in a sort of balance between the artistic side and the problem-solving or the technical side. I always think that designers are slightly schizophrenic. You have to not be quite sure whether you're a problem solver or somebody who's doing something beautiful, and perhaps if you're flip-flopping between one and the other, it's the right way to be.

GH — What was your design education like?

BM — I attended a school called the Central School of Art and Design, which is now part of London University. But at that time, it was more of a vocational program that didn't award a degree; rather, it awarded a certificate, so it was very much training. I went to school and learned all the things in the shop and all the different kinds of drawings and did lots and lots of design projects. It was very much a learning-by-doing process that suited me particularly well because I had a pretty good high school education in a more general educational sense. I was already able to write pretty well and do math and physics and things like that. I just really wanted to learn the special things that a designer needs, and there was a good course for that.

GH — Did you enter the professional world right after school?

BM — Well, my idea was that I should get some experience when I graduated, both in consulting and in a company. When I was still at college, I won a couple of traveling scholarships. Toward the end of my program, I used a scholarship to go to America and arrived in New York with no money, maybe a hundred dollars in my pocket, and tried to find a job. I didn't actually get a job in New York. Eventually, I ended up in Pennsylvania, working for a hospital equipment company. That was my first year and a half of experience. One of the things that happened to me there was that they asked me to do the corporate identity as well as the industrial design. I did such a bad job of it that I decided to go back to school and learn about graphic design and came back to England and studied typography in an advanced program, and at the same time started consulting. I got just enough work, in parallel with study, that I was able to start my own business.

GH — What were some of the projects you worked on early in your career?

BM — My first major client was Hoover, the American company, but in Europe they had a much more diverse range of products. At that time, they were manufacturing washing machines and dishwashers and steam irons and toasters and even stoves. There were a lot of consumer items that I had an opportunity to work on. They had an internal design department as well as using a little consultant help, and when they had too much to do, they asked me to help them. It turned out they had a lot of too-much-to-do, so I was able to expand the amount of work I did and get some other people on board to help me.

GH — Could you describe the role of an industrial designer at that time?

BM — I think the big change that happened was that, after graduating, I had expected to design products for the local market in Britain, but there was a kind of miniature version of globalization that happened in the late sixties and early seventies. It was the time when Britain joined the Common Market in Europe, and instead of having a couple of competitors in every industry within the country, they got spread out all over Europe, so the best manufacturers and R&D units for most of the things that I was expected to design turned out to be in a different country. Most went to Germany or Italy or France or Scandinavia. It turned out

Britain was actually very strong with the service industries like banking and insurance and design, so most of my clients, in my early years as a consultant, were offshore. I found myself traveling around Europe in order to do work for European companies rather than finding work in Britain. With my first team in the seventies, we designed telephones and computers in about 10 different countries in Europe.

The other half of the big change that happened was the nature of the complexity of solutions that designers were expected to solve. So the expectation of my contribution, as I was educated, was designers would be solving problems in terms of the way things are manufactured or made—figuring out how to solve a business problem, to create something that had a unique appearance and appeal to people and was very usable in terms of its simple human factors. And it's really pretty possible for a single designer to handle all of that. You know this great tradition we have of the Renaissance designer who's perhaps an architect and able to design buildings and things and do everything, chairs and lights, the sort of very versatile designer who has the authorship of the complete solution? That was very possible.

But then what happened was that, as technologies started to become more advanced, when they started to design computers or anything that contained electronic or digital technology, the scope suddenly got enormously more complex. And the idea of a single person being able to design something—which included the user interface and the software, and the behavior of the digital elements as well as the physical—it really became enough to hurt anybody's head, to the point that they probably wouldn't be able to do it. So then you have this need for a team to start working on a solution rather than an individual designer. Then when we connected everything together, you know, as we've done now with the Internet, there's another layer of complexity that gets added to that picture.

So you go from physical object, then you add digital technology, then you add connectivity. In that kind of complexity you have to have a team in order to problem-solve. So if you take the things that are still simple today, like the chair or the lights or the piece of pottery or the glass, then certainly a designer can do the whole thing. But if you take new technology, like a telephone or a computer or some element of something which has got all those things mixed together, then, really, you have to have a team approach.

GH — But does it seem like whoever ends up designing the physical form of a product—whether it's simple or complex—ends up getting most of the credit for the authorship of it?

BM — Well, I think in the generic computing world—because the software and behaviors are rather separated from the design of the physical object—the form of the object is still thought of as separate. So the people who design a new laptop are going to be industrial designers, and they're thinking about the form and the portability and the way the human factors work in a very simple way, like, where is the display? And then the people who design the operating systems or the applications that run on the thing are another set of people. But if you take a more integrated kind of product which has all those elements together, like, for example, a cell phone or possibly a piece of medical equipment or anything which has got physical form and digital technology integrally connected, then the same designers have to do all of it because the two elements are intimately related and not separated in the way that they are with a generic computer.

GH — Who would you say are your design heroes?

    BM — I really admire Charles and Ray Eames. They're my heroes for the kind of mixture of media, doing film as well as design, but also for the incredible depth of sensitivity to materials. And the other one is Henry Dreyfuss. I admire him and his organization for the combination of human factors and design problem solving.

GH — I'm sure over the next couple of days when we're at IDEO, the term "human factors" is going to come up many times. I'd like to get your definition of what that means.

    BM — For me, human factors is about the science of understanding people. So if you take a designer's understanding of people, the most important thing is the subjective or qualitative aesthetic, things that people care about emotionally. But they're not necessarily very good at the scientific aspect of really understanding how people operate. So if you then take the science of understanding people, you have the human factors discipline.

You can think of those in increasing levels of complexity. There's the very simple element of the sizes of people—anthropometrics. That's at the lowest level of this hierarchy. Then if you think about the way people's bodies work—perhaps you're designing the feel of a keycap or the way a bicycle fits your body—then you have to understand the mechanics of the body, the physiology. And then if you add this technology to it, you know, with the digital chips and software, then you have to understand how the mind works to the extent that the man-machine interface is about humans' way of thinking and the way that they think in an abstract, digital world. So then cognitive psychology becomes very important. And then connect everybody together, and perhaps we're more concerned now with sociology, you know, sort of how people relate to each other when they're in a connected set or community. Then if we think of people in a very holistic, global sense, there's an even higher level that has more to do with anthropology or perhaps even the world itself—sustainability.

So you can think of that as a sort of hierarchy where you start with the simplest, which is the sizes of people. The next step is physiology, how the body works. The next step is cognitive psychology, how we think about things. The next step is sociology, how we connect to each other. The final one is anthropology, you know, how communities or societies work, and then sustainability is the whole planet.

That was a bit more than you bargained for?

GH — Yeah, there are a million follow-ups to that. I definitely want to talk about sustainability, the issues surrounding the impact of what designers do. What would you say are the challenges facing designers now?

BM — In terms of challenges that are facing designers nowadays, I think there are two main categories, one of which is this complexity issue, which we've been talking about a bit. If you decide that you want to try and solve the messy, complicated problems, which include digital technology, the fact that everybody's connected together, that we have to design systems, that we have to design connectivity, that we have to design HCI, Human Computer Interface—those are complexities which can mean that it's too much for any individual to do, and you have to start, then, having collaborative teamwork and making different roles work in terms of solving those problems. However, that is limited by the context. I mean, you only need to worry about that if you're dealing in the messy-problem world, and there are still lots of opportunities for designers to operate in a simpler way where they just don't have to face those problems because they chose to design the simpler things. They keep their context relatively simple.

And then the other big thing that affects everything, both the simple and the complex, is more to do with the sustainability issue, you know, how the world is now being thought of in terms of what we do and what we design and the materiality. If I think of my admiration for Charles Eames, it was an admiration for his ability to identify the qualities of new materials which could be used to create new objects. But nobody worried about whether fiberglass was going to cause disease or going to be difficult to dispose of. I mean, life was a little bit simpler for him in that regard. He could just think about using the materials for their best design attributes.

But now we have to face this idea that what we do is not just the way we create some individual design. It's what happens first, before we start operating on the material—how does it get created, and is the material being made in a way that causes other forms of damage or other issues that might be of concern to society?—and also what happens afterwards when we finish our design, when people have used it. How do we design for what happens after? So this sort of cradle-to-cradle concept—what happens before we operate and after we operate—becomes something that, really, every designer needs to face. You know, there's a much bigger picture to deal with, and it's actually quite a challenge, I think, to come to terms with that.

GH — Since a lot of times there's a client involved, how much can the designer really affect what the manufacturing process ends up being? Does it feel like it's a little bit out of the designer's hands? In the designer-client relationship, how is that being played out?

BM — There is a sense of frustration very often when a designer has an idealistic view about wanting to do the right thing in terms of sustainability. So yeah, there is sort of a difficult challenge for designers, perhaps a frustration that they don't feel empowered to make a big difference because they're working in an organization or for an organization. For a consultant, there would be a client. For an employee, there'd be a company. There would be the rest of the organization, the bosses, the management. And if they feel that they can't influence the decisions that really matter in terms of sustainability, that can be very frustrating.

What we find is that there are some pretty simple things that you can do that at least improve the situation. One of them is asking two very simple questions: "Where did it come from? Where does it go?" And it's surprising how effective that is. You know, if you say in every meeting to the client or the management team, the decision makers, "Where does this material come from? Where will it go when it's finished?" then everyone's conscious of the need for sustainable design. Just that reminder seems to make everyone on the team take a little more notice, so they'll make a more careful choice of a material, or they'll think about design for disassembly or disposability, and so on. So I think just those very simple awareness questions can make a surprising amount of positive difference.

GH — Are there any examples of things that you've done, either you personally or through IDEO, that have made that type of change within the client's thinking or product? Are there examples having to do with products that people might be familiar with?

BM — Well, I think having a materials scientist on our staff helps us a lot to deal with that. There's things like packaging for some of the soap that we've designed. There's a lovely pink papier-mâché package with a little hole in the top so in the store you can see if you like the scent of the soap. But then buried in the papier-mâché are seeds of flowers, so when you finish using the package, you can just put it in the earth, and it'll turn into flowers, which is kind of a nice idea. So instead of having something that you need to throw away and put in a landfill, you can put it in the earth, and it creates something nice.

We did a concept project on shopping bags, which is actually rather relevant here in San Francisco because there's some political stuff about banning plastic bags, which is happening locally. And one of the issues, of course, is what is the true story about them? Is plastic using more energy than paper, and where does the paper come from, and where does the plastic come from, or what kind of plastic is it? So one of the concepts we did in the plastic bag project had material that's biodegradable so that you can actually have a plastic bag, but then you can be sure that it'll be biodegradable when you're finished using it. I was in Denmark this summer, and I found a milk carton that's made of plastic which is 40 percent chalk with a bit of plastic material as a binder, and you put the milk inside it, and then you put a bit of air in the little handle section so that it makes it possible to pour. So there's very little material, and it's made of this Ecolean plastic, which then biodegrades into chalk and CO_2, so it's a very clean material. So you can have a plastic bag and still have something that's very good for the environment.

Another approach was to take a ripstop nylon material, which is very fine and very strong so that you can reuse it all the time, and you can put the shopping bag into a tiny little container that you can fit easily onto your key ring and then use it many times, so you don't have a question of throwing it away each time. And the third one was using a recycled material—car tires. So you can take something that's already had a first purpose and repurpose it to make a shopping bag. So I think there's lots of examples like that.

GH — I would like to talk very quickly about designers today, young designers or the currently working designers who you think are doing important work, many of whom we'll probably talk to in the course of this film, but do you want to throw out some names?

BM — Yeah, I think fuseproject is doing some pretty wonderful stuff. There's a philosophical connection there, I feel, in terms of thinking of a designer's narrative and the need for making something which is connected in terms of those levels of complexity that we talked about. I think they're doing really nice work. I presume you'll be talking to Yves Béhar. He has a relatively small practice, which is really focused on industrial design, so it's a form-giving practice in the traditional industrial design sense, but I think he also has a very intelligent sort of broader scope in terms of his point of view about connecting things together. There's an interesting young guy named Branko Lukic who's just recently formed a company called NONOBJECT. He has worked at frog and also at IDEO, and he's doing some very interesting stuff. I think you might enjoy looking at that website.

GH — Do you have any client nightmare stories? I mean, you don't have to name the client, but has the process ever gone wrong in some crazy, horrible way?

BM — Well, I've always had a struggle about which projects to turn down. Why would we not want to do something? As a consultant, you spend a bit of energy trying to make the phone go. I mean, mostly you're just trying to do good work, but then you also try and win some awards or put your name out there or get recognized in the press as doing that good work, and then you hope the phone will go and people will come and say, "Can you design this for us?" And so if that's working, then the question arises occasionally: "Do I want to do this sort of work?"

One of the examples, the most obvious I think, is military. At IDEO, we have a very simple principle about not doing anything that's going to harm people. And we use David Kelley, our chairman, as the arbiter if something is uncertain. "So is it really going to harm people or not?" "But it's for the military." "But it might not harm people." And the philosophy there is, okay, well, if you're in doubt about whether the project is something we should be doing or not, just ask David Kelley, and he'll always say no. So it's a simple way of dealing with that.

I think we also have a philosophical thing about the use of materials. Now, I've always been interested in honesty of materials, and so there's a question of, do you want to do something that's clearly forced? So I remember struggling a little bit with a project where I was asked to design a log-effect gas fireplace and thinking, "Do I really want to do this?" You know, you can get nice ceramic logs. People do like to look at something and not have to worry about the smoke, but I couldn't quite bring myself to do that.

GH — You might have designed a hell of a log. What do you think the role of the consumer is in what designers do?

BM — I think doing things with the people you're designing for is a hugely wonderful concept, and there's several different versions of that around now. One of the human-factors techniques that has evolved is to try and participate with the people who are going to use the final design—participatory design. An example where that's worked particularly well is a surgical product for sinus surgery, which you'll probably see when you're down at IDEO, but the idea was to actually have the surgeons who specialize in this particular form of surgery on the design team the whole time. And the nice thing was that they felt so motivated by this that they actually felt that they owned the design themselves, rather than the design team or the consultant. That's particularly useful in a world where the designers themselves have little experience of what it's like to use that thing. I mean, none of us are specialists in nasal surgery, so it helps a lot.

I think if you look at the tradition of many industries, particularly in Silicon Valley, they were started by people who thought of themselves as being the customer. Hewlett-Packard was developed by guys in labs who designed stuff for guys in labs. It was only when they tried to design things for the general consumer that they had a little bit of trouble, and they had to kind of evolve their techniques and learn to understand people in a different way. So if there's a natural participation, then you perhaps don't need that focus on working with the people who are going to finally use it. But if there's an opportunity to work with the end user, whether it's a kid or a surgeon, then that's actually very powerful and helps the design team enormously to sort of realize what might be right for those people.

But I think there's a whole different, new form of consumerism in design, which is based on our new media, on the electronic revolution, the fact that you can actually now find something like Wikipedia where the consumers are the ones who are creating the content and editing it. The big difference, perhaps, between old media, mainstream media, and the new media is that, in mainstream media, you had experts who were responsible for making the choices, creating the content, editing it, deciding whether it's right, and now we find there's this possibility, with this newly connected world, that we can have all of us do it in a sort of democratized way, which is very exciting.

GH — Which leads to my next question: what's the future of design in terms of, well, everything you were just talking about? How do designers change the world?

BM — Well, you know, if designers can change the world by making the world more sustainable, that's obviously a benefit. I think there is a general awareness and movement everywhere to make that happen. Certainly Northern Europe, Scandinavia, and Germany are way ahead of America and Britain in that regard, but now there is a strong movement here as well to make that happen. So I think we will see it happen in a big way. The new generation will come along and make the change.

Another thing is, the connected world means that societies are connected in a much more intimate way, so the idea of designing something for a different community in a different part of the world is now becoming very much more prevalent. So that's a sort of social-benefit type of design: designing something for water for people living in Africa, as with our aqueduct product. That's becoming much more normal, I think. Before, there was a sense that Africa was so far away you couldn't do anything about it, but now there seems to be a sense that, because of the connected world, we can make a big difference there. And so that's one of the super benefits of connectivity.

In terms of the sort of democratization of design, I always welcome that, because I think every time you find a new technology getting inexpensive enough that lots of people can do it, then you find the overall standard rises. A good example is desktop publishing. You know, if you think about what was happening before the eighties with desktop publishing, most of the informal graphic design was done by people with just handwritten notes, and they really didn't have any awareness of typography. But then desktop publishing came along, and suddenly everybody was able to do the notice for their picnic or their baseball game. And they looked horrible for the first years. They had too many typefaces and too much type on the page, and it looked dreadful, but it didn't take that long for them to shake out and find that they could actually make it at least not too bad. At the same time, they got to admire when it was really good, so they recognized the quality of excellent design because they got far enough in terms of awareness to succeed at least at a level which was acceptable, but they could also admire the excellent.

I think that's happening now with video, that you find that everyone's able to make movies now, and so the whole standard is going to rise, and people will sort of appreciate more good movie making. And it's obviously happening in terms of connectivity with the democratization of informational things as well. Software, open-source code being written by multiple people, the open-architecture kind of ideas.

GH — But how does that relate to product design and object design?
BM — Well, I think it's a very interesting question, you know. When would I have an open architecture to design my product? And when would it feel okay to me that I would actually have other people do it for free in the way that we see in some software? When would it seem that I need the control in order to achieve the quality? And I don't think we have that answered yet, but that's a question we're going to have to face in the future.

GH — So, I want to talk about the objects that you've brought out. What are they and why do you like them?
BM — Well, one of my favorite objects is this spoon that was designed by Ettore Sottsass for Alessi. A spoon in itself is a dramatically interesting problem. I think a spoon is a wonderful design object because it's so multisensory. It's very intimate, so you pick it up, and you hold it in your hand, and you have this need for a balance, or you'd like it to be perfectly balanced when you hold it on an edge. That's what makes it feel

comfortable in your hand. But you also have to be able to pick it up off a surface very easily, so it wants to present itself, and then, as you hold it, you're holding it in a sort of delicate way, and then you're bringing it up to your lips. Then when you touch it with your lips, you have this incredible tactility of the actual feel of it, as you slide it into your mouth as well. Because it's bringing some object that you're going to consume, it also engages the taste and also the smell. So you have the look of the thing; you have the tactility; you have the smell and the taste, so four out of the five senses are really engaged with the design. You could even say it has a little sound as well. What does it actually sound like when you put it down on a glass surface or a wooden surface? So this may be a five-sense design.

The thing that Ettore did so beautifully is to make this sort of three-dimensionality of it, which has got these very complicated curves in terms of the sections. And rather than being a flat piece of metal, which most of them are, where it's stamped and pressed, this has got a three-dimensional quality that makes it very sensuous in terms of its form. So everything flows. You know, it's a shape that's complicated as you turn it around in space, and you find that every element of the form is completely three-dimensional. It's sort of organic in its quality and very sensuous.

It's interesting that it's designed by Sottsass, I think, because he's known best for his Memphis Group contribution, and he's always been a fantastic joker. I mean, all his jokes are great. But this is not at all jokey, and in a way, if you think of the pre-Memphis time when he was doing all that work for Olivetti, those were pretty serious designs. But this is just in between the two. It's got both. It's got a sort of sensuality, but it's not taking the piss out of anything. It's really just reveling in the beauty of the thing itself.

GH — I'm also interested in the kind of emotional qualities that people invest in certain objects.

BM — Yeah, actually, I have a lot of emotion invested in spoons because my major project in my middle year at college was a thesis on cutlery, and I got to be involved in cutlery and flatware at that time. So I have some Georgian spoons as well that I have a long-term relationship with, and they are really great, very refined silver spoons, but they don't quite have the sort of final result that the Sottsass one does.

So, when it comes to more technical objects, another thing I chose is the iPod touch. This is, of course, a very recent product, but it's very magical, I think. To take the idea of an interface for something like an iPod and combine it with so many of the aspects of a PDA that we value most and to find that it really works so well for us, along with the fact that this has got this sort of wonderful materiality—you know, it's actually glass, and it's got this lovely beveled edge and then the shiny back of stainless steel—makes it a very jewel-like object in itself.

And then if you start to play with it, rather than having the clumsiness of a mouse or something, which is very computer oriented, we've got the sensing availability of being able to move things with the finger and expand them. So the sense of touch and lightness and that being integrated into the input—what a contrast to a regular cell phone where you've got all those little buttons and a sort of pseudo-joystick which you have to struggle with, and here we've got this fluent ability to play with things.

And look at the actual content. Take, for example, this map. Here I am with an iPod, and I can see where I am right now on the Google satellite map. Pretty amazing. And also all these other applications, which of course we can go back to and get email, et cetera. In fact, the only things I can't do with this are the phone functions. Otherwise, the iPod touch is just as proficient as the iPhone, but because it's not got that phone stuff in it, it's incredibly thin and delicate, and it has that sort of superior elegance to it. So it's a wonderful combination of beautiful graphic design, in terms of the screens; behavioral design, in terms of what you can do with touch; and physical design, all working together. What an achievement.

GH — How do you think a well-designed object like that changes the people who use it? How have our lives been impacted by products over the past decades?

BM — Well, you can certainly see the huge difference with the invasion of the telephone. Think about the original telephones being tethered to the wall. You'd come up and grab something and spin a handle and then speak to an operator, sort of human to human, but the object itself was a very simple piece of almost furniture. And then the telephone started to reside on the desk and be dialable, and so you were going person to machine and then machine to person. Then we had, suddenly, this untethered quality, the release of the telephone, where we could carry it around with us all the time, and you could then communicate in a completely different way. Whereas people used to make appointments with each other, now they don't. They just say, "Okay, I'll see you maybe. Call me and tell me where you are seven-o'clock-ish." So that the whole social interaction for a Friday night out is a much more fluent kind of thing based on that cell phone.

And the same sort of thing is really true of the computer. If you think about the big mainframe moving to the desktop, the desktop was still very chained. You had to sit in front of something and use this keyboard, move this mouse, look at this screen. The laptop released you to be able to carry it with you, and wirelessness allowed you to communicate anywhere, and then PDAs miniaturized that so that you get this quality we find here. So again, it enables new behavior, the ability to do things in many different places. Those technologies definitely changed the way people do things. Work, for example. So many people work from home or don't have regular office hours. You know, they can sort of lead much more fluid lives.

GH — Do you want to talk about your truck outside?

BM — Yeah. When it comes to the sort of more overt, expressive design, similar, I suppose, to postmodernism, I think of Americana having a wonderful flowering in the fifties. This was a time when most of the world was recovering from World War II, and the rest of the Western world wasn't really very developed at all; it was just concentrating on having enough food. Whereas in America you had this very rich society. We had this flamboyant period where so many exciting, extraordinary things were happening. You think of all the cars with their fins or racing stripes. This kind of thing was very exciting visually and entertaining, although sort of a challenge, perhaps, to modernism's idea of form fits function. Well, it's more than that. It's more form fits fun.

I think this truck that I managed to find is a very interesting example of that because it's a 1955 GMC Jimmy. It's the second series from '55. It actually has more glass in it than any other truck before or since, because in '54, they still had two windscreens, which were split down the center. Then in the first series in '55, they managed to get a straight-across windscreen. But in the second series, they managed to bend the glass around, and they were so proud of that that on this particular truck they bent the glass around the windscreen, but also at the back, so you have an almost complete surrounding of glass. On the front, you'll see the form is amazingly overstyled for a truck, even for a car perhaps. It has this huge sort of chrome grin on the front, which makes it look very flamboyant. And I've managed to find one that's almost all original, and it's not been repainted. It's got the same inline-six engine, and it's really just the truck it was when it was made in 1955.

GH — When you're driving the truck, how do you feel? What do you think you're expressing?

BM — I don't know what I'm expressing, but it certainly can be pretty entertaining. Of course, there is no power steering or anything like that. Particularly before I had some work done on safety issues, it was quite an adventure, because one didn't know whether one could stop at any moment in time. I just, you know, I suppose there is that sort of tradition about America that you feel like you belong to when you're in that truck.

GH — Can we talk a little bit about the concept of people expressing themselves through the objects that they surround themselves with or buy? I wonder if you have any thoughts about that.

BM — Well, I think it's important for us designers of everyday objects to be modest about the effect they have. You know, if you think about self-expression, it happens so much more powerfully with things like fashion or even environment. The way people deal with expressing themselves through their furniture or the decoration of their rooms or what they wear is a much stronger emotional expression than what they have as objects. And certainly people do have an emotional attachment to things they love, like my spoon or my iPod touch, but at the same time, I don't think it's so overpowering as some of the other more fashionable areas of design.

GH — But things are maybe more permanent. Clothes tend to wear out, and you just said you love your spoon and your iPod touch.

BM — Yeah, you have a close relationship with things. I mean, I like the concept of wearing in rather than wearing out. If you're going to have a more permanent relationship with an object which is supposed to last a good amount of time, you'd like to get more fond of it as it gets worn. For example, on the laptop that I designed, the effect of the dings that it has—it's actually a magnesium enclosure, but it has paint on the outside, and when it gets dinged, you know, if it's dropped, and a bit of paint chips off, and you see some of the magnesium showing through, somehow it feels better because of that, because it's sort of got the quality that allows it to wear in rather than wearing out. Whereas other things, if they haven't got that quality, then they just look damaged when they have a little bit of wear. So I think you'd like to create something where the emotional relationship is more satisfying over time. You may not worry about it or think about it very clearly, and people don't have to have a strong love relationship with their things, but they should grow sort of a little more fond of them perhaps over time.

GH — Excellent. Speaking of the laptop you designed, can you talk about that?

BM — One of the most exciting things that happened to me soon after I'd arrived in California, in Silicon Valley, to start our second office was I had the opportunity to work for a new start-up company called GRiD Systems. This was started by John Ellenby, who had been working at PARC, but he was originally from Scotland, where he'd worked with Ferranti, and he was determined that it would be possible to make a computer that you could actually carry with you conveniently. And he was inspired to do this by a meeting he had with somebody in Washington who was talking about the fact that his job was really to be out in the field and he needed the computing power to be with him. So he said, "What I really want is a laptop. What I really want is a computer I can put in my briefcase and take with me." And so John set out to design that device.

I got to know him incidentally and introduced him to the work we'd done in our London office, and he asked me to be the designer for it. I did the industrial design and worked with an industrial engineer whom I'd hired to do the kind of mechanical engineering of the enclosure. And the thing that was pretty amazing about it was that it was so dramatically innovative. This was in 1979 that we started work and 1980 when we did most of the design work. At that time, the computers were, at the best, luggable. They were things the size of suitcases or sewing machines and with tiny little screens. Here we were trying to do something that really was going to fit into half a briefcase. We signed a patent for the design, which had 43 items of innovation in it, of which I only signed one, which was the physical geometry.

We called the computer the GRiD Compass or the Compass Computer. It had a processor inside, a power supply. It was connected by a modem to a server—which was a little bit like current servers we have now—called GRiD Central, and you could carry it with you. We designed it to be thin enough to fit in half your briefcase, so you could put papers in as well, and then there was a leg at the back that flipped down to put it at the right angle for using the ergonomically preferred angle of 11 degrees, then a hinge, which would allow it to open so that you could look at the display and type and use it directly.

One of the things we did was a test about how robust it had to be in order to be shipped back for service, because one of the things they wanted to do was make sure that it could be serviced in 24 hours using Federal Express. We sent an impact recorder through Federal Express to Washington and back, and we found that at one point where it was being sorted in the central St. Louis sorting center for Federal Express, it saw 60 g's, which is the equivalent of dropping the thing from about 35 inches onto a floor covered in linoleum. So we designed it with that as the spec. That was what drove us to use a magnesium housing, so it's a metal housing in order to resist that impact.

One of the interesting design challenges was the hinge. We wanted to devise a hinge that would allow it to rotate so the display could come up but also would form a simple geometry when it was opened, which looked appropriate, and also not let things into the electronics behind, so to avoid something like a pencil falling into it. What could happen is, if you put a pencil in the back, it could roll down and drop inside. I designed a scoop that would then self-eject the pencil when you closed it. There's a little trick.

And of course, we didn't have enough battery power to run this thing. It's 80 watts, so the battery you needed in order to run it was sort of a belt-operated, heavy thing, so you did have to plug it in as you went. And one of the things that we did was to create a little folding device for a cord, and we made a little leather thing with some Velcro on it, so you could just fold the cord conveniently and drop it into the case next to you.

Now, the history of laptops is a little interesting in terms of its complexity because Alan Kay at Xerox PARC came up with the concept of a laptop a long time before this, in the seventies. But arguably, the first laptop that was actually ever produced was this one, if you define a laptop as having an electronic display, an input device, and the computing within it. So there are other devices that are sort of flat and one which had a telephone modem attached to it, but I think that this is definitely the first laptop, and that's probably proven by the utility patent, because the part of the patent that I signed was for the geometry, the folding geometry, and it was that that allowed them to gain license income from the laptop manufacturers that followed like Toshiba and Sanyo. And so they got seven million dollars for the licensing for the geometry.

Maybe we should plug this one in? You might be interested to see the display itself. I just turned it on, and it has an electroluminescent display, so it's very bright; it still works after all these years. It was the first graphic display with pixels to be used in a device like this, rather than a character display, and it was made specially by Sharp in Japan. It's on an operating system, so they designed a suite of applications that all operated on the same system, which is very similar to what you have in a PC or a Mac now, but it didn't happen again for many years. And the GRiD OS was designed for that connectivity between applications, but also the connection to the server that backed up the information. Let me just see if I can get you something nicer on the display.

GH — What do you think when you look at its OS now?

BM — In a way, you know, the OS was the thing that made the company not so successful as it might have been because soon after, well, in parallel really with it being launched, the IBM PC came out, and that was something that was immediately popular in the industry and became the dominant product. So GRiD then had to modify their own OS to take the IBM operating system DOS, and it took them a little while to catch up with that.

But the big revelation for me was in late 1980 when I'd gotten the first working prototype. Maybe it was the beginning of '81; I can't remember, but around that time. I took the machine home, really thrilled about wanting to use it myself, and it was with great pride that I opened up the display and put it on its leg and thought how clever I was to have designed this latch and this hinge and all this stuff. Then I started to actually try and use it, and within a few moments, I found myself forgetting all about my physical design and realizing that everything that I was interested in was happening in my relationship with what was happening behind the screen. I felt like I was kind of being sucked down into the machine, and the interaction between me and the device was all to do with the digital software and very little to do with the physical design. Maybe five minutes of my day was physical design, and eight hours was the interactive software.

That made me realize that, if I was going to truly design the whole experience from the point of view of a user, I would really have to learn how to design this software stuff. And that made me search for a name for it, and we ended up calling it interaction design. In the mid-eighties, I actually found a very good person called Bill Verplank, who'd got a lot of experience with Xerox and designed the icons for the Star user interface, to join me in the San Francisco office, and he was a kind of guru for us in terms of being able to do this stuff. Then I got a team of people from all over the place to come and contribute. Originally, we thought we might call it "softface," meaning software interface, but then, talking to my friends, they said, "Well, it sounds a little bit like a Cabbage Patch doll, Bill." You know, "soft face." And then we came up with this idea of calling it interaction design, which seemed to stick and then grow, so that was sort of the origin of that. A mixture of Bill Verplank and myself.

GH — I wonder if you could talk about what people's initial reactions were to the GRiD Compass.

BM — Yeah, when the GRiD Compass was originally launched on the market at COMDEX in 1981, there was a tremendous interest in the industry of course. People crowded around the stand, because they had never seen anything like this, and they were very excited about it. And then the question was, who's going to buy it? Because it was so expensive. It was nearly nine thousand dollars at the time. Who would be able to afford that? Well, an executive. But of course, at that time, executives thought they had to have a big mahogany desk and a secretary to take all their dictation.

So it was only those few individuals who really were like John's original inspiration—the guy who was a high-level individual, needed to be out in the field, who would really be willing to learn how to type, learn how to do the interactions, and would be wanting to take it with him. And there were applications that emerged. Sales was very powerful because, you know, the sales force that had these devices with them could come in and modify an offer in real time and compute a new price or a new offer in front of their client, whereas the competition who didn't have this device would have to go back and come back the next day with new paperwork. So that kind of application emerged as something possible for it.

They also put them on Air Force One. They sent them up in the space shuttles for the astronauts to use and navigate when they were going behind the shadow of the earth and they couldn't see the signals from base. So it found its few applications, but it never became an everyday product just because of that price-performance issue compared with the kind of use that people expected for something they carried with them.

GH — And nowadays ...

> BM — Now laptops are everywhere, aren't they? They are. And actually, if you look at the big differences, I think, of course the display is the most important thing, and this was a huge step forward in that we had a rich, graphically capable display that was able to show images as well as type. But it was still tiny, and if you think of it by comparison with today's laptop, that's got this enormous display covering the whole surface, so you really feel you're looking at the same kind of screen as you could do on a desktop. And the input device, you know, there was no mouse attached to this, so something to steer and point with other than the cursor keys—that was obviously a next step, as well as all the technological stuff.

GH — How much does it weigh?

> BM — Eight and a half pounds.

GH — Really? Wow.

> BM — That was another story, actually. As part of devising the specs when we were first deciding what this should be, I did those things like finding the spec for the drop test by sending it through Federal Express, and we also wanted to figure out how much it could weigh, the maximum that would be acceptable. So what I did was I made some weights up that were small and heavy in one pound blocks, and I gave them to all the members of the company (there were seven people at the time) and said, "Okay, carry as many of these as you can, and tell me when it gets unbearable." And they said they really couldn't stand it above eight pounds, so we made that the spec for the weight.

GH — Do you want to talk about the wear on it? That was what you originally brought up about it, the idea of wearing in versus wearing out.

> BM — Okay. So first, the experience of taking it away: there's something rather satisfying about the fact that it's very robust, so you can slam it shut. You can grab the leg and slam it shut. It sounds more like a gun, in a way, than a computer, because of this magnesium housing. And you

can see, after years of using it, if you look closely at the design along the edges of the computer there, you'll see little marks where the paint has got chipped away, and you can see the magnesium through it. In a way, I think that's one of the characteristics of a design that you enjoy. If it actually looks sort of more sympathetic and perhaps better as it gets worn, wearing in rather than wearing out, perhaps it makes the heart grow fonder because you feel it's really more yours.

—

Tim Brown (TB)/ April 9, 2008 Palo Alto

Tim Brown is the CEO and president of IDEO. An industrial designer by training, Tim takes special interest in the convergence of technology and the arts, as well as the ways in which design can be used to promote the well-being of people living in emerging economies. His book on how design thinking transforms organizations, *Change by Design,* was released in September 2009.

—

Gary Hustwit — How did you get started in design?

Tim Brown — I'd always wanted to go to art school. I knew when I was quite young that I wanted to go to art school, but I didn't really know what design was, at least not product design. And my father was a photographer, so I had some experience and exposure to graphic design and photography through his work. They have a great system in England, where they send you off to art school to study everything for the first year; you are not allowed to go and decide what you want to study. So, I did that and found workshops and started building things and loved it and followed that to industrial design—at least what they call industrial design in England.

GH — So, you were building things as a kid?

TB — I think if you ask any product designer what was the most important toy of their childhood, it's going to be Legos—at least it was for me. I mean, I was building stuff with Legos. I remember when I was very little, we had big power cuts in England and I remember I built all sorts of lamps and torches for my mother so she could cook our dinner while we didn't have any power. So, I was kind of designing products; I was certainly younger than 10 at that point. I built airplanes and all of those kind of things. I spent my whole childhood building stuff.

GH — When you first started out as a professional designer out of school, what were the types of products you were you working on?

TB — While I was going through school, I got very interested in the role of electronic products. Obviously, this was pre-Internet, pre-a lot things we have today. It seemed to me the electronic products were redefining our lives. I got very interested in those when I left school and started working for Bill Moggridge. Actually, that's what I started doing—designing various electronic things like fax machines and laptops and telephones, that kind of stuff.

GH — So if you had to define what an industrial designer did then and what they do now, how are they different?

TB — I certainly, at that point, saw industrial design as the process of giving form to function, if you will. Normally, the technical aspect of the product was already defined to a large degree, especially if it was electronic. So, my job was to create meaning and usability, as it were, for the object or the product. Allow the user to figure out how to operate whatever it may be, but also give it some form in order to make it appealing and attractive to people. It was a very simple idea, and I thought of my role as a designer to be a form-giver, when I left school. It has evolved a lot since then.

GH — Can you talk more about that evolution?

TB — Sure. Today, I see my role as a designer as to help define what it is we should be creating for people. So, not just giving form to the thing that has been created, but understanding what people need, how they operate in the world, and what kind of experiences they need to have in order to live the lives they want to live, and therefore, what products or services or experiences ought to be created to serve those needs.

Where I spend most of my time today is much further upstream in the process. I think we as designers spend more and more of our time there. So, now we have many more pieces of the puzzle that we have to think about. You know, there was a time when I didn't have to think about technology very much. I didn't have to think about a business model very much because they were already kind of figured out when I got to do my piece. Now, I do. Now, I have to think about what makes sense from the technological perspective as well as what meets people's needs and desires. Does it all make sense as a business for a company? If they are going to do something new that they have never done before, some innovation that we are helping to create, does it makes sense for them as a business? Is it going to be sustainable for them? We have to think about those things. We have to contribute to that part of the discussion as well as the piece that we are trained to do as designers.

GH — Can you give the cocktail-party definition of design thinking?

TB — My aspiration as a designer is be able to tackle as many different kinds of problems as I can. I mean, that's what fascinates me, and sometimes the output is not necessarily obvious in design. It's not obviously a product. So, what we have tried to do is to understand what we bring as designers to a problem that makes us relevant in terms of what the ultimate solution will be. We call that design thinking. It's the way that we were trained to problem-solve and so it has certain characteristics to it. It's obviously visual, because we are visual people. So, we look at a problem and we pull it apart visually and put it back together visually— we think that way. So, it has got a lot of synthesis involved in it. We take a lot of separate pieces and put them all together in some whole form, which is what visual thinking is all about. It's also very human-centered, it's about trying to solve something for a person or for lots of people. Again, that's what I was trying to do as an industrial designer, where you can apply that human-centered approach to any problem.

It's very much based on trying things out through prototyping, through building something, seeing if it works, trying it out, building it again and again and again for as many times as it takes until you actually get to the right or appropriate solution. It's also based on storytelling. The translation of ideas and concept into a kind of narrative that we all understand. I mean, we used to have to do that with products. We used to have to explain how our products worked or why they were that way. Storytelling is incredibly important when it comes to complex ideas—to navigate their way through an organization and then out into the world—so storytelling is a part of design thinking.

GH — Can you give an example of how you've applied that design thinking to your work or projects IDEO has done?

TB — Well, often when you're working in innovation—when you're trying to decide what it is that you're trying to make—you have a lot of ideas. They're all sort of complex and in some complex context, but you want to tell a story about them. So, for instance, a couple of years ago we were helping Intel think about what the future of ultra-mobile computing is going to be like. How are we going to live in this mobile world? We could and did create a whole series of future-oriented products, software, interfaces, devices. But on their own they didn't tell the story of what people's lives were going to be like. So instead, we made a movie about it. And we made a movie that told three different scenarios of three different sets of users and consumers interacting with this technology in different ways, to give a sense of how those products and services would sit in the world. That, in a sense, was the outcome of our piece of work—not really the products themselves, but the story. The products might actually never exist in the marketplace, they may never get built.

GH — Do those theoretical exercises happen often?

TB — We handle strategic design in two different ways. We do the kind of work where the output is the strategy, or the output is the vision of the future. We do quite a bit of that. We also do that as a precursor to then actually developing products or actually developing services and putting them in the marketplace. So the work we do has these two big phases, if you will. First, this strategic phase where one is trying to determine what one is going to potentially put out into the world. Often there are a lot of choices. Then we take one or two of those choices and do the next iteration, which is to develop those real products and services and get them out into the world. In the end, I think that's what drives us as designers, is to have a direct impact in the world. Now, you can do that through organizations by influencing them, but I think most of us as designers, certainly myself as a designer, I get the most satisfaction from actually making something that gets out there and affects somebody's life or, hopefully, many people's lives.

GH — Do you have any examples?

TB — Wow, I can think of lots of things. It's as varied as when we designed some of the early pieces of technology, like the mouse for the original Apple Macintosh. A lot of people have used that. It's affected a lot of people's lives. More recently, we designed a new banking service, a savings account for one of the big banks here in America, Bank of

America, and there are two and a half million people using that savings account today. That's affecting a lot of people's lives. We're working on some projects about farming and clean water in India and Africa. You know, when those things get out into the world, I think they're going to affect a lot of people's lives. So yeah, we try and measure what we do by the impact we have. It's hard to do; I mean, it's hard to really be objective about the size of the impact you have. Also, to be objective about what is positive impact and what is sometimes not so positive. That's one of the things we have to grapple with as product designers, I think.

GH — We were talking to Bill Moggridge last night, and he said the test was if it was going to hurt someone—in terms of designing something, whether to take on projects—and he said that for IDEO, David Kelley was the arbiter of whether it was good or bad.

TB — Yeah, we've chosen to make all of our lives easier by letting David decide. But in fact, we all kind of know. We very rarely have to ask those questions. I think there's another form of impact that is designed that we are having to grapple with today which has really shifted since I started working as a designer. That is the unintended consequences of what we do, around issues of sustainability, for instance. If one's really honest with oneself, if you look at it from purely the product perspective and if you only think of the product that you are designing to put out into the world, then in a relatively short time most of what you design ends up in a landfill somewhere. I'm pretty sure most of the products that I've designed in my career, most instances of the million things that are being produced, are probably in landfills today. And that isn't something I was conscious of when I started working as a designer. It didn't even really occur to me because it didn't really occur to us as a society, I think, to consider the implications of what we did in that way. At least we didn't worry about it too much. It was like, "Okay, yes, things get thrown away. We deal with it."

Now, to be a designer, you have to take that into consideration, and you have to think about what you do in a much more systemic way. That's one of the big shifts, in my opinion, in design. It's just a lot more complex than it was, because we have to think about these complex systems in which our products exist. We have to think about the upstream piece of that, which is, how do things get made, and where do those materials come from, and how do they all get assembled together to make something as efficiently and sustainably as possible? How do you make choices which say, "Actually, we're not going to use those materials because they're kind of bad for us," or "We're not going to use that process to make something because it uses way too much energy"? You've got to think about that now in a way that we didn't think about it before.

Downstream, too, how things get used, where they get used, where they end up when you're finished using them. Can they be disassembled easily so that the materials can be reused or reintegrated back into the supply chain? Can you just design them so that they are used for a long period of time? It's about the effective use of the energy and materials that we put into something so that, as a society, we get more effective use out of it. Should things be disposable, or should they not be disposable? Should you be using virgin materials, or should you be using recycled materials? These choices aren't always easy ones, and they're ones that we have to think about now when we're designing products. Should we even be making a physical product at all? Should we be trying to make a service? Because a service is less tangible, it uses less energy. Even then there are considerations that aren't always obvious. For instance, every megabyte you download off a server somewhere uses energy. It's not free in terms of energy; that energy can add up to as much as a physical product might use. There's a big argument going on in the publishing industry today about whether magazines are better physical or digital. The amounts of energy that get used in each system are equivalent to each other. So, it's complicated.

GH — Could you give an example that expands on this idea of "where things end up"?

TB — It's this idea that design has unintended consequences. Every design problem starts with some kind of frame. It says, "Okay, what's the question that we're trying to answer?" And you can ask a question and then find out sometime later that maybe you weren't asking the right question. So, one example of that is several years ago, we set out along with a client to design a toothbrush or a set of toothbrushes that were better for kids, that were easier for kids to use, that allowed them to do a better job of cleaning their teeth because the client rightly wanted to improve dental health, and that's one of their missions. So, we designed the first-ever big, rubberized, toothbrushes—easy to grip. We had some really great observations out in the field and watched kids trying to use toothbrushes and realized that their hands couldn't grip something small. They needed something big. So we designed this nice, big, soft, squishy, fun looking, attractive toothbrush for kids to use. It was great. We were really pleased with it. And it went out into the market and was incredibly successful. To be honest, it became the standard approach to designing a toothbrush.

Two or three years later, one of our designers who had actually been involved in the project with us was on vacation down in Costa Rica, wandering along one of these endless beaches they have down there, and noticed one of those toothbrushes washing up onto the beach. And it had been in the ocean for quite a while, actually, because you can see when you see the picture of it, it's got lots of little barnacle-like pitting going on in the rubber. Yet it really looks like it's kind of new. You know, obviously it's a used toothbrush, but it looks like the one you might have just grabbed out of your bathroom cabinet. This thing had been in the ocean for years. And it just brings it home, that this is one out of probably millions of these toothbrushes that got manufactured, and they're all somewhere. They're in landfills, or they're washing around in the ocean, or wherever they are. That, for me, and I think for us, is a strong reminder that maybe we need to expand the frame of the question a little bit and say, "Okay, not only are we trying to improve kids' dental health, but we're also trying to do it in a way that is as sustainable as possible, that doesn't create waste that we can't deal with."

GH — What do all these objects mean to us, and how do we give them this meaning? And should we become so attached to these things? I'm interested in this kind of fetishism of the object; there are certain objects people just are obsessed with.

TB — I'm as much of an object fetishist as anybody, probably more so given that I'm a product designer. I still love objects even though I like tackling problems and I'm not only about objects anymore. You know, I love my iPod and I love my old 1960s Porsche. I love beautiful objects. I love the Eames chairs I have at home. I have all these objects because I enjoy them. I enjoy using them; I enjoy looking at them; I enjoy being around them. I think it's more than just the form of the object. I'm trained as a designer, and therefore I can enjoy the form of the object in a way that's a little different than perhaps most people in the world might enjoy it. But I don't think that's the main reason why we adore our objects, to be honest. I think we adore objects because they somehow become part of our behavior. They become part of our behavior out of function. They do a job we enjoy getting done all day; they do something we enjoy doing. Also at an emotional level, they do something in a way that somehow sits with us and suits us, something we feel good about. So, for some people those objects therefore are very unique. And you'll see people fall in love with objects, and they're completely one-offs, they're craft objects, objects that only they would see beauty in. That might be because of the way they behave and the way they think. Others fall in love with things that are mass-produced and yet can somehow relate to those things individually and personally.

Again, I think it's because these objects become part of our behavior, become part of the way we are, and the way we think. I believe that that's a basic human trait. We do that with our spaces that we live in. We do that with the objects and the tools and the stuff that we have, at least some of them. I think the issue we have today, of course, is that we have so many products around us that none of us can elevate all of them to that same level of thoughtfulness or consideration or emotional attachment. It's getting harder and harder for objects to do that because we're kind of bombarded with them. These products have to be pretty special, I think. So, more and more I think people are turning to products which have got some other emotional attachment to them or they do something that has an emotional attachment. I believe, for instance, the reason people love their iPods—some people love it because of the object. Most, I think, love it because of music and the way it delivers music to them—that whole thing is attractive to them. In fact, my daughters have iPods and are busy disguising them and putting stuff all over them because the actual object is not what they're interested in. It's the music that they're interested in, and actually creating kind of personal versions of those objects. So, it does vary across individuals. I do think it's this emotional and functional component of objects that we get attached to.

GH — But has the business side of it changed from manufacturing objects to almost kind of manufacturing needs? Do you see that taking place around you?

TB — Well, there's a competing set of objectives you could argue that business and industry have, compared to what we have as consumers. Companies need to distinguish themselves and differentiate themselves and attract our attention in order for us to go and buy the things that they make. In order to do that, they have to serve our needs in the best way they can, which ultimately is good for us. But, it also means businesses are looking pretty hard to try and figure out what our needs might be, and sometimes they do a good job of that. Other times, they don't do such a good job of it. Sometimes, they literally manufacture a myth about what our needs are, and kind of sell it to us through advertising. Other times, they really get under the surface of us and our society and provide things that we had no idea that we needed, but once they arrive we can't help ourselves from wanting them.

The cell phone is a great example of that. I mean, nobody knew what needs the cell phone was ultimately going to satisfy. But once it appeared, we just wanted it more and more and more and more. Now, you go to every country in the world today and cell phones are playing a really important role. So, I think smart companies, companies that use design well, actually get under our skin and figure out what needs they should be satisfying, even if that means moving quite a long way from the things that they're doing today. I think they're the companies that use design best.

I would say in order to do that, we've had to bring new skills to the design process. When I started as a designer, I thought, "Okay, I'm the designer; I tackle this problem." Maybe I'm working with some other designers and we're synthesizing all the various pieces of the problem and deciding what the response should actually be, what the product should be. Now, at IDEO, a design team is made up of quite a complex, interdisciplinary group of people who've come from many different backgrounds, some of whom are professionals at understanding people's needs. These are people who've got backgrounds in psychology or anthropology or linguistics or ethnographic research—all kinds of different human science fields. And they work with us on the design teams; they don't go off and do the research and bring the research back. They take us designers out into the field, so that we can really look at people and understand needs, not just on a superficial level, but really try to dig down and understand them in many different ways—physically, but also emotionally, cognitively, all the different ways that we all behave in the world.

GH — Give me an idea of the types of people you're talking about?
TB — I stopped counting at about 50 different disciplines at IDEO, but yeah, we've got most forms of technical folks—software engineers, mechanical engineers, electrical engineers, manufacturing people. We've got most forms of designers—industrial designers, graphic designers, architects, interaction designers. We have various forms of human scientists. We even have people who come from a business background, although normally they have some other kind of practical background as well, as an engineer or an architect or a designer. We have food scientists; we have filmmakers; we have writers; we have

this really eclectic group of people who work together in relatively small teams. We don't put 50 people on a team. These are small teams where we can bring this really eclectic group of perspectives, all using design thinking, to tackle the problem.

GH — Who are some designers working today that you really admire?
TB — There's a collection of designers who I have a lot of respect for, and there's also a collection of design thinkers who I think are very influential in the world. People who wouldn't even think of themselves as designers. I see them both as being important. So, on a design side, absolutely Naoto Fukasawa in Japan—I've had the chance to work together with him for many years. He influenced my design thinking a lot, and I think I influenced him a little bit too. He's got a level of depth of understanding about our relationship with products which is, I think, second to none. I've also got lots of respect for those working in Europe today who are taking a more, shall I say, humorous, skeptical look at the world of products. Humor is an important part of design, and asking questions in kind of skeptical ways through products is a great, great way to force us to think about what we do as designers, and I think it's a tremendously important piece of what goes on. You see more of that in Europe than you do in America.

On a design thinking side, for instance, working in India today, there are people that are running an incredibly exciting health care system. There's a hospital in the south of India that's called the Aravind Eye Care System. It was originally set up by this wonderful man, Dr. Venkataswamy. He recently died, but he built the biggest eye care operation in the world today. It serves over a million patients a year. It handles 250,000 cataract operations a year, and it is an incredible design. The way he has designed the service has made it possible to do this and serve over 60 percent of his patients for free, and yet it is still self-funded. It's an incredibly clever use of smart technology, space, services—everything is designed to be really efficient yet still really effective. He, in my opinion, and actually his family that now runs over 20 of these clinics, they're all great design thinkers. It's the kind of design that's going to come back and affect things we do in the West.

GH — What would you say are some of your favorite design objects?
TB — So, this is a product that I actually found in England last year that I absolutely love. I always love chopsticks, and I think chopsticks are a great expression of both the functional and emotional sides of design, and I have lots of chopsticks that come from Japan. But I was at a great little restaurant chain in England last summer called Yo Sushi, and they had these; they're chopsticks for kids. There are two pieces of wood, sort of like ice cream sticks, and you put them together and it creates a little spring, and it's perfect. And it's perfect as a product in two ways. One, functionally it is incredibly simple, and incredibly inexpensive; they give these away. It's exactly what kids need to use chopsticks when they haven't got the dexterity to use regular ones. But also, visually, it's lovely. It's soft; it's simple; it tells you what it does with no need for instructions. It is really obvious how to put it together and use it. For me, it is a great piece of product design, and it creates a great experience.

It's kind of invisible design at some point, and I think that's what a lot of good product design is. It's not showy; it's not about the big expensive luxury products; it's about things that do a great job and deliver a great experience for the end user.

Here's another product which, when I first saw it as a design student, it made me realize what great industrial design was all about. This is the Valentine typewriter by Ettore Sottsass, designed back in the 1960s. He took a very mundane, ordinary object and thought about what should it be like if it's not about business anymore, but it's about, maybe, a reporter out in the field, or maybe just an ordinary person who needs to type some stuff and wants to have a typewriter around their home. It has this incredibly simple and elegant design and this absolutely outrageous red color. He took a product that is still serious, that worked very well, but he made it human in a completely surprising way. It's got a lovely case that goes around it, so you can carry it around easily. I still think this is a great piece of product design, even if we're not using typewriters today, and I keep it in my office just as a reminder that great design can be pretty simple. It doesn't always have to be a complicated idea.

GH — Fantastic. Is there anything else you'd like to talk about?

TB — I do think this challenge as designers today—to operate more globally, where we're trying to work on problems that are not just for ourselves; they aren't even for societies or cultures that we are necessarily familiar with—means a couple of things. One, we have an absolute imperative to get out into the world and really try to understand it the best we can. We have to get out of our studios. We have to get out into the world and really spend time in it and spend time in people's homes and people's businesses and in their lives.

I think the other thing is, the best designers in my opinion have always done a good job of framing the question, of asking the right questions that the design project follows from. I think, as designers, we are being asked to frame much more complex questions, much more systematic questions, and that is something we're not always trained really well to do, and we're having to learn how to do it. I think that's going to be the challenge for designers as new designers come into the field, as kids go through school. It's really learning how to ask the right questions as well as learning how to actually design once the question has been asked.

—

David Kelley (DK)/ April 10, 2008 Palo Alto

David Kelley is a cofounder of IDEO, and has a long history in the field of industrial design. David serves as chair of IDEO and is the Donald W. Whittier Professor at Stanford University, where he has taught for more than 25 years. In 2013 he published the book *Creative Confidence: Unleashing the Creative Potential Within Us All.*

—

Gary Hustwit — How the heck did you get involved in this stuff?

David Kelley — So, I'm a kid from the Midwestern United States, right? And so the notion to be a doctor, lawyer, or venture capitalist never came up. You know, my parents and relatives were farmers before, and so the highest aspiration I could think of was to be an engineer. My father became an engineer, and so I went to engineering school, but I was really bad, I mean *really* bad. I tell my students now that I failed classes and got Cs and Ds. They think that's hilarious, that their professor didn't do well in school, but they don't actually believe me.

So, I was kind of a bad engineer out in the world doing these things and thinking that I was going to have a job to make money and then on the weekends I would do the things that I really enjoyed. And then I ran into a guy who explained design to me; I didn't really know what it was. I realized that's what I'd been doing since I was a kid, you know, tearing things apart and rebuilding them or welding bicycles together to make a tandem, or my mother would give me a bicycle for Christmas, and by the end of the day I'd have it stripped and was repainting it. Well, normal people don't do that, she pointed out.

I found this program at Stanford, which was about making you an expert at the process of design, and so I ended up studying at Stanford, and it was the first time I actually excelled at anything, so it felt really cathartic. You know how that is, when you're kind of bottom of the class and then all of a sudden, wow, you find your fit in life. That's really what I try to help people with now, to find their fit. I was just lucky that this design stuff is where I really fit well.

GH — What was the role of an industrial designer when you started out?

DK — Well, when I first started the company, the role of industrial designer was primarily about the aesthetics or cleverness around function. It was always a minor piece—it was as if the company was in charge of the major piece and we were hired guns to complete some aspect. We were experts in a narrow field, let's say. One way I look at it: In the early days, it was about how good we were with our hands. You know, drawing, building, presenting new images for the client to look at.

GH — You came right out of Stanford and started your own company?

DK — So, I went to the Stanford program, and I really fell in love with this design stuff, and it became my religion, and I wanted to teach it. I wanted everybody to be lucky enough to hear about this stuff. So I thought I'd get a PhD, because I was at the university, and I spent a year taking the coursework and stuff, and then it became pretty clear that I wasn't much of a reader or a writer, and so I wasn't going to do a PhD. But right then, out of school, one year after I graduated with my master's degree, I decided that I really wanted to work with my friends, and I wanted to make a difference in the world. And so, in 1978, I started the company with a partner who stayed for a short while, and the company has just grown from that. Those were the humble beginnings 30 years ago.

GH — In what ways is your role different now from back in those humble beginnings?

DK — Years ago, designers were thought of as commercial artists or people who could help you spruce up your design or your product at the end—you know, make it look pretty, make it look better. In some ways that was a lot of fun, because we were doing things that people saw. So, you'd go into the store and see the thing that you've done, and the first thing that you see is the overall appearance of it, and that was important. My background being engineering, I was working with all kinds of designers, and I was sometimes doing the engineering part of the design as well. We got to do some functionality, but it was usually peripheral stuff compared to the main meal of the thing—whether it was the electronics or the mechanics, we were doing some small part of it.

As time went on it became clear that the companies were happy for us to do more and more of the actual design of the overall product as well as the help strategize what the product should be, because it would just free them up to do more products. I mean, if they were going to come out with two products next year, and they could come out with three if we took a big piece of the work, that made them more profitable. So, it became more and more clear that as clients started to trust us more, we could take on a bigger and bigger role as a part of that. I would say that the most interesting thing that happened all these years ago, though, was that clients figured out that we had a different way of thinking, so we were liable to come up with different ideas than they would. I think of it as: they do the analytical thinking, and we do this innovative or design thinking, where we're more focused on user-centered ideas, stuff that will resonate with the people that are going to actually use the product. We come in from the point of view of like, "What do people value? What are their needs?" and it just results in different products.

So, our company will look at it from this way and see if we can't come up with something different, which leads to a different kind of innovation than the client would normally come up with. That's good if they're trying to come up with many different products.

GH — Can you give me the kind of cocktail-party definition of design thinking? What is design thinking?

DK — If you think about defining design thinking, it's of course a methodology for being. I look at it as a methodology for getting comfortable and confident in your innovation ability, whether it's an individual or a company. Look at it this way: people don't learn to play the piano by just walking up to it and all of a sudden playing it, but people think you either are innovative or you're not. As if it's a kind of God-given right. So we don't have a lot of methodology around somebody who synthesizes. We have a lot of methodology around people who analyze, but not who synthesize. Design thinking is about synthesis. Design thinking is a way to systematically be innovative, routinely innovate.

But the main thing it does is, once you buy into having a methodology, which we call design thinking, then you can improve it. You have these buckets of steps, a kind of step-by-step process, and those buckets are full of your ideas on how to do that step in the methodology. So, before we got hip to this, we would just do the creative process, and then we had no way of evaluating what happened. But if I have a framework to hang my methodology on—design thinking methodology—then every time I do a project and I find a new way to do a prototype, or I find a new way to interview people, or I find a new way to test something, I have a framework I can hang that new idea on, and the next time I do it I get better and better and better. So design thinking is a methodology for helping you improve your creative, innovative acumen.

GH — What are some past IDEO projects that still resonate with you?

DK — If you think back to the early days, we were in Silicon Valley, so we were doing mostly technology-based things, but the really exciting part was they were new to the world. When you were working on a laptop, there were no other laptops in the world. So, it's clever to make the keyboard cover the display, or the display cover the keyboard. We invented the technology that's in Apple's mouse. There weren't any—you know, mice just weren't a big deal then. Xerox PARC invented the concept, but they weren't on the market. So all those things—you know, a joystick, or a new way to make a hinge for a display monitor so you can move it around. All those things were new to the world, and they were going to be adopted fast by the world. You'd go into a store, and all of a sudden people were buying the stuff it seemed like you'd just designed yesterday, especially stuff like the Apple mouse, which really took off as a "change people's lives" product.

A lot of things come to mind that were just kind of personal. I designed a camera, or I designed a toothpaste tube, and it impacted my mom. The feeling that you were doing something that made a difference in the world was cool. Today we do much bigger things; something we did for Kaiser has improved the way nurses deal with patients. Or there's this Bank of America thing we did, Keep the Change, where it helps people save, and the bank matches their savings. I really like projects that can have a big impact. When I was younger in my career, I just liked things that were cool. If it was cool and it was out there, that was great. But looking back, what motivated me were things that made an impact, where a lot of people ended up using them.

GH — What would you say are the enemies of good design?

DK — I think that the enemies of good design are really people who jump on the first thing that's on their mind. The enemies of design are the clichéd answers that come into people's minds when you give them a problem and they jump to a quick answer and then they just implement that. I think real innovation comes from that little bit of perspiration, a little bit of digging deeper and deeper. We do these things—you know how some people make lists? Designers make what I call "mind maps," where they keep going further and further; something leads to something else, which leads somewhere else. As you're branching out, you're getting to new ground where your mind has never taken you before, and that's where interesting design happens. If you keep everything close to the vest and somebody says, "Design a new toothbrush," and you just say, "Okay, I'll put toothpaste in the handle," and then just implement that, that's the enemy of design.

Design is iterative, over and over, refining and refining. I mean, I could spend my whole life designing anything. I'll get a hair dryer, and once you've designed a hair dryer, and you've completed it, and people are using it, there are always little things wrong with it. So, you could fix those things, and you could keep designing, and when you got that one done and you showed it, there are still going to be things you'd change. It's got to be the same as making a film—once it's done there'd be a few things you'd like to change, and when you showed it again, there'd be a few more things to change. It keeps going in that way. The problem is that clients don't like that notion. You know, I would send a little note that would say, "Geez, this hair dryer is really nice, but if I had more time, it would be a little better." Clients don't want to send that note out to the public.

GH — What about the more external, outside enemies of design?

DK — I think the outside enemies of design are people, customers, who think it's their fault that things don't work. What really needs to happen is that people need to demand that things work for them. So, when you sit and you can't make your GPS work in your car, there should be a riot, because they're so poorly designed. Instead, the person sits there and thinks, "Oh, I'm not very smart. I can't make this GPS thing work." I can't make them work. This is my field, and I can't make them work! So, I think that complacency is kind of the enemy of design.

It's really interesting that in this country, in the United States, people are not as critical of design compared to places like Europe and Asia, Japan in particular. Anywhere in Europe, people demand that design perform for them and that it's special in their lives, these objects that they buy. We are more laissez-faire, you know, like plastic wood grain tables are perfectly okay with us even though they're fake. The enemy is this complacency, that you don't demand a lot out of these things you own. It builds into the sustainability issue, right? I mean, if you design something that's precious that you really love, you're never going to get rid of that; that's never going to be recycled. Whereas if it's done without care, then in a short period of time that's going to be thrown away, and it makes a landfill. My father's briefcase, made out of a beautiful piece of leather, gets better with use, and I've inherited it, and I'll pass it on. I'm not making a landfill with that. It's a really interesting thing. Sometimes I give my students the task to design something that gets better with use. There are very few things, but things like this briefcase get better with use.

GH — Let's talk more about the future. What are the next challenges and the next phases of industrial design?

DK — So, presently design is expanding into being design thinking and design strategy and all that kind of stuff. I really think the next step has to do with this globalization aspect around taking the whole world into account when you make something. A lot of times we think we're designing this for the people in our town or designing this for ourselves. And I think that's the axis that we're moving along, that we're designing this stuff for the whole world. How does it fit in the world? It's happening that way because we're going to design it here, but it's going to be made in China, and it's going to be shipped to Europe for sale. The empathy that we have to have for the entire chain of where something's going to go is going to change what things are. We're going to have to learn about their cultures; we can't get away with making stuff that's offensive in another culture because we don't know about that culture.

It's kind of sad in some ways because I used to love to go to Italy and find things that I'd never seen here before, or go to Japan and go to the Tokyu Hands store and find things I'd never seen. I don't think that's going to happen for very much longer. Designers are going to have to be more aware of the life cycle of the product and where it's going to go and who's going to use it. It's similar to what we're doing now, which is this human-centered design, but we're going to have to be citizens of the world instead of isolated. In Silicon Valley it's easy to be really isolated, because even your babysitter has a PhD in electrical engineering—that's not true everywhere.

GH — Why do you think Europeans are more sensitive or appreciative of design than Americans?

DK — I think Europeans are more into design because of their schooling. If I talk to my colleagues here who came from Europe, when they were in grade school, they learned about painters and the names of architects and those kind of things. We didn't get that in school here. At least in the fifties when I was in grade school, we didn't get who painted what and who sculpted what—that just wasn't in our curriculum. We got who invented what. We learned that Eli Whitney invented the cotton gin and Alexander Graham Bell invented the telephone; in fact, we believe everything was invented in the USA. We have an American name associated with stuff that wasn't even invented here. But we think that, so we have this kind of innovation and invention bias. People like Thomas Edison, they were the heroes, and so we were taught all about them. It wasn't macho to think about the artistic side of things in life, so we didn't get that. The Europeans got all that in school. I'm not sure that's right, but I really believe they've cared for a long time, for their entire lives they've been interested in aesthetics; Americans don't get it ever. Now, if you become a designer, you figure it out—even though you can't explain to your mother what you do, you understand it.

GH — Could you talk about sustainability issues, both in America and other countries?

DK — I'm actually not an expert on this, but the sustainability issue is taking off in a way I hadn't expected. I mean, I never thought that people were going to take shorter showers and eat food that tastes like cardboard and put a brick in their toilets willingly. I feel like we've got to actually solve the problem through technology or design where it's okay to take a long shower because we figured the solution out—we recycle the water and all that kind of stuff. So, I still have hope for that. I think the world's been scared enough into making progress. You see the dollars being spent in venture capital on all this stuff; it all looks like it's going in the right direction.

I think that the developing world is more of a challenge for that because they're—it's not like they're trying to have low salaries, they're trying to have salaries the same as in the USA, right? I mean, it's not like that's their competitive advantage. When you're struggling to make a living and feed your family, in Maslow's hierarchy of needs, sustainability is lower on the list. So, I'm nervous of course about how that will play out in the developing world. Here, I'm actually quite positive that our clients want to hear our story, our sustainability story about the things we're doing and what our ideas are for how we can make this product more responsible—like what's the cost trade-off of that, and what's the long-term benefit of that? That's really quite new. It's been an academic discussion before, and now it's an actual business discussion, which I'm very positive about.

GH — Wild card question: is there anything we haven't touched on that you think should be talked about in a film about industrial design?

DK — This stuff, as I've said, is kind of my religion. We could talk about how IDEO helps their client companies with design thinking and how to do it. I'm actually very interested in the individual. I think that there's a lot of kids in K–12, even college students, who walk around thinking of themselves as not creative or, on a more positive note, that they're purely analytical. You know, doctors and lawyers, a lot of them do. So, when I engage them and they say, "Oh, I can't draw," or, "I'm not good at this, the creative stuff. I'm good at the analytical things," I don't think that's true. I think people are inherently creative, and that's trained out of them in K–12. But they inherently have it. I see it in my daughter; I see it in other people. So, one of the dreams I have is working with people to get them confident in their own creative ability.

That's what's really cool about design thinking. If you can teach them this framework, this methodology, and have them do a few things, whether it's plan a dinner party or something at work where they need a creative solution, once they do it a couple of times, they get so excited. Once they flip from thinking of themselves as only analytical and learn that they can be both analytical and creative in the same body walking around, it's so gratifying. I get so many letters from people and students saying, "It changed my life. I was thinking that I wasn't going to be that kind of person, and then I did it." I'm starting to sound like Tony Robbins or something, but I really think that if people think of themselves as creative, they'll do different things than they were going to do before. They'll do things that are more out of the box, that will result in innovations in the world or in their personal lives that are really quite amazing, and all they have to do is have confidence in it.

So, by taking them through a few exercises and allowing them to see that they're capable, with a little help, of coming up with ideas beyond what they thought they could do, it's so gratifying. It seems like it's really good for these people and good for their companies and good for them as students. So, I'm really excited about design thinking as it applies to the individual.

—

Jane Fulton Suri (JFS)/ April 10, 2008 Palo Alto

Jane Fulton Suri is a partner and Chief Creative Officer at IDEO. To increase the accessibility of human-centered tools, Jane created *Thoughtless Acts?: Observations on Intuitive Design*, a book of snapshots that depict the subtle and creative ways in which people interact with the world.

—

Gary Hustwit — How did you get into design?

Jane Fulton Suri — I came from a background in psychology, which was all about my excitement about what makes people do what they do. If we could understand that better, could we design a better world, better stuff? So, it was from psychology that I went into architecture, which was the design profession I was interested at that time, and that's when I found Bill Moggridge. Since then, I've been connected with IDEO and pushing this idea forward, and it's been 20 years. The idea is about understanding people and the fact that people are at the center of design. It's a human activity, and most of the work we are doing is for people.

GH — Can you talk about the approaches of designers 30, 40 years ago compared to now?

JFS — When I came into design, they would give you give a brief and the designers would work at their drawing boards. They would have some magazines to look at to inspire them. One of the things I did when I came was drag people out from the studio into the environment, and put designers into the position of looking at people and going through the steps that other people were going through as a source of inspiration. I'd come from a background that was called "human factors," and I think much of that was Dreyfuss anthropometrics, which basically told designers, "You've done it wrong," or "You can't do that," and my ambition was always to make people and what people do a source of inspiration as opposed to a limiting factor for design. I think that's really changed now. I don't think there are many designers who wouldn't, given a brief, first thing want to go understand what the world is like and what people are doing. They wouldn't just sketch.

GH — In a project like that, what would be the first steps you would take?

JFS — This is in the realm of thinking about designing for people. I want to emphasize that this isn't necessarily about asking people what they like to do and what they find exciting. It's really about making a connection with people in their context so that, as designers, we are picking up on the vibration of what they are about. We want to somehow identify with that and have that spur our creative thinking and our creative response. Not literally translating what we're hearing—listening to people is important, but a lot of it is about watching and then empathizing. Not just looking at the behavior, but thinking "Why are they doing that?" It's about understanding what they are thinking and feeling, as much as what they are doing and saying.

GH — This is sort of off-topic, but why are there so many British people at IDEO?

JFS — [Laughs.] I have a theory about that. I think the background that I and my contemporaries had in education in the UK had a much stronger affinity with design thinking. I think it was a lot more about demanding that individuals value their own experience and communicate it, and much less about getting the right answer or doing it the right way. I actually think that has been changing as British education is becoming more metric driven, more to the test. It used to be very much more open-ended and creative. It was the essay question not the forced choice, you know?

GH — That's interesting. Could we talk about the *Thoughtless Acts?* book, and how that project came about?

JFS — Sure. You asked me about how design was when I came into it in the beginning, and like I said, I think it was about designers as experts providing for people. One of the things I think I brought into IDEO was, in order to design for people, let's go and look at them and see what they are already doing. How can we fit in and be inspired by what they are doing?

In the course of looking at what people are doing, it's hard to overlook the fact that people are creative by nature and always solving problems and not quite satisfied with the design of something that they have, that they bought, that they've adapted. That's what lead to the book *Thoughtless Acts?*, meaning the things people do without a lot of thought. If you just look around you, there are examples. A music stand is out in the wind, so people have to use clothespins to hold the music to the music stand. Reusing things, using spaces in really interesting ways, like a street just turning into a theater—adaptations. One of my favorites is where there are a whole range of appliance plugs and people can't remember what they all connect to, so they write little notes on them. It's all about making the world work for them.

This is inspiring to designers, but also makes us recognize that everyone is a designer at a certain level and that could become a clash or tension. Like, "Hey, I'm a professional designer, I'm suppose to come up with the answer and you're suppose to buy it," and i think that's been the model for quite a long time. So, when you start to think in this way, it offers a new opportunity, or it forces us to respond to an opportunity, which is: people are creative. Is there some better way to engage with people's creativity, as professional designers, to make more of it or enhance what they can do for themselves. It's changed, so it's much less of the "Tada! We've got the answer," both to our clients and to consumers. We involve them in the process with us now. We take them out with cameras and have them look at their own behavior and the behavior of people around them, and together we will come up with ideas. We will even help them make things—rough prototypes—but with their expressions of what they care about. When we are designing with people in that way, we are still in a very professional stance with them, because what we are doing is using their creativity to inform the way we design.

It still means we have to have designers who are taking the models they have made from cardboard and take the spirit of that into something that only a really professional designer can give form to, give shape to. So, that's moving from "designing for" to "designing with." And I think we're being challenged even beyond that right now, by Web 2.0 and a revitalization of craft that is taking place and is partly enhanced by the Internet. People who thought they were just doing this embroidery for themselves can now share that and show it and have people respond and get very excited about their own creativity.

So, there is this democratization of design and a conversation about design in the marketplace which is more sophisticated than it has been before. I think it is still something of a challenge, that design is being done by people, so what is our role? Part of it is getting on board with the idea to design with them. Some of it is exciting and interesting—that the role of the professional designer may be more to give voice to a vision, or create a vision that other people can aspire to, or create the tools or platforms from which people can operate. You know, we start talking about designing the theater and not the play. That is, design the place for this to occur, or the box that you can put your stuff in, but don't try to fill the box with all the things that a person might need because, going back to *Thoughtless Acts?,* people want to make the world around them.

GH — I think it's especially interested how people express themselves creatively through objects.

JFS — Yes, and I mentioned craft, and I do think that the increase in people's confidence around craft is an important thing today and it's taking people's creativity to a more formal design level. It was that, I think, that made me excited about what Paula Dib is doing in Brazil because the people that she is working with are very poor, and they are creating a living through their own creativity. I mean, they are doing things like taking old magazines that other people have thrown away and rolling them up into little straws and then using those straws to weave baskets and then painting them black or red or something.

When Paula saw this happening, she went in and helped them see that actually, if you don't paint them, they are even more beautiful. Then of course that saved them a step, and it saved them materials, and helped them provide something to a developed-world market where people could enjoy the look of it instead of it looking like a school project, not to diminish school projects. It had a sort of fine craft about it because it was celebrating the material, this rolled-up paper. She is a professional designer who has found a way of using her design skills to really elevate the level of regular people's design. In a way, it is profitable for them and evidently enjoyable enough for her. That, to me, is very inspiring as a model of what a professional designer can do.

GH — What would you consider the enemies of good design? What are designers up against?

JFS — What designers are up against is a different question than who the enemies are, I think. Resolving that tension that I'm talking about—about everyone as a designer—I think that is a tension that is yet to be resolved in a happy way. I do think it's a huge opportunity. I really think the idea that everybody's creativity can be inspiring to everybody else's creates this sort of mutually reinforcing cycle. I think it is, ultimately, a very positive thing.

What's working against design? Everything that works against design works for design. I think we are going through this phase of changing from a society that consumes to a society that is asking questions about consumption, like, "Well, do I really need another one? What do I do with this thing when it breaks or when it wears out? Is wear adding value and making it more precious, or is it something to throw away?" We are, as a culture and society, beginning to ask those questions, which is challenging to designers, but it's also clearly a really positive influence for designers as it forces a new form of creativity, which I think will ulti-mately benefit us all.

—

Karim Rashid

(KR)/ May 2, 2008 New York

—

Karim Rashid is a prolific designer, with over three thousand designs in production. He has created products, identities, surfaces, packaging, exhibitions, and interiors for companies such as Christofle, Veuve Clicquot, Alessi, Umbra, 3M, Samsung, Sony Ericsson, Morimoto restaurants, Method, Kenzo, Hugo Boss, Deutsche Bank, and Audi. He also has plenty to say about his vision for the future of design.

—

Gary Hustwit — So how did you get involved in design?

Karim Rashid — Well, my first memory of it was when we were coming on a ship from London to Montreal, on the *Queen Elizabeth* in 1965 or 1966. It was a huge ship—10,000 or 15,000 people on it, and there were 300 or 400 children. There was a drawing competition for children up to the age of 10. So, I was sitting there drawing, and I realized at that moment that, well, I was fascinated about the way my parents somehow could manage to put all of their belongings from our apartment in London in a few crates, how we were moving our entire home as if it was just knocked down. So, I started drawing luggage. I was drawing a way to make things compact and put things into boxes. I won the competition. The majority of the other children's drawings were of people, their families, boats, and landscapes. I had this page full of luggage. I think at that moment I was really aware that I could somehow contribute to the physical landscape—that I could actually have an imprint on it, that I could change it somehow.

Then there was another time too. My father used to take us sketching all the time and we'd draw churches. We would take a few folding chairs, sit in front of a church, and draw it. He taught me perspective, and I remember starting to shape my own windows on the church. So, a lot of times when you draw, the way to learn is to, basically, draw exactly what you see. What I realized is that I was starting to already kind of reinterpret what I saw. So, I had a moment, let's say, when I realized that I could actually be effective in changing this physical landscape.

GH — And then you went to school for it?

KR — Yeah, and then when we got to Montreal it was Expo '67, so here I was, seven years old; my brother, I think, was nine. We would go to Buckminster Fuller's USA Pavilion and see all these aerospace things, and the Italian pavilion that had all these furnishings. There was the *Man and his World* exhibition and they showed a vacuum cleaner that could vacuum by itself—which actually just came out literally 3 years ago. So, that took about 40 years, almost, to come out. So, with all that I realized it was a utopic period. This was a very, very pivotal period in design because this is when you had Buckminster Fuller and George Nelson and Charles Eames—many of these players who were at the most prescient period of this utopian vision that the entire world was starting to embrace. This notion that we are going to go live on another planet, that our progress is critical to the survival of humanity. There was this idea that we will evolve to a point where our lives will just get better and better and more technological, or even more techno-organic in a way. So yeah, there were discussions in the late sixties of nanomechanics and of bioengineering modifications of food. So, I was kind of brought up in that period where the world looked like it was going to be the most advanced, most digital, most beautiful, most seamless place. That was what the future held for us.

I remember a really nice little story. In 1969, we were driving around on vacation in a Ford station wagon in the mountains in Vermont, and we got lost. It was about midnight. There was fog everywhere, and it was a little bit like a John Carpenter film. We drive up to a diner, and the diner's got a Pabst Blue Ribbon sign hanging in the window and a bunch of cars parked outside. We walk in, and there are all these relatively hard-core redneck hunters sitting at the bar. And up on the screen, on the television in the corner of the bar, right at that moment, Armstrong put his foot on the moon. I remember that moment so well.

Thirty-some-odd years later, it dawned on me why that utopic spirit, where everything was going to be contemporary, where we weren't going to live in this postmodern condition of revivalism and derivations, disappeared. It was because we realized there's nowhere to go but here. It was like, "Oh, we landed on a dead rock." So, a huge turning point in my life was 1969, because I was watching for my first nine years a world that was talking all about the cosmos, about building spaceships that we would live on, about moving into outer space. Design language was very, very instrumental in the sense of that vernacular. We had transparent chairs, and we had acrylics and glossy finishes and chrome, all the things that were going on, this kind of seamless language was about this notion of living in a really positive future.

My father was a designer, a set designer for film and television, so he designed the furniture in the house that we were raised in, and he was designing dresses for my mother. He was doing set design for television and film and painting, so I was brought up in a pretty creative environment. My brother and I were constantly drawing. We were obsessed with sketching and drawing, and we would draw our utopian vision for that time. I remember hiding under my bed. I used to spend hours under the bed when I was five, six years old, escaping the world and drawing my own world, drawing a world that I would like to see. I remember at that time being so afraid of adults, because as far as I was concerned adults were these really conservative, frightening creatures—the smell of tobacco and alcohol and all that. So, I was hiding under the bed drawing a kind of utopic nirvana of the way the world might be, my world.

By 1978, I had enrolled in industrial design school, and it was a very unheard-of profession; if you told someone you were an industrial designer, they thought you were designing factories or designing industrial buildings. I didn't know much about it at all; I had a book on Raymond Loewy that I got when I was 14, and I was really interested in design. But the term "industrial design" was so, so marginal— it was amazing. I applied to the school of architecture, but I applied really late, in August, and enrollment was in September. So they said, "Architecture's full, but we have a department called industrial design. Would you like to take that?" And I thought, well, it's kind of interesting, but it's not really what I wanted to do. Then they said, "Well, if you take industrial design, what you can do eventually after two years is move into the architectural program." So I took it with the intention of moving into architecture and then found myself in the place I really always wanted to be.

It was interesting too because I think design crosses this beautiful boundary of many disciplines. I was actually taking engineering classes, and I was taking architecture classes, and I was doing all the liberal arts, and I was taking psychology classes, and I was taking theory classes. It was, in a sense, a very broad education. At the time, I started getting frustrated thinking, "Why is it so broad? I should be in the shop making a chair, or producing a lamp." But really, it couldn't have been a better education because what it was saying was that design has the power to touch our souls and to touch our emotions, to touch every part of our physical and psychological and immaterial existence. It's amazing the affect these physical objects in our lives have on our psyche. Over 10 years with my students, I've studied how many objects we come into contact with on a daily basis. The average was 658, which meant here we are interacting with 658 objects a day, and we never speak about them. There's no real critique of them. There's very little discussion on how these things really, really affect us in so many different ways.

So anyway, by the time I finished university, my school was a Dutch-German school, a modernist school, so I remember that every model that we made had to be black or white, which I was always so frustrated by. The pedagogy, the methodology was very linear too. The idea of creativity was really suppressed in design, and it is quite suppressed in industrial design and in design schools in general, because there was something about the profession that was so much about conformity: the way a designer should draw, the way a designer should behave, the way a designer does business, the way a designer should think. You know, the process of designing a product. I realized I was just way too artistic and brought up far too much by an artist. It's in my DNA to be an artist, and then I find myself in such a contrived and banal profession. I could argue maybe in the last 10 or 15 years it's broken out a little bit, and more artistic people are in the profession.

In 10 years of teaching, I always found it interesting that there was an industrial design floor in a fine arts school because we teach industrial design in this country mostly in art colleges, not in universities that are about engineering and architecture. So, you know that floor was always referred to as, "Oh, there's the floor with the suits," or "There's the floor with the ties," or "There's the floor that's about business." Whereas all the art kids with the piercings and tattoos and everything, they would almost laugh at the industrial design floor, and it's true: you'd get a lot of industrial design students—most of them had some sense that they could draw or be creative, but they were a bit more engineered. You know, they were nerds. You didn't get really artistic people enrolling. I was always frustrated as a teacher. I was wondering, "Where are they? Why don't the artists walk in here?"

It's because they think industrial design is a very technical field, just like we used to think that architecture was a very technical field. You couldn't go into architecture if you didn't have a science and math background. But we all know now, I think, that architecture, in a sense, is so much more about the kind of emotional and anthropological kind of spatial sensibilities of how we navigate in space, and how we live, and how we see, and all these sorts of more abstract issues. The real technical part of architecture is not being done by architects, and the real technical part of product development isn't really being done by product designers. So, this has really opened up now in the very recent years, and I think maybe it's because we're exposing the real role of what we do. And we are creative players. Ideally, you need a good left-right sort of balance to be a really, really good designer because you also have to be extremely practical, and you have to really understand human needs, human performances, human functions, et cetera.

When I was a teenager, I had this white bubble stereo with these two bubble speakers. It was probably very inexpensive, it was a really democratic product, and it was a turntable with the whole thing built in. It was a beautiful thing because it was very self-contained. The message was very strong and very simple, and at the same time it was very human. It has this quality about it: it was like a womb; it was like an extension of us somehow—it was engaging. I used to have this alarm clock radio that Dieter Rams designed for Braun in the late sixties, and it was orange plastic, perfect. It's probably not much different than an iPod in the sense of its language. But it had this kind of orange gloss finish about it. And it's these objects in my life that I was really, really kind of in love with. They brought so much to me. I can remember going through the teenage angst thing, feeling really depressed and lying on my bed, and I'd just look at the alarm clock or look at the stereo and felt better immediately somehow.

So I always had this really strong relationship with physical products. I became more and more and more obsessed with it. I really loved the idea of industry and loved the production of goods, and I loved the idea that we could produce goods that can add so much meaning to people's lives. I loved the idea that I could actually somehow add meaning of my own, messages of my own. Some level of communication, some sort of personality, some sort of character, that would then be interpreted by hundreds and thousands of other people. You can make a dish soap bottle, and it's touching 9, 10 million people a year and more—that's the power of design. It's really a beautiful thing if you're doing work that's positive, that can really elevate our banal lives a little bit. Because I really think the digital age has increased our experience, elevated our experiences, but the physical world is not increasing our experiences.

I have this theory that the digital age is bringing us far greater experiences than the physical age. I think at one time the physical age was so engaging. Now, I think we can do so much more and we can be so much more creative. We can disseminate so much more of our own sensibilities or views or values to the world through the digital age, and we can have these heightened experiences that we can't really have anymore in the physical age. With that said, I always think about whether objects can come up to speed and really be competitive to give experiences like the digital age gives. It's a theory I've had in the last 30 years because I think that I started doing Fortran and COBOL-80 and all these weird programming languages in the seventies when I was studying. The computer age was coming, and I knew it was going to be a fantastic time, and I knew that what I saw in 1965 on *Star Trek* in Captain Kirk's hand was going to be my Motorola Razr. It was obvious; it just took a lot longer than I thought as a child. I was hoping it would happen tomorrow.

Now, we're living in this age that is fantastic because I can use LiveJournal and Myspace and Facebook. I can basically tell the world who I am. Technology has democratized creativity so we can all participate too. On my laptop I make fabrics and I make music and I do everything—I can make 3-D objects and I can basically run around the world and do this seamlessly. I can work in 35 countries. I'm working on about a hundred projects, and I can Skype with my clients everyday and it's fantastic. You know, even today, before this little discussion, I spoke to 9 countries. This is a fantastic time.

With that said, this digital age allows you all these experiences, and you say, "Well, then what's happening to the physical world?" I mean, if you make something just very, very simple like a chair or a vase or a watch, can you somehow capture this time we live in? Can that object speak about this moment in which we live? Because as far as I know, during the 50,000 years of history and humanity, objects spoke about the time in which we lived, and those objects spoke about the stability of the time, the religion of the time, so we would kind of unearth or excavate an object, and we'd learn so much about the time. We know about the Ming dynasty through some vases—at the end of the day, it's kind of amazing, this idea. Right now it's 2008—if you design an object today, is that object going to communicate 2008 and touch the time that we've lived in?

GH — When I saw you speak in Toronto at the DesignThinkers conference, you talked about archetypes, that people have preconceptions of what objects should look like. I was wondering if you could run through your thoughts on that. You brought up examples like coffee cups, lapels, the digital camera, the wine glasses on planes, et cetera.

KR — Well, I actually want to write a book called *The World Sucks*. I've been thinking a lot about this, and it's a critique on these absurd, ridiculous commodities that we have and human social behaviors that are irrelevant to the age in which we live. We just kind of carry on and on and on with these things, and we don't question them at all. We just accept them. It's amazing, the notion of conformity. I always wonder if it's built into our DNA that we are, as human beings, here to conform, or that we're here to be individuals. Thank God for the diversity of the fingerprint. You know, I think it's about the individual, not at all about conformity. But we move through life, and we just start to do what everybody else does, and we don't question it, and the next thing you know, 78 percent of the world is completely impractical; 78 percent of the world is uncomfortable. When you run around the world as you do when you travel, you feel it. Hotel rooms are poorly designed. You sit in chairs at conferences that are very uncomfortable—it's craziness. Imagine how many chairs have been designed in the world—why on earth would we have an uncomfortable chair? There's no excuse whatsoever.

So there's this strange thing, and I think design as part of the mechanization of the 20th century has become a bit of a machine to propagate, seduce, and address desire. Design is becoming very much like fashion design, in a way, where there's an expectation from the buyers and the consumers to have new, new, new, new. In fashion, that's what it was all about. Fashion was also very, very disposable. Is design disposable? That's the big question. No one's ever talked about this number, but there are probably 40 to 50 thousand new pieces of furniture designed every year. How many furniture fairs are there around the world? And why do we feel like we need to keep revisiting the archetype over and over and over again?

Without sounding like a hypocrite—I've designed many chairs, I revisit archetypes, I'm sitting on a couch now that we could argue is still yet another variation of a couch—the question is, "What are we doing with these things?" We have the demand to do something new for a company—this company needs to survive after all; it needs to continue making sales; it needs to feed three, four hundred families. There's the chain of economic issues, right? So with that given you say, "Okay, I'm going to design a chair. I'm going to design a couch. What can I do here? How can I put my fingerprint on it and differentiate it from every other designer? Am I playing a game to show that I can differentiate, or am I really doing something that is contributive? Am I taking on responsibility? Am I doing something that's really going to affect and touch people's lives?"

About 15 years ago, I used the word "design-ocracy," democratic design. I was so interested in the fact that, when I was brought up as a child, that little inexpensive stereo that was a fantastic product, or that little inexpensive clock radio, or the watch my father and I ordered from the back of a comic book that came delivered to you in water because it could go five hundred meters underwater—these are mass-produced products that really, really touch all the people out there. Because this is a big issue with designers: are the things we're doing really making change? And I think that the mass market is where designers should really be much more rigorous. I try to do everything I can in the mass market to really change the goods for people who know nothing about design. Although we all know a little bit. The people who say they don't care about design or the people who don't buy into design or the people who don't believe that their world should have contemporary goods in it—those are the people I want to touch. Those are the people that I think design can have such an amazing effect on. There's nothing more rewarding for me right now than to walk into the home of a person who says they know nothing about design and see three or four or five of my products or other products that I think are well-designed in their home.

I think that landscape is starting to change, obviously, drastically, and the movement of democratic design which ironically came from 165 years ago and the Industrial Revolution—the whole premise of the Industrial Revolution was to make mass-produced commodities accessible to a larger, broader audience. So, what happened with design? Did we forget that agenda? Did we forget about being socially responsible, ecologically responsible? Did we forget about making life better? The betterment of society in general? Have we gone off and decided to be esoteric, or have we decided to be to poetic? Or maybe too intellectual? I think that is what happened. The design profession, all of a sudden, is bifurcated with industry. Next thing you know, people who are actually called designers are talking about design; they are doing very sculptural things, more artistic things. Meanwhile, industry is still doing this without us. With or without us, industry is moving very, very fast. We have to run past industry, catch up, get in there, and make some change. We need to do some serious things that can really make everyday life better.

I remember, 25 years ago, designing electric drills for Black & Decker, snow shovels for Black & Decker, mammography equipment, x-ray equipment. I've done all kinds of real products, hard-core—what I call hard-core—product development. Peter Dorner, who's fantastic, wrote *The Meaning of Design*, and he used to draw a line, saying there's "below-the-line design and above-the-line design." Below-the-line is design, but where most people are not aware of it. Like designing a plane, for example. Most people just expect to get on a plane and things just work. Whereas above-the-line design is something like a vase or something that has so much more character and something that can be more personalized, something that is part of daily life. Well, that borderline is a very, very important part of design, a critical part of design.

With that said, those companies that I worked for at that time were all very afraid of design. In fact, a lot of the time the firm I was working for wondered why they had even hired us. Most of the time they never listened to us. We were just kind of there. They changed everything that we designed. Why? Well, number one, they thought that it would reduce their market. Number two, they thought designers would make things that cost more money, and designers were expensive, so it would to add to the R&D cost. Most large companies just stayed away from design and designers altogether. Every time a designer got into a large company and did something and it was a failure, they would think they didn't need designers. Now, what's happened? Now, a company can't exist without a designer, because the world has changed so much. I think with free enterprise, with free trade around the corner, global free trade around the corner, the new kind of entrepreneur, this global phenomenon of the entrepreneur with global competition, every company in the world now has to have design. You could even argue that design is the only brand differentiator. That's it. That's the power of design.

GH — I'd love it if you could talk more about that whole archetype concept, why things look the way they do when they don't have to.

KR — I think that we're all brought up to live and exist in a world that's already been designed. So, immediately we just accept everything that's around us. But in fact, the world could be a very, very different place. A lot of times, I think about how the world could be completely flipped upside down. We've built all these paradigms that we just buy into on a daily basis and we don't even discuss, and we don't critique, and we just accept, completely accept it all. I always really have to question what I would consider the archetype of everything in our lives. There are so many of them, and I wonder why we just continue with them. You know, I could mention digital cameras—their format, their proportion, the fact that they're a horizontal rectangle—the majority of them are models built off the original silver film camera. The silver film camera, which is a rectangle, had a roll of film that would have to travel across the aperture. So, it was the film that defined the shape of the camera. All of a sudden, our digital cameras have no film. Why on earth do we have the same shape we always have? Then there are these semantics of silver and black symbolizing technology—metal refers to technology. You could also argue the shelf life of a high-tech object is less than 11 months, so why on earth does anything have to be built to be permanent? It should be all 100 percent disposable. I think my laptop should be made of cardboard and my mobile phone could be a piece of cardboard. They could be wild, these objects.

I've always wanted to design a mobile phone. Nine years ago, I was working on a mobile phone that I wanted to make out of silicone rubber, it would have been this translucent thing. You'd see all this nice stuff inside. But if you're talking to somebody, and you're so fed up, and you can't stand them, and you turn the phone off, and you just kind of throw it against the wall, you could go pick this rubber phone up, and you could use it again. Instead, we built this kind of fragile, over-engineered world of very, very old languages. In the sixties we had so-called "spy equipment." When you look at these little micro-cassette recorders, they look no different than the Apple MacBook Air. We're not moving ahead. The technology has moved tenfold, but the actual, physical design has barely moved ahead.

This idea of archetype goes on and on to the point where I could name thousands and thousands of things that we keep hanging on to. On airplanes, if I'm in business class or first class, I'm getting silverware, and I'm getting a tablecloth. I'm getting a piece of china, and I'm getting a delicate teacup with a little handle. A little handle on a teacup is useless—not just on airplanes, anywhere. It just doesn't really work anymore. Instead of getting on an airplane and having a beautiful, really efficient, very aesthetic way of dining, I end up with all these old archetypes that go back hundreds of years. I'm drinking out of a wine glass with a stem on an airplane. The stem was there so you wouldn't touch and warm up your wine. I think with the majority of wine we consume now, it doesn't really matter whether you warm it up or not. It's not that great a wine. In turn, why do we still have a stem?

It's preposterous, in a way, a lot of those glasses and those goblets and chandeliers. There's a movement in design now of a kind of weird, Belle Époque, rococo revivalist thing going on where I have to keep seeing chandeliers and outdated chairs that are completely ornamented and embellished. That's just not at all the world that we live in today. A chair and the fabric on a chair should be smart and efficient and some sort of great fabric, like we have in the technology of our clothing. Jockey makes a T-shirt that doesn't smell. I wear it when I travel. Imagine that! You can wear it three, four times, and there's no scent that's captured in it. In turn, when I design some couches and use a fabric, some aerospace fabric from Japan that wouldn't absorb anything even if you poured soda on it, that's the world we really live in now.

There's so much technology, and we have advanced so far technologically, somehow there's almost some paranoia. We're afraid to admit that we live in the third technological revolution. I have an iPod in my pocket, I have a mobile phone, I have a laptop, but then somehow I end up going home and sitting on a knockoff of 19th-century Thonet bentwood chairs. This is not our world today. So, in a sense, if we really critique this world, we would say, "Well, when I walk into a restaurant in New York that looks faux French 19th century, it is no different than going to Las Vegas and going through fake Venice." In other words, it's all a stage set. You could argue that we're building all these really kitsch stage sets that have absolutely nothing to do with the age in which we live. Strange—I find it completely perverse, in a way. It's like, I'm sitting at my laptop, and then what I am I going to do—go out and get on my horse and carriage? We live with a very, very absurd way of thinking. I think that if we were educated and brought up to just think much more freely, so all of us could individually develop our own values and our own meaning in the world we live in now, the world would be a completely different place.

I'm talking not from just a designer's perspective, but from an everyday consumer perspective. Let go of these notions of the archetype; leave them. Feel freer. Be free in this world. Be who you are, and go deep into your soul to find out who you are. I was reading an issue of *Fortune Magazine* four or five years ago on a plane, and there was an in-depth article about the tie industry in America and how it went from a billion dollars to something like five hundred million a year. Half the industry. It's amazing. You don't really think about how many people lose their jobs because all of a sudden we aren't wearing ties anymore. The big question is: why aren't we wearing ties? We're not wearing ties because we're living in the casual age. This is the age we live in now. Eighty percent of the shoes in the world right now are running shoes. In that same issue of *Fortune*, four pages later, was an article on the dry cleaning industry, how it's gone down 40 percent because we're not getting our suits dry-cleaned anymore. A lot of us are not wearing suits anymore. If we're wearing suits, they're either ripped or they have holes—they're more expressive. We just do what we want, in a way. So the industry just disappeared from America. We were the number one country in the world in making hats at one point. These things disappear, and we have trouble letting go of them. I think we should just let go of them.

I was flipping through a book the other day about Pierre Cardin from the sixties, and the outfits for men were so cool and so simple. It looked like something from sci-fi films from the sixties—they were basically like jumpsuits. We don't need lapels; they don't do anything for us. We don't need buttons on the end of a jacket sleeve. We don't need any of these things anymore. We can go much, much further. When the Europeans developed the euro, they spent $160 billion to make the euro dollar—and they dropped the word "dollar" eventually—but why? To compete with the dollar. Euro cents today have the word "cents" written on them. Why? The word "cent" is so foreign to Europe. I don't know why we wrote "cent" on a coin. Why coins and bills? Coins and bills are centuries old. All they really do is carry germs, and we don't really need them. So we could all be living with electronic money. I travel the world with a credit card to be as simple as I can. I hardly ever carry money with me, and I've rarely had a problem.

We are so hesitant as human beings to move forward fast enough, so we end up moving in these tiny little increments of change. Airlines, for example. There are still only two airlines in the world that have high-speed Internet. Why? We're about to be able to use our mobile phones on the airplane. I always think about this: I'm sitting at my office eight hours a day on an Aeron chair by Herman Miller. I never think that I'm uncomfortable. In fact, it's so comfortable, it's incredible. I get on an airplane, and within two hours I'm super uncomfortable. So maybe Herman Miller should make chairs for Boeing or for Airbus. Why don't we do these things? So, if you look at the airline chair, it's the archetype—we've stuck with the archetype of that airline chair for 60 years now.

Where does the word "beauty" enter the conversation? This stuff is really ugly. The world is full of really ugly things. This is another subject that design never talks about. After I finished my undergraduate studies, I went off to Italy to do my master's in design. I only heard the word "beauty" in school in Italy when I was studying, but in general, it's rarely used. That word is rarely symbiotic with the words "industrial design" and "design." Really, we've got to shape a more beautiful world in a way. Make a more beautiful life for all of us.

GH — How would you describe your style, in terms of the visual impact of your designs?

    KR — Other people see a style. As far as I'm concerned, I don't see a style in my work, because every project has its own set of criteria. A lot of times, I try to follow a lot of the criteria. Let's say an object has 10 criteria. There needs to be an efficient production method, or it has its own kind of market, or it needs to provide a function. If I go down that list and I hit 8 out of 10, chances are I've got a really, really successful project. So, that means the criteria are really starting to inform the form somehow. I'm not just making form for the sake of form. And at the same time there's something that moves through a lot of my forms. That is, to speak about a kind of digital, technological, or techno-organic world. Somehow, if I do things that are very, very organic but I'm using new technologies, I feel like I'm doing something that's a real extension of the human body and an extension of the human mind, in a way. There's a relationship when I look at something and it feels right; it feels comfortable; it feels engaging; it feels like it could really become part of me, part of my life—an extension of me.

The other part that I'm very inspired by is creating ornamentation or decoration that is a physical interpretation of the digital age. A word I used many years ago, "info-sthetics," is the aesthetics of information. Can I make an object like a table and somehow talk about the digital age or the information age? Is that possible? I struggle and try in that way to develop a language, a physical language or languages that speak about this time in which we live. That's my inspiration.

GH — Is there anything we haven't discussed that you think should be mentioned?

KR — In my last 25 years working, I've always been concerned with the words "style" and "design." There's even a broader discussion about art versus design, and what those words mean. Design is not art, and art is not design. At the end of the day, if you have to define it, design is about mass production. Design is about using industry to produce serialized goods. Hopefully, with new technologies we'll be able to use a production method that creates nonserialized goods so that everything will be different. I would love today if the seat of my car could conform to my body. I would put in the dimensions of my body, and when I get my car, the driver's seat would fit perfectly. The rest of the seats could be generic. I can push a button on my computer and create 1.6 million colors. Why can't I have my car in 1.6 million colors? In fact, it would be quite easy to do. The car can move through a spray booth with 160 little spray guns, just like a bubble-jet printer on a large scale. Boom—1.6 million colors of car.

Those sort of notions of variation are symbolic of how design is moving. I've had a great interest in this, how it really allows you to express yourself on an individual basis, for you to personalize the objects or spaces in your life. I think more and more of this is going to happen. On the Internet today, you can design your own shampoo; you can design your own running shoes; you can be very, very involved in shaping your own world, and design is going to move this way. We're going to have much more of a say. The public realm is really going to start to shape its own world too.

With that said, let's talk about style and design. When a movement ends, we call it a style. The minute that expressionism ends, we call it the expressionist style or after-expressionism, fauvism, fauvist style, et cetera. When we're within a movement, we're not even aware we're in a movement. There's probably some sense of collective global reasoning. We're all working on a similar pattern where somehow, when that period is over, we want to categorize it, to place it in history in a chronological way. We label it style, and we shut the door. So, in a postmodern world, what do we do? We open the door, we go back into styles, and we start to take and take and take and take. If we're taking from history, we're really styling. The Italian word for fashion design, *styliste*, means stylist. Everybody knows that's what they do, they've already accepted that. They have no problem with it. Constantly, constantly, constantly creating derivatives of history, mixing and remixing it. So through some of that, some of them move forward, but a lot of it is regressive. It keeps going in a big circle. Through that there are a few fashion designers who are obviously innovative and have really moved things forward too.

In design, we were all about moving it all forward. That's what design was about, it was about moving the world and making it a better place. But all of a sudden, if we're going to show a chair that's rococo-like, we're styling; we're not designing. As soon as we go into the vaults and take from history, we're styling. This is the difference between style and design. So, design and working with contemporary material—I make a chair today, and maybe I have to think of how I want the chair to flex or move in a certain way. I make a chair, and I want to make it out of some responsible material. I want the production methods to be efficient because I want it to be low-cost. You know, make it out of propylene because it's a really good plastic. If I burn it, it turns into a vapor—it's one of the better polymers to use. These are contemporary criteria. So, in turn, if I use all of the contemporary criteria, I am going to create a contemporary product. That's design. That contemporary product is going to shape the future. That's how we as designers shape the future. If I go back into history and I say, "I'm going to make a chair that looks a bit Mission-like and be inspired by the Missions," I'm starting to do a derivative of Mission furniture; that's not designing at all. I think that definition is rarely, rarely considered and spoken about. Design has started to move into trends, and these trends sometimes lose the real raison d'être of the profession itself.

—

Alice Rawsthorn (AR)/
May 20, 2008
London

Alice Rawsthorn writes about design in the *International New York Times*, which syndicates her articles worldwide. She is also a columnist for *Frieze* magazine and an author, whose latest book, *Hello World: Where Design Meets Life*, explores design's influence on our lives: past, present and future.

—

Gary Hustwit — Can we talk about the history of industrial design? What are the first examples?

Alice Rawsthorn — Industrial designers have existed for centuries. One of the earliest examples would be the first emperor of China. He was waging war to try and colonize more and more parts of what would eventually become China, and one of his problems was that each of his archers made his own arrows. So say, if an archer died, a fellow archer couldn't grab the arrows from his quiver and start shooting at the enemy because the arrows literally didn't fit his bow. So the first emperor and his advisors came up with a way of standardizing the design of the arrows so that each arrow would fit any bow. That is one of the earliest and single most effective uses of industrial design. But industrial design as we know it now is really a phenomenon of the Industrial Revolution. It was the transition from individually made products to ones that were standardized in huge volume and huge scale.

So the goal of industrial design has always been mass production—it's been producing standardized objects for consumption by millions and millions of people. The intellectual goal of industrial design has been to use standardization, technology, and mass production to build a better world for as many people as possible. And that's a very laudable goal. We've now, however, had a century of modernism which has been underpinned by that ambition. And it has achieved tremendous things for a lot of us, but has failed in many ways. We've been left with a crippling environmental crisis. We're in a ludicrous situation where 90 percent of designers are spending most of their time designing products and services for the 10 percent of the world's population that already owns too much—when 90 percent of us don't even have basic products and services for the things we need to lead a subsistent life. Clearly, the old school of industrial design has its limitations, and now it's trying to come to terms with them.

GH — What would you say are the other big challenges facing designers today?

AR — Well, arguably the biggest single challenge facing design, and most areas of contemporary life, right now is sustainability. It's no longer possible for designers to ignore the environmental crisis or the implications of continuing to produce more new stuff that we don't always need in a world of depleting resources. Now, this is a very difficult issue for design to come to terms with, because design has always been a culture intellectually rooted in innovation and in the notion that technology can build a better world—that there is always a solution to a problem and that the new is almost always better then the old. Once you start questioning those things, the underpinnings of design start to weaken and fall away. So, although a lot of designers believe emotionally and intellectually in sustainability, they and the manufacturers they work for are finding it very, very difficult to come to terms with. Sustainability isn't just a sort of a pretty, glamorous process of using some recycled materials to design something that may or may not be the color green. It's about redesigning every single aspect of a company's process, from sourcing materials to designing to production to shipping, and then eventually designing a way for those products to be disposed of responsibly. That's a mammoth task, so it's no wonder that designers and manufacturers are finding it so difficult.

GH — How do you see the consumer's role in that issue?

AR — Well, one of the most interesting aspects of the sustainability issue is that it's absolutely been driven by consumers. A lot of designers and manufacturers talk the talk, but really it is consumers that have forced them to come to terms with it. For many years, it was fairly comfy and cozy for designers and manufacturers to say, "Yeah, a minority of people are interested in environmental issues, but it really is only a minority. But the majority still wants new products, new things." One of the most interesting aspects of sustainability is that it has been driven by consumers rather than designers and manufacturers. There have always been mavericks in the design world who embrace sustainability, going all the way back to Buckminster Fuller in the mid-20th century. But, it has tended to be a maverick minority. In recent years, the awareness of sustainability issues of consumers, particularly in Europe, has grown and grown. Take the plastic bag as an example: you know it was once a ubiquitous part of daily life. No one thought anything about stuffing as many plastic bags as possible at a supermarket check out. Now they are absolutely taboo. In many countries, people feel completely comfortable telling you off for even asking for one. That shows how quickly consumer attitudes have changed. That's been followed by big retailers like Marks & Spencer in the UK and Walmart in the United States who again have embraced sustainability issues long before design and manufacturers. And so, they are forcing design and manufacturing to follow their lead.

GH — So the second part of that would be whether consumers understand the influence of design in their lives. Do you think the general population sees the impact?

AR — Design is an absolutely fundamental part of daily life, and designers are agents of change. They take the changes in our lives, whether they are technological, social, or economic, and they make sense of them, but more importantly turn them into products and services that enable us, at their best, to live more efficiently or more enjoyably. Now, what people expect from design evolves all the time as social and cultural attitudes change. So, if you asked a couple years ago what good design is, somebody would pretty likely say something that fulfills its function efficiently and looks great. Now, there is another part of the equation. It's whether it is environmentally responsible in the way it is designed, made, sold, and eventually disposed of. That is just one example of how our attitudes toward design, and good design in particular, change all the time.

GH — In America, it seems like people shopping at a Walmart in Kansas are generally thinking about the cheapest option that will suit their purpose. If it's the cheapest and it's environmentally responsible, there's no issue. But it seems like price is the leading factor.

AR — By applying intelligent design to mass manufacturing, it's created inexpensive products and services from ones that were made in such tiny quantity that they were so expensive, they were completely unaffordable to ordinary people. And so prices have been driven down by design. I mean, good design isn't just about making something visually more seductive; it can be about making it more efficient, cheaper, more environmentally responsible, or simply more enjoyable to use. It's a whole bundle of different things.

GH — What excites you about design?

AR — Well, I find design endlessly exciting because it touches so many areas of our lives, often in strange and unexpected ways—it is an inherently dynamic discipline. It's all about change. It's all about embracing change, whether it is changes in technology, or in society, changes in our behavior—making sense of them and turning them into something that can enable us to lead our lives more enjoyably, more efficiently. Now, that's very complicated, and an often inherently contradictory process, but one I find endlessly enjoyable to observe and write about.

GH — What do you consider the most interesting, exciting parts of a designer's creative process?

AR — Design is about ingenuity, great leaps of the imagination and finding unexpected solutions to problems. That is sort of the crux of design. It's also about illusions. Sometimes you can look at a product and what you think of as a straight line, what looks like a straight line to you, is actually a complex series of curves that creates the optical illusion of a straight line—that is an extraordinary piece of art in and of itself. But more importantly, often the products that look the simplest, the easiest, the most natural, that make you feel sort of relaxed and laid back by just looking at them, are the most neurotic. Industrial design, product design in particular, is an endless battle against the laws of physics. Struggling against mathematics and science to try to make things lighter, cheaper, more flexible, more versatile. And so the creativity of the designers is often found when dealing with the most mundane of problems, endlessly trying to find ever more unexpected and ingenious solutions for them.

GH — How does design art play into what you've said about the status of the industry today? It seems like a lot of design you tend to see now is almost kind of created for that market rather than for mass production.

> **AR** — Well, if you look back through the history of industrial design, there's always been this duality of designers succeeding in designing for mass production and others doomed by their work being produced in tiny limited editions. Many of the most memorable examples of 20th-century furniture were originally produced in tiny, tiny quantities. I mean, no more than a couple of Le Corbusier's famous chaise longue, for example, were actually produced during his lifetime. We now have the illusion they were mass-produced because they have been reproduced in such large volume, largely for advertising agency and investment banking foyers, ever since. Recently, limited editions of furniture have acquired higher profiles and even new names.
>
> The brand name of "design art" is universally despised by just about everyone; artists are furious because they think designers are trying to borrow the intellectual trappings of art to build respect culturally, and designers are furious because they don't think design needs the intellectual trappings of art to be culturally complex and important. Design art has been a very successful brand name, and these limited editions of furniture are frequently impractical and often uncomfortable, but in some cases uniquely interesting, examples of design which have been sold at huge prices to collectors by galleries or at auction. So, they are classic examples of what an economist calls a positionable good; in other words, a product whose financial value bears no relation to its essential properties, but whose value is found purely by the inflated demand for it.
>
> There are many reasons why people in the design world are irritated by design art, but perhaps the biggest of all is that it dominates the media's perception of design. So the real problem of design art—some of which is well designed and unfortunately an awful lot of which isn't and is simply designed to make lots of money—is that, increasingly, the general public sees design as a very expensive, probably uncomfortable, and almost certainly impractical chair that is doomed to be auctioned at Sotheby's, when of course design has so much more to offer than that.

GH — We were just at the International Contemporary Furniture Fair, just two days ago.

> **AR** — Always a rather dispiriting experience.

GH — Well, it was funny to see how much of what was shown there—the objects were sort of one-liners, you know? They were ironic or jokey design objects made in limited editions. Someone would have a stand with one trick design object in it and that was it.

> **AR** — I mean, in fairness most design is mediocre whether its mass manufactured or limited edition. It's just, the one-trick limited-edition design is much more visible.

GH — Yeah, yeah.

> **AR** — But it can be depressing.

GH — It seems that the role of the designer is sometimes difficult to define, or at least most people don't have a clear conception of what they do, if they're inventors, or stylists, or artists. Can you speak about the role of a designer today?

AR — Industrial design is all about teamwork, but the specific roles of the different team members tend to blur depending on what company they work for or the time in which the objects were produced. Almost always, if you look at stunner examples of industrial design, it's a period when each member of the team is blazing. But if you looked at Braun's electronic products in the fifties and sixties, for instance, you have incredible styling by Dieter Rams and his design team, and phenomenal engineering by the geeky engineers at Braun. You can see exactly the same thing at Apple today, where the software designers are working in tandem with the hardware designers who are working in tandem with the engineers and the marketers and everyone else at the company who has anything to do with that product. Now, the balance of power between the different parts of the company made between those different teams may change over time, but always you tend to get great design when everybody is really contributing to it. And often the tension between the teams can be as creative as it must be frustrating for the individual players at the time.

GH — Speaking of Apple, could you talk about them a little bit, in terms of how they've influenced other designs, and how they've changed the relationship between design and the consumer over the past few decades?

AR — Well, if you look back through design history, there have always been stellar examples of companies that just caught on at the right time. Today, if you ask most people, certainly most designers, which is the single best example of corporate design in the world today, they would say Apple. And it has been absolutely phenomenal. I mean, Apple has designed that sort of gorgeous, glacial aesthetic that looks very simple. All the details are superbly refined. It's always easy to use and that's because the user-interface software is incredibly complex, beautifully resolved, but also the marketing of Apple is just brilliant. If you look at the iPod, people have made MP3 players before—Apple didn't invent that product sector. But by inventing iTunes, they managed to add that additional component to the MP3 player that made the iPod really the stellar product of its time. It's absolutely changed the way people listen to music, certainly the way people buy music, because the record companies would all complain. So it made a huge impact on our lives.

If you ask most people why Apple is a great design company, they would say it's because the products look gorgeous. But it's not just that. That in itself is never enough. It's that they are so rigorously engineered; the marketing thinking behind them is so original and so sophisticated; and the user-interface software, the technology that dictates how we use the product, is absolutely stellar. It's this combination of things. And it's a very neurotic combination of things. I mean, all of those simple, seemingly effortless products that Apple produces are a nightmare to design, to engineer, to manufacture, to develop. That's what makes them so great.

One of the most irritating clichés about design is "Form follows function," which people tend to prattle off as a great design saying. It's popularly misattributed to Mies van der Rohe, when actually it was the American architect Louis Sullivan who coined the phrase. And in the old days of what are called analog products—in other words, they are not digital; they are not electronic; for instance, a chair or a spoon—"Form follows function" tended to work. So, say you imagine being a Martian, and you just land on planet Earth, and you've never seen a spoon or a chair before; you can guess roughly what you are suppose to do with them—sit on them or eat with them—by the shape of the object, by the way it looks. Because its form follows the function. Similarly, if you look at the first generation of electronic products—record players, television sets, radios—you can guess roughly what you were suppose to do with them, simply from the way they look.

Now, all that has been annihilated by the microchip and the advent of digital products, because now we have a new generation of products, arguably the most useful products of our lives, where the form bears absolutely no relation to the function. Look at something like the iPhone and all the things it does. It's a phone, a mini-laptop computer, a clock, a watch, an alarm clock, a weather forecaster, a personal GPS system; the list goes on and on and on. How on Earth could you possibly guess, if you didn't know already, what it did from that tiny, gleaming, glass and metal case? So, form may no longer follow function.

There are fewer and fewer clues in the shape of digital objects to what they actually do, but a critically and increasingly important component to good design, or what we think of as good design, is how an object works. It's that invisible user-interface software that determines whether your cell phone is a nightmare to work because it's so tricky, so neurotic, or so overcomplicated—sadly, that's 90 percent of all cell phones.

GH — Could we talk a little bit about design thinking, in relation to companies like IDEO who use innovation and design methodology to look at health care or topics we wouldn't traditionally think of as design?

AR — Well, one of the most interesting areas of design at the moment is called strategic design, and this is applying, not necessarily the physical design and the process in which a three-dimensional object rolls out at the end, but this sort of lateral thinking designers have used for centuries, to new areas. So, you would have socially motivated consultancies, like Participle here in London, who apply design thinking—the innovation, the ingenuity, the lateral thinking—to the education system, caring for the elderly in the community, and health care systems. Commercial consultancies like IDEO do a similar thing, particularly in their case in terms of health care. So, this is sometimes loosely called the "new design." At its most ludicrous and open-ended, you can argue, "What on earth can't be designed in our lives?" As a verb, "design" is so loosely defined. It almost becomes pointless. But it is also a very interesting way of applying the very positive things designers have learned how to do over the years to areas of life design hasn't touched so far but which suddenly can benefit from design thinking.

GH — What are some examples where design has dramatically affected people's lives?

AR — An increasing dynamic area of design is humanitarian design—literally using design to save people from disaster and improve the lives of the people in the world who need the most. There's a long history of this, all the way back to Buckminster Fuller in the mid-20th century with his Dymaxion shelters, which have provided emergency shelter for hundreds of thousands of people in absolute desperate circumstances whether it's typhoon, hurricanes, storms, tsunamis, whatever. The Dymaxion shelter has proven very useful and life saving for many, many years. There still numerous examples of design helping people in desperate circumstances. For example, the design of more sophisticated mosquito nets which protect people throughout Africa from the risk of malaria. Or little tubes that automatically clean and disinfect water as you are sucking it up, even from a fairly infected swamp. Or the One Laptop per Child project, which is trying to cost-engineer down an educational laptop cheap enough to be bought by governments across the developing world in hopes of transforming the educational potential of millions of poor children.

GH — It's interesting to look at all the creativity and talent that designers have, but in many ways it's serving consumerism and materialism. Those two sides seem at odds.

AR — When people think about industrial design, they tend to think of the fantastic examples of stellar success, whether it's Apple with the iPhone or whatever, but the big truth is that 99 percent of all new products are startlingly mediocre at best. They are not great leaps of innovative thinking in terms of technology; they don't help in terms of building a better world; they don't even help to make our lives a little bit more enjoyable. They are simply mediocre, and that's because design is very, very difficult to do. The design process in itself is tough enough, but if you are designing for industry, navigating through the needs of the marketing department, the finance team, the engineering department— all these other vested interests who possibly have different objectives and priorities—it is a very, very difficult job to do, and very few companies succeed in getting it right. For the ones that do, the rewards are extraordinary, but most don't. I don't think anybody wakes up in the morning and thinks, "I'm going to design a mediocre product today," but the bleak truth is the odds against them designing something really extraordinary are very, very high. But of course, it tends to be the successes or the dismal failures that color our perceptions of design.

GH — What about the consumer who wakes up in the morning and decides to buy a new iPhone? He doesn't really need one, but he's got to have it.

AR — Design has always been a culture of plenty, intellectually and commercially. The underpinnings of design have been about this belief that the new is almost always better than the old. There is a solution to every problem, and everything can always be improved upon. That lends an almost moral imperative to design that makes designers feel happier about the virtuous part of what they do. Also, for consumers, it makes us feel justified in spending what may be money we don't necessarily have on things that we don't necessarily need. It's this sort of vicious cycle. But that cycle is coming to an abrupt end because there is an increasing recognition among consumers, suddenly, in the West that we already have far too much stuff we don't necessarily need and we probably don't even want in our lives. That is a very difficult change of attitude for design to come to terms with.

Now, the obvious answer to that is to only design really extraordinary things for which there is a genuine need, that genuinely make our lives better or enable us to do something that we couldn't do before. But all the forces of the capitalist cycle militate against being able to do that. There are so many pressures on many companies just to design a sort of mildly modified version of the same old thing and to produce something that they can label new, again and again and again. The sad truth is that most of that stuff is pretty mediocre.

GH — How does a nation like China figure into the future of design?
AR — Well, the emergence of China as the workshop of the world has been the phenomenon of industry in recent years, so when most people look at a gorgeously designed, impeccably realized iPhone or iPod, they think of groovy Apple and northern California. What they don't realize is that it rolled off a Chinese factory line. China has an incredible history of innovation as the country that invented silk, the umbrella, the tooth-brush, gunpowder—so it has this extraordinary culture of ingenuity. The critical question for design is when China will stop simply manufactur-ing but will start designing too, and that moment can't be far off. The Chinese government has poured millions and millions of dollars into building new art and design schools in China. I think there were two hundred under construction at the latest count. So, all those design graduates will eventually start designing in China as well as manufac-turing there.

Design tends to be a sort of indulgent medium in a developed economy and a matured culture, and so if you look at the pattern of development for emerging economies, they begin by being manufacturers, and actu-ally adding value by designing comes a little later. China has the financial clout to invest in the education system it needs to train a new genera-tion of designers. And what is going to be absolutely fascinating over the next couple of decades is to see the degree to which they incorporate a Chinese sensibility—the Chinese expectation of how objects work, the Chinese view of the world that will be urban rather than rural—into the products that are produced in the Chinese factories.

GH — It's interesting that with the computer, and CAD software, it's almost like some designers are divorced from the material now. Like they do something on the screen and zap it off to a fabricator in China. What are the benefits and drawbacks with this reliance on design software?
AR — Design software has absolutely transformed the process of indus-trial design, and it's given far greater power to the designer. In the past, the designer would sketch their sketch or do their technical drawing, and a model and prototype would be made, generally by the manufac-turer. So the risk of compromise is much lower now, with model makers

imposing their sensibility over the final product. In the past, the designer may have had to argue a way to bring it back to their original vision. Those risks were really quite high, so the probability was that through the course of the design process, because so much of it was physically outside the designer's control, the final object would look less and less like how the designer originally imagined it.

Now, thanks to design software, the model-making and prototyping process is taken care of by the designer on the computer screens in their studios, so they literally send the specifications for the prototype directly to the manufacturer, erasing a couple areas of risk that the designer previously wouldn't have been able to control. Obviously, this process differs dramatically from designer to designer and company to company, but the broad end result is that the designer has much more control over the physical process of their work. Now what tends to characterize what the eventual product will look like is how the designer works. Some designers, like Marc Newson, always begin with sketches, and then someone in the studio will transfer those sketches into digital specifications on screen. Other industrial designers, like Konstantin Grcic, actually work with their hands. Konstantin actually makes very rough, handmade models of the end product. That's what he begins with, because he visualizes his products like that rather than in the form of a sketch. Then, again, they are turned into digital specifications on the computer and then sent to the manufacturer.

So, the end result is that, although most designers are still working with mainly the same software programs, their starting points are dramatically different. They all find very different ways of imposing their own visual and tangible sensibility on their end result. But also, they have far greater control over the end result, and that's why the products you buy for not much money in shopping malls today tend to be more flamboyant, more emotionally and visually expressive, than products were in the olden days, pre-design software.

GH — But on the whole, do you think it's a good thing or a bad thing?

AR — Well, it depends on the designer. I mean, a great designer will find a way of using the tools that are available to them at a particular time in order to impose their sensibility on the final product. That involves the whole process of negotiation with the manufacturer, their engineers, their model makers, their marketing team, and the people who design the packaging in order to ensure the end result is as pure as it can possibly be. Bad designers lose heart or courage during the course of that process, and they give in; they compromise, and that's why the vast majority of new products look startlingly mediocre.

GH — It seems that the general public doesn't fully process the relationship they have with all of the objects in their lives. Why do you think that is?

AR — Well, one of the problems with design is, when people think about design, they think about something that looks pretty. Now, design is much, much more than simple prettiness. Also, people tend to think something hasn't been designed unless it's been styled in a very seductive and alluring way. Many of the best examples of industrial design are things that people don't think are designed at all.

Take the Post-it note, for example. 3M had developed this weird glue that was sort of slightly sticky but not so sticky that it stuck permanently. It took decades before someone worked out what to do with it. Legendarily, when a piece of paper fell out of the prayer book of a 3M scientist who happen to be a member of his local church choir, he realized that this sticky-but-not-too-sticky glue could attach the piece of paper to the prayer book so he would never lose his place again. Now, that is a brilliant example of design ingenuity. But a Post-it note is so cheap; it's so everyday; it's something we take for granted that people don't think of as being designed. What they don't realize is that, from the moment they wake up, almost everything that fills their world, and all the artificial components of their world, have been designed. Some of them have been designed badly, and a tiny, tiny handful have been designed very well. But all of it has been designed one way or another.

—

Marc Newson (MN)/ May 22, 2008 Paris

Marc Newson is one of the world's most influential designers, and has worked across a wide range of disciplines, creating everything from furniture and household objects to bicycles and cars, private and commercial aircraft, yachts, and various architectural commissions. His iconic Lockheed Lounge has had the distinction of being the most expensive piece of furniture by a living designer, since it fetched over $2 million at auction in 2010. In September 2014, as this book was being edited, Marc joined the design team at Apple.

—

Gary Hustwit — How did you start out in design?

Marc Newson — I began when I was around five years old, because in my mind, my career began as soon as I felt the urge and compulsion to make things. Not design things, but actually *make* things, which I guess is a precursor for designing things. But in terms of what most people think of as when you start a career, I guess it was when I went to art school. I didn't have the grades because I got expelled from high school, and I don't think I even tried to get into design school, because it seemed far too academic for me. I just wasn't cut out for the academic routine, so I went to art school and ended up in the jewelry and silversmith department because it was the only department where you were actually taught how to do something. Other departments like sculpture and painting were quite esoteric, to their credit. You would find yourself in a room with a lecturer, puffing away on a joint, telling you to get busy but not telling you actually how to paint, which is a complicated thing to do.

So I'm in the jewelry department learning how to be a silversmith, which I thoroughly enjoyed because I really learned a lot of skills in terms of how to build things, especially in terms of metal. I learned how to use a lathe; I learned how to solder; I learned how to weld; I learned the difference between ferrous and nonferrous metals; I learned how to rivet; I learned how to glue things—it was a fantastic place. The jewelry department was essentially a massive workshop where I could just go and have fun. I'd always dreamed of having a workshop. That's where I started.

And then, at a point, I made some furniture. I was always really interested in furniture from a historical point of view. I was interested in how iconic the chair, in particular, was, and how as an object it was able to represent certain periods in architecture and design, for example. I started making furniture in the jewelry department; I managed to convince the lecturers that a piece of furniture was just as much a piece of jewelry as a ring or necklace, because it related to the body in essentially the same way. It needs the body to function. I'm not sure if I believed it myself, but they loved it. So I kept make furniture in the jewelry department. From that point onwards and after finishing college, I just kept making chairs.

GH — I like that your career started when you were five. I just read something recently where an artist was talking about that sense of play and creating when you were a kid. Sometimes that continues on and becomes your "career."

MN — Yeah, it's hard to know, really, why I was like that—why I felt this compulsion to build things and consequently design things. I think it may have had a lot to do with coming from Australia. It's a place where you were obliged to build your own fun. It wasn't as if there were loads of Toys"R"Us stores around. It was a very much do-it-yourself culture, for all generations. The culture of design doesn't really exist in Australia, but the culture of invention exists. It's really fervent and very dynamic there still. People are always coming up with mad ideas. There was also this surf culture thing. Kids would make surfboards in their backyards, and so everyone knew how to work with fiberglass. I was just mucking with polyester resin. I've been inhaling polyester resin since I was 10, chopped up with bits of fiberglass. But I graduated up to carbon fiber, which is much better for you. [Laughs.] But yes, it started early on.

I remember making my first object in my grandfather's garage. I tried to make a wristwatch, which was hysterical because I could barely tell the time. I remember my uncle said that as soon as I could tell the time, he'd give me his cruddy wristwatch that he never wore and that I promptly pulled to bits and decided to repackage, so to speak. I found an old bit of Plexiglas in my grandfather's garage, and I started hacking away at it, drilling holes, and transplanting the movement from this once-working watch into it. That was my first design, I guess.

GH — Nice. Do you still have the wristwatch?

MN — It must be somewhere in one of the many boxes that my mother has in storage that she's dying to get rid of. Now that I have a 9-month-old daughter, I'll probably go and rifle through all of those things to see if there's anything good that I can give to her. But I'm sure it's there; it must be around.

GH — This reminds me of what the graphic designer David Carson said. As a longtime surfer, he's convinced that there's something about surfing that puts people on the path of design, even if it's non-surfing related.

MN — Well, for me it was more about surf culture. In a way it was the prevailing and indigenous youth culture that I was exposed to. What we did was go and watch the surf films and muck around with fiberglass and attempt to make surfboards. And this was actually at a point when the Billabongs and the Quicksilvers and Rip Curls were barely making board shorts; maybe that's all they were making. So that whole aspect of surf culture, or surf apparel, had not been exploited, I guess. It did seem, not rebellious, but really vibrant, essential, and interesting, and every kid in Sydney was energized by that.

GH — Do you think surfing has had any formal influence on your work as a designer? The fluidity . . .

MN — Well, yeah, I guess. People have always referred to my work as being organic, which is always a term I've struggled with. In a very simplistic way, you could say it's organic, but I've always seen it as a question of symmetry and bright colors and things like that. But then I guess if you go back a few steps, perhaps it is about the surfing, about landscapes and about nature, atmospheric conditions. The waves, water, and the light you're exposed to in places like Australia and California. So, yeah, that must have had a huge influence, but also combined with this DIY philosophy that's more of a necessity really, it's just sort of the way people are in Australia. If you go to Australia, even now, you'll notice that all the cars are about 5 years older than anywhere else. It's one of the first things that strikes me when I land at the airport in Sydney, that few very people are driving brand new cars. I mean, if you go to New Zealand, they're about 10 years older than that. It's really funny. And so people are forced to fix things.

GH — If you had to talk about the role of the designer in our world, how would you describe it?

MN — It's a complicated question, or maybe not so complicated, but it's obviously very subjective. I mean, I can only ever really use myself as a reference for that, and my role I think is half compulsion and half trying to create choice for myself. Because ultimately, what I want to do is be able to have things that don't exist, things you can't go out and buy, or to replace things that irritate you. I've spoken to Jony Ive about this; we always talk about how anger, or dissatisfaction at the very least, plays such an important role in motivating us to do what we do. My role is to create choice, to create a good choice. I honestly feel that a lot of the time people are being ripped off with the choices they're being given. I mean, if you look at the automotive industry, for example, it's a pretty woeful state of affairs, I think. And I don't think you'd find many design-ers who would argue that if you had 50 grand to go out and buy a new car with, you'd be struggling to find something good. I'd go buy an old car. I always have.

I had a crack at designing a car with Ford, but unfortunately it never got made. But yeah, I think it's about choices, and maybe it's just me; maybe it's just all selfishness. It's about creating choices for myself. But at least there will be people out there who respond in the same way as I do. And they may be a little bit happier that I've been able to expose them to something a little bit more exciting than the stuff that would otherwise get rammed down their throats. I'm working a huge amount in the aviation industry now—commercial interiors, private planes, some spacecraft even—and that's a really good case in point because, particularly with commercial aircraft interiors, when you see the stuff that people are subjected to when they're traveling—it's extraordinary really. There is an enormous amount of work that's needed there, I think, far more than designing furniture for the luxury furniture industry, for example.

GH — It's funny; you're also describing my documentary film process. It's the same thing. There are films that don't exist that I want to see, and there's nothing out there.

MN — Yeah, and it's always about me, of course, and I know that sounds very selfish, but it's my point of reference. And I always say this to clients, because the larger the corporate client you get—you get to a certain point in your career where all of a sudden you start working with these big corporate clients, and you think, shit, you've finally arrived. But in fact, it's like you've finally regressed. Because what happens is you have to start dealing with things like consumer market research and focus groups. And I'm constantly fighting with executives about the validity of using focus groups and things like that. Sure, sometimes it's interesting, but ultimately my job as a designer is to look into the future. It's not to use any frame of reference that exists now. My job is about what is going to happen, not what has happened. And the focus group is based on what has happened, and what does exist. So yes, it's all about me, but I'm the one that has the ability and the opportunity to look into the future and try to bring the future here, or expose people to what I think the future may be.

GH — It's your conception of it, and some people are going to get it, and some people aren't.

MN — Yeah, absolutely, some people get it and some people won't. But at the end of the day, I've created a little bit more choice, and that can't be a bad thing.

GH — Can you talk a little about your creative process on a project, the typical steps you'd go through?

MN — Well, it doesn't matter what I do or who I do it for, my process is always the same. It never changes, the way that I work. It is always an absolute constant. It's all about thinking. It's thinking and thinking really, really hard about how things should be. Trying to resolve things as well as I can in my head. So when an idea is born, it's fully formed—I feel very strongly that you can't chase an idea; it's got to be there. It either is or it isn't. I really feel your mind is the best thing to visualize things in three dimensions and really knock out all the details.

Of course, there's a process after that which enables you to get the idea out of your head. At some point, it's got to come into reality. You know, I sketch; I draw pictures. Actually, I don't use computers myself, never have. I graduated in 1984, and I think the first computers were just starting to be used in my art school. In any case, I was in art school, not design school; no one really used computers in art school anyway. I just missed out on learning about computers. I'm glad, in a way, because I've never felt encumbered by it.

So, I'm quite content to draw. I feel that the computer, despite being a very, very powerful tool, is still not as intuitive as we are. There's just no way that they can mimic what you can do with a sketch. A simple stroke on a piece of paper has so much character, so much richness that you can't replicate with a spline. Or some really sophisticated curve plot that'd take you days, hours at least. Nevertheless, I do use computers, my office uses computers, and they are a very central part of the process at some point. But, it's the end part of the process, so the whole thing can start in my head; I go to paper, and then from the paper, I go into the computer. We use all the same kinds of software, really, as everyone else. Which is a great thing about computers, because everyone tends to speak the same language no matter where you are in the world. That's one of the great things about design, actually. If you're working in the US, if you're working in Japan or China or Europe, it's all the same. We all speak the same language. We all communicate the same way.

GH — In terms of materials, do you have a material in mind when you come up with an idea, or sometimes do you find a certain material and then figure out a use for it?

MN — I think it's absolutely both of those two approaches. They are both completely valid. Basically, the way I see it is that you have a problem to solve, a design problem. I'm a troubleshooter. That's what they employ me to do. I'll find the best material to help solve the problem. So I'll explore the material as best I can in order to achieve a goal. In the process—and it's a long journey—I'm fascinated by materials, as most designers are. It's really all about the materials, the processes, and the technologies. I'll identify and develop a project that is based around a particular material just so I can use it, because I think it's so cool. It's often the case that when I do more artistic endeavors, like having exhibitions of art and design, I tend to identify materials that I want to use and never had an opportunity to use, and I'll use those materials and exploit those materials so that those materials can do the talking, can communicate.

GH — Carbon fiber seems like one of your favorites.

MN — Well, I think composite materials in particular, like carbon fiber, are popular for two reasons, for me. One is the fact that the majority of what I do is in the aerospace industry. So, whether I like it or not, I'm obliged to work with composites, particularly carbon fiber; it's pretty much the material of choice in that industry. Strangely enough, though, composite materials go way, way back. When I was in my teens and building surfboards and things, that was early composite stuff too. I can remember using carbon fiber in the early eighties, getting my hands on the first bit of carbon fiber. It was this incredibly rare material. There was always this fascination with those materials because they're plastic. In a weird way, they are backyard materials as well. All the things you can do when you are laying down carbon and composite materials, you can do it in very low-tech situations. It's not like injection-molding plastics; it doesn't require enormously expensive tooling. And coming from Australia, it's always the technology that was on my doorstep. The boat building industry was right there. There were all these technologies that I was exposed to as a kid. I've been fascinated with those materials for a variety of reasons, but it stems from there. And as luck would have it, composite technology is where a lot the big leaps are being made.

GH — Well, you did that suborbital craft for EADS, and there's this space thing you brought up before . . .

MN — The space thing is life imitating art in my case. I grew up in a generation where I can remember when they landed on the moon, I was six years old, and I can't deny that was a massive event in my life. I was just old enough to begin to comprehend the enormity of that. There was an incredible sense of utopia at that point in my life. I guess maybe in everybody's life, through the sixties and all through the seventies, the future was still *the future*. The future was futuristic. It isn't futuristic anymore. The future is pessimistic somehow. At least there's nothing particularly utopian about it. But the future was all mixed up with my childhood, with my typical boyhood ambitions and dreams. So for me, it's completely inextricable.

All of my dreams were about the future, the same as a lot of kids would have been at that moment in time. I was growing up in a place that was big and open and didn't have masses of historical baggage. I think being a creative kid in Europe would have been a completely different thing, growing up with all that history. I was always unafraid to pick and choose my history; it was like a big library. I could have this or not, but none of it was rammed down my throat. I grew up in a very, very liberating environment. It was very pure and it was utopian; it was good and it was fun, and I think what I'm doing now is just trying to really live through all of those ambitions, somehow. Bizarrely, they are all coming true. All these things I really wanted to do when I was a kid, I'm doing them—it's really weird. People always ask me what's the one thing you'd really like to design. And, without sounding conceited, I'm doing it; I'm doing all of them.

GH — The whole concept of sustainability and materials and where things come from and where they are going to end up afterwards is part of the discourse now. What are your thoughts on that issue and how it applies to some of the work you do?

MN — Well, there all these particular issues with regards to sustainability and the environment. There are many, many different aspects to how you can deal with that and how you approach that and how you assimilate that into the way you work. I think it's important first to stress that, as a designer, my philosophy is fundamentally non-disposable. That, for me, is the big idea. I love the idea of designing things that are really well made, that have a fantastic and innate sense of quality, and that you can have for rest of your life. Somehow deep down inside me, that's the most sustainable way of approaching anything, regardless of what it is, what material, whether it's made in wood or whether it's made in plastic, whether it's biodegradable or not. The fact is, if you are creating quality and you are creating objects of desire that you can imbue with a real, emotional quality, then good. People will always want them. They won't want to throw them away.

You know, the whole problem is because we are making shit that we throw away all the time. There's nothing wrong with plastic, but the problem is disposable razors, disposable pens, disposable cultures. One of the things that really struck me when I first moved to Japan, when I was about 25 years old, was that certain Japanese people I knew used to take their chopsticks everywhere with them. I just thought that was such a cool idea. You could travel with your own chopsticks. It has to be said, of course, that Japan cut down an enormous amount of trees to make disposable chopsticks. But there are so many ways—it's such a confusing debate, you know, it's such a massive debate. I think it would be trite to say, "Well, I'm only interested in using wood that is sustainable and plastics that are biodegradable." I mean, somehow it has to be a more wholesome, philosophic approach, at the same time bearing in mind that we live in a world where we need to travel.

GH — It's a behavioral thing; it's like how people just assume that they're entitled to get a plastic bag when they buy something at a shop, at least in America. They don't want to change.

MN — At least if we could address the issues like light bulbs, plastic bags, disposable razors, and maybe just eradicate 90 percent of the shitty choices . . . I'm all for improving quality in people's lives, and somehow trying to offer products that are better and nicer and more enjoyable, and products you want to keep, and products that you feel, most importantly, will stand the test of time, that won't get outdated. I love that idea. We have the ability to create objects that hopefully won't date as badly as other things. It's all about wanting to have new things, isn't it? Ultimately, we can all still be using the mobile phone we had three years ago, but we've all had about five in the meantime.

GH — I'd like to talk about this whole idea of the "democratization of design." I think it's one thing to have everybody be able to afford better-designed objects, but it's another to justify selling cheaply made stuff because it has the sheen of "design." What are your thoughts?

MN — It's a conspiracy in a lot of ways, especially for designers because, unfortunately, it's not us designers that decide how much things cost. I'd love for there to be a report on the cost of production and the cost to the public. There are so many variables between those two ends of the spectrum. The designer really has no control over it at all, and sometimes it's a literal and logical relationship. Other times, it's utterly arbitrary. Particularly when you work in the so-called luxury goods industry. That is complicated, especially for designers. Of course I fundamentally believe that something that is well designed shouldn't necessarily cost anything or cost more; arguably it should cost less. The problem is that design has become a little bit of a cliquey byword for a lot of companies, particularly big multinational organizations who try to commercialize or add value because something is designed and therefore you can charge more money for it. When in fact it's probably not a better product, and probably looks worse. If you look at the appliance industry, for example, there are some good examples of that.

GH — In the States we've got Target, with this "design for everyone" campaign, and when I look at all the stuff—wait, you haven't done anything for Target, have you?

MN — No, I haven't.

GH — Well, when I look at the stuff I just think they're using the gloss of design as a way to market things that people really don't necessarily need.

MN — Absolutely, a lot of people are using design as a way of merchandising things. It's another way, a new way. It will become more and more pervasive. Things will be marketed in terms of design for the future. If you look at the luxury furniture industry in Italy, you'll ask yourself the question, "Does the world need another chair?" There are many facets of the design world that are hard to rationalize in the world we live in right now. I think one of the reasons I'm designing airplane interiors is not so much that I like flying, but surely it is a more valuable contribution to the world of seating than designing another chair for a luxury company. I've spent many, many 24-hour-long trips in airplanes and it's not fun. But people have to fly, that's the point. People have to spend a lot of time, people want to spend a lot of time moving around the world. The world is becoming a smaller place. So I think that seems like one way of addressing one of those issues. It's not to say that I won't design more so-called luxury furniture. In fact, I've taken it to a new extreme; I just design furniture in art galleries, so I've taken it to new heights, where you don't even sit on the stuff, you don't even touch it. You're not even allowed to look at it. Like the guitar in *Spinal Tap*. [Laughs]

GH — I ask this question a lot: If you were watching a film about industrial design, what's the one thing that no one talks about that you'd want to hear someone say?

MN — Oh, wow—I wish people would be more critical of design and designers and the people responsible for some of the nasty stuff. Of course, we can blame consumers ultimately, but I don't really think they're responsible. Everyone is nervous about saying the right thing, me included. I think that's something I'd like to see: a critique, a professional free-for-all. That would be really fun.

GH — Does that ever happen at design conferences?

MN — I've never been to a conference where people have really and truly been frank about what they think about other designers' work or the state of design. It's rigged. All the big design awards are sponsored by major corporations, and they get prizes. It just happens all the time. It's just so cheesy, the whole thing. I mean, it's an industry like any other industry, and when you go to those conferences and those forums, which I don't anymore, you really understand it's not much different than any other industry, really. But I think it could do with a dose of reality, a bit of a health check.

GH — Can you tell me about Ikepod?

MN — Yeah, well, I was always interested in designing watches, but I've also had a go at making watches. I set up this company in 1994 with another guy to manufacture one of my designs. That was the whole reason for the company existing. It grew and grew, and I designed another watch. It just grew organically and then went bankrupt, as a lot of things do. And then, it came back to life three years ago, and my new business partner, Adam Lindemann, reinvested in the company, and now it is flourishing again. So we are putting a few of the old designs into production, designing new things. So yeah, my little foray into the watch business turned into a watch company. Which is really interesting for a designer because it's like being on the other side of the camera, being the actor. You are the director. It gives you a very interesting exposure to what it's like, the realities of actually running a company, bringing things to market. Designers never really have to deal with commercial realities. We do, with this watch company, and it's fascinating. Very interesting.

GH — Did it give you a new appreciation for manufacturers and the other businesspeople involved?

MN — Yeah, it gives you a better understanding of how the whole process works. The whole process of merchandising—although I hate that word—the whole process of making things available to people and how that process works, and the process of publicity and marketing. All these things that they do that designers typically don't think much about. They're all really, really important parts of the picture.

GH — You've done some automotive design work with Ford. Why aren't cars designed better?

MN — I don't know. I'm stumped. I can't figure it out. It's not for lack of good designers. I mean, it's mad, because we all buy cars; we've all had cars. I grew up in a car culture—cars, for me, they run in my veins. I love cars. They represent freedom for me. But like I said before, if you gave me 50 grand, I couldn't go out and buy a nice new car. It would be really, really hard.

I think the reason cars are so badly designed is simply because the industry is so myopic; they just don't care. I think it's generally one of the worst examples of where there are simply too many cooks. There are lots of designers, of course—when you see the way it works and the fact that there are no less than 50 people working on a single car—so there it is. I mean, when I designed a car, I designed the whole thing. I even designed the tire tread. Which is not to say I should get a pat on the back for doing all those different things, but it's to say there was a consistency in its conception. When you look at contemporary cars, they are clearly designed by so many different people, with so many different agendas. Some parts are very driven by engineering; some parts are very driven by styling. Computers have a huge part to play in the way cars look. You can almost tell which software was used to design what car. And the people who work in the big creative jobs in those industries get to live in really horrible places that you would never otherwise want to live in—Dearborn, Michigan.

So it's just a weird, bizarre thing, and I feel it's become so myopic in its inability to incorporate any other form of contemporary culture into the culture of car design. It's just all about cars, and it's all about car styling cues, and there are certain languages that all car designers will use over and over and over again. Consequently, all the cars end up looking somewhat similar. So yeah, a very unhealthy situation, I think. That is a perfect example of what I was talking about—a cool car costs the same to manufacture as a shit car. I mean, there's really no difference. A sad state of affairs, really.

GH — It's funny, really, like you said, it doesn't cost any more to manufacturer the poorly designed car. Like with graphics, it doesn't cost any more to print something that's well designed.

MN — Absolutely. Graphics are a perfect parallel. When you are talking of such economies of scale, it would make no difference. The problem is the management systems that are in place in those organizations prevent anything interesting from happening. Ultimately any good idea will or will not be vetoed by anyone in a senior position for maybe the right or the wrong reason, and like I said, it's a recipe for disaster. Design can't really flourish in that environment, I don't think. People think it can; people in those environments think it's functioning perfectly and that's the way it should work. But when you go in from the outside like I did, you really see how utterly dysfunctional it is. The results speak for themselves.

Bad design is everywhere, but there's this thing known as "bad-good design." It's only when you attach a personality to something—then, of course, it's designed by a person. There are bad designs out there; there's some really, really ugly stuff. As I was saying before, I would love to be in a position to point the finger, but don't quite feel like this is the forum to do it. I can tell you what I really like. Of course, I think someone like Jony Ive is doing a terrific job. Apple has an extraordinary ability to be able to reinvent themselves all the time, to come up with not only a new design but a new concept, a new paradigm shift, which is mind-boggling when you consider the influence that they're having.

Back to bad design—bad design is gratuitous design, I think. It's just lazy design. The thing that irks me the most is when I have to buy badly designed stuff. I have no choice; I'm given no choice. I have a nine-month-old daughter, and I've got to tell you, the state of stroller design is just, I mean, it's got to be seen to be believed, it's so bad. Anything, absolutely anything associated with children is just crap. It's so bad in every way—it's bad morally; it's bad design; it's bad for the environment; it's bad for the kid; it's bad ergonomically. We are sitting ducks. You know, I feel like I've been exploited. I feel like I'm being ripped off blindly. I have to have this stuff. I've got to buy this stuff; I have no choice. My kid has to sit on one of these stupid high chairs, whether I like it or not, and I'm dying to throw the thing out, you know? Knowing full well I've just purchased a piece of landfill. There's an industry that really needs a shake-up, that can really, really, really do with some help.

GH — There's a lot in the media right now in the States about fire retardants. The amount of fire retardants that they put in those baby chairs, and baby car seats, it's just ridiculous.

MN — Toxic.

GH — Totally overkill, versus using some other materials that don't burn, that are naturally fire retardant. Instead they use all this cotton, and they just soak it in chemicals.

MN — Clearly that can't be good for a kid, because kids just chew everything they can get their mouths on.

GH — It doesn't make sense.

MN — Unfortunately, it has had the opposite effect on me—instead of doing something about it, I feel utterly repelled. I just want to have nothing to do with it, you know? I just want to get through this period and throw it all away.

—

Ronan Bouroullec (RB)& Erwan Bouroullec (EB)/ May 23, 2008 Paris

Brothers Ronan and Erwan Bouroullec studied at the École Nationale des Arts Décoratifs in Paris and at the École des Beaux-Arts in Cergy-Pontoise. Ronan began independent design work immediately after completing his studies, while his brother, who was still in school, assisted him. Since 1999 both brothers have worked together as joint partners in their own design firm. Their work ranges from domestic and office furniture to small utilitarian objects to architectural projects. A primary focus of their work is the design and organization of interior space. I spoke with the brothers in their Paris studio.

—

Gary Hustwit — I guess let's start with the beginnings, how you guys got involved with design.

Erwan Bouroullec — We started our company more or less 10 years ago, when we stared working with Cappellini, the Italian brand. That was the formal start of our industrial design work. Of course, there were other things after college, things like that.

Ronan Bouroullec — The most important thing is that we never had to work for someone else. We did very little work, just enough to survive, and then very quickly we started working for important companies: Cappellini, Issey Miyake, Vitra. They came to us—even though we were a very young company. We went very quickly from project to project; we never had to go knocking on doors for work. The clients came directly to us.

EB — We were very much self-taught, and for that reason we never had to work for someone else, as my brother said. We had a lot of tools, software. We created fashion shows. We learned a great deal ourselves—in fact we learned everything just by actually doing it. That gave us a unique style; we were creating work that had a certain simplicity. Our work does not look like the work of engineers. We never studied how to make bridges and things like that.

RB — It's true that we have a certain philosophy that's applied throughout our work. In many ways, a designer is like a chef. There are a great number of elements that are necessary to work with to be sure that the result is a success. There are a great number of different methods to learn design— that is to say, the people that you have in this film mostly have come to design by accident. Marc Newson learned design by making jewelry. For

Jasper Morrison, it was something else. There are these very different and complex paths for arriving at what one does.

EB — For us, from the start it's always been a dialogue. It was Cappellini and us. It was Ligne Roset and us. It was Vitra and us. Working with Giulio Cappellini was very important. We were very young, we were very new to the field, and he found just the right way to bring our work to fruition.

RB — When we started working with Cappellini, it was a little like suddenly being on the Chelsea football team or Manchester United. So after that a lot of companies came to us. Our career is very linked to the fact that we met some very important people early on, and the fact that we love what we do.

EB — We really need to have a strong relationship with a client, which is what makes design different than—

RB — It could be the same relationship that a painter has with his gallery.

EB — No. No. No.

GH — What are the negatives, the downsides to the client relationships?
    EB — There have been no downsides in our work relationships with the companies with which we've collaborated so far. The most fundamental thing is to have the strength to be true to the project. If the project goes in another direction, you need to have the strength to stop it, which can be tricky. Projects always ask for an investment of time and research, but we go into these projects knowing that they may not always work out. Which is sometimes what happens—it is possible that we cannot agree on an appropriate solution. And that can be the most unpleasant part, when we have to say we cannot continue working on a project.

There are always rules that we're subjected to—technical constraints or marketing objectives or some other thing. But the reality is that these constraints are no more complicated than the rules in a soccer match, like don't kick the ball off of the field or touch the ball with your hands. There are rules that can limit the scope of the work, but there is always a place to express our freedom.

RB — We are very lucky to have a studio that is very small so that we can limit ourselves to only a small number of projects with the type of companies or the type of clients that we choose. That makes it possible, as Erwan said, to work for clients that we can collaborate with, engage with, and act from a position of strength with if we feel a certain way about how a project is going.

For example, today we are still very young as a company, and we would have difficulty working with a huge company where there is no direct intermediary. We work with companies that we can discuss all phases of the project with in a very informal way. With Vitra, we can call them anytime and have a conversation in a very simple and direct way, which for us is crucial to our process. We have great difficulty when our work must pass through different departments, such as marketing, et cetera, which makes us uncomfortable.

GH — Would you ever do something independent, like manufacture a product that you designed and work completely on your own?

RB — At the beginning it was like that because, when you are starting out as a designer—and now that's more complex because there are 10,000 people who get a design degree every year—you start in a very simple way. Like a painter who paints canvases, we started to make objects. We would find money, a little from here and a little from there, and produce physical things that allowed us to participate in group exhibitions. That gave us the opportunity to learn and develop and to allow people to notice our work.

EB — We also have a strong desire to create objects that have a mass appeal, but that is not the only thing we would like to achieve. It's a little like, if you want to make movies and you want them to be shown in thousands of cinemas, you have to find partners who will help you to produce them. I believe that philosophically this has a fundamental role in our approach to the development of a design. There is also the heavy burden of the time the project takes and the technical work involved; it requires that we be commercial at certain times, and in my opinion that is the struggle within our work.

RB — That brings up another point: why make design? I believe that this field corresponds well to my nature, because if I have a good idea, there is no reason not to produce the design. That is the reason that brought me to the field of design—putting ideas into production. At times you can get great feedback, and sometimes it is less related to the industry, and for us that creates a relationship with the entirely of the production.

EB — The industry is related to the needs of the market. And the market—for lots of good reasons, not for bad reasons—has a reactionary force. There is a tendency to stop the development of new things. So we have a responsibility to look for—like haute couture for fashion, we are motivated to create things that are also for a specific audience and outside the realm of mass-produced products. That's always a tool for finding new clients, a tool for research. Our role as industrial designers is to think of what will be needed in the future for mass production.

GH — I am sure that this is a question that you hear all of the time, but working with your brother—how is that relationship?

RB — We mentioned before that the relationship is usually a team consisting of a designer in partnership with a manufacturer. From the beginning, Erwan and I have had a relationship that was a team mentality. Our relationship is very complicated, and at the same time, it has a great strength behind it. When things go well, everything is very simple; it is exactly like playing a game of ping-pong. We both say, "It would be great if this went like that." And little by little the project develops very smoothly, very naturally, and it works very fluidly. Other times, Erwan has a terrible idea, and everything falls apart. Erwan thinks his idea is good. I think my idea, which is different, is good, and we reach an impasse.

I believe that the strength of our work is that we are each a little different, and our projects come into being via two minds. A good project is a combination of lots of different elements; the thought process that forms is something quite formal and at the same time quite simple. And to have two minds working together to develop these types of projects is something that's very important. But, at the same time, it's a complex process because it's important to find the commonality that runs through the ideas.

The creative process, as I see it and as I interpret it as expressed by others, is a procedure that is very tumultuous; there are highs and lows, big moments of highs and big depressions. There are moments when you go home thinking, "That was a great idea," and then later after further reflection you look at the project again and say, "That is a terrible idea." And that is the creative process. It has a force of its own, in any event. That was a long explanation.

EB — What is good is that we're both inspired by the same desire to make things that are very, very strong. We did not create this agency to make money; we did not create this studio to become famous. In fact, I think we both come from a very romantic understanding of art that is very "old school." In the deepest sense, the heroes who are the most influential to us are painters, such as Cézanne and others, people who have arrived at an absolute form in their work.

I think that we both approach our work with the same fundamental philosophy to create strong, honest work even in the simplest of projects. And that puts a great deal of pressure on us. This is a desire that can also be very tricky. Sometimes when our projects are completed and we did not go all of the way, or projects are delayed and delayed, that gives us the incredible frustration of waiting and hoping that we can go as far as we want in our work, and it is a constant frustration to never arrive at that level of purity. The only, not defect, but strength of our work is that we are very emotionally tied to it, because of the deep attachment to what we do.

RB — Also, what Erwan is trying to say is that we have what is maybe a naive hope in the absolute sense that in the end we could have been painters or we could have been writers; we just happen to be industrial designers. This is the medium we have come to to express ourselves. So, perhaps it is the best choice for us, and that's why it's also interesting to be a team of two. The creative experience, looking for purity in the solution, is sometimes a very painful process, so being together gives us perspective after the emotional highs and lows experienced through the nature of the process. It is always our sense of camaraderie that bolsters us.

EB — We rest on each other.

RB — We rest on each other. As Erwan said earlier, we can be working on a long-term project over many months or even a year, and we still realize that the solution is not strong enough to present. It does not reach our own internal expectations. So, since we are a team, it is easier to accept that result.

We have approaches that are very different—Erwan is very talkative; I am more silent—so in that way there is a very subtle game that goes on, not at all in a way that is Machiavellian, but that helps to push the process to its conclusion. Erwan has a way that is very direct in talking with the engineers. Erwan can be brutal with the engineers, when he wants something technical, and that can create tension. And then I can arrive to smooth things out, to make sure that we end up with the result we wanted in the first place.

EB — He is the fox, and I am the porcupine.

RB — There are two profiles in the basic understanding of psychology. There are the porcupines that move forward with an idea head-on—

EB — That's me.

RB — And there's the fox, who is cunning enough to get everyone to see things his way. That is the difference between us, and that is also our strength.

GH — Let's talk about materials and the relationship that you have in terms of inspiration. Are there times when you have an idea for, say, a piece of furniture covered in black mesh, and then you go out and find that material? Or is it the other way around? Do you see a piece of black mesh lying around and that inspires you?

RB — It is really everything at the same time. There are certain projects where we will find a piece of plastic and some fabric—

EB — Often.

RB — And from that departure point, we are able to create something.

EB — For me, more than the materials, it's about the process, the transformation. I'm very interested in textiles and ways of sewing fabric, or how to assemble pieces of fabric by finding a way of gluing them. We also work with plastics sometimes, and we enjoy the challenge of finding new ways to work with injection molding.

RB — There are four or five departure points for approaching a project. Certain machines allow us to do something that has never been done before. Sometimes it's a little screw or some unimportant detail that inspires us. What is important is that this element helps us to produce our ideas.

EB — I would say that we put a certain amount of confidence in the logic of the materials and their transformation. For me, it is this process that has a direct connection to the design of the exterior of the object or the piece of furniture.

We have a sort of dogma, and it's that we're against design for decorative reasons only. We are never going to go back and add an unnecessary flourish on a project for aesthetic reasons, or print something on an object to make it turn into something else. We would never use a formal reference for an object, like Philippe Starck did by creating a small table in the form of a garden gnome. It's not that we are against other designers doing that, but we would never do something like what they do at Alessi, create an object that looks like a person to represent something.

To create a kind of balance or beauty or honesty in the object, we try to follow the logic of the materials, the logic of the transformation. And we often find details and uses within the materials—for example, there is the Facett sofa we made with Ligne Roset which is based on a detail from the sewing of the fabric that allowed us to go in a certain direction, to communicate in a very detailed and specific way. Or, for example, when making the Steelwood chair, we knew that it was going to be bent metal, and we knew from the start that when you work with bending metal there is a delicacy of form and all sorts of rules that are related to the manufacture, that would give us the cleanest lines. In the end, we try to push the manufacturing to exploit the greatest use of the materials, so that the final form is very pleasing to the eye, which people notice.

It's true that this is our interpretation of the concept "less is more," which comes up again and again as a dogma in contemporary design, which is to make the object's form with the least amount of materials and with the least technical operations. But we are not trying to make a minimalist object; we are trying to streamline the process to make the product the best, treat it the most carefully, to put the most depth into the design of the object at the moment of the transformation.

This creates a very particular relationship with the materials and with the transformation of the materials. How do we work best with these materials? How will they be best exploited, and how can we make this detail superb? How can we show off the details, to bring them to prominence, to find the beauty and the characteristics of the materials in the most simplistic use of the forms, to bend the metal in this way, or to use sewing in that way? It is very different from the way fashion works, for example, which is very often a work of addition, adding materials, colors, or details to remind us of a certain time period.

RB — Our point of view is that we do not have the need to use new materials or new techniques to create something radical. We can work very well with a fine piece of wood, a piece of metal, and a vise. We can bring something extraordinary to that. We are always happy to discover something new. The materials are only a part of the global vision that is the object.

EB — It is true that we've never made tables or chairs in carbon fiber. Because, yes, it would be lighter, but it is not very suave as an approach. It's too, how can I say?

RB — I think there are objects whose only justification for existence is that they're made from these nice materials. Sometimes a new material is available, and someone refined and extremely intelligent makes something great with that material, and we are of course happy for that development. The iPod exists and now we have access to digital music; someone created something that never existed before.

EB — It's true that these new materials are being used to make things that are "the longest in the world" or "the lightest in the world," but at some point that becomes a bit comical or too trendy.

RB — It makes no sense. Very often there is a technical development that is completely unnecessary; for example, the painter who paints in the most superrealistic way is not necessarily the most interesting painter in the world. The quality of an object or of a sculpture is much more rich than that. Often there are nice materials, but it is more about the thinking behind it or the concept behind it; the product should not be dependent on the molecular formation of the object.

GH — I'm interested in how the end users of these objects form these relationships with them. There's emotion invested in the object because there's a history or story behind it. What are your thoughts as designers and also as users of objects yourselves?

RB — I am going to respond differently from Erwan, but for me, in a certain way, I separate myself from what will happen after we've designed an object. If I were a chef and I had a restaurant, it is obvious that I would prepare meals and then people would want to eat them. As a designer, I have a certain ideas for products, and it would be natural that the consumer wants to use them. I do not really have an interest in thinking about it beyond that point. I am often shocked by the relationship that people can have with objects, and very often I am disturbed when people purchase things that I have designed and they consider them sacred. It's really strange.

I find that I need very few objects to survive, and I am happy to have them, but I can also live without objects. I do not feel any need to make certain objects sacred. And to be able to think clearly about the work I'm doing, it is important that I am not surrounded by other objects.

EB — There is always the question of: why this new chair? For me it is simple. We are constantly evolving, and the reality that things change is the only thing that moves us emotionally. An object must be right for a particular usage, and it must be right for a certain philosophy of living. After that, all we can do is to suggest something. If people don't like it, they will not buy it. There are plenty of other chairs and things that people can purchase. We have to find things that speak to us, that respond to what we need, to what we feel, why we are here, and that is linked to the question of diversity. There is nothing worse than these ready-made solutions. Nike, Louis Vuitton. They are not things that respond to our individuality—these are things that make us the same. That make us look like other people. We try to do the opposite—we try to make things that are meaningful, that are unique. In designing furniture or shelving systems that are more flexible, more customizable, we give people the ability to make their own statement and define what their own needs are.

—

Hella Jongerius (HJ)/ May 26, 2008 Rotterdam

Dutch designer Hella Jongerius has become known for the way she fuses industry and craft, high and low tech, traditional and contemporary. After graduating from Eindhoven Design Academy in 1993, she started her own design company, Jongeriuslab, through which she produces her own projects and projects for clients such as Maharam, KLM, Vitra, IKEA, and many others.

—

Gary Hustwit — Okay, let's talk about your background and how you got involved in design. What was the path?

Hella Jongerius — I started late with my studies, because I didn't really know what I wanted to do when I finished high school. I didn't know about design as a profession when I got out of high school. After some wandering, I eventually knew I wanted to do something creative. I had actually been studying ergotherapy, where you're being creative in a caring way. That's when I thought, "I really want to be creative," and I could choose between art and design. I felt that I really wanted to find creative solutions within boundaries, so that's why I became an industrial designer. But I started late, when I was 25.

GH — And what were some of your first projects?

HJ — The first projects I worked on when I graduated were in polyurethane, in rubber. Vases, mats—those were the first things I wanted to do. The first theme I studied was copying; materials played the design role, and the formal aspect was copying what was already there. So I didn't design, and I still don't. The form doesn't interest me so much, but the materials—materials form the product. That was instantly the first theme. So, copy/paste was the first theme I explored, using rubber as the material.

GH — What's the scope of design that you work in today?

HJ — I work in various materials, so, ceramics, textiles for furniture, furniture, and now also colors, consulting on color choices. I do this in one-offs for galleries, and I do it in mass production for IKEA, and everything in between.

GH — What were some of your other projects when you were starting out?

HJ — The first part of my career was self-initiated, as there were no clients, and that was when

I started collaborating with Droog Design. So, for the first 9 or 10 years I was doing self-initiated work, and then Droog took it all over the world and showed it in various places.

The first self-initiated project that eventually became mass-produced was the B-set porcelain plate set. This was about imperfection, and it was the first of my projects to be mass-produced in the Netherlands by Royal Tichelaar Makkum. By firing the clay at too high a temperature, each piece deforms slightly, making it unique. After that I got an assignment from Maharam, the textile manufacturer in New York. Their request was: can you make one textile for eight different chairs? I started with the idea to make a repeating pattern that's longer than 30 centimeters. Usually, a motif or design is 30 centimeters in size and is repeated. This is how you buy it in the furniture industry; it has to fit one chair and one backrest. Now, I just wanted to make a huge repeat, it's two or three meters that repeats, so that you get a different piece every time on a couch or chair. It looks like you've got a unique textile, even though it's really mass-produced.

In the Maharam series I first discovered the idea of making individual pieces that still are mass-produced. That's what interests me, to make individual pieces en masse. To give something that's produced industrially an individual character. The idea turned out to be very successful.

GH — Are there other ways you've found to add character to an industrial process?

HJ — I always want to show that there are multiple layers in a product— it's sort of a puzzle that builds itself, and one of the layers is to try to make an individual piece in that industrial work. Sometimes that's a matter of craft, so you can just see that human hands made it, so every piece is really different, like in the B set. Sometimes, like with the sofa I made with Vitra, at the last minute buttons are sewn onto it, as if they're just there for no reason. I wouldn't call that imperfection; it's adding crafted details. It makes you feel you're buying a piece or seeing a product that has paid attention to the human details.

GH — Could you talk about the perception of design versus art? There are all these designers doing limited-edition work; is it art or is it design? What contradictions are associated with the two?

HJ — I made limited editions from the start. Now there's a word for it, but at that time I made things without clients. They were trials in the design process. That was in the early nineties. We threw those pieces out; they were merely experiments to get somewhere. Some, like the embroidered plate I made in '95, are now real "editions." I think that when I make a limited piece, there needs to be a reason why it's limited; then it really is a study to get somewhere else. I'll use it as a reference to apply to an mass-produced piece later. It's great to get a request like that once in a while. I also have a gallery, and I still work there because I think it's interesting to do research in that way. That's how I use it. Period. That's how I work.

I've always said I don't want to make art. I want to make an object that has functionality. It has to be functional, because I'm terrified of making bad art. I think I see a lot of bad art being made by designers right now, and they call it "editions."

GH — Can you talk about what you see as the role of a designer in our world? How do you see what you do affecting people's lives?

HJ — I find it very hard. That's already such an existential question for me because I think that the profession in itself has very little weight, very little meaning. It doesn't solve any global problems; it's not curing AIDS. The only thing you can do is sustainability. That's a way you can be useful to the world. Personally, I like to bring beauty and to do it in an innovative way, or to try to do something innovative in my profession and in that way create a meaning for myself to keep doing this.

GH — I'm interested in how the objects you make have this life of their own after people buy them; they go on to change other people's lives. Even if it's bringing beauty, like you said.

HJ — Beauty is something that is almost an understatement; it's hard to say about your own work. But if you look at art, you're touched by something, and it can change your life because at least at that moment it moves you. You hope that an object will also do that to someone. Because you use the objects in your house, they become part of your family, and you'll want to inherit them. It'll become "that one chair that Dad always sat in." That's what's fun about it.

GH — I like the idea that somebody is passing that chair down to someone else. They're all having a relationship with the objects that are surrounding them, so by extension they're having a relationship with the creator of the object.

HJ — The reason I work with very good clients, with companies that deliver very high quality, is partly that I believe I bring a lot to the process in the sense that I really want to innovate. So, if I make a couch, it really needs to be something new; there's no use in making just another couch. I don't want it; a lot of people don't want it. So, if I take on an object, it has to bring something new, bring a new language, in that field. And I want that to happen with a company with high production quality, someone who really wants to give the product a long life. Then a chair really can live for two or three generations. That's a way you can try to do something about overconsumption.

GH — Can you talk about your relationship to ceramics? Why do you work with them so often?

HJ — Ceramics are one of the more serious craft materials that exist, with a very long tradition. Everything that's been around since before Christ is pottery and ceramics, so there's a big tradition, craft-wise. The seriousness of the material, because of its hardness—it's almost precious. It doesn't have the qualities of gold, but porcelain has something serious about it. It starts with something very, very soft. When it's clay, it's so free to form, and when it's done, it's very rigid. Those two aspects of ceramics I find very interesting.

If you then add all the traditions, that makes you able to play with people's memories. I find that to be an interesting aspect—a lot of people have memories of ceramics that they used at home in the past or ceramics from certain movies or ceramics that you think queens drink their tea from. People have a lot of memories, which makes it possible to give layers of meaning to the material.

GH — Does that sense of memory and history appear in other areas of your work as well?

HJ — I want to speak a new language in a design, but you shouldn't innovate everything. It's a recipe I work with. Don't innovate every aspect when you're designing. So, some of the things I use are parts of design that come from people's memories. I either use a craft that everybody's familiar with or something from a certain culture that we can all accept easily—something in which you see a human scale, something sewn or where an icon is used, so that you've already reassured someone with the object, and that's when you can do something very innovative. That's when people are open to saying, "Oh, of course, you can do that too!" That's when the product can communicate with the user. If you innovate everything, people will disconnect. They'll just think it's funny, and you'll lose their attention. So, I use memories in innovation.

GH — Speaking more generally, what are your thoughts on companies like IKEA and the concept of democratization of design?

HJ — When IKEA called me about doing something for them, I doubted a lot if I was willing to do it because I can see that, in some projects, choices are being made solely for economic reasons. I see that in the products that are being sold at IKEA, so I was afraid that I'd lose my quality standards if I wanted to do something with IKEA. On the other hand, I thought it was such a challenge. I'm commenting on mass production and on the high quantity of products. I really wanted to collaborate once with a mass-producer, to see if my signature style would stay intact. Can I bring individuality to such a company? That's why I took the job. I think it turned out to be a very good project. My ideas stayed intact, even while working with a producer like IKEA. I also think that IKEA is the first educator in taste for a lot of people. IKEA's furniture is made for a younger audience. They're actually educators in taste, which is a very good role. It's incredible if you can do that. So I'm happy there's an IKEA.

GH — What about your relationship with Vitra?

HJ — The collaboration with Vitra started with a list of potential projects from Rolf Fehlbaum, the owner of the company. On the wish list he gave me of things I could work on, number one was a sofa. I was very surprised, as up to then I'd been working at a completely different scale—a lot smaller and a lot of tabletops and textiles. Also, the subject, a sofa, is boring in my opinion. If you own a sofa, you're done. So I told him, "What should I do with a sofa? I don't even have a sofa myself!" To which he said, "Why don't you make a sofa you'd want to own?"

That inspired me to start working with them. Really, from the first day, it went very smoothly. We really fit together—the two cultures, the Swiss culture and the Dutch culture are very similar, I felt at home there. I've already done a couple of furniture pieces with them. In 2005, I was asked if I wanted to be responsible for the colors, textiles, really all the finishes there. That's what I'm doing for them now. I told them I wanted to work on all the pieces, not as a stylist, but as a designer. I can't approach it only as a stylist; I really wanted to do it as a designer. I've thought for a long time about how I wanted to do that job, how I could come up with the theme colors from clichés, like red is the color of traffic signals but also of love. You know, the world of color is so superficial; so often it's only used as a marketing trick. You know, "We'll give everything a new color and we can go on for a couple more years." I wanted to do it in a different way and tried to find a way I could approach it as a designer.

We just started making the famous Eames lounge chair in white leather, and that was instantly right. I'd been asked to make a softer version, and the first time I walked around that chair, I thought, "How could I?" After all, Eames is the master of chair design for all of us. Everybody's always talking about the lounge chair, the icon of the profession. But slowly, I felt enough liberty to change things in it, especially together with Rolf Fehlbaum. He knew Eames and can be sort of the conscience of the old master. He knows what you can't touch, when it's the essence of Eames. I was able to move freely as a designer; I didn't have to be Eames's conscience. That was the first product, and now we're working on all the fabrics of the Eames Aluminum Group and slowly the whole plastic range. There's a Panton color world; there's an Eames color world; there's a Prouvé color world. Very slowly, we've done all the old masters. The ones who are dead are very easy because you don't have to take an ego into account. There is always a family foundation, but we're approaching these changes seriously, so that always works out.

Slowly, we're building the range of colors into a color library that'll also be available to the consumers, to see what those colors are and what your palette could be. Also for the designers who are still alive and are working for Vitra now—the Bouroullecs and Jasper Morrison—for that group it's also a sort of laboratory or library from which they can take samples and from which they can see, for instance, what a certain red looks like on aluminum, or a red on wood, or a red in glossy plastic. All of that needs to be present in the samples.

GH — That also kind of plays into what you were talking about before: taking something familiar but changing it while still keeping its iconic form.

HJ — Right. I give color advice and design new colors, but it's being used on an old piece, on something that was already created. I often work with archives. When I start working with a company, the first thing I do is look into their archives. I just have to open them and I already see such beautiful objects. There's such a DNA of the company in an archive, something you only have to dust off and show in a new way so that it becomes a product again. I don't believe in starting with a blank sheet to design a product. It's always based on something old. With Vitra, I make colors for old masters, for chairs that are already good and made well. They only need a slightly new color.

GH — What are your general thoughts about approaching color?

HJ — When I started the color job at Vitra, I started with the fairly radical idea that there are reds, there are greens, and there are grays; all the rest are tone derivations of those three colors. Now that I'm completely immersed, it's very hard to keep to that conviction. But it's still a starting point for the work I do. Color is so subjective. It has everything to do with intuition and the way it's being used. A plastic Panton chair was made in a certain era, with a certain background, in a material that was very important at the time. So for that, you're looking for a color. It's very hard for me to say what is color inspiration, because it's all about the usage, the surroundings, and the shape.

GH — Wild card question: if you were watching a movie about industrial design, what would you want to have someone say that we haven't talked about yet?

HJ — If you're talking about furniture design, that's only a very small part of the business. That's what always intrigues me, how everyone in the business operates differently. If you look at electronics, for instance, there's a completely different way of looking at design. It's always just a splinter of a profession. That's what I find interesting.

One of the questions I always ask when I'm designing with my team is: would you buy this? Would you spend money on this? That's an important idea, because you're working for a target audience. Despite that, I take myself as a starting point. I ask myself, would I want to have it? Would I want to buy it? Everyone always wants to have it, but would you open your wallet for it? Would you sweat to spend the money? That's an important question to ask.

—

Jonathan Ive

(JI)/
**June 8, 2008
Cupertino**

There are few designers whose work is so closely associated with a single company that it's impossible to imagine that company's products without them. Jonathan Ive's work at Apple, including the iMac, the iPod, the iPhone, countless desktop and laptop computers, and now the Apple Watch, has made him arguably the most influential designer of our time.

In 2007 I was invited by Apple's graphic design department to screen *Helvetica* at the Apple campus in Cupertino. As a lifelong Apple user (we got an Apple II+ at our house when I was 14) it was a big honor. The following year, when I had the idea for *Objectified*, I knew that the film would only be complete if Jony was part of it. Through some friends I'd made at Apple, and a lot of patience, I managed to secure the interview. I was also honored to be the first filmmaker ever allowed to film inside Apple's design lab.

Funny sidenote: the airline lost some of our filming equipment on the flight to San Francisco. With no time to buy replacements, we were forced to go to Home Depot and construct our own DIY substitutes, like a microphone boom pole made out of PVC pipe and duct tape. Let me tell you, we felt pretty silly walking into the most design-centric company in the world with our crappy, makeshift "gear." But it did the job, and I guess that's all that really matters.
—

Gary Hustwit — What have you got here on the table?

> **Jonathan Ive** — Basically what we've got are some of the stages we go through to make the MacBook Air.

GH — Maybe we can start by talking about the manufacturing process?

> **JI** — Sure. We had a really clear goal designing the MacBook Air, and that was to try to design and build something that was not only remarkably thin but also very rigid. Those two things usually don't go together very well. Traditionally how you solve that problem is that often you have an internal structure and then you have an external shell, which actually contributes much less to the overall structure of the product than you would imagine. What we've been working toward is removing a ton of those parts and all the inherent risk, inaccuracies, weight, and complexity, and trying to solve the structural issues with fewer parts. The real breakthrough we had that enabled the MacBook Air is that the structure of this product is almost

entirely derived from this palm rest. This palm rest is the backbone for the entire product. Normally when you have a palm rest, you cut this great big hole that makes it completely hopeless in terms of having any structural integrity. What we discovered was that, instead of one big hole, if we machine a whole bunch of small holes, the structure remains largely intact.

This part actually starts out as this extrusion. So this is an aluminium extrusion that goes through multiple operations, most of them CNC machined operations, to end up with this part. So you can see there's just a dramatic transformation between this raw blank and the final part. What's fantastic about aluminium is that, at each of the different stages we go through, we're harvesting the material we're removing; we are actually recycling all that material. What we end up with is a part that has all of the mounting features, all of the bosses, all of the undercuts. They're all integrated. So this is just one part, but this one part is providing so much functionality, and this really does enable this product. I don't know, as a designer, how you can design a product like this without becoming intimately involved with all the processes to make this one part. This isn't just about building a model and just hoping and stamping your feet; just belligerence isn't going to get you there. It's about taking the time to thoroughly understand.

It's interesting: we look at a finished object, we look at a physical product, but the design of this in many ways wasn't the design of a physical thing. In many ways, it was figuring out process; it was figuring out all the processes that would eventually enable this. And by definition, if you're doing something that hasn't been done before, if you're trying to solve problems in a new way, you don't have a precedent that you can refer to. So much of the effort behind a product like the MacBook Air was experimenting with different processes. This is completely nonobvious, but the way that you hold this to get from this blank to this part—there is an incredibly complex series of fixtures to hold this part in the different machine stages. And we end up spending a lot of time designing fixtures. So we are designing physical objects that hold a component to eventually enable this product.

And that's what I love about what we do. In a way, you could say you're designing a process for an object; then that object defines a whole slew of other processes for the users of that object. If you design an object in a certain way, you're designing the way that we'll hold it, the way that we'll use our hands. You can be working on what can seem like very abstract parts of the problem that you eventually realize will culminate in the object. It's certainly been my experience that the more profound and significant your innovation, it's just a requirement, a necessity that you get involved in a depth and a level that you would never dream exists.

GH — It totally makes sense that you spend as much time designing the methods that you are going to use to manufacture the object as designing the actual object. It's all intertwined.

JI — Yeah, that's why I'm still struck by how hard design seems. It's just … this is really complicated. In some ways, the products that were developed years ago—because production in high volume was so hard, I think there was a sense of reverence before you launched a new product. And I think that is one of the reasons that so many of the products that were designed many years ago seem to have an integrity and a significance that a lot of products now don't have. Today, as a designer, it's easy to get so far removed from the actual product. You can design virtually with sophisticated CAD tools, and prototypes can be made remotely. The actual product is usually manufactured on another continent. It used to be that the product was manufactured downstairs, and you would develop that product in such a fluid, natural, organic way with how it was going to be made. That's not the case anymore, but I think you have to make it the case if you're going to do something interesting.

We're just getting more and more disconnected from the physical, more and more disconnected from the product, so we end up being surrounded by ideas. They're sort of three-dimensional ideas, and some of the ideas are really compelling and interesting, but because there is nothing more than the idea, I think they just don't last. They don't work, and they very often don't solve problems.

GH — It's funny. This is a lot like conversations we were having with designers in *Helvetica*, because the same thing happened in typeface design. In the 1950s, you didn't just walk into a shop as an apprentice and make a typeface; you had to work for years to get to the point where your designs were deemed worthy enough to be cast in metal. The investment was just so huge to tool up and manufacture a typeface.

JI — Yes, whereas now to develop and launch a product in volume is relatively easy. It's like pressing Command-P. It's like printing. The incredible rigor, significance, and gravitas aren't there anymore. That's why I think a lot of the products we're surrounded by, a lot of our manufactured environment, seems too easy and too superficial. There's an incredible disconnect between the designer and how the physical thing is being made, and there's a disconnect between the shell and the guts of the product.

GH — Are there benefits to the ease of designing and prototyping now? Does it help with experimentation, for instance?

JI — I think that there are fantastic benefits to being able to prototype ideas. When sophisticated tools let you do something you could never have done before, that's fantastic. But those tools, if they're used superficially, all they really do is get you from one point to another point really fast, and then it just stops there. If you're not experimenting, and you're just using those tools to get things done fast and rush to launch a product, that's a tragedy. That is very, very sad.

GH — Can we talk about materials? Where does the inspiration come from in terms of what material to use? I don't know if here at Apple it's kind of like, "Oh, we're gonna use aluminum on this," and then you start machining, or sometimes do you see a certain material and say, "Oh, I know the perfect use for that"? Do you want to talk about that process a little bit?

JI — You know, I think when we're designing a product, we start by developing the criteria for what we need a material to do, and so that would drive the way we think about our material selection. Very often, exactly what we want isn't available, so that sees us developing new materials or modifying existing ones. So definitely we see the necessity of the requirements of the product driving what we're looking at. But of course, also, we see materials that we find completely intriguing and seductive, and we sort of find out more about them. And so I think it happens in both ways, because very often we're trying to solve some very practical problems about, say, we want something to be small and durable, and we want something that may be transparent to radio frequency, you know? Or you're developing a phone with some very specific requirements of materials.

But again, it's an awful lot for us to just start with the material and understanding the material, not defining a form, and then sort of annotating the form and saying, "Oh, this will be wood, and this will be metal." You know, they're so closely coupled, what the material is and the form of it, and also the architecture of the entire product is a huge part of what we do. Just figuring out how a product's configured, how it goes together, that's a very big driver in where we end up. And that's not a constraint, you know? We don't see it as, "Well, this is ideally what we would like. Oh no, now we've got to figure out how we make that real." How do you actually make that a real thing? What we like is driven massively by how you would make it and how you would architect the thing. And again, I think that's a lot of what we try and do: see design in a broader sense. It's how a thing works, and I don't mean by the usual definition of "how it works." It's not just how it works for me as a user but what the product is. That's partly your experience of it as a user, but also a big part of what it is is how it was assembled and how it was made.

GH — What about form? Where does your inspiration there come from?

JI — When it comes to form, I think we're mindful of a number of things. Definitely the architecture of the product and how it's going to be made. The materials we're working in play a huge role at a part level, and there's what the object is and what's just appropriate and what's just a truly simple, almost inevitable solution. And then what's inside a product has a big influence if you're going to try and be connected to the truth and honesty of the internal components. So for example, the first iMac that we made, the primary component of that was the cathode ray tube. And that was a big component, but the part of it that really had an impact on the external surface and form was the display, which was spherical. And so we would have an entirely different approach to designing something like that than the current iMac, which has a very thin, flat-panel display. So I think it's a mixture of things that really drive the way we think about form. What it consistently isn't is an arbitrary shape that we then try and figure out how to make and try and figure out whether the components inside actually bear any relationship to the shape, whether literally or at some sort of philosophical level.

GH — Can you show me the battery enclosure? Is that from the 15-inch MacBook Pro?

JI — Yeah, I think it's right under here. So much of our achievement here is completely nonobvious. I mean, clearly one of our goals is to try and simplify, and that's not just applying a simple appearance. It's not putting a simple sticker over something that is inherently complex and sort of sloppy in its development. It's that we figured out a whole new way of building the product. We didn't accept the fact that it's been done this way for years; we developed a new architecture, a new way of building it. And the reason why simple is a good goal is that you get rid of clutter and you bring a sense of peace and calmness to the object. So you can focus on what really matters, and I think, with these products, there is a hierarchy of importance. You establish something as being important, very often, by removing distractions.

When you look at an object, there are so many prominent artifacts that are only there because apparently there wasn't a better way of solving the problem. But the amount of work that went into just developing the way you remove the battery on this product—there is this lever here that pops up that removes the battery door. You can see that we've laser etched the instructions for how to take the battery out there, and then there's this tab to take the battery out. But just the work on this, the enclosure itself, I mean, this is a big project. Right down to all the structure that you can't really see. This is sort of like finishing the back of the drawer. Whether you're going to see this or not, we would still do this. And we would be thinking, does anyone really see this? Does anyone really care? Does this really matter? I really do believe at some level that, when you touch and use a product that is the product of that obsession, I do think that in some way you do know about the care that went into it.

That's the one of the reasons we don't develop a huge number of products. We want to focus on a few things but go into this fanatical, obsessive level of detail. It's like there are all these discreet, self-contained little worlds inside the product. And you can just get lost with the amount of detail and care you put in. It's really remarkable.

GH — And most people would just take that for granted.
JI — I think that most people—they might not be consciously aware of it, but at some level, I think they are aware. And I think if you try and understand why we gravitate toward some products over others—somehow a product can assume some sort of significance in your daily life, and I don't think that that happens very often when the product is ill-considered or was developed as fast as possible to a price point. Those sorts of products don't ever assume that significance, you know? You don't end up loving them very much.

I think one of the things we're becoming really aware of right now is just how much design is about learning. It's just a huge part of the process. There's a group of us here that have been doing this together for a while now, and because we're at Apple and not working independently, we get to live with the consequences of what we do. So we get to learn, and sometimes that learning can be interesting and predictable and straightforward and exciting, and sometimes it can be pretty painful. I think products really benefit from you having to live with the consequences of what you did the year before and the year before that. A lot of these innovations are based on something we've done previously, and then we get to extend it and explore it more thoroughly. But we needed that stake in the ground from what we did last time. We couldn't have designed this product if we hadn't figured out some of these core architectural problems and solutions that we were grappling with on the MacBook Air. Each victory affords a new understanding, and a new level of opportunity for the next challenge.

I think it's important that we don't just accept. I mean, why is simplicity a good goal? I remember sitting in a lecture, years ago, where somebody was talking about consistency between products. And it was just assumed that that was a good and glorious goal, that the products from one company should all look the same. I remember thinking that I understood the premise and I understood that there were some assumptions about that and that maybe, as a consequence, it's a pretty cool thing that they look the same. They all look the same because they are the fruit of the same people with the same design goals. But I remember thinking, I don't actually see the virtue in it. Consistency was really important; they talked about that a lot. But they didn't talk about the products being good or not, so all the products could have been consistently crap. But consistency was seen as this wonderful and noble thing.

We spend so much energy trying to find the essence and the very simplest form of an idea and the simplest way of solving a problem. And because it's hard, whenever something is hard, I think you're given pause to say, "Well, does this really matter?" Or, "Is this goal right? Is this as important as we clearly think it is?" So very often we get absolutely stuck trying to find that completely quintessential idea. I am absolutely convinced it's the right goal, even if it can be difficult to achieve. The product is inherently a complex thing; it's complex in how it was conceived and developed. So I think our simplicity, in some sense, is just the outworking of the way we develop the product and the way that it's built.

For example, we're surrounded by so much clutter when you actually stop and look. I mean, there are so many distractions, even within a single product. And I think it's really important to remove those distractions, to remove those things that are all vying for your attention. An example of that is the way we've developed indicators. An indicator has a value when it's indicating something. But if it's not indicating something, it shouldn't be distracting you; it shouldn't be there. So very often you've got an object, and there's all this stuff that's clearly of no use at that point in time, but it's still all distracting you. It's still competing for your attention. One of the ways we solved that problem here was that we figured out a way, with a laser, to cut these tiny, tiny holes in the surface of the aluminium, so that when the indicator is not on, you have no sense of these holes in the aluminium, but when the indicator comes on, then it's there.

That's one little example. When we cut these tiny holes, because of the ratio of the diameter of the holes to the thickness of the material, because of parallax, you couldn't actually see the LED behind the holes.

We spent months developing a bubble-jet printing process, essentially filling these microscopic holes with a resin so that you could remove the issue of depth and essentially bring the light readout to the external surface. That hadn't been done before, and I am very aware that that might sound a little bit fanatical. There are so many examples like that. But that's how you make something that just seems obvious and inevitable and simple, and I wouldn't expect anybody to point to that as a feature, but on some level you're aware of a calm and considered solution that therefore speaks about how you're going to use it and not the terrible struggles that we as designers and engineers had in trying to solve some of the problems.

That's quite obsessive, isn't it?

GH — Yeah, but like you were saying before, it lets the user not have to think about it.

JI — I mean, look at the features that are on here. If you look at other laptops that some of our competitors make, they have more than four feet on them because the bottom isn't flat. And rather than figure out how to make the bottom flat, it's easier to add another foot. But if there's an element on this product, it's because we really can't think of how to solve the problem in any other way. Like the fact that there isn't a button that you have to press to release the display. I love when you can add tremendous utility and solve problems by taking something away. We haven't added a feature; we've gotten rid of the latches. But again, that's not because of some abstract goal that we've got that speaks to our preoccupations. This is all in the service of trying to make a simple product, and in some senses, arguably, it's about getting the designer out of the picture. I think it's about deferring to the user. When you see this, you don't see a designer wagging their tail in your face. It's not about self-expression. It's not about trying to be different. It's about trying to solve problems and make a product that people like using.

GH — Let's talk about the iMac screen too. I like that story. Let's slide some of these parts over.

JI — This is the bezel for the iMac. This is made from a pressed, forged, and then machined aluminium part. When we were developing this, we were struggling to find precedent. Again, we found ourselves in this somewhat lonely place of not really being able to point to processes or parts where this had been done before to achieve this level of quality and to make it in the volume that we need to. But one of the stories of how we make this is, when we remove the aluminium for the display in the center here, we actually take that material, and then we can make two keyboard frames from it. So this is the primary part that then makes the keyboard that goes with the iMac.

GH — So taking what would normally be waste and using it to make something else.

JI — You can have the attitude about manufacturing that you need to be engaged so that you can police what will come out at the end, to make sure that your intent makes it through the development process. I think we see it as completely polar opposite to that. It shouldn't be a necessary evil that you have to endure the process but that it's absolutely fundamental to what you do as a designer. It can't be this disconnected process that just has to happen. Time and time again, what we've found is, what you learn from being so connected and spending so much time in the actual process of making this stuff is not only that you increase your understanding of the material and the process to help what you do the next time; you also spot opportunities. When you see the material that we just removed to create the display, when you see that all stacked up, it talks to you very succinctly. Look at all that aluminium. Why don't we take that and make our keyboards from that material rather then just taking it right to be recycled?

I find that so much of what gets us excited and is so provocative and really gives us pause to think about the context of what we're doing is being so involved in the making. I don't know what design means; I don't know what designer means. I don't know where the design starts and stops and making starts and stops. We just make products, and that sees your involvement take so many different forms. But you can be consumed for two months trying to solve a problem relating to how to hold and fixture a part for machining, and nobody will ever know about that.

GH — But like you said before, somehow you'll get the essence of that. It's like closing the door of a really nice car.

JI — I think that's one of the reasons this design thing is so hard— because at one level, you're trying to solve problems that relate to the fundamental way in which you perceive an object. So you're dealing with stuff that's quite abstract and is not very tangible. On the other hand, we're preoccupied by magnetic force, so that the MagSafe connector will break away just at that right point, through to our thinking about what should the nature be of the sleep light. You know, you could argue that if it just blinked on and off, it would be doing its job. To have it breathe is much more complex and time-consuming, but there's a humanity to that, isn't there? Again, it's one of those funny things; you spend so much more time on something to make it less conspicuous and less obvious. And when you think about it, so many of the products we're surrounded by actually speak to the antithesis of that. They want you to be very aware of just how clever the solution was; it's just right in your face. And so much of what we're trying to do is to have our contribution to the product not be obvious, not be evident.

GH — But when you find those details as a user, it's like a treat; it's a discovery. The things that you find that are well done, that aren't obvious, when you understand the thinking behind them, it's like, "Wow."

JI — Yeah, and I think it's very interesting that when you first discover a little detail where there is a lot of care, then you do pay attention. But part of me thinks what you pay attention to—as much as it is the actual feature—is that somebody cared, that somebody gave a damn. And that's conspicuous, isn't it? "Look, they cared." That's one of the things that is interesting about that product. When you see it, you have a connection to who made it. That product does speak to the goals and the motives of the collection of people who designed and manufactured it.

GH — Can we talk about the iPhone a little bit? We'll probably have to use yours as an example. A lot of people in the film talk about interaction design, like, "What is good interaction design? Well, it's good if it works, and if it doesn't work, then it isn't." I'd like to get into those intangibles about what makes something feel natural to use.

JI — Right.

GH — And it also speaks to what we were just saying. Letting you do what you need to do with the object in the most direct way possible.

JI — Well, I think an object invariably defines an experience, even an object that you don't touch. When you see something, you're trying to figure out—of course, not consciously, but I think you're trying to place that object. You're trying to make sense of it. So even something you don't touch defines an experience, and it's engaging you and forcing you to try and come to terms with what it is. Those products that you touch, as the degree of interaction increases, the object and the user interface sort of combine to define your experience. And I think with the iPhone, from an industrial design point of view, I think we had a really clear sense of what the object needed to do and needed to be relative to that overall experience. Of course, you can't disconnect the user interface from the physical object, but if you aren't developing them in tandem and sympathetically, you can completely undermine things and end up with a product that just seems not clear. It seems confused.

GH — Maybe we can talk a little bit, just to carry on from that, about the way the interaction design works together with the form. It's not really about the form following the function anymore, because if you look at an iPhone, it could be anything. You don't realize that it's a GPS device, and it sends emails, and all these other things.

JI — I think one of the big challenges working with such sophisticated and technologically complex products is what you base the product's story on. If you go back 50, 60 years, normally the function of the product was a good place to start. For example, with a printing press or a chair, you understand the nature of those objects, and you understand their function because their function is reflected in their form. And the problem with an iPhone is you can't express, really, GPS and its mapping capability and its communication capability. There's not a specific formal story that you could construct that would help you understand that. And even if you could, one of the amazing things about the computer or the iPhone specifically is that it's constantly changing its primary function, which is pretty remarkable if you think about it.

So we have to construct a story and look to the different attributes of the product, and some of those attributes will be the materials it's made from and the form that's connected to those materials. Other issues would be, just physically, how do you connect to the product? So for example, with something like the iPhone, clearly the big story there formally is that everything defers to the display, because it's a huge percentage of the surface. Clearly it's the focus of the product; it's the focus of the interaction. And so what we start to do there is really establish a hierarchy, because you make that important by making other stuff unimportant by trying to remove clutter, trying to remove distractions.

So the formal story and the construction, the architecture, really does defer to the display. And in that sense, a lot of what we seem to be doing in a product like that is actually getting design out of the way. You know, the physical nature of the product really should be at the service of something much more important. You know, that's not an end in itself. The content, or what's on the display, is more important than the form of the product in many ways.

From a structural point of view, I mean, it's a really significant challenge to have a display that large, with such a large piece of glass that is going to be strong and robust. The glass is very hard. It's the hardest material we could find that was appropriate. Our preoccupation, right down to the structural architecture, was with this big display, so that drove so much of it. This bezel is one of the key structural parts; it's actually a forged stainless steel part that goes through multiple processes from forging to machining. But that enables the product to be this strong and this thin.

GH — Can we talk about working with software engineers on the interface design? You mentioned how one side is informing the other. Even the visual motions of the interface, like stretching an image on the screen, are meshing with the form of the object. How does the visual component to the interaction design and tie in with the physical form?

JI — So often I am struck by the collaboration that is necessary to produce incredibly complex products—the collaboration between an engineer with a certain expertise and a design team with an expertise through to a fixturing design expert through to the user interaction designers. You do sometimes get this sense of how important and how fluid the collaboration and the connection needs to be to make a product that will be cohesive, where you have a sense, at some level, of the big idea. There's a sense of alignment; you understand it. Sometimes it's remarkable that we can even begin to engage with these products at all. They are so sophisticated and so complex. I do think that part of the comfort and ultimately the affection we have for an object is because, at some level, we understand it. There's just a sense to it. That doesn't just mean that it's easy to use. It's deeper than that. Every component and every attribute is somehow meshing together to define the user's experience with the object.

I mean, the expertise that ranges from the software teams to the people developing the silicon for the central processors to the electrical engineers to the experts who are figuring out how to design the cutter that will be used in the CNC machines for mass production—the breadth and the depth of the expertise is fantastic. It's incredible to be a part of that effort, because ultimately the place where that all clicks, the place where each of those contributions are suddenly tangible, is with the object.

GH — Excellent. Do you want to talk about some of these other parts?

JI — Yeah, I was just going to show you a couple more stages. It's just under there, Gary. Just at the bottom of that pile.

GH — Got it.

JI — So you can see what we've gone from. These are literally just a couple of the stages of how we make the MacBook Air, going from the extrusion to rough cutting. This is for the keyboard well. You can see that, at one of the stages, we've started removing some of the material from the underside of the palm rest and then actually created some of the boss features. There is a remarkable efficiency and elegance and beauty to just how much a single part can do, and one of the things that we try and push ourselves on is, how can we do the job of those six parts with just one? And you get into some really interesting trade-offs, but at a certain point, it makes complete sense.

GH — Can you talk about the tactility of objects, these objects in particular? People think of interaction design as the software, but much of it is what you are actually feeling in your pocket when you aren't even paying attention to what you're doing with it.

JI — It's really interesting. It's hard to talk about just those attributes of an object that define what it's like to touch and hold, because it can sound so trite. Well, we can measure in a very sophisticated way the torsional rigidity of something. And one of the reasons it really matters is that you know when something just has that structural integrity to it. So your experience of a product like this is partially its form. And in many senses, it's the material and the structural architecture that will define your experience, whether you think this is a nice thing to touch and hold.

GH — Even something like how round the corner is and these little details.

JI — You know, there is that sense when you define an object—perhaps this is way too esoteric, but you could argue that you're defining the way that you hold something; you're defining a physical process. Because it's this shape, we define the way that it will go in and out of your pocket. One of the specific examples on the iPhone is the way you change the ringer switch. It goes . . . sorry, I was just checking my messages.

GH — Ha!

JI — The ringer switch actually moves in this direction, between having the ringer on or off. You could argue that it would be more intuitive to switch it up and down, but we noticed that when you put it in and out of your pocket, it would catch, and so inadvertently you'd be changing the mode of the ringer. And so I think it's fascinating, the way that, at one level, you are very deeply involved in the minutiae of how you make something, and at another level you are completely preoccupied by a surface and transitions and forms. And then at another level, you're trying to figure out what's the right mechanism and the right approach for a single switch.

GH — This is kind of a jump, but it seems like design is used as a selling point or as some sort of marketing tool now. Everything is "design." Like everything at Target is suddenly "designed." Well, obviously everything is designed, but what do you think of people using it as a branding term now?

JI — I struggle to get my head around what that means when people are pushing that something's designed. Of course it's designed, and design isn't important. What's important is good design. And I think many people are skeptical, if we have to say, "Design's designed," that it's really designed. With the sort of products that we develop and design and manufacture, I hope, in a way, that the solution feels almost inevitable, that it feels almost undesigned, that it feels almost like, "Well, of course it's that way. Why would it be any other way?"

GH — Are you a consumer of design as well as a producer of design?

JI — No. I mean, I'm a consumer of objects. I'm not interested in who designed them and where they were made, per se. I'm just interested in the final object. And I don't own a lot of objects. Certainly not as would be typical of someone described as a consumer of design.

GH — I'm interested in what the objects we own, or buy, have to say about us. I'm interested in what that relationship is.

JI — I think the objects that we buy do speak to the criteria that we have for the things that we think are important. But again, I think that, with the objects I buy, my interest in those would be very similar to the way we work here, which is about the way that they solve problems. I think products that you buy are different from, say, art.

GH — Unless it's design art? What about design art?

JI — I'm so focused on what we're doing here and the issues that we're wrestling with. It's odd, but I don't really have much time to lift my head up from what we're focused on, the product that we're working on right now. So I guess one of the by-products of this is that you don't get distracted super easily. Developing and making really complex products is completely absorbing.

GH — But it seems like, with the current trend of design as art, most young designers that I see are somehow doing these things that are almost like one-liners. You can burn a chair or something, and that gets classified as design.

JI — Yeah, I think when design becomes a one-liner, if it's a phenomenal one-liner, that's great. But, as we know, there is the danger that it might not be particularly good or work particularly well. And again, I'm really so absorbed by what we're trying to do, my biggest concern isn't that shift in the way that people approach and practice design. The shift that's occurred away from designers being intimately connected to the physical object is, I think, much more concerning for what our manufactured environment is going to be in 5 or 10 years' time. If the people who are defining our physical environment, our made environment, the made objects around us—if they don't really understand the real nature of objects, we're going to be living in some three-dimensional picture book that has no intrinsic depth or beauty. And again, I think this goes back to having to be very clear about what's the goal. What is it that we're trying to do? For us, it's not a photograph in a book, and it's not a product that's going to appear on screen. It is the physical product. I think we're still learning so much about what that really means.

That's what's so remarkable about the object: you know, when you see an object, you make so many decisions about it's nature; you immediately form a perception of what it is, what it does, how well it's going to do it, how heavy it is, how much you think it should cost. You immediately have a sense of it relative to history, to culture. You make so many assumptions about that object in seconds, and the physical object is then incredibly complex, ranging in issues from form to material to its architecture to how it connects to you, how you touch it, how you hold it.

GH — And just from a behavioral standpoint, the way that in the past 10 years—we can talk about Apple's products specifically, but look at how these products have changed the way we live.

JI — Yes, in the last 10, 15 years, we've seen the way that we've done things for, in some cases, many hundreds of years dramatically changed. And that can either be something where as consumers we're forced into that change, or we can be drawn and compelled to change. A good example is music, just being able to change the way that we consume music, you know, the way that we browse and buy and then ultimately listen to music. So much has changed in the last 10 years; it's absolutely remarkable. I think, as a designer, it's very important to be really aware of what's going on and the consequences of what you're doing. I think you can't help but feel really quite humbled by being involved in that process.

GH — Is there anything that you have always wanted to design that isn't in Apple's product range?

JI — I think a big definition of who you are as a designer is the way that you look at the world, and I guess it's one of the curses of what you do that you're constantly looking at something and thinking, "Why is it like that and not like this?" And so, in that sense, you're constantly designing, you know? You're constantly redesigning, very often. It can be really frustrating, because I do think that so much of our manufactured environment seems arbitrary and seems not very well considered.

One of the things I think is so interesting about the object is, of course, it speaks to what it is and what it does. Whether it's being considered or not, it speaks to all of those things. But also the object testifies to who put it there. It testifies to the people who conceived it, thought about it, developed it, manufactured it, distributed it. It speaks to a value system. Every object, intentionally or not, speaks to who put it there.

I remember the first time that I saw an Apple product, and I remember it so clearly because it was the first time I realized—when I saw this product, I got a very clear sense of the people who designed it and made it. It was the first time that ever happened to me. I was in art school in the late eighties, and I remember the connection to the product was quite remarkable. But what stayed with me was this sense that I really wanted to know who made it, because I just thought it spoke so clearly to a set of values and to a set of preoccupations, and I just wanted to know who those guys were that made that.

GH — I'm wondering, if two hundred years from now, when archaeologists are looking back at the objects of this time period, what are those objects going to say about us?

JI — I think that in a few hundred years time, when people look back at the products that are being produced now, on one level they'll think—I mean, my guess is that there will be the comment on the current state of technology, which right now we think is just absolutely remarkable, just breathtaking, but there will be that. I think also, as is always the case in archaeology, people are interested in the object, but they are terribly interested in how that speaks to society and terribly interested in how that means that we connect and relate to each other as well as the physical things around us. And I guess, somewhat sadly, I think there will also be a sense of just the huge amount of stuff that seems to have been developed with no more care than just trying to do something that's maybe a little bit new or a little bit cheaper but has no real substantial reason for existing. And unfortunately there are a lot of products around, I think, that are like that.

GH — You know, there's always this question of what's the future of design; what's next? I'm trying to get a feed on where these things are going. Industrial design now seems like it's branching out into many different things, like environmental design and interaction design and design thinking.

JI — I think if you wanted to get a sense of where design's going, what I would do would be to look at what's motivating designers. And if motivation is about trying to design a better product and actually not see design as a beginning and end but seeing design as just playing a role in that, you can get and predict one sort of future. If design is about huge design consultants trying to figure out another way of selling a design surface, ultimately the product of that activity is billable hours, and you're going to see a different future. If it's about self-expression and just the object being an embodiment of the designer, you're going to see another future. I have no idea where we're going to end up. I do see, though, less and less interest in young designers that I talk to in how you make a product, less interest in the actual object and in solving problems.

GH — Do you think consumers in general should be more critical about what they're given?

JI — I actually think consumers are discerning and very critical. I think as designers we let consumers down by not always providing great choice. But I actually do have an awful lot of faith in the people who we design for. I just wish that there was more choice. Actually, no, I don't wish there was more choice. I wish there were better alternatives.

GH — In the film, we may segue from you to Newson, so do you want to talk about Marc?

JI — I think, if you look at the way we practice design and the way Marc practices design, so much of it shares this same preoccupation with the physical object, with how it's made. You know Marc knows how to make his stuff too. It stems from this very direct connection with the object. What's so interesting is that our preoccupations are so similar, and yet we can practice design in very different ways. But the foundation is completely common—unnervingly so sometimes.

GH — Do you ever find yourself wanting to design an airplane?

JI — Nah. I'm happy.

GH — Okay, last thing: if you were going to teach a class on industrial design, what would be the first thing you would teach?

JI — It sounds so naive and so obvious, but it begins and ends with the object. It's a physical thing that is so remarkably complex but wonderful in how you can relate to it on so many levels all at once. But your obsession has to be with the object; you can't just live in a little virtual world and develop forms in CAD and then remotely prototype and manufacture something and expect that it will have any significance. A three-dimensional idea is not a product.

—

Dieter Rams (DR)/
June 27, 2008 Kronberg

Dieter Rams's influence on design has been massive and well documented, and it seems that in the six years since I interviewed him his influence has only increased. And like Massimo Vignelli, Dieter's home is a reflection of his design philosophy, from the Vitsœ shelving he designed, to the Braun stereo system, to the beloved bonsai trees he tends to daily.

—

Gary Hustwit — Can we talk about how you got started as a designer? What was your training?

    Dieter Rams — I began my studies in architecture at the Wiesbaden School of Art in 1947. I was interested in interior design, but always the emphasis was on architecture. After I finished school, I joined an architectural firm in Germany, Apel, which was doing work with Skidmore, Owings & Merrill, so I came into contact with what was happening in architecture in the US. It was a very interesting time after the war; it was like a new beginning in Germany.

    One day a colleague of mine saw an advertisement that Braun was looking to hire an architect. He said, "Why don't you write them? Maybe you'll get the job." I wasn't interested at the time, but he kept pressing me, so I wrote them. I met with the Braun brothers, and I got the job. Later, in 1956, I became more involved with the industrial design there. So that was the beginning. But I never lost my connection to architecture, in spite of the design work I did for Braun and other companies.

GH — Can you talk about how architecture influenced your design work?

    DR — Without a doubt, architecture did influence it. Especially architecture by the people who'd been chased to America by the fascists: Mies van der Rohe, Walter Gropius; these were very influential architects for me. Then and now, I consider their work remarkable—in Chicago, in New York.

    But it also influenced me in other ways, like the procedural methods. The principal architects of Apel and the Skidmore people, they studied every detail. It was all clarified in advance. That influenced me a lot when I got into the industrial design sector. In industrial design, everything for the production has to be clarified in advance with models and prototypes, all the details, for multiple parts. Otherwise you don't proceed to the production stage. You have to think carefully in advance about what you're making and how you will make it, because for both architecture and industrial design, the cost of changing things afterward is much higher than the cost of better preparation. So I learned a lot from architecture.

GH — How would you characterize your design philosophy?

DR — I always strove for things to be sustainable. By that I mean the development of long-lasting products, products that don't age prematurely, which won't become "out of style." Products that will remain neutral, that you can live with longer. I summarized my philosophy in 10 points, and I'm actually very surprised that people today, especially students, still accept them. I didn't intend these 10 points to be set in stone forever. They were actually meant to mutate with time and to change. But apparently things have not changed greatly in the past 50 years. So even nowadays, they are still accepted.

GH — Can you tell me those 10 points?

DR — Yes. Good design is innovative. Good design must be useful. Good design is aesthetic design. Good design makes a product understandable. Good design is honest. By the way, these are just the short versions; there are longer explanations for each rule. Good design is unobtrusive. Good design is long lasting. Good design is consistent in every detail. Good design is environmentally friendly. And last but not least, good design is as little design as possible.

It's summed up in the title of the book I'm working on: *Less but Better*. That is my basic philosophy. It's about going back to purity and simplicity. Fewer products which constantly stimulate our lust for consumption but are then useless and put aside, put away, thrown away. Fewer products which break quickly, which wear out, age too fast. And less information overload. We are constantly swamped with information. That, too, requires reduction. We need more things that actually are and perform as users expect them to. Because value, and especially the legitimization of design, will in the future be more and more measured in terms of how it strives to enable us to survive—and I really think that's not an exaggeration—to survive on this planet.

GH — Can you talk about how design has changed in the last 50 years?

DR — What I am especially bothered by today is that, particularly in the media, design is being used as a "lifestyle asset." I'm bothered by the arbitrariness and the thoughtlessness with which many things are produced and brought to the market. There are so many unnecessary things we produce, not only in the sector of consumer goods, but also in architecture, in advertising. We have too many unnecessary things everywhere. And I would even go as far as to describe this as inhumane. That is the situation today. But actually, it has always been a problem.

We need to deal with our resources differently, in terms of how we waste things. We have to move away from the throwaway habit. Things can, and must, last longer. They must be designed so that they can be reused. We need to take more care of our environment. That means not only our personal environment but also our cities and our resources. That is the future of design, to take more care of these basic elements. Otherwise I'm not sure what the future of our planet will be. So designers have to take on that responsibility, and to do so we need more support from government. We need political support to solve the problems with our environment and how we should shape our cities. As designers, we shouldn't be doing this for ourselves, but for our community. And the community needs support, not only to interact with each other democratically, but it also needs support to live democratically.

That is something I learned very early on, by the way. The Ulm School—founded as a successor to the Bauhaus, with American help, with the Marshall Plan in the fifties—was founded with the intent that people interact more democratically with each other with the help of design. And I still find that idea very, very interesting and important, and it needs to be rediscovered today.

GH — Are there differences in how design has evolved, country to country?

DR — There is a very easy answer to that: good design is international. Of course there are always some regional influences. But really good design which has established itself worldwide . . . well, there is very little. In Italy it was Olivetti in the fifties. In the USA it was Herman Miller and Knoll. In Germany it was, maybe, Braun and also smaller companies. And today, you find only a few companies that take design seriously, as I understand it. And at the moment that is, again, an American company. It is Apple.

The combination of Jonathan Ive as the designer and Steve Jobs as the businessman—it's a very close connection which reminds me very much of the connection that I had in the fifties with Erwin and Artur Braun. It was very close and very reciprocal. And without that, it won't work. We designers, we don't work in a vacuum. We need the entrepreneurs; we need the producers. We are not the fine artists that we are often confused with.

GH — If you were to design a computer now, what would it look like?

DR — It would look like one of Apple's products. In many magazines, or on the Internet, people compare Apple products to things which I designed, with this or that transistor radio from 1965 or 1955. In terms of aesthetics, I think their designs are brilliant. I don't consider it an imitation. I take it as a compliment.

GH — Can you talk about the user, and their relationship to design?

DR — The users—and in German I say, "users," not "consumers." There is a big difference in German. To "consume" is to consume, it's gone; whereas to "use" is to utilize. In my experience, users react positively when things are clear and understandable. Otherwise I can't explain how Braun, with products for daily use, could be so successful all those years. I spent 40 years with Braun, and they became more popular every year. This proves to me that the products were accepted by the users.

Basically, I find that when design is honest, when it follows my 10 principles, it has a chance to be successful. Apple is an example of that today. I have rarely experienced that, when a company launches a new product, people wait in line to get ahold of it, for example in New York. The only time I'd seen queuing for products was during the time of the German Democratic Republic, when you couldn't get anything, there was a lack of things. Or during the war, when you couldn't get hold of certain things, that's when people queued. But I have never experienced people queuing for a new design. That's what Apple has managed to do.

GH — Speaking of design objects being sold in New York, do you want to talk about Murray Moss and his shop?

DR — I like Murray Moss because he is an incredible aesthete. I think he has done a lot to introduce people to design. I mean, in America, 20 years ago, you couldn't get a glass of wine. You could get a bottle, but not a single glass. There were hardly any galleries. There were galleries for fine art, but not for design. And Moss played a huge part in suddenly making these things more popular in America.

GH — What's your reaction when you see objects that have been poorly designed?

DR — It angers me. What winds me up most is the modern kitsch. Older things make me less angry; they are the past. But I'm angry at the many bad, false things of which there are still too many of in this world. Unnecessary, false, dishonest products; these are the things that make me angry. Of course I'm also angry that there isn't more design happening in the environmental area. For example, I think solar technology has to be integrated much more into new architecture. We need renewable energy in the future, and it has to be A) integrated into existing structures and B) articulated more clearly in new structures. We are guests on this planet, and we have to do more to keep it healthy in the future.

GH — I wonder if you could talk about how the process of design has changed, in terms of new technologies.

DR — I've always been of the opinion that new technologies—for example, when I said in the first of my 10 principles that innovation is an important aspect, I meant that technical innovation will get us further, not innovation in terms of appearances. Innovation has to come from the inside and then influence the outside. That's what I understand as innovation.

That's why new technologies are extremely important. We should not condemn them or detest them. We have to live with new technologies. But, please, they shouldn't be wasted or used to kill one another. Instead, they should be used to improve our lives on this planet. I don't know, in 10 or 20 years we'll fight about whether we even have enough water on this planet. Or whether we are wasting the little that we have. So there will be different challenges and priorities, which we will only master with new technologies.

GH — Is there anything else you'd like to talk about that we haven't covered so far?

DR — Well, I'm not very active in the design field anymore. I have only a few things to do, mainly in the furniture sector, because I have certain commitments. But I am still very interested in what's happening, and it is my wish that we really do deal with our surroundings more consciously in the future. That is really my wish, because I believe it contributes to living with one another more peacefully. That's why, if I had something to do in this world again, I would not want to be a designer. Because I believe, in the future, it will be less important to have many things and more important to exercise care about where and how we live.

[At this point, we walk outside into Dieter's backyard to see his garden.]

DR — My garden, as you can see, is strongly influenced by Japanese gardens. It's not a real Japanese garden—obviously the climate is different here and the plants are different—but it's influenced by them. I like to work in the garden myself. I like to work with the bonsai.

GH — They're lovely. Can you show us your bonsai trimming technique?
DR — Yes, of course. These are my bonsai-trimming scissors. Japanese gardeners, they have to cut the bonsai in a way that a small bird can fly through it. That's nice, isn't it? My wife helps me with these, because they have very small roots, and every day you have to water them. So we can't ever travel! We have to find someone to take care of them if we leave. But all the other trees, you also have to cut them. So that's my garden. It's small. I'm sure in America you have much more space, but here in Europe, it's expensive. It's very rare to have a garden like this. It's much more rare in Japan, that's why they have this culture of small trees. They have to cut them; they have to, we would say, to design them.

But why are we doing all this? We are doing a lot to design our world now. We even design nature. But we have to do it better, and more carefully. We can't leave nature alone, because we have to live together with nature. Look at the American Indians, for example. They had, as far as I know, a much better relationship with nature than what we have today. They were very careful with their surroundings. I always wonder why we aren't able to learn more from what others have done before. It's the same with design, and with architecture!
—

Anthony Dunne (AD) & Fiona Raby (FR) /
July 1, 2008 London

The work of Anthony Dunne and Fiona Raby is provocative and invites us to reexamine our preconceptions about the roles objects play in our lives. What drew me to them is that they're approaching design from a completely different point of view, and with different goals, than the commercial product designers we'd spoken to for the film. Their most recent book, *Speculative Everything: Design, Fiction, and Social Dreaming*, was published in 2013 and proposes a kind of design that is used as a tool to create not only things but ideas.

—

Gary Hustwit — So at a dinner party, if you had to describe what you do, how would you do that?

Fiona Raby — Oh God, I hate that question, partly because it's so impossible to say what we do because it doesn't fit into any category.

Anthony Dunne — I'd say we use design as a medium to try and explore ideas, find out things, question, that sort of thing really.

GH — And how would describe what you do from a practical, day-to-day standpoint?

FR — I think in many ways design is about solving problems, sort of essentially. It's about looking at the diverse kind of range of problems and synthesizing and solving them and trying to be excellent at that. What we're very interested in is how design can start to ask questions so that, you know, by making a design, it starts you questioning. Our designs are actually not solving anything in some ways, but they're opening up other ways in which you might start to ask more questions. It's a bit like the way you talk about your filmmaking. It's a method of trying to understand more. That's why I think a lot of the work we do is very much about new technologies, because we don't know what these technologies are capable of doing, and I guess that's why we're very interested in thinking about what we don't know. Design is a way to explore that.

AD — I guess on a really practical level, because a lot of our projects are either self-funded or they're based on grants and things like that, we spend a lot of time setting up the projects, a short amount of time doing them, and a lot of time afterwards communicating them through exhibitions and lectures and publications and stuff.

FR — And so projects can take a long, long time. You know, years. It starts off from very simple things, something like a piece of technology we found, like in vitro meat culturing, but then we start to say, "What is that, and how does it work?" And then, "How could it be a part of a design?" Then that project might go on over four years, and we might do a student project on it, and so these projects take a long time to develop and kind of emerge.

GH — I'm interested in the fact that our environment, for most of the time we're alive, is completely artificial; it's totally manufactured and designed. And so I was wondering if you could maybe talk about that fact a little bit.

AD — I think that's one of the things that attracts us to design as a medium for raising issues: it's completely neglected as a reflective medium. We've got cinema, fine arts, literature, craft. Every other medium seems to have a part that's dedicated to just reflecting on important issues, yet design, the thing that's responsible for so much of the built environment around us, doesn't do that. And if you turn that familiarity around, the kind of everydayness, then things start to become more provocative and thought provoking. It's very exciting. I think that's one of the things that attracts us. So even though our design ideas are never really put into mass production, we always try to suggest that they could be mass-produced or they could be on the scale of hundreds of thousands, because that's part of what we're interested in, really.

FR — I was thinking more about how there's this kind of nostalgia, which I think we don't particularly like. We're quite forward-looking in the way that we work, and we really love the synthetic, like the designer, very modern house. There's a lot of nostalgia in our world still. I think the complexity of today, as well, does sort of somehow make us want to cling more on to the past and not change anything and look back at nostalgic things. For us, you know our favorite city of all is Tokyo. We absolutely love Tokyo and the way that the culture comes from the synthetic. They embrace it such that it really becomes a cultural aspect. You don't get that here. We live in a kind of museum in London in some respects. It's all very historical, and you don't have that play of the synthetic that you do in Japan. So I think we're hugely influenced by things in Tokyo. Our favorite architects are Japanese, and we love the design in Japan. We lived in Japan for three years, and I think it had a huge impact on us: this sense of the future, a sense of a kind of artificial world as being the real world that we live in, as opposed to a nostalgic world of the past.

AD — I would just go back to the mass-produced nature of the things around us. Recently we were in a debate about critical design or using design as a medium to raise issues, and we ended up discussing critical shopping, because it's only when you buy something that it comes out of that virtual world into this world and becomes part of reality, and the power of shopping, I think, is completely underestimated as well. In a way, we get the reality we buy, and there's something quite interesting about the role design plays in that sort of presentation of different options through shops.

GH — What do you think that role is?

AD — Well, I think at the moment our role is to make it happen faster and smoother and more enjoyably, you know, to make things cool and sexy and easy to use. But I think we could also press pause and start to design these other possibilities that maybe are a little bit more dystopian or more complex and offer those up as well so people can see, well, here's the reality we can buy in the shops, but these other realities are possible as well. Maybe they're not the most desirable, but they kind of broaden the spectrum. But at the moment, the fact that everything has to end up in the shop really dominates the possibilities of design and narrows them as well.

GH — About Japan: there seems to be also a different relationship that the Japanese have with objects, technological objects or just any object. I wonder if you maybe have any thoughts on the reasons for that.

FR — Well, we lived in Japan, and there's a kind of, to me, very healthy relationship to technology. It's there, you can play with it, or it has seriousness about it. But when we came back to the UK, there was definitely a sort of, not exactly antitechnology feeling, but there was a sense of it being . . . I don't know. Somehow in Japan, it tends to be very playful, and there's no sense of threat that technology's going to take us over or anything. It's there to be enjoyed and, you know, there's a lot of pleasure in technology. I think maybe we in the UK see pleasure as coming in a different way.

AD — You see images of the woman in the kimono with the mobile phone. That is so true. There seems to be a continuum between the traditional aspects of Japanese life and the modern. There's no cutoff point where suddenly it becomes technological, new, and so on. Whereas in Europe, there is a feeling that technology is always posing a threat. You know, it can destroy communities; it can dehumanize us and so on. I do think, with technology, one of the interesting things in Japan is, after the war, the brightest and best inventors couldn't really invent weapons. They sort of had to turn their attention somewhere else. They've got all these amazing forms of entertainment and pleasure and leisure, and I think that definitely has an impact on the technological landscape of Tokyo. The imagination and intelligence that goes into trivialness and fun is fantastic.

GH — But that Japanese relationship with objects is beyond just technological. I mean, you were specifically talking about technology, but there's also something else there that's maybe somehow a thread from traditional Japanese culture. They're very reverent about specific objects.

AD — Yeah. Yeah, I mean, we never learned to speak Japanese when we were there. We were always sort of skirting on the surface of this idea of Japanese poetics and aesthetics in relation to the object, but there is definitely a hypersensitivity to the thinginess of things. Have you come across *In Praise of Shadows*? The book talks about how electricity destroyed a whole chunk of Japanese aesthetics. Originally these black lacquered bowls with silver particles in the lacquer were supposed to kind of glitter in the dark, and then when you had clear liquid in them and a little bit of fish, it was supposed to be floating in this cloud of silverness. And of course, when you switch the light on, it's all gone, and most Japanese lacquerware is displayed in contemporary museum settings, which are quite bright, but it's actually designed for these extremely dark environments.

GH — There's also this kind of sense that objects are living or that they have a soul.

AD — Yeah, definitely. The traditional Japanese attitude is that everything has a soul or something inside it. I think there's a very different way, somehow, of thinking about the relationship between the soul, or the idea of it, and the object, that goes throughout Japanese society. I'm not sure—I think it's Shinto temples that are rebuilt every so often. The first time we were shown one, someone told us it was 1,000 old or something like that, and we said, "It looks quite new," and they said it had been built 50 years ago. As long as the site was there and the temple was there, that's how old it was, but the physicality could be renewed again and again and again, and it didn't challenge or contradict the idea that the essence of the temple was 1,000 years old.

GH — We'll switch back to the Western world. When you think about our relationship with objects, you might say that 200 years ago we related to them in a certain way in our society; then with the Industrial Revolution, and mass production maybe things changed; and now there's a still different way that we relate to these things. Like today, we were filming, and we stopped at a market at lunch break, and it was interesting just to see how everyone on the street—and this is no revelation—is guided around by their device. And it was pretty interesting to film them in slow motion. It's really striking when you watch people with these objects sort of like divining rods or something. They're looking up and down, and they're bumping into things. It's fascinating how that object has changed their day-to-day life. What are your thoughts on our relationship with the object, past, present, and future?

AD — I think it depends on what kind of objects you're talking about. Historically, there's one object that we always or often like to start talks and things around when we're talking about how objects function in culture. It's a walking stick that was designed over a hundred years ago for an alcohol salesman to sell drinks to hoteliers and barkeepers. When he used to go in, of course he'd always get offered a drink, and if he took too many drinks, he'd get drunk and couldn't sell. If he didn't take any drinks, he'd insult the customer and lose business. So this walking stick was designed to sit on the bar counter. Then you could lift it up and slip the handle into the drink when the host was gone, siphon the liquid out, and then discreetly release it into the gutter when you left.

You're talking about mediated relations and things like that with the modern technologies, but I think they always had this strange role sort of allowing us to navigate difficult social situations and overcome potentially hazardous situations and so on. Today is just a lot more complex, you know, with networked electronic devices. Of course more and more of our everyday lives is mediated, shaped, and determined by them, but I don't know; I think it's always been there. I think objects have always had this kind of pivotal role.

FR — But there is this whole thing about superfunctionality, this fiction of the product that's going to turn you into this superbeing who's going to be in control of your life and able to cope with anything because you've got this supergadget in your hand. A lot of the things that we look at ourselves focus on the sort of fragility of people and how they do all the wrong things. I love the fact that most disasters are caused by human error, and it's this idea that the person is not quite up to the technology and although science may put forward these very radical ideas, in the end, people are kind of a bit lazy and a bit stupid. There's a real separation between the ambition of who we think we are and the reality of our psychology. And I think some of the things that we design are looking at this fragility in some way.

AD — It's like, when you design mass-produced objects, there's always a user in mind, and that user obviously is a stereotype or a caricature. I think, in our projects, we try to design for people's eccentricities and uniqueness and even their neuroses and weak points. Ultimately, we all have that, and we often wonder what it would be like if mass-produced objects had these kinds of qualities in them. If the material world became more neurotic, maybe it would also become more humorous or more human.

One of the things we see in the students' work is, as they embrace biotech, they're starting to make things or propose things that are semi-alive. They're made from tissue, and they don't have a nervous system; they can't think, but these things need to be fed and looked after.

FR — Tissue as in flesh. As in, sort of, meat products.

AD — I think that's interesting because it's a whole other layer to the material environment, and then from that, students also start to see insects as components in devices, like living sensors, or they start to see animals as machines that can be used as well. And I think we're in a really interesting phase where the nature of the material environment is about to undergo this really radical change, but I'm not sure if we are ready for it or if we know how to kind of deal with it. For us, that's also a really exciting aspect of designing at the moment.

FR — So in technology, there are a lot of kind of techno-utopias about this way we're going to be these superbeings, when in fact, we're not. We've got these frailties, and we're sort of slightly damaged and neurotic. I think that we're not quite up to the technologies, even bio-technologies and things like that. So I think, when we're designing, we try and encourage the students to design a multitude of different outcomes, from the best possible outcome to something that's more dystopian and everything in between. So there's a real diverse range of thoughts about where this technology might go—not always the best solution, the ideal solution, but also the kind of more realistic solution, which might be actually pretty distasteful, and that's equally as valid as something that's the ultimate optimistic ideal.

AD — I'm thinking of the in vitro meat, meat that's grown in a laboratory from animal cells. So the animal doesn't die. The cells are just taken out and grown. And an artist called Oron Catts developed a real piece of this meat about three centimeters in diameter for an exhibition. We saw it, and we were very excited about it but started to wonder—I mean, it looks horrible; it's a yucky little blob of something—how designers would approach this to maybe look at the commercial exploitation of it. And so we ended up getting into things about, could you eat yourself? Could you eat pop stars? Could you eat presidents? Could you do it out of love or malice? Because, you know, it's just grown.

When we set the project for students, some of them looked at it quite seriously, because what this means is animals would no longer have to be slaughtered; farming would be reduced; it would have a huge impact on all sorts of ecology. Maybe even vegetarians would feel okay about eating this meat. So one side of it was about trying to make the meat more presentable, more aesthetically interesting, to try and engage people in this technological possibility. Then other students saw it as very dystopian, and they were even imagining sex toys that were made from the flesh of their favorite film star and things like that.

FR — Or your lover.

AD — Or your lover, or yourself. I think this spectrum's really interesting, that you just take one little technological development like that, and we just don't know what's going to happen. And there are very good, beneficial aspects to it and also scary ones. That was done about three or four years ago, and recently I heard there was a huge conference in Norway exploring the commercialization of this technology. So it's on its way.

FR — One of the nice projects that came out of this was Michael Burton's project where he sort of looked at the material as kind of semiliving, so is it animal—but it's not really—or is it plant? You know, what kinds of objects might start to emerge out of this materiality? So he had this idea. He found out that apparently you could take a piece of hair, and you could start to grow it in this meat. You could take a piece of hair from someone who you loved or a lover who'd left you. So he had this scenario where you, first of all, start to grow this piece of hair like a plant, but then eventually it ends up, when it's all long, on your lap, almost like replacing a human, replacing a pet; you could somehow stroke it to make you feel secure, and it's this strange kind of hybrid object.

AD — It needed to be washed.

FR — Yeah, so he had the whole practicality of washing it. So it's not a pet, and it's not a living—well, it's living, 'cause the hair is growing, and it's got a bit of meat that's helping it, but it opens up whole different scenarios. Some people will think, "Well, yes, that's a very comforting thing to have. Why is it different from a pet?" And others will see it as a kind of shocking, horrific thing. You know, "How awful is that?" But the idea that you could start to think of broader scenarios of what this semiliving material might lead to, whether we like it or not, I think is very important.

AD — That particular student wasn't advocating that as an ideal future but just saying, in the kind of world we live in where everything's commercialized and there's a market for almost everything, this could happen. How would you feel about it? And if people are really opposed to it, what can we do about it? Can we block it? Should we block it? There are also these other benefits to this technology, and that's the kind of space I think we like to work in.

FR — Revital's project is a good one. I mean, in many ways, Michael's project is quite extreme, and you can see it's quite an awful project, but Revital's project—from a graduate who's graduated this year—is on the balance between being quite a strong project and less sensational. It deals with the idea of using animals as material.

AD — She did some investigations into patients on kidney dialysis machines.

GH — And this is one of your students?
AD — Yeah. So one of our students who's just graduated this year, Revital Cohen, did a project called *Life Support* where she started off looking at the relationship between people and technologies that keep them alive, and, you know, there's the cliché of these medical machines beeping and bleeping and outputting data that we just can't possibly understand, but people are absolutely dependent on them. So she went into a hospital and interviewed all the people using kidney-dialysis machines, for example, and made this really beautiful video about the emotional connections and attachments that people have with these machines. And in fact, the authorities wanted to commission her to make a higher-production-quality version of that video to distribute through the NHS to make people aware of that.

But she moved on into, at the same time, discovering that, for example, greyhounds, which are commoditized and used as these racing products basically, for betting and so on, once they've done their job, they're abandoned, and thousands of them are abandoned each year in England. And she's proposed a system where they're linked up with people who have breathing difficulties, and the greyhounds are placed on these treadmills, and they have this attachment that changes the rate of their breathing to the human rate and then connects to the human to regulate their lung movement. It's just a really useful project, and it's creating interesting discussion around it because it's not really sci-fi-ish and horrific. It's kind of reasonable, and it opens up this other way of thinking about health, and in a way these dogs are sort of mass-produced or mass-trained.

FR — What's nice about the greyhounds is that they're quite needy. These dogs actually love to be next to people, and there's this relationship between—rather than you and a machine (that's the kind of medical situation we have at the moment, where you have an attachment with this machine)—she's sort of putting the animal in there as an emotional machine in some ways, and it's really interesting.

AD — Also, she had kidney-dialysis sheep that were genetically modified so the blood could flow over from the sheep to the patient during the night, and then the sheep could urinate out the by-products. And she has these lovely photographs of the person in bed with the sheep and the special device next to them. They're almost romantic and utopian and ideal, with this perfect harmony between these animals and humans, and I think, when you talk about technology, I guess at the moment that's what we get excited about. It's not strictly technology but maybe the technologization of animals or animals becoming objects, but not in the horrible way, in some kind of strangely symbiotic way.

FR — So there's this whole area of biology where animals, particularly insects, are being used as sort of sensing devices. So, you know, at the moment, they train bees to look out for explosives and things like that. One of our other students who graduated last year, Susana Soares, she did this great project where she was training bees to look for certain diseases or certain illnesses or particularly fertility—imagine the idea that a woman could actually become more connected to her biology and her fertility cycle through the use of these bees to smell where she is in her reproduction.

So there are a lot of our students looking at how the human fits into a bigger macrocosm of biology, which I find fascinating because it's almost as if, within the NHS or within health situations, we've separated ourselves. This is the opposite, actually, from the synthetic. It is actually going back to a sort of biological connection, and I think the more technology is now going into genetics and into microbes and into synthetic biology and how we might manipulate microbes at a microscopic level, you know, it's sort of looking at a different model of the human. Biology is opening up again into a new kind of space that I think we need to explore as designers. Previously, you probably never thought designers would be involved in that kind of work. I think there are some very strong projects and organizations who are trying to bring designers in at this very early stage, when we don't actually know what this stuff can do, to start speculating in this way and thinking about all the different possibilities, from very utopian ones to very dystopian ones, and seeing what we want.

AD — It's what happens when you start to design with living tissue. It's not metal or plastic anymore. How do you train designers to work with those materials? And even if they are working with them, is it about making new products from those materials, or is it about supporting debate and discussion around it?

GH — Do you want to talk about some of the projects you've done? Like *Robots*?

AD — Last year we were part of an exhibition at Z33 in Hasselt, in Belgium, with two other designers, called *Designing Critical Design*. And as part of that show—we showed about five, six projects from our pasts—we were each commissioned to do a new piece, and Fiona and I decided to focus on robots. We only had two months to do it, so it was a very, very sketchy project.

FR — We were in Japan at the time when we were starting the project. Being immersed in that kind of culture of synthetic things was really inspirational to thinking about—robots! We need to think about robots.

AD — Well, oddly enough, design doesn't really address robots that much. There are lots of art robots and obviously technical robots and everyday robots. I wanted to look at it from the point of view of not making them humanlike or animallike but looking at our relationship to robots in the home and how, if we rethink that, different forms might come about and different configurations for the robots. So we zoomed in on a few different types of interactions and then made these sketch models, which were then used as props for a video with Noam Toran.

FR — I mean, we really wanted to look at the materiality of what a robot might be, and so one of the key things we wanted to do was, when someone saw the robots, we wanted them to go, "Oh, that's not a robot," as if it's not even within the robot language. But the minute they say that, then they're immediately thinking, "Well, what is a robot?" You know, asking what a robot should be, what kind of an identity it might have.

AD — There are four of them altogether. They're not really, strictly speaking, robots. They're sort of supersmart electronic devices, and we didn't even really specify what they do, but one of them, for example, might become the interface for important data you keep online or on remote servers. And as we do that more and more, how we access that information becomes a security issue. So it's a strange-shaped, wooden object that you pick up, and it has two holes in the top, and you stare at its eyes for about five minutes, and when it's checked it's you, it releases the information. We wanted it to seem almost as though it's a new type of furniture. Why should furniture stop evolving at tables and chairs and cabinets? It could just keep going on. So this is like a sentinel that allows you to access online data.

FR — But it's also about that idea of accessing something, you know, that we've got so much information about ourselves within these computer systems, and we've got numbers, endless numbers and passwords. Because there are so many, they're actually saying that people tend to just use the same ones, and I was reading recently that they're saying maybe we should just have some kind of identity card. So there's the issue about accessing through our identity, and suddenly the eyes or irises become the thing that could access it. At the moment, in Heathrow, you can enter the country by getting your irises scanned. You're standing there, and it scans you very efficiently. There's something about the idea that if you could hold this object and stare into it and stare and stare and stare until it really is sure that it is you, that's kind of entering into the machine. There's something about identity being a really strong thing rather than something that's just functional—you know, you just zip in a barcode or an RFID. And then we want to open it up a lot more into something a bit more meaningful—well, not meaningful, but something more powerful.

AD — I count that as a form of interaction. So it's not just a quick glance at a retinal scanner but a meaningful stare into this machine's eyes. And also, you feel better. You feel like—

FR — "Yes, it gets me." And then you access it.

AD — You know, "There's no chance it mistook me." Another thing we became interested in was, as devices become more clever and smarter, people seem to worry about them and what they're doing behind their backs. So we thought it might be interesting to design one that's hobbled in some way; it's not quite as efficient as it should be. So it's a small white blob on a little wooden box with a string, and again, in this scenario, we don't know what it does. It's like a supercomputer trapped in a child's body. It's just something amazingly clever, but it can't move. It has to call the owner over to it whenever it wants to move, and so it makes this robotic noise, and then she sort of drags it to the place it needs to go. And possibly in the future, when we're dealing with very smart technologies, one of our roles as designers might be to handicap the technology and make it dependent upon us in some way or needy so that we still maintain this feeling of power over it. We haven't gotten to that point yet, so it's hard to imagine, but I think it is possible we'll just want to limit the technology in some very tangible way so that we know we're still the boss, and it can only do things as long as we let it do it.

FR — Then there's another one, which is a black can. The idea is this object has lots and lots of eyes on its surface. It's kind of the idea that now we can sense so much; we can sense to like .000 accuracy. So if a gadget was to sense a room, or to sense what's going on, or our sweat, or a sudden light change. But then again, if you have all of these sensing devices, it's going to make you paranoid, so we make this object paranoid. It's sensing all this stuff, but it doesn't know what is important and what's not important. You know, who's judging it? So in our scenario, we thought, in the end, it might think that if it's human, then it's a problem. So in our scenario, this object, when it sees a human, it just kind of freaks out, and the closer you get to it, it's very irrational and starts to kind of shriek at you.

AD — The final one is a red ring that sits on the floor, and again, we don't know what it does. It could be managing the home system or something like that. But it would be sensitive to electromagnetic fields because they can harm the circuitry, so it'll move about the home to the quietest electromagnetic point and just stop there. And because it's a ring, you could put your chair into the center and just sit there and enjoy the fact that this is the least e-smog-filled part of the home.

GH — E-smog?

> **AD** — E-smog, you know, is the pop term for all the electromagnetic radiation that's being produced by mobile phones, computers, microwave ovens, cables, power lines, everything really. A lot of people, though it hasn't got a physical presence, they imagine it as something smoggy clogging us up. So this device lives in that, but it finds the least harmful part of that space. But that one was about how, if it's just a very smart control center, it could just disappear into the fabric of the home, and you'd never see it, but you might want to know it's functioning and doing its business. So it becomes an object, but at the same time, if it's an object in the space, it's important to have some kind of relationship with it, and in this case, that's completely nonfunctional because it's fully automatic. So the relationship's based on it offering you this potential to sort of enjoy a space that only it, as a machine, can find. So although, again, very sketchy, that idea was about cohabiting with a robot and what you can get from it if it actually becomes physical.

GH — Great. Is there anything else you want to talk about on that project?

> **AD** — I mean, I suppose the reaction was quite interesting. Like we said, it was a very fast project for us, a very enjoyable one, and we just scratched the surface. But we were approached afterwards by a consortium of Swiss robotics engineers who invited us to join a huge European Union–funded grant proposal, and we joined it with them. It was unsuccessful in the end, but it was quite exciting for us that something we were afraid would expose our ignorance on the topic was actually appealing to them because of the different way of thinking about our relationship to robots.

GH — It's interesting. Again, this brings us back to different approaches and opening up and asking questions that maybe the Swiss robotics guys would never have thought about. Is that part of the designer's role?

> **AD** — Well, I think it's an emerging role. Maybe because historically industrial design has been so closely tied to industry and meeting the needs of industry and working within the constraints set by industry, it doesn't seem to take on the independent role that other professions, like architecture, for example, do, where architects will imagine whole scenarios for towns and cities based on, you know, social and moral ideals rather than just commercial ones. I suppose we believe that it is possible and more than possible—it should happen that designers take on this role as well and, in that role, ask questions through design about the effects technology will have on our lives, especially industrial designers, because we're the ones dealing with all this stuff. And I don't think it happens enough at all. So in our teaching capacity, I think that's something we strongly encourage: to try and go beyond just making concept design for the sake of it, where it's very whizzy or seductive or a showcase for someone's design skills, and to also embody some kind of ideals about everyday life that can be discussed in some way. Pose a question, I guess.

GH — Can you talk again about how objects affect our daily lives? Or how we express ourselves through the object we buy?

> **FR** — I think it's a bit like cinema or literature. You're reading other people's stories, and it doesn't really connect with you. And I think we love

the idea that, with a product or shopping—we love showrooms, because what is a showroom? You go in there, and you imagine this is in your home. You project yourself into this other space, but you could actually buy the thing and have it at home, so it's a very strong idea about bringing something into your own life. Then you adapt to it, or you change it.

AD — You just reminded me: that's one of the reasons why, for us, products are such an exciting medium, because when you walk into a gallery, you don't imagine that sculpture in your home and how it's going to impact your life. But if you walk into a shop, whether it's electronics or furniture or a car showroom, you do imagine yourself experiencing this thing and enjoying it. And when you then shift that into a more critical space and you want people to think about issues, this becomes a really useful mechanism. When we're doing conceptual products, we're hoping that people will imagine one of these robots in their home, and how that will impact the way they live their lives. I think this is something that mass-produced products as a category offer that's really underexploited, especially in relation to how technologies impact us.

But I think in other areas of our work, we do try to use them in a more aesthetic way. As you say, all products have this kind of story or aura around them. When you wear a particular suit or use particular products, you're entering into the brand imagery of that particular product and the stories that come with it. But there's no reason why it can't be used in a more poetic and expressive way, and that's something we try to do as well, so that the products somehow provoke the person who owns them to project a narrative onto them. That's quite difficult, because you don't want to limit what the people are projecting, so you can't be too precise, but equally, if we step back too much, the products become so generic or abstract that they just feel empty.

FR — One good example we always show that we love was the knickers. There's a site about electromagnetic radiation and how you might protect yourself from radiation, and they had these kind of his-and-hers knickers made out of a metallic netting material that obviously doesn't work. It's a placebo. But if you get these knickers and you wear them for a day, it's going to change how you walk around. Everything electronic you see, you're going to be so conscious of it in your everyday world. That was a kind of switch. A light switched on when we thought about that, you know, how something as simple as electromagnetic knickers could suddenly change everything you see in your everyday life and make you think about things in a very different way.

AD — I think we started to think of these products as noir products, you know, like "design noir." Most design is kind of Hollywood-like. You know what you're getting when you buy the products, and why and so on. They're mass-produced and mass culture. We wonder, why can't companies produce these more niche-like products that provide the equivalent of art-house cinema experiences? And the noir product might provide these moments of dilemma and anxiety and anxiousness and things like that.

That was partly inspired by an existing product we came across called the Truth Phone, I think near the end of the nineties. It was a little black phone with a red disk on it, and when you're using it, the disk reads out the truthfulness of the person at the other end. It was used as an intimidation tool for employers, for example, to ring up someone in the stock house, say that something's gone missing, and do they know anything about it? "And by the way, I'm on the Truth Phone." And we thought, if you could live with the Truth Phone for a while, would it sort of start to transform your experience of everyday life? So you'd ring up your mom and discover she's lying, and then you'd have to confront her or maybe just deal with it. Or your girlfriend's lying, or your boyfriend. And I think that really opened our eyes to the possibility that electronic products can transform the relations you have with other people in an everyday setting, and that's quite interesting, just aesthetically and conceptually. And I guess, for us, we just go as far as proposing these ideas and making prototypes, but we're still interested in noir companies that might spring up and mass-manufacture these things.

GH — *The Secret Life of Electronic Objects* fits in there too. Can you talk about that?

AD — Well, I guess, yeah, that's where the phrase comes from. A few years ago we gathered together loads of examples of that kind of thing, products that create these quite exciting experiences unintentionally. We called the book that gathered them together *Design Noir: The Secret Life of Electronic Objects*, and it was trying to set out an alternative way of designing everyday objects that wasn't about the look and the aesthetics and the usability but much more about the experiences they provided and how you could mass-produce and distribute quite exciting experiences of everyday life through electronic products. The Truth Phone was one of them. The electromagnetic knickers were another. There were many, many more.

FR — In that project, we really wanted to test out some ideas on other people, and it was this idea of how other people could make their own scenarios and stories about an object that they might have in their homes. Because we would go on and make stories forever; you know, that's obviously what we would do. But how could you then put an object in someone else's house and have them kind of see what stories they would make? So we had a series of furniture-like objects, which had different functions, which were trying to make an awareness of electromagnetic radiation in people's houses.

Some of them are really ridiculous. Like we had a GPS table. Tables don't really move that much, and so this table would tell you exactly where it was in the world. But the technology at the time was still quite primitive, so it would have to search for three satellites before it knew where it was. And if it couldn't find three satellites, it would just say "lost" on this object. So we were doing this project where we were sort of getting people to adopt furniture and put it into their homes and see what living with these objects would be like and what kind of stories they'd tell us about how they imagine their electronic world around them. And so, with this particular piece, we were very anxious that someone who took it have either a skylight or a conservatory or somewhere where the object could at least sometimes know where it was and it wouldn't be lost all the time. We were really interested to know whether people would feel an obligation to make sure the table knows where it is so it wouldn't be lost. But actually, we showed it recently in a gallery indoors, and the technology's developed so much, it's hardly lost now. It knows where it is most of the time.

AD — But that was quite interesting, taking a thing like a very simple table—in this case, it was like a diagram of a table, four legs and a square top with a blackened display—and just by adding this extra level of awareness to an object, it encouraged the people with it to project all sorts of stories onto it about it being there physically but absent electronically, about it being lost, about it being frustrated and unfulfilled.

FR — They told us great stories, actually. That particular interview was really interesting.

AD — It really opened our eyes again to the potential of products not to tell stories but to provoke stories in the viewer. And we took that to quite a lot of manufacturers, that project, to see if we could put it into production somehow, but they all said, basically, there wasn't a market for things like that. I think, for us, a very disappointing thing at the end of the day about mass production is that, very quickly, you come to the edges of the spectrum of choice, the official choices about what kind of things companies, I guess, who produce these products, believe people want. We know people want a lot more interesting things. So far we haven't managed to cross that gap.

GH — Well, I guess it's like you were saying—most manufactured objects already have that narrative. The narrative is there already, and people are really buying it because it's easier just to buy the narrative that you want and then bring it in and somehow adapt it versus getting something that you project your own narrative onto.

> AD — Yeah, the things we're interested in invite you to tell a story around them. Going back to the thing about objects asking questions, again, it seems that when people encounter these kind of devices, they can't help but say, "Well, what is it for? Why does it have this?" And that process initiates a chain of storytelling in the person's imagination. I think that's definitely something we're interested in, but so far on a one-off prototype kind of level. Someday.

GH — I love the shopping thing and, again, the kind of ethics about it. I mean, in America, we have Walmart and stores that just mass-produce things in China, and it can be difficult just getting through to people that some things are well designed and that some things are well made and ethically made, and they might cost a little bit more, but they're going to last much, much longer.

> FR — Yeah, this whole thing about buying things and putting value to things: I think a great example at the moment has to do with the obesity crisis here in the UK. You can try and kind of encourage people to eat in certain ways and be healthy and get them to exercise, but the only thing

that's working at the moment is they're paying children to lose weight. That for me says so much about the attitudes. In the end, money is the thing that makes it happen.

AD — It seems like that's one of the reasons that we're attracted to products as a medium for debating ideas, because there's an implicit price inside these things, and because of that, people connect with them in a very different way. It brings out the consumer in people, not in a negative or trivial way, but because that's the society we live in. We live, at least in the West, in a kind of consumer society. We want to access that aspect of us in this debate and not present the objects in a way that people set aside that side because it's trivial or dirty in some way and take on the purer citizenship-type hat. And products have this amazing power to do that, but it seems neglected.

FR — When we were doing the bio project, basically we did a survey of all the various products that were being developed in industry and the promises that were coming out of the labs. And we felt that, in the end, the products that we'd all consume would end up in some big warehouse building next to IKEA. We called it the *BioLand*, and it was supposed to be this mall on the outskirts of the city, and that's where the real products of biotechnology would kind of hit us. Those are the ones that we'll be consuming, and they'll probably be the ones that are a little bit dodgy and distasteful and not, perhaps, ethically sound. And that's a reality that, when these things are being developed, isn't really acknowledged. Not that we should design inappropriate futures, but in many ways that broad sort of sense of what is possible should be acknowledged, I think.

AD — I guess as a kind of a weird pragmatism, we were thinking, "If you can't buy it, then it's not going to happen." So these alternate realities have to somehow be designed in a way that can be bought or offered through shops and supermarkets, and *BioLand* was our attempt to, conceptually at least, offer a different idea of everyday life through the mechanism of products, whereas if you step outside of that, it seems utopian or fantastical or highly unlikely to ever happen.

FR — But there's a kind of irony to that, isn't there? Because all the things that we think you should be able to buy, you'd never be able to buy. Because you can't control the marketplace. So that's difficult. There is no market for this stuff.

AD — There is! It's funny: people, especially students, often say at the end of lectures, "But you just design things that get shown in museums and galleries. Shouldn't you be trying to mass-produce?" And because we're more interested in designing to deal with ideas, actually putting things into a museum like MoMA reaches hundreds of thousands of people, more than if we made a few arty and expensive prototypes. So I think it depends. I think we're interested in maybe mass communication more than mass production. I don't think we'd want to fill the world up with loads of objects. It's nice if you can just make one or two and dis-tribute them in other ways. We just eliminated ourselves.

FR — Funny enough, we don't have many objects.

AD — But we love the idea of mass production, but it's kind of dealing with it more as an idea through our work rather than really mass-producing things.

FR — We like emptiness. We don't like loads of stuff.

AD — But if one of our objects was mass-produced, I think we would feel uncomfortable that all those resources, materials, consumerism, everything just kicks into place. For what? Is it worth it as an experience? Whereas, at least when you offer up a kind of one-off thing that maybe is about mass production, people reflect on it.

FR — So it's consuming ideas that we like. Producing immaterial imaginings. It's like watching films, I guess. We love films and ideas that are intangible.

AD — If design could be like publishing, I think that's what we'd like. If mass production were like film distribution or publishing books and an object somehow had that quality, then I think it would be exciting. But at the moment, we'd have to sneak those qualities in.

GH — What would be your take on the state of contemporary design education?

AD — I think generally it is in a bit of a state, because I think a lot of the ideas that sort of inform the training of an industrial designer come from the early 20th century, and obviously things have moved on a lot since then, but design education hasn't really moved on with it. And there's all these mutating courses, like interaction design, the one that we're involved with, and experience design and surface design and information architecture. I think a lot of these should have happened within industrial design as industrial design kind of evolved in relation to the situation and opportunities around it. And these mutations have occurred, like interaction design, but I think somehow the education of a designer really does need to be rethought at the moment.

FR — I guess we love the architecture model, that, in the end, you know, in architecture education, you consider many different possibilities of societies, of cities, and not exactly futuristic but totally impractical ideas about what architecture is. There's a broader education so that there's a kind of a critical inflection as well, and I think we love that idea of students still being educated in some ways, not just being trained to do skills. Those skills are really, really important, and they should learn their skill sets, but through thinking projects or small, challenging projects.

AD — But I just can't believe that students can go three or four years through industrial design or product design and not have done any electronics or software, yet most products that they'll be working on will be based on those technologies. It's not that they should become makers and engineers; it's just so they understand how electricity, programming, software, and things like that work. And even to think that today, at the beginning of the 21st century, an MA course is the first time that students have a chance to think about nanotech, and they're design students, or to think about biotech—I think that there's something wrong with that. Students should be pouring out of BA education familiar with what their views are on synthetic biology, nanotech, where the commercial opportunities are, what they think about it ethically, but it's just not happening. They're still being exposed to a very narrow set of possibilities in relation to technology and industry and commercialization and so on.

FR — It's complex, all of this stuff to do with education.

AD — It's funny for us because, on the one hand, we're critical of design education, but we're total optimists, and that's why we teach. We believe it's changing, and there are many extremely talented students.

FR — But I guess we treat our students like the research lab. In many ways, we're learning with them, and we're always asking questions. So we don't go there and teach them. In fact, we want students who want to find things out. And in fact, we have our antennas up: "Okay, what's going on over there? There's some new technology happening over there. Let's go and explore. What does that mean ethically?" I think we don't have this traditional sense of teaching students. It's more opening doors for them to go off and ask the right questions and find out which skill sets they should use to look at which problem. Sort of more creating an awareness.

AD — I think that's true with a lot of postgraduate courses already. I guess what we're trying to do differently is focus in on the relationship to technology as a designer. What do they think? So we look at different roles for a designer. One is as a problem solver and that kind of more commercial thing. Another is as a provocateur, or another is as a critic. And then, once you decide that, what context? Where can that happen? Does it need to happen in industry or in a think tank or independently? Then, also, what kind of new design approaches and tools and methods do they need in order to do that? So I think, in our course, a lot of students are trying to design at a very small and modest scale for themselves. But I don't know. I mean, I'm not optimistic generally about design education, but I don't really know what the solution is. I just know we're very lucky to be teaching a very small course where we get very talented students and it's flexible and we can experiment. But when I step back and look at the broader spectrum of possibilities, I find it less exciting.

GH — Okay, I've got a semiacademic question: what do you think are the important philosophical influences on design?
FR — We love Ballard, don't we?

AD — Yeah, J. G. Ballard.

FR — J. G. Ballard is one of our heroes.

AD — And I think, design-wise, we point a lot of students toward the sixties and seventies in radical design, so people like Andrea Branzi, Superstudio, Archizoom. All of the sort of writing and ideas that floated around at that time were almost like a starting point. But a lot of the references are from outside of design, so writers like J. G. Ballard particularly. Although it could be a bit of a cliché, it's still really, really interesting when you're looking at how society and technology and consumerism come together.

The other area is there are very specific thinkers like Frank Furedi, who talks a lot about what's going on with society today, and one particular area he focused on was the idea, in a book called *Therapy Culture,* that we're losing the ability to listen to ourselves. Also, we're losing our network of close friends and family support as we start to work all over the place. And so we're turning more and more to experts to help us cope with heartbreak, or losing a job, or disappointment, and things like that. A lot of our students, we find, find those people quite interesting.

But within design, we don't really point them toward anyone contemporary, I think partly because we assume they must know the key thinkers, especially if they've done their bachelor's degrees in design. But also because we want them to spread their net a bit wider and find these other types of influences.

GH — I think we've kind of talked about this in different ways throughout already, but just to maybe crystallize it, what is the biggest challenge facing designers in the future?

AD — I think the biggest challenges for a designer at the moment are twofold. One is to stay relevant. It can't just be about styling and presenting and user-friendliness. It has to take on a bigger and more significant role and somehow be relevant to what's happening. I think the other is that design somehow has to become more responsible. I don't mean that in a boring, preachy sort of way, but as a profession, I think we need to support more reflective activity through the medium of design where we do question what's going on in society and offer up possibilities through design ideas, scenarios, competitions, exhibitions, and so on. Most design competitions, for example, today are aimed at students, or they're very much promoting a brand. Whereas in architecture, a lot of competitions are about how you rethink a particular city or a particular aspect of London, for example. When the Olympics were being conceived and developed here, there were all sorts of competitions for architecture, but in those were implicit ideas about sports, celebration, people, community, cities. I'd love to see, in the future, more things like that happening in design that were less commercial and less tied to the narrowly industrial agenda and much more social and kind of cultural. But I don't mean that in a boring, moralistic, preachy way.

FR — I think also designers will need to be able to communicate their expertise to bigger groups of people. In the end, I do think that, to make anything work amazingly, they're going to have to have amazing teams of people who are specialists at what they do. And actually, the architecture model is quite interesting, and the film director model is quite interesting too—the idea that there are lots of disciplines of people who are experts and the project manager who can bring all that expertise together. I'm not saying the designer—it would be nice if a designer could do that, but they're part of that team. Maybe it is like a film when you have your cinematographer working very closely with the director. I don't know. I think it kind of needs to jump up a notch. Design needs to come in at an early level, and maybe the young designers have that ambition of doing more ambitious projects. But you can't do it on your own. You know, in the end, big, ambitious projects will never be about one person. They will always be about a certain group of people who just come together and do amazing things.

—

Chris Bangle (CB)/ August 16, 2008 Monterey

Automobile designer Chris Bangle was Chief of Design for BMW Group from 1992 to 2009. His work at BMW was controversial, but undeniably influential. After resigning from BMW in 2009, Chris moved to Clavesana, Italy, where he founded Chris Bangle Associates, a design consultancy.

We met with Chris during at the Monterey Car Week event in Northern California in 2008. We couldn't find a suitable room there in which to film the interview, so we thought, "Why not just film it in a car?" It seemed appropriate.

—

Gary Hustwit — It seems there's a nostalgia associated with automobile design today. Brands like Chevy, with the new Camaro—they always seem to an echo the golden era of car design. Yet other companies don't adhere to that, and seem to be criticized because of it.

Chris Bangle — Maybe it's helpful if you take a kind of longer look at it. The automobile has been around for over a hundred years. But the idea of car design, per se, may not be so old in people's heads. Probably most people associate it with something that matured in the 1930s. And so from the thirties until, let's say, the nineties or something, there's an enormous amount of progression in the automobile technically, and because of that, and with that, aesthetically. Come the eighties, nineties, this progression technically began to get so sophisticated that milestones were being made, but invisibly. Electronics, valve technologies, structural things, crash, airbags, stuff you didn't see.

This wasn't about who put the engine in the front, who put it in the back anymore; we'll make the people sit this way or make them sit the other way, that kind of stuff. This super-sophisticated advancement, but not the kind that drives new forms, and therefore the whole mechanism for the formal logic of cars began to lose its sense of need for newness. You might combine this with a general social trend toward a look away from the future. People began to think more realistically, more rationally; they weren't so interested in that. Anyway, all these combined to the point that I would say sometime in the eighties, this whole idea that every year we have to see newness in this same sense of jumps began to dial back. Cars began to, in many senses and for many companies, almost stop in their design evolution. I think I'm pretty happy that at BMW we were able to maybe jump-start that evolution a few times in the late nineties and as the century progressed in the 2000s. But for a lot of car companies, it almost stopped for them. And then the questions were, "Well, now what do we do? And what do we show people? And what do people want?" There was no more sense of progress driving that need, and people began to look backwards.

Probably one of the critical things that happened in the nineties was that Chrysler basically rediscovered a huge chunk of DNA of automobile design in hot rods. Fantastic, purely American, something that only they as an American car company could exploit; the Europeans couldn't do that. And they did a really good job of it. And that infused a huge amount of newness into car design, coming from the past. The idea that we will take hot rods from the fifties and inject them into car design, this was kind of a new idea. And people liked these shapes. The particular shapes, sizes, their forms, they remind them of things, et cetera. And the Europeans didn't have this hot rod culture, but they have a great heritage. They have a fantastic heritage. And the idea that you always have to come up with a new car as opposed to keeping a heritage car alive took on new impetus.

Some car companies, like a Porsche with a fantastic car like the 911, could keep this going over many generations. For example, we had the Mini, and the Mini had never really ever been evolved from its original concept. So we kind of had to make up lost time. Still, the car maintained a huge amount of connection to its past, which is nostalgic as well. But let's not say retro as most people tend to use it, which is to reinvent a lost car. So, all these factors probably came about to fulfill a need to create cars which are very nostalgic, but at the same time probably drove an alternate route of, "Well, let's see where car design can really go if it really does answer the problems." Because nostalgia doesn't really answer aerodynamics, and nostalgia doesn't really answer problems of lightness and technical issues and safety and crashing. You're not going to solve those purely with nostalgia.

GH — Nostalgia satisfies some sort of an emotional need, I think.

CB — Well, you kind of have to be careful about that. There are emotional needs, but they're also very generationally hooked. You or I may be in a particular nostalgic mode, but my son certainly doesn't have those same hooks. He does see cars perhaps differently, through cartoon eyes, the eyes that his generation's grown up with to see proportions of cartoon vehicles. And so the cartoony-ness of them is really inspiring, really exciting. That's cool because they have these funky shapes and sizes. Big wheels as opposed to big eyes, and a kind of a happy face, and things like that. There are issues which maybe you or I might say, "Well that's nostalgia-related because it's from the past," but another generation might see that entirely differently.

GH — Today we found a lot of people on the track just looking at cars. Just the act of looking at cars—it's amazing to see people's faces when they're looking at a vehicle that they're lusting after. We've also filmed one-year-olds looking at an object, a toy, with the exact same look. I'm interested in those kinds of revelations about design. I'm not sure why I like the look of this car, but I like it. Is there a language of automobile design that maybe I as the consumer am not privy to, but that I totally react to? Can you discuss those concepts?

CB — Certainly that's standard studio discussion. Yeah. I mean, what is it that makes people get excited about cars? You could probably categorize them as well. There are some things like the dynamics of cars. You know, you put enough wedge into it, and you make the wheels the right proportions and it's going to have this certain amount of excitement. There are other types of sex appeal. There are certain formal languages that appeal to people. Softness, curvaceous shapes. It could be an exploration of what we know from the human body and feminine forms or masculine forms that we think are really sexy. Cars are big sculptures that, although they're reproduced by machines and computer-built stamps that make them, every one of them was originally carved by hand by men and women using techniques not a whole lot different from Michelangelo's. They went in iterations into a computer, of course, and it regenerated the surface in computer geometries. But the real design work is still being done in this loop that involves hand carving. That has literally not changed for the duration of humanity.

If you look at it that way, cars are the biggest and most abundant set of sculptures that we come in contact with every day of our lives; they're everywhere. As such, they play those kinds of roles as well, probably half artistically and half industrially, as an object to move you; they play that role between your emotions and your logical thinking needs and requirements quite well. But people don't really buy cars just to go from A to B. For that they buy *auto-mobiles*. You know, *auto-mobile, self-moving;* an elevator is automobile. No, people buy *cars*. Cars are emotional; they're sexy. It's a word that goes back to the Romans. It's not just an *auto-mobile* invented 110 years ago to satisfy some journalistic needs; these are *cars. Carro, carra, carzeria*—it just tugs at emotions that are involved in these sculptures that go beyond just simply, "How do I put a couple of people behind some wheels and get them from A to B?"

GH — How did you get involved in automobile design?

CB — I always liked model cars and built model cars. Today, I was out at Laguna Seca at the racetrack looking at all these Can-Am cars, with the first wings on them, these fantastic McLarens, and I was remembering putting wooden wings on the go-karts that we used to push down the hill; fantastic. There was always a fascination for me with cars, but I didn't know car design existed until I was ready for college. It wasn't so obvious like it is today. They weren't publicized; you really couldn't find out about it unless you had some sort of in, and I discovered that there were some colleges where you could actually learn how to design cars. So I went to one in Pasadena, Art Center College of Design—fantastic place, amazing place, a real eye-opener. I was lucky that my roommate and his friends were all young car design students that were ahead of me in the school, but were extremely talented and could show me the ropes. That was really good. And after that I had a break: I got into GM. And after that went to Europe, and I've been there ever since.

GH — You mentioned there's a big difference in terms of the tradition and the styling of American cars versus European cars. How has that transition been for you?

CB — It's fascinating. I like to think the car design group is a reflection of the company, because the company, whether it's the upper management or the company per se that makes decisions, they operate sort of like the Medici for Michelangelo. They give us a job, basically: "I need this, so please do the artwork side of it and make it work," but if they're not there, then cars don't get made. So it's much bigger than just car designers. And because every company has a different personality—the upper management has a different personality—my feeling is that the cars you see tend to be more a reflection of them than the designer. The European companies tend to have engineers at the helm, tend to be engineering-driven companies. BMW, for instance, is very much the Bayerische Motoren Werke. So, it has that sense of a complete, rational, driven product, very tight. They're not going to mess around and leave you a lot of space to do styling in, no. Very clean, very orderly, stay on it, and form will follow function—that type of an approach. The Americans probably have a perhaps more marketing, commercial mix in their management, which looks at the aesthetics from a different viewpoint. And they give a little bit more allowance for some things. Let the design have a hand; it can do fantastic things, but under less, perhaps, dramatic engineering constraints.

GH — So you might have a bias, but is the more advanced engineering in Europe? Or in America? Or in Japan?

CB — I'd be very careful about speculating on advanced engineering. But I would say the relationship between design and engineering is a lot tighter and much more disciplined in many European companies than I've seen in other companies.

GH — How would you sum up your design philosophy?

CB — Well, I have a couple of guiding principles, let's say. I believe very strongly in the emotional authenticity of the product—it should reflect what it is; it shouldn't be fake. So if the car is a performance object, you should have that feel. I'm very fortunate to work with a company that tends to do those types of products, so that helps. But I also feel there's a relationship between the creator and the object that is very intimate, and it's not very good to split that up. We keep our designers very tied to their cars. We don't hand a design off from one designer to another as it progresses. We go to lengths to make sure the designer comes with the car and works with it. And when you have a team spread out all over the world, sometimes that means you're going to move people around, but by doing so you make sure that the integrity of the design stays intact. Authenticity and integrity are strong components of a good design.

Along with that, of course, goes the whole relationship to the customer, that it has to be a positive one and an exciting affair, one that answers his problems but at the same time makes him excited about getting into his car every day. I mean, that's the whole idea. If we can do it in a way that he discovers something every day, that makes it a little more interesting—washes the car, sees it differently, the sun goes down in a different way, sees it in a different manner—that's then really when we're hitting our stride. We have the current designers making extremely dynamic, sexy objects in theory. But in reality, they're bending metal, plastic, glass. This isn't like a woman coming down a catwalk where she's swooshing the dresses and showing a little bit here and here and really getting your eyes to goggle. This thing is frozen in time, which means we have to create it in a way so that you, as the observer, look at it and you put the motion into it by the way you scan it. And you get the swish in the dress, and you get the opening and revealing of whatever the catwalk model would do, but you do that right here in the car. Because that car has to be a reflection of that emotional energy that you want to see in it, if it's that kind of a car.

GH — There's something about when people sit in certain cars and it just feels right. Can you talk about the thousands of people who spend thousands of hours to invoke that feeling?

CB — Well, the interior is probably the most complex part of car design. Exterior car design is a little bit like painting a gorgeous painting and then having people come in and chop it up into a puzzle and maybe take a puzzle piece out, and you really have to work hard to make sure that the painting stays integrated to its original idea. Whereas interior design is often working with a lot of disparate puzzle pieces, and you have one picture in your mind that you want to come together. You have to use a lot of technical elements to make it happen like that. It's a very complex object, the interior of a car. Most of the safety elements that are most intimate to the passengers and the driver are located here right around me. Right around me are airbags and explosives and seatbelt retractors and knee crash bags and everything else. Particularly crash elements—everything that, hopefully, can maintain a safe environment should you have the misfortune to be in an accident. All of those have extremely tight technical parameters which have to be maintained, and despite that, the interior has to have one elegant look.

Among these issues is the whole issue of orientation to the driver of the user interface, which is mostly focused on the person doing the driving. It's much more complex than flying an airplane in that sense. In an airplane, you can actually take your eyes off the sky for a while; in a car you can't. Within milliseconds, this car is gone on its own in a different direction than you intended it. So, basically you want to keep the driver's eyes up there, and you would like to keep his hands on the steering wheel as much as you can, which means you tend to orient things around here, put some buttons on the steering wheel if you can. This starts to get rather complex because that's also one of the crash zones, so you've got to be a little bit careful about that—perhaps swing some of the other elements so that it makes it a little bit easier to reach. As cars become more and more complex, we have to add things to this interface like heads-up displays, the controllability of navigation, of the entertainment interface, so that it can all happen, and you'll still have your eyes on the road. At the same time, the other people in the car don't feel excluded.

Any one of these elements here is really, really, really complex. If you take something as simple as a speedometer for instance, it has to work day and night; it has to work under different lighting conditions; it can't reflect back to me even though I'm wearing a white shirt. At night we use a very specific orange light because that's the light color that men and women react the best to. There's a high percentage of color-blind men, which tends to put a hole there for some wavelengths, but orange is the one that matches all of them. So we have to ask, "What is going to happen right there?" and on top of that we say, "By the way, it has to be able to tell you 20 different things should an emergency come up, give you this symbol, this warning, this element as well." Somehow, all of that has to be packed in there at the same time. It gets to be kind of complex, but that's what makes cars interesting.

GH — When it works, it's invisible.
CB — That's the idea. At the same time, you really want to have a brand experience. This is another element that's come up in the last, say, 30 years, this idea of the brand experience. And in the past it was, maybe, a lot of smoke and mirrors because cars were extremely styled, and so the brand experience was a styling experience. But in the meantime it's become rooted in the authenticity of the company itself. There is a way you sit in a BMW. BMW makes sure your pedals are oriented to your body in the best way possible. These cars, if you really see them at the heart of it, they're designed from the test-drivers on up, because it's the test-drivers that say, "No, that goes there. No, that goes there," because they're the ones that put thousands of miles on these things. At the end of the day, that's best for everybody.

GH — This doesn't have to be specific to any car manufacturer or model, but are there things that you see on other designs that just drive you nuts conceptually?
CB — Oh, you see lots of things on cars. Well, on one hand, I think all car designers should be happy if they see something new that they can react to. Say, "Wow, okay, they did it a different way." Probably the thing that irks me the most is when I see this repetition of the known because it shows people have comfort zones that are too tied to themselves and they're really afraid to walk out of those. Then somebody comes up with a new idea, and everybody has to do that because their comfort zone has been expanded. The work that we did in the last 10 years has been a lot about expanding those comfort zones for many people. And on the one hand, it's heartening to see when it does work. On the other hand, you kind of wish that other people would go out and do different things so we could see other ideas on how to approach it. So, that's a little bit frustrating sometimes.

It is quite bothersome to me when I see the humanistic elements of a car being strangely handled. For instance, cars have a face. You could say we have lots of faces. You could smile, you could be sad, you could be aggressive, but when you put that one face on a car, it's there forever. It's just one expression, so you would think you would tend to pick the expression which best reflects the character of the car or driver, one would think. And because cars have evolved to having two elements—big taillights, a thing in the middle, a license plate, which can be related as a nose or mouth—the backs of cars have also evolved a face. Very interesting. Some of those are awfully challenging; let me put it that way.

GH — I'm always fascinated by the creative process. Maybe there are inspirations from outside the car world that you take and sometimes transfer or that influence you? How does that inspiration come to you? Is it all just modeling new shapes and trying out different ones, or are there things from outside the automotive world that come in?

CB — As far as inspiration for car design goes, on the one hand, you have this huge history of the automobile, which you look at and try and find things from there, which is also quite exciting. You, at somewhere like Pebble Beach, could really find interesting things to see. At the same time, we live in a world full of products, furniture, everyday use, products that are handheld, whatever, that offer new interpretations of aesthetics, of functionality. They are very inspiring. They tend to sometimes be a bit short-lived for cars, of course. It takes us a while to do one of these cars. And that doesn't always work if the product cycles change so fast that we design it to look like what was in 10 years ago. So, that doesn't always work so well. But, there are many things also in nature and in the nature of art and the crafts that humanity has developed over its existence which are very inspiring. We look at fashion strongly to see, do we need to always make shapes? Like, you would make shapes of a hull on a ship—that's generally where car shapes come from—or can we look at how fabric stretches, how it moves? We even went so far as to look at fabric itself as a part of an automobile exterior.

Then, we looked at things like origami. What shapes come out of folding? If you can fold, you don't need a stamp press to make it. Maybe we can make cars lighter, or less expensive because we don't have to put the same investment into them? We began to look at folded shapes, and suddenly a whole set of formal logic, of aesthetics, of forms, of vocabulary, if you will, was revealed to us. All because we took another look at something that is really ancient—the art of folding. So things like that are also very inspiring. I have part of my team all the time researching for themselves, but also trying to inspire each other along these lines. We'll go to another culture. For instance, we just brought back a set of designers that had done a large tour in the Middle East. And just to look at calligraphy from the Middle East, from the Arabic world, is fascinating. You can learn so much about shapes and forms by studying their types of calligraphy. And some of it you could directly interpret into shapes that are usable for cars. I don't know if we will in the end put that into a car or not, but it certainly was inspiring to look at a culture—what can they offer to us; how can we look at that in a certain way which is more automotive than it would be from an original-culture point of view?

GH — What would you say the challenges are for automobile designers going forward? Obviously, there's everything from sustainability and energy to economics. What do you see as the ones that are important in terms of the thinking and practice of automobile designers?

CB — Well, there are a lot of challenges out there for us. Some of these challenges are purely technical. How do we solve problems of lightness? How do we solve problems of efficiency? How do we solve problems of sustainability? These are technical on the one side, but they all need a design solution as well. That, I think, is the craft that we know well. We can address that. I think these are things that are going to be difficult, but we can solve them. But there are other challenges out there that are not so well addressed by car designers today. They have to do with how people perceive cars. If you and I perceive cars as a sculpture, and we think this is fascinating and wonderful, that doesn't necessarily mean that a generation of 15-year-olds see it the same way. And if they don't perceive cars like that, how will they perceive car design? Why will they buy cars? Is the idea of personal ownership as important to them as public ownership?

We did a very interesting project with young students, and we were very fascinated to see how the social interaction of the people in the car took prime importance over any kind of aesthetic direction. For them, most important was that they could talk to each other. Not, "Well, I want it to look sexy or interesting." There will always be space for sexy cars and dynamic cars and sporty cars. The real challenges of car design are going to be addressing the future generations' perceptions of what they want cars to be in their lives. Do they want them to fade into the background and just be there when they need one? Or do they want them to stand up and be a representative of them like, basically, how we grew up with them? They're kind of like avatars, you know? I show myself to the outside world with this car. It will be very interesting to see how car design answers that.

GH — What would you like to hear from someone in a documentary about design that we haven't spoken about?
CB — I'll tell you what the one thing I'd like somebody to say is. What I would love to see happen is for people to get the idea that, you know what, they're all designers. Or you are all designers, or you're going to be all designers. The tools with which we design today are our tools. We make the shapes, and people buy and use the shapes. Tomorrow, this'll be different. The tools to make things and define your world will be available to everybody. It was only about maybe two or three thousand years ago that reading and writing was an elitist act—only the elite could read and write. And now we think everybody should go to 12 years of school to learn this. Why? I mean, are they all going to be good at that? I don't think so. It's because we know that reading and writing makes you an active member of your society. This is important, because without that, you lose something. Society loses something and everybody in it loses something if you're not proactively involved. You have to read and write. Today people do it on the Internet. Tomorrow they'll be doing it in reality. And therefore the tools of design, the ideas of design, it's important that people understand them in the future. They're for everybody.
—

Naoto Fukasawa (NF)/
August 26, 2008
Tokyo

Japanese designer Naoto Fukasawa has worked on product development for many well-known brands and companies around the world including Muji, Herman Miller, and Artemide. He started the household appliance and sundries brand Plus Minus Zero in 2001. Naoto finds inspiration for his designs by observing human behavior and the way we unconsciously interact with objects. I spoke with Naoto in his Tokyo studio.

—

Gary Hustwit — First, I'd like to ask about how you originally got involved in industrial design. Did you like to make things when you were a child?

Naoto Fukasawa — It's true that I liked to draw and make things when I was a child, but it's not that I had wanted to become a designer then. As a child, I liked strange things. I definitely liked to draw, but another factor was my health. I got sick quite often and couldn't play outside, so I often found myself drawing. And I also liked to make things. When the time came to enter university, my parents told me to take advantage of the fact that I was going to school and to study what I truly wanted to pursue. I had to come up with an answer, and I started to think about things that I could lose myself in and what I was better at doing than others. Around that time I happened to pick up a guidebook in the library about professions and careers. The section introducing product and industrial design described the profession as bringing happiness to people through industrial products. I had a good feeling about it, and I decided right then and there to become a designer. I remember that moment very clearly. So the foundation was there, but I actually made the decision to become a designer when I was 17 years old.

GH — In terms of drawing, were you drawing from your imagination or sketching what you saw?

NF — For me, to be good at drawing was to draw a photographic copy of what was in front of me. So I was constantly drawing everything that was in front of me, from the correct perspective to the tiniest detail. Later, I started studying different ways to depict space and depth. Take a newspaper, for example. I thought it was better to be able to perfectly copy the font and text size of an actual newspaper than to create what many would consider a great children's newspaper, with lots of illustrations. It's a curious way to go about drawing, but that's what it meant to be good at drawing to me. So my goal was to create the most accurate copy of the real image that was in front of me.

GH — So you've never changed your mind since deciding to become a designer at age 17?

NF — No, I've always been a designer and never even thought that perhaps I should have done something else. I've always believed that that was the correct decision.

GH — That's great. And after you graduated?

NF — At that point I still didn't know what kind of designer I wanted to become. And although I had studied design, I hadn't had the time to really understand what industrial design was. You absorb all this information, but you don't really have the opportunity to think about it. Thinking back, I'm not even sure whether I knew what industrial design was while I was studying it. I didn't know what kind of designer I wanted to be or what kind of products I wanted to design either.

GH — So is there anything that you learned back then that directly influenced your philosophy as a designer?

NF — When I first began designing my own products in university, we were given a basic training assignment to make a clock that was to be hung on the wall. We were to use four triangles to create a squareish clock and place the needles in the middle. When I created the paper prototype, I found that the four paper triangles did something unexpected—they became warped. That gave me an idea, and I created the product with the warped shape. My instructor and the other students were impressed, and at that moment I realized that inspiration comes to you. You don't necessarily create it, but it can be drawn out of an accident. I would say that was the first time I sensed that this unexpected element was an important part of design.

GH — So how did you choose Seiko Epson after graduating? And what kind of design did you pursue there?

NF — There's a hierarchy of popularity among the fields that industrial designers work in—cars, home appliances, et cetera. The design graduates with the best grades get placed professionally along that hierarchy. I just wasn't interested in cars or home appliances though. Around that time, I found out that a clock manufacturer was recruiting. I was told that they would be holding a hands-on exam. Well, I showed up and there were many great designers that had come from all over the country. I experienced my first competition where you're put in a position to try to win.

GH — Did it kind of energize you?

NF — Exactly. My abilities were recognized there, and they decided to hire me on the spot. The offer was made before I even had time to consider my options, but I knew I needed to start working. Clocks are a very particular field within industrial design, a field where your thoughts are focused on a very small target. I've come to design larger products, but I'm fortunate that I started in a field where I had to consider the molecules that comprise the universe.

GH — And after that you went to America, to IDEO?

NF — Right. I actually didn't work on clocks very much at Seiko Epson, but mostly on development products. Now Epson is known for making high-technology printers and LCDs, but I was there at a time when the company was just starting to shift from clocks toward these products. As a young, cocky designer, I was made responsible for the products in development, so for eight years I had the opportunity to be constantly working on something new. Fortunately, my portfolio became full of really unique projects. For example, I worked on interaction design when that wasn't well known yet.

I had designed clocks, but in addition I worked on products like mobile phones. We were still in the stage preceding actual use of products like these, which were very high-tech and unique. The fact that I had these designs in my portfolio became an important catalyst for me to work in America. Not necessarily just in America, but it made me realize that I could be an international designer rather than just an in-house designer. I realized that there were better places for me to continue my career, and I applied to a few of them.

GH — What was it like moving to America and working at IDEO?

NF — I started seeing what lay beyond the horizon, and wondering what was out there. It was a very natural progression to feel that motivation. So then I applied to IDEO and was accepted. At that point I already had the ability to design a particular product, but designing within the culture of America was a unique experience. Industrial design in America is more directly connected to business, and product development often determines what direction the industry moves in. So in America, there is more to industrial design that just designing the final product. I had to design more innovatively, on a bigger scale so that my designs could affect the culture of the field and tackle its problems. I learned a great deal about extracting the issues and using them as keywords to create designs that would thereby lead to change. I learned a lot about this system.

GH — And is the way designers work different in Japan and America?

NF — First of all, almost 100 percent of industrial designers in Japan work in-house. The original position of the industrial designer should be freelance, working within the framework of receiving commissions to design for specific clients. In America, even large projects are outsourced. In the case of IDEO, I was in a position to oversee the entire process of creating a product, and my role as a designer was directly related to R&D for these outsourced projects. One of my first projects was a controller for an artificial heart. I had to go to the hospital and observe surgery on a dying patient. I then had to study how to synchronize a healthy heart, an artificial heart, and an unhealthy heart. So in one sense my realm of design expanded greatly. If you work for a clock manufacturer, you get used to designing clocks. As a design consultant, you're always working on a different project and studying anew.

My most unique experience at IDEO was observation—the process of drawing out the essence of design through observations of people and their lifestyles. Industrial designers used to use the term "consumers" to refer to the client, but there was a movement to redefine them as "users." I eventually got to the point where even the term "users" seemed inappropriate, and I started using "humans." So for me, I changed the term from "consumer" or "client" to "user" to "human." It's a reflection of the fact that I picked up on the phenomena that arise by focusing on our essence as human beings, and started transforming those ideas into in my designs.

IDEO is very interesting in that they are always pursuing the new. The knowledge they gain in achieving that new frontier becomes one of their selling points as well. They don't solidify past methods, but their innovations become their future business and services. They didn't like marketing. We rejected the idea of making products just because they sold. IDEO is a company that really gives a lot of thought to how to create change by providing the essential elements that were necessary and identifying those that were missing. That was a great lesson for me.

GH — Can we talk about form? Your products always seem to have unique shapes. Where do you find inspiration for that?

> **NF** — Part of that is related to the training I received at IDEO in observing what is essential to human beings and human behavior. But also, after I returned to Japan, I thought about how people don't think about the tools that they're using while they're using them. Taking it a bit further, we designers create products to stimulate people's minds and souls. But in reality, I'm not thinking about this pen at all when I'm writing with it. Rather, it's when you're least thinking about how to hold the pen that it can be held most naturally. Or it's when you're not aware of your shoes that you're walking the most naturally.
>
> That's when I started thinking that perhaps it's not about stimulating people's psyches. Walking and writing characters are natural actions, right? That's why we do them without thought. I thought, perhaps there is an enormous hint in this natural state that doesn't require thought. So I decided to stop trying to create something very "special" that would leave a mark in people's minds. This is the most important factor in my current design process. So uniqueness is not simply to be unique, but when something mysteriously fits perfectly with you; this is the other side of uniqueness.
>
> I found something that the users themselves hadn't realized. It's hard to catch on to things that we do naturally, whether it's with ourselves or with others. We try to see into each other's hearts, but stripped of thought, we become mere bodies, animals. Then we're basically all alike. Good people, bad people, people with personality, people without— we're all alike. We all try to interact with our environment, because it comes naturally to us. In recent years I've become sure that if I don't lose sight of that, since we're only capable of creating simple tools anyway, I would never miss the mark.

GH — Could you talk about the mobile phone you designed that was inspired by the shape of a peeled potato?

NF — Well, the act of peeling a potato wasn't the inspiration for the phone design. It was more of an afterthought, but I was remembering being a child and peeling potatoes. You can peel most of it, but you're always left with small bits of skin because of the "eyes," no matter how careful you are. And the more you peel, the dirtier the potato becomes even if you're trying your utmost to be careful, because dirt gets on it. When you put that potato in the water, it washes off and suddenly becomes clean! The surface, which was originally round, transforms into a composition of blunt, faceted edges due to the knife.

To me, this sensation of blunt edges emerging as I put the peeled potato in the water just felt right. And I was sure that it must feel just right and good to everyone! I might have been a bit precocious, but I wanted to incorporate these sensations that felt good to everyone into my own designs. So of course I never forgot this moment, and when I received the request to design a mobile phone, I was thinking about how much time we spend handling and touching our phones in our pockets. At the time, mobile phone designs were becoming rounder, but I thought that perhaps there was something else. I felt that there was a starting point for communication in feeling the sensation of these blunt angles, and I thought that would be interesting.

GH — Many of your designs are manufactured using plastic. What are your feelings about plastic as a material?

NF — I'm not particularly stuck on plastic as a material choice. In most cases, plastic meets the most conditions to create the particular product, so I end up using plastic. I don't start designing from the material. There are many designers who do, but I don't.

GH — Have you ever been inspired by a certain material?

NF — Of course, I have, but that's not the way I go about designing. Our relationship with materials isn't clearly established yet, so I feel that it is a bit unnatural. It's preferable to base your actions on experience from actually interacting with something. It's more important to choose the material carefully when the material has to draw out a certain relationship between the user and the product. For example, perfecting the blunt edges means getting the exact roundedness of the edge that reflects the right light, so the material's surface needs to be polished immaculately.

GH — You talked earlier about things that you noticed after returning to Japan. I read somewhere that you said, "Being surrounded by American culture really got me thinking more about Japanese culture and its sense of beauty, not of Japan today, but of the Japan that is on the verge of being forgotten." Can you discuss that?

NF — I must have been feeling a bit nostalgic when I said that. Living in America for a long time made me want to extract a Japanese-ness in design. I think that was quite natural. As a result, I was in America spending all my time studying Japanese design rather than American. What that meant was studying and contemplating the Japanese aesthetic, sense of beauty, and spirit. It was a very important time for me.

GH — Even more than when you were in Japan studying design?

    NF — There's no comparison. I also had a lot of time. What I came up with was that the Japanese aesthetics was in the tools. Put in extreme terms, art and beauty were not about placing and hanging things as decorations. Beauty was sought after in tools that were actually being used, even separate from the function for which the tool was initially created. Taking it further, it's about creating a completely harmonized universe using the one tool. The tea ceremony is a great example. You use one cup to drink one cup of tea. It can be a beautiful cup, but in the end it's just a teacup. But while having a cup of tea, the mountains are changing beautifully, the moon is coming out, and waterdrops are falling, and it has to be one teacup that is used amidst all these moments. I started thinking, what is it that stirs up all of these thoughts and sensations derived from a single object, like a teacup? As the designer who creates these items, I learned that my designs could have the immense power that causes transformations of the moments and lifestyles associated with one object.

Another lesson that left a powerful impression on me during this period was the term *kyakkan shasei* (objective sketch) from the haiku master Takahama Kyoshi. I came upon the term in his writing, "Susumubeki Haiku No Michi" ("The Proper Direction for Haiku"). It was a very important turning point for me. Poems like his are written with the intent of communicating the writer's emotions, but a poet's excessive awareness of the need to communicate could have the adverse effect of giving the listener or reader a sense of corniness. When the poet's sentiments are overly visible, the audience may become uncomfortable. Japanese ritual is the opposite. By writing simply and only about what is actually there, the audience is drawn into the poet's world, their imagination is stimulated, and a silent connection is established.

I started thinking that this is where the most important aspect of the Japanese sense of beauty lies. So I began shying away from any kind of design that would be exclaimed as "great" or that plugged directly into a certain emotion, because it seemed so corny to me. I started considering mobile phones simply as mobile phones, pens simply as pens. Nothing else. I approach a mobile phone by asking myself, what is most "mobile phone–like" about it? The focus shifts from design to simply using a mobile phone or a pen. All the unnecessary elements fall away very smoothly, and we're left with an underlying "good feeling." I've been able to design products that communicate this good feeling subtly, so that the good feeling rises to the surface gradually, rather than putting it out front. So *kyakkan shasei* remains important to me to this day. IDEO was essential in starting me on the path of observing people and behavior objectively, without subjectivity.

GH — Does humor play a role in your designs?

    NF — It doesn't, really. I don't strive to express humor through my designs at all. But I'm asked about humor and the role it plays in my designs often. I think it's because I understand human behavior better now. I have a strong desire to actually see human instinct and not just the psychology behind it. As a result I'm able to see beyond what the person himself can see or feel. When the person realizes that I've seen beyond what he's conscious of, he's taken by surprise. And when human beings realize something new about themselves, the new self-awareness can be a bit embarrassing. That moment of self-awareness and embarrassment can be humorous as well. It's the same with jokes. You can make a joke and create humor because you know the timing at which your audience will laugh. People will actually laugh before the joke hits, because we can usually detect it, you know?

GH — Yes, I do.

NF — That's what it's about. I don't try to create products that are humorous; I'm actually quite serious. I'm serious, but many people experience an "aha" moment of realization when they experience my products, and that is sometimes translated as humor.

GH — Like the moment you can't help but laugh at yourself when someone points out something about you that you hadn't noticed before?

NF — Exactly. But while humorous, it's actually a very sensitive and important interaction. If the expression is too harsh, it can come across as sarcasm, so it has to be smooth and just right. Then people end up scratching their heads and having a shared moment of wonder and recognition. This ability lies at the foundation of my current activities. It's the key to being able to take off the armor and enter this shared moment.

GH — In addition to designing, you've also started conducting workshops. Can you discuss the concept of "without thought"?

NF — Using a product but not thinking about it, a concept that I talked about earlier, was very interesting to me. I managed to develop the ability to find this world made only of actions that human beings take subconsciously, things that exists behind the world of hard reality, very quickly. I realized this is an essential element of design that exists in famous products that have been considered industrial design classics. I thought that superior products all had the "without thought" element and that it was very important. I wanted to share this concept with young designers in the industry who were accustomed to designing only for a specific set of criteria, so I created the workshop program and named it Without Thought.

This workshop is a way to provide a certain organized activity around this philosophy. I've extracted the richest parts of my essential philosophy and used the workshop to share them with young designers. It's something that's hard to understand unless one experiences it, so the designers must change their way of thinking within the two to three days of the workshop. They are given a set of criteria that requires them to actually experience finding the cue to design. What's interesting about training and giving a group of designers the same exercise is that it always leads to a design that everyone thinks is good, even if it is by chance. It's unrelated to my presence or the presence of an experienced designer. At that moment, everyone can share in the understanding of a concept. Everyone, including the designers who didn't understand it before, can share the understanding, and the process is accelerated when the group is larger. Then some people start understanding that what they are doing is wrong, and the process continues as another person produces a design that gets it in the next exercise. This is how the designers' existing philosophies start changing radically.

GH — What do you think are the biggest challenges facing designers today? What advice do you give young designers starting out?

NF — Well, I don't feel that I can give advice, since I still feel that I'm in the same position as them. I haven't done everything that I want to do with design, so it's hard for me to give appropriate advice. I believe that design must always keep pace with society's movements. Our current society moves very rapidly, but we can't get swept up in these strong currents. It's necessary for us to continue seeking what people truly consider "good." The world is full of things that aren't truly good but delude us into thinking that they are, so it's tricky for designers also. It complicates matters even further when designers, being unsure, create products that are similar to the deluding products.

So if one first nurtures the ability to spot the true essence and quality in good products, that should serve as an example. Then one can design toward that example and always compare one's own designs against it. That part should be easy. It would be extremely hard to aimlessly pursue this search as a designer without that ability.

GH — That can be hard when there are so many products being produced these days.

NF — Of course. It's a fact that becomes clearer traveling back and forth between America and Japan as well.

GH — How so?

NF — Life in America is much more simple and systematic. In Japan there is a greater feeling of passivity. There is a feeling of being moved by the environment at large in our daily self-consciousness. So our interaction with our environment often involves us adapting to it. America, to take one example, is a nation of people with different backgrounds. There are many smart Americans who prioritize creating a simple, efficient system to accommodate everyone. Once a system is established, people will complain if it doesn't work, putting into motion a corrective mechanism.

Japan is the opposite. People sense the particular space and environment they're in at every moment and attempt to adjust to it. So the system is pretty useless, since people don't complain but try to work with it. Some people adjust to the system, and some don't, so the system loses its center. As a result people end up going this way and that, but at the same time comprise a coherent group. It seems rough, but things end up running pretty smoothly. A situation that is fairly common in Japan is probably hard to understand for those from another culture.

GH — Okay, last question: how do you think these differences are manifested in American and Japanese design?

NF — I would say that the Japanese have a keen interest in building tools to make their lives better. There's always a drive to improve the quality of tools and the interaction and communication afforded by them. I think "quality" lies at the pinnacle of what Japanese consider their culture to be. One aspect of quality is service. Manufacturing products is a service also. At one point, economics produced a system in which we pay for better service. The belief that paying more gives one access to better quality is becoming a worldwide platform.

Japan, though, is based on a very strong foundation that, no matter what the price, the utmost service should be provided. This is so difficult to understand for people who can't receive good service unless they pay a price for it. But in Japan, even the most delinquent service person would most likely give you a certain level of service that's clearly higher than the standard in other cultures, however begrudgingly. The Japanese are constantly striving to perform better than the standard. In Japan, extremely high quality can be found in individual products and situations that at one glance seem chaotic, outside the realm of a formal system. I think this is one big difference between the rest of the world and Japan.

—

Davin Stowell (DS) & Dan Formosa (DF) / September 22, 2008 New York

Davin Stowell is the founder and CEO of Smart Design, a multidisciplinary design consultancy. Dan Formosa is cofounder of Smart. Over the last 30 years, Smart has focused on consumer products, services, and experiences for a broad range of clients including OXO, HP, Johnson & Johnson, and Gillette.

—

Gary Hustwit — Let's start with the basics. How did each of you get involved in industrial design?

Davin Stowell — I grew up always wanting to be an industrial designer. When I was in seventh grade, I was making things, and nobody knew what an industrial designer was at that time. I have a sister who is a commercial artist, and she told me about it. I convinced the guidance counselors in high school that it was a legitimate profession. I went to school at Syracuse University to learn how to do it.

GH — Were you making things as a kid?

DS — I was taking apart things. When I was a kid, I was always curious how things were made, and one day, I took my mother's sewing machine apart. I did pretty well; I got it completely apart and back together, but then it didn't work. I didn't really say anything, but she took it to be repaired, and the repairman said, "I just can't figure this out. There's a part in the middle of the machine that was put in backwards. I don't know how that could possibly have happened." That was the beginning. After that I built a go-kart and accidentally killed it with weed killer, went through all those experiences, and figured someday I'd have to learn how to do it right.

Dan Formosa — I was caught between art and engineering when I was in high school. I had never heard about design until the very nth hour of getting out of high school when someone told me about a profession called industrial design that I could go into. I'd say as a kid I was curious about a lot of odd things, design-wise. For example, at a very young age, I noticed that you needed two one-way signs on the street. You've got to make one for this side of the street and one for that side of the street, even though they're both pointing that way. Why I would even care at that age is a mystery, but it's the fascination with those odd things that led me to design school. I went to Syracuse, along with Davin, which means we've been working together since our teen years. I won't pinpoint the year, but it goes back to age 19, right?

DS — Much before that.

DF — We go way back, and we've been working together since.

GH — How would you characterize the profession at that point in terms of the types of work you're really learning and the scope of what you were doing as opposed to now?

DS — Back then, not many people really knew what it was. I think the state of product design was all about putting lots of chrome trim on something and some wood grain, and it would sell, at least in the United States. That wasn't really what I wanted to do. I saw the design of some of the great masters from years before. I thought that we really needed to bring design back to its purest form and back to its real meaning.

DF — Being born in the fifties and growing up in the sixties—an era of great change and a lot of social reform—had something to do with it. By the time we got out of college in the seventies, we were radical student baby boomers just like everyone else. We weren't amazingly radical, but the entire baby-boomer population was there looking for some sort of social change. When we got out of school, we were thinking about, how could we use design to enact that change? "Is there something different we can do? Rather than just shape products, can design actually have a social impact? Is there something we can do to change the world from our own corner of this profession?"

DS — I think that it's common among designers to have that desire to change the world even if it's just their personal world around them. I think designers want to do great things. Today, I think we want to design products that are better for the world. I don't think we thought about it that much back then. I think we just wanted to make beautiful things. For many designers, the goal was to have products sold in design shops revered by other designers. My approach was always a little bit different because the products that were sold in design shops didn't really sell to anybody but other designers, and that didn't really seem like changing the world. It was self-serving. My goal was always to make products that could sell in Kmart to millions of people but still be liked by designers. That way, you really are changing the world little by little.

Products that are designed for designers don't sell because only designers appreciate them, and the designers always think that, well, that's the consumers' problem. They're just not smart enough to understand. In reality, designers aren't really understanding the consumers' needs and how to bring them forward, how to get them to understand more than they do today.

DF — Early on, Davin was always out at stores like Macy's or the electronic stores, and I was kind of back with things in the studio. The point of view there was that design is for everybody and can be applied to day-to-day products, not just to esoteric products. At the same time, I was into both psychology and biomechanics. I was interested in perception and how people understand products and use them and also in how to make something physically easy to use or less damaging to the body.

GH — Tell me about some of the first products you designed.

DS — The very first product that I ever designed that went to market was user centered. At the time, I worked for Corning Glass Works. They made CorningWare and Pyrex and different housewares. I grew up in Corning, New York, so this is where I worked during summers when I was still in college. The design manager said to me one day, "We don't really have a project for you, but why don't you design something that you need?" As a student, I was thinking, "I like to cook, but I don't want to mess up any dishes . . . I like dinners, tossed salads . . . Let's hold a wedge of lettuce over the sink and pour some dressing over it and cook some soup in a pan and eat right out of the pan; then you're done."

I thought about CorningWare. It was white. It looked nice. Maybe I could make a pan that I could heat the soup in and cook in and then eat out of it. In colonial times, there were porringers, these little metal dishes with a handle on them that you could set next to the fireplace to keep them warm. I put that together and came up with this little CorningWare bowl that had a handle on it. You could heat up the soup and eat out of it. Everybody thought that it was a great idea. The marketing manager said, "Okay, let's go do some focus group testing to see if people really like this idea." We took it into the focus group. We were behind a mirrored wall and watched the moderator poll consumers about whether they liked the idea. They absolutely hated it and said, "Cook soup in this dish and then eat out of the same thing we cooked in? No way. We'd never do that."

GH — How did it get manufactured then?

DS — Luckily, the marketing manager was a recent college graduate too, and he thought that he would use it, so we went ahead with it. Back then you really had to prove everything in these focus groups. He set up new groups, and to half of them, he would say, "Here's a nice single-serving saucepan. You can heat up one serving of soup so you don't have to dirty the big saucepan when you're only serving one person." Everybody loved it. They thought that was a great idea. To the other half he took it to, he would say, "Okay, here's a bowl that you can take to the table. It's got a little handle on it so you can hang on to it. You can tip it up, and you can eat your soup out of it. Do you like that idea?" Everybody loved it. Never asking the two questions at once, he had the justification to make it, and it became the largest selling product in CorningWare history for over 30 years.

That's one of the things about designing for people. People will never tell you exactly what they need or what could be better because we're creatures of habit and we just do things the same way over and over again. Whenever anybody asks about a different way, it doesn't really register. It's like, "No, that's not what I do." This idea of heating soup up and then eating out of the same thing that you heated it up in, you just wouldn't do that. If you give somebody a product that's designed to do that, like the big saucepan with a big plastic handle on it, it doesn't look right at the table. If you give them a little saucepan that looks like a dish you would eat out of, of course they'll do it. It's just shifting the paradigm so it's a new way of doing things. That's what we're really always looking for whenever we design: ways we can improve the way people do things or improve their daily life without them really even knowing it or thinking about it.

DF — I think since that time, we've shied away from the definition of an average consumer. Oftentimes, we would have clients coming to describe their target buyer. For instance, "Female, 34 years old, 2.3 kids. She drives to work." On and on and on. They would very proudly describe their average consumer.

We'd listen politely and say, "Well, that's great, but we don't care about that person." What we really need is to look at the extremes. We want to know who's at the one end of the scale. Maybe the weakest or the person with arthritis or the worst-case scenario or someone who's having breakfast in the morning and is under a lot of stress, real-world situations. At the other end, we may want to know the tallest person or the athlete or the strongest or the fastest person, because if we understand what the extremes are, the middle will take care of itself. It's really a cultural clash between marketing and their traditional ways of defining consumers and the way we think as designers, which is more based in reality. Let's think about a range of people, not an ideal person, because we can't find that ideal person.

GH — Do you still do focus groups in that traditional sense?
    DF — We always do one-on-one interviews. There are times when we'll do two people at a time because, if they know each other, they may get into a discussion that we wouldn't normally be privy to. We tend not to talk to people in groups just because it seems to get watered down.

    DS — We really like to talk to people in their natural habitat, like in their kitchen or living room, not in a mirrored facility with fluorescent lights.

GH — Then you can observe them.
    DF — Yeah, and they can point to things. Sometimes we look at other parts of their life. If we're looking at something in the kitchen, we may look at their living room or their garden. Again, it's a reality check, because our idea is, if we're working on something in the kitchen, for instance, the idea may come from something in the garage or something that they're doing somewhere else in the house.

GH — What makes bad design bad, and what makes good design good?
    DS — I think really bad design is pretty easy to identify. It looks bad; it works bad. Everything about it is bad. Something that's attractive but doesn't work is confusing. That's my definition of bad design because it lured you in; then you're truly disappointed that it just doesn't do what it's supposed to do. I think good design is something that attracts you and that you're emotionally connected with, and it exceeds your expectations

in terms of performance. You take it home, and it works better than you could ever possibly imagine. That's what we're really striving for.

DF — Yeah. People expect things to work. If you go to a store and you buy something, you basically bought it because you expect it to work. That's good, but it's not necessarily special. What makes great design is something that surprises you after a period of use, like after you've been using something, then you discover a week later that it's better than you previously anticipated.

DF — There are many things in our everyday lives that are just begging to be redesigned and rethought. Sometimes we've used things all our lives and just never thought about them. For instance, here's a basting brush that is designed to hold oil just through capillary action. This holds oil much better than standard bristles do. It's an "aha" moment that you can get the oil to hold in there.

Another thing that I'm kind of proud of, again, in its dumb simplicity, is this cheese grater that is the first cheese grater that grates in both directions. When you grate cheese, you're going up and down, and usually you grate just on the downstroke. We doubled the efficiency by just putting our cutting edges in both directions. Sometimes it's the simplest solutions that are sitting right in front of us and can be most fun to talk about once they're out on the market.

DS — It's kind of dumb, simple. That's why we're called Smart Design, because we see those simple things. I think everything we do is really inspired by what people do and what they need.

One of my favorite products we've designed was inspired by my own grandmother and the memory of her baking cookies. She was over 100 years old at that time. She had a big, old ceramic mixing bowl, and she would stir cookie dough that was pretty thick and heavy. She'd tip the bowl up on its side and try to stir it, and the bowl would skid across the counter or sometimes even fall on the floor. She was over 100, so what do you expect? But she really liked making cookies.

So I designed a mixing bowl for her; we put rubber on the sides so, when she tipped it, it wouldn't move, then gave her a big handle so her thumb wasn't down in the cookie dough and made the bowl really light. I think she was about 102, maybe even 103, when we finally finished it. This was her favorite product because her grandson designed it. She was making cookies until she was 105.

GH — Can you tell me about your designs for OXO Good Grips?
    DF — Davin got the first phone call.

DS — A good friend of mine, Sam Farber, had a few housewares companies. One of them was Copco, a place where we had worked at for a number of years. We became good friends. He had retired, and he was never really that comfortable being retired. He kept telling me he wanted to be making and selling things, and he wasn't one to lie on the beach and relax. I got a phone call from him one night around 7:30 p.m. He was vacationing in the south of France with his wife, Betsy. If you do the math, he was calling me at 1:30 a.m. in the morning his time, and he was so excited. He said he couldn't sleep.

What he was excited about was that he'd been cooking dinner with Betsy, and she was making an apple tart, and she was complaining about the peeler that was hurting her hands. She had arthritis and she just couldn't hang on to it. It hits him at that moment that here's a product that nobody has really thought about. The fact that we call these kitchen gadgets—it isn't really paying a lot of respect to them. There were peelers that were nicer looking, but none of them really worked very well.

He said, "Here's something that I could be doing. I could be making kitchen tools, kitchen gadgets that are much better, that would work for anybody, whether you were young or old or have arthritis or not. Let's get started on this right away. I'll be back from France in another month. I'd like to see some progress by the time I get back." I think, Dan, you go involved at that point.

DF — Yeah, because the concept of designing for everybody was definitely within our school of thought. Previously we were looking at biomechanics, perception, psychology, how people use things, and, like I said, how to think about the extremes of the population, not just the average person. The idea of design for everybody used to be a very uphill sell to clients. We used to have to explain why we're looking at extremes of the population, for instance. But when this project came in, it was a complete 180-degree reversal. Now it was a client coming to us and saying, "Hey, let's look at the extremes of the population and understand how to make these gadgets perform better." Luckily for us, this was an ignored category. It wasn't that hard to improve on.

That being said, we did a lot of homework. We looked at people with arthritis, because that's an extreme of the population, very early on in the process. Our thought was that, if we can make it work with people who have arthritis, it could be good for everybody. It was a great project to be given, because we were able to do what we'd been talking about for a while.

GH — What were the first steps?
    DF — Rather than to jump in and design something, which we could've done based on our preconceptions, we actually went out into the field and very specifically walked up to the Arthritis Foundation. We knocked on their door and said, "Hi, do you have any books we can look at?" We didn't really want to look at books when we went there. We knew they had a library in there, but we didn't really want to look at books. We really wanted to talk to people who worked at the Arthritis Foundation because they had arthritis as well. They were really knowledgeable about the topic.

So we weaseled our way in there. As we were looking through their books, we started talking to people sitting at their desks, one of whom

I remember very specifically was an enthusiastic cook at home. Luckily we connected with her and got into a great conversation. This was on the first day of being out on the streets. During the conversation with her, we were talking about the handle a lot, and what it's like to hold, and what makeshift items she or other people with arthritis used to compensate. But she kept pointing at the peeler's end, the metal end, saying, "That's got to be sharp." We replied, "Fine, okay, great, but now with the handle, what sort of things do you have to do to deal with arthritis?" And she kept saying, if it's not sharp, it's really hard to use. We realized then that it needed to be a sharp tool in order to work. It's not that we didn't know that, but the fact that she kept going to this end just really drove the point home.

GH — I see a bicycle grip in that box. Was that initially the inspiration for the bigger handle?

DF — We were doing this project here in New York City, and I remember saying, "Hey, let's go out and get a bicycle grip." It was probably Davin's idea first, but I thought, "Fine, I'm commuting. I'll walk into the shops or run down the street." It was very, very hard to find the old, traditional, school-aged rubberized bicycle grip because most of the bike shops in the city catered to messengers, and they're not using this stuff. Eventually we found a rubberized bicycle grip like this and stuck a peeler in it and made a very quick mock-up.

DS — We knew that it had to have a bigger handle. It's like how kids have big crayons because they're easier to hold on to. It's the same thing for people who might not have full mobility of their hands. They need something a little bit larger that's a little easier to grip with a little bit less force. They won't have to close their hands as much. We did a lot of studies around the shape of the handle, the size of it, to come up with that optimum size that would be perfect for everybody.

Then we realized it still needed something. There are places where we wanted to be able to squeeze in a little bit more or have it change shape depending on what you're doing. For peeling, you might have a light grip on it, but if you were coring an apple, you might be pinching it hard and twisting it in. That's when we came up with this idea to put rubber fins on it like this bicycle handle. It's one shape when you hold it lightly, but if you squeeze into it, it takes on a different shape. Eventually, we realized that we didn't need the fins everywhere, and we settled on having them just on the sides where your thumb and forefinger would be. If I pinch in hard, I'm able to get a better grip on it.

As designers, we're always thinking of other ways of doing things. We thought, "Well, maybe it shouldn't have the fins because maybe food can get caught in there or something, or it'll be harder to manufacture." We designed a handle that just had soft areas that were hollow inside, so you could still squeeze in, but you didn't see any fins on the outside. But we realized is that it didn't communicate anything to anybody. One of the things that's been really pretty remarkable about this product is that, whenever you hand it to somebody, the first thing that they do is they grab it, and they start squeezing the fins and playing with it. When they do that, they've made an emotional connection with it. They understand what it's all about. I think that was really one of the secrets for its initial success, that people got it instantly when they saw it. It was all about a better grip.

GH — How many prototypes did you make before you arrived at the final design? You've got a box here with dozens of them.

DF — We literally made hundreds of models, tried them ourselves, and gave them to others to try. As you can see here, we were trying many different things with shapes and with contours. Like Davin said, it was very important to have a mechanical indent, because we want fingers to nest. If you're pushing or pulling, it's important that your fingers get into a recess, not just rely on a squeeze force. The fins allow us to do that. It really went through many more iterations than you would think to do a handle that looks relatively simple in the end.

DS — We made hundreds of these prototypes, because it's easier to make something and try it than to theorize whether it's going to work or not. There are a couple of very early ones that have the bicycle grip built into them. You can see we've literally cut apart a bicycle grip and then glued it to a piece of foam so that we could try it and see if it worked.

DF — Here's a story that I probably have never even told Davin. One of things we needed to do was design a hole in the handle so you can hang it up on the rack in the kitchen. We were looking at small holes and big holes, and none of them seemed quite right. They just seemed awkward. I was in the workshop with the one of the designers on the project, and we were talking about, what are we going to do about this hole? Back then I was commuting from New Jersey and going through the Lincoln Tunnel every day. If you notice, the Lincoln Tunnel has an extremely big entrance, but for a tiny little tunnel. I said, "Why don't we do what they did with the Lincoln Tunnel? Let's just start larger on the outside and narrow down to a smaller hole, and, on the New Jersey side, make it big again. What this does is make it easier to hang because it's a bigger target to slip over a hook, and visually it works. The proportion seemed about right.

DS — We got another benefit from that too: by putting a big hole in the end of the handle, it made the back end like a spring. So when it's in your hand, it's softer. It even bounces. I've never heard the Lincoln Tunnel story before. Did you just make that up?

DF — No, I've been saving that for the right moment with the camera.

GH — What was the reaction when these hit the shelves?

DS — Well, Sam was coming out of retirement to make this product, so of course he wanted to do it in a hurry. He's very impatient. Before we'd even figured out how to make it, he had already reserved a space at an international gourmet conference. We were still talking to manufacturers who didn't think they could get the rubber to go into the little fins on the grip. We spent a lot of time in Taiwan looking for manufacturers. We were looking for very low-cost sources, because we knew it had to be priced right. We went into these factories with dirt floors and people sitting on the ground in sandals filing metal tools with an old rusty file. It was a just a horrible scene.

Finally, we realized we couldn't get something like this made there, and we went to Japan and found this manufacturer that had a history of making samurai swords from the 1800s. I just remember sitting in this conference room with all these Japanese businessmen in their suits and them looking at it and saying they weren't sure whether they could make it or not. They finally said that we had to go to their factory and talk to the people there. We all got into their limousines and went down the road to their factory. There was a man in green overalls in the middle of the factory, and he had a remote control to this gigantic piece of steel that was hanging from the ceiling over our heads. He stopped it, and they handed him the model that I had made of this peeler; it was just a hand-made prototype. He looked at it and thought for a minute. All of a sudden, he said something in Japanese, and everybody started smiling and laughing. They confirmed that they could make it. I asked Sam what he actually said, and he told me he had said, "If you can make it, I can make it."

This was just two months before the gourmet show, and they promised they would have production pieces ready for us. A week before the show, we'd gotten nothing. We'd made big photographs for the show of our model, so that it would look like we actually had a product. Then the day before the show opened, the boxes arrived from Japan, and we pulled the peelers out, and they were perfect. That was the beginning of it.

It was the talk of the show because everybody knew Sam; he was such a prominent figure in the housewares industry. It was front-page news in the trade journals. But we barely sold any. Just a couple of stores took it. It didn't really sell at all. People had never seen anything like that in a kitchen store before. But we'd get letters from people saying it was the best peeler they'd ever used. They were buying them for their friends as housewarming gifts—just incredible, passionate stories about it.

Then we got the idea that people really need to try it to understand it. There was a chain of stores. I think it was Lechters at the time. They're no longer in business. We had them put out bowls of carrots in front of the display of the peelers in every one of their stores so people could try peeling the carrot. When they did that, sales went up tenfold. It was like this viral thing. Everybody started trying it, and they would buy it, and they would tell their friends. That's really what made it take off.

GH — Were they called Good Grips from day one?
    DS — When we designed the product, it was designed for everybody. We made the design with the fins so that people would understand it was all about a better grip and the black rubber. We wanted to be really straightforward and take no chances. We decided to call it Good Grips. If they didn't get it by looking at it, they'd know by the name that that's what it was all about. We made the special packaging so that the handle hung below the card that was fastened to it so you could try it and you could hang on to it.

The name of the company was OXO. A lot of people asked, what does OXO mean? It means nothing. The only reason the company's name was OXO was because Sam liked the combination of letters. He liked the way Os and Xs looked together. The best part is, since it's symmetrical, O-X-O, you can turn it upside down and it still says the same thing. We thought if it was going to be on a kitchen tool and you're using it this way and this way, you should still be able to read it. That was his idea of how the logo should be—universal design that works any way you put it.

DF — Early on when it was first named OXO, we kept calling it hug-kiss-hug.

DS — No, it's kiss-hug-kiss.

DF — I don't know what that spells.

DS — If you look at the logo, it looks like a little face where the X is the nose in the middle and Os are the two eyes.

GH — How many products are in the line now?

DS — There are now over a thousand different products, and they're sold everywhere. Virtually everybody has tried to copy it. It's really changed the housewares industry. What's surprising is nobody has really been successful at copying OXO. The mistake they always make is they think it's about the handle, about it being a black rubber handle, and they forget that the blade has to be sharp. That's really the secret of why the product works well. It's not just the handle; it's that everything about it works better. If you put a dull blade in this, it wouldn't work any better than the old metal peeler. If you have a really sharp blade, you can stick it to a wooden stick, and it would work great.

DF — We now have clients who come to us and say that they want us to do what we did with OXO, because OXO grew from nothing to a giant company. We tell them we'd love to, but we're not sure you have the nerve, because OXO—as ubiquitous as it may be now with the number of products available, at the time, it was a tremendous risk. While we were passionately behind this idea of design for everybody, when those samples showed up to the housewares show and we were saying, "Yeah, they're perfect," we were also thinking, "Hope this goes okay. Hope people adapt to this," because it was a tremendous departure from what was out there before. Not only that, but the price was also higher than what was out there before. For all the work that went into it design-wise, really the big part of the story was the audacity to take this point of view. It's to Sam's credit that he said, "Let's design these things for everybody." He gave us permission to do that, and it was a tremendous risk.

DS — At the time, we probably didn't know better, so we just did it.

GH — What year was it?

DS — It was in 1990 when it was introduced. It took a few years before anybody knew what it was.

DF — There's been no advertising. There has never been advertising with OXO. When it launched, the company relied completely on word of mouth. There've been newspaper articles, or magazines may do an article about it, or it may show up on the Food Network, but it's really grown from that. It brought some sort of surprise or delight once you got back home and started using it. You realize that you like it so much that you may even buy it as a gift for someone else, or tell someone else about it. You might say, "Hey, you should try this. It's cool. I bought two of these. Now let's peel some potatoes."

GH — You mentioned the emotional connection and the physical connection to the object. I wonder if you can talk more a little bit about that, both in terms of this product and in general.

DS — We probably can make a connection between that topic the printer that we designed for Hewlett-Packard recently. The printer is an electronic gizmo. When we started designing photo printers, it gave people the ability to go from a digital camera directly to a print without going through a personal computer, which is a great advantage. Again, this device became a little bit of a workstation. The printer itself took the place of a personal computer because now you're working at it. There are a couple of steps that you need to do to get it up and running like load the paper in the back and open the door in the front.

One of the things that we did to make that whole operation a bit more pleasant was we created a printer that was white, very friendly looking at home in the kitchen, and when you pressed the on button, the back door opened up, the front door opened up, the screen popped up, and the welcome screen came on. With one touch, it had this sort of flowery effect which was really an introduction to the product. Of course, the engineers were saying, "Well, it's not that hard. You open the back door. You open the front door. You open the screen. You turn the button on." We felt that the simple gesture of a flower opening started an emotional connection with the consumer. It gave them the impression that this was going to be easy. Again, it gave people incentive to take the next step and actually get photos out of the printer.

DS — When we're thinking about the products we design, the people who use them, we have to step out of our own way of thinking. Most industrial designers are a bunch of guys. When we look at something like a printer, we're thinking about how many dots per inch it's going to print? How fast is it going to be? How many ink colors are there? All the technical specs. But guys don't really use personal photo printers, they're actually used primarily by women. The mothers are the archivists of the home. They're taking pictures; they're printing them and putting together the albums. They could care less about how many dots per inch this prints. They just want to be able to share memories. They just want to be able to take a picture and as quickly as possible share that memory with somebody else. When they look at the printer, they're thinking: Is it something that is going to be easy to use?

We came up with this idea making it white and making it so that you could grab it with one hand. It's like a little clutch purse or something.

You could take it into the living room when you weren't using it with your computer. You might use it in the kitchen. You might use it in the living room. You might even take it outside and use it at the soccer field or something. When you come up to it, you go to turn it on, just push one button, and it just opens up by itself. That was just a very easy one, two, three that you start with the button. We had a goal that we had to have a print coming out of this within 30 seconds from the time somebody takes it out of the box.

GH — Is it simplification of things? I don't know if this is true or not, but it seemed that, for a while, it was about having more features. Everything's got to do more things. If a product can do a million things, the more detailed the gadgetry, the better. Now it seems there's a trend that we're going toward simplicity, like the Flip camera.

DF — Throughout the eighties and nineties, a lot of product design and consumer interest had to do with technical features. It was about how fast it is, how many dots per inch. What's the speed? What's the baud rate? What's the resolution? By the 2000s, people pretty much reached their threshold with technology and with what that technology has promised or maybe overpromised. We started to see a greater interest in personal meaning, like this phone is great, but will it fit in my pocket? What does this do for me? This printer is great, but if I can't get prints out of it, it doesn't matter how fine the resolution is. We saw this shift from consumers looking at features to really thinking about their own lifestyle and the benefits. We're in the midst of that now.

GH — Is simplification part of that?

DF — To some extent, it's simplification, but to the product itself can be extremely sophisticated. Really, the more technically apt the product is, the easier it should be to use. There's no sense filling a product with technology if you can't understand how to use it. You would think that's what the technology is for. It should solve my problems, not create them. Sometimes products are faster so that you can go play with the dog or play with the kids, not because the product is faster, but because it may free up time to do something else in your life. That is a benefit. It really has nothing to do with the product. It has more to do with the rest of my life.

GH — That's interesting. Tell me more about that.

DS — We want products to do things for us, and you could think, "Well, that's adding more features, making them do more." When we get products that do more, we actually don't use them. We all have video cameras. We buy the ones with the greatest zoom lens with the best resolution in the tiniest package. Then when we want to use them—like when the kids are doing something funny—we can't figure out how to turn them on. They end up just sitting there in the drawer never being used.

One of our clients came to us with the idea that we should make video cameras that are a lot easier to use, that anybody can use, are ready when you need them. The concept was the Flip video, and it's basically this. This tiny little box does the same thing as a great, big video camera. It just has one button on the back and you just push that button and it turns on and it's taking video. I'm videotaping you now as you're videotaping me. Push the button and it stops and that's it. To get the movie out of there, you just push this one button, and you see a little USB connector. It plugs into the side of your computer, uploads the video, and it starts playing. That's it. It doesn't need anything more than that. In just a year, this has become the highest-selling video camera on the market now, outselling all the fancy, big cameras. It costs a fraction of the price, and it does what people need with just one button.

DF — It may not be technical, but the resolution is as good as anyone else's camera. Also, the ability to fit this into your lifestyle or literally fit into your pocket without too much thinking is the point. It's an unassuming, precious thing. It's not as expensive as most video cameras, but the ability to capture video of whenever is the key benefit. This leads to people taking more videos because the camera is with them much more often.

GH — We talked about industrial design as a discipline in the seventies. I wonder if you could just talk about what the challenges are facing designers today.

DS — I think the most challenging thing for us today as designers is that we've already designed everything, and everybody has enough stuff. Everything that they have works pretty well. What we're finding is, most of the companies that come to us now don't want a new or better product. They want to know what they should be doing. Should we be making what we make anymore? Should we even be making things? What do people really need? How should we be thinking about the future, the environment? Should we continue to make stuff that just goes to people's home and then the next day straight to the dump? The issues are really quite a bit different today than they were 10 years ago.

DF — Initially, industrial design was about taming the machine. It started in 1930s and 1940s, the industrial age, when people wanted to make better products on a mass-consumption level. The industrial design profession focused on, how do we tame that machine, the metal stamping machine or the injection-molding machine? That's where, really, the history of industrial design has been. It's only recently that attention is being shifted from the thing to people. It's been going on for some years, but we're at a critical point now in industrial design where the focus needs to be on understanding people. It is a dramatic shift in what designers should be learning and focusing on. It's not in the background of a lot of designers and certainly not in the history of design to really understand people's psychology, biomechanics, social issues, lifestyles, and cultural issues.

If designers don't make that change now and embrace this new frontier for design, then the design industry may be controlled by people from other professions who understand people better. They'll just tell the designers what people need. It's an amazing and interesting time for design.

GH — Obviously, you need smart people. You're making progress for other companies that are in manufacturing. Talk a little bit about the client-designer relationship, specifically your experience with OXO. They seem to be open to anything, and you seem to have more of a working partnership than with other clients. Are there stories or issues around that relationship you want to talk about?

> **DF** — I would think the key to innovation is reducing the risk or the fear of risk. A thing that we've been doing all along is taking our projects in a path that is very person focused. It's very user-centric. Along the way, we've collected images, photographs, and videotapes of people responding to products or prototypes or mock-ups or models or existing products. By doing that, we take our projects along a path where I think everyone is behind us—our whole team, the client team, project development, engineers, et cetera. Once they all they get on that wavelength and have that point of view and that vision of where this product could be, then the fear of risk is reduced, and the chance for innovation is increased. If we've done our homework right, we've actually created more innovative products that actually would be more successful, so it actually reduces the risk.

> **DS** — I think the traditional way of doing things doesn't work anymore. You can't design in a vacuum and then launch something entirely new and ask people to accept it. That's usually what kills innovation. We might create a great product, but before it ever makes it out in the marketplace, somewhere in the big corporation, it gets killed because they ask the questions: Did you test it with a focus group? Did you do quantitative testing? How many people liked it?

> We found that it's just so much more beneficial that, when we're trying to do something new, we're not looking for whether people understand it immediately. We want to understand if there's a potential for them to understand it. We work with our client teams to look for these opportunities. We go out in people's homes and see what they're doing, see what might help them so that the clients are thinking the same way that we are, that, "Hey, if we made this, this probably would really work." It might take a little while for them to understand it, which may mean that there are some needs for communication or some way to help tell people about it. Once we get past that, we'll have something that really makes a difference.

GH — You've had a lot of success. How about failures? Does doing a lot of prototyping help you avoid those?

> **DF** — Typically, we do hundreds of prototypes. We're not afraid of failure, which is part of our charm, I think, making those mistakes and admitting them. For instance, we knew that our peeler handle was going to be applied to products that not only would have a sidewards action but also stirring or in this case pushing down. We had it be somewhat generic in the types of actions. We have so many explorations about handles because the tools that these were being applied to were really varied in their action and use. For manufacturing concerns and cost and tooling, we had to keep our number of parts down. Ultimately, we used the same handle in a lot of different products.

DS — We try to use less material. Here's one that's hollow inside, so it'd be a lot lighter and less expensive.

DF — It's not unusual for us to do lots and lots of models. The way we describe it is that we make a lot of little failures along the way. We do little iterations, so we design things in little steps: trial, error, trial, error, trial, and error. At a lot of companies, the projects take a big design step and maybe end up with a large mistake, at which point it may be too hard to back up. We make just as many errors, maybe more because we're doing iterations, but we're solving them as we go.

DS — We can do 10 variations of something in the same amount of time that somebody might do 1. Each time we make something, we can instantly find out whether it works or not. We just make it and try it. If it doesn't work, we make it again and fix it.

DF — I mean, look at all these peeler handle prototypes. Here's a mistake right here.

DS — These are all mistakes.

DF — Why are we showing these?

DS — Here's a good one.

DF — Generation three. Nice. We get a lot of inspiration from eBay too. Like Davin was saying, with the original bowl, we used to go through old patents to see what people did in the 1700s when they had nothing. Again, it's partly how to conserve resources because people 100 or 200 years ago were doing things with very minimal materials and being very efficient. We used to go through very, very old patents or antique stores. Now we just go to eBay.

DS — Actually, the products that we designed, people would use them for a little while, and then they went straight to the dump. Now they live forever on eBay. They just keeping getting recycled over and over again.

DF — We have done things like this before to experiment. Here's an example of a handle that we know isn't going to work. It's not quite right. We've done this in other projects too. We would deliberately make something that we know is not going to work because we want to see how people cope. How does the hand compensate? Because if you find people holding this a funny, different way to compensate because of the way this doesn't work, it may trigger ideas on what we should be designing or how the hand actually wants to work. In some cases, it seems counterintuitive for us to tell the design team to try things that we know are not going to work, but it's actually very educational.

GH — How do you make your prototypes?
    DS — When we used to design things, we'd have to carve a piece of foam or make it out of clay, and it's quite a long laborious process, and then eventually you'd have to do drawings of it so you could have it made.

Now much of the design is done on a computer. One of the drawbacks of doing design on the computer is you can't really touch it and feel it. You can see it. You can rotate it. You can look at your design from every angle. You can enlarge it and see every detail, but it's not the same as actually being able to feel it and use it. Today we have machines that can make things for us. We design it on the computer, and then we can print it. The same way as you might write a letter on the computer and then send it to the printer, we can design an object and then send it to the 3-D printer and have it made.

DF — But even though there is a lot more sophisticated equipment out there, sometimes we need to do things quickly within a day or two, so in some cases, we just go get a fish scale down the block; hook it up to the grips and make a very, very quick, rudimentary test just to start to experiment and understand exactly what advantages or disadvantages different shapes and sizes are giving us. In this case, it's a fish scale that's very simply hooked up to different sizes of handles. If you make something small and round, you've got to squeeze it really hard, and your hand is much weaker. If I was going to squeeze this, I wouldn't be able to get nearly as much torque on it, really as much pressure, as if I took a handle that was larger and oval shaped so that my hand can get around and really get some force on it. So we're measuring how much torque is possible using the various designs. Understanding exactly what that means to people who may be weaker or have physical challenges, like arthritis, can make an extremely significant difference. It's fun and interesting and great for the design team just to make clear things like this very early in the process and just experiment.

Again, we may try these with people with arthritis, with kids, whoever may be within that wide spectrum of people who may encounter the product just to make sure that it works for everyone. These trials remind reminded us that different shapes and forms do create significant differences. In some cases, it's able versus unable. Disabilities are defined by a person's ability to do something. In our minds, a disability is, in a way, also a function of the environment, not just of the actual person. By creating environments that are more friendly or usable, then we are enabling more and more people.

GH — Talk to me about your philosophy of interaction design.
    DF — With interaction design, we basically follow the same philosophy, I'd say. It's about understanding what people need and anticipating their motivations.

    DS — It's all about taking away everything except what you actually need. There may be many different paths you might follow when you upgrade a product, but if you can get rid of everything that you don't need and only have what you're likely to need or do need, then it just makes it so much simpler. One of the best examples of that today is the iPhone, where the interface completely changes depending on whether you're using it as a telephone or as an email device or a text messager. It really gets down to, what do you need?

DF — We work as consultants. This means we work with a lot of different companies and a lot of different fields. If somebody asks us what we do, we say we design kitchen products and medical equipment and this computer printer, and we're doing some food products. It sounds mind-boggling, but our common interest is in understanding people and what their needs are. If you start to think, "Well, really, what these guys do as consultants is focus on people," then it's easy to think about what's needed design-wise in the kitchen or in the hospital or in the car, whether it's a physical device that we're designing or the interface.

I think from our point of view, we typically don't think of interaction as a separate project from the physical product, because to the person using it, it's all one story. It's all one thing. They went to the store. They bought this thing. They don't want to think, "Oh, this interaction is pretty good, but I'm not sure about the button." It's all one experience.

GH — But at the end of the day, it's about companies selling things. Do you have thoughts sometimes like, "What does all this stuff really mean? Do we really need all this stuff?"

DS — Our job is to design stuff. Our clients want to sell stuff. That's why they pay us. If we can design stuff that has lasting value that people don't want to replace a year from now or two years from now or maybe even five years from now, then I think we've made a little bit of a difference.

DF — We're working with a large software company to design a package for their software. Ultimately, what our team responded with was, well, you don't need a package because in most cases those discs that you're selling are going to be obsolete as soon as you do an update, which will probably happen three weeks after the launch. Secondly, what you're really buying when you buy the software is a membership, the right to use the software. In many cases, people can download the software more easily than they can go to the store and buy the disc, or order the disc online and wait for the package.

Not only that, but with the download, it's instant. You can do it anytime— like at twelve midnight, you can download this package, and then you own it. We're not exactly there yet with all software companies working that way, but there's a move that way. That's our thinking. A lot of times when we start projects, we question whether or not the product itself is necessary or, again, whether what you really want is the benefit of that product as opposed to the physical thing.

We don't want to design things that are obsolete early on. We don't want to design things with too much material. We want to reduce weight. There are processes that are friendlier than others. Painting plastic for instance is not as friendly as using the raw plastic. We'll look at every step of the manufacturing process. We look for ways to be friendlier in any way possible to really lower the impact at any step along the way.

It's very hard when you do a project like this to come up with an equation that says, this product is more friendly than that one because of this,

this, and this, because there are different steps along the manufacturing route. Anything from sourcing the materials to shipping and the weight required with shipping and distribution is part of the big equation. What we tend to do is just look at every little step and try to make improvements every step along the way to lower the impact on the environment.

GH — Anything else you guys would like to add?

DF — We talked about making design available to everyone, but there's of course a huge movement to see if design thinking can solve problems in other parts of the world—the bottom of the pyramid story.

DS — There's this great, great opportunity to apply design throughout other parts of the world where design can have an impact on people's lives in a very significant and serious way. For instance, solving problems with farming in Africa or problems of disease in places like India or different parts of Asia. There's great, great, great opportunity for design thinking to have a great impact in other parts of the world.

I think designers have a different way of looking at a problem, that often these problems become unsolved because people look for the obvious solution. Let me think of a good example. We need to get water from the bottom of the hill up to the top of the hill, so that means we need a pump, and we need electricity or something. Maybe the real answer or the solution is they just need a better way of carrying the water up the hill or something to help them do that. I think often our creative ways of thinking are very underutilized.

DF — For instance, we've looked at issues in Asia, and it's interesting to understand how people cope with taking care of an infant when they need all the same products—baby powder, shampoo, towels, blankets, et cetera—but their water supply may be down the road. That's fine. They've certainly existed in parts of the world with that method of doing things, but there's a lot of opportunity in the area of childcare in different parts of the world if we start applying some design thinking to how to make it safer, reduce disease, reduce infection—really public health in general.

GH — Are there specific projects that you guys have been involved with, or even ones that you haven't been that you think are exemplary, that address some of these issues?

DF — We've done a lot of work with some healthcare companies where we've encouraged local and regional groups within the company to get more inventive and creative. In other words, don't necessarily take what's being offered from the corporate headquarters in the United States and distribute that around the world, because really, what a lot of companies have is not the product necessarily. It's the knowledge about how that product functions and the realization that those products may or may not fit in different parts of the world in the same way as they do here in the US.

We see a lot of companies who want to be like Coca-Cola: one product. It's the same here as it is in South America, Canada, Europe, Africa, and

Asia—the same exact thing. That's great for Coca-Cola, but there are a lot of products that don't fit that model, and there are so many cultural issues that are significant or even economic issues that are significant that would have an impact on actually what we would design if we were going to design what's appropriate for that part of the world.

GH — I'm interested in this area and in trying to get it across to people. Are there other great examples you can think of?

DF — I saw a picture recently of a bicycle-powered machine. That's cool, right? I'd love to get involved in that, but, again, the whole idea of it is to apply design thinking—how to transmit energy from a human body into something that will clean clothes. I think that sort of stuff is just fascinating and gets us really excited.

GH — What are your thoughts about China as a manufacturer or maybe soon designer of products, but also even as a consumer?

DS — For quite a long time, designers here felt threatened by China in that China is the manufacturer of all the products that we design, and now much of the design work is going to China. It has changed what we do here. China graduates thousands and thousands of designers a year. Many of them are very, very skilled at their craft. They're as good as designers here at creating objects. They read the same magazines as we do. They're in touch with the world to some degree.

What they may not know, though, is that they can design a product that's equal to other products that exist in the world today, but they're not in the right position to be able to identify new opportunities. New opportunities are really culturally based. A designer in China might have trouble identifying what I need in my house here, in the same way I might have trouble identifying what someone needed in China because of how differently things are done there, for example. There's still a need for designers to understand their own cultures. As designers, we're not going to make a living by doing things that can be done elsewhere for less money than we can do it for. Although that may be changing. The Chinese economy is growing, and it won't be long before the world is equalized in terms of standards of living and the expectations people have.

A big surprise is in how China is becoming a major consumer. It's going to greatly affect what's available to us because recently material costs have doubled, tripled, gone up by four times because the Chinese market is absorbing world supply for their own needs. We don't really even think about that here. We don't realize that the price that you pay for something here is being directly affected by the fact that the Chinese are driving cars now.

DF — Integration of design thinking from around the world would be extremely beneficial. I don't see a limit to where design can go. I'm not thinking, "Oh, all these designers in China, we're going to hit the ceiling, because what are we going to do next?" There are so many opportunities for design to take different paths and to address issues not only in this part of the world but in all parts of the world.

If anything, it's going to keep us all on our toes to constantly change and evolve to stay ahead of the curve. I think for consumers worldwide, the ultimate result will be beneficial.

—

Paola Antonelli (PA)/
October 7, 2008
New York

Paola Antonelli is the Senior Curator of the Department of Architecture & Design as well as the Director of R&D at The Museum of Modern Art, New York. Paola has worked on exhibitions such as *Humble Masterpieces*, which celebrated traditionally unheralded design icons such as the paper clip; *Design and the Elastic Mind*, which considered the relationship between design and technology; and *Talk to Me*, which looked at design and the communication of people and objects.
—

Gary Hustwit — Okay, for starters, I'd like you to define what design is.

 Paola Antonelli — Oh God!

GH — Industrial design, product design, what they both entail as an industry. I'd also like to get a better idea of what a designer's role is.

 PA — Well, I've been collecting definitions of design, really, for a few years. I have about 172, and yesterday I found some more on a website. It's so encompassing, just the noun itself, that you can say anything you want about it. I have my own definition, the one that works for me and the one that also shows which kind of design I'm interested in.

 To me, really good design is what takes revolutions and progress and makes them into objects that we can use. I like that push forward that designers give to us by taking innovation and bringing it home, in a way—making it into things that we can use. That's my kind of design.

GH — And how would you describe the role of the designer?

 PA — Designers are at people's service, in an ideal world. What I tend to say is that designers almost take a Hippocratic oath, as if they were doctors. That's how they differentiate themselves from artists, because sometimes what they do formally looks like art. They come up with prototypes, with scenarios, with concepts, but in truth, they always have this idea of servicing people, sometimes their clients.

 They have different ways of working, but what they have in common is that they bring together teams, and they act as synthesizers of goals and of means. There's the goal of the manufacturer, and then there's the means: the kind of production plans that you have, the budget, the marketing plan, the object, the function. It really is an amazing role that they have of bringing things together, and it's quite unique. I don't know too many other professions that have the same kind of modus operandi. Maybe architects, but architects do it for one thing, and designers have to have an idea and then see this idea realized in sometimes millions of objects.

It's a really, really tough job, because the distance between the perfection of the idea and the final object is really big. You have to be able to defend your idea and at the same time understand the needs of everybody around you so that, in the end, your idea is still in the object.

GH — What are your feelings about objects in general?

PA — Objects are fantastic. I discovered early on that I was much more comfortable with objects than with people, so I decided to just lose myself in them. That's what I'm trying to teach people around me through my work at MoMA, through these interviews, any way I can. Behind every object, there is so much. We've gotten to understand more about music and more about movies, because somebody explained to us what tracks are, what arrangements are, explained to us what a production designer does and what a director of photography does. I just want people to have the same array of critical tools and of understanding that we have for other expressions of creativity. Because once you have that, you can really spend your life entertaining yourself endlessly throughout the day. You can stop in front of a traffic light and just start wondering—you'll understand that's a new light; it has LEDs; it doesn't have the old lamp; therefore, "Oh my god, it wastes less, and they have to change the lights less. It costs more at the beginning, but it's an investment."

What I'm always telling people is that my idea of the perfect location is to be in a city that I don't know, on a bus, with a window seat. I just look at the trash bins, and I look at the traffic lights, and I just think that I understand the culture. Maybe it's a bit of an illusion, but I think that you can understand a culture that way.

GH — What's the relationship between the object and the user? We invest so much emotion in these things, and I'm interested in trying to explore that a little bit. What are your thoughts?

PA — You know, sometimes we forget that objects were not born in the nineteenth century. When we study design, it's as if we're starting with the Industrial Revolution, but in truth, designed objects have existed forever. From the beginning of civilization, people have had an emotional relationship with objects. That ranges from using them as status symbols, to investing them with memory, to investing them with function. The emotional attachment and the functional need has not changed, but at different times in history, we've been highlighting different needs.

If you look at the modernist period and the famous motto of "Form follows function," that was an interpretation of what it is that makes objects not only useful but also desirable for people. It's only lately, through many philosophical upheavals—poststructuralism, postmodernism—that we've gotten to highlight the emotional bond we have with objects instead. Nothing's really changed. We're still designing them pretty much the same way, and good designers do a better job than bad designers. Some people have actually coined slogans like "emotional design," and so on, and so forth. In truth, objects need to have a language and a relationship and rapport with people that goes beyond the function.

GH — When does that develop into rampant materialism?

PA — I don't even know what rampant materialism is. I think that very often we underestimate people. Of course we're consumers; of course we tend to buy; but at the same time, something's happening to everybody. It's not only the fact that the economy is not doing so well. I think it has to do with an ethical ocean that's sweeping people. I always use the example of the smoking ban. It started out as legislation, but then it became peer pressure, and it really changed the landscape. I was actually very resistant to that. I think that the same is happening with consumerism, or at least with waste. We still buy objects just because we like them, without any specific need, but I don't think anyone approaches buying a car without thinking, and maybe rejecting, the idea that it should be environmentally responsible. You can reject it, but you know what? You're going to come to terms with it one way or the other.

I think that ideas spread, and they become moral concerns, and they become concerns that people express back to the designers and to the manufacturers. That's what I think. Materialism is good and it's bad, but no matter what, people will be the ones who will change the balance.

GH — Is more knowledge of design part of that process, because then you're understanding more about where the object came from?

PA — Knowledge of design is very, very important. It's so empowering to people. To me it's almost outrageous that there are no design critics in major publications. There's only one, that you've interviewed, Alice Rawsthorn at the *International Herald Tribune*, but she's the only one that really sits as design critic. Otherwise, nothing. You have critics for perfume; you have critics for dance. It's time to understand that design is not only style; it's not only decoration; it's part of our lives. It touches every single aspect of our lives, including the moral sphere, and tremendously so. It's just necessary to spread that knowledge. I think it's time that publications just get with it.

GH — It seems like when major publications actually do something about design, it's just a photo spread about new objects, new furniture coming out.

PA — In major publications, you find design either in the style section or in the business section. Sometimes you have special issues that treat design comprehensively, but it's the exception and not the rule. I am talking about a weekly column, like that one in the *Herald Tribune*. It's necessary.

GH — We've talked to a few designers for this film. Could you give your thoughts on them? Let's start with Dieter Rams.

PA — Oh, Dieter Rams. Dieter is such a pillar in design history. He established a type of design, an approach to design, that is bare-bones functionalism. In reality it's almost baroque. The minimalism and the perfection of those objects—objects that always elicit a reaction from the user and the viewer—is just endless. You know, it's interesting: when you have the kind of historical span that you have here at MoMA, you realize that the Braun alarm clock was designed initially by Marianne Brandt at the Bauhaus. It was iron, but it's here in the collection; it really has that face. Dieter Rams was able to, at the same time, continue this amazingly innovative tradition of German design and also make it hugely popular and make it into a style. At that time, it was important to have a style for that kind of functionalist design. It was endlessly important.

GH — We went to the Braun Museum with Dieter, and in one display case they had products from the pre-Rams era, and everything was brown. These very old-fashioned, Bakelite-looking appliances. The case next to it was post-Rams and everything was white. It still looks very futuristic.

    PA — It does. It was very, very futuristic at that time, and it's very contemporary today.

GH — And influential.

    PA — Enormously influential. Dieter Rams, I think, really had the same influence that Mies van der Rohe had on architecture: he changed the landscape of the world. He really exported a language that was totally universal and applicable to almost everybody. It was very, very identifiable with an idea of progress and of technology.

GH — What about the concept of design as a language that can tell a story. Could you talk about that?

    PA — Every single object has a story behind it. One of the biggest masters of this kind of storytelling was my teacher Achille Castiglioni. When I organized a show on his work here at MoMA years ago—I think it was '98—the wall labels were all illustrations. I hired an illustrator who, using the same style, illustrated the object and then a little design tale telling that object's story. I wanted to make sure that people would read this story. It was incredible, because people really understood, after somebody explained to them, the story behind each object.

There's the famous example of the Arco lamp: the Arco lamp was designed the way it is because the two Castiglioni brothers wanted to have a dining room lamp that fell in the middle of the dining room table, but they did not make a hole in the ceiling because they were renting a flat. They thought of street lamps, but of course, you can't dig a hole in the apartment, because it would be self-defeating, so they thought of something really heavy and cheap that they could use. Carrera marble in Italy at that time was not very expensive. You have the big base. You have the telescopic launch that throws the light about seven feet away so you're able to sit underneath it. You had space to sit. Somebody could serve behind you without running into the base. The last final touch, which drove everybody crazy, was the little hole through the base, because nobody understands why there is a hole in the marble base. It's so that two people can stick a broomstick through it and carry the lamp around, because it's too heavy. This brings a smile to everybody's face. It's such a beautiful story. When he designed light switches, the most important feature was the sound: the click of the light switch.

The same thing happened with another show, *Humble Masterpieces*, which was a sleeper. It was a very small show, but it was about every-day objects that don't cost much money. We made the effort to tell the story behind the object. Once again, you just give people the narrative behind an object, and they just eat it up. We just have to start doing that more often.

GH — What about Jony Ive?

PA — Oh my, he's done more to change the world than anybody I know almost. He's a great designer. Also, you have to understand that some-thing that people don't usually talk about when they talk about Jony is the kind of structure he works in: designer as a synthesizer. Jony participates in this gigantic production that is Apple. Of course, the vision of Steve Jobs is apparent everywhere. What Jony's been able to do, working together with the software designers, interface designers, with technical engineers, is to create an object that has established a new benchmark for consumer products.

Of course, he's designed beautiful objects even before, but with the iPod, in particular, all of a sudden everybody's expectations of what an object should look like were raised. The world will never be the same. You cannot design a crappy anything anymore, because people will think of the sublime iPod and expect that you do something nearly as good, or at least try to. That's the gigantic function that Jony has had in design history. He's the best designer, but he has this social role that is incommensurable.

GH — And Marc Newson?

PA — Marc has also had a very important role in design history, for a another set of reasons. Marc is a really, really fine industrial designer, and he's been designing heavy duty industrial objects for a long time. He has a flair for style that also has established a new stylistic archetype in the world. You can immediately recognize something that is inspired by Marc; it has a certain kind of organic shape.

Also, he was able to heat up the debate on design and art with his famous exhibition at the Gagosian Gallery in New York a few years ago. That was possibly the most controversial display of design, if one wants to call it design, that I can think of. You cannot talk right now about what's happening in design and the market for design without quoting that particular show. Whether you think about it in positive terms or in negative terms, it's one of those controversial moments that really will remain in history.

Of course, he's reestablished himself with the amazing program that he's doing for Qantas, where he's able to influence everything from the industrial design and the engineering of the seats all the way to choosing the chef and the perfume for Qantas. It's interesting, because he's still really able to do great design at an industrial level, and also he created that amazing controversy.

GH — Let's talk more about the range of someone like Newson. The idea that a designer can do anything and also express their creative vision through this limitlessness range of different objects.

PA — There are few designers that become auteurs. In our contemporary world, it began with Philippe Starck. Before, you had Raymond Loewy; you had other designers. When they rise to the status of auteurs, they can pretty much write their ticket and design anything, even pasta. Starck tried to design pasta—it was not good. Pasta cannot be designed, but he tried.

Starck was one, and Marc Newson is another. Ron Arad is another one, and Karim Rashid. They are at a certain level where people might want their signature. Who cares if that's the reason? They still get to have the widest range of products possible. They certainly have to have a strong style in order to do that. They are the kinds of designers who sometimes are accused by other designers of being stylized. In truth, it's a very interesting phenomenon.

GH — What are your thoughts on Naoto Fukasawa's work?

PA — Naoto Fukasawa is an excellent designer. I met him many years ago, around 18 years ago, when he was working at IDEO in California. I loved IDEO, so I was always looking at what they were doing, and I immediately had a rapport with him and with David Kelley, but with Naoto in particular. We've worked together on several shows here at MoMA. One of the best ones that I can recall was *Work Spheres*, which was a show about the changes in how people work. It was in 2000, so it was the time that wireless technology had started to become ubiquitous but didn't really work well.

I commissioned IDEO, and in particular Naoto, with a single brief. Let's say you have your cubicle; there's nothing you can do about it; you have a cubicle. How do you make it more livable? I wanted him to use his Japanese sensibility, and the capability of making the best out of small and confined spaces, and also his amazing poetry, and his knowledge of engineering. He came back with this great installation called *Personal Skies*. The idea was that you could have a screen on top of your cubicle, nearly as big as the cubicle, where you could project your own favorite sky in motion. Friends could send you a sunset in Vienna. It was video, so it was not just a picture. You could have this hole above you that would relieve the pressure.

After that, Naoto went back to Tokyo, opened the IDEO office in Tokyo, and then opened his own office. In a way, he's the Dieter Rams of today, the Japanese Dieter Rams. He is at the same time very synthetic and very minimalist, but also full of ideas. It's when minimalism becomes baroque. The work that he did for Plus Minus Zero is emblematic. The same goes for what he did designing telephones. You can tell that his objects are very compressed and about to explode with creativity.

GH — What I love about Naoto is there's always this kind of humor; there's a sense of fun in the designs that don't necessarily look fun; but when you experience them, you begin to understand.

PA — Humor is important in design. Some designers don't really want to mess with it, but the ones that do have one more way into people's souls.

GH — How about Hella Jongerius?

PA — Hella is really unique. She is the one designer I know who is able to take two polar opposites and merge them into a seamless design that is just groundbreaking because it opens new horizons. For example, many designers from the West, or from the Northern Hemisphere, have gone to Africa, and they've seen the Kasese stool: the three-legged stool with the high back. They've fallen in love with it and come back and tried to repeat it. Most of them have kind of mimicked it, a form of copying that meant that the cannibalism was not really digested. Hella's the one person who was able to bring back the Kasese stool and make into an object that looks like it could be from the West. But at the same time, you feel like it comes from outer space—it's made in carbon fiber; it has neoprene or a strange synthetic fur on it; it's foldable so you can make it even more utilitarian. And voilà!

For the exhibition *Work Sphere* that I mentioned, she was also commissioned for that. Her brief was about working at home. That was the time where everybody was saying, "Oh my God, if you work at home, you have to careful. You have to mimic a walk around the block as if you were going to the office. You have to make sure it doesn't interfere with family life, you have to put the computer on a timer so at 9:00 p.m. it shuts off, and you can't use it anymore." Hella said, "Paola, look, this is ridiculous. People are not so childish. It's really paternalistic and condescending. I'm going to make objects that can be used either for work or for pleasure, objects that are going to be totally seamless." She made many different things for the exhibition. Particularly, she did this TV dinner tray that was a computer keyboard with a dish in the middle, so you could have your pizza there and still work on your computer. She's quite fabulous that way.

GH — Great, let's keep this going. Tell me about the Bouroullec brothers.

PA — The Bouroullec brothers have been able to interpret the most innovative and contemporary bourgeois style one can think of. If you think of a well-to-do family home, and you think of what it should look like to be really up to date, it's Bouroullecs. I think that they've been amazing in the furniture that they have designed, especially for Cappellini. But there's another aspect that I love about their work, which is their focus on modular. They have not only done furniture, but they have also thought of the entire interior space, which is something that most designers don't do. Most designers usually design the object, but they don't think as much about the space that the object is going to fill.

In the Bouroullecs' case, the tiles that they did for Kvadrat (felt tiles that you can compose together) their work on the Algue screen system (the plastic, seaweed-like forms that can be put together to make these beautiful, organic-looking screens) or Clouds, which is this kind of bookshelf system that is very organic and can also act as room dividers—it all speaks to a notion of space that is almost architectural, that really transcends product design or furniture design.

GH — What are your thoughts on the so-called democratization of design. Stores like IKEA or Target, are they democratizing design? Or are they using design as a marketing tool to bring people in?

PA — Democratization of design is an empty slogan. It really should not even exist. There is design that costs more, and there's design that costs less. Some of it is good; some of it is bad. I always tell people that I grew up with good design in my home—with all the Joe Colombo and Achille Castiglioni pieces—not because we were rich or because my parents were educated in design, not at all. We were totally middle class, and my parents are doctors. It's just because those were the products you would find at the corner store. Whether you could afford it or not was the same issue as affording a pair of shoes that cost more or less.

I've found this discrepancy here in the States. The United States has one of the best traditions of utilitarian design that one can find, an amazing history of design. But for some reason, Americans neglect it, or push it aside, and look to Europe and the rest of the world as if they needed input from the outside in order to be elegant and really tasteful. It's ridiculous. The idea of elitism and the idea of design here in the States have merged, and it's out of this culture that the idea of democratization of design emerges. In other words, okay, IKEA sells objects that are affordable. That's such a novelty for Americans, but it shouldn't be. It should be the normal thing.

I hope, once again, that by making people more aware of design, by making people understand that beauty is a right—you should not pay more for something beautiful—by making people understand that, they'll just demand that this so-called democratization of design becomes the norm.

GH — That brings me into the idea of utilitarian design and how there is nothing that is not designed.

PA — It's interesting. Of course, we always have very subjective thoughts about design objects. I'm lucky, because I work in a museum where I'm forced to pretend that my subjective thoughts can be objective—I have to make that effort because we have a collection.

Lately, we've been installing recent acquisitions to the collection. As wall text, we decided to try and explain to people how we choose objects. That's not easy, because you can't really talk about a form, because that's so personal. Once again, after poststructuralism, there's no absolute beauty; it really is not even in the eye of the beholder, but in the personality of the beholder. You can't talk about function that much, because these days emotion is also considered function. When you have an object like Tamagotchi, the little toy, how do you talk about function? You can certainly talk about environmental responsibility, but it can't be the only criteria.

We concluded by saying, "Look, there's one litmus test that you can use, anybody can use. Think about it: if this object did not exist, would the world miss out?" And we're telling people, "Try this at home with your objects." The missing of an object can even be based simply on beauty and cannot really be about utilitarian value. It is very powerful, because once again, it's the economy of thought that we need in order to deal with economic and environmental issues.

GH — Can you talk a little bit about the concept of the consumer or user expressing their identity through objects?

PA — I'm always reading a column that I really love in the *New York Times Magazine* by Rob Walker, called "Consumed." As a social commentator, he talks about brands and objects that are signifiers. He talks about the hidden power of objects to make you an early adopter or a late adopter. It's all about what you project. You used to be able to say that about clothes—what you wear is how you want to present yourself to the world. Now it's also happening with objects. For instance, right now the iPod is so ubiquitous that people who are using the Zune are considered weirdos. It really is interesting to see how people modulate their personality and the communication of their own identity through objects.

GH — You talked about automobile design a little bit, and on one hand, I think it's probably the most intricate of all the different types of design. The thought that has to go into any vehicle, and also how it's marketed to consumers, seems to be the epitome of that identity.

PA — Automobile design is really a world unto itself. It doesn't really follow the normal design rules or the normal marketing rules. The sheer size of the investment and the outreach is totally different from almost anything else.

I remember interviewing Giorgetto Giugiaro in the 1990s, and it was the moment when Japanese cars were becoming much more ubiquitous, and therefore that particular organic look for cars was also adopted by Western manufacturers. I told him, "I'm having trouble recognizing cars lately. They all look alike." As the great designer of the Fiat Panda and the VW Golf, he told me, "You have to think about cars as human beings. They all have two eyes, one nose, and one mouth, but, boy, if you really learn to read faces, you can tell one from another instantly." I've never forgotten that. Lately, I think that cars with personality have become much more ubiquitous. In some cases, the personality's unbearable, but you know what? As my mother would say, "Not all flavors are strawberry." You need to have cars for everyone. It's much more fun this way. There are cars that you would not touch with a stick because they don't express your personality. There are others that you fall in love with.

I think that in the realm of car design, the emotional side of the design process is even stronger. Also, car designers tend to show you the exceptions rather than the rules. Chris Bangle showed me this amazing car with a cloth skin that can change shape, and it almost looks like it can fly like a bat. Then, you have the famous $1 million Lamborghini. Those are the objects of desire, the dream cars. Right now, personality and customization are available pretty much to almost everyone, even at lower prices.

GH — Can you talk about China? Of course, many of the world's mass-produced objects come from China, but there seems to be a shift—will Chinese designers start leading instead of following?

PA — China is an extremely interesting design case study—seeing how fast it's developing, the economic boom, how it's using architecture, the art market. I expected a few years ago to see a Chinese language of design forming very quickly. What happened in Japan in 15 years could happen, I thought, in China in 3. Instead, even though I continued to see really great, forward-looking, poetic, instinctive ideas in Chinese design schools, I didn't see that filtering down to the market. I couldn't really understand why until I read an article in a business magazine talking about the fact that the Chinese government, and the Chinese economic system, is so shrewd that they understood it would be better to slow down the establishment of a real Chinese design language in order to be able to continue manufacturing designs from all over the world.

It was an economic choice in order to maintain a certain advantage and use the other cultural advantages of art and architecture but not really capitalize on design just yet. I still don't think it can be contained. The students there are really good, and you can tell that they have ideas that might be adopted in the West. There might be this strange circle where Chinese designers will go to Western companies in order to get back to being manufactured in China. It's interesting. It gave me renewed admiration for the ability to modulate expansion and affirmation on the part of the Chinese.

GH — What do you think, or hope, the future is for design and designers?

PA — I think that what designers will do in the future is develop this really unique capability of being shrewd generalists. In order to be able to keep up with the world and do their job, they need to read business magazines at the same time as *People* or *Us*. They need to be curious about everything. Then, they need to be able to call upon the right people in order to achieve the task at hand.

My hope is that they will become the reference point for policy makers, for anybody who wants to create a link between something that's high-brow and hard to translate yet also real and communal. I almost envision them becoming the intellectuals of the future. I always find it really funny that the French, whenever they have to talk about the price of gas or the cheese war with Italy, they go to a philosopher, right? Philosophers are the culture generators in France. I want designers to be the culture generators pretty much all over the world, and some of them really can. No matter what, they should become really fundamental bricks in any kind of policy-making effort. More and more that's happening. I see designers as designing not just more objects per se, but also scenarios based on objects. Scenarios that will help people understand the consequences of their choices. People like Dunne and Raby do exactly that. They call it "design for debate." Anthony Dunne actually sets the basis for his course at the Royal College on exactly this idea.

I also think that virtual platforms, not really Second Life, but others that are in development, will help people test design before it goes to production. I think phenomena like 3-D printing will enable designers and people to make objects on demand and therefore diminish waste and diminish trucking and warehousing. There's so much. I just think it's a golden moment for design, if not a platinum moment. I see designers as growing in their importance for society and growing in their intellectual and cultural capabilities. I'm just really happy to be here now, and to be able to help this process through.

GH — If you're sitting in a theater and you're watching a movie about design, what's the one thing that you would want to hear somebody say that we haven't talked about yet?

PA — I would like to hear a pledge from somebody that is not in the design world. For instance, it could be the mayor of New York, or it could be the editor in chief of the *New York Times*, or it could be the education commissioner. Someone to say that they understand the need to make design part of people's cultural and educational curriculum. I would like to see, for once, somebody that is in high power in the way our society's structured acknowledging the importance of design. Not the importance of style, not really cute and very expensive chairs, but the importance of knowledge of the process and how much it influences society. Get me one of those people and sit him—it's usually a him, unfortunately—sit him down on a chair, and make him give us a pledge.

GH — We need a design czar for the country.

PA — We need a design advocate. We can be the czars ourselves. We can get into the White House and do our thing; we just need somebody to open the doors.
—

Andrew
Blauvelt
(AB)/
December
2, 2008
New York

Andrew Blauvelt is Curator of Architecture and Design and Chief of Communications and Audience Engagement at the Walker Art Center in Minneapolis. A practicing graphic designer, his work has received more than one hundred design awards. As a writer and critic of design and culture, his essays have appeared in numerous journals and publications. I spoke with Andrew at the Norwood Club in New York City.

—

Gary Hustwit — What do industrial designers and product designers do? What's their job?

Andrew Blauvelt — Well, it's kind of hard to pinpoint when we first get an industrial designer in history. Some people trace it to the late 19th century as a natural by-product of industrialization, especially in England. Some people look at it as the rift between the engineer and what we used to call the stylist; giving function to the object versus giving form to the object. The modern designer operates between both realms. They're not wholly in the engineering realm, and they're not wholly in the aesthetic realm anymore, because it's too complicated for that now. The industrial designer is trying to give form to the object, but their awareness of its functionality and how it needs to be produced and manufactured is a key to being successful in the field. A lot of that goes back to history and the separation and specialization of labor.

You hear of people like Christopher Dresser, who was doing all sorts of household objects in the late 1800s, as being an early industrial designer—he's the proto-industrial designer. Or even manufacturing concerns like Wedgwood, with the industrialization of ceramics production. In the US, most of the history seems to be around the twenties and thirties during the great age of streamlining, for example, where the form of the object took precedence. You could have a streamlined locomotive or a streamlined iron, and it didn't really much matter; it was all streamlined. Norman Bel Geddes figures heavily in that history.

But the modern industrial designer is often just so connected to companies and corporations, either in-house in product development or as a consultancy working for companies to develop new products. That's another new facet of the product designer—it's not simply a company coming to them and saying, "I have this idea for a flashlight.

Can you make it sexy?" It's almost psychoanalytical now. The designer is concerned with what the consumer wants. They're being probed by the company. "What kind of ideas do you have? How do we bring this to fruition in the marketplace?" So a lot of product design is actually conflated with product development.

GH — Could you talk more about in-house designers versus consultants?

AB — Some industrial designers work in-house at companies, say like Apple. They happen to have a very high profile of head of design. Other designers work in consultancy situations like at an IDEO or Frog Design. Those firms obviously don't work for anyone who walks through the door; they pick and choose what clients they'll take on.

GH — You mentioned IDEO, which makes me think of this whole field of "design thinking" and innovation. How do you define design thinking?

AB — There are different camps about what design is or what design thinking is, because design thinking is already a newer subarea. Traditionally people think of designers as form givers—what shape will this object take? More recently that equation has been modified and is so close to product development in the various phases; everything from engineering to research to how to get the product into the marketplace, including branding. Those are new developments that have made the idea of design much bigger and much broader.

Design thinking is design as a synthetic process. It's different for different people at different companies, but it attempts to take information and research from different areas and give it some sort of form, and that's the real power that design has. A lot of these ideas that came out of England in the 1980s and the research about what makes design different or special. They likened it to the idea of modeling—that designers have the power to model things, in other words, to make things real or tangible, to make them into objects. That's a specific skill that, oddly, designers themselves don't think is very special. I think laypeople are absolutely fascinated by this ability to visualize. You've probably heard that most people who buy real estate, looking for houses, can never read a floor plan. Realtors know this. It's a shockingly high number, because they're not intrinsically visual. Of course, this is not a problem with people that end up becoming designers. Oftentimes designers end up not thinking about their own gifts and powers in that way.

GH — In terms of how a company like IDEO uses design thinking to, say, rethink the flow of a hospital emergency room, is the term "design thinking" used to refer to the act of borrowing from industrial design methodology and applying it to areas outside traditional design?

AB — There has been an expansion of the problem that the designer receives or formulates. Sometimes it's been called "experience design," because it's moving away from just solely an object. You might have a client who comes to you to design some new medical equipment that's used in emergency room situations. But when studying the problem, naturally you have to study the larger context. Once you start doing that, where does the design stop? Your solution may not be an improved medical device; it may actually be cleaning up the chaos in the emergency room. Clients come with these bigger issues, especially to a place like IDEO, a practice that presents itself as capable of solving those big, complex problems. It's when somebody comes to you with a simple problem that turns out to be not so simple. That's how you get this expansion beyond the design of the object.

It could be the design of the whole voting system like in Florida in 2000. The butterfly ballot design was a really interesting occasion, not only because of its failure as a piece of graphic design, but for how people started thinking about solving that particular problem. You had more of the technologists looking into electronic voting, for example. There were a lot of graphic designers and experience designers looking at the whole voting system. How do you register? What is the experience like? What happens afterwards? Looking at the complete cycle of voting, for example. It's much bigger and much broader.

GH — When a company approaches a product designer, what are they typically looking for?

AB — The myth is that the client comes to you with a problem. But often their problem isn't clearly defined. One of the designer's roles is to play detective and to figure out what the real problem is, and then also what the variety of solutions. Perhaps the dirty little secret in design is that there's always more than one solution, but there's only one that's being offered up as the solution. Other people have defined design as a never-ending series of solutions to never-ending problems. It's this constant cycle of change and innovation and boredom. These are all factors that contribute to why somebody wants something new.

In product design, it's often about designers adding value to the original idea the client brings them. It's the old notion of the tinkerer or the inventor having this idea, then getting it massaged and developed in a very specific way by a product consultancy firm. They're adding tremendous value to that equation.

GH — And in terms of the average person, how aware do you think they are of these designers?

AB — I remember somebody once asked me, "Well, what isn't designed?" I was stumped, because when you think about, the human-built environment is a designed world. Sometimes we know who these designers are; sometimes we don't. But anything that's touched by man, or is transformed by man, is by its very nature design. Even the definition of design is now changing. It's become a generic verb. When you can manipulate molecules, you can manipulate science. Does that become design? Someone like Bruce Mau may say yes; others may say no, that it goes too far.

Everything in the world is designed to one degree or another. Sometimes it looks undesigned or it's anonymous or it's vernacular, but it's all designed in the end. If you think about it, just in your daily life, in your normal routine, how many objects you come into contact with— you wake up in your bed, your sheets. You can just go through the daily rituals of everything that you come into contact with. It's not surprising that there would be hundreds of objects in a single day that a consumer comes into contact with.

GH — What do you think the word "design" means to the average consumer?

AB — It's funny; it depends how old you are, I guess. Back in the day, when you told people you were designer, they thought that you were a fashion designer because that's what they thought designers did, and some still do. Then in the eighties, we had designer water and designer jeans. Design was this adjective used to connote a kind of specialness within that product. People bought that idea; it became a sellable quality. In the nineties you had a proliferation of "designed" ordinary objects, things like tennis shoes, for example. Nike revolutionized the design of a tennis shoe; they really employed product designers to think about all aspects of the shoe—its sole, its laces, its performance, and so on.

You can see that in things like toothbrushes too. It was happening around the same time actually. In the late eighties, early nineties, there was this fascination with toothbrushes. If you go to any Walmart, Kmart, or Target, look at the selection and the array of toothbrushes that are available. It's mind-boggling. It isn't just about smooth, hard, medium, long head, short head anymore. It's now more like picking your sneakers; like blue gel, flex, cross action, different brush shapes, different performance options.

GH — Do you think that was just for marketability, like providing color options, or were those designers trying to innovate?

AB — During that same time, you had the launch of the iMac—the teal-colored one, the very first one—which introduced the element of color as if it had vanished from the world of objects but suddenly came into the world of computers, and it was a big sensation. So sure, color does some of that. But I think a lot of it was also performance related in the sense that you didn't just have tennis shoes anymore; you had training shoes; you had cross-training shoes; you had running shoes. It's all very much adapted, and you find that same kind of infinite niche within the toothbrush.

GH — And where is this concept headed?

AB — Well, in terms of where design is headed, I think it's about this notion of what I call relational design. I think there are really three phases of modern design. The first phase was preoccupied with form giving, form begetting form, developing a visual language of form. It's something that we take for granted today, that we can talk about the texture or weight of an object, its visual weight, or the rhythm in a building facade. These are all concepts that were developed and articulated at places like the Bauhaus. Design schools today still use that same vocabulary.

I think that next phase happened in the sixties and seventies when designers became more obsessed with the idea of the content of the subject matter. Architects became interested in the vernacular, particularly if we think of Robert Venturi and Denise Scott Brown and their famous study of Las Vegas, the old Strip of Las Vegas. That was really a content analysis of the symbolism of architecture. Architects during this time, and especially in the postmodern phase, were really interested in the symbolism of classical architectural languages and recycling those. That's an example of content-based form giving. It's the symbolism and the content of what you're dealing with. The little rituals that make up making coffee or using a fork and knife or the cultural symbolism of a particular object. Those come back to inhabit and give form, help give guidance to the designer about how that form should be or how it should look.

The third phase is really looking at design in a contextual sense, in a much bigger picture scenario. It's looking at the typological context for that object. It's looking at the human and object relationship, the user's relationship to the object. It's looking at all sorts of constraints—cultural constraints and social constraints—around the object. It's a different kind of approach, but how I think about it, as a designer myself, is that design is really the search for form. It's just asking yourself the question, "What form should this object take?" Designers have asked that question, and they've used different processes. I think sometimes the answer's a formal solution, a formal logic. Sometimes I think it's a content-based logic—what is the subject, and how appropriate is this form for that? This new phase seems to be guided mostly through developments in interactivity and social networking, like Web 2.0 or the idea of an open-sourced model for product development, for example.

When I think about these three phases, I think of them as ripples on a pond, and they're moving outward and radiating outward. If you start at the object itself, you have this formal logic. Then moving out from there you have the meanings and symbolisms that are associated with that object with the user involved, interpreting it or using it. Then the largest thing is the world in which the object exists. It's not surprising that things like sustainability become major issues now because designers are really looking at the whole relationship. It's the whole cradle-to-grave idea behind product development now. The idea of what happens. We used to design for the point of purchase, and now it's really about the afterlife of those objects. How can the parts be recycled, perhaps, or how do they live on in a secondary sense, and how can new consumers give new life to old objects?

GH — What would some objects be that represent these three phases?

AB — An example of the first phase would be a very modernist conception, something like the Braun Aromaster 10-cup coffee maker. It very much embodies Dieter Rams's approach. It's white. It's pristine. It has the smoothened body. There is a little bit of articulation around the process—the coffee goes here; the water goes there; it comes out down here—but basically it's a streamlined object and a classic one.

You can see the ideas from the second phase, the content approach, in something like Michael Graves's teakettle for Alessi. There, again, it's about geometry, but the geometry he's playing with as an architect comes out of his own research and interest in the historical forms of architecture. Graves is playing with classic shapes of architecture. But more importantly, the kettle's whistle is articulated by a little plastic bird at the end of it. The bird is supposed to be a kind of stand-in for the whistling noise that comes out of the tea kettle. It's obviously a cultural reference and a symbolic reference, a fairly literal one.

Then you have something like Naoto Fukasawa's rice cooker for Muji. What's interesting about that product is that, if you know about rice cookers at all, they typically have a curved top that helps return the water back down into the rice while it's cooking. If you've ever served rice, especially if you're Japanese, the rice paddle has always been the problem. What do you do with this paddle? Usually, you had a plate to put it on, so you scoop out the rice, and then you put the paddle on this plate, because you can't just leave it on the counter. That's very bad manners in Japan.

He solved this problem by flattening the top of the cooker, at least on the outside, and then incorporating a rest, the same principle a chopstick rest, as a place where you could put this implement. I think he came up with that design after looking at the whole process of eating rice—not only just cooking it, but also serving it, eating it. He's already moved the object away from its sole function and is looking at the way it's used, almost ritualistically, within his own culture. That's a good example of this third phase of relational design.

At one point Fukasawa did work for IDEO in Japan, and IDEO's approach is an ethnographic user-oriented approach. This is how I explain this concept to people, we used to have these things called focus groups where they'd put people in a room, and you were behind a two-way mirror, and a moderator would ask them questions like, "What about this? What about that?" but what IDEO does that's different is ethnographic research, which really means observing people in their natural environments. It's a study of behavior. You can either tell somebody what you think they would want to hear, or you can really see how people behave and perform.

GH — But the study of human factors informed design before IDEO.

AB — Absolutely. You know, human factors really came out of designers working in the mid-century. Not surprisingly, a lot of it is connected to furniture design, particularly chairs, because the chair becomes the support for the human body in space, if you think about it that way. There's this really intimate connection between the scale of the human body and the scale of furniture, or a simple chair. It's not surprising that designers like Niels Diffrient would be involved in this burgeoning field of development. Or even more intuitively, designers like Charles and Ray Eames or Eero Saarinen when they were collaborating together were really looking at the body position in a chair and that chair being a kind of symbol for society, really, and social rules. They were battling the entrenched Victorian era of furniture—big, heavy furniture—that was really about keeping your body in one position.

Later on, Saarinen developed the womb chair, which was really a revolution because it's much more lightweight and much more generous in its scaling, which meant that you could have a different kind of body posture while sitting in it. It's no coincidence that this is also the advent of cocktail culture. This is leisure America; it's postwar America, so there's a relaxed environment for that to happen in. That's why it resonated. The womb chair's been in constant production by Knoll since 1948, which is really quite remarkable for a piece of furniture.

Today, however, it's really about studying behavior. Not about the ideal sitting position or the ideal this or that or even the average, which is really what human factors was about—a person at such and such height has this kind of average thing going on. Today it's much more specific. When studying behavior, you can look at how people modify things themselves. Can you move in the chair? Do you add a pillow? Do you not add a pillow? Do you develop all sorts of quick fixes for problems with the chair? These are the little telltale signs that ethnographers study that really help product designers think about innovation within those contexts.

GH — I know you've talked about the evolution of the vacuum cleaner as a mirror of the evolution of design. Could you give me some examples?

AB — If you look at an object like a vacuum cleaner, you can see these three phases at play. For the first phase, you might actually have something fairly new, like Karim Rashid's KONE vacuum for Dirt Devil, the handheld vacuum that's "so beautiful that you can put it on display." You can leave it on your counter, and it doesn't look like it's a piece of crap. It has a very simple geometry to it. It's very integrated, the base and the actual vacuum, so it's a very beautiful thing.

Conversely, you could look at James Dyson and his vacuum cleaners. When they first came out in the early 1990s, they really looked like the language of high tech from architecture applied to product design. Dyson approached the design of the vacuum in a very functionalist manner. It was about improving the nature of the vacuum through thousands of prototypes, or at least that's the legend. But if you look at the form of it, it's really expressing that; it's expressing the symbolism of functionality. Color is introduced into the design, and Dyson is not a frivolous person, so it's really there to articulate the various components of the vacuum, particularly the cyclonic chamber that he invented, the transparent chamber that got rid of the vacuum bag altogether. That's the big innovation there. Or you could look at his newer vacuums like the Ball, named for the yellow ball that is actually the articulating device in the vacuum that allows you to maneuver very quickly and nimbly around furniture and such.

A more recent manifestation of the contextual approach would be something like the Roomba vacuum cleaner created by iRobot. There, the relationship to the vacuum is very different. First of all, there's no more human interaction relationship. The relationship is to the room it's cleaning and maybe an occasional house pet that it tramples over and gets into a fight with. That is a really interesting mode. I think it's even more interesting that the company has kits available on the market called iCreate, which is essentially the Roomba vacuum cleaner kit that's made for hacking. People are really wacky. They've created things like Bionic Hamster, which is attaching the play wheel or dome that the hamster uses as the driving device for the Roomba. The hamster's controlling the direction of the Roomba, so it's the ultimate revenge of the animal on the vacuum cleaner.

GH — Awesome! I'm going to have to get one of those. I'd like to talk about interaction design and how that figures into all this. Because with so many of today's products, it's more about the software than the form.

AB — Within that realm of contextual or relational design, there's been a revolution with interactivity which allows designers to have instant feedback. I know this is particularly true for graphic designers who are entering interactive design and web design. When you create a poster and you put it up, you don't really know what the feedback is. You can do fake feedback sessions like when you pull somebody in off the street. But this technology allows an instantaneous communication back, to help either improve the object or modify it some way. Being able to interact digitally with products was one of the big problems as products were shrinking; as chip sizes got smaller and smaller, there was suddenly a human interface problem. You can see that manifested in digital wristwatches that had calculators embedded into them, or the text messaging that used to happen on old cell phones, where human beings and their fingers were just simply too big. It's a problem with the miniaturization of electronic products, this problem of the interface, the relationship between the designer and the user and the object they were trying to manipulate.

GH — How would you define interaction design?

AB — Classically speaking, interaction in product design means the control of objects—by pressing a button, for example, a certain function will happen. This is the command-control mentality that originally came out of engineering cybernetics to create a rationalization around what the expectation would be with the humans interacting with machines and the ultimate predictability. You punch the button; you get the end result.

Digital technology created other interesting complications, because sometimes the functions weren't so exactly related. In other words, the mechanical connections presupposed or established some sort of expectation along the lines of "I pushed this button; I get this result." It's not a one-to-one relationship in digital technology, or at least it doesn't have to be. That's where you have the development of screen interfaces and the use of metaphors, the idea that one button could have multiple functions. It's a much more complicated set of relationships, and then you pair that with the idea of feedback or of the object pushing data at me like a Blackberry or iPhone. Those kinds of products are much more than just the telephone. The keypad—good luck finding the keypad on a phone; it's buried somewhere in there. A telephone is the obvious function, but most people aren't using the device for that, at least not initially.

Design has always had this problem, though, of, how do you control objects? Everyone has the classic experience of the old VCR and the nightmare scenario around programming it. With something like a screen, a digital interface, it's not a one-to-one relationship. It doesn't have to be, so you can layer in a lot of the functionality. Those screens can also tell you what to do, which is how a lot of it works now.

GH — Let's talk about the concept of simplicity. What do you think of the idea that finding the simplest solution defines great design?

AB — I think it builds off this idea of the interface. If it's a button, a lever, or a screen, it doesn't really much matter. It's really the connection between the user and the machine, whether it's a computer or whether it's a mechanical machine. This is the nature of the design of interface, whether you mean it in a predigital sense or postdigital sense. That idea of manipulation, expectation, result, is extremely difficult, especially as machines get ever more complicated and complex and have so many multiple functions embedded within them. Then it falls upon the designer to create this interface so that it's the Holy Grail of interfaces.

The classic digital example is Google, right? It's a stripped-down box, and the basic premise is really quite brilliant, I think. I don't know if anyone even remembers searching and search pages before that. Certainly it wasn't that complicated. All you needed was a simple box to type into to get all of that working. It's a classic example of simplification being really difficult to achieve, but when it's achieved, it's actually quite brilliant. You can see that in a lot of products too.

GH — Let's talk a little bit about how people use objects to express identity. How do you think that manifests today, and what is our relationship to all this stuff?

AB — Design has really become synonymous with the idea of conspicuous consumption. Historically, people have always longed for these objects. It's fascinating. If you look at Dutch still-life painting from the 1600s and the opulence of those really ordinary things, in today's perspective, like fruits, vegetables, this orgy of materialism is really what it's celebrating. There was a shift in the economy in the Netherlands that contributed to the surplus of material goods. Those fruits and vegetables were brought in from other markets around the world and as such were exotic, and that same basic human impulse still exists now in the sense that people want well-designed objects. Of course, what's "well-designed" is open to a lot of different interpretations. It could look nice, but function okay. It could function brilliantly and look banal. Of course, you have a lot of bad design that also looks bad. The notion of good design itself is a heavily contested field.

I think today there's this emphasis on design being an extravagance, or related to the idea of status symbols. It's kind of ironic because a lot of the designers I know really want to produce things at cheaper price levels and for more people. It's just a question of what the market can bear. Then you get into issues about quality and craftsmanship. Do you judge something on the price over a lifetime or the price of each individual unit? That's where it gets really complicated. A lot of people don't think about that question: "Will I spend $5,000 on a quality sofa, or will I spend $1,000 on a sofa and buy five over my lifetime?" It's really the commitment to those objects that maybe gets designers into a little bit of hot water, because the other pressure is the idea of planned obsolescence. Surely it came through loud and clear in the United States with the introduction of the automobile. There was the classic story about Henry Ford, who said, "You can have any color, as long as it's black." He only had one product to sell you. General Motors, on the other hand, offered a wide variety of colors and style changes every year. That's what pushed GM over the top of Ford in the marketplace. It's interesting that they're both on the bottom now.

GH — All this creativity and all this work and thought and energy is going into some of these things, but it's really about selling stuff, right?

AB — Yeah, that's the traditional equation in industrial design, that the designer is there to help embody the object and imbue it with certain qualities that will differentiate it from other objects that are just like it in the marketplace. But of course, that's not the only role for industrial design. There are just now starting to be other movements within product design. We had a flash of it in the sixties with Victor Papanek and his *Design for the Real World* approach, but that started to disappear in the hangover of the seventies and was gone by the eighties. That was the era of conspicuous consumption that a lot of people associate with Reagan and the boom in the markets back then.

Today a lot of designers, especially younger designers in school, are looking at other issues like sustainability. It's a huge factor within product design and architecture—what role can design play in that equation? In school you're always reenacting the mythology and the fake client-designer relationship in terms of: here's the brief; here's the problem; here's my solution. What are the other ways of tackling that kind of problem? Most people think of design in this conspicuous consumption mode as being exclusively a product of capitalism. Of course, design has existed since the beginning of time, and it's existed in different economies and different countries and different time periods. The idea that industrial design only exists within the universe of capitalism is historically false. If that's true, then how can you use design differently, and how as a student might you approach design?

There have been different takes on that. This may sound kind of goofy, but I think some of the more interesting ones are within the realm of science fiction—people are creating imaginary machines and objects for roles that don't really exist yet. Some even use science fiction films as the basis for their work, and they start suggesting objects that would occupy that cinematic space, and it's really interesting, because it throws it into a whole new context, and you get rid of the status quo assumptions about who's the client, what's the problem, what's the solution.

The other big movement is what's called the "Next Billion." That's basically taking the lessons of base capitalism and applying them to the developing world, looking at billions of potential consumers. Your price points are different; they're a lot lower, but you sell in higher volume. The problems are not the same problems found in the First World, or whatever we're going to call the industrialized world. Something like transporting water is a big issue, not only because it's often using recycled containers, sometimes even gasoline containers, which is a contamination problem, but it's also the distance that's involved in going to the water source. That involves a lot of time, and that's time away from learning, time away from working. It also causes a lot of injuries because often you're carrying the maximum amount of water that you can physically carry, and it's done several times a day.

There have been some Western designers who have looked at this issue and have proposed different solutions, like the Q Drum that was developed in South Africa. It's basically a drum cylinder that's shaped like a donut. It has a hole in the middle where you put a rope through to help pull it; it's like a wheel that rolls along. Then there's the opposite approach, the push approach instead of the pull approach, with the Hippo Water Roller. It basically looks like a little lawn mower with a cylinder, but you're pushing instead of pulling. They both carry about the same amount of water. What's interesting is that they're both priced at seventy-five or a hundred dollars, which is way too much for individuals in villages that need them. Now there's a conundrum: do you end up subsidizing these products through foundations, or do you somehow expand the market so you can drive down the price point so it's cheap enough? Or what are the other solutions? Is there a sharing or cooperative approach that could be possible? Or could it be fractional ownership over time? They're trying to figure out what the right balance is.

You have different camps trying to solve problems for this very large base of customers that is basically ignored by modern industrial design because there's no way that they fit into the equation as it exists now. I think especially for Western designers, instead of solving the same old problem with a slight tweak or variation, it's much more interesting to encounter a problem that's very foreign. Of course, the challenge then is how do you begin studying it? Is it even possible they would be empathetic enough in those kinds of scenarios? At least they're interesting and they're different. I think that's where the appeal is there, but also because it's something that's needed. We have needs and we have wants, and those are two different things. Sometimes it's hard to judge in the developed world what is a need and what is a want, but it's very clear when you're out of that context which one is which.

GH — You've brought a few objects in to discuss, what did you bring?
AB — This is actually from my office desk drawer. It's a Muji calculator, but the reason I brought it is more because it's solar powered, and I think this is interesting when everyone's talking about solar this and solar that; these actually were introduced decades ago. It's really a great application for the solar cell technology that existed at the time that still functions today. Of course, it's a Muji product. The fact that there's no logo, that's the most attractive thing to so many designers, ironically.

Actually I was reading something in the paper today, about the new McDonald's in Japan. It's a special McDonald's restaurant that only sells the quarter pounder, with no McDonald's branding at all—just red and black packaging. Maybe it's not a surprise that it's a hit in Tokyo considering the sway that Muji holds there, with the no-brand promise. Since brands are supposed to be promises to consumers about what they'll do, the no brand, the no logo, is definitely something that I'm surprised hasn't grown larger in the US. The idea that you could actually charge more for stripping away the identity is quite fascinating to me and, obviously, quite compelling.

GH — Beyond the logo, there's an aesthetic embedded, right?

AB — Right. The aesthetic of simplification, of reduction, of clarity, is there. It's like Jasper Morrison's work for Rowenta, the toasters and coffee makers. Or Naoto's work for Plus Minus Zero. Those objects are what Morrison refers to as "super normal." They're beyond nondesign. They try to be as elemental as possible.

GH — And you've got a toothpick?

AB — Yeah, it's one of these funny objects. There's actually a whole book written about the toothpick by Henry Petroski, who is an engineer at Duke University. His other book was called *The Pencil*. It was really about the history and the significance of that object. This particular toothpick is a Japanese toothpick, but obviously, it's manufactured for sale in the US. What's interesting about it is the evolution of a type of object that happens over many, many years. You'll notice at the end of it the tip is serrated and grooved. It's that way so it can be separated, so you could break it off. This was to signify that it was used, but it also creates a tiny rest for the toothpick, which is again a very Japanese custom in that you don't allow objects that have been in your mouth or that are dirty to be placed back onto the table. You'd see this kind of rest with chopsticks, for example.

Of course, that kind of functionality is culturally specific. It arrives from a certain cultural context but is eventually displaced. I'm sure most people don't use it in either one of those fashions here in the US, but I think it's the kind of cultural encoding that is brought to objects. There's this quote from Henry Ford, who said, "Every object tells a story if you know how to read it." Ford was thinking about this in the context of this giant museum he built in Dearborn, Michigan, which is really a history of industrial design. There are printing presses there, automobiles, locomotives. That was a place we went when I was in graduate school at Cranbrook to get a sense of the history of some of these objects. The craziest things are there. A recent addition is Bucky Fuller's Dymaxion House, the only one in existence.

GH — Speaking of Ford, what are your thoughts on automobile design?

AB — I think the automobile is the quintessential status object in America. It's like people and their dogs—what kind of automobile should you be owning? It's just the kind of object that everyone relates to and most people own.

The thing I find most fascinating isn't really the shifts in car design over the last few decades, but it was the flip key. My introduction to it was through a purchase of an Audi, though I downgraded to the VW given the current recession. What I think is interesting about this little object is the history of its development. Apparently, it was developed by the nice folks at Audi because they were concerned about traditional keys tearing the pocket linings of their customers. It turned into much more than that, of course. You have all the electronic functions for the alarm and for the truck release and for unlocking the vehicle that could all be embedded in a small object. This is the part of the car that's always with you. It's always in your pocket and becomes a touchstone.

The marketing folks latched onto this, and it became its own status symbol because it was the most different kind of key at that time. Now it's a little bit more common. It does provide a direct connection between the owner, actually, of the vehicle and the vehicle itself. The latest phase seems to be, especially with proximity detection and keyless automobiles, that the object has taken on almost jewelry proportions. I think this little piece of design is actually one of the biggest revolutions within car design, in the last 10 years at least.

GH — Can you talk about your theory about the recession and how it impacts the design industry?

AB — Well, designers today are in somewhat of a quandary. They're emboldened by the hope the Obama era brings, but on the other hand, we have the collapse of the markets and what was actually described yesterday as the first year of recession in the United States. What's interesting—having lived through so many recessions as a designer—is that there are often moments when designers can take stock of what they're really interested in. It's untested, but there seems to be a theory that there's a proliferation of new design firms that emerge in the recession, mostly because people are laid off from other jobs, so why not make a go of it?

Within realms of architecture, much of the theory that fueled later practice came out of the paper architecture that was generated when there was no actual building going on during the recession in the seventies. On one hand, it might look dismal from a product development standpoint, but it actually might be a very interesting and lively time for people to take stock of what direction they want to move in.

GH — So what's next?

AB — The digital age has changed things in so many different ways. It has changed the process of how design is done, in terms of the visualization and the various kinds of tools and gadgets that are available. Basically, it's just collapsing the distance between sketches, visualizations, and actual products. Models used to be made out of clay and foam; that is all going by the wayside. There's always an upside and a downside. It affects the process; it affects production.

Today, you can make your own Levi's for exactly your body, or your own Nike tennis shoe within the constraints that they allow on their website for mass customization. But the biggest category has to be the idea of cocreation—in some instances, the user is becoming the designer. Those are more like DIY, hacking-type projects. There's a funny website called IKEA Hackers. I think it's more of a fan site, but users are trading tips for how to purchase things from IKEA and use them in an adapted way or customized way. One of the funnier posts in the last few months has been from someone who bought a typical storage unit—I think it's called the Helmer drawer from IKEA—and used that as the box, the tower, for the Linux-based computer they built. Good examples like that abound—evidence of how the whole do-it-yourself movement has permeated so many aspects of society. We're not surprised to see that also influencing how companies can maybe tap into this creative potential.

This is the destiny of companies like Threadless, right? It's where there's this collapse, and everyone's a designer; everyone's a consumer. Where is the design in that equation? Where is the designer in that equation? It's really everyone; it's a mass collaborative example of how people using technology can create their own production and their own consumption marketplace.

GH — What is the professional designer's role in that?

AB — Wow, one of the opportunities for designers is to begin to think of design in a much more expanded way, in that really you're designing design. You're designing systems. If you think about Threadless as a model, it's a designed system, and so the designer has to think beyond just the individual object. People can contribute to something, they can collaborate, but how are they doing that? What brings them together? What are the rules? It's almost like game theory: if I do this, then maybe this happens; then that happens. It's a slightly different construct of what design is, but you'll still continue to have discreet objects. Those will never go away.

—

Rob
Walker
(RW)/
December
10, 2008
Savannah

Rob Walker is a technology/culture columnist for Yahoo News. He is the former "Consumed" columnist for the *New York Times Magazine* and has contributed to many publications. He is coeditor (with Joshua Glenn) of the book *Significant Objects: 100 Extraordinary Stories About Ordinary Things* and author of *Buying In: The Secret Dialogue Between What We Buy and Who We Are.*

—

Gary Hustwit — Can you talk about companies that use design as a brand marketing tool?

Rob Walker — Target, in particular, is the one that I associate with really using design as a slogan—"Design For All," or something along those lines. I'm not sure how far back that goes, but probably 5 or 10 years now. I think that campaign and their advertising fell right into line with, and influenced, a lot of pop culture thinking about the importance of design—the virtue of good design, whatever that means, as being something that you, the consumer, would want in some way. They had it available to you in a very attainable way, and they would show you that in the advertisements: here are some examples of good design. They were, I believe, a path breaker in doing these kinds of deals with designers like Michael Graves, where they're kind of announcing that this is what good design is and good design is something that you want.

It fits really well in terms of how magazines and media think. Right around that time, it dovetailed with a huge number of articles and essays in a wide variety of publications touting an idea of a design democracy and the availability of good design. Again, the term "good design" was never really defined with a checklist to determine what was good design, but it became a selling point. The basic idea was that good design is something you want. Good design is something that distinguishes you. It's a mark of progress. If you are a person who recognizes good design, it distinguishes you from all of the naive and corny bourgeois of the past, the past being everything up to that minute. You can now buy into that. You can buy into progress, good design, and good taste simply by purchasing the products that we happen to have.

GH — How does a company like Apple position itself in terms of selling good design?

RW — When you talk to designers, what they will often say is that design doesn't have to do with looks; it's about how it works. You're always corrected when you confuse design with style or aesthetics. I think that Apple, before they were celebrated for the way their products looked— and that really came about with the iMac and then the iPod—Apple was positioning itself as a good design company. I think that they were better positioned when that idea hit the zeitgeist. They were offering stuff that looked different; it was exciting, but it was also that they were coming out of nowhere. Their graphic user interface was called a revolutionary innovation. They were associated with the idea of ease of use. When they came up with the iPod, there was a real marriage of function and design that everyone recognized immediately. It was a really elegant-looking, exciting-looking, different-looking device that really hit the sweet spot. It hits exactly those notes of cleanliness, minimalism, simplicity, and almost a starkness. The iPod was established as a kind of an icon of what good design meant.

It's a product that many designers will also point to. They'll say, "Well, it's not just about how the iPod looks; it's also about how it works," and they're right. However, in the marketplace, it's often about how it looks, and the look of the iPod is not that difficult to reference or to allude to. It's a spatula, but it sort of resembles the iPod somehow. So it becomes something that any consumer can easily attain.

GH — That's funny. If it's not about how it looks, then why are there twenty colors of the new iPod nano? The whole marketing campaign is something like, "Look at all the colors you can get this in!"

RW — Absolutely. If you go back and look at the past, there was a popular notion of good design as it's defined today. You can read things about design in a book called *The Taste Makers* from the fifties, and the author refers to industrial designers as "taste appeal artists." That's such an insult. I mean, his goal is to dismiss these people as if all they're doing is adding the fins to the Cadillac or adding the basic elements that will sell this year's model. They say all designers are doing is building novelties that will get attention and have shelf appeal. Designers today resist that thinking. That's why they will always correct you and say what they do isn't about style; it's about function and style.

It's just one element of it, but it remains a crucial element. There aren't many examples you can point to where something is venerated by the design world, is a successful product, and is very functional but also is ugly. There aren't that many examples of that. Style is built into the definition of good design. Frankly, the problem with the design world of both critics and designers who like to talk about it is that they've let that word "design" and that phrase "good design" become way too amorphous. It's as if you were going to talk about writing and said something like, "Well, good writing is important. Writing matters." Well, sure, writing matters, but what are you talking about? Are you talking about William Faulkner? Are you talking about the *Star*? Those are both writing. You've thrown the term so wide that you're sort of talking about nothing, and then you get mad when people use the term "design" in an all-encompassing way. You've let that happen.

GH — There really hasn't been a product that's commercially successful and hailed by design critics and is ugly?

RW — I was going through some files the other day, and there was an article that would have been from the mid-to-late nineties. It was giving examples of good design for all, and one of the examples was the PT Cruiser, which was pretty funny to encounter seven or eight years after the fact because I think now the PT Cruiser is kind of seen as a kitsch object by serious design type people. It looks very corny, but it was once seen as good design. Now, we look at it and say, "Well, that was an example of bad design that we've gotten over." I think that's a challenge for many designers. In a lot of ways they're hired to make something seem very "now" and very "next." The problem with spending a lot of time focusing on what's very now and very next is that it isn't very forever, and that means that it doesn't last. There's someone else coming along trying to design what's now or next after that, and part of their agenda, whether it's overarticulated or not, is to make whatever used to be "now" look like "then" so that people will buy the new "now." That's the name of the game.

GH — Can we talk about car design a little more?

RW — Well, cars have played a crucial role in the history of industrial design because they are associated with the introduction of planned obsolescence, which I think is a pretty important part of understanding what design is in the marketplace. Planned obsolescence has very negative connotations around it, so my saying that doesn't mean that I'm condemning every designer as a stooge of late capitalism, but actually, this is an important point. People have talked about planned obsolescence and the role of design as being somewhat insidious. There's a critique that it's insidious, that we don't really have anything new to offer you with these cars, so we're just going to make these cars look different.

The thing that gets left out in that critique is that consumers tend to be complicit in planned obsolescence—that is to say, we tend to want new things, and that's not a function of late-stage capitalism; that's a function of human nature. People are drawn and attracted to novelty, and there is research on that. An interesting psychological study wired people up to a machine that dropped flavored water on their tongues. If you're told what the pattern will be, your brain shows one set of reactions. If you're not told, and you're sort of straining, and you don't know what's going to come next, the reactions in your brain are different. Your senses are raised with a rush of dopamine. That's the way novelty makes us feel; it's exciting. There's also counter-research about the ways that we're drawn into the familiar, but I'll come back to that later. We like something new and something different, and it often feels like progress when you get a new thing.

Another interesting question is, why are so many SUVs four-wheel drives when there's no compelling reason for that to be the case? The answer is that research showed that consumers really wanted four-wheel-drive SUVs to drive around the suburbs. That wasn't something that the car companies knew; it wasn't a design decision that was imposed on consumers. That was a design decision that was imposed on car companies *by* consumers. That's seen throughout the history of the relationship between auto design and the marketplace. It's a dynamic. It's a dialogue. It's a back-and-forth relationship.

GH — Let's talk a little bit about the car as an expression of identity.

RW — Cars are big decisions. With the exception of the house, it's probably the biggest individual purchase a consumer will make. And there are a lot of choices to make. When you're buying a car and when you own a car—even the decisions about, are you going to put a bumper sticker on it? Are you going to put a "Support the Troops" magnet on it? Things like that. There's an idea of an audience for the decision that you've made. It's an interesting version of an audience though, because it's a highway audience; you don't actually know them, and they don't know you. Whenever they think of you, you'll really never know. It's interesting that we have that relationship. Now, I don't think anybody starts the car-buying process by saying to themselves, "Well, now it's time for me to get a car that really reflects the person that I am and broadcasts the person I am to an audience of strangers." No one goes through that thought process. On the other hand, few of us walk into the car market totally blind. By the time you're buying a car, you have ideas about what your priorities are, and maybe your priority is just good mileage, maybe it's something beyond that, maybe it's more about style, or maybe you just want it. We live in a world where the marketplace stretches from the Prius to the Hummer. That's quite a range of identity options.

It's such a large purchase that it would be weirdly dissonant if you bought a car and you didn't have an answer when someone asked you why you bought it. Everyone has some sort of answer. "Well, I bought it because . . ." And that could be a style-related question or an economy-related question. It could just be that they liked sports cars. It could be a number of things. The interesting thing though—and I feel pretty strongly that this is true not just for cars but for almost everything we buy—is that our real audience is just ourselves. You are the person that you're really speaking to when you're speaking about why this car and why I'm putting a sticker on it or choosing not to put stickers on it. You're making a statement to yourself about yourself; it has nothing to do with what other people think. In sort of an abstract way, you're thinking about what they might be thinking about you and whether or not they like your Obama sticker or your Christian fish or whatever it might be. Because the truth is that no one cares on the highway. None of those people around you are actually paying any attention to you any more than you're pay attention to them.

I'm guilty of this myself, most notably when I'm traveling somewhere and I'm in a rental car. I really want to know what state the plates are from. I'm originally from Texas, and I've lived in New York, and I have my certain sort of prejudices about what plates I want. Especially if I'm traveling in the South, I don't want Massachusetts plates. Now, does anybody really care around me? No, but I just don't want to be the guy driving in Mississippi with Massachusetts plates. That's not who I am. I don't want to be that guy. So you can take that and put it in terms of the commercial realm and say, "I'm not the guy who drives the Hummer," or, "I'm not the guy who drives the Prius." There are people who really dislike the Prius message because it can come across as eco-snobbery, but the crucial thing is the self, your own life story. That's what really matters when we're making decisions about what we're consuming.

GH — And the same is true with all the stuff we surround ourselves with, the objects in our homes?

RW — Right. In those consumable object decisions, we've been able to see how they communicate our identity. There's a personal story applied to all kinds of objects: consumer electronics and dish soap and spatulas and teakettles and trash cans. So it becomes, "What does your trash can say about you?" The theory is that we invite people into our homes and entertain, so you want to have all of your objects reflect who you are in the same way that you want your car on the highway to reflect who you are. I think the reality is that, again, the real audience is yourself, and I think it's really underscored by the movement of those ideas into really mundane objects like dish liquid. Because there's no plausible scenario in the Thorstein Veblen theory of conspicuous consumption of proving your status by way of having a high-end dish liquid—there's no way that can happen. You're not going to be having a dinner party and say, "Oh, by the way, have you seen my awesome dish liquid bottle?" Again, I think it comes down to the story you're telling about yourself, to yourself.

GH — I assume you're talking about the Method dish soap bottle?

RW — Yeah, Method is a really interesting story for a couple of reasons. One is that they applied that "good design for all" aesthetic to a very workaday category of goods. It was very much in line with the idea of democratization of good design; it was an attainable piece of good design, whatever that means. The interesting thing about Method was the strategy was almost a Trojan Horse strategy. Their functional design difference was the materials that they were using—they were using fewer synthetics, and everything is eco-friendly. It was really an interesting decision that they made not to echo that selling point graphically, because that's a common decision in the marketplace now, to say, "Here is a synthetic-free toilet bowl cleaner," and communicate that by putting a picture of a tree on the bottle and calling it green something or eco-something.

And Method, I think, made a very interesting decision in not doing that, saying instead, "We're going to speak to the idea that this is almost a luxury. This is an attainable luxury, and that's reflected in the look of this thing." I don't know how many people who buy Method products are really attracted to, or even aware of, the materials or the backstory. It was kind of a rare case of a strategy of aesthetics as a marketplace tool that underdelivers. You bought it for the packaging, and you know what? The packaging is basically what you got. Method actually told me when I interviewed them for a column that they got letters from people who expected that, who bought it being skeptical that it would work. And that's a fascinating consumer moment, to imagine the consumer at a shelf, looking at a bottle of hand soap and saying, "This probably won't work, but it looks so good. I'm going to buy it anyway." Then they would write a letter to the company saying, "Wow, I can't believe it worked. Great job."

GH — We've talked to a lot of designers about what they do and the objects that they make, but do we really need all of this stuff? As consumers are we being driven to push the economy by buying this stuff we don't need?

RW — I had an interesting conversation the other day with a young designer who was telling me about an advertising agency that was creating products. They had a client that made sponges, and it was a start-up that needed more products for real distribution. They needed more SKUs and the advertising agency said, "Don't worry about going through that industrial design firm. We'll help you develop some of your products." This designer sounded indignant about it. This advertising agency, they're just going to come up with things, and they're not going to have the consumer in mind. They're not going to be developing for the consumer. They're not going to be consumer-centric products that an industrial designer would come up with.

At the end of the day, what advertising agencies and industrial designers have in common is that they are both in the client services business. Neither advertising agencies nor industrial designers work for consumers. They are not paid by large groups of consumers to create things that consumers have asked for. They're paid by companies to come up with new stuff that consumers might want, and there's all kinds of research involved in determining the details of that to make sure that the product is consumer-centric et cetera, but at the end of the day, there's a company that's writing a check, and what the company wants is new SKUs. They want more stuff, and they want more people to buy it, and that's the name of the game.

Designers are often excellent at talking about the theory of design in general. This goes back to the word "design" being so amorphous. It is sometimes as if someone who's doing a celebrity blog or gossip blog started invoking Faulkner. The theory of good writing is important. People create good writing. It is true that good writing changes people's lives. The same is true with good design. When you talk about it at the theoretical level, design solves problems. However, often the way that a product comes into being isn't because a bunch of expert designers sat down and said, "What are the most important problems that we can solve?" It's that the phone rang, and a company said, "We need more products in this area. What can you do for us?"

I read once about a new design for a fire extinguisher, and it was really interesting because it was a very sleek-looking, iPod-esque, fire extinguisher. It won a lot of design awards. The idea was sort of rational as well. Fire extinguishers as they are now are ugly. Because they're ugly, people forget where they are; they leave them places; they forget to replace them. By having a really beautiful fire extinguisher, they're excited about it, and they'll leave it on the counter. This is supposed to be a fire extinguisher that you leave on the counter. It got a lot of positive attention.

Designers are constantly lecturing that it's not how it looks; it's how it works. This, however, won a major design award based on how it looked because the judges never handled the object. They just looked at photographs of it and the description provided by the company. I'm sure it worked fine, but what was the core problem that brought it to life? Not enough people have fire extinguishers. Who are those people, and what is the best way to get them fire extinguishers, and is the best way to start making fire extinguishers look like iPods?

Maybe what's really going on there is introducing an interesting novelty into the market. It gets a lot attention, and the margins are pretty good, and they sell, and all of a sudden people who probably already had a fire extinguisher are buying it because it's a new, interesting object. Sales are made. You can sort of rationalize it as it's solving a problem, but I would wonder whether it was a problem that was invented after the fact. That's their starting point. You can have a conversation about what's the best way to solve that problem. I'm not sure that a really stylish fire extinguisher would be the winning answer in a non-marketplace-driven discussion of how to solve that problem.

I would think that the dilemma for designers who are in client services must be: what's the difference between progress and novelty? What designers want to do is participate in and create progress. Consumers want progress. The trick is that the difference between progress and novelty is often very hard to discern. All progress entails novelty, but not all novelty entails progress. Novelty, at the end of the day, isn't that difficult to achieve for a talented designer. They can do something that has a different look, a fresher look, a newer look, a "new now/next now" kind of look that suggests progress. It often doesn't entail progress. The tension is that a designer might want to be only involved in authentic progress. The client might not care. The client might want to move units. If they had a choice between thriving on authentic progress or thriving on novelty, they would all choose progress. Then, if you ask them if they had to choose between thriving on novelty or going out of business, they would tend to choose thriving on novelty.

The marketplace is flooded with novelty, and designers are a crucial part of that. It couldn't happen without them. For every designer you talk to who says they turned down that job because they didn't think it was contributing to the common good, there will be 20 other designers who are also very talented, who are waiting in line to take that job because there are a lot of talented designers out there. I think that we're living in a boom time of design talent. There's just a tremendous amount of it. The schools are bringing out more talented young people every year. The aesthetic vocabulary and mastery of different forms of graphic and industrial design is unlike before. It's a buyer's market for the companies that want to hire someone to create an exciting new look, a redesign for something, for instance. They're not going to have any problem making it happen.

GH — So because there are so many designers, companies will never have a problem getting what they want design-wise?

    RW — Yeah, there's enough talent out there that there's always going to be a designer. Designers are just like consumers in some ways, and they'll find some rationale for why it's okay to do this particular thing. First of all, everything is designed. Therefore, a designer is involved in almost every product you can imagine. Even cigarettes, arguably the most demonized product out there. Well, cigarette companies have done some really great looking packaging in the last 10 years, really great looking stuff. I don't know if it wins awards or not, but they found talented people.

At the end of the day, there's a lot of competition in the profession, and there's always going to be someone who says, "Well, if I do this, it will perhaps help me to get into a position where I can turn down things like this in the future." I don't think you can come up with a way to say designers should be the ethical policemen of the marketplace. I think that would be silly. On the other hand, designers as advocates are not necessarily in a position to claim the moral high ground of saying they're problem-solving artists. They're in the client services business. They're looking for clients by and large who will pay them handsomely to make things look and function well.

GH — So here we are in December 2008 in the middle of this economic downturn. What happens to designers when people begin buying less? How do their roles change?

RW — Design always matters. It just might matter in different ways in a more unpredictable economic environment. There are times when consumers are really open to novelty, but there are also times when we're drawn to the familiar. There's a whole line of counter-research on that. There was an interesting experiment in the sixties where they showed people random shapes, and they'd rate each shape on how much they liked it. They would repeat shapes. The exit questions would include whether or not they noticed that shapes had been repeated, and they hadn't noticed. They weren't aware of it, but when a shape was repeated, each time they would like it more. The rating would get higher. There is an attraction to the familiar.

At an uncertain economic moment, this can play out in two ways. Sometimes you're drawn to novelty, and sometimes you're drawn to the familiar. This could happen when you're in the marketplace and you're confronted with this bewildering array of washing detergents. There's the Tide box, and you know what it is, and without thinking about it, you just reach for it. Then you kind of blow that out onto a broader level of thinking: there's a lot of uncertainty around; I reach for the familiar. It's the comfort-food theory. It becomes a challenge for designers because you're not getting that venturesome spirit in the consumer where they're out specifically looking to be surprised. They've been surprised all day long by the bad news that they're bombarded with. So they're less likely to take a risk.

That has a potentially serious impact in that, as the idea of green, eco-friendly, sustainable practices have come into the marketplace, they've done so by leaning very heavily on the idea of exciting novelty that is also progress. It will cost you a little bit extra perhaps, but you think that's okay because it's exciting, and it shows you care about the world. It's worth the psychological risk, and it's worth the money. But it remains a risky strategy to tie those together, the ideas of sustainability and trendsetting chic, because trendsetting chic is the first thing you can live without, whether on a personal or societal level. When situations change, your priorities get reordered. The first thing you cut is the need for trendsetting chic. If you've put sustainability or eco or green in that same basket, it's going to rise with that, and it's going to fall with that too.

GH — Some of the people we've spoken to think a recession could be a good thing for design. They think that it'll give designers time to try new things or start companies with friends who also got laid off.

RW — I like the theory that there's a lot of talent and creativity and intelligence in the design world. I'm using design defined as broadly as possible—graphic designers, industrial designers, all kinds of people. A lot of people are somewhat frustrated by marketplace limitations, and I think it would be interesting to see some of their intelligence and smarts turned on to projects and subjects that were not marketplace driven. I can't say exactly what they would be, but it would be an interesting experiment to see what they came up with, what they did with their creative talent when the question of who to work for was removed by the fact that they couldn't work for anybody. They'd have to find some way to do their own thing. It could be really interesting.

GH — So we've talked about Target and their approach, and about design as branding, but what about IKEA? Where would you put them in this context?

RW — IKEA is interesting because about five years ago IKEA furniture was unusual in the United States market. Now it's widely known; it's widely distributed; and in some ways, it's become an example of this novelty process. The novelty has worn off. There is certainly a case to be made that IKEA makes good, well-designed products, but I'm sure you wouldn't have any particular trouble finding design expert types who would essentially sneer at IKEA and dismiss it as too mass-produced. It's a very interesting topic to me, how design identities change based on a changing environment.

We talked about the PT Cruiser earlier. The PT Cruiser and an IKEA chair are the same as they were when they were first created, but the context has changed. This is something that people have a lot of trouble with, I think—understanding how the context will change what is new right now. It may not only seem not new and not exciting, but at some point it becomes kitsch. This period of good design as an approach into the mainstream was a period when design became associated with exciting progress, material progress, open to all.

Something is innovative; it's exciting; it's novel; it's new; it's for everyone; and then it sort of becomes like, well, it's for everyone. What else have you got? What's new and what comes after that? Maybe Muji from Japan is one answer to that right now. Muji is a very mass-produced line. It covers an astonishing breadth of product offerings. It's positioned with no brand identity. In the United States, it's positioned as or it's thought of as almost high design. Their initial entry to the US market was in museum design stores. That's a particular context that's very different than a no-name brand; it's not generic; it's coming through the sanctified context of a museum design shop. You could argue that some museum design shops are more interesting than some museums.

GH — Where do you see design going from here? What's the future?

RW — It's hard to figure out what we are doing now that will be looked back on with amazement, and perhaps ridicule, by future generations. But I think the interesting new development is this rise of the DIY, handmade crafting movement, in particular its rise as a marketplace phenomenon. Independent, single creators making things and then selling them, and because of the Internet, they're finding a significant number of consumers. Being able to compete and be available, being able to sell a wide variety of things to a lot of people, that introduces a lot of creativity. It adds this dimension of individuality to the consumption process, because it feels very different from buying something from Apple or Target or IKEA or Muji. In those cases, you're still buying something that's mass-produced.

There's something compelling and interesting about the idea of buying something from an individual, on an ideological level—I'm supporting an independent creator—but also, there's this other level, which is that, often, an object that means something to you has some kind of a story to it. Maybe the story of how you discovered it or the story of the relationship you forged with that individual. It's just more compelling than saying, I bought it at Best Buy, or Sears, or the mall. It's more compelling to say, "Well, this woman makes ties, and she lives in Detroit, and I found her on XYZ website, and she's also a DJ, and isn't that cool?" There's a story to it. It becomes an object that has a narrative life on its own that feeds into the narrative of your own life. It fits in.

This is one new development in what I think is a big dilemma for any designer who's working for any company that's in the business of creating novelty. We've all had the experience of buying the next new thing, the new iPhone or whatever, and we've all had the experience of getting over it. After a while, it just becomes another object that's in your house. At the end of the day, if you're looking around your house and asking, "What here has value to me?" the things that have value to you and the things that have meaning to you are not going to be the same things that were venerated in the marketplace or by design critics. They're going to be the things that have some meaning in your life. If we looked around whatever room you're in, and we said, "The hurricane is coming. You have 20 minutes. Get your stuff and go," you're not going to be saying, "Well, that thing got an amazing write-up in this design blog." You've forgotten about that. You'll need that book that no one else would want and has zero value on eBay, but your father made a drawing on the back cover when he had the book as a kid.

Those are the objects that mean something to you, and no designer can touch that. They can never recreate that. Those are the true objects that reflect the true story of who you are and what your personal narrative is and the story that you're telling to yourself and no one else because you are the only audience that matters. This DIY stuff can't completely replace that, but it can go a little bit of the way in that at least you have the feeling that it was touched by someone's hands who you had some quasi-relationship with through emails. But still you've learned something of the narrative, and it didn't just roll out of a factory on the other side of the world. That's just not much of a story.

GH — At a certain point, with the technological advancements like 3-D printing, do we all end up becoming DIY designers of objects?

RW — As design becomes democratized in the sense of people having the tools more widely available to design things, there are two ways that happens. One is that it happens through these sanctioned methods where Nike says, "Here is this easily usable website where you can design any color combination. Make your own sneaker any way you want, as long as it has a Nike swoosh on it." That's one form of design democratization.

The other form is that the software is more broadly available. People can look on the web to figure out where to find suppliers. It becomes easier for people to do this stuff themselves. Does it represent a threat to the professional designer? I think that we're seeing this go on in every creative endeavor that you can think of, certainly including writing and journalism and filmmaking.

I think it's probably safe to say that there are always going to be differences in skill levels and execution levels and that there will be things that rise higher than everything else. Jonathan Ive is not going to get run out of town by an undifferentiated crowd of designers. Even if you look at things like Threadless, one of the interesting things about it is that it's an open, democratic system, and what has happened—and no one wants to talk about this; they just say, "Oh, it's democratic. It's the wisdom of the crowd"—is that champions have emerged, and there are people who have won over and over again. There are people who have emerged as stars on Threadless. I think that's human nature, that we recognize skill and talent and reward it, and it's human nature that we want those people to lead. We want a best seller; we want the blockbuster movie; we want the thing that we all have in common and we all know about.

So I don't think the design profession is going to go away. These applications are giving more people the tools to just understand the process and to appreciate and learn how to look at things. The design world differs from some of these other categories; the design world has much more of a recognized hierarchy to it than many other creative professions do at this point. I'm not totally sure why that is, but I feel like there is more of a willingness of people at the top to make pronouncements about what's good and bad, and their pronouncements seem to make more of a lasting impression than in some other creative professions.

GH — It seems like a lot of this probably has to do with the relative lack of real design criticism versus writers just championing new products and selecting a clique of designers who should be noticed. If you look at film criticism or book reviews, it seems to be a lot more vibrant and critical than in the design world.

RW — Right. My impression is that there are about 20 people in the United States and maybe 50 globally who have the authority to make pronouncements about what makes good design. They mostly just agree. There's not a lot of dissent. A movie can come out that critics will disagree violently over. A book could come out, and they'll disagree violently over that too. You'll see some disagreement among design critics, but by and large you see a lot of agreement. Maybe that's because there aren't a lot of critics operating in that world.

I don't know. I've never understood the design criticism world. I wasn't familiar with it at all before I started the "Consumed" column. And some of my early columns were criticized by design world people because they thought I was writing a design column and thought that I was doing a very bad job, and I guess I was, but I didn't really know what that meant. I didn't know what they were talking about, and I remember one critic saying that I made a poor choice if I wanted to say something useful on behalf of the importance of design. He was right, because that wasn't anywhere near my agenda. I wasn't thinking about saying anything on behalf of the importance of the world of design. A great deal of what gets said by design critics, seems to me to be fundamentally a statement on behalf of the importance of the role of design. They are still in that mode of trying to make this case that this is important and should be taken seriously.

GH — Do you have specific moments where you see a piece of design that you really hate, and you imagine how you'd recreate it?

RW — My wife and I talk about it all the time. If there was something that I thought should be redesigned or that designers should take a look at or something that makes me wonder why this lousy manifestation of design continues to exist, it wouldn't necessarily be any particular object, but it would be the packaging and shipping materials and all the waste that seems to be inevitable in those things.

When you get the box from an online retailer, you've ordered a book, and it's mostly a box of air and a bunch of plastic packing, or you go to the store to go buy a tiny USB flash drive, and it's in a big, impossible-to-open clamshell package, and you've got this big pile of plastic shards, and then you feel sort of guilty. It just seems like such a bunch of waste. It's hard to believe, and part of me understands the systemic reasons why it's still around. One of them is that it's not an easy problem for the marketplace to solve. It is a problem, though, and it is a design problem. So you would love to see some kind of solution introduced into that because it just seems to be a waste, and it's just so frustrating as a day-to-day consumer. It's something that you have to either confront, and then you're sort of bummed out, or you just put it out of your mind, which I think is what we do most of the time.

GH — It's interesting; I think that's the first time in all our conversations for the film that someone has talked about packaging waste. There must

be packaging manufacturers out there lobbying to keep everyone quiet.
Anything else that bothers you?

RW — I don't know if this is an issue designers have to address, but I think it's a really interesting thing that is a really relevant part of our relationship with material culture. It isn't represented in the traditional design-marketplace process. And that is the forgotten role of the things we already own, the thing that becomes obsolete. Obsolescence is an area of frustration for some consumers when talking about electronics. You know that if you're the first on your block to buy this device and you're the kind of person who always needs to be the first, you're also the kind of person who's the first on your block to be dissatisfied because it's been surpassed by something else. There's a very practical side to that because the marketplace and design's role in the marketplace is so heavily focused on the new, the next, the novel, the progressive; it kind of marginalizes basically everything you already own.

If I had a billion dollars to fund a marketing campaign, I would launch a campaign on behalf of things you already own. Why not enjoy them today? Because we all have so many things that are just around—they're in the closet;, they're in the attic, whatever—that we don't even think about it anymore because there's not enough room left in our brains. We're so busy processing all the exciting new developments, such as the Michael Graves spatula, that are just coming out day upon day. We appreciate the material at the moment during the process of antici-pation and at the moment of acquisition but then nothing. It's basic behavioral psychology. We lose interest in it. It becomes less of a focus of our attention, less a source of pleasure.

That's too bad because we all have things that we could sort of redis-cover in our own material lives and find a way to find pleasure in them again, which would be a more satisfying way to think about the relation-ship we have with material culture, and also maybe economical because you wouldn't have to constantly keep getting your hit of material plea-sure by going to the store.

GH — Can you give a firsthand account of a purchase you made? The process you went through and what ran through your mind?

RW — This is a treacherous area for me, because as a person who writes about objects every week, I'm exposed to many objects and have to really think about them and dwell on them. I go through a process often of falling in love with something. I'll hear about something like the Flip video camera. I'll decide to write about it. I'll borrow one from the company. I love it. I can't get enough of it. I've got to buy one of these things. By the end of the week, I've written my story, and I'm over it, and I send it back, and I never buy one. Now, every once in a while, there's something that I talk myself into, and this is when I think about or talk about my own consumer decisions.

I had two experiences. One was with the iPod when it first came on the marketplace. I was very resistant to it because of the price point. It was $400. It's a lot of money. I thought it sounded like a really cool thing. I'm not a big gadget guy. I had been a longtime Apple consumer even when

I was in college. I thought they made good stuff, their stuff worked, and it was ahead of the curve. At that time I didn't even own a cell phone, so it was like, "Well, what am I really going to do with this? Four hundred dollars is so much money." It sounded good, and I remember going into the Apple Store at Mall of America. I don't usually talk to store clerks, but I found myself telling the clerk at the Apple Store that it was too expensive and that I was going to wait until the prices went down. Not even two months later, I had talked myself into getting one by a process that I still don't totally understand, but it was sort of, "Well, I really am a music fan, and I have to travel, and it would make air travel so much more bearable. It's really more of an investment." So I bought it.

The second example is related, but comes from the column. For various reasons, the topic that I landed on was noise-canceling headphones. I had never given any particular thought to noise-canceling headphones, but now I had to do this research. What I found was a particular brand and particular model. It was supposed to be the best. They were kind of expensive, over $300 or something. It seemed like kind of a lot of money. But, it was the one. I did the interviews, I did the research, I wrote the column, and I couldn't get it out of my head. Again, it came back to, "Well, I like music, and I travel," and at that time I was on airplanes a lot, and it's such a nightmare when you get stuck in a seat behind a screaming kid, and it was just like, "Wow, this is really the thing that I never in a million years would have bought." I did end up buying them, and I have to tell you, I love them.

GH — I love the internal justifications we all use to convince ourselves to buy these things. I've started thinking, "I'm going to buy one of these things and keep it for the rest of my life. I'm going to buy the best version of this thing instead of buying five of these cheaper versions over my lifetime, so I don't want to get bored of this thing."

RW — It's tough to find those things though. But I've heard designers make that argument even on an aesthetic level. A professor was telling me about a student who had asked, "What's the sustainable aspect of this product?" The sustainable aspect was basically that it looked so great that you would never throw it away. That's kind of the ultimate aesthetics-as-function rationale for the ethics of good design I guess.

GH — Do you buy that argument?

RW — There is actually a logic to it, that if you really did make something that was so great that you would never throw it away, that would be good. In practice, I think it's a rationale though. For starters, style changes, and the arrogance implicit in the idea that you have created an icon is sort of stunning. It's just unpredictable what becomes an icon and what doesn't. You think about even the things like the McDonald's arches. Is that an example of great design? I don't know, but it's iconic. Same thing with something like the blue USPS mailbox. It's an absolutely iconic piece of design; it's good design. But there are reasons why the blue mailbox hung around for so long, and there are reasons actually why blue mailboxes are now being removed from cities, and nothing will change that. It's basically a rationale to give a sheen, a moral sheen, to taste appeal.

GH — It's funny: I look at my friend's one-year-old and the look in her eyes when she's looking at a shiny toy is exactly the same look we saw filming people at a classic auto show looking at a Ferrari. I don't know if it relates back to our survival instincts or the prehistoric era. We see a bright thing, and we're sort of programmed to notice differences in different objects, and maybe our survival depended on that, on accumulating stuff.

RW — I believe it is actually rudimentary and plays into evolutionary survival instincts. If you're foraging or if you're even looking out for danger, your senses would feel a rush at the spotting of something that was a break in the pattern, whatever the pattern is. That's sort of what interest in novelty comes down to. We feel that rush, whether it turns out to be danger or whether it turns out to be pleasure. Now, in the marketplace, it's generally going to be a pleasurable result.

You don't really have to force consumers to be interested in novelty. We're humans and we're interested in novelty in a lot of ways. A more interesting challenge for a designer would be to resist that. It plays into the designer's own motives as well. Whatever icon you're looking at, the natural thing is for you to want to change it so that you can put your own mark on it, so that you've reinvented the icon and now this icon is something you created. Again, I think that's human nature. If you're hired to make the new version of a film or take over someone else's newspaper beat, what you want to do is put your mark on it. You don't want to do exactly what's already familiar and done; you want to have some authorship. That dovetails with something that consumers are looking for—they're looking for something new.

There's a school of thought that the best strategy in a lot of ways is to try to resist that and just stick with it. That's how you really build an icon, and that would be the secret. If McDonald's had changed their logo every five years, it wouldn't be the iconic thing it is today. Or Coca-Cola, how they're playing off of familiarity and tweaks of novelty here and there, but they sort of drill the logo into someone's mind. The temptation of novelty is that it creates the need for more novelty. It leaves you vulnerable to someone else's novelty when that comes along.

—

Urbanized:
The Complete Interviews

32 Interviews/307 Pages/
164,836 Words

Alejandro Aravena (AA)/ September 6, 2010 Santiago

I met Alejandro at the Design Indaba conference in Cape Town in 2010, when I was invited there to screen *Helvetica* and *Objectified*. Alejandro's talk on participatory design and social housing moved the audience to a standing ovation, and I knew then that I wanted to include him in *Urbanized*.

—

Gary Hustwit — We're standing here in front of the Lo Barnechea houses. Could you talk about how you approached this project?

Alejandro Aravena —What I would say to start is that it's pretty obvious that we live in a country of inequalities. It's pretty much the case in the entire second and third world. There's just one discourse that one hears throughout the world about correcting inequalities, which is redistribution of income, and I guess in the city, we have found an extremely efficient vehicle for correcting inequalities without touching income. A city, in a way, is a shortcut toward equality because it can ameliorate quality of life of people without having to improve family income by strategically using housing, public space, and infrastructure. In this project, or this group of projects, families at the bottom of the pyramid are now living in a part of the city where they can find education, transportation, even public space of a very high standard. If we followed the normal way to improve quality of life through public policies, we might get a new housing solution, but two hours away from here.

What we were looking to do was to try to take advantage of the city as this network of opportunities, because if the city is anything, it's a concentration of opportunities. To do housing here, we needed to be able to find a way that, with a modest public subsidy, we could keep the networks that families have built over decades, of jobs, of education, health, transportation. They should not have to spend two hours a day crossing the city to come here where the jobs are or where higher education is. In that sense, I would say that what we're systematically trying to do with housing is to be able to pay for better land, which in the end is the reason why the poor are usually expelled to the outskirts of cities, because land is a scarce resource, and everybody wants to be as close as possible to the good parts, and therefore it's expensive.

We have found some design keys and design tools that enable us, within the public policy and within the system of subsidies, to be able to have the poor in the best part of the city, ameliorating the quality of life without touching income.

GH — How long have people been living in the slum behind us?

AA — That slum is maybe 60 years old, and what it expresses is not just an incapacity of people to have a decent home; it also expresses that they're willing to pay a very high cost, meaning very bad living conditions, for location. They are looking to be close to this network of opportunities.

What we have found is not that the poor do not have an income; they do not have a regular income. If they don't own the land where they're living, they're not going to invest. They will maintain their very bad living condition—I mean the house, the physical condition—but be close to the opportunities, and unless they're owners of the land, they're not going to invest. So one of the things about the projects that we're working on, because the policies in Chile are property oriented, is that beneficiaries of these subsidies end up owning their house. So they become owners, and therefore, if they don't lose their jobs, they can invest in their houses.

The other thing is that, if they do not have regular income, they're invisible to the banking system, so we have to do everything with subsidies. There's no debt. There's no loan, and that means that we're talking about, for the solutions we're working on, $10,000 per family with which we have to pay for land, the infrastructure, and the houses themselves. That $10,000 is the biggest aid these families are going to receive from the state in their entire lives, and we would like it to perform as an investment and not as a social expense. It would be highly desirable for a poor family that their asset, their house, gain value over time, because then it can have a parallel life as capital. They can go to a bank, ask for a loan for a small shop, for paying for the education of their children, or a car that can be used as a taxi. It can generate income, and the more value those properties gain, the better they can do against the legal system of banking and, in general, of capitalism, which in the end is the rule that we see in this system.

All of us, when buying a house, expect it to grow in value over time. There's no reason why this shouldn't happen in social housing too. How do you make a family's life easier in the process of achieving a middle-income standard? That was definitely not the way social housing was being measured, not the way it was being designed. What we're looking to do is design and build housing as an investment and not as a social expense.

GH — Maybe we can talk about the other houses here. These families haven't moved in yet; they'll move in during phase two, right?

AA — Yes. We tend to work in phases. The density we achieved during first phase of the project freed up some land. It was extremely expensive land, so our design had to be dense enough to be able to prorate the very expensive land between more families, but without overcrowding, and with the possibility of expansion.

When I say $10,000 per house, we're talking about 40 square meters, and that's not a home. The market tends to look at 40 square meters as a small house. What the market instinctively does is, it looks at a middle-income-standard unit and scales it down until it matches the amount of money that is available in the system. What we're trying to do is to reframe that set of constraints, actually rebuild the question given those constraints. We asked, "Well, what if instead of looking at 40 square meters as a small house, we look at that 40 square meters as half of a good house?" With public money, we thought it was efficient to make the half that a family would never be able to achieve on its own, and then allow families to do the other half on their own, on their own timing, according to their own needs, within the framework we're offering them.

We did 150 homes in the first phase of this project. That liberated some land because of the density we achieved, and then that will allow us to build out the second phase, which is the households that we're looking at the back of. That will liberate more land; we'll move to the third phase and so on and so forth. So we're able to keep the families within the neighborhood throughout a process that has, in this particular case, one thousand families involved.

Behind me, you see a group of families in the situation before, meaning they live in a slum in very poor-quality, wooden-panel houses. What we were trying to do is—knowing that the location is so important, because schools, transportation, jobs, are in this part of the city, which is actually the richest part of the city—was to be able to find a design that would allow us to be able to pay for very expensive land but keep all those networks. We were trying to find a way to achieve enough density in low-rises without overcrowding, and with the possibility of expansion so that we could solve the difficult equation of having the poor in the best part of the city.

GH — What do you see as the responsibility of architects in the larger context of the city?

> AA — First of all, I think it's important to make very clear that this is not charity. It's about professional quality. I mean, social housing or working with public money—be it infrastructure, public space, or housing—in a country like Chile is a difficult issue. What you don't find, in the chain of professionals involved in using public money, is quality. Nobody pays for that quality. So we thought that if there was any difference to be produced within the public system, it was to introduce more quality in the professional chain involved. More than responsibility, I would call it professional difficulty that we were trying to deal with, complexity, which design can deal with without reducing it so that it makes complexity operable. We can move from the current state of things into its potential without reducing the initial complexity.

Normally, architecture is seen as just a way to make things prettier or as a profession with better taste than the average, and we thought that the power of design lies in its capacity to synthesize complexity without reducing it but still make it simple enough to be able to operate over it. In the conversation, the starting point is never architecture, not even urban design or design in general. It's the conversation that society at large is having. What do we do with the poor? How do we avoid segregation? How can we produce development for the country knowing that the city is a very powerful vehicle to create wealth and also shortcuts toward equality? So the starting point is a conversation that anybody can have: a politician, any other professional, but families too, families that might not even know how to write or read.

The only thing that we tried to do with architecture is translate that initial starting point into a form, into a strategic design than can make things move forward and that then is afterwards verified outside architecture. Value gain is not a design that is more beautiful than another or a space that has more tension than another. Value gain is a very objective thing that anyone, from a bank to a family, can verify. What we tend to do is redefine notions. Like, what does quality mean? Value gain? That's something that everybody can engage. The only thing that we're trying to do with architecture is to use its power of synthesis to enter difficult issues, like the city. We do like complex questions, and naturally we design the question a lot. We talk actually of equations, not because we think design is a science, but in equations, the terms that you have to deal with are explicit, are in front of your eyes, so that then, after the design, you can ask whether the design did well or not in trying to satisfy the terms of the equation.

I would say that, if there's any responsibility in design, it's not to take a tool out of complex questions—design itself and its power of synthesis. That's the responsibility of design: not to be away from a discussion that starts and ends outside design.

GH — It's great to see all the children playing here. How does it make you feel to see families settling in now?

AA — When you live in a slum like the one over there, if there's anything in a slum, it's this notion of a network that allows you to survive better in a fragile socioeconomic environment. That is, an extended family—not just father, mother, children, but grandparents, uncles, aunts, nephews. That notion of an extended family, when relocated into a new project, tends not to find that space where the extended family can develop. So we wanted to have the physical space where the social network of relatives, of friends, or of solidarity can develop over time. Because that's crucial in the economic development of poor families—not just location and closeness to opportunities, but also the amount of people around that allows you to survive better.

When we go into the project, you'll see, in those places, children can play safely. It's very important that you have enough scale that a space can be maintained, that there is an agreement among families, and that those children's parents know their children are playing in a safe environment. Security's a major issue in impoverished environments, and you can deal with that not only through control and police but also through empowering people to be responsible and to have a physical translation in space of how those social agreements can be maintained over time.

GH — All the families that were in this phase were also in the same slum before, right?

AA — Yes. The other thing is that this is participatory design. When you have money to pay for just half of the house, it would be very inefficient not to have the ones responsible of the second half of the house sitting at the table from day one, so that we can split up tasks. In this case, you don't see that self-construction maybe in the facade as you do in other projects that we have done, but it's inside. I mean, because of the rain and because of the weather, it's the inside that families tend to continue completing. In the desert, it was expressed in the facade.

Anyhow, families are responsible for part of the house. In many of the cases, as much as half of the built environment is self-built, so you better have those people sitting at the table and helping the group of professionals to establish priorities. If money cannot pay for everything, then who knows better than the families what has to be delivered on day one? That set of priorities, it's crucial, and families do know extremely well what is important for them.

In that sense, what we're looking for is to involve families in the design, but not in the hippie, romantic way of asking, how you would like your house? What we're trying to do here, first of all, is have more symmetric information. You should know as much as I know regarding the set of constraints that we're dealing with, and once you know, once you're informed about the constraints, you help us to establish priorities. I do know very well, as a professional, the kinds of things that I cannot negotiate. I do have some knowledge, and when I think something is important to be done, it's done. It's not negotiable. But there are many other things in a housing project that can be negotiated, that can be better understood and informed by the background or families, and that's another thing that is very important in these projects—the families having a say in their built environment. There's also a guarantee that over time they will take more responsibility for how it will evolve in a more positive way, more than if they just got a subsidy, everything for free, and then the only thing that was left for families was to complain about the poor quality of what can be done with $10,000.

What's unusual for Chile, in the end, is the standard that can be achieved. We cannot pay at the beginning for too many square meters, but that doesn't matter. The discussion of how big the unit should be, what is reasonable, or the "existence minimum" that we have heard a lot about regarding social housing doesn't matter. I mean, size matters, but not the initial size. The real question is, how big can these homes end up being after the families' intervention? The standard that we should try to achieve is at least double that, 80 square meters.

In the end, more than a technical thing, the key question is, for design, how do you measure quality? Would you live in one of those houses? If the answer is yes, then it might be okay. More important than the laws and all the codes and everything, the real key question is, would I live in one of those houses? If the answer is yes, then the design is okay.

GH — Let's talk about the challenges facing Santiago.

AA — This is the case in Santiago, and I would say it's pretty much the case everywhere in the world. Cities are going to make or not make the difference in competitiveness. Cities will need to attract knowledge creators, and knowledge creators choose where they want to live depending on the quality of life that cities are able to offer. These elite knowledge creators pretty much earn the same everywhere in the world, so they're choosing where to live depending on urban quality of life. The more knowledge creators you are able to attract, the more competitive you are going to be, so to create urban conditions, urban amenities, the quality of the public space, of transportation, of services that can attract those knowledge creators is going to be one challenge.

On the other hand, a city is a shortcut toward equality. Societies are not going to be competitive unless they can provide quality of life for the poor. If the only solution is about income redistribution, then that's going to take too long. By doing housing the way we're doing, by doing public space, which is then redistributed, people can enjoy themselves in a very democratic way. The quality of air, the wind, the nice weather of this city, which is very democratic, are the kinds of things that we would like to capitalize on through projects. For both ends, for the bottom of the pyramid as a shortcut toward equality and for the upper part of the pyramid, for the elite able to create knowledge, we need to create the living conditions in the city so that they're able to coexist. I would say that's what we've been trying to do, trying to operate in the city at both ends of the pyramid.

[The next part of our conversation took place in Alejandro's office at ELEMENTAL.]

GH — How did you get involved in architecture? What's the story?

AA — How did I start studying architecture? I have no clue. I've been asked this several times, I swear. I'm unable to identify why or how. It's like an involuntary start.

GH — Did you take a class in college?

AA — Not really. I started when I was 17. I guess at 17 you have no idea what you're looking for, so at school, there's like a guidance counselor who will say, "Looks like you're good at math and drawing. That equals architecture. Go for that." But I really have no clue what it was. Nobody in my family was connected to architecture. I don't know. I really have no clue. I guess it was not very scientific. It could have been any kind of science or engineering. It was really not a conscious decision. But I kind of guessed that architecture combined something that was very clear and rational with something that you don't talk about, but just know, kind of an unspeakable certainty. At that time, I really have no clue.

GH — Then after school, did you think you would go into traditional practice? What happened, basically, when you left school?

AA — I guess I took it for granted that I wanted to work independently, so I never really thought about working in a big office. You have to imagine, I started studying architecture in '85, so we were in the last years of Pinochet's dictatorship. Very few things arrived in this country in terms of information; it was a rather closed country. Even the big names in architecture were not part of what we were hearing about. I didn't choose to go to work for a big firm because I didn't even know that there were big firms. To start working on your own was the natural thing to do. It was combined with a need—and this was not just architectural; it was a more personal thing—to leave Chile for a while.

I started studying in '85 and finished in '92, but in '91, an invitation arrived at the school from the Venice Biennale, and they wanted the school to present a small pavilion, and they chose some students, and I was among them. So I said, "Okay, I'll put this on hold and go to Venice." It was unusual to receive such an opportunity. I thought, "I'll keep on working there," but when I arrived in Venice, I was completely shocked. I mean, all my life I'd studied architecture from books, with photographs, and then all of a sudden you have those buildings on the street in front of you, one-to-one scale, with weight, with gravity, with people using them. I decided that I had to get back to Chile to finish my thesis as soon as possible, and then find a way to go back to Italy because I needed to swallow the buildings themselves, not the theory of the buildings, not the disciplinary body of work on paper, but in stone.

So I came back, did my thesis, and then went on a scholarship back to Italy, mainly to draw and sketch buildings. Of course, because it was a scholarship, I had to make as if I was studying, but my real interest was measuring and sketching—I mean walking in the footsteps of the decisions made by the architects. Circular or square? Distance between columns? How many columns? How wide? How thick? My intuition was, "Okay, I will have to make decisions in front of a blank piece of paper. I would like to walk in the footsteps of those that had to make those choices before me, and better than me, as a way of being trained properly by the buildings." I went to Europe in general, to old Europe, to Sicily, to Greece, to Turkey, to understand that. Then, after that, I thought, "Okay, maybe it's time to start my own practice." So I guess that's how it began.

GH — Fast forwarding, can you describe ELEMENTAL?

AA — I would call ELEMENTAL a "do tank." There are think tanks, and think tanks do care about a reality that matters. They study and try to understand themes that are relevant to society, that are important. But as an architect, I guess our training prepares us more naturally to operate in that reality more than just study it, so instead of doing papers, it was natural for me to try to do projects and, before even doing concrete projects, at least while understanding a problem, to be more concerned with, okay, what do we do with this? How do we move forward? To organize information in such a way that it tends toward a proposal.

When I was invited to teach at Harvard back in 2000, I faced the problem of, okay, what do I teach here? It was the first time I'd left Chile to even give a lecture. I'd never given a lecture in Chile before that, and then all of a sudden, I found myself invited to teach at Harvard, to choose a theme that would be inviting to the best students. So I took a look at who else was speaking at Harvard: many big names at the time. That's a natural magnet for students. Also, there were studios that were offering field trips. I had to compete with that with no name, and no capacity to offer any field trip. So out of a strategic need, I was required to think, is there anything that I can talk about where I know more than these big names? And even though I was completely ignorant, I kind of guessed that on the subject of scarcity there might be something that I knew that the others didn't. I didn't have any idea what a subsidy was at the time, but still, being trained in Chile under scarcity of means, my guess was I might know something about how to do everything with nothing.

Actually, the name of that first studio at Harvard was Otherwise-ness. It's a word that I was trying to avoid in the sense that I was concerned with the fact that architecture, in operating, could do things in this way and this way but also otherwise, and that arbitrariness was a failure of the profession for me. When you're trained under scarcity of means, the level of arbitrariness goes down. I decided to deal with a theme that left no space for that arbitrariness, for this otherwise-ness, and emergency housing was an actual field where you don't have time or money to answer with too many complicated responses. One chance, one shot, that's it. It was naturally close to social housing. Out of a strategic need, I decided to overcome my own ignorance in the field of scarcity and social housing, knowing that it was a very powerful filter and antidote against the superfluous.

Simultaneously, I met someone who ended up being my partner at ELEMENTAL, Andres Iacobelli, a transportation engineer doing his master's at the Kennedy School of Government, who was, I would say, one of my mentors even though he's two years younger me. He's one of the people I have learned the most from. His approach to the themes that we were discussing was so precise, so original, and so clear. I mean, he was not even using a word of architectural terminology and still being able to throw light over things that I didn't have a clue about, like social housing or housing policy or that kind of thing.

So the strategic position of saying something that others might not know about, combined with Andres's ability to frame the information and the problems in a way that the natural tendency of architecture to make proposals was a natural match with, made us say, "Well, why don't we do something with social housing?" If this question had come only within architecture, this "do something" would have meant a conference, a congress, a book, a paper, things which don't even scratch reality and are really inoffensive. For my partner, "do something" meant go out there and build social housing. For that, we had to understand housing policy, the market, meet decision-makers, so he said, "Let's ask for a meeting with the minister, and let's go and understand families. The effort that it would take to ask for a million pesos, which is what we would need to do a conference, is the same amount of effort that it would take to ask for a million dollars to actually build the buildings." Actually, $10 million. I was naive enough to believe him, and it was natural that that initiative would end up being what today we call a do tank.

I would say that, from the very beginning, we were comfortable going into the gray areas to make things become real. This was not going to be a pure approach where a clear outcome and eventually even an elegant answer would be at the end of road. We were interested in going into reality with all its friction, with all its areas where we would have to negotiate, but where we could get things done. Then we'd have a photograph of something that was built to prove our point. We thought that was much more powerful than having the most exquisite, intelligent paper or rendering on a screen, because that was the only way we could actually improve reality.

GH — What do you think are the biggest challenges and problems facing cities? Santiago or any city?
AA — I think there's a challenge in cities, and there's a challenge in architecture, and then I think there's a challenge in design.

Regarding cities, you know that we just crossed the threshold of having more people living in cities than in the countryside, which, in principle, is excellent news. Cities are the most efficient way to improve quality of life, even if it's very counterintuitive. If you measure quality of life from birth rate, to access to healthcare, to sanitation, sewage, water, jobs, education, everything is better in the cities than in the countryside, particularly for the poor, because cities are more efficient in distributing through public policies all those elements. The more people we have in cities, the better, because we're going to be able to, in a more efficient way, improve quality of life. That's for the poor.

One of the things that is particularly important in the future, given the global economy that we're living in, is, as I've mentioned, that the difference in competitiveness of countries will come from knowledge creation. In the recent past, it came mainly for investing in infrastructure because countries were more competitive not because of the cost of goods and services but because of their efficiency in moving those services and goods. The more a country had invested in infrastructure, the more efficient it was to move all those goods and services, and the more urban a country was, the more efficient the investment in infrastructure was. The new thing will be the soft areas of infrastructure: knowledge creation, which in the end is about face-to-face contact and critical mass. Knowledge creation requires personal contact. It won't happen over the Internet. Cities are a big magnet to these knowledge creators that will come and eventually produce that difference in competitiveness because they will have enough critical mass, which tends to happen in more dense environments.

So that's the good part. What's the challenge? That the scale and speed of the process of people coming to cities now has no precedent in human history. The mass of people that will come to cities will be mainly in the poorest countries in the world, in between the tropics. There are some papers that say, if you want to put a number to this, in the next 20 years, we will have to build a one-million-person city per week with about $10,000 per family to be able to host the floods of people, both poor and rich, coming to cities. We do not have enough knowledge to respond to that challenge. So more than money, it's knowledge, speed, and coordination that we're lacking. So we're in an urgency—because in principal, it's good news—to be able to generate the conditions so that flow of people into cities happens in a good way.

This is another difficultly: Today, six billion people live in the world. Three billion are urban dwellers. Out of those three billion, one billion are living under the poverty line. By 2030, we are going to have five billion people living in cities, and two billion are going to be under the poverty line. Unless we do something, the way people are going to come to cities is going to be in the form of squatters. Slums. That will create big challenges regarding quality of life, regarding security, regarding public health, and eventually people coming to cities are going to miss the point of having access to opportunities. They might end up even in a worse condition than what they were in before. That's the urgency of gaining the knowledge we need to create reasonable solutions for this flow of people. I believe it's a great opportunity that we shouldn't miss. That is going to be the challenge for cities, which is a great challenge.

For architecture, I would say that back in the sixties and seventies, there was a kind of forking path. On the one hand, there was a big movement of a part of architecture more connected to art that claimed a space in which to operate with more freedom, creative freedom, to prove that talent was important. Society allowed the architectural discipline to be creative, to be free. The price architecture paid was irrelevance. Between freedom and irrelevance, there's a very tiny gap. I guess, in the last few decades, we've been existing in that moment where we're paying the cost of that irrelevance, and the strategy of shock has been one of the pieces of evidence that we see. If you're irrelevant—because it's a major threat—to make as if they're not, architects use a strategy of shock. You try to impact people to show that you're not irrelevant. I think that was one trend that started in the late sixties and seventies, and I would say postmodernism was a very clear expression of that.

On the other hand, there were those willing to enter reality with all its complexity and roughness and hard issues—poverty, underdevelopment, segregation, violence, all those issues—and actually interest society at large. One of the things about the first approach is that architects deal with things that only interest other architects. These other issues interest society in general. Everybody is eventually interested or eventually can have a say regarding poverty or underdevelopment or creating more opportunities. There was a group of professionals interested in entering that reality, and they actually did, but the price they paid was abandoning design. It was about being consultants for international organizations, for NGOs, for think tanks, and to diagnose was the main thing that you could get from that. The power of design, of synthesizing alternatives as a possible future, was abandoned.

We had those that still were doing design, doing proposals, but with themes that interested nobody but other architects, or those that engaged issues that interested society at large but then did not have any proposals. I would say that the challenge today is to be able to start from outside architecture, in those themes that interest a society at large, and to be able to operate within that reality using specific architectural tools—design. In a way, it's nonspecific issues treated through specific knowledge that then, again, is verified in a nonspecific way outside architecture. Do we overcome poverty after doing our projects? I guess this is the challenge today for architecture: to be able to cross nonspecific problems with specific knowledge, which until now have followed separated paths.

Finally, the third challenge is this attribute of an architectural work being simultaneously a mirror and a cloak. A way, I would say, to measure the success of an architectural project is in its capacity to perform simultaneously as an object that you pay attention to—a mirror—and an object that you don't even pay attention to while doing what that object enables you to do.

In the mirror dimension, an object should be able to resist a careful look. If you interrogate that object, that object should be able to answer those questions up to the point that it can eventually reflect, as a mirror, a society, a cultural moment, an author, a moment in time, a zeitgeist. So you pay attention to the object, and the object resists that careful look. Simultaneously, that very same object should be able to disappear in the corner of the eye to allow you to live your life in the most unconscious way. The ultimate verification of a good design is that it disappears and enables a situation and activity in a very smooth, natural, silent way, as if it was a cloak around you, something in the background, not in the foreground. But it should be both. It's not just about a false modesty of doing things that systematically disappear without a capacity to be a reflection of that moment in time when that cultural object was produced, and also it's not about doing something that has no capacity to disappear and get dissolved as a mere background.

GH — Can you give me like an example of a building that's a mirror or a cloak, or both perhaps?

AA — A good example of this is a window. You can pick a window from the old times, and it tells a lot about the technical capacity to span a void, the amount of decoration, the amount of ventilation, the transparency of glass, even what role it plays in the facade as a composition. It is a word in that language, and actually, if you pay attention to the window, it is an object able to reflect. It's a cultural object. Simultaneously, the ultimate purpose of a window is to be able to disappear completely, to let air, light, and view go through. Finally, the best window is the one that completely disappears around what you're looking at or the air that it allows to enter a room.

All of us have in mind objects that work perfectly as a cultural object, they reflect their moment in time, but if you want to use them in a very casual, ordinary, daily-life way, they can't disappear. They are always saying, "I am a cultural object." Everyday life requires a level of neutrality. On the other hand, there are many objects that make your life very easy and comfortable, but once interrogated, they do not contribute to the history of art and the architectural history of a culture in the end. I would say that everyone could do the exercise of analyzing an object and test that capacity of being a mirror and a cloak simultaneously, depending on which eye you look at it with.

There are many examples: the Guggenheim Bilbao, the Barcelona Pavilion, the Pavillon de l'Esprit Nouveau by Le Corbusier. They're great cultural objects. Are they able to disappear, to be part of your day-to-day life? I don't think so. Actually, I don't even know if they were built or not, but the courtyard houses by Mies van der Rohe: they are for sure a reflection of their time. I mean, the capacity of producing thin slabs, minimum structure, that appreciation of reduction, of the minimum amount of elements to build a space, are a cultural thing. Simultaneously, because they are so subtle, a nice courtyard, I guess, will always be a great courtyard, and it's about the air in between things.

I would say that Louis Kahn is a great example of that. I was in Bangladesh not long ago, and the National Assembly Building—if interrogated as a cultural object, it's very dense. It has a huge specific weight. It not only talks about that moment in time, in art, or even about the architect but also that moment in democracy, the cultural discourse around the building, the capacity of a country to build a capital. The discourse around the building can be extended to an entire nation. Simultaneously, you go there on a Sunday, and you have people exercising, families going around, sports happening. People do like the building. It is just a nice place to go on a weekend. They might not even pay attention to the building. It's just the generosity of the open spaces around it and the lagoon. There are many examples, but I'm just thinking about that one recent visit and that capacity to capture attention and disappear simultaneously.

GH — Can we talk about informal housing in slums? What can we learn from informal housing that can applied to the bigger picture in a city?

AA — I think it's very important while looking at informal housing and slums and squatters to learn from them, to understand their power and their logic but not to be romantic about them, not to be romantic about poverty. There's an incredible amount of energy for sure, and the capacity of self-building is a huge resource that, while trying to solve the problem of people coming into cities, shouldn't be overlooked. Trying to respond to the problem of accommodating the poor within cities with public funds is not the only way. The huge capacity of people themselves, if they're given the right frame on top of which they can build, should be considered and integrated into the initial equation. Otherwise, there's really no way to respond to such a scale and speed of people coming into cities in a proper way. It is better to take advantage of that power and energy and capacity of self-investment of people.

There are also very precise rules in that. Actually, I would say that we can learn precision from slums and informal building. When you're dealing with scarcity, you are very close to the limit of what is possible in terms of structure. What's the minimum thickness of a wall that you can use that won't collapse? Eventually, they take advantage of the walls of the neighbors. So it's a very precise structural operation at the very limit because you don't have enough resources. How do you maximize internal space while still allowing public circulation on the outside? I would say that there's a deep notion of order that we can learn from, an order that does not lead to regularity. It's the notion of order in the sense of, what's the law that explains the position of parts and elements in space? Those laws are very precise, and so there's a deeper notion of order that is not connected to regularity.

But it's important not to be romantic about that. There are coordinated operations that do not happen. There's the incapacity to ventilate properly, very poor sanitary conditions, or the incapacity to guarantee public space. Everything is eaten up by private individual space that is claiming as much as it can from the public sphere. The individual quality does not have any guarantee over the common good, and that's the kind of thing that requires coordination that, individually or spontaneously, has not happened. A very key, strong, effective professional public operation is required to be able to combine individual energy with public good.

I would say that the most important thing regarding slums is also to understand the economic logic behind them or that missing potential that is in there that is extremely well described in the Peruvian economist Hernando de Soto's book *The Mystery of Capital.* He says that the amount of resources that are invested to build slums is huge, but by being informal, by not being able to have access to a system of rules that allow that asset to be interchanged and, "have a parallel life as capital," they're losing the capacity of households to be the foundation of becoming something else. In the formal world, you have access to ways of getting income: go to a bank and, with your property, ask for a loan for a sewing machine, a taxi, or to run or start a small shop at home. The informal world has no capacity to make that individual asset, your household, have a parallel life as capital, and that's an obvious opportunity that we're missing.

I think it's extremely important that we're able to combine the set of rules, the coordinated, shared set of rules that allow public good to exist with the individual energy to complete open systems, because there's not enough money, time, and, in general, energy from the public sector to be the complete answer. It is actually not desirable. In the end, the individual himself knows better what is needed, and that isn't able to be provided by a centralized system. Open systems are the only way to react to diversity. How do we combine both so that you capture the energy of individual performances but do not affect the common good?

GH — Could you tell me about these paper models on your desk? These are for Lo Barnechea, right?

AA — Yes. I would say these are some examples of what we mean by participatory design. What does it mean to get people involved in the design of a housing project? One thing is asking them to anticipate some operations that we expect are going to happen. Just to start, the idea of having people involved is not only a choice. It's mainly a constraint. There's not enough money to deliver the entire house, so it's only about 40 square meters. That means that families will meet on their own to keep on building to achieve a higher standard. In order to be more efficient in the use of resources, both from the family and from the state, we do these workshops with the families so that we can anticipate some problems, get some information from them, communicate to them the constraints, and anticipate some operations and coordinate them more properly.

In one of those workshops, we start, for example, with this piece of paper where we ask families to write their name and the date, because in the end, it's actually an agreement that might have a legal consequence. It's going to be the set of rules and codes that are going to guide this community. We explain what we're expecting from them here, also remind them what the house is going to look like, and then we ask families: Are you going to paint the facade? Are you going to change the width of windows, have fences or expand toward the courtyard in front? This piece of paper is then cut and folded, and it's transformed into, even though it's a very fragile model, a 3-D model. Very modest, made out of paper, but it still gives the notion, first of all, of a space. It's hard sometimes for people who are not trained to read plans and drawings to understand what we're talking about, and a model is more self-explanatory. That's important.

Simultaneously, it goes from the individual scale—what this family is saying that it's going to do, like add balconies and terraces or fences or change the width of a window, as an individual initiative—to what the consequence over the entire block might be. Are there things that we would like to do in a more coordinated way, as a community, or is it fine to give complete freedom for individual initiatives? How is that going to affect the value of the community? Or am I more concerned now about trying to gain those spaces for my own reality, more bedrooms, a shop at home, or a car that I need to park inside because of the way I generate income and so on and so forth?

GH — It's interesting because it also seems like it can make the residents stakeholders in the whole community versus just their individual house.

AA — I mean, what we're doing here has many objectives, many goals. One of them is to communicate what the project is going to be in the future. Families have been waiting for quite a long time. There's a lot of anxiety. We need to do things in the meantime to lower that level of anxiety, to anticipate what they're going to do once they move into the houses, so we want to communicate what we're doing.

Simultaneously, we would like to already know what kind of things they expect to do in eventually modifying the design. One of the things that is pretty clear here is that there are many families changing the width of a window, and that information is crucial for us. There are cases, for example, where, if we're on time, we try to react and already change the width of the window. A wider window is more expensive, so part of the workshop might be asking, "Okay, what do we not do in order to pay for a wider window? It will mean less trouble for you, but we have to pay for that. What are you okay with not receiving from the very beginning in order to allow us to do a more difficult operation like making a wider window?" This trade-off, establishing priorities in spite of what *we* think, is the part of the notion of participatory design that we're dealing with.

Finally, it is very important to understand that in many cases we're dealing with a person who comes from an informal world. They're invisible to the formal system. They're living in a slum, and they're a squatter, and they will, after receiving their home, become a citizen. They're going to begin to be an owner of a property that is a legal property. They're going to begin to pay bills, and there's a certain discipline that the project itself can help to build in that transition from informal dweller to citizen.

GH — When we were at Lo Barnechea, we didn't get a chance to talk about the "water heater versus bathtub" question.

> **AA** — Again, as a consequence of scarcity and not having enough money, it is important to establish priorities. Establishing those priorities some-times is a technical thing, so it's not really a choice. We communicate to families what is a very high priority, but there are other cases where families can tell us what is more important. We went many times through this decision—having to choose between a water heater or a bathtub. There was not enough money for both. If you ask this question to, let's say, decision-makers or politicians or professionals, they normally tend to answer: the water heater. And in 100 percent of the cases, when we ask these families, they prefer the bathtub over the water heater.
>
> There are few reasons for that. You have to understand that they're coming from a slum made out of cardboard panels, with no water, no sewage. So to take a shower meant having a can with water in the court-yard and pouring water on themselves; that was a shower. Moving into these houses, they're going to have privacy. The most important thing is privacy. If you choose a bathtub, you're not only going to be able to take a shower with a certain intimacy in a private room, but It also allows you to give your child a bath, not just a shower. And in the bathtub, you can also wash your clothes.
>
> More important than that is the fact that when they move in, they do not have money to pay the gas bill to heat the water. So if you give them the water heater, it's going to be there without the capacity of heating water because there's no money to pay the bill. Instead, the bathtub can be used from day one. There is a subsidy for water, so you get water for free if you're poor. The use of the bathtub is from day one; with the water heater, it's not clear if it's going to be used at all. There are many cases where families sell the water heater to generate income to buy other things. So knowing that in their priorities bathtub is much higher than water heater, we say, "Let's do the bathtub." And over time, they might be able to buy the water heater and connect it easily afterwards.

GH — I'm interested in the idea that you can have planners and architects and all these other professionals trying to guide the design of cities, but it really comes down to the people who are living there. I was wondering if you could maybe talk about your thoughts on that.

AA — I think it's important to recognize that the starting point of any urban design is a dispersed thing. It's a complex thing. It's about people and the average citizen, yes. It is also about resources, be they public or private, which factor in. It's about the environment, the weather, politics, decision-making, the capacity to maintain coherent decisions over time, eventually over periods that are beyond policy modules or political modules. A city is made over more than the four years of a presidential term. It's about technicalities. It's about so many things that inform the form of cities.

The biggest threat, I would say, is that, in the face of that complexity, you're paralyzed and at the most tend to give a diagnosis of what is going to happen if we don't do this or we do not face this bad issue. I always say that, as architects, with that complex starting point and set of constraints, we like to offer a proposal as soon as possible. Risk a possible state of things—what would happen if?—and throw that into the discussion so that, afterwards, we might even change the initial proposal by 180 degrees, but at least align all those interests along a proposal instead of a diagnosis.

I think there's an incredible amount of power if you understand what you have to gain or, phrased differently, if you're able to frame a proposal in the city in such a way that every stakeholder understands, feels, and sees what there is to gain in quality of life, votes, money, you name it. That's the only way to keep moving, because cities are such a complex reality that, if there's not alignment, if the energies are not oriented in the right way, they're going to be chaotic. If we're able to frame the problem and, first of all, have a proposal, risk a proposal, with all the fears and threats that that might mean, and in such a way that every stakeholder sees what there is to gain, then we're going to be able to mobilize the amount of energy that is required to make cities flourish and develop and not sink and become impoverished as a result.

GH — Okay, anything else you want to get off your chest that we haven't talked about?

AA — I don't know. I've been thinking actually for the last week about adding a chapter to the book that is about to go out about ELEMENTAL. We'll eventually modify at least a sentence in there, because when we talk about cities and want them to become this nice place to be, that are able to ameliorate quality of life and correct inequalities in a good, efficient, friendly way, it's the kind of thing where everybody looks at you and says, "Yeah, okay. That's a utopia." I was thinking that—it works particularly in English—if we're smart enough and we create the right solutions for facing the challenges of an urban world, we might go from utopia with a *u* to youtopia, like *y-o-u*. Besides being an architect or an urban designer or a planner, I'm a citizen. The power of youtopia is the capacity of having your say as a person, and eventually wearing as many hats as you can: as a citizen and as a politician, as a citizen and a designer, as a citizen and a citizen, because you're nothing if not a citizen.

It's an interesting moment in time because we crossed the threshold to being an urban world, an urbanized world with the amount of democratic tools to be able to have a say so that we can transform utopia into youtopia.
—

The High Line/ September 2010 New York

Robert Hammond (RH)& Joshua David (JD)/ Cofounders, Friends of the High Line

The High Line in New York City has been almost universally hailed for repurposing a piece of obsolete urban infrastructure and revitalizing a large portion of the city. During the process of making *Urbanized* I was living in Manhattan just a block from the High Line. So this project was literally in my own backyard.

I spoke with Friends of the High Line co-founders Robert Hammond and Joshua David, landscape architect James Corner, and architect Ric Scofidio of Diller Scofidio + Renfro about the project.

—

Gary Hustwit — Let's start out with the easy stuff: we need one or both of you guys to give us the history of the High Line, what New York was like at the time, the reasons they built it.

Robert Hammond — Can we talk about Helvetica and the Vietnam War?

GH — [Laughing.] Sure.

Joshua David — There is a Vietnam War quote about the High Line. A city official, who I won't name, said that the High Line was the Vietnam of old railroad trestles, referring to the endless battle that was unwinnable and went on forever.

GH — So what's the history?

JD — This thing that we're sitting on was built from 1929 to 1934. It was actually part of a much bigger system. It was called the West Side Improvement Project. It took the trains off the street levels of Manhattan all the way from Spuyten Duyvil above the northern end of Manhattan down to Lower Manhattan.

One of the things that used to happen right around where we're sitting is, on the avenue right below us, 10th Avenue, there were so many conflicts between the trains running on the streets and horse traffic and truck traffic and cab traffic and pedestrians that people got run over all the time, and it was called Death Avenue. There were these public committees that were put together, the Committee to End Death Avenue, and this discussion went on for many, many years before they figured out what to do and ultimately came to an agreement to build the High Line, which, as I said, is part of a much bigger system. This is the only elevated part of it. Much of the West Side Improvement has the tracks below ground, going under what's now Riverside Park.

That's why it was originally built. It carried freight. There were no passenger trains on the High Line. It was designed to interact with other buildings. It was designed to take the trains directly into factories and warehouses, which I think is the really interesting thing about the High Line, both at the time that it was built and today, this interactivity between this structure and these wonderful industrial warehouses on the West Side. At the time it was built, it meant that you had a very efficient way of transferring goods from the line directly into the factories.

For now, in the situation that we find ourselves in, it means that the rail line, which is now a park, has this interaction with these buildings, and you have this very unusual circumstance where a New York City public park actually runs through a piece of private property, surrounded by private property, like a doughnut and its hole, and as you move through that void in the private building, you're in the public realm. It's a very unusual thing.

GH — What are the dates again?
JD — It was started in 1929, and in 1934 it was completed and trains started running. It was active for about 30 years until interstate trucking began to take traffic off all freight lines all over the country. As rail freight traffic declined, it declined on the High Line as well, and they began to tear down parts of it. It used to go much further south, down to almost the tip of southern Manhattan. They tore it down up to a place in the West Village in the early 1960s. Then there was another teardown in 1990, bringing it to where it ends at Gansevoort now.

Trains ran on it until 1980, and then they stopped entirely. That's when the real story of what happens to the High Line next began, because, basically, all of the property owners underneath the High Line, at one time or another they either sold an easement to the New York Central Railroad, or the New York Central Railroad actually bought the property to allow the easement to run over private property. When the trains stopped running, all of those underlying property owners began to sue to have the High Line torn down. There was a very strong opposition to the High Line's existence for a long time that we didn't really even know about when we started Friends of the High Line. There was a court battle that went on for over 20 years.

RH — Another part of the history is it was built at a time when there was the city-of-tomorrow image, where people thought that the city was going to exist in all these different levels. It was built at the same time the Empire State Building was built, where passenger blimps were going to dock. The Starrett-Lehigh Building was built at the same time, where freight cars were going to go up on elevators. It was just at the very end as the Depression hit when all these different kinds of multilevel structures and ways of moving things through the city happened. It turned out not to work that way.

GH — Tell me about the start of Friends of the High Line and how you guys both got involved. You're not, I assume, real estate developers or architects.

RH — I've lived in the West Village since I graduated from college. I'd always seen parts of the High Line in the Meatpacking District, and I thought it was interesting but didn't give it a lot of thought. Then I read an article in the *New York Times* in the summer of '99 that said it was going to be demolished. It had a map, and it showed the whole line from 34th Street all the way down to Gansevoort, that it was all connected; it was a mile and a half long, still owned by the railroad; and that it was basically set to be demolished.

I assumed someone in New York must be working to save it, some civic group or community group, and maybe I could volunteer or help out. I started calling around, and pretty quickly found no one was doing anything. I did hear it was on the agenda of a community board meeting, and I'd never been to one, never had really wanted to go to a community board before that, and I went. I happened to sit next to Josh—we didn't know each other—and discovered he lived in Chelsea and was interested in the High Line in the same way I was. No one else in the meeting was interested. Everyone was actually not just disinterested but very much in favor of demolition. After the meeting, we exchanged business cards and said, "Why don't we do something together?" We didn't have a grand plan in the very beginning.

JD — I was a freelance magazine writer and I was doing an article on changes that were happening over on the West Side of Manhattan, particularly in this area of West Chelsea. I'd lived about a block away from the High Line for over 15 years and never paid it any attention at all. That's partly because of the very unique way that it interacts with the street and with buildings in Chelsea. Most of the High Line is hidden. You don't really see it from the street. You see it as it jumps over the street crossing, and then it hides behind buildings again. It's very easy to be in this neighborhood and not really pay it much attention or think it's a remnant or just a piece of something. I think it was the realization that that thing that I thought was just little pieces of something was actually this monumental structure that ran 22 blocks, three neighborhoods, connecting the Meatpacking District, going all the way up to West Chelsea, and landing at the side door of the Javits Center. It just seemed like this amazing opportunity to experience the city in a whole new way.

I ended up at the meeting in the same way that Robert did. I think what struck me in that meeting was the depth of passion of the people who wanted to tear it down. There was one person who spoke who I think was literally frothing at the mouth about how terrible the High Line was, just the worst thing you could possibly imagine, and it was killing people, and pieces of it were falling off, and it was all going to come down. I think the depth of that antagonism to what seemed like a relatively harmless thing was something that really interested me and made me that much more eager to see if there was something good to do with it.

GH — And that man is now a billionaire because he owns something under the High Line.

JD — Indeed. You got it.

GH — What was the first time you each got up here? Had you seen Joel Sternfeld's photos? What was the first time that you experienced it from this level?

RH — When I first fell in love with it, it was because of the steel structure. I just loved the steel girders, the rivets, that it was this industrial relic in the middle of Manhattan. Then at that community broad meeting, there was a representative from the railroad there, and we just asked for a tour. Everyone assumes that we both were sneaking up here, and it's not that exciting really. We asked permission, and they took us on a tour.

When they first took us up here, it was in the fall of '99. It was this field of wild flowers stretching through the middle of Manhattan, with views of the Empire State Building, the Statue of Liberty, the Hudson River, the city. It was not just this steel artifact, this industrial relic then, but it was nature, and that to me is what I think is the strongest appeal of the High Line, these juxtapositions of hard and soft, nature and steel, in the middle of Manhattan. Because there's probably millions of miles of abandoned rail tracks all over the country with wild flowers growing on them. It's that it's in the context of the city, that you look right over the side and there's 10th Avenue; there's the Empire State Building. I think that's what I really fell in love with.

JD — We really did conceive of this project from the ground. We hadn't been up on top of it at all when we began to lay out the direction that we wanted to take it in. Before we'd gotten the tour of it, we'd assembled a small group of people, named the organization, decided that we thought that probably some kind of park use was the most viable reuse for it, all without being up here at all, all without actually seeing what it was like up here.

That moment when the railroad representative brought us up here and we actually—you used to be able to get up to it through Chelsea Market, the building that's in the background over there. There used to be a freight elevator that took you up on this big old loading dock where the trains used to load and unload into this Nabisco factory. When we came up that way and came out almost right directly behind us and walked right along here, I just remember, almost as you get to this point where we are right now, you see this incredible 13-block-long straightaway, this incredibly expansive corridor of open space that's in, really, the middle of Manhattan. Just the idea that there was this secret space that was a block away from my house that I'd never seen before, that there could be this incredible resource so close and unused, was just amazing.

RH — My early elevator speech, when I would call people up trying to get them interested before they hung up, was, "It's a mile and a half of Manhattan. How often do you get a mile and a half of Manhattan to think about?" When we came up here, we realized there was something magical up here already, and we knew that we needed to capture that because it wasn't enough to just see it from the street. We knew we needed to get it photographed. Someone suggested Joel Sternfeld, he had done some photographs of aqueducts in Rome. I looked him up in information and just cold-called him and said, "You want to come up?" We brought him up, and after the tour, he said, "Don't let anyone up here for a year, and I'll give you some great photos." We almost think of him as a third co-founder because those photos were so much more powerful than anything that Josh and I ever said because people could make up their own minds.

Early on there was a lot of pressure. People would say, "What do you want to do up here? Show us some designs. Show us some renderings." I think the power of using Joel's photos was you could see whatever you wanted. Some people saw it as a preservation project. Some people saw it as gardens. Some people saw it: "Oh, wild flowers, native grasses." Some people saw it: "Oh, a site for new architecture." It enabled people with a lot of different ideas to come in and help us. Joel's pictures also helped influence this design, because at the end of the day, people finally said, "We want it to feel like this." Early on, we were open to it being completely different designs. One of the finalists for the design competition was Zaha Hadid, and she didn't have a plant in the whole park. I asked her in the competition interview, "Do you not like plants?" She said, "Trees are things architects put in when they don't know what to do with the space." I love Zaha Hadid, but we realized she wasn't right for this park project. But in the early days, we were really open to a lot of different ways that this could look.

GH — At that point, you started Friends of the High Line. Did you use private contributions to get it started?

RH — Yeah. We started Friends of the High Line back in '99, right after we met. We gave it a name, and Paula Scher designed our logo about a month after we started. Early on, the first thing we had to do was, we wanted to print a brochure with some photos and to explain what it was, have a little map. We had to raise—I think it was $5,000. We started by really just sending an email to everyone we knew saying, "There's an old elevated railroad, and we want to do something with it. Will you give us $100?"

JD — Then we did our first event not that long after that, which was in, I think, winter of 2000, and I think we made $60,000 from that first event. Then the next one made $200,000. After that, it slowly grew, but one of the things that I found really interesting about the whole process of beginning to raise money for this was the link between fundraising and people contributing to a project like this and their sense of ownership of it. I think that we have thousands of friends of the High Line, people who consider themselves friends of the High Line and consider themselves people who've made this project possible who haven't given us a penny, and we've really cultivated their sense of ownership, a large sense of public ownership. Those people who have contributed year after year, they have created an organization that now, after having brought this project through a place where it had city approval, through raising all the money to build it, through construction, now has an organization in place that is well positioned to maintain and operate it for many years to come. It's a great example of the role that philanthropy can play in organization building and in changing the shape of a city.

RH — At the ground breaking, we gave people little buttons that said, "I saved the High Line," and there were hundreds and probably thousands of people wearing this button, and it really is true. I think Josh and I get a lot of credit for this. We're getting interviewed for it, but I think the most important thing we did in some ways was raise the flag to start it. It allowed other people to come along with the expertise, because a lot of times we get asked, "Oh, how did you have the expertise in the politics, the city planning, the fundraising?" We didn't, and now we maybe have a little more, but it was all these different people and most of them volunteers and a lot of them that didn't give any money but gave their time and expertise to not just get this off the ground but to *get* it and, in a lot of ways, to continue to help us run it.

GH — Is it safe to say that when Bloomberg came into office, that was when it really got traction and city funding and started to happen?

RH — That was one of the early things, we always were trying to show momentum, because early on I thought the chances were one in a hundred that this would ever happen. I always thought, if it did happen, it would happen in 20 or 30 years, and if we were lucky, we would get it started, and someone else would finish it. Early on, it was a lot about fighting. Our maiden slogan was "Save the High Line," and with Giuliani, we were suing. The second fundraiser we had was to pay lawyers to sue the city of New York and Mayor Giuliani for trying to demolish it. Two days before he left office, he signed the demolition agreement—because he knew Bloomberg was going to be supportive—to try to lock the city in to demolition. It took a while for Bloomberg to be able to change that city policy. That's why we did things like the ideas competition and publications, to try to keep building awareness. The other thing is, no one knew what the High Line was, even people in the neighborhood. You'd say, "Oh, the High Line, that elevated railroad." "What?" You would say, "Oh, you go under it, and sometimes there are pigeons." "Oh, that. Yeah, I hate that." It was about building awareness.

Some people saw the Joel Sternfeld pictures and got it, and said, "Wow." A lot of people would be like, "It's rusty. It has weeds. Why? What's the big attraction?" That's one of the reasons we did the ideas competition in 2003, to just show momentum, but also to have people think about it in different ways. One of my favorite entries was turning the whole thing into a lap pool. It was such a beautiful graphic and idea, just this mile-and-a-half lap pool. Another one of my favorites was a roller coaster. Leave the landscape alone; build a roller coaster. You never walk on it. It's this idea of this urban experience. You already have this elevated, but imagine going even further, looking into rooms, zooming. I think it helped people think about the opportunity in a different way, and it engaged the public.

GH — I'm interested in the fact that you guys, like you said, you raised the flag. You're both residents of the city, of the neighborhood. Raising that flag allowed other people to come in. It's really a citizen-driven project. At some point then, the government sees the light or doesn't see the light.

> JD — I think the idea that the High Line is really driven by, at the very start, Robert and me, but very quickly a large group of neighbors, community residents, New Yorkers, and then ultimately people from all over the country—that it's really a grassroots, community-based effort—is something that very much affects the place that it is today.

One of the inspirations and models that helped us develop the High Line is a similar structure in Paris called the Promenade plantée, which was already completed by the time we started our work. We didn't know about it before. We thought, "Oh, let's make a park on the High Line," but as soon as we started talking to people about it, they said, "Oh, there's one of those in Paris." We went to it, and we visited it and learned a lot from it. It's very impressive. They did it 10 years before we did it, and it was a model that was extremely useful to us in advancing our own. It showed that people would go to it, that access is possible. You can use elevators. You can use stairs. People don't get killed up there, and it becomes a well-used park. The thing that's really different between the Paris elevated rail park and this one, aside from its design, which is also very different, is the fact that this is a community-based, community-driven project, that its origin comes from the community, because the Paris project was government driven. The government said, "We're going to make a park on this." There was never a call to action to get people involved to make it happen.

RH — It's just a park to them. They were surprised: why were we so interested? To them, it was just building another park like the city does all the time.

JD — Because of that, it didn't have this massive community group, city-wide attention, and all of this design community attention. Long before this park got completed, we had all of these members from Tokyo and Finland and all of these places who were emailing us all the time about the High Line from all over the world. We were nowhere near getting it done. The fact that there was this community spirit that extended that far, I think, has really imbued the park with a different kind of sensibility, a real communal sensibility that very much affects the environment that is up here. People are really passionate about this place. Whether they know that story or not, I think they can just feel it here.

RH — This is a true public-private partnership. A lot of people use that term, but this really is, from how it was paid for—part from the city and federal government, part privately raised by individuals—to how it's run—it's a New York City park, but Friends of the High Line manages and operates it under a license agreement with the park—to how it was designed, which was a partnership between the city and Friends of the High Line. I think neither one could've done it without the other. I think it makes for a better project than, say, if Josh and I had the money to build it. I think it would be a very different experience. I think it would feel more private, and that's what this partnership with the city enabled us to do, is create this public park that's so special and different. Now we've proven we could do it, but back then it was Josh and I and some other volunteer saying, "Oh yeah, we can do this." That's why we had Paula Scher do that early logo: we wanted to show a commitment to design from the beginning, that if we were going to go to all this trouble, we weren't just going to throw up a plant or a stair and some asphalt and call it a day, that attention to design was going to go all the way through.

GH — Let's talk about the public reaction from the ribbon cutting on. I live on 24th Street, so I'm in the neighborhood. I'm amazed at how many photographs are being taken on this thing. It's not like any other park. People are constantly snapping photographs of everything around. It's amazing.

RH — When I was away in Rome, my favorite way of keeping up was on the Flickr page where people were uploading photos. You could literally see the park change every day and the seasons change just in people's pictures. People are taking pictures of everything, not just the plants, but the details. Now with cell phones, it's the new way people capture things, but yeah, the response, I think, has been overwhelming.

We've had over three million people already come up. I would say it's 5, almost 10 times what we ever expected. On a busy Saturday, you have almost 20,000 people come up in one day, and it's a very small space. It's probably the most heavily used space per square foot of any park in New York City.

JD — The thing that amazes me about the way people are experiencing the High Line and what they're taking away from it is there are people who are passionate about this place in a way that I'm passionate about it. I've spent the last 11 years of my life on it, but they far outdo me in their obsessive zeal about the High Line. There are people who are just totally freaks about it. They really, really, really love it. They come over and over again. They're up here every day. They use it as their walk to work. They bring all their family here. You get these messages: "I was up there again." It's striking some kind of nerve in people that is making them react in a really enthusiastic way, and it's wonderful to see, a little astonishing, but really, really wonderful.

GH — It's a good thing that it works on a couple different levels because some people are very aware of the history and the place. Other people have no idea. They could care less actually. They just love being able to experience the city in this way.

JD — There's one thing that we haven't touched on that I think deserves just one note. We've talked about the effort to save it and the fighting to save it and the lawsuits. We've talked a lot about the design and working with the design team and the architects. But underneath where we're sitting is I don't know how many blocks of land, lots of blocks of land that were part of an urban planning process that went through the Department of City Planning, a rezoning.

The neighborhood between 16th Street and 30th Street was already scheduled to be rezoned before the High Line came along. They were going to rezone it, assuming that the High Line wasn't here, for residential development, all west of 10th Avenue. As the High Line became more of a certainty and a new administration came in, they took a different approach to the zoning, and that was under the leadership of Amanda Burden who understood the value of the High Line the moment that she saw it. What was really created by the Department of City Planning—it's a zoning plan that's gone on to win every top planner's award that exists basically—was an incredibly complex plan to allow the property rights under the High Line to be utilized in other areas. It's a very similar system to what got used to save Grand Central Terminal and also the historic theaters of Times Square. It also created all of these other provisions: setbacks to ensure light and air on the High Line, places where access would be built, provisions that would ensure creation of affordable housing, other provisions that would encourage the art galleries that had moved into manufacturing districts to remain.

As design and construction went forward, there was this urban planning base that was happening underneath it that was coming out of city hall, which was really extraordinary, and it's a really amazing piece of planning work viewed by many as one of the most nuanced and detailed pieces of zoning that's ever been done. A lot of what we see today is the result of the care and attention that went into that process.

GH — The success of the High Line has now changed the entire real estate picture of the West Side of the city. Did you foresee that? How do you see the way that's developed?

RH — One of the arguments we made for saving the High Line and doing this project was that it made good financial sense for the city. One of the reasons that I think the Bloomberg administration and the city council really got behind us was that we did an economic feasibility study in 2002 that showed this made financial sense, that it was going to increase the amount of property taxes the city would take in, because one of the arguments we made is proximity to small parks increases value. We also said it's going to create a neighborhood, a district that people are going to want to live in, work in, shop in, visit. I think that's happened beyond our wildest dreams. We're in the process of updating that economic study to show what the economic impact has been, but there's just been a lot of articles recently about how this neighborhood is recovering faster. One of the local restaurant owners said the recession ended for them when the High Line opened. There are less vacancies in apartments that can say they're in the High Line district.

The other thing that I think we're happy about is that it's inspired a lot of developers to use better designers and better architects. Actually, this spot we're standing in, looking here, you can see buildings by Frank Gehry, Shigeru Ban, Jean Nouvel, Annabelle Selldorf, Neil Denari. You go through four historic districts, so you're seeing all this old industrial architecture and then some of the best new architecture in New York.

GH — What do you think the impact of that continued development, even up the line, will be on the actual park?

RH — Before we opened, people said, "Don't you think the new development will ruin the High Line?" The High Line's a big steel structure.

It's a big industrial structure, and I think the design had that in mind, that it can hold its own next to new and old buildings. When you walk by buildings like the Caledonia—it's a big, new building—it can hold its own with it. What also makes it interesting is you're not in the middle of a wheat field in Kansas. You're in New York City, and that's part of what I think makes it exciting, is you're seeing all these new buildings.

The development that's going to happen up at Hudson Yards is going to dwarf anything that's down here. They're looking to put 12 million square feet of development, two downtown Seattles, squished into that small space with the High Line running around it. I have a feeling it's going to be able to hold its own.

GH — I was wondering, how close or different is the High Line now from '99 when you guys had the idea of it? When you look at it now and think about what you imagined then, what do you think about it?

JD — I never could've imagined this, never in my wildest dreams. We've been sitting up here talking to you, and I've seen my neighbors go by, people I see at the gym in the morning go by, people I know from just up here that I don't know why I know them go by, and all of these hundreds of people that I don't know. Just the amount of people who've walked past us in a half hour sitting here with you is just mind-blowing.

The thing that I'm always struck with, also, is just that you can get up here, that there are this many people up here. That was one of the main things we wanted to do. Even before the design and before all of these other complexities, the whole thing was, this is a great place from which to see the city, and nobody can get up here. They're not allowed up here. We used to have to jump through all these hoops to get up here. There were permissions and waivers and hard hats and special shoes and all of this stuff. Still, every time I come up a staircase, and all I have to do is walk up the stairs or even ride an elevator to come up here, it just blows me away that that's possible. I always hoped it would be possible but never really could totally imagine it.

RH — When I was first telling my mother about it on the phone, I was describing it and what we wanted to do, and she always supports crazy ideas, but she said, "What do you think the chance is of it happening?" I said, "Oh, like one in a hundred." She said, "You really think you should be spending your time on that kind of project?" For me, I'm a dreamer, but a pretty practical, realistic guy as well. For me, it was always worth it, just the process. Because working with these interesting people—it always attracted interesting people, smart, creative types, and so I was learning a lot and getting a lot out of it even if it didn't happen, but that it actually did happen.

A while ago, I developed my personal goals for the High Line: One, that it becomes well loved by New Yorkers. The fancy design didn't matter because it just needs to be well loved, because you can have fancy and great design; if people don't love it, it doesn't matter. And that it inspires other people to think that they can start these kinds of projects, and they don't need to have an idea how they're going to do it. They don't need to have all the money. They don't need to have any expertise in it. Josh is a travel writer. My background was in business and as a part-time artist. Neither one of us had any background in this.

What's exciting to see for me is that it's working. Not only is the High Line working as a great public space, but it's inspiring other people all over the country and all over the world. I mean, there's a lot of old elevated rail lines that people are now turning into parks, but what's more interesting is just the rethinking of old industrial sites. To me, this is the ultimate recycling project. The best way to do something good for the environment is not to just build a LEED Silver green building, but it's to reuse old buildings, to not have to tear them down, to rethink how you build open space, instead of trying to start over and build these rural oases, doing something that integrates the history and that industrial character into the project.

—

James Corner (JC)/ Field Operations

Gary Hustwit — When you think about the role of public space within cities and the lives of people in those cities, what do you think is important to talk about or to think about?

James Corner — To me, it seems so obvious. It's perhaps harder for others to figure it out. Cities are about people. The great cities that we all like to go to traditionally, like Rome, Paris, or London, these are great places that have great restaurants and great cafes and a vibrant street life. They're also about people. They're also about the kind of people you see and the kind of people you bump into and the kind of people you have chance encounters with. They're just very exciting, vibrant places to be and take part in the citizenry and the culture of the city.

I think a lot of American cities have been more about economics and engineering infrastructure, more about roads and parking and economic development. There's nothing wrong with that; cities have to function. But only recently have American cities begun to recognize that, if they really invest in the creation of amazing public spaces, the design of those public spaces can add real value to the city, value not only in terms of culture enrichment, social enrichment, social equity, but also environmental improvement, air quality, water quality, biodiversity. Also, economic development. Especially central parks and public spaces add real value to the economic development surrounding them. So all win-win, but it's surprising how only recently this has been understood. Perhaps in some cities that's still yet to become something that they understand.

GH — Did you ever notice the High Line before you started working on this project?

JC — Oh yeah. I'm also a professor in the School of Design, University of Pennsylvania, and very much a studio critic in the context of a design school. For many years throughout the eighties and nineties, the High Line was a subject for design schools. It was interesting to speculate, for many students, as to what the High Line could be. It was definitely on people's radars.

It obviously became much more highly visible with the formation of the Friends of the High Line, who overcame early efforts to demolish the entire High Line and open the space up for private development. The Friends of the High Line and all of the communication initiatives certainly raised the visibility and the importance of the project.

GH — And how did you get involved?

JC — Once Mayor Bloomberg made the commitment to funding the project and the city was organized and had made a commitment to develop this as a public-space project, they had a call for proposals from a number of companies around the world, and we were fortunate to be short-listed. We had to actually develop a design as part of a competition. We were one of five that were short-listed for that competition, and we were lucky to win.

GH — Could you talk about the design you did, or the inspiration for it?

JC — Well, I think when I first came up here and visited it, I was struck by how amazing it was already. Something I'm always very much aware of, especially because it's landscape architectural work, is that it's always site specific. You're always working with sites. A question I always ask is, "What will design actually mess up here? What, through design, will you anesthetize, will you destroy?" A lot of these, especially, postindustrial sites have a charm to them, an innate charm that, really, I'm always looking to try to capture and to actually amplify. Well, that was super intense with the High Line. The High Line was this extraordinary postindustrial artifact: rusting steel, a railbed landscape where grasses and flowers had taken seed naturally and were growing in a diverse and colorful and dynamic way. It's totally charming. Very striking by virtue of the fact that it runs for a mile and a half through urban fabric. It's just doing its own thing. It's a green ribbon.

At the very beginning, it was really, how do we make this a public place? We have to get people up here. We have to have stairs and elevators. How do we do that in a way that dramatizes a sense of arrival? How do we create pathways where people can safely meander and stroll? How do we bring back the sense of an amazing, natural, wild found landscape in a railbed context? It really had to do with the close reading of found conditions to amplify those and to create something quite poetic and quite special.

GH — Let's talk about the types of planting that you did. How did that echo the natural growth?

JC — I mean, what was very striking, again, with the original High Line as a found landscape was that it had a quality of consistency and yet variety. In other words, you could stroll along it, and you'd actually find very different settings, very varied settings as you strolled, but it would always be consistent, still be a railbed landscape.

We were very interested, in the beginning, in developing a paving system, a path system, that people could stroll along, that we could make them meander and actually slow their pace down. What's nice today is people really do stroll slowly. They're not bounding along. We wanted to create a path system that would also bring a sense of consistency but also a variety. You'll notice that some of the design details are these combed fingers of paving that go into the planting. It was really the idea of having the grasses and the flowers come up through the paving like they did in the original High Line. It's obviously an abstraction and an intensification of a certain phenomenon, but this idea of the paving just combing into and blending into and texturizing the landscape and this intermingling of organic life, finding its way through cracks and emerging out, was a big part of the design idea, the design intent.

A lot of the plants that you see are mostly grasses and perennials with a few shrubs and trees, but we're very restricted here with very shallow soil depth. It's quite windy, and it's exposed to the sun. It's a very dry and stressful environment for plants. A lot of the grasses and the flowers are drawn from the prairie—American prairie—landscape, which is also a very arid, windswept, high exposure to the sun. It's really drawn from a native prairie meadow that is very seasonally dynamic.

Another factor here is, how do you get visitors to come back again and again and again? One of the things about the planting palette, it's very different from week to week to week. It's not just different in winter and fall and spring and summer. It's really a weekly thing. Different things are coming into bloom. Different textures are being foregrounded. It's extraordinarily dynamic. A number of visitors are just repeat visitors A) to enjoy strolling with fellow citizens, but also B) because the plant life is so unusual. They always say that: "It's amazing how different it is every time we come."

GH — What were the biggest challenges? I always think it's interesting A) how long the project's taken and B) how much political drive it takes on the part of the people that are trying to develop the project or design it.
JC — Well, I would say that, compared to many other public-space projects in the US, the High Line has been enormously successful in terms of getting it done in a reasonable time. I think we started this in 2003. It was opened in 2009, or this first section was. Six years for public process, agency review and approvals, design development, bidding for construction, and then the actual construction is not bad. I think a lot of the success there is owed really to the mayor and to the various agencies. He literally said, "It has to be done by a certain time, and that's how it's going to be."

Having said that, there's lots of challenges on the way. Many challenges are technical. Technically, this is a very difficult structure to build public space on. There are safety issues, code issues, regulatory issues. It's a difficult ecosystem to get a landscape to grow in. We have very thin soil. It's very dry. There are drainage issues, irrigation issues, maintenance issues. There are issues of safety, security, how this is a secure public realm. All of these challenges are formidable. It's a testament to a design solution that I think is relatively simple, relatively easily adapted. As we find local conditions that pose a challenge, the design system actually is flexible and can adapt. I think that we made it through in a great way. Many other public-space projects in this country take much longer. Double, triple the time.

GH — Could you talk about the idea of reuse? This is a prime example of that, but it seems to be something that's occurring more and more. I think that's the case in other cities too.

JC — A big boom in my practice, but I would say in landscape architecture generally, is the rise of these postindustrial sites—old landfills, old airfields, and pieces of infrastructure like old railbeds—whether they're at grade or, in this case, elevated. These issues have come about only in the past 30 or 40 years in cities, and people don't know what to do with them. They also are perceived very badly. People are skeptical that they can ever be anything productive. They think that they're derelict. They're abandoned. They signify decline. They should be removed and erased and replaced with something perfect, pastoral, ideal.

I think what we found over the past ten years is that you can actually take these postindustrial conditions and, through creative design, produce something that people love and that celebrates the reappropriation or the reuse of these historical and these postindustrial conditions, that is a little bit of comingling of new with old. It's not one erasing the other, and it's not one overriding the other.

The inverse of what I'm describing is, perhaps, a strident preservation movement where certain historical infrastructures, historical situations, should be preserved. Well, that's not our philosophy either. It's not erasure, and it's not preservation. It's really transformation, where the old is made into something new. There's clear evidence of those postindustrial conditions, but they're now something totally new. They're on a new lifeline.

GH — Yeah, I love how in section two there's still graffiti on the buildings. You still feel like you're in New York and not somewhere else. It's like what you're saying: comingling of old and new, past and future.

JC — Yeah. I think another point you are bringing up about public space generally is, again, for a period a time, there was a trend in American cities in particular to make public spaces all the same, just standardize them, to make parks look like every other park, to make plazas and streets and public spaces like every other public space under an idea that that's what people are familiar with and, therefore, what they're comfortable with. Well, I think, interestingly and excitingly and correctly, in the past decade, the trend has shifted now to producing, creating very unique public spaces that actually in some way foreground and celebrate and bring forward the innate characteristics of their location, of their city.

Another thing that's successful about the High Line is it only really works in New York in this context. The views, and the vistas, and the panoramas, the perspectives you have at the 10th Avenue Square looking at the yellow taxicabs, the elevated perspectives into certain neighborhood streets in Chelsea—the High Line is totally connected to its context in a way that adds to its uniqueness.

GH — Can you talk a little bit about sections two and three of the High Line? It's just mind-blowingly beautiful out there, looking out at the water. It's amazing. It's still open now with the train yard, but in the future, who knows what the space will become?

JC — Right. Well, the High Line is a mile and a half long, equivalent to roughly 30 blocks. This first section is the first 10 blocks, section two is the next 10 blocks, and section three is the piece that wraps around the rail yards.

Section one has interesting anomalies. There's not a dead-straight line. It twists and turns. It goes underneath some buildings, through various tunnels. It has a number of spurs and offshoots. It's quite wide in certain sections. Section one has a lot of variation as you're walking along it. It's quite episodic. You go from episode to episode to episode because it twists and turns a little bit. You do really have interesting vistas and panoramas across the city. I think we've created a series of really dramatic or theatrical settings for public life. The sundeck at 14th Street with the big chaise longues is more popular than any of us ever thought it would be. It's popular with individuals, with couples, with groups, with families, with young people, old people. It's enormously successful, but it follows from a simple formula of, look, it's southwest facing and people like to sit in the sun; it's a great view. If we can simply provide the furniture that theatricalizes that moment, people will come. The 10th Avenue Square is the sunken amphitheater. It theatricalizes the frame, looking along 10th Avenue. So section one has these interesting twists and turns and this interesting sequence of places.

Section two is a little different. There's 10 blocks where it's absolutely dead straight. There are no twists and turns. There are no tunnels. There are no spurs. There's not much variation. It's also quite narrow, typically ranging from 35 to maybe 50 feet. Section two, I think, will have a much more melancholic feel, less theatrical in some ways than section one, but maybe more powerful in terms of strolling along the line for 10 blocks that slice through the city. I think it will feel a lot more intimate because the spaces are more intimate. The adjacent buildings are more tactile, more intimate.

We do, again, have a sequence of episodic chapters, if you like. The first part is a garden we call the thicket. It's really designed as just a transition from this section into that section. We then have a large sun-lawn area that is on one of the wider areas and opens the space up for people to just put a towel or a picnic cloth down on the lawn and just hang out. We have a very dramatic feature called the flyover, which is actually just an elevated catwalk eight feet above the High Line that will walk you through the canopy of a stand of magnolia trees that we're putting in there. That should be a little abstract, a little quirky, a little strange and will certainly be dramatic by virtue of the elevation above the High Line. Then we get to the bend at 30th Street where there's a big cutout and the structure, the raw structure, of the High Line is revealed. I think it will be dramatic, episodic, and sequential like section one, but I think it will also feel much more intimate, much more tactile, have a different sense of scale.

Section three, as you know, has another character altogether, partly because it runs east-west toward the river. When you get to the river, you have an amazing sense of the river and river space. The sun sets to the west. I think the challenge there is how to retain a sense of that big urban Hudson River Valley scale and, at the same time, make it more palatable to people to stroll, and hangout, and find places to sit.

GH — If you're looking out to the west on section three and the sun is setting, wow. It's one of the most unique and powerful things I've done in the 10 years that I've lived in New York City.
    JC — The quality of light there is very powerful.

GH — Are there things that you learned from section one and the use of it that you can apply or are applying to section two and section three?
    JC — I think we underestimated how much people really do want to sit and linger. I think in section one we always thought it would be a place for strolling, and we would accommodate sitting at certain key locations where we thought there were particular views or sunny spots where it would be nice to sit. I think what we've found is that the demand for sitting and lingering is much greater than we thought. People want to come up here and stroll, but they also want to hang out. Some of the more successful public spaces where people are really there en masse are areas where we provided dramatic, overscaled furnishing and we've made a sort of a stage setting for people to hang out. I think, in sections two and three, that remains a challenge: to maintain these pathways and gardens for strolling, these overlooks for viewing, but also to accommodate the desire to sit and to sit theatrically—not simply a provision for seating, but to actually catalyze socialization through how we furnish the place.

GH — Have people been using the High Line in any interesting ways that you had not anticipated?
    JC — Oh yes. It's funny, because when we were doing renderings in the early design phase, we would put in a lot of hipsters doing sometimes questionable things. We were told by the client group to normalize people in the views, so the people are relatively benign and behaving in a relatively benign way. Sure enough, we designed and opened the High Line, and some extraordinary things have come about.

Firstly, the sheer variety of people: You get old people, young people, wheelchairs. You get people strolling, sitting, jogging. You get individuals. You get couples. You get families. You get groups. There are lots of locals in terms of people here from the neighborhood, but there's a lot of people from afar as well as from abroad. It's now very popular with tourists. It's on the tourists' itinerary. The sheer diversity, range, and variety of people is unbelievable. I think it adds to its success. When you think about it, if you've got a couple of hours to kill in a city and you want to embrace public life in that city, a huge draw is going to be being with lots of different types of people. It's what makes it cosmopolitan. It's what makes it urban. It connects you to the world in a strange way. There's that. I would say there's simple diversity and variety.

Secondly, there's a lot of "illicit uses." There are people who bring bottles of champagne and strawberries and have a picnic. Now, that's not allowed. There are people who strip down to their bikinis or their swim trunks and sunbathe. There's a lady further down who stands on her balcony, her fire balcony, adjacent to the High Line and does opera performances free of charge.

Life is larger than you ever think it is. I think part of the success of the High Line is just the sheer freedom of expression and the wide variety and scope of how people appropriate spaces, some in ways we partially anticipated, some in ways we could never have imagined, but it's all wonderful. That's part of the draw. The draw is just being in a public space and seeing other people. People watching or just being with other people is what cities are all about. I know we've had this sub-urban-sprawl phenomenon for probably close to a hundred years now, but it's beginning to reverse. Parents, baby boomer–generation parents, their kids have left home, and they're now looking to return to the city so that they can take part in public life. They can have the restaurants and cafes, and the theater, and the museums. They can also simply stroll the streets. They can enjoy the sounds and the life of being with others in a collective environment. I think this is extraordinary. It's been the way of life for many cities in Europe, and it has not been the way of life for many American cities. Fortunately, that is changing. American cities are rein-vesting and looking for the magic ingredients and the magic dust that brings more people into their cities, attracts businesses and residents for economic reasons, but also enhances the cultural life of the place.

GH — Great. Are there other public spaces in New York City that are inspiring? Or globally are there other public places that inspire you? Or just natural sites? It doesn't have to be just man-made sites.

JC — Interestingly, for me, some of the more vibrant public spaces that I've encountered around the world are often not designed, or if they are designed, they're designed in an almost empty way. You think of Piazza San Marco in Venice or some of the Italian or Spanish historical squares and plazas. These are really just residual voids in the fabric of the city. They're not overly designed for sure, and I think that emptiness encourages a certain amount of appropriation and use by people. That's one type of thing that I think we can learn from. The other is the sort of undesigned environment where people just appropriate the space in unusual and imaginative ways. We've seen examples of seawalls or pier walls where people are doing climbing, or scuba diving in little bays, or kayaking out on little water bodies.

I do believe that design can often kill a place. I think when design is focused on what it looks like, on a certain look, that doesn't necessarily mean it's going to be a great public place. Design is really about cho-reographing how people interact and finding the ingredients to really encourage, instigate, activate interaction and participation. In a sense, you're much more like a movie director or a stage-set designer. You're trying to create settings for people. It's a little different from understanding design as just looking good.

—

Ric Scofidio (RS)/ Diller Scofidio + Renfro

Gary Hustwit — You've lived here for a long time. Did you know about the High Line before this whole project started?

Ric Scofidio — The High Line, it's interesting, because when you teach architecture—after I graduated, I went to Italy, came back, and then I started teaching at Cooper Union—one of the things that you do when you're in the design studio is you're always looking for both projects to give the students and sites that you can do these projects on. When you start looking at urban sites in Manhattan, there aren't that many. So you're either tearing something down or saying, "Look at the sites as though they're empty." Of course, the High Line was there. It was this empty strip in Manhattan. Steven Holl actually started using it for projects for his students, and he did a number of projects of housing and things on the High Line. So the High Line was pretty well known in academic circles as a site you could do projects on with students. We were aware of it, but we never thought about it more. Actually, I'd say we never thought about it outside the classroom.

GH — It's interesting because I've lived here 10 years. If I came here to go to a gallery back then, I'd notice there was a billboard on it or something like that. I never really thought about it at the time. I guess most New Yorkers, maybe they'd seen it, but they probably hadn't really thought about it or thought about a future for it.

RS — Yeah. Even when we gave it as a site, we always assumed it was almost a tabula rasa. It was an elevated rail; it was a certain width. We didn't even accept that there were rails or anything up there. It was just a strip of land that you could do something with. In fact, it was a big surprise, when Joel Sternfeld published his photographs, that all that was up there. I'd never snuck up onto the High Line before then.

GH — When was the first time you got up there?

RS — The first time I got up there was when Friends of the High Line had a competition. It reached the point of where, actually, if you did go up during daytime hours, you'd probably have the police there pretty fast because of the whole security consciousness that happened in the city. Even going up there with permission, because of the FBI and its relationship to the High Line and Homeland Security, you would immediately have police checking you out to find out why you were up there and what you were doing up there.

GH — What's the FBI's relationship to the High Line?

    RS — They have headquarters right across from Chelsea Market.

GH — Really? I didn't know that.

    RS — Yes. They'll probably come and arrest me if you put this on film. I'm revealing their headquarters, right? [Laughs.]

GH — When you started the project, what were the things that inspired you and contributed to the design?

    RS — A number of things contributed to the way we thought about the High Line. Probably one of the prime ones was Joel Sternfeld's photographs of this postindustrial, melancholic landscape that had occurred up there. When Friends of the High Line decided they wanted to turn it into a park, you realized that it would be destroyed by bringing people up there. How would you bring people up there and still maintain that atmosphere that everybody fell in love with? We had looked at Promenade plantée, which was one of the first elevated train rails that had been converted into a park in Paris. It was very formal and had a straight path with very formal gardens along it. It could've been on the ground. It could've been in a park. There was nothing special about it. The nicest thing about it was what they did under the arches, those brick arches, allowing artisans to move in and open shops there. But that was the big question for us.

New York City is a city of many city-states. If you live in the East Village, you dress a certain way; you talk a certain way; you are a certain kind of person. If you live in the West Village, it's another group that inhabits that. Then when you go to cultural performances, operas or concerts, then everybody knows everybody, and everybody dresses a certain way. There are times it's been wonderful, and I've gone to an event, and I look around, and I don't know those people. It's interesting. I don't know those people. What I'm saying, in a way, is they're dressed differently; they talk differently. This idea that public space is always democratic is not always true. Public space caters to certain types that will use it more than others. Lincoln Center is a cultural institution, and for years it was a walled fortress. They didn't want people that lived in the housing projects to enter Lincoln Center. There was always this kind of segregation, this degree of undemocratic but interesting space in the city.

So there were a number of things twirling in our brains as we thought about the High Line. The other thing that's interesting is, looking again at Sternfeld's photographs, initially you could say, "Ah yes, the jungle is going to take over the city. The plants are going to come in, and in no time the city will be gone. The High Line will be gone. It will just be a green, eroding mass." I don't think that's at all true. I think there's a new paradigm that existed in those photographs that Joel Sternfeld took. It's much more about a symbiotic relationship between nature and civilization. You see that in an interesting way. It hasn't really fulfilled itself yet, but you've got peregrine falcons living on the top of office towers and churches in the city. Recently there was a coyote that running around and captured in Tribeca. The curious thing is it's not an isolated case because in the Bronx there are huge families of coyotes that are living there. The city is a messy place. There are lots of places for nature to move in and not take over but form a relationship with the urban infrastructure in a really interesting way.

So we were looking at the High Line and thinking about, how do you marry this soft-scape with the infrastructure, with this postindustrial artifact? How do you bring people up there and not destroy it? We came up with this idea of digitizing the paving. By the way, this is a competition that we did with Jim Corner of Field Operations, and we worked together on this. The whole idea was, with this planking then, it wasn't a paved area, a hard-scape and planking beds, but it was, as we say, digitized. It was a series of elements that could be dropped down, and they could feather out. You could have 100 percent hard-scape or 100 percent green. It kept a relationship between both the greenery and the hard-scape, between the greenery and the rails, between nature and civilization. It was that kind of blend, and I think that's what we were striving for and trying to create. That's what has been really successful up there. In a curious way, I think that's what people relate to when they go there. They don't feel that either the hard-scape is taking over or the plants are taking over. They realize there is this new way of thinking about nature and infrastructure and the city and public space.

One thing I want to add is, I think that the High Line is very much about the city, that if you took it out of the city, took it out of its location, it wouldn't be as successful. I could say it more intelligently, but I really enjoy saying that people living in the city are like mice. If you've ever lived in a space where you have a mouse, the mouse comes out and always runs along the baseboard. Mice do not run into the center of the room. Maybe when you're not there they do, but they run along the baseboard. They always run along edges. We come out of buildings, and we run along the baseboard. We never get into the center of the room. What's so beautiful about the High Line is, when you're up there, you can stand in the center of an intersection of two streets and not get run over and look at the city and the space of the city in a way that you can't do when you're down at street level.

Also, you locate yourself physically. You know where you are as a presence within the city, which is really unique. Generally, if I come out of a building or if I come out of the subway, I invoke a map in my brain, and I go, "Oh yeah, that's north, that's south, and this is that." I have this map that tells me where I am, and I can move around. When you're on the High Line, it's a little bit like being in a public piazza or plaza. You can look around, you see the important landmarks, and you know your relationship to them. There's something very strong about that. The fact that, equally, you're a voyeur to the city, as well as being a member of the city, I think is quite good.

GH — How did you think people would use this space when you were working on the design?
RS — I must say that I'm completely overwhelmed by the public reaction to it, the strength of the public reaction. I think, on projects, you bury yourself in them. You don't look up that often. But you are in fact

choreographing space. You're choreographing the way people move, and there are ways that are very clear so you know exactly that's what's going to happen and how people will use it. Then of course, you know there are unexpected consequences that will happen, but you're not quite clear on what they will be. You spend a lot of time thinking about what might happen. For example, we made the sunken overlook and cut it down and said, "Okay, we're going to look at traffic going up 10th Avenue." My fantasy is it's pretty much like looking into a fireplace. It's like staring out a window. Either you're sitting there talking to somebody and it's background, or you're sitting there by yourself watching the cars go up. The thing that happens when you're sitting at the fireplace or looking out the window is you start to daydream a little bit. Your brain goes someplace else. You're on the High Line, but you're also mentally in another location, another space. There are things I expect to happen. Whether they do or not, I believe they do.

The High Line, for me, has been a source of a number of unexpected consequences, such as the Standard hotel and the voyeurism that occurred at the Standard with people standing up at the windows and flashing to the public down on the High Line. The fact that the day it opened you had married couples in their wedding dresses and tuxes running up to take their photograph on the High Line. The branding that's happened now, between the desire to tear it down—Giuliani said, "Tear it down," signed papers to have it torn down; every real estate agent and developer wanted it gone—and now when you have this High Line symbol that's on tote bags. I think it was in Sex in the City 2. It's like everybody is cashing in on the High Line. I guess they say, "Success has many mothers." I guess that's the quote. I didn't expect it to have quite as many ramifications as it did in that respect.

The fact that New Yorkers would literally go someplace with the intention not to do anything. Whenever you went anyplace in the city, you'd say, "I'm going to the movies. I'm going to a concert. I'm going here. I'm going there." There's always a reason for it. When you go to the High Line, you're just going to the High Line. For New Yorkers to go someplace without an intention of what they're going to do, I think, for me is a major transformation of public attitude in the city.

GH — Have you learned things from the High Line project that are maybe now being applied in other projects, or are there things that have been carrying on from what we were just talking about?

RS — Our practice has always been involved in thinking about public space, how public space is used, even when we did the Brasserie restaurant, the whole idea of the public entering, being on display so people can meet each other. In a way, it goes back to even when we started thinking about glass and architecture and the whole issue of voyeurism and the whole issue of surveillance and what has changed over the years in relation to that, going from, "I don't want to be on camera; Big Brother's watching me," to now, "Nobody's watching me, that's the problem. I want to be on camera. I want to be seen." There are a lot of things we've always been thinking about. I think the High Line was really a great source of being able to implement some of those ideas and really verify, in fact, that they are substantial and have meaning in public space.

GH — Do you see the attitude toward public space changing over the last several decades? I think it's interesting to look at from the public's perspective. How have the attitudes changed? Or what are the attitudes?

RS — It's interesting. In New York with Mayor Bloomberg, we have a lot of support for what's happening in the city, although the money has always come from developers and private sources. The High Line—in fact, there were a lot of individual, private donations that made that happen. I accept that the controlling influence is going to be more the developer, the investor, than the city. The city will support it, but the idea that this can be accomplished will come from other sources.

I think attitudes have changed. I do think it goes back to the fact that we have a lot of what I'll call city-states, areas in the cities where individuals congregate, and that's their home territory. Curiously, I think the Internet also supports that because websites are very particular, and they bring in a certain audience to that site. Certain people watch Fox News. Certain people watch Keith Olbermann and Rachel Maddow, and they won't watch Fox News. There's already this parceling and morselating of public space and activities. The question is, how do you break that down?

GH — Another thing about the High Line is the success of it: it's really interesting to see the real estate, how much building there is now along the entire corridor.

RS — Yes, from that desire to tear the High Line down, to creating real estate value, to branding. It's become the golden mile and a half now for development. I think we'd see much more happening if it wasn't for the recession right now.

One of the things that, in fact, we've had to be very careful about is of course every developer would love to have his building open on the High Line. Every time you allow access to the High Line, you have to have paving, more hard-scape, for people to enter, which begins to cut down on the green. I think right now we're probably about 50 percent green and 50 percent hard-scape. It's really important that we don't give adjacent buildings entrances onto the High Line. It can happen in a few locations if the developer provides a public entrance to the High Line, so there's an elevator and stair and the general public can enter the High Line. Then he can get a door onto the High Line. You're already making an area for the public to enter, so you're not changing the amount of paving or coverage for a particular developer. It's for the general good of everybody.

GH — This is a case where, like you said, the Bloomberg administration got involved. Something that keeps coming up is negotiating the politics of a city. There's going to be a new mayor maybe every four years, but some of these projects could take a decade or longer. It seems like a challenge for a lot of architects, developers, anybody trying to do a large-scale project. Things move so slowly sometimes, and there are so many players involved, it's almost more political work than actual design work. What are your thoughts on that?

        RS — I think the critical criteria is the success of the project. Much to Mayor Bloomberg's credit, the High Line has been a big success. When we open the second section, which will be in the spring, again, there will be, I'm sure, more interest and publicity about what's happening there. I think if another mayor comes in and there's still the third section to be done, he's going to look at the value of it to the previous mayor and absolutely be on board and in support of it.

GH — I'm sure you've spent time on the third section?

        RS — Yeah. The city actually is, I think, purchasing the third section so that it will not be torn down. The Friends of High Line would like to be able to open it in at least some temporary way to the public so they get a sense of things to come.

GH — Yeah, that's amazing. I'm sure the first two sections were much different than the third section. There's such variety, it seems like each section had a certain character, and different plants, and a different eco-system or something.

        RS — I know. It's been quite amazing, the plants. Certain plants grew where there was always shade. Certain plants grew where there was sun. In a way, we've taken advantage of that in our design also. We have a sun deck where there's a view of the Hudson, and it's always open to sun. Plants that were growing where it's shady will be the same plants that will be put back. We've increased the species.

        Parks take time. It's pretty amazing. When you open a park, it's probably at least five years minimum before it starts to become what it was designed to be. Everything had to be removed in order to check the structure to make sure it was sound, repair the concrete slab. Everything was brought back. Meanwhile, the birds said, "Okay, this is not a place for us," and they disappeared. This year we expect the birds will be coming back. The butterflies came back last year. The birds will be back this year. Other plants will grow in. The biodiversity will continue to increase. In five years, it'll be visually totally different from what you see there now. It should be an extremely rich and beautiful place, both in terms of plants and the city, which is changing around it.

        An interesting thing about the High Line is that once it crosses 10th Avenue and starts north, it's a very narrow line. The dimension changes from maybe, I'd say, 18th Street down: it's fairly wide; it goes through buildings; it's a totally different experience. It was difficult for us to think, as you move north and you move into a more constrictive zone, how to both make that interesting and hold on to the spirit of what we established in the framework in phase one of planting and paving. We have a few events that will happen along there. There will be a flyover where you'll actually go up on steel-grating decking. You'll be about eight feet above the High Line. You'll be able to look down on the High Line and see the planting from rail to rail. It will be a green zone, and it will be pretty much like what it was before anybody came up and touched it and changed it. There will be a few things like that.

It's interesting that when you're down on the street, and you think about what the High Line was before, and you walk along, and you look up, there's just a fairly dense, black lump of steel. You can understand why, for most New Yorkers, that was the High Line for them. That's all they thought of, this lump of steel that nobody uses, that's there, has no value, and it puts another shadow down on the street. Why not take it down? Why not remove it? I think, by the way, that's one of the things that's very important about the overlook. That's the one place that, when you're down in the city, you can look up and see people on the High Line, see plants, and be aware that something of interest is up there. It's very important.

GH — You spoke earlier about how this could only exist in New York and also have the relationship between the buildings and the weaving around of plant life. Could you talk about that more?

RS — I mean, at one point, the Hudson River was in where the High Line is. It was an industrial port area, ships coming and going. Then slowly, as warehouses built up and industry evolved, landfill came in, and eventually we know there was a freight train running on 10th Avenue, New Yorkers getting run over by the freight train. They finally, in 1929, decided to elevate the train, bring it up, and put it on the High Line. Because of that, the High Line was servicing a lot of light industry. The buildings adjacent to it were not residential in nature. They were office buildings, light industry, and meat-packing industry. That's changing now. Because of the success of High Line, you're going to see more residential occurring there. It allows activity to occur that can blend with the city and be part of the city on the High Line.

I think what's important here is the fact that we've taken this industrial artifact that should be torn down and said, "You can reprogram it and get something new out of it." I think a lot of preservation occurs by simply trying to hold on to something and not reprogramming or thinking about the fact that reprogramming can produce new results. Preservation, I think, is as much an act of design as building something new. That is, for me, probably the lesson that is of interest to a lot of areas pretty much around the world. For example, we had the Danish contingent here. They were interested in the High Line. I've heard that people come in and fly into JFK and grab a taxi, take the taxi to the High Line, walk the High Line, get back in the taxi, go back to the airport, and fly home. They've heard about it. They want to see it. They want to think about it, in some ways kick-starting something else. I think only time will tell us how that will change the urban infrastructure and public space.

GH — When you walk on section one, now that it's completed, how do you feel?

RS — Walking on something that you're responsible for is always a mixed blessing. The first thing I feel is a little bit of sadness that I could never experience it the way somebody who doesn't know what it is and has walked up there for the first time does. I love when I see something I've never seen before. I go to see somebody else's building; I go, "Wow." There's that wonderful surprise. That's an experience that's denied any creator, whether it's a book writer or a filmmaker. They're too much embedded into it. Then the second thing, of course, is that you're looking at things that you wish had been done a little bit more carefully by the contractor. Those are things nobody else will see other than me or people who have been involved in the project.

Then finally that goes out of my mind, and I just look at it, and I probably look more at the people and how the people are using it, their activity, and their mood, and what they're talking about. I become a little bit of a voyeur and eavesdropper. That gives me a great deal of pleasure.
—

Jan Gehl
(JG)/
September 28, 2010
Copenhagen

For over 50 years, Danish architect and urbanist andm Jan Gehl has been an influential voice for creating cities on a human scale. A proponent of pedestrianism and bicycling, his book *Cities for People* was an influence on our team during our research for the film.

Gary Hustwit — How did you get involved in architecture and urbanism? Did you go to school for this? Were you interested in cities when you were a child? What was the impetus?

Jan Gehl — That's one of my favorite stories. This year, 2010, I have been a full-time architect for 50 years, meaning that I graduated in 1960. In architecture school at that time, we were taught about the glorious new idea of the modernists that, in cities, you should always separate housing, workplaces, recreation, and communication. Streets were bad; squares were bad. What you should make were freestanding buildings surrounded by trees and lawns, and preferably high buildings, because then you could have more people and more grass. That was my training, and I left architecture school as a young architect really looking forward to working with the city as a machine, as the modernists had instructed us to do.

Then a few months later, I married a psychologist, and then suddenly there were new tunes being played, and the story goes more or less like this: My wife and all her friends, they always asked us young architects, "Why are you architects not interested in people?" We would say, "We are very interested, for God's sake, in people. That's what it's all about. Aesthetics, spatial sequences, the texture of materials, the volume, the design of the facade, all this is really something which people are urging for." And they said, "You know very little about people."

That was the start of many years of very valuable collaboration with my wife. We actually got a big grant from Carlsberg Beer to go to Italy and sit and drink Chianti and look at what the spaces between the buildings were being used for. Because I had this inkling that the real difference between the old stuff and the new stuff was that with the new stuff, the suburbs, there was no life between the buildings. They were empty. While in the older parts of the built-up areas, there was always life and people doing whatever. I thought, maybe I'll go to Italy and see what a piazza is used for. We found that there is endless literature about piazzas, but it's all about what style they're made in: this is a rococo piazza; this is a Renaissance one; this is a baroque piazza. There was hardly anything about what piazzas were used for.

We did this very basic study about what the Italians use their piazzas for and found a fantastic number of regularities and behavioral issues: how people use the spaces, where they are placed. Based on this, I wrote an article in an architectural magazine in Denmark just called "People in Cities," about how people used cities in Italy, and then I was invited to a university to elaborate this study into a PhD, which I did by studying public spaces in Copenhagen, and found, much to my surprise, that the behavior of the people here in the northern part of Europe was exactly the same as it was in Italy. The Italians have more hours to do it because the weather is better, but the basic pattern was the same.

Later on—but this is another story—I had the opportunity to meet up with William H. Whyte in New York. I met him in 1976, and he had been doing a lot of studies about how people behave in New York. When I met him, he said, "I'll show you something because it's fabulously interesting: how the New Yorkers use public space." And he showed me all this stuff about what they were doing, and I said, "Oh, by the way, I saw the same things in Italy and in Denmark. Maybe we are onto something global."

The more I've studied, the more I've realized that we are really talking about the urban habitat of *Homo sapiens*, and there are not that many differences. It's the same *Homo sapiens* all over the world. Cultural circumstances differ, economic circumstances differ, and also climatic circumstances differ. But basically we are the same little walking animal with the same senses and the same way of moving, and there are so many things which are the same that we can really talk about some patterns that are universal.

I do think 1960 was about the time when the knowledge of how people use cities, the knowledge about the size of man and how far we could walk and see and whatever, all that knowledge was left behind, because then cities had to be expanded in a great haste. We were able to industrialize the building. We mass-produced single-family housing. Instead of just adding to the existing cities, now suddenly planning became a big profession, and the architects were more and more concerned about the freestanding building. Actually, the idea of the freestanding building was a godsend for many architects, because then they didn't have to look to the right and the left. They could just do their funny things. We also got a new profession—the traffic planners. They started to be really active around that time when the car invasion took place.

So we had a number of professions now, looking after all the new buildings—planners, architects trained as modernists, and traffic planners. None of them had been instructed in how to look after the people in the cities. The traffic planners were asked to make the cars happy, and they became very good at that. But nobody in this process was asked to look after the people and make them happy, and that has been overlooked and forgotten for a long, long time.

When I look at my work, it is very much about trying to take an interest in the life part of architecture, or the interface between life and form, or the borderland between architecture and psychology and sociology. There is a very excellent quote from a British architecture critic, Ken Worpole. He said, "It's bad luck for you architects that your means of communication has always been the still photo and the two-dimensional drawing. That focuses all the attention on the form. You guys, you continue to communicate form to each other. You give each other medals for the form. Form, form, form. But good architecture is not about form only. It is about form and life and the interaction between form and life. Only if this interaction works is it good architecture." Then the problem with the architects, and also planners of course, is that it's so easy to start this, to make this, to design this, and it's so complicated to find out what this is and how the built form influences this.

You can build a new town where you can be absolutely sure that nobody will ever sit on a bench out there of their own free choice. You can build another one where you can be absolutely sure that they would hardly waste their time by sitting at home because the city would be so lovely that they would like to spend a lot of time out in it. All this we had to find out through many decades of studies, but in the sixties it was just a big jump from small-scale projects and additions to the city to big-scale planning and big-scale projects and big-scale freeways and whatever. It was all mechanized and all at this enormous scale. The concern for people was overlooked. It was taken for granted that people would continue to enjoy being in these places, but then it was found out the hard way they that were not enjoying it. Now the wind is really blowing from a different direction.

GH — Interesting. It's almost like maybe they concentrated on what they could control, and what they couldn't control had to sort of conform to what their designs were. Was it a control thing? You can't control life, and they maybe didn't even try or didn't even think about what the life was.

JG — I wouldn't say that at all. I would just say that there have always been a lot of assumptions about how people would use these places. There's also been a number of moral ideas—this is how you ought to use it. If we make a big grass lawn, you ought to come out and sit on the lawn, for God's sake. There were a number of other assumptions: that this would be within walking distance because it was five hundred meters away from there. But whether something is acceptable for a walking tour is not a matter of meters. It's very much a matter of quality. You can easily walk a full kilometer if what you're walking by is very interesting. If you have to walk two hundred meters, and it's absolutely boring, that's very tiresome.

There's always this quality issue involved also, and what we have found out about people's use of spaces is that it is incredibly predictable. It is very logical. Much of it is related to the body, our senses, how far you can see and how far you can hear, how your eye is always on the horizontal. You see very little upward. You see much more downward, and you see much, much more out to either side. That is a leftover from the evolutionary process, when the walking animals were walking on the plains. The enemies were out there and in front of you, but they were not up there, but you should look out for snakes and scorpions and boulders where you are trampling. All this is part of something which we have, all of us have, together in common.

I would say that man is a linear animal. That means an animal moving linearly. We have feet, and with those feet we can walk along a path, and actually the path is a movement space, and the path is one of the two elementary building blocks throughout city planning history. We have two of them: the street, which is the linear moving space, and we have the square, which is what the eye can command, and the eye can't command more than about an area of 80 meters by 80 meters or 100 meters by 100 meters. That is the distance where you can see other people and movement. That means everything inside a hundred meters you can command and see what's going on and have an idea about. But if it gets bigger, it gets hard to see.

You can find this hundred meters, very interestingly of course, in all spectator sports. All the stadiums are built up in this way so that everyone would have, maximum, one hundred meters from where they're sitting to the middle of the field. If it was bigger, you could not see if it was the green or the red team who was running, and you could not see the ball at all, so it wouldn't make sense. And that is why all stadiums actually can hold about one hundred thousand people, because you can't make stadiums bigger, or people couldn't see.

All these things are very logical, and they are bound in the body of mankind. If we look at all the squares in all the old cities, they will, nearly all of them, be smaller than this 80 or 100 meters. That means that, by standing in a corner, you can see everything. You can see the market. You can see the procession. That is what we can accommodate.

The other thing is that people waiting in public spaces will always be standing up against the wall. We talk about wallflowers in the dance hall, and it is the same thing. Out by the wall, you can see everything, and everybody can see you. That means you have full command of the space, and your back is protected. It's not very nice to be standing in the middle of a space and suddenly somebody comes and claps your back and says, "Hey ho!" Then you feel less comfortable. Standing in the corner, preferably in a niche, is very comfortable, and that can be found all over the world. That's because of the way our senses are organized.

So knowing about *Homo sapiens* and the kind of creature he is has, to me, been a very important key to understanding why some places work and some places don't. In all the old cities, like Venice, or the

Greek Island cities, or many little villages, or places that have not been invaded by automobiles and where everything has not been blown up in scale, you can see this—I call it the 5-kilometer-an-hour people scale—at work. You'll always feel very comfortable in those places. It's when we have this fast, 60-kilometer-an-hour scale and people are pushed out to walk in that place that we feel it's very boring and it's very cold and impersonal. Because it's not at all made for people. It's made for vehicles going 60 kilometers an hour. It's no wonder that we don't feel comfortable there.

All this about scale is something that the planning profession, the architecture profession, has been extraordinarily confused about over the last several decades as we were able to build bigger and bigger and higher and higher and move at faster speeds on the streets and have more and more vehicles. So everything was blown up, and we forgot that man still has the same size and the same senses that he has had for millions of years. That's why so many people feel not only slightly but grossly uncomfortable in many of the so-called modern surroundings; modern environments; modern, new towns; high-rise downtown areas with a lot of towers and big spaces.

GH — I think it's interesting because people feel uncomfortable, and they know that they're uncomfortable, but a lot of times people don't understand why they're uncomfortable. Even as a normal citizen, if you understand the reasons behind the design or why the design is affecting you, then you're more critical.

JG — I do think that the reason why there has been quite a big interest in my research and my books is because of this idea of the point of departure: the departure point is your body, the *Homo sapiens*, and the development story. If we go back to the time before around 1960—because that was when it exploded and we started really to move from an old society with a slow speed to a big society where the cities were expanding with enormous speed—throughout all the centuries before that time, there was a lot of life in the public spaces. People were promenading; they were talking; they were carrying stuff; they were using the public space for a lot of things. And a number of basic demands for good public space for people were built in because of experience and because of tradition.

It was not something that you talked about. It just had to be that way because that was how it was organized. It was when we started to professionalize the planning, the architecture, the traffic engineering, as big, strong professions that all these traditions and experiences were not carried over and professionalized. They were never taught in schools of architecture or schools of planning, all these things about people and senses and *Homo sapiens* and how we talk to each other. When we are very close, we talk about important issues. If someone starts to cry, if my little grandson starts to cry, I would go right up and grab him and pat his hand and say, "Oh no, you'll be all right. Let me blow on the wound, and you will be all right." Now, we have all these distances between us.

One of the things we've done in these studies is go out and sit for years and years on streets and squares and just see what was unfolding and try to put it down in a systematic way. Then, very quickly, there's a fantastic order to what is happening. It's very logical. It's also very rhythmic. Every day is like the day before, is like the day after. Unless there is a festival or a heavy rainstorm or something. It just goes on and on, and that means that, in a city like this one, Copenhagen, we know pretty well what will be happening. Today it's a September day, and the weather is fine, and I know pretty well how many activities you will find in most of the downtown spaces, because it was like that last year, and the year before, and last week. All this, that it is very unpredictable, and people go in all directions, and it's completely mumble jumble, and everybody makes their own decisions—fine, they do. But the whole sum of it is a very foreseeable pattern.

All these studies had to be done so we are now able, in a big way, to introduce the notion that, just as we have landscape architects and furniture architects and lighting architects, it is my very firm belief that we certainly need some people architects. Even better, we could educate the people who make the decisions about how to care for people in their designs. That's a grand task, but it's very, very interesting that that education is not forthcoming in hardly any of the schools for architects, planners, and traffic engineers. They have to look after other things, and nobody looks after people.

GH — This sounds like the "Brasília Syndrome" that you talked about in your book. Could you talk about Brasília?

JG — Around 1960, city planning really took off. That was a time when industrialism really started to demand a lot of workers to come into the cities, and that was when we started to see the big expansion of cities, all the creation of new cities, and the demand for new cities. We have seen new cities in a number of places. Most of the cities in Western Europe made new suburban towns like the ring around London. But there are a few cities that were made completely from scratch at that point, one of them being Brasília.

Brasília was especially famous, because that was the ultimate, the ideal modernistic city, built on all the ideas of the modernistic manifests. It was started in 1955, when a big world competition about the plan was concluded, and then they started building. It has all the things that are part of modernistic ideology—the workplaces are separated from the institutions are separated from the dwellings. Everything is organized in various quarters where these things should happen.

In city planning, there are actually three levels of scales or plans. There will be the city-plan scale, which would be sort of the big story, or, we could say, the city as seen from the airplane. If we talk about London, the only thing you can see from up there is the Thames going through the city. That's the big story about London. Then when you come further down, you can see more. So there's the big story, and there's the intermediate story: that is sort of closer; that's the individual sites, and we could talk about that as the city seen from helicopter or from rooftop height. Then there is the people scale. That is the city at eye level, the city you move around in. What is typical of the planning done after 1960 is that not all three scales have been addressed.

Brasília was the first and, by far now, the best example of this. It looks fantastic from the airplane. It looks like an eagle or an airplane, with wings, and the cockpit is the government. From up there, it's fantastic. Also, the individual quarters and site plans were done carefully with competitions and whatever. That also looks fine from a helicopter. But if you are down there on your feet and going from one place to another, it is really rock bottom, because nobody ever started to think about, what would it be to be out in Brasília, between all these monuments? Everything, every distance is too wide. All streets are too wide. Things are not connected. There are big holes in the city. You have to travel for endless miles and miles along completely straight paths.

Down at eye level, Brasília is a disaster, and that's what I call the Brasília Syndrome. In my new book, I say that what we've found out about good cities is that, if you only have the time or the energy to do one scale, make it wonderful where the people are. Then it doesn't matter if it doesn't look that nice from the helicopter or from the airplane. That is also the most complicated scale, the people scale, that five-kilometer-an-hour scale where you should be comfortable. It's much easier to discuss how many dwellings do we have, and how many square meters to each dwelling, and how many schools per square kilometer? All this is easy. But how we should make the scale for little children and old people and people moving around—that is much more complicated, but that's much more important.

All these things, of course, should have been embedded in many, many new city districts, be they in China's fast growing cities or be they in the suburbs of the North American and European cities. That art was not carried over when we started to professionalize all the designs, and that art has to be reinvented now, because people are sick and tired of most of these things that have being built.

We can see in the cities how the populations and the politicians have started to revolt very rigorously against the dominance of only one profession, namely the traffic planners, as the ones who decide everything. And for many, many years, a major concern in city planning has been finding capacity for more traffic and more parking. As this has been going on, it has been made obvious for a lot of people that there could be other qualities to look at in city planning. That is why, now, so many cities are turning around and starting to push back the unlimited access for cars, starting to make one-way streets into two-way streets, widening the sidewalks, realizing that other people are also using the streets, so maybe we should have wide sidewalks and some bicycle lanes and maybe some street trees.

There are a number of things helping us with these decisions. One is that we know that we have to do something with the climate challenge, and just letting in more and more cars, as they do now in China, is not the answer to anything. The answer to some of these challenges is to use people's own muscles more and also to introduce more well-functioning public transportation systems, which can take on some of the transportation work and also relieve some resources so we don't have to use so much.

We can see this movement very clearly now, but there's also another part of that movement. That is, we have more leisure time. We live much longer. We live in smaller and smaller households, and the public realm always was an important part, throughout the history of mankind, of our social opportunities. What we can see now is that whenever we make good quality public spaces for walking, for bicycling, or for public life, people will generally come streaming to participate. We can just see the enormous growth in the number of outdoor café tables around the world. I can give you a figure here: in Melbourne five years ago, they had 7,000 café chairs; five years later, now they have 15,000 café chairs outside in Melbourne. That is the same pattern we can see in all the industrialized cities in the Western world.

That shows that there is an enormous interest in spending time among your fellow citizens, because there's one thing that has been constant for years and years and centuries and centuries, and that is that other people are the most interesting objects in our lives. There is a saying in an Old Icelandic *edda*: "Man is the greatest joy of man." And if you go and study what is happening in any place in the world, you will find exactly the same pattern: that the children will play where other people are. The youngsters will hang out where they can watch what's going on. The old people will want to go and see what is going on in the community, in the city. The boys will look at girls, and the girls will look at boys, and they'll continue throughout their lives to do that. We watch people all the time. That's our greatest interest.

GH — When I was in Brasília, it wasn't even about the distance between things, I think. It was about how actually, from one street to the next, there was no pedestrian walkway. My girlfriend, who I was doing the filming with, almost got killed by an oncoming bus because we had to cross a highway basically. All you're doing is walking through those large grassy areas in the middle of the highways, and to get from one patch of grass to the next you have to cross a highway off-ramp, and she was almost killed by a bus.

    JG — I had a broken leg when I went there, and waddling across with crutches was interesting, it was the same experience. It was never meant to be that way, but everybody in Brasília is not born with a Volkswagen or a helicopter at their disposal. The vast majority don't have that, and so the people have to fend for themselves. Then comes the question of why nobody was tasked to look after their interests. They have to fend for themselves, but a number of other issues were addressed.

GH — Can you talk about the concept of invitation? How do you design a space to invite a certain use?

    JG — In my studies of people in the city, I make many comparisons between how you plan parties and how you plan cities. Of course, if you want to have a very good party, you are very careful. You will organize the space carefully. You place the seats carefully. You will want to have the best catering, which will make people enjoy themselves while they're eating. You can actually influence what is happening at the party in a number of ways.

My old professor used to say, "Always make sure to have everything happening in a space which is too small. It will be much better." He would mention the example of the auditorium: if you expect two hundred students, get an auditorium for one hundred students. Then, well before the time when the lecture has to start, it's full of students, and then the next batch is standing out in the corridor and is looking enviously in at the one hundred who got in there, and they'll start to file in, and it's standing room only with some still in the corridor. The expectations will be sky high, and the lecture will be great because there's a fine, intensive atmosphere and the distances are short. Everything is compressed and focused. On the other hand, if you expect a hundred students and get a room for five hundred, they will be scattered all over. You will come and look around, and it will look like the end of the year, and you will sit there thinking that there must be something interesting happening somewhere else in the university, something you didn't hear about. You will have started the whole thing on a wrong note.

I say the same thing about parties: it's about always making spaces smaller than you think there is need for, and that is a very good thing. We always, in modern cities and modern city buildings, make too many spaces and make them too big and for too few people who have too little time to come out anyway. Almost every time, we start by doing everything to make the party never take off.

I also think that a good city is like a good party because we normally will refer to a good party as one that lasts a long time. If you ask a guy, "Was it a good party on Friday?" he'll say, "Ah, no, not quite because at eleven o'clock everyone left." And you ask another guy, "Was it a good party on Friday?" He'll say, "Oh, my dear, I didn't get home until five thirty in the morning." The time the party takes has something to do with the fact that, if people get involved in social and recreational activities, they will forget place and time and just enjoy. That's what I mean by saying that a good city is like a good party. People stay for longer than they plan to because they're enjoying themselves. It's interesting; it's joyful.

That's also why I would say, always when you look at a city, do not look at how many people are walking in the city, but look at how many people have stopped walking and started to stay and enjoy what is there. You can always recognize a very nice city. Go to Rome and see the relation between the number of people walking and those who are not walking. There's a great number of people who are not walking but are sitting in chairs, sitting on fountains, standing about talking, taking in the sun, taking in the views, looking at the girls, whatever they are doing. To me, Rome is a very fine city because it's so inviting for stopping. You will not stop unless you feel it's worth stopping.

It has been known for almost a hundred years now that if you invite more car driving, you will get more car driving. If you make more roads, if you lay out more asphalt in a city, it is an invitation. It makes it easier to drive. It makes it easier to get the idea that I can drive more; I need another car for my family so that everybody can get around. There is not one case in the history of mankind where adding another street to relieve a traffic situation has actually brought relief. It's just brought, for sure, more traffic. Way back, Henry Ford even lectured his employees, saying, "Go home to your community and demand that more roads be built, because then we will sell more Model Ts." He realized this connection.

There is also a little anecdote, it must be from the North American continent. This guy had a bad problem. There was a skunk that had moved into his basement. He was desperate, asking everybody, "What do I do? I have a skunk in my basement." Finally, one of his friends said, "Take some bread and crumble it all the way into the woods during the night." So he crumbled a trail of bread into the woods. The next morning, he had two skunks in his basement. It is the same thing with inviting vehicles. We know that.

We also have a number of interesting stories where the amount of asphalt has been limited. It's very difficult to limit the amount of asphalt in any city, because people believe that the amount of asphalt is given by God and is protected by United Nations human rights. If there is an earthquake and a freeway collapses, that is an act of God. We had such a situation in San Francisco in 1989 when the Embarcadero Freeway cracked and had to be closed. It was believed in the beginning that it would be the end of San Francisco as a lively place, as a vibrant business city, because now the blood vessel had been severed. Before they were even finished with making the plans for what they could do, they realized that there wasn't really that problem, because very quickly the traffic had adjusted to what other opportunities it had. People started to go by public transportation. Maybe they had carpools or whatever, drove with more in each car, and then they realized they didn't need that Embarcadero. If you go to San Francisco today, you can see that the Embarcadero is now a boulevard with trams and people promenading up and down.

There are several stories around the world of the facilities for cars being diminished for this reason or the other, sometimes by a strong government, like a strong mayor who closes a street. Then very quickly the traffic finds a new level. If you had two more avenues in New York, you would have 20 percent more traffic for sure. If you had two less avenues in New York, you would have 20 percent less traffic. In either case, New York would be fine.

We also know that, if we invite more bicycling, what will happen then? No big wonder: you will have more bicycling. In Copenhagen, we have—for 30, 40 years—had this very distinctive policy to invite people to bicycle as much as possible. There has been a complete network of very good bicycle lanes made, which are proper lanes with curbs to the traffic and curbs to the sidewalk. They are really citywide. The crossings have been made so there are pedestrian crossings and bicycle crossings, and there are special lights for the bicycles.

Gradually, it's become more and more safe and comfortable to bicycle. And there are a number of other things that have been done to make it comfortable and nice to bicycle, and we can see from year to year that more and more people take up the invitation and realize that maybe it's smarter to bicycle because it's the easiest and quickest way to get anywhere. There are fewer parking problems, and also it's better for the environment, isn't it? And finally, it's very good for me as a person, because I need to do some exercise every day.

In Copenhagen, in 10 years, parallel to all this infrastructure going in, we have seen the bicycling doubling. We have seen that now we have 37 percent of everybody commuting to work arriving on his bicycle. That is going up every year, and the goal is, at this point, for every other person to arrive on a bicycle to work. That's a case of inviting bicycles. In Beijing, in Shanghai, to have room to invite more car traffic, they have, in many areas, forbidden bicycling. Beijing used to be the city of bicycles. Now it is the city where you would be very lucky if you saw a few. So they have done an anti-invitation to bicycles.

We also know, equally, that if you are really sweet to pedestrians and make the city so that it's a good city to walk in and also has good opportunities to stop walking and start to have some fun, then we will come back and see that walking has expanded. More people are waking, and many more people are sitting and stopping and enjoying. In the city center of Copenhagen, we have found that, over just 20 years, the number of people you find when you go through the city has gone up by a factor of four. That means going through the city on a summer day today, you will find four times more people in the city center than you found 20 years ago. That is because they have gradually stepped up the quality and put out more chairs, which is a good invitation to sit, and they have made it easier and more safe to walk and also more interesting and comfortable. Gradually they have changed from the mindset of "Let me drive wherever I want," to "I can have a lovely walk through here," and "I can rest here and here and have a cup of coffee there, and there may be some interesting things going on on the way, which will make it very exciting to walk through the city."

So you can invite people activities, or you can invite traffic activities. All this is well documented now, and also it's documented that we have for many years in most of our cities invited more traffic and have actually discouraged people from walking in the cities and from bicycling in the cities and from developing a bicycle culture.

GH — In your book Cities for People, you talk about how this idea of invitation has a lot to do with the ground floors of buildings. Can you talk about the importance of that?

JG — The really important thing for the quality of any city or built-up area is what you experience at eye level when you move about between the buildings, when you move on the sidewalks or you move around in the developed areas. We have found that, of course, the configuration of the ground floors, the way the buildings meet the city, is extremely important. If we have a building, the architects may be very obsessed with how the skyline will look and how it will look from the sky, but what really matters is how it lands in the city and how it addresses the surrounding streets. I do think that, if you look at older buildings, you'll find that, historically, there was always a special treatment of the ground floors. There were bigger stones. There were more details. There were carved doors and stained-glass windows and fine things, and also there used to be many shops for each stretch of street, which gives you a fantastic experience when you walk along. You can see all those things put out in the shop windows.

We know that man's vision is horizontal, and the only thing you actually see if you walk on the sidewalk is the ground floor. I would always say to my students, use all the money and all your energy to make the ground floor fantastic. Forget about what's above, because you don't see that very much. You see it at a distance. Some of the skylines, you need to be five kilometers away to enjoy them. Really, what is important is the ground floor. That is both in shopping streets and in residential areas. In one of my new books, I suggest that all the schools of architecture introduce a department for ground floor architecture, because the art of making fascinating ground floors, the art of landing buildings so they are fantastic in the street, has more or less been lost or forgotten. I would say, to paraphrase a famous president of the United States, "Never ask what the city can do for your building; you must always ask what your building can do for the city."

I will also say that the way we can do dense new city districts and wonderful new city districts would be using the strategy of making a fantastic city at eye level. Make the two lowest stories fabulous, and then plunk the high stuff on top of that. But don't make the high stuff go down and interfere with the people scale. Because the high stuff and the dense stuff is not in people scale at all. That is what gives us such a confusing city landscape, that so many big towers and big buildings just plunk down into the sidewalks like Norwegian mountains going into the fjords, with a bang. Make a wonderful city at eye level, and put the high stuff on top of it, and you'll be all right.

GH — Can you talk about the concept of the soft edge?

JG — Yeah, we call it soft edges. Especially in residential areas, we have all the porches in America; in Australia, we have the forecourts; and we have the front yards in front of the row houses in many cultures. Generally there will be quite a bit of greenery there that will be part of the private area, but it will be between the public and the private. It will be semipublic or semiprivate. You will be the one who can put out your chairs there. You can put out your groceries there, and you can put your bicycle there, and the kids can put their playthings there, and you can plant some bushes and beautiful flowers, whatever. That can be a little zone that is a transition zone between no man's land and my land and the building.

The definition and the detailing of this transition zone is very, very important for the overall functioning of the streets and also for the visual image you have when you walk through the streets. It makes a great difference if you walk down and it's completely closed. It is like a person standing completely closed as opposed to one who stretches out his arms.

When I use the phrase soft edges, it's because, if it's just a blank wall, nobody can call that soft, I guess. But if it is something with signs of human activity, with furniture, with bushes, with flowers, with playthings, you will pick it up as inviting and welcoming and soft.

GH — I live in New York City, and I've seen the changes even in the past year or two in the bike lanes there, and I know you consulted on some of those developments. I like your concept that, in a normal bike lane, it's the bicyclists that are protecting parked cars.

JG — In many cities, you find that there has been quite a lot of pressure from the bicyclists to have better infrastructure for bicycles. The good mayors have been out there on the streets and have painted bike lanes for the bicyclists to use, but they will generally be painted on the outside of the parked cars, as opposed to what we do here in Copenhagen. Because in Copenhagen, we always have the bike lanes next to the sidewalks. We say, sidewalks are the slow traffic; the bike lanes are also slow traffic but a little bit faster; and then there would be parked cars; and then there would be traffic.

Of course, this is a much smarter thing for the bicycles because, in this way, you have the parked cars to protect the bicycles, while in the first mentioned system, you have the bicycles to protect the parked cars. Of course, having the bicycles on the outside of the parked cars involves a lot of problems. Every time a guy has to park, he backs out into the bike lane, and the bicyclists are pushed far out in the fast traffic. Every time there is a delivery van, the driver will stop bang in the middle of the bike lane and go and do his thing. While in what we call the Copenhagen-style bicycle lane, it's all protected by the parked cars. The cars are used to going into traffic, and they can do it without pushing any bicycles out. Also, delivery vans will have to stop out in the flowing traffic of cars, which the cars are used to, but they will not be taking up the bicycle lane.

I do think that, in many of these cases where we see these bicycles on the outside, it's because the bicycle lanes came after the parking. It would be a little bit difficult to shift the parking a bit further out, while in Copenhagen, we had an older tradition of having the bicycles next to the sidewalk. In this case, it may have been easier to keep that.

In many cities now, they want very much to invite more bicycling, because it's a very smart mode of transportation. It keeps people fit. It doesn't pollute, and it doesn't take up much space, and it doesn't use any nonrenewable energy sources. It's a really smart way of getting around, and you can see this urge to make these changes to the city.

Like in Melbourne, they are shifting from the old system to Copenhagen style, where they have the bike lane, and then they have a little buffer so that you can open the door of the parked car without hitting a bicycle, which is smart—and you can do that in wide streets—and then you have the parked cars. It is basically just a matter of asking a painter to come down and do a line on the inside of the parked cars. It won't take more space. It just saves a lot of lives, and more importantly, it helps invite a lot of people who would be too afraid to bicycle to get the idea that, I can actually do it also, because now it's much safer. We know that the more bicyclists you have, the safer it is to go by bicycle.

GH — We're also going to interview Janette Sadik-Khan or Amanda Burden about the developments in New York and how it's changed. That's another situation where, like you said before, less lanes means less traffic, not the other way around.

JG — That's what they have done here. They have constantly taken asphalt from the cars and given it to the bicycles. As there are more and more bicycles, they have, in certain areas of the cities, just doubled the bicycle lanes by taking another lane from the cars. Because if there is enough interest in bicycling, it gives you a much higher capacity on that street because, in the bike lane, you can have five times more people moving through than you can in a car lane. If there are enough bicyclists, it's good traffic economy to give them more space so you can invite even more. Then you can have more rush hour traffic going through that street.

GH — Can you talk about your involvement with the bike lanes in New York and some of the issues?

JG — Of course, the background in New York is that the mayor, Michael Bloomberg, took the initiative to make PlaNYC, a rather visionary plan about how to make New York much greener. This is somehow linked to the initiative of the C40, the meeting of the mayors, and the realization that, if the climate situation is going to be changed, the big cities of the world must be active, because most of the consumption of oil and all the pollution comes from the cities. Mayor Bloomberg, he took, really, some very interesting initiatives, partly for his own city and also together with all the other mayors, and sort of made it a joint commitment that we must do something.

Of course, in connection with this, it was promised that New York would be the greenest metropolis of them all in no time to speak off. That resulted in PlaNYC. But then the next phase, of course, was delivering the results. The delivery took a big step forward when Janette Sadik-Khan was brought on as commissioner for transportation. Already at that point, there had been a number of contacts between New York and Copenhagen. I've been over there a number of times to explain what Copenhagen had been doing and also what we had been doing as consultants to the city and how we had influenced the development of Copenhagen by providing the different data about how, when you did something for the bicycles, there would be more bicycles; if you did something for the pedestrians and the public life, that would grow. The whole idea that you could actually have a city policy saying, "We will have more of that, and more of that, and less of that," that has been documented for quite a few decades in Copenhagen. That was known in New York.

It happened that my firm was commissioned as a consultant to New York, and I was lucky enough to be able to include on my team the traffic engineer for Copenhagen who had done all the wonders in this city and who had just retired, and we just grabbed him right from the town hall and said, "Now you come down and work for us. Now we're going over to New York, and you use all your experience in doing these people-friendly things to cities. We'll use it over there."

We did a number of studies in New York that are the same ones we've done in this city and many other cities. I would say that we are so used to studying how cars use cities—we have figures for how many cars there are in all the streets—but we are completely unused to having knowledge about how people use cities. That is one of the things we have worked on in our firm and in my research: making people visible and finding documentation about how cities have been used. Because then, when we have this documentation, then we can say, "This is how it is. How can we improve it?" Or, "This is how it is. What kind of policy would we like in this area? Would we like it to be less of this and more of that? Would we like it to be here 5 years from now, 10 years from now?" Then we can start to talk about how we can do it. Just like the traffic engineers. They count all the cars and say, "We have a prognosis. We'll need two more lanes in two years' time." We actually have used the same process, but now with people and street life and bicycles as the things we have focused on so that we can make policy and also so that you can make a strategy about which things we will try to introduce here to give a stronger invitation for that and a weaker invitation for that.

That was exactly what we were involved in in New York based on our experience from a number of big cities like London, Melbourne, and Sydney. Also our experience from Copenhagen, and from European cities, and also cities in other parts of the world. We made a number of strategies for Department of Transportation in New York: a strategy for what a bicycle plan could look like and a number of strategies about how to make better sidewalks and also how to introduce more nice urban spaces so you do not only have the parks here and there but also some urban spaces like they have in Paris and in Rome and in European cities, Melbourne, whatever.

We made strategies for how that could be accomplished, but these strategies were not carried out. They were used as inspiration for the Department of Transportation, which looked into the political opportunities, where the stakeholders wanted some changes, what could be done? They also introduced sort of a staged plan: let's start here, here, and here, and here; then we can unfold the strategy. The idea the whole time was that you could not just do 8th and 9th Avenues and 1st and 2nd Avenues if you did not have a strategy about how you could make a complete system.

These strategies are there. They will be changed, and things will be picked from them, but for me it's very important that you know what you want before you start to make the changes. Then you can also go in and check what happened and say, "Was this what we wanted to accomplish, or how can we further that goal? Can we do more?" Or you can be surprised, say, "That was fantastic. We never thought it would work this fast."

—

Stuttgart 21/ October 2010

I've always thought that the Stuttgart 21 project and the protests against it represented the culmination of many of the ideas we were exploring in *Urbanized*. Public interest versus private interest, the role of developers and local government in shaping the city, mobility and environmental issues—it seemed to have everything in a microcosm.

I actually discovered the project through Twitter. I had tweeted something like, "Any interesting DIY urban design projects happening in your city?" and one follower replied, "Well, it's not a DIY urban design project, but it's a DIY opposition to a project. You should check out what's happening with Stuttgart 21." Within two weeks, my team and I were in Stuttgart, and we happened to show up the day the police began a violent crackdown on the protesters.

Shortly after the film was released, a statewide referendum was held on whether or not the project should continue. Voters in Baden-Württemberg ultimately approved the project, and construction has continued with completion planned for 2022.

We've included expanded text from the three main interviews in the Stuttgart 21 section—Gangolf Stocker, Udo Andriof, and Fritz Mielert. Special thanks to Ben Kempas for all his help with our filming in Stuttgart.
—

Gangolf Stocker (GS)/ Opposition Leader, Living in Stuttgart

Gary Hustwit — What's the Stuttgart 21 project about?

Gangolf Stocker — Stuttgart has a railway terminal station, and it's state of the art in Europe. That's because there are three levels of access tracks, meaning the trains' routes don't block each other. With the Stuttgart 21 project, they want to bury the station, rebuild it underground, and change it to a through station. This will include 40 miles of tunnels that need to be drilled into unstable geological formations, among many other things. And now the citizens of Stuttgart and its metropolitan area are fighting against this plan.

It is not only the station that is to disappear—they already demolished the first side wing, and the second one is to follow soon. A big section of the park with two-hundred-year-old sycamore trees will vanish; memorial sites will vanish, all falling victim to this new station.

The current station is a listed national monument designed by Paul Bonatz. Whatever you think of it, it has historical significance as it was built during the transition from classicism to modernism. You could also see it as sort of a predecessor to Speer's architecture for the Nazi regime, but that would be very unfair to Bonatz, as he was simply trying to accomplish modern architecture at a time when classicism was still the order of the day.

GH — The destruction of part of the park seems to be the biggest issue with a lot of the people protesting.

GS — The Schlossgarten park was created by the King of Württemberg. It is two hundred years old, and it gave the city of Stuttgart its name. It used to be called the Stuotengarten, which translates to "the mares' garden." I don't know of any major city in the world that would destroy its own namesake. Something like this could only happen in Stuttgart! And people love the Schlossgarten. They've taken it into their hearts. During the war, everything was bombed. Firewood was needed; there was a lot of logging in the surrounding woodlands. But they didn't touch the trees in the Schlossgarten. Nobody would have dared to cut down any tree there, although it was bitterly cold in those winters.

GH — What is the project going to cost, and who's paying for it?

GS — In 1995, the station was projected to cost $3.6 billion, according to Deutsche Bahn, the German railway company. They stuck to this figure for quite a while. We said early on, "That's never going to be enough." Deutsche Bahn later estimated costs at $4.05 billion, then $4.62 billion, and then they jumped up to $5.9 billion. Of course, that's only the beginning of the truth. We had surveys done—for example those by Vieregg-Rössler in Munich, renowned experts on transport—that say this project will cost somewhere between $9.98 billion and $12.59 billion, and these numbers should be closer to the truth, if sufficient at all. And those billions are to be spent on a train station which won't reduce journey times any more than a mere two minutes and which scales back the capacity of this railway node compared to today's terminal and may interfere massively with Stuttgart's mineral springs. Stuttgart is one of the places with the highest occurrence of mineral springs in Europe, second only to Budapest, so these may be threatened as well.

It is very difficult to find out why Deutsche Bahn is doing this. If you ask someone working for the railway, they will throw their hands up in horror. Their top management wasn't recruited from railway experts. Dürr, the first CEO in the mid-nineties, came from the automotive industry, and Dürr AG is still the largest manufacturer of automobile paint. The next CEO, Mehdorn, has a background in aviation, and the third and current one, Grube, came from DaimlerChrysler, or Daimler-Benz as it is now called. They all come from industries that compete with the railway, so you could be suspicious and say that the competitors are taking control of Deutsche Bahn by providing the corporate management.

The problem with Stuttgart 21 is that, on the one hand, surface area will be vacated, but—assuming a construction period of 15 years, which should be a pretty good guess—this area won't be utilized before 2025. At that point, the demographics will have changed, meaning we will no longer need as much housing as we need right now.

GH — Is there an alternative plan for the station?

GS — Yes, we've put one forward, which we call "Kopfbahnhof 21" (Terminal 21). With this plan you could start residential construction today. However, since real estate revenues help fund Stuttgart 21, their urban planning scheme in fact aims at a maximum return on investment, so house building needs to be as tall and dense as possible. With K21, we would keep the terminal station, modernize the track field, and add a fifth and sixth track toward Ulm. As for urban development, K21 means we could start building today—we would need to change the master plan again—and we could develop social housing there. But first and foremost, we would be in a position to develop a showcase urban quarter with the participation of the citizens, without any rush. Surely, the supporters of Stuttgart 21 promise the same thing, but it just wouldn't be possible before 2025. We could make it happen today.

GH — How would you characterize the parties on either side of this issue? Is it the mostly the government versus environmentalists?

GS — The profiteers of Stuttgart 21 are the major construction groups, the banks that provide the loans and, for example, Herrenknecht in Schwanau, the European leader in mechanized tunneling. The protest involves people from all walks of life in the urban community of Stuttgart, now representing a cross section of the population and all age groups. People participate for various reasons. Some want to protect the Bonatz station building. Some are fighting for the park. Some are concerned about the mineral springs that may be threatened. And then there are people like me who don't want to see a functioning rail hub be scaled back.

Whatever their motivations are, the protesters have one thing in common—they are no longer willing to accept how the government treats the people and how they use brutal force against the population, such as last Thursday. That was no anarchist group in the park, it was the population of the city that stood there. The police action seemed a bit desperate at the beginning but then turned into a military-style operation, including water cannons clearing the area and policemen pushing the people back. There were truly violent scenes, and they used mace against the people of this city. On one side, you've got the police in full riot gear, their visors down, and next to them, old and young citizens. Some kids who came from a students' protest were really beaten up by the police forces, shot down from the trees with the water cannons and things like that. It was horrific. Nobody would have been able to imagine this. I'm sure this will eventually mean the end of this state government.

The first thing I heard here that best describes the local mentality is the phrase: "No in nix neikomme." It translates as: "Don't get caught up in anything." I think this is a result of the Peasant War in the 16th century, when the Swabian farmers got screwed so badly. This experience must have been passed down through generations of Swabians. Every time they're confronted by an authority, they'll duck their heads. But those times are over now. I guess you could be mischievous and say, "Finally, the Swabians have left their Peasant War trauma behind."

GH — When did you start opposing this project, and how has the situation changed over time?

GS — I've been helping to organize the opposition to this project for 15 years. At the beginning, we didn't think we would be able to stop this project. We thought we would just throw a wrench in the works, and we would educate the population about the project, as they had only seen glossy brochures. That's what we did, and it took a while. You need to be patient. Half a decade later, we had turned public opinion around. At the beginning, two thirds were in favor of the project. Now more than two thirds are against it. What's needed is education, and knowledge. I always say that the average knowledge of the population is significantly higher than the average knowledge of the decision-makers, of the politicians.

The other thing was that the project was dead for a long time, and it was only resurrected in 2007. This took the population by surprise, as no one had expected it to resurface. We had ridiculed it; we had made jokes about it. And then the anger kicked in. A citizens' petition with more than 70,000 signatures was submitted and subsequently rejected by the city council. Ever since, there has been a big division between the population and the administration.

The resistance is growing in surges. People who've previously stayed at home are coming out and saying, "Now I need to go there as well!" When the first excavator started wrecking the north wing, it really drove the people to come and support us. I always say, "We don't need to recruit more protesters. Our adversaries do that for us. They automatically boost our protest."

What happened on Thursday failed to intimidate the citizens. It failed to make people drop this cause. On the contrary, it is intensifying the protest. We are confronted with a large contingent of adversaries and institutions, which have come up with the same spin for 10 years. Sometimes the mayor of village A tells it, sometimes the mayor of village B. People aren't listening to that anymore.

GH — What is the plan for protest going forward?

GS — We've been running mass protests for about eight weeks now. Following these mass rallies, politicians are suddenly starting to take the protest seriously. Our events created a sense of urgency, a lot of pressure. The SPD (Social Democrats) are now falling to pieces over Stuttgart 21, and they had always been ardent supporters of the project. I'm expecting a similar development with the CDU (Christian Democrats), in spite of Mappus (first minister) and Rech (minister of the interior) playing the tough guys. But they won't be able to continue, as they will lose the state elections because of this issue.

Considering that, ever since World War II, the CDU has always been the ruling party in government, there is a hell of a lot of insider dealing going on among all these elected officials who are faced with losing their seats. So I'm just waiting for the first big blowup within the CDU. For that to happen, we need to increase the pressure even more. We are going to continue with our protest marches every Monday and hold large rallies every Saturday as well.

GH — Is there any chance for direct discussions between the two sides?

GS — Both sides of this conflict have only talked to each other via the media. We told them we can meet for talks, we can participate in events, but at the very least you need to stop the demolition. The answer from the other side came in the form of a bulldozer that kept destroying even more of the north wing at 7:00 a.m. the next morning. That simply eradicated the basis for any talks. Through mediation by Pastor Brock, talks were held nonetheless. So we said, "Fine, we can tell them directly what we've been telling them through the media." And so we did. We went to certain lengths with that but noticed that the other side hadn't even made an effort to coordinate things. They had no leeway or anything. That's why the talks were totally pointless. We said that under these conditions we shall not continue with them. On Saturday, the theme of our mass rally will be, "Freeze construction before we talk." We're going to adhere to that policy.

In my experience, the politicians think, "People will back down at some point, and we're going to push things through. Or we'll frighten them a bit. That works sometimes. We'll just exert our authority with the police." None of that has worked! It doesn't work at all. Citizens are so fed up with politics. Words can't describe this.

What a new state government can do—and this is the first chance for a state government here without the CDU—is they can introduce legislation in order to enable real referendums like in Bavaria or in Switzerland. What Mrs. Merkel said is getting more and more likely—the state elections will effectively turn into a referendum on Stuttgart 21. I can't wait to see that!

—

Udo Andriof (UA)/ Spokesperson, Stuttgart 21 Project

Gary Hustwit — Can you tell me the idea behind this project, and who will benefit from it?

Udo Andriof — The concept for this project is to bring better connections between Europe's major cities, which can happen if we reduce journey times. The high-speed mainline through Europe goes from Paris, the capital of France, to Budapest, the capital of Hungary, and we want it to go through Stuttgart, the capital of Baden-Württemberg. However, the tracks we've got are 150 years old and are not suitable for high-speed traffic, so we'll need to build a new mainline.

This concept has been in place since the 1980s and was further refined in the 1990s, when administrative proceedings determined the best routes. The second part of this project is the new train station for Stuttgart. The new station will have a new mainline that will run along the autobahn and allow trains to travel as fast as 155 miles per hour, not just 40 miles per hour like the old tracks.

The other part is an urban development project that will put all the tracks underground on a lower level of the station. That opens up an area of 250 acres, more than a hundred football fields, where the old tracks used to be. A new city is going to rise there, which will be attractive for recreation with an enlargement of the park, but also for living and working.

GH — The people opposing this project have said that the current station is one of the most efficient in Germany. So why fix something that's not broken?

UA — The train station in Stuttgart is working fine at the moment, but it's not ready for the future. It was built a century ago, and its track field is totally cluttered—a sea of tracks in the middle of the city. Stuttgart is surrounded by hills, and the valley is cut in two by this train track field. We want to eliminate that and let the city grow together again.

The station here in Stuttgart is a terminal station, so the trains go into the station and stop there; it's a dead end. When trains enter or leave the old train station, their routes may cross, and this limits its functionality. We want the trains to travel through the new station in Stuttgart, so its capacity will be much higher than the old station.

GH — Do you think the government has done enough to include the residents of Stuttgart in the process for this project? Should the public be allowed to directly vote for or against a project like this?

UA — In the 1990s, we started the approval procedure and involved citizens. More than two thousand of them told us specifically about their objections and suggestions, and the proposal went through land-use planning in 1997 and was approved in 2005. A few court cases dealt with this, but in 2006, the courts approved the plan as well. We've talked about funding ever since, and now that we're starting the project, the debate about financing resurfaces: should the money be spent for this or something else?

In addition, people are fed up with politics, or to say it positively, people want to have their say in these matters much more so than in earlier years. In the 1990s and early 2000s, we had matter-of-fact discussions with citizens. Some were affected directly; others may have been worried about a loss in value of their house. But the current situation is totally different. Many people who are not directly affected want to have their say, and they call the whole process undemocratic. This is a cause for concern for us, as the project was approved, and the developers must be able to rely on such an approval so they can go ahead with the project and not need to face a renewed debate in the streets.

For large and complex infrastructure developments such as this one, it is necessary to go through an approval process, which reviews the reasoning of the project and checks available alternatives and which also looks at anything that may be affected, such as the environment, and then assesses the benefits. Such a process is not really suitable for a referendum. Also, our constitution and our legal system don't allow for this kind of poll. Consequently, a call to "clear the way for a referendum" may not be successful. A referendum is generally possible in local politics where citizens are directly affected and the matters at hand are straightforward. A major project like this affects not just one city but the entire country and even interest groups beyond that, so it would be difficult to determine who should be consulted. The process is also very complex and needs to be understood objectively. I don't think this would be suitable for a referendum.

A government planning to realize a certain project needs to face up to the electorate again and again, so elections will determine if people are happy with the government and the progress of the project. I think the protest has many layers. You can't profile "the protester" as such since there are so many causes, some just general, some very concrete. So I think this project will influence the next election, but it won't be the sole factor.

We're in this situation where the disadvantages and interference due to the 10-year construction period appear imminent, but the benefits, such as the development of a new city, the expansion of recreation areas, construction of new houses, and creation of new jobs, are still far away and are not yet perceivable. The current claim that citizens had not been sufficiently involved might be due to fact that some can't recall what we did 15 years ago. A protester who is 30 years old now surely didn't understand this whole process when he was 15. In the 1990s, we let citizens have their say in working groups across the city, which addressed a diversity of questions. There were public hearings and information events during the approval procedure. However, once the project was approved and its funding still being discussed, there was a definite lack of communication of what all this will mean for the citizens. So it's no surprise that they perceive it as encroachment when parts are removed from the old station or when trees need to be cut down, and yet they can't see the good that this project will bring with it. What's happening in Stuttgart is a great opportunity for the city, and we need to promote it so that will be recognized.

GH — So what is your solution to the massive protests happening now?
UA — Surely, the worldwide attention to this project as national and international media are reporting on it was triggered by tens of thousands of people taking to the streets, many of them middle-class citizens who had never gone to a protest before. But it's still only one part of the population. In the meantime, supporters of the project have come forward, and they're rapidly gaining in numbers. Ever since both the state government and the federal government announced their unequivocal support for the project and since leaders in politics, business, and society backed it, we've been

approached by many fellow citizens who want to get involved in support of the project. It is extraordinary how people took the initiative and got together of their own accord, saying, "We want to show the public that there is not just protest against the project. You'll always find people who are against things, but there are people who are in favor it." So this started with a handful of people and, within a few weeks, grew into a crowd of several thousand.

We can only call on the opponents of the project to look into its objective reasons and to enter into talks, to listen to each other. One needs to learn from the other side about their suggestions, worries, and fears, but at the same time, they also need to realize that many surveys and inquiries combined with a lot of experience from earlier traffic projects are the basis of the project. So not only will this project have no disadvantages, but it will also have significant advantages. The project has been examined thoroughly over many, many years, so we're not guessing or estimating now. We know a lot about the actual costs. Of course, with any large-scale project like this, you can never exclude additional costs. For example, safety requirements for such a project may change, and this may increase costs. However, you need to realize that the whole project is worth the money indeed. The costs have never been obscured but have been updated constantly, adjusted to actual developments. So there's nothing that could take people by surprise.

GH — Protesters seem to be most angered by the plan to cut down the ancient trees in the park.

UA — We have a wonderful park in Stuttgart, which is unique in Southern Germany and which I really love, including the trees, and it also hurts me when old trees need to be felled, but it was already shown during the approval process that many new trees will be planted in their place. We are going to plant as many as 5,000 new trees for those 280 that have to be cut, and we're going to extend the whole park by 50 acres. That's another 30 football fields. So the overall balance will be positive.

Stuttgart is very lucky to have natural mineral springs here. After Budapest, this is the second largest occurrence of mineral spring water in Europe, and of course, this mineral water needs to be protected. For me, this has always been a knockout criterion, meaning the project wouldn't go ahead if there was a chance the mineral water would be harmed. That's why it was very important to explore the bedrock over many years with drilling tests. In Stuttgart, every building with underground parking needs to deal with this problem. With this experience and these explorations, we can be sure the mineral water will be sufficiently protected. On top of that, there will be a sophisticated, very complex monitoring system, which will make sure that nothing will happen unexpectedly during the actual construction period since appropriate action can be taken right away.

I think the protest has intensified a lot through the perception in the media. This is a self-escalating process. When the *New York Times*, the BBC, and the entire national press from Hamburg to Munich is covering this matter, then they're surely not doing it because they're worried about the groundwater or trees in Stuttgart. What they see is that tens of thousands of people took to the streets. And the other thing is, this becomes an interesting adventure for many people, and the young people say, "Let's meet there. Something's happening there, and we'll be on television." For many, it's a big performance. I don't mean to belittle the protesting of those who are truly worried. Yet these other factors contribute as well, and the interest of the media has made this protest surge so much.

GH — Can you talk about the violence that happened on Thursday? Do you think it was justified for the police to use pepper spray and water cannons?

UA — I took over my new task as spokesman for the project on Monday. On Tuesday, I'd already presented our concept for the trees, showing that, in the end, the balance will be a positive one for nature and the landscape. But on Thursday, we had to secure the site for the upcoming construction of a groundwater management system, and it was necessary and permitted to cut trees for this. This stirred up emotions amid the population. The police were going to secure the site on the first possible day, hoping that their intervention would come as a surprise and happen fast enough that there would be no protests on the actual site. Certainly, the police were surprised how quickly protesters blocked access to police vehicles and construction workers, and that's why the police resorted to direct enforcement. Those images then traveled the world, and they have certainly harmed the project.

It is our task to convince people by providing factual information. Images like these enrage everyone and make our task more difficult. I think it has not yet sufficiently been reported how protesters go beyond what's covered by the right to demonstrate. Many think that civil disobedience or blocking vehicles is covered by their right to demonstrate, but this is not the case. You can always proclaim your opinion. You can announce it loudly as well, and you can sit down in the street or in the meadows in order to voice your views, but you can't block an official process. That's illegal.
—

Fritz Mielert (FM)/ Activist, Park- schutzer

Gary Hustwit — What's the history of the Stuttgart 21 project?

Fritz Mielert — Deutsche Bahn, the German railway corporation, has several projects with the "21" name. There was Munich 21, Frankfurt 21, and Stuttgart 21. They've looked into various ways the company could utilize the track surface areas it had obtained from the state as part of their privatization process and how these could be converted into urban development sites or real estate projects in order to fill their coffers.

We never knew whether Stuttgart 21 was being developed any further or not. It was called off at some point. Then they said: "Yes, we're planning again!" Then other parties became involved in the project, as the funding had never been secured. In the beginning, we were told the project would finance itself through the proceeds of sales of the real estate. The locals like promises like that, so they welcomed the idea: "Yes, this means renewal of the city without any real cost to the public." Of course, this has changed a lot over the years as cost estimates for this project have now reached catastrophic levels of up to $21 billion in a worst-case scenario. This whole back-and-forth made it really difficult for citizens to enter the debate.

Back in 1997, I participated in an initiative called Local Agenda, which happened across Germany and was meant to empower citizens to have their say in urban development. They printed high-gloss brochures, and every citizen could really get information on the project. But even then they were already saying, "The basic principles of this project cannot be challenged." It was a done deal, and only bits and bobs could be adjusted. Political debate about this project had already become immensely difficult.

At that time, an association called Living in Stuttgart was founded. It investigated Stuttgart 21 and raised awareness in the city, and it changed public opinion over the years, asking, "What are they developing here? What kind of urban district are they designing? What type of housing is there going to be? What does the city really need? And what ecological and social risks come with this project?"

Stuttgart 21 requires a radical change of the train station. At the moment, this is a terminal. They want to put it underground, turn it by 90 degrees, and make it a through station, changing it from its current 16 tracks— ideal for short-distance public transport to fight congestion and make traffic more eco-friendly—to an 8-track through station with much lower capacity. And as part of this process, surface track area will be vacated. The current track field also includes a marshaling yard for preparation and servicing, which is to be moved out of the city. At the moment, this train station has the second-best punctuality rating in Germany. As they say, "Never mess with a good thing," but that's exactly what is going to happen here. Many traffic surveys have told us that the new station would be less efficient than the current one.

The railway corporation is looking at profits, period. They're making a lot of money from this. You're not dealing with a single company here. It's a corporate group with lots of limited companies that compete with each other. Before privatization, this business served the public good. Today, while it's still controlled by the government, the not-for-profit times are over. In my eyes, it's a redistribution program. The railway corporation invests almost nothing and receives a lot from the public. The aim is to financially strengthen this corporate group, Deutsche Bahn AG, to let it become more commercially viable and expand across Europe. That's what this is about.

Then they're going to cut into the park. Stuttgart has a long green corridor in the middle of this basin leading all the way to a major river. This green space defines the cityscape; it is transparent and almost level. Now, this is where they're going to heap up a huge embankment to hide the lower-level station. It's not like the entire station would be underground. They're really going to raise this rampart, which will obstruct visibility. This park is a central point in the city and of enormous importance. The city heats up a lot, and the park is a cold point at night and helps cool down the city. It's home to many young people. The goths meet here once a month. There are punks and many different groups who use this park and make it theirs. We also have families who use this park during weekends, who are simply saying, "Yes, this is my space!"

We need housing for people who don't have that much money, and that is not the kind of living space being created here. We're looking at luxury apartments here. So they're going to build houses in these restructured areas, but not the kind of flats the city needs. They are creating luxury apartments on property funded by the city, which again leads to a process of redistribution. There is no city without change. Yet it really matters how careful you are—or have to be—with a city, with this incredibly fragile structure, so that it'll still be possible to identify with the city and your community.

GH — How do you think this situation should be resolved?

FM — There already is an alternative proposal for this project, but I would recommend that we analyze what the real transport needs of the city are. I would like to make an argument for a reassessment by specialists, carried out separately in various areas of expertise. A sociologist needs to look into this in as much detail as an urban planner and a traffic manager. And then you combine it with a big referendum. If we really want to enable a city to identify with its urban development, we need to involve the citizens from the beginning. Not only did they completely miss out on that, it was probably thwarted as well. Trust in politics is at an all-time low here.

GH — What's the future of the protest?

FM — We are holding training sessions where people can practice things like a sit-in protest. There was a lady, about 75 years old, who showed up and said: "I've been well behaved all my life. This is an end to that now!" People are waking up. If we show them now that they can actually achieve something, then this will benefit the city in the long term. Citizens are going to wake up and say, "I can start projects in my neighborhood. With a nursery or traffic-reduction measures, I can really improve quality of life for myself as well as for my fellow citizens!" If this project goes ahead, you won't be able to keep this spirit in the city. Many people will be really frustrated and will abdicate their social responsibilities.

—

Ricky Burdett (RB)/ October 5, 2010 London

I spent about six months doing research in 2009 before I started filming *Urbanized*, and early in that process I attended the Urban Age Conference organized by Ricky Burdett and the LSE Cities program of the London School of Economics. The conference was held in Istanbul that year, and brought together mayors, city planners, architects, and policymakers from cities all over the world. It was at Urban Age that I first came into contact with Enrique Peñalosa, Bruce Katz, and several other people who would be instrumental in making the film.

—

Gary Hustwit — What do you think cities are doing wrong in response to today's major challenges?

Ricky Burdett — I think you can talk about cities as being sick patients. There are a lot of sick cities, and there are a lot of cities which are going wrong, and you can see the negative effects on them on their bodies themselves. So cities—what's gone wrong? I think the first thing that strikes me, as someone who has now in the last seven years been going to parts of the world where I never thought I would be—I'm thinking of Johannesburg; I'm thinking of São Paulo; I'm thinking of parts of Asia and India—what we are seeing there is the increasing ghettoization and the creation of a city of difference, on the whole, for those who are well-off and those who are not well-off.

There are many axes along which this happens, but perhaps I sound a little bit romantic in feeling that the great 19th-century city where everyone was sort of jumbled together—with some problems, of course—is an interesting model. I think it still is. I think some of the most livable cities in the world, among which I would throw in London, New York, Milan, or Rome, and Buenos Aires for that matter, work because the boundaries between difference aren't opaque. You tend to live, even if you're quite well-off, relatively close to people who are not like you—different communities, as James Jacobs writes about, of Jews, Koreans, Italians, and Hispanics mixed together in a cauldron of difference—which is exactly what makes up parts of New York or East London. What has gone wrong is trying to separate all these differences out.

No one is really deciding that Johannesburg should be a city of difference, but people are fearful. No one is deciding that São Paulo should have all new developments have six-meter walls and security, but people are scared about coming home.

The bizarre thing is that, you go to Istanbul, which is one of the safest cities in the world together with Cairo, and the same typology is being repeated as a model of some sort of lifestyle. The same in Bangalore, on the outskirts of Mumbai or New Delhi. I think that is worrying when the private sector effectively determines what to do without any public sector strong hand. I guess I do believe that cities, to be fair, need to have a strong democratic base. I think the two are connected. You don't get this fragmented environment in a place where there is a system of shared values, which goes through, for example, the mayor and elections, and if it doesn't work, they kick him out, and someone else comes in. That, for me, is a really big problem in the emerging and changing landscape of the city.

The second one must be related to the use of the car or the increasing dependency on the car as a form of transport to do the most basic thing, which is to get from home to work. Now, I have nothing against the car. I don't. But I have a lot against using the car for the wrong purpose. If I can earn enough money at the university or as a consultant and I want to have my car to go somewhere in the evening, that's fine. But it doesn't make any sense that I should be able to drive my car into the center of London. In fact, I've been priced out. I can't. The mayor decided that it would cost me the equivalent of basically thirty-five dollars a day, between congestion charge tax and parking, to do that. So I drive a scooter, and I'm a very happy citizen, and I got here 2 minutes late, but I live 11 minutes from here. People adapt, and I think that's important. If the system is available, you can adapt.

Just think of this: in Tokyo, 80 percent of the population uses public transport to get to work, in the world's biggest city, 80 percent; 20 percent use cars. In Los Angeles, it's the flip: 20 percent use public transport, and it's only the very poor people using buses, if that; 80 percent take the car. The impacts on the environment are clear: the more you are dependent on a car, the greater the environmental damage is, particularly if they're petroleum based. There are also social costs, which is often not talked about. In Bangkok, it takes something like four hours for some families to take their kids to school and get to the office. I've been told that some families therefore deal with this by putting their kids, in their pajamas, in the back of their car at four or five in the morning, taking them to school. They wake up and they have breakfast in the car. When they pick them up, they have dinner in the car too.

Now, leaving aside the sort of immoral dimension of this and the environmental aspects of this, think of what this does to the family relationships, what the children think of their parents? Where do they talk? Imagine if you're a policeman on duty and you have to spend—as you do in São Paulo, Mexico City—those sorts of hours commuting. What is your efficiency? How good are you going to be, if you're a doctor or a nurse, after spending that amount of time commuting? There are social costs and environmental costs to do with this.

I think many cities, and unfortunately most of the new cities or the expanding cities, are taking our models, Global North models, mainly

American models, the Los Angeles model, the Phoenix model, and just applying them because that's where the market is taking us. I think the city of exclusion and the city of car dependency are the two problems.

GH — On the social cost, there's something about being on public transportation in New York and the number of people that you come into contact with on a daily basis in that sort of city, from different cultures and economic strata. Do you think it's a factor in people's views, politically or socially? You maybe tend to care about other people more if you're in that kind of daily contact.

> **RB** — There's no doubt, taking this view, that perhaps car dependency should be diminished; that cities should be more limited in terms of their growth, should not sprawl; that perhaps you shouldn't have as many suburbs as the market would like to deliver because it makes a lot of people very rich very quickly if we have to build a house on land on the fringes of whatever it is, LA, or Liverpool for that matter.
>
> A number of things are going on there. One is that actually the state ends up subsidizing the private sector. Apparently, in the States, every house that is built in the suburbs effectively has got $20,000 of indirect subsidy, because the city has to build sewers; the postman has to collect the mail. Think of it that way. The lighting has to be connected. There are actually some direct costs that you can calculate.
>
> It does, if you think of this vision that I'm talking about—it's not a vision; you see it everywhere—it does go with a sort of social democratic notion of life, that something's got to give, that you do share in some collective values. Having the freedom to choose that you want to sit in your car and spend five hours a day in it and listen to radio or not, as opposed to being crammed with people who are different than you—that's a social choice, and I think it's a different one.
>
> I think the reality, the unhappy reality, is that in most countries of the emerging world, in most cities of the emerging world, public transport, including the underground or the subway system, is mainly used by the lower end of the social scale. Therefore, one way of establishing difference is not just by wearing Prada but by taking your kids to school in a Jeep. By that way, that doesn't just happen at those extremes, it's a very, very subtle shift where you sort of celebrate your independence by not using public transport.
>
> Of course, if you have a good public transport system, as we do here in London, you can afford to manipulate the market by raising taxes so that you basically price people off the streets. But you also have to do something that is very important and that requires political investment: invest more in the quality of that public service so that it isn't only used by those who can't afford to get to work in any other way.

GH — Do you want to talk about the origins of cities, the birth of cities?

> **RB** — Sure. I guess I would immediately think that cities today have been doing the same thing that they've done for three, four, five thousand years, which is they've been the place where the flows of people and

the flows of money, the flow of goods, have coalesced. People have just moved there to take advantage of that place of encounter of all these things, of human beings, who come to exchange goods, ideas. Ultimately cities are markets in one way or another and obviously not just of fruit and vegetables or meat, but in global-city days they're measured more by which goods, like coffee or beans or something else, are traded, or gold or stocks. That accounts for how important they are in the international rankings. Two, three thousand years ago it would have been something else. It would have been sheep. In that sense, it's really about the same thing.

But they're not temporary. The city, ultimately, is not a tent encampment. Making a city is about garnering resources, putting them together in such a way that they resolve the long-term stability of a larger and larger and larger and larger number of people who are going to stay there. So issues of what you do with water, what you do when it rains, what you do at night, what you do when it's very cold, are ultimately the fundamental urban design problems at the heart of any town which then becomes a village.

The world today is changing pretty dramatically, shifting toward more and more people living in cities. I don't know what it was like in 1000 BC, when already a lot of people were living in cities, what percentage of the world was living in cities, but it must have been 0.1 percent. All I do know is that by the beginning of the 20th century, so 110 years ago, it was 10 percent, which sounds like quite a lot. Only two years ago it was 50 percent. If we continue at the pace we are, which we will no doubt, it will be something like 75 percent in 40 years' time, which is not that far away. It's when my son will be just a little bit older than I am, so it's sort of around the corner. It's half a lifetime away, so to speak.

The pressures are different today because of one, I'd say, fundamental thing. The pace of change is very different. Cities accelerated relatively slowly from let's call it pre-Greek, pre-Roman times to the time that they became the biggest metropolises of the world, which are Rome, Athens, et cetera. Then it took a very, very long time, centuries, for many cities to reach those numbers which might be something like a million. It was gradual, very gradual. Today if you take a city like Lagos, for every minute that I'm speaking to you, there's a new person who has moved in. Every minute. Multiply out. That means there are hundreds of thousands of people moving into the city, looking for what? Looking for the same things that we were talking about before. Looking for jobs. Looking for security. Looking for that not-very-tangible notion of "making it."

GH — Just going off that, I've always wondered if you look back at those ancient cities, are there things that we can learn from the way that they were designed that speaks to today's cities?

RB — There are many, many different types of ancient cities. Few of them were planned. A lot of them just happened. Very organic. I think that is something that you have to consider when you're talking about cities today: What bit of the city are you talking about? Are you talking about the bit that is planned, the formal city, or the bit that is unplanned?

Ancient Rome was planned for completely clear purposes, military arrangements: the famous structure of the one line, the *cardo*, and the other line, the *decumanus*, which is the regulating axis. It's like 57th Street and 5th Avenue, let's say. It's the same sort of principle, all to do with how you make the encampment actually work as efficiently as possible. That's a planned city. It goes with some sort of formal social structure, economic structure, political structure. The more cities we talk about, the more cities you visit in this film, the more we see that actually a lot of them are unplanned, or large chunks of them are unplanned. In Mexico City, 60 percent of the city today, still more or less the biggest city in the world after Tokyo or greater Tokyo, most of it is informal. There are no planning regulations. People make decisions on their own, but they have water; they have electricity; they're just connecting to the system illegally.

I think that the lessons from the ancient cities, if there are any, are more relevant to the planned side. There, I think, are actually today one or two lessons. I'm totally biased. I was brought up in Rome. Whatever I say will probably be affected by that. The notion of a very simple grid, ordered streets, like on a square, which allows a city to grow over time and adapt but also to contract and change, and that buildings, whether they're houses, whether they're parliaments, whether they're temples, whether they're shopping centers, are aligned on these streets and sort of face out onto them—I think it's one of those incredibly simple lessons. It would be fantastic if a new town in China or India just looked back at some of these, what I would call, visceral relationships between a human being and public space.

Not all planned cities are like that, and not all ancient cities have those qualities that I'm talking about. I mean, they are, of course, completely different in South America and in other parts of the Mediterranean Basin. If you go back to parts of, say, North Africa, Turkey, the eastern Mediterranean, North Africa in particular, there the organic city, the hill city, the built-out-of-mud city is done in a completely different way. There it's not about dealing with enemies in terms of troops, but dealing with enemies in terms of the environment: heat, lack of rain, long periods of drought. How do you make a benefit out of bringing people together and keeping a shaded environment? There you see a totally different way in which the creative human spirit is able to construct the most extraordinary things.

All those issues apply to the contemporary city in a completely different way, you could say in a sort of gigantic way or a monstrous way at times. Also because there are other forms of movement, which are not just to do with the way the body moves and moving on foot or on horseback or whatever it may be, but using vehicles, which makes a dramatic difference to the shape of the city. I'm sure we'll talk about that.

GH — When cities do take something from the ancient cities, it seems like this kind of quoting. It's like, in China or in Asia maybe, they'll say, "Well, we also have the canals of Venice here." What's the draw of not developing something original but taking from these other cultures and plopping down New York's Central Park in the middle of a new city in Korea or something?

RB — Well, I think it's a wider issue within cultures and what their references are, you know? It's more an issue of how important Coca-Cola is there than what the models of cities are. The sorts of examples you're talking about, the Venice canals somewhere in the middle of China, is more to do with a value system and icons and branding than it is with the reality of city change. I would say that's a very tiny percent of what's actually happening.

I'll never forget how Shanghai, when we studied it about six or seven years ago, had just abandoned a completely insane plan. Shanghai is still today one of the fastest growing cities in the world. It was then probably the fastest. It decided, to expand, it would build a number of satellite towns, eleven in fact at that point, beyond the last ring of the motorway. Each one of these new towns was going to be designed "in the style of." When I spoke to the chief planner, I asked, "What does that mean?" He said, "Well, we're going to have a German town." I said, "Well, what's that going to look like?" "Well, it's going to look like a German town." "Which means what?" "Well, it's going to have a campanile and a steeple and a church, and right next to it is where the Volkswagen factory is going to be so the German engineers can live in a German environment." There was an Italian town. The German town is partly built, actually. I did go and see it. The Italian town was built, or designed anyway, by the Italian architect Vittorio Gregotti, so it looked more like something out of Poland in the thirties than anything else. So it went on. Then they decided this was not a good way of making cities and abandoned that venture, I think very wisely, and are now thinking of other things.

GH — That's crazy. That expanding outside—is it Cairo now that's doing these massive megacities just outside of the city as an expansion?

RB — Yeah. I mean, one thing is intent, and the other one is what actually happens on the ground. Cairo is—first of all, for me, as someone brought up in Rome, it's difficult to say that any other city is as beautiful as Rome, but it's one of the most beautiful cities in the world. Together with Istanbul, Cairo and Rome are sort of up there. It's totally chaotic to actually live there, but it has exactly those essential qualities of a city that we were talking about a moment ago. You're never alone on the street. You're never at risk. Cairo has one of the lowest levels of criminality of any city in the world. You can leave your door open anywhere. You don't hear of people getting mugged in Cairo. You do in Buenos Aires. I'm putting aside terrorism. That is another issue, which has got nothing to do with it.

Over the years, the authorities have said, how do we get rid of this congestion because it's unlivable? Too much traffic, too many taxis, too much noise. They've created these new things: New Cairo. I visited a gated garden community the name of which was more appropriate to the West Coast of the United States than anything else. You know, watered gardens and I'm sure the most unsustainable stuff in the world.

What's interesting, in terms of this aspiration of creating new cities or new megacities, is that the people who are supposed to move to these places, which is the middle class effectively, don't. The just don't want to go there because they miss the hubbub. They'd prefer, naturally, to do something which is now considered in New York or London the cool thing to do, which is to stay in the center; retrofit an old building, old flats, or whatever; put some air conditioning in; try and squeeze another place for a car; actually stay there. These new developments around Cairo have been uniquely unsuccessful in terms of absorbing growth. The numbers of people who move there is tiny. I mean, I can't remember what it is, but it's something like the same number of people who moved to these new developments outside Cairo over three years moved into Cairo in two months. It's even more dramatic than that, the numbers.

GH — Can you talk about the pre–World War II and post–World War II eras? The modernist experiments in cities, and how and why those came into being?

RB — It's interesting. I teach a class here at the London School of Economics. It just started yesterday. It's called Cities by Design. Most of the students are sociologists, lawyers, a few architects, mainly people interested in social, economic, and cultural processes at large. There is this prevailing feeling in the room with the students that—when you start showing pictures of projects from the 1920s and '30s—architects are just mad. Who would want to demolish Paris and get rid of all those wonderful little streets with brasseries at the corner and flower stores and all that magic and everything else and replace it with maybe forty tower blocks all surrounded by open space and green and Le Corbusier's *Ville Radieuse*? That's one of the important shifts in the early part of the 20th century. The other one was the garden city movement.

What were they about? It's absolutely important to understand: it was a knee-jerk reaction—actually, not knee-jerk, a thoughtful reaction—to the problems of the congested, overdense city which was coming out of the 19th-century Industrial Revolution. If you think of Paris; if you think of London, of course, more than any other; Barcelona; Milan; Berlin, these are cities that, within the space of 30 or 40 years, just mushroomed. The effect of this mushrooming was that the living quality inside became unbearable. In a room like mine here, there were probably nine people sleeping. Haven't we heard that somewhere else recently? In the slums of Dharavi. Haven't we heard about that in the favelas of São Paulo? That's exactly what's happening there. People are attracted to the city because of jobs but living in unacceptable conditions in the hope that something happens. There was a benevolent reaction to this on the part of the civic authorities, the architects and planners, which was, how do we create a new city which is healthy? I think we sometimes underestimate how health was a driver of so much physical and social change 20, 30 years ago.

Anyway, October of 2010 is the 150th anniversary of Baron Haussmann's replanning Paris. That was an attempt already—and that's 150 years ago, not at the early part of the 20th century—to say, we've got to civilize and improve the city and provide sewers and gas lighting. Well, the only way to do it is you rip things up, make straight lines, and then you cover them up again. Once you've ripped these straight lines, you might as well keep them the way they are, plant a few trees, and put an opera house at one end and a parliament at the other, and, hey, presto, you've got Paris.

In the early 20th century, Le Corbusier and others are not dissimilar in terms of having a geometric idea of purity where people would be living in high-rise buildings, 20, 30 stories, where you could open windows; you could have daylight; you could have fresh air coming in one side of the house and going out the other. This is an extraordinary improvement in the conditions of people who were living in dark, damp places full of coal. Let's not forget, at the end of the Victorian era, life expectancy of a man in Britain was something like 40 years old. I'd be dead a long time by now. Certainly housing conditions, together with health provision, hospitals, and all that, made a massive difference. I think this is important in the context of your question.

What's changed? I think what's changed is the shift of where that growth is geographically. What I've been describing is very much a Western-centric, Global North phenomenon, while large parts of India, China, and the Far East as we know it today were probably, relatively speaking, static. South America in particular. From before the Second World War to let's say the sixties and seventies, then, you had this extraordinary acceleration of these new economies. South America's the most dramatic. I mean, cities like São Paulo grew by—I think I've got the figures right—970 percent, so 1,000 percent, in the space of a century, just from a village of nothing to a city of many, many millions. This is the pattern you find in Santiago, in Mexico City, in Buenos Aires, et cetera, where a lot of, of course, European money connected with whatever the trade was, coffee or oil later on in Venezuela, allowed these economies to grow and, therefore, the cities to grow because they were offering jobs.

I think the visual landscape, the physical side of what happened in the postwar era—now I'm extending that to where we are now—as opposed to the prewar era is really quite different because of the scale, because of the lack of control at one level and the growth of the informal economy. I don't know whether in 1930s South American cities there was a large amount of informal settlement, but I doubt it. Today the numbers, I've said, are 60 percent of people in Mexico City living informally—which doesn't mean slum conditions; it just means without regulation—but similar numbers elsewhere. As you go east across the world and south—so I'm thinking obviously of Asia, but I'm also thinking of Africa—that phenomenon becomes even more sharp in terms of the landscape of change.

We know from Lagos, from beautiful films about Lagos that have come out recently, how people live around rubbish dumps, and that's their market. They're recycling stuff that has already been recycled. There's a barber shop. There's a little town hall. There's a jury system. Totally informal but within the community that lives on this dump. Now you would say, "Why aren't they living in the village five hundred miles away?" Well, because they make more money there by recycling the garbage that someone threw out. I think those are interesting twists in the way cities are manifesting themselves in relation to these big economic changes, social changes, and then I'm sure we'll talk about the climate change issues.

GH — It changes the way you think about how buildings are oriented or what the traffic pattern is or what the public space is like or if there isn't any. Are there any people, jobs, that are in this chain that are particularly influencing these things?

RB — There are two groups of people. It's the politicians. There's got to be someone who says, "This pisses me off. I really don't like this. Why should I arrive in London from Paris and come out of St. Pancras and find this horror of this roundabout or whatever. Can't we do something about it?" There's got to be someone with the eye who cares about that, at all levels.

Then there's got to be someone who can design that and do it well. I think what you're tending to get now is, first of all, in the West anyway, most public-sector-designed apartments don't exist anymore. London used to have the GLC. The Greater London Council had a thousand architects in the seventies. Now each local authority might have five, if that, or zero more likely. Therefore, things have to be farmed out, and then designers come on.

The other problem is that in the design community, I think, there are very, very few people who know how to design good public space. It takes a modesty which most architects, landscape architects, just don't have. I mean, sometimes the best thing—again, I think of Rome, some cobblestones and some beautiful marble where you can sit on the edge underneath a church. You need absolutely do nothing else. Well, now if you get landscape architect *x* or *y*, you know, you're bound to have three diagonals and some circular pools and some symbol which reflects something, which you probably end up tripping over, and it gets in the way of getting from *A* to *B*. It does come with a sort of overdesign. It's like an overcomplicated typeface, which tries to say something fresh about itself and create this identity.

Where it's worked is this synergy between a politician with a vision and someone who wants to do things. I'm fascinated by a New York experiment now with the park pedestrianization of Times Square and Herald Square and Union Square, which I was at the other day with my daughter. It's incredible how badly done these spaces are. I mean, it's really a bit of a paint and a few plastic bollards and chairs, but I can see why, because it's got to be seen as, let's see whether the city likes it and adapts to it. Bloomberg is very shrewd, and Janette Sadik-Khan, the transport commissioner, knows not to go too far. In Barcelona, you'd start at exactly the opposite end. You would just say, "Let us get some 25-year-old kid out of university"—which is what they did in the eighties—"and have him create a completely, undoubtedly modern piece in front of the 13th-century cathedral. Let's make a statement about ourselves that way."

GH — Can you do a little bit of a breakdown of the different roles that government plays in urban design?

RB — I think when you talk about who decides and what governance is in a city, the first question is, what is the city? That may seem a banal question, but the administrative boundary of a city may be very different and out of step with what actually is the collective consciousness of what is a city.

Here's an example: New York City has five boroughs with one mayor. If you superimpose those boroughs on where people actually live, in New Jersey and beyond Queens, in the tri-state area, the bit that feels like New York, not Manhattan, extends well beyond. A lot of the decisions about New York supposedly are, in fact, not made by New York. They're made by New Jersey, or they're made by the Port Authority, or a lot of them are made by the state of New York.

I'm using one example. I could say exactly the same thing in Mexico City, where you have one area, which has around six, seven million people, called the Distrito Federal, which has a mayor. When we talk about the mayor of Mexico City Marcelo Ebrard, he's actually the mayor of a bit of Mexico City. Quite a big bit. It's as big as London. But it's much smaller than the other bit, which is governed by the state of Mexico. (It's like saying the state of New York.) That has, whatever it is, 13 million people. And these two people don't speak to each other. They don't like each other. They're from different parties. The first thing to say, before we even go down into the system and what happens inside it, is that there is often a conflict of interest between what is the metro area where people live and the city proper and who decides what happens.

London is different. These are concrete examples which are important to see the difference. London actually has this thing called the Green Belt beyond which the city cannot grow. The mayor of London, since 2000, is responsible for all the land, all the transport, all the key decisions, the police and fire service, and everything else within that outer boundary. There's one territory. Underneath that, we have 33 boroughs, which are smaller units. So first of all, there's that big issue.

Then when you move inside the city, there's three levels. One is the level of the jurisdiction of the mayor or the municipal authority. There, for example, whether the mayor is actually elected by the people or appointed by the central government begins to be very important. In India and in China, these are not directly elected people. They are chief ministers in India, or mayors appointed by, effectively, the Communist Party in China, with no accountability to people. That makes a big difference in terms of what happens. These are the cities where you tend to see lots of stuff happening which gets central funding, for obvious reasons. You get lots of flyovers; you get new airports, things like that. Big hospitals suddenly arriving on the scene. Probably not dealing with some more complex issues such as regeneration or housing. So you have the mayoral authority, and it's either directly elected or not. If you're directly elected, you're thrown out after four or five years, or you stay in, or as you do in New York, you change the rules, and you stay for another four or five years, which is always interesting to me.

Then underneath that you have the boroughs, which will be units which have their own, depending on where you are in the world, democratic system and sort of mini-governments. Let's call it that. The mayor will have a minister responsible for, let's say, the environment, a minister responsible for transport called the transport commissioner or something like that. Then when you go down into the boroughs—which may be units of, for example, in London, 230,000 people is the average; in New York, it's going to be much higher than that—these have their own mini-structures, their people responsible for transport, the environment, and schools or whatever it may be, at that level.

Then you have—and these names change enormously depending on where you are in the world, and the unit numbers change enormously —the community level. In the States or New York, it's the community-board level. In London, it's the ward level. Where I live in my house, there is a ward councilor who we elect every election. He's the guy who knocks on the door, says, "Is everything all right? I see that your bicycle chain is snapped," or something. It's that level of contact.

Now, there are some cities in the world which don't have this bottom level. There are some cities in the world that don't have the middle level. There are some cities in the world that don't have the top level. All of those situtations have very different implications. Indian cities tend not to have that lower level of democracy because, even though it's a profound national democracy, there isn't that level of engagement. The middle level in some cities, like Johannesburg or Caracas, practically doesn't exist, or it's completely controlled by what happens above. Some are just—what is the word I'm looking for?—some of them are just titular, they don't really have power.

Then a lot depends on the power of the individual. Some individuals come along, incredibly powerful mayors who totally overtake the structure. Then often what happens is significant in terms of the status of cities. Mayors increasingly move from being a mayor to being a national politician to becoming then a president or a prime minister. This is Bloomberg in the United States. What's going to happen? The man who has done actually very well in the national elections of Brazil—he's still second at the moment, but they have the runoff next week—José Serra, was the mayor of the city of São Paulo, then the governor, et cetera, et cetera. Marcelo Ebrard in Mexico will be running for president. You use this as a platform. Jacques Chirac in France became president, and so it goes on.

GH — What about on the other side, the private side? Developers obviously play a big role.

RB — If you look at any city, you just look around you, and you realize one important thing: that 90 percent of it is private capital. Some cities have more public buildings than others or more public investment than others, large structures like schools or universities or hospitals or housing blocks. In many cities, certainly in Europe, you would see that something like 80, 90 percent would be private. People building things because they want to make money out of them at one level or another.

The private sector is absolutely vital to the way they are shaped and the way they are developed, socially and environmentally and economically. It is essential.

I think there the relationship between power structures and private interest can go one of two ways. Often the pendulum swings in favor of corruption and very negative associations between political structures and private interest so that basically land deals are made through zoning regulations on bits of city, which makes some individuals lots and lots and lots of money but ruins the fabric. Or it can swing the other way, which is that actually the private sector, like in Holland, like in most of Scandinavia, Northern Europe, Germany, and Britain to a degree, plays the game and negotiates with the public sector to get planning permission and to do things on the whole by the book. That doesn't mean there isn't corruption as there is perhaps elsewhere. To give permission as a mayor to a piece of land that changes use from, say, industrial to a shopping center is going to make someone a lot of money at some point if the economy is good.

GH — Social housing projects—can you talk about why those didn't work? We can talk about Jane Jacobs too.

RB — That's actually this week's lecture in my class. Should I get out my PowerPoint?

GH — [Laughs.]

RB — The projects in the US were, as social housing estates were here, an attempt to deal with improving the living conditions of a large number of working-class people. The idea wasn't to provide a bad-quality environment. I think most of the architects involved in doing these projects had very noble intentions. I just don't think they had the intellectual tools to really think through what the impact was going to be.

I think the great weakness of nearly all these projects—I don't want to generalize it enormously—of Cabrini-Green in Chicago or any of the housing estates a few miles away from where we are in London in South London, the poorest part of London, is the design of public space, or the absence of design of public space. That so much effort and interest, perhaps rightly so, went into creating the house unit, existence minimum as it was called in Germany in the prewar era—how do you make a space as efficient as possible, with a fridge, with a kitchen, with an extractor fan, all the mod cons you need for people to live?—that little attention went into, well, what happens on the outside? Where do kids play? Where do mothers, which was then a more common question, look at their kids playing? What happened in the rush to knock down perfectly decent terraced housing, which today anywhere in any of these cities would not only be preserved but would be lapped up by the middle classes—in this rush to get rid of them because it would have cost more money to refurbish them, some basic lessons about the relationship between a street, the pavement, and the front door were lost.

I would say that one of the greatest problems, why many of these projects didn't work or didn't work socially, is the distancing between the public realm and the private realm. People became invisible. Richard Sennett speaks a lot about this. What Jane Jacobs was able to describe, I think, incredibly accurately in her book *The Death and Life of Great American Cities*—which was 1961, so we're talking about 50 years ago—she described how the typical New York block, whether it was in Greenwich Village or the Lower East Side, had a very simple quality. Yes, they contained lots of people in apartments, private, public, or whatever, but the ground floor was always activated with stuff. That stuff was either a Chinese laundry or an Indian take-away, an Italian grocer, a shop front for FedEx or whatever it would have been then. If you think of it, the experience of walking down any street in New York is that continuous visual stimulation, commercial stimulation. The minute you take everyone out and put them in a housing block with absolutely no commercial activity, you lose that relationship.

I would say that 80, 90 percent of those estates (we call them estates in England; you call them projects in the States) that have failed to create community—they've put roofs over people's heads; that's true—failed because of that. And then the other thing is the absence of the fundamental social infrastructure which makes life possible: schools, health centers, where people meet informally. Everything then was done by numbers. For every x thousand units, you have to have a primary school and then a secondary school. They weren't necessarily close to where people were living, so then you've got that distancing mechanism. You multiply that forward. The attempt now, in many cases, where they try and, instead of blowing these places up—which for 20 years was the thing to do, right? Think what a waste of resources. You built that much stuff. You're going to blow it up? The attempt now is to retrofit these places. I think that's an important word: to retrofit, to use what's there. You begin to find some of these projects actually beginning to look like normal pieces of the city.

The most extraordinary sight for me was in Moscow: one of these desolate out-of-town tower blocks where people had been moved to about 20 years ago. With the relaxation of Communism there, suddenly private commerce came into being. You have the bus stop, and where the bus stop was, obviously there were more people hanging about. Then on the facade of the ground level, where there had been nothing, there was a newsagent, then next to the newsagent, a butcher. You suddenly actually saw, because there was no pavement, the footsteps of people walking to these places, hanging around, having a cigarette, smoking, and you began to see the essences of communal life.

This is exactly what Jane Jacobs observed. She was the first urban ethnographer. I mean, up until that time, anthropologists, ethnographers, looked at what happened in the West Indies but not at ourselves. William Holly Whyte, another great American sociologist, and Jane Jacobs just said, "Let's see what people are doing, what works and what doesn't work, and very importantly in those cases, relate that to the physical fabric itself and try to connect the two things." I think that's why those ideas are still very, very powerful today.

GH — It sounds like that contact that you get in the city, of different socioeconomic strata, is imperative to an architect, for instance, or urban planning. Understanding that ground level.

RB — Yeah. There's something about the DNA of the cities and the relationship between physical space and social fabric which I think is very clear and little understood by the design professions. That has to do with the notion of whether you divide up people who are different in plans and in sections.

So thinking architecturally, do you have the ground floor where you can see stuff happening and people you know, or don't know, on a daily basis? But then, what happens above? Who lives there? Or is it a monofunctional activity? Is it just an office block with reflective glass and there's no sense of what happens on the street? I think many designers just do whatever their client wants to do without questioning that. It's taken years in London to try and bring back the American or the New York model of having offices over shops, because the people who owned the offices didn't want commercial tenants because they make noise, and they're smelly, and they sometimes don't pay their leases. All the things like that.

I think recognizing that difference between peoples and different activities have to actually be pushed together is what a city is about at its best, and the successful design or the successful designer can, in a way, play with all those different components to make it work. Often working against the interest of different groups—and those groups would be private developers, investors, or sometimes the public authorities themselves—who have a sense of an overcleansed city as being the right place to be. I think more complexity is what we need actually.

GH — We touched on this in the opening question, but the challenges facing cities now. Can we break them down into mobility or public space or housing and discuss those?

RB — I think it's important to frame any discussion at literally a global level before you go down to what the themes are. Cities today consume something like 75 percent of world energy and therefore contribute 75 percent of CO_2 emissions. Why? It's obvious. The wealth and money and activity is generated there. A small reduction in the environmental footprint, the energy footprint of the city, has a massive impact on the planet. I think there are a whole series of issues which need to be discussed around that: issues of sprawl, issues of car dependency, the issue of inefficiency of resources. So that's one cluster.

The other big issue, which balances the 75 percent of energy and pollution, is that 33 percent, roughly, of new urban dwellers today live in slums. That's a third of the world's population, which is vastly urbanizing, living in unacceptable conditions. That means, according to the UN, without the most basic amenities, without sewers, without water, without sanitation. Of course, as the urban population continues to grow, if that number remains the same, we do face a massive problem. I think about it this way: today Mumbai has the same number of people as the whole of London living in slum conditions. The whole of the city. Mumbai is set to become the biggest city in the world in 2050 if it continues the way it is, therefore, bigger than Tokyo. That means that the slum population, if it were to be the same or roughly like it, would be New York and London put together.

These two parameters of the environmental and the social, I think, are the meta-issues for any city. Any city. I think what Copenhagen or New York does is as important today—it's not a drop in the ocean—as Mumbai and Bangkok. I think it's as important also because cities, one of the great things about them is, unlike nations, they learn from each other. Mayors know each other's telephone numbers and call each other and say, "I've got a problem in Barcelona. What do I do?" They do that. A political leader would never do that with another country unless they belonged to NATO or something.

Now, within that framing, I would say that there are three or four big issues that cut across the health of all cities, and by health, I mean in the widest sense possible. One is the size of the city, how sprawled it is or how compact it is, the distribution of the population and its footprint. That has ramifications obviously on both parameters.

The second one, which is very much linked to that, is how do you support populations of a certain size through infrastructure? There's what you don't see underground, that's water, sewers, electricity, but what you do see, mainly above ground, is movement patterns. How do you get people around, and how does that relate to environmental and social inclusion or exclusion? That is important.

The third must be housing: where you actually accommodate people, where they go back in the evening to live. And what are the new ideas which are coming up after a hundred years? Not many, is my quick answer. I've seen very few radical things, some which you're filming in this program, such as Aravena in Chile or some of the inventions of the mayors of Bogotá or Barcelona in making the most poor areas of the city better. By doing what? By investing.

This is a fourth point: the necessary social infrastructure to make, I guess, mixed communities. Cities die if they are just exclusive areas of very rich people and very poor people, business areas here and shopping areas over here. That's not a city. That's just a planning dream, which makes some people happy because of the efficiencies, but most people who inhabit that space, not so.

If we take those four headings—the shape of the city, the infrastructure, housing, and mixed quality of it—they come up to . . . A colleague of mine who I'm a great admirer of, who you might be interviewing in the film, Saskia Sassen, says, "Cityness." How do you describe cityness? Urban isn't enough. Urban sounds a little bit middle class and European. We're working with the Brookings Institution, with Bruce Katz. He says, "No, no, no, we can't use 'urban' in the States. It's sort of froufrou. It's for New Yorkers. We've got to use 'metro.' We've got to talk about 'metro.' How do we solve the problems of 'metro'?" The problems of metro have to do with, I think, these four issues. There are different shades of importance wherever you are in the world. I think those are probably the four big themes, which we can talk about.

GH — I guess it varies by country and political system, but in general, let's just say in Western, democratic societies, can you talk about the importance of citizens being involved in the way their cities are shaped and the consequences if they don't get involved?

RB — It's a catch-22 situation. There are many reasons why citizens involved with anything is a good idea because you have a sense of people's values and what they want. The down side when it comes to cities is what we call NIMBYism, the "not in my backyard" syndrome, which I think can stop some of the risky and difficult choices being made by politicians which might in the short term be negative in terms of the interests of the few but of great value to the interests of the many in the longer term. Here, obviously, I'm thinking about transport systems, or air quality issues, or social provision of one sort or another. Sometimes people don't want to have a school right next to their front door. On the other hand, why not? Someone's going to make a decision about that. I think I have to say that the central-European, modern-European model is outstanding in what it's achieved, and I include Switzerland, Austria, Germany, Denmark, and Sweden in that cluster of countries where civic participation has effortlessly created places of incredible quality of life.

I think the key thing here is information and communication. Many of the things you and I are talking about are actually quite complicated. They're not one-liners on a television debate, which looks good, and they require, really, absorption into what the issues are, the pros and cons, cost-benefit analysis at all levels. I think there's a lot of space needed for that and some evidence that it's happening. I've been involved, as others have, in actually making exhibitions which talk about some of these issues so that the public awareness rises.

GH — How aware do you think most people are about the design issues in their city? Or is it something where you either like this area or you don't like this area, but you're maybe not sure why?

RB — I would say people anywhere have a very, very good sense of what they like and what they don't. Maybe they don't know why, but unlike typography, they feel it more. It is very much something everyone will have an opinion about in neighborhoods in a city. They'll either go there or not go there. Or will they cross the world to go and see a city? That speaks for itself. Low-cost airlines, I think, probably can tell you more about this than I can, the opinion people have. It relates to climate and other things.

I think there's a relationship between the human body and our senses which respond to certain conditions in cities. What we respond to is a sense of closeness and compactness, being enclosed in public space without being claustrophobic, having a sense of what is around you without feeling that you are in a completely windswept plaza. There's some basic things that make the human mind feel comfortable wherever you are from. If you look at basic urban forms that work, they all have those qualities about them, whether it's a baroque city in Germany or

Renaissance Florence or the best of contemporary design. I think those qualities are there.

It's got little to do with the aesthetics, though. It's more to do with the physical shape and notion of, as Richard Sennett speaks often about, how the body relates to the natural environment, and how close do you feel to people who you don't know? I think that's the great quality of cities, that you can feel safe in a crowd. You feel alone. You don't have to be worried about being surrounded by people you don't know, because actually that gives you a sense of, hey, I'm part of the collective; this feels good. That's an essential quality of all cities. In the middle of Mumbai, it is really clear to you, while if you're in a slightly desolate place and suddenly someone comes up to you, you might feel threatened. Those are the two extremes.

I think there are the macro statistics of what's happening across the globe that I've alluded to, and then some very specific things about what's happening, which maybe capture the day-to-day experience of individuals in cities themselves. The macro ones we've talked about: the mere fact that only a couple of years ago half the world was living in cities—100 years ago it was around 10 percent of the population of the world living in cities, and 40 years from now we'll be 75 percent—is a macro issue with enormous consequences. Added to the fact that when three quarters of the world's population will be living in cities, they will consume more and more energy, and more and more people might be living in slums. At the moment, it's one third of the urban population of the world that lives in slums. This raises a whole series of macro questions. I have to stress, I'm optimistic about cities finding solutions. It's just a question of what model we choose, and you can actually begin to shift. If all cities consumed energy like Copenhagen, that graph would drop overnight. That's why, if all cities consume energy like Phoenix, it will just go off the top of the radar screen.

Moving further in, let's think of the pace of growth. At the moment, a city like London or New York is roughly adding 1 person per hour to its population. While many cities in India are growing by something like 35 to 45 people per hour. The peaks at the moment are Lagos, Kinshasa, Dakar, cities that are growing at something like 58, 59, 60 people per hour. That's why I say, every minute that I speak there's a new person entering Lagos. That's one thing.

There are other facts and figures which describe the environmental use footprint. Without going into exact details and numbers, suffice to say that someone who lives and wakes up and washes him- or herself and moves from A to B in an Indian city will probably be using something like 30, 40 percent less energy, less water than someone in China, in one of the new Chinese cities, who in turn will be using something like 30 or 40 percent less than someone in a European city, who in turn will be using something like 30 or 40 percent less than in a typical American city. New York, compared to some of the cities like Mexico City or Johannesburg, uses something like 67 times more energy per person.

GH — You said you were hopeful for the future. That's my next question. What do you think is the future of cities?

>**RB** — I think it's very important that, despite sometimes sounding like doom and gloom—cities have these horrible statistics—it's very important that one stresses the great potential of cities to civilize humanity. They've always done that. People who come to cities speak better languages, appreciate art, eat better food, and live longer. That's what happens. That is, the human development index, as the United Nations calls it, improves in cities. In that sense, I feel that, as long as cities can work on those aspects which improve people's lives and more and more people are moving to cities, that could be a good thing. That means investing in avoiding sprawl, avoiding social exclusion, avoiding the sort of issues we talked about, such as car dependency, but being very positive. Investing in what? In a compact, mixed city, which we see everywhere. You don't have to go that far. It doesn't have to be very rich either. Mumbai is a pretty good example of a compact, mixed city. It has its own problems. Not everyone has to have the income of a citizen of Copenhagen or Oslo to do things well.
>
>I think there's a very simple set, a clear set of emerging principles, which can make cities more civilized, more sustainable, both socially and environmentally, which you begin to see. You begin to see them being talked about. They are to do with the way they're managed. Also how they're governed. Democracy helps to a degree. It's to do with governing the amount of land they actually occupy, who lives where, and where different functions are distributed.

GH — Could you speak about what one can do individually to affect one's city? Do you have any good examples or anecdotes that address that issue?

>**RB** — I guess this raises the issue of the public realm. There's no doubt that the changing urban landscape of cities, in the last 50 years, is leading to a greater sense of alienation of the individual. What I mean by that is, as you come out of your front door in the cities we might be used to, there is a sense that your eye feels comfortable because you can see around you the facilities you know, the places you like, maybe trees next to elegant buildings and all that. I think the cities, the emerging landscapes of the cities that we've been talking about, have very different conditions as people look out of their front door. Often they don't see anything because they're out there, living in some new development on the fringes of Bangalore or Lagos in a newly developed piece of city which has no public transport to get to it. You might have to walk four hours to get a job, which is still the case today in Soweto, for example.
>
>I think the other thing is that you will see an emerging landscape of walls, of boundaries, of fences, of things with barbed wire on them and a sense for a child, for example, of not having the rights to have access to that, whatever it could be. It could be a shopping center. Istanbul, São Paulo: kids there, if you're not wealthy enough, you don't go in. Therefore, you're just left with that structure which invades your state of being. I think much more profound than any of this is the family that lives in a slum or

lives in a purpose-built new piece of housing, which is trying to resolve the problems of the slum but sometimes actually reproduces them.

Let me give you two examples, which are really the flip side of the same coin. Many of the pavement dwellers in Mumbai, people who might have eight or nine children, live in maybe a space not bigger than this table, which doubles up over night in a tent form to house the kids. Many of these people work there; their job is being on the street and dealing with passing trade. One of the communities that actually lived there made baskets; they were basket weavers. They needed the space on the pavement to work with the bamboo. Then they'd make their baskets. Then they'd put them there, and they'd sell them.

The Mumbai authorities decided to build a massive new motorway in the city with World Bank money. They moved all these people into purpose-built housing. The buildings are 12 stories high. The distance between one window and the other is the distance between me and the camera, so it's close. They were designed at lower standards than the national building regulation allowed because it was for poor people. Therefore, there was no ventilation in these concrete bunkers. The heat of Mumbai was unbearable. The families moved in. The rooms were too small to actually do their craft; therefore, they lost their jobs. They didn't have the money to pay for the electricity. They had to walk up and down on these lifts. These lifts were used for rubbish; they started throwing rubbish in. Within the matter of three months, the lift shafts became infested with rats. From a horizontal slum, you have a vertical slum.

GH — How would you approach that differently?

RB — That's where design is absolutely central. I mean, there are different ways of designing housing for poorer people, which go back to the part of our conversation about how you organize the public realm and access to streets from doors and all that without having to repeat all of the problems from the last 30, 40 years.

GH — Okay. We've covered a lot of this stuff, but if you go to the cinema to see this movie, what's the one thing that you hope that somebody up on that screen talks about?

RB — I guess the sorts of projects you're going to show in Bogotá or Chile and more are exactly the sorts of things I want to see and say, "Can I bring some of those ideas home?" Most importantly, I would want to see the positive, that cities are positive generators of great new ideas, as opposed to the concentration of depressing news and statistics. Unfortunately, part of my, not job, but the effect of my job has to been to sort of—ah, my God—create a sense of fear of cities, that everyone should stay huddled in their little villages and they'd be happier. No, not at all!
—

Enrique Peñalosa (EP)/ October 25, 2010 Bogotá

Enrique Peñalosa was the mayor of Bogotá, Colombia, from 1998 to 2001. During his term in office, he created the Trans-Milenio bus rapid transit (BRT) system, a network of green spaces and bike paths, and other reforms intended to make Bogotá a more livable and equitable city.

—

Gary Hustwit — Could you talk about the challenges of cities?

Enrique Peñalosa — The challenges of cities are the challenges of how to live happier lives, because a city really is only a means to a way of life. We cannot decide what kind of transportation we want for a city before we know what kind of city we want. It's very different if the city we envision is more like Houston or, rather, if it is more like Amsterdam. Even before we know what kind of city we want, what we really have to know is, how do we want to live? Because a city is only a means to a way of life. I think that cities can be very powerful in creating environments that are more fertile for human happiness.

One of the things that they can do is to make people less inferior, more equal. A city that works well will have rich and poor meeting as equals in many circumstances: on public transportation, in parks, on sidewalks, at cultural events, in libraries. In cities which do not work well, in cities that are a bit sick, shopping malls replace public space as a place for meeting people. In developing countries, shopping malls tend to be almost like country clubs, to exclude people. A city should comply with that democratic principle that public good prevails over private interest.

The first article in every constitution in the world says that all citizens are equal before the law. This is not just poetry. This is very powerful. It means, for example, that a bus with a hundred passengers has a right to a hundred times more road space than a car with one. Also, this means that public good prevails over private interest so that things that will benefit the majority should be done. For example, if you have a golf club, a country club with a golf course in the middle of a dense city, clearly, millions of people today and in the future would benefit if this were to be turned into a public park.

A city is a powerful instrument to create more equality. You can charge more taxes to higher-income people and invest in better services for the lower-income people, so they can have great sports facilities, parks, libraries. We cannot have equality of income in today's market economy, but we can have equality of quality of life for children. All children should have the same access to green space, and the same access to water. A truly democratic city should have all these waterfronts as public spaces with easy access for everybody and with pedestrian infrastructure.

Clearly, if we have a true democracy, we should not have slums as we have in most developing country cities. Almost half of Bogotá and half of Colombian cities have been developed illegally. Because, even though we have hundreds of thousands of hectares of flat, perfect land for the city's growth, this land is in the hands of a few landowners, speculators, and the poor people have to go to crazy places where there is flooding, where there are steep hills, sometimes even landslide risks.

Clearly, the market does not work in the case of land around growing cities. Private property and the market work when supply increases as prices increase. For example, with tomatoes. If the price of tomatoes goes up, then people will grow more tomatoes. The supply increases, and the price goes back down. If the price of land around a growing city increases, then clearly, you will not have any more of this land. You will not increase the supply of land that is accessible to water, to transport, to schools, to jobs. Therefore, there is no justification, in my opinion, for this land to be in private hands, the land around growing cities. It should belong to the government, and we would have much better cities if this had been so in Latin America. Hopefully in Asia, in India, in Indonesia and the Philippines, they will have much more radical government intervention in the land around cities to avoid the mistakes that we made.

Parks. Are parks some kind of luxury? I mean, do people need to play, or is it just some kind of frivolous, useless activity? I believe that play and access to nature is a need for healthy, happy lives. Central Park in New York differs from European parks, which used to be the gardens and playgrounds of kings and nobles who had to be overthrown or changed somehow in order to turn this land into parks. Central Park was created in the 1850s by a democracy when New York was smaller and poorer than hundreds of developing-country cities today, yet very rarely are we are doing anything now that is close to Central Park.

We have had cities for five thousand years, and for five thousand years, all streets and cities were for people. A child could walk several blocks away without any fear. Today, you tell any three-year-old child anywhere on the planet, "Watch out, a car," and the child will jump in fright, and with good reason because there are more than one hundred thousand children who are killed by cars every year. It is shocking not that that happens but that we think this is normal, that this is progress. I believe the 20th century was a very bad detour in the construction of human habitat. It will take us hundreds of years to correct the mistake. We made almost everything wrong. We made cities for cars, not for people.

I think that continues to be the essence of the conflict between what a good city is and what it is not. We have a very large conflict for space and for funds between people and cars in developing countries. Either you spend your money making highways or you spend it make wonderful libraries and schools and housing and parks because, unfortunately, you cannot do both.

Also, there is a conflict for space. How do you distribute road space? Road space is the most valuable resource a city has. It's more valuable than if a city were to find oil or gold or diamonds in their rich soil. The question is how to distribute this road space between pedestrians, bicyclists, public transport, and cars? I think that it's clear today that it does not matter how much space you give to cars; they will fill up all spaces. If there was more space for cars in London or Paris or New York, there would be more cars. If there was less space for cars, there would be less cars. The mayor of Paris over the last five years or so has eliminated more than 14,000 parking spaces to make bigger and better sidewalks or bicycle ways.

I believe we are on our way to improving our cities. At least the issues are clear. But I think developing countries in particular could do things which are completely different than the cities we find today. For example, we have here in Bogotá some interesting experiments. About 70 kilometers of streets are for bicycles or pedestrians only. Some of them link some of the richest areas to some of the poorest areas, and there are more being built. I believe in the future a really good city should have hundreds of kilometers of streets that are for pedestrians and bicycles only, sort of bicycle highways where people can easily go by bicycle anywhere. Now electric bicycles makes cycling accessible in cities which have hills or to elderly people or for longer distances.

This completely changes life, to be able to be in a city in an environment without noise, without the threat of cars, without the noise of cars, and it does not matter whether cars are electric or not because this is not the issue. Electric cars and gasoline-powered cars kill children just the same. The issue is to create networks of pedestrian and bicycle streets. I imagine some of the Colombian cities in the tropics with this kind of infrastructure of hundreds of kilometers of pedestrian and bicycle streets and giant tropical trees. Our cities will never be able to have the Egyptian pyramids or Notre-Dame Cathedral, but London or New York or Paris would never be able to have something like that. They could do this also in the Philippines or in Indonesia. They would work like fantastic public transport systems but much more pleasant.

They tell me in many places, "Oh, public transport is a priority." What do they do? They put public transport users underground like mice, and they give beautiful highways with trees and gardens and the sky and sunlight to cars. I believe that the best public transport could be surface transport. I think buses have been completely underrated. You could also do trams if you want, but they are much more expensive. Buses have a great flexibility to change lanes without people having to get off and walk to the next line.

I think we could do completely different cities than we have today, with many more parks, with much better public transport, much better sidewalks. At the intersections, the sidewalks should continue on at grade, almost always except maybe at very large intersections, so that it's clear that it's cars that are entering the pedestrian space and not the pedestrians entering the car space. We have to make a city for people. This sounds very obvious, but it's not.

Clearly, we are not making a city for equality. In New York, for example, we are talking about democracy, and we have thousands of kilometers of the Long Island Sound waterfront that are privatized for a few wealthy house owners, but even those wealthy owners of those house, I think they would enjoy it much more if they could ride for dozens of miles on a bicycle next to the waterfront and millions of people could have access to it. This is not communism. This is basic democracy.

Societies have been used to doing very powerful government intervention, to make airports and roads and ports, and they use eminent domain, but now we have to use the same instruments to create pedestrian spaces, to create parks or to create this pedestrian and bicycle promenade along the Long Island Sound waterfront if we have true democratic principles. Democracy is not just the fact that people go vote.

GH — So what exactly is the government's role in bringing about these changes?

EP — I mean, we live at a time when the market is considered supreme. We live at a time in which Adam Smith and market principles reign triumphant. Clearly, communism failed, and we think that most things done by the private sector are more efficient, better quality, and all this, but government is necessary in cities. We cannot just let anybody make buildings any height they want. There needs to be some regulations. What is most fascinating is that these are relatively arbitrary regulations because there is no scientific law that says that a building should only be 4 stories high or 40 stories high or that sidewalks should be 12 meters wide or 2 meters wide. It's not only that government intervention is necessary, but it's a very peculiar kind of intervention because it's very subjective, very ideological because there's no way to prove that this is better. It's something that people feel in their heart and in their soul, but it's not so evident that it should be one way or another, that we should have a park every 3 blocks or every 30 blocks.

Clearly, parks would not exist if it were not for government's intervention. The private landowners will not be nice and kind and create these parks. There must be a shared vision of how we want to live, how cities should be, and then government has to intervene. Government has to intervene, and government has to say, "We are going to give priority in the use of road space to buses and to pedestrians and to bicycles." Government has to intervene and say, "We are going to get rid of parking."

Parking is a very fascinating issue because people seem to imagine that parking is a right, almost a fundamental right to be included in the United Nations Charter. For example, in Manhattan where there are a lot of cars parked along the streets, I believe the city would work much better if they would eliminate such parking and instead make very high-quality protected bicycle ways. Who decides? Why don't we ask the citizens of Manhattan? Regardless of what is done, if a mayor is making sidewalks bigger and the people who used to park there say, "Now where should I park? You have to solve my problem," the mayor can tell them, "Look, in our constitution, there are many rights—the right to housing, the right to education, the right to health—but I don't find the right to park. I don't see any constitution which includes the right to park. If you ask me where you should park, it's almost as if you're asking me where you should put your food or your clothes. This is not a government problem. This is a private problem, which should be solved in private spaces."

Moreover, in many advanced cities, parking is progressively restricted. I think in the future, we should have cities where pedestrian spaces are ever better; bicycle infrastructure is better and better and better, and bicycles are admitted, for example, in any elevator or they can easily find parking; and people will not have cars, but they will have shared cars, a lot of shared cars, or car rental. Or even if people have cars, they will mostly save the car for going out to the countryside. I mean, people will not use the car to go to work or to go to study.

When we are talking about these cities without cars, when we are talking about the conflict between cars and people or if we talk about reducing car use, at first it sounds like some kind of crazy, hippie proposal or something like that, but in fact, today we have cities like London or New York or many cities which are the most attractive cities in the planet. If we ask the best university graduates from India or Latin America or most places in the world if they would want to go live a few years in Manhattan or Paris or London, most of them would jump at the opportunity, and they would go to live in very small spaces and without cars. Limiting the use of cars is not some kind of crazy, hippie proposal. These are cities which not only already exist, but they are the most attractive cities in the world, the cities that attract the most tourists, investors, highly qualified people, have the most valuable real estate on the planet. We are not talking about something crazy. We are talking something which is not only possible but that already exists and it is extremely successful.

Clearly, government is necessary in cities. If we just let the businessman and the market work freely, we will have no parks, no sidewalks, no public transport. It will be a disaster. A city is an area of human life where we cannot simply hand everything to the market. We have to create a shared vision of what it is that we want, and through a collective organization, which is called government, we have to enforce that vision.

GH — A lot of these initiatives and a lot of these things that need to be done, they're unpopular, at least in the short term if people can't see the benefits as easily. Nobody gets into office saying, "I'm going to do something really unpopular." Maybe you could talk about that negotiation?

EP — Many of the qualities that are necessary to be a successful politician are defects when you are in government. People, in order to be elected, many times they have to be really nice and say yes to everything and promise all kinds of things even if they are not true. When they are in government, they have to be responsible and make difficult decisions.

In this case, in the developing countries, what's more worrisome is that, in fact, a developing-country city, almost by definition, is one where the majority of people do not have cars. This minority of car owners—which may be 20 percent, 10 percent, 30 percent, 40 percent—they have all the political power. The low-income people, they do not participate, so even if you were to propose to them measures that are favorable to them, like making better pedestrian space at the expense of parking, they would not support you or they would ignore you.

All of these things are difficult. Many things are not obvious, and they take learning. Many things about cities and particularly about transport are very counterintuitive. For example, it seems to us that it is the sun that goes around the earth. I would have never discovered it myself unless I was told. It seems to us that making bigger roads or flyovers or elevated highways will solve traffic jams. Clearly, this has never been the case, because what creates traffic is not the number of cars but the number of trips and the length of trips. The more road infrastructure you do, you'll have more trips and longer trips, so the traffic will become even worse, but this is very difficult to convey. Especially when people are in a traffic jam, the only thing they can dream of is an elevated highway above them, despite the fact that these high-velocity roads— they become very slow velocity after a while—but these wide roads or elevated highways do great damage to urban quality of life. I mean, values of real estate next to a highway go down in many places. You get crime under these elevated highways. The upper-income people in cities, they want these highways, and now it's very dangerous because these highways are being built privately.

Now in Bogotá, some of the most powerful groups in society in developing countries get together: some of the big civil work contractors, big financial institutions interested in the business of private highways, the upper-income groups who usually don't even walk in the city—the only thing they care about is traffic jams—and big landowners who own land outside the city, who also want the highways to go there. Of course, these highways will not go through the upper-income neighborhood because it's too expensive to put them through there, so they will go through low-income neighborhoods, and the low-income people are not even conscious of the damage it will cause to their quality of life to have these high-velocity roads go through their neighborhood.

This is a great threat to developing-country cities. In advanced cities, for a long time, it has been clear that this does not solve the problem. Maybe some of the biggest political movements in the second half of the 20th century in advanced countries were against the construction of new highways, in London, in New York, in San Francisco. Many highways were demolished, but in developing countries, they still see these elevated highways as great symbols of progress when I think they are great monuments to inequality and to the failure of the city.

It may take a long time, and some of those may be built, and they will be demolished again later on. That's one of the great challenges for cities. When we talk about cities and we say, "The great challenge is to make a city for people," it sounds so obvious, but yet, what we have been making is not cities for people. We have been making cities for cars. We should make cities for the most vulnerable citizens, for children, for the elderly, for the handicapped, for the poor. If we design cities that are great for them, they will tend to be good for everybody else. I would say that every detail in a city should reflect that human life is sacred, that human beings are sacred, but we mostly see that cars are sacred.

GH — How do you deal with the role of private developers? Obviously, you need private development in the city, but it seems like their influence on government is problematic in the case of getting things like eminent domain to build a new shopping mall or a stadium or things like that. Maybe talk a little bit about the role of private developers.

EP — Private developers will do what they can do within the parameters that government sets. Of course, they're very valuable. Many times, they have great ideas, but we are learning. For example, clearly, shopping malls are a sign that a city is ill. If you go to a city that you don't know, what is it that you do? I mean, tourism is pedestrian. One of the great economic activities of our time is tourism. Tourism is a pedestrian activity. What people want to do when they go as a tourist is to walk, and you find that in the tourist magazines, there are no cars in the pictures. Even when they have streets in the picture, the photographer gets up at five in the morning, and then they take the picture before there is any traffic, because cars seem to generate some tension.

If you go to a city, when you ask the concierge at the hotel, "Where is a nice place to walk and see people?" if they tell you, "Go to the shopping mall," you will never go back to that city and never recommend that anybody go to that city. If you are blindfolded and you are put into a shopping mall somewhere in the world, you will not know if you are in Bangkok; in Houston; in Barranquilla, Colombia; in Istanbul, because shopping malls are all the same. With globalization, even all the shops are the same. They are kept at the same temperature everywhere. In the mall, you won't see the mountains. You won't see the vegetation of the place. You don't feel the weather. You don't see the birds.

The private sector can do things that are good. They can do shopping areas which are great for cities. For example, a mall which has shops on the first and second floor but then housing and office space above where the halls are not closed but more like an open network of pedestrian streets. I mean, Venice is a giant shopping mall, except that it's a good shopping mall because it's an open mall and it has shops on the first floors and then offices and residential above. Clearly, private developers do great things, and they can do great things, but society has to intervene through government in order to create some things.

We are seeing horrible things happening when just the market works. For example, in Mexico, they are doing these gated communities 20, 30 miles away from the cities, totally car dependent. Many of these things which failed in the United States, such as low-density suburbs, totally car dependent, are being reproduced in many developing countries but worse because, in the US, they didn't used to be gated. Now they tend to be gated, very far from the centers, completely car dependent.

There are many discussions in cities which, in my opinion, are not the right discussions. We have a lot of discussions, for example, about what the minimum area for low-income houses should be. I mean, of course it will be greater if we have a larger area, but in many cities and societies, it's not possible. But more important than how large the area of social housing should be is the location and the quality of the public space around it. Maybe a very small house, it even can be 30 square meters for a young person who buys his first apartment; it doesn't mean he's going to be or she's going to be living there all their lives but for a few years, and then they will save, and they may buy something else or even the apartment next door and make a bigger one. More important than the size of the housing is the quality of public pedestrian space around it. Does it have nice sidewalks, plazas, parks, sports facilities, access to shops, to the libraries, to public transport? Location and quality of public pedestrian space is much more important, but the discussion that is usually done is about the size.

Another big discussion is the height of buildings. I tend to like cities which have buildings less than eight stories high better, but I also love New York, and it has 40- or 60-story-high buildings. I think more important than the height is what happens at the ground. I remember the words of Richard Rogers. He says, "We must remember that buildings do not end when they reach the ground." I find many times that buildings that are horrible for the city win architectural prizes. The real way to evaluate a building is, does it make the public pedestrian space around it more attractive, more pleasant to be in? After we make a building, is it more fun to be around there, to walk by, to kiss there, to talk there, to play there? I believe this is the way we should judge much of what the private sector does. Does it improve the public pedestrian space around it, or does it do the contrary?

Another example, here in Bogotá all the rooftops of all buildings should have a common area on the roof. Many regulations don't allow a roof to be used by people, and other times it's the penthouse that owns the roof terrace. It should be a terrace for the whole building. We should begin to judge the buildings.

GH — You mentioned architects, can you talk more about their role?
EP — Many times architecture prizes have done some damage because they are giving prizes to some kind of sculptures to create some star architects, but they don't give enough importance to the interrelationship with the city. It's very often that you find architecture books where they have pictures of the public spaces without any people. I think the most important criteria to judge whether a park has good design or not is not whether it wins some kind of architectural prize but whether it attracts people, whether people want to be there and stay there, whether many people want to be there or not. The same can be said about even

private buildings. A very important consideration is, does it improve the public pedestrian space around it?

GH — That seems to be a movement now in architecture.

EP — Yes. In developing countries, for example, one thing that is funny is that people in the upper-income neighborhoods, they don't want to have shops. They think this is low-income thing, but it's crazy because you find in the most successful cities like Milan or New York, you can have a $10 million apartment on top of a deli, bakery, or a restaurant, but in the developing world now, they don't want anything that is commercial near, but actually, it's necessary to have shops near the buildings. I would say for almost any building that is more than 20 stories high it should be mandatory to have shops on the first floor so at least the people can meet there.

I love a definition of a good city by Jan Gehl, a wonderful Danish urbanist who said, "A great city is one where people want to be out, not inside their homes or inside the shopping mall, but where they have fun." With any pretext, people like to go out and walk, but in order for people to have great sidewalks and shops and destinations—because you may have a 10-meter-wide sidewalk with very nice light and trees and benches and everything, but if there is no place to go ... We need shops and restaurants and places where people can meet to be much more intertwined with the residential areas.

In the 18th century, and especially in the 19th century, we had industrial development, which was very polluting and very bad, so we invented zoning, and we zoned that an area should be only residential, only industrial. But happily, modern industry is very clean. Actually, today we can mostly mix everything, and clearly the more intermixed these parks and residential areas and shops and offices and even industry, all the better.

GH — Maybe now we can just talk about Bogotá a little bit. Can describe the urban design of Bogotá circa 1990, 1995, that era.

EP — I have never been in a city which hated itself more than Bogotá. People thought that Bogotá was horrible and not only that, that it was going to be worse and that there was nothing that could be done about it. There was a total lack of self-esteem and lack of hope. I think we were able to turn it around, a group of mayors and the things that we did, basically making a city for people, doing parks, sidewalks, quality public transport, libraries, great schools. Much of what has to be done to improve cities is not a matter of high technology or a lot of money.

Of course, high-income people, especially in developing countries, they want subways. Usually not because they have the slightest intention of getting onto the subway but because they think this way they would put low-income people underground and they would get rid of these buses so they would have more room for their cars. Of course, subways are great if you have the money for them, but the issue is, beside the fact that this is an extremely expensive form of public transport—most things that the city needs are not generally very expensive—it's mostly a political conflict that arises. For example, you have to buy land around the city. I think all growing cities should have very large blocks of government-owned land, which should be bought in the best locations voluntarily or through eminent domain in order to be able to do quality planning, high-quality housing for low-income citizens and, in general, to do a good city. I mean, clearly, the market does not work in the case of land.

In Bogotá, when I was elected mayor, I received a transport study by JICA, the Japan International Cooperation Agency. They are very dangerous because I see them doing the same all over the world, proposing elevated highways and subways so that there is more room for cars. Of course, they are one of the great sellers of cars in the world, so you would not expect an agency of the Japanese government to propose restrictions on cars.

What we did was the contrary. We started to restrict car use. To get cars off the sidewalks was a very difficult battle, to make bigger sidewalks, to restrict cars through a tag number system so that cars could not be taken out on some days at certain peak hours. Instead of making huge investments in giant elevated highways, which is what they proposed all over the city, we started investing in people, in sidewalks, in parks, in great schools, in libraries, in improving slums, in making all kinds of investments for people.

We had a war to get cars off the sidewalks and to make nice sidewalks. Of course, we had a long way to go, but this was something that taught people. Today, in every little town in Colombia, there are at least a few good sidewalks. Instead of following the Japanese advice of creating giant highways, one of the places where they suggested doing an elevated highway, for example, we did a 35-kilometer greenway only for bicycles and pedestrians, which links some of the richest to some of the poorest areas in the city.

Also, we created a public transport system, but clearly, it's not possible for any city to solve its mobility needs with rails. It's too expensive. So we created a bus-based public transport system, and today I think Bogotá has the best bus system in the world and has a lot to improve. Basically, we copied a system from Curitiba, a small city in Brazil, but then we implemented it in this very large city, with seven million inhabitants. It's a very powerful symbol. We wanted our system not just to be a transport system but to be an urban improvement project. We wanted our bus system to attract even car users. It has been quite successful at that because about 20 percent of its users are car owners today. We called it TransMilenio. We gave it a name because buses in most places have a stigma, bad image of being for the poor, so we had to raise the bus's status. Also, we improved the public pedestrian space around it. We built sidewalks and trees and lights.

GH — What was the bus system like before?
    EP — We still can see it very easily because TransMilenio only covers about 25 percent of the city still. The rest is a total chaos of individually

owned buses racing against each other like mad and actually almost at war. I mean, actually, I've seen sometimes when a bus driver would get into a fight with a driver of another bus, and he would get out with a cudgel and break all the other bus's windows, and with the passengers still inside the buses. These were almost all individually owned, about 30,000 individually owned buses racing like crazy for passengers, dumping the passengers, even a woman with three or four children, in the middle of a highly congested road.

TransMilenio is a completely different system where buses go on exclusive lanes. It's like a subway but with buses. People pay when they enter a station. When the bus arrives, the four doors, or even six with these extra-large buses, open, and so the station doors open simultaneously. You can get a hundred people out of the bus and a hundred people into the bus in seconds because they have already paid. In stations, there is an extra lane so that express buses can go by. This is a very high-speed, very high-capacity system. It's moving almost 50,000 passengers per hour per direction, and it could be much better. It could be improved with more underpasses at intersections and bigger stations, because it's too congested now. If we had some subsidies, we could make the buses less full.

Basically, this is a powerful symbol also of democracy because low-income citizens who take public transport have never imagined that the cars would be in a traffic jam practically not moving and the bus would just zoom by. This is a powerful symbol that public good prevails over private interest. Also, it's part of the city's identity today, the same way as bicycle ways are. When we started, there were almost zero bicycle ways. Bicycles ways, protected bicycle ways, are also important not just because they protect cyclists but because they raise the social status of the cyclists. Today, we have about 5 percent of the population using bicycles every day, about 17 percent using private cars, so it's almost one on a bicycle for every three or four that go by private car. This could still increase much, much, much more. We are only beginning to advance in the right direction.

Now Bogotá is a complete traffic jam again. The US dollar value has decreased, the peso value has increased, cars have become ever cheaper, incomes are growing, and people still dream that they can solve traffic problems just by making bigger roads or elevated highways. What we have to learn in developing countries is that even high-income people will have to use public transport. What is funny is that the high-income people in developing countries, they go to New York or Paris or London, and there they take the public transport. Moreover, they feel proud that they are experts at using the New York or the Paris subway next to perhaps the poorest people in those cities, but when they go back to their own cities, they don't want to get near where the low-income people are. That's what we have to understand: that advanced cities, not the ones where everybody goes by car but the contrary, advanced cities are the ones where even high-income people use public transport.

I will say that the most important difference, the most important element in a city's infrastructure is sidewalks. What really makes a difference between an advanced and a backward city is not subways or highways but high-quality sidewalks. In the developing world, you can almost see it. If you just saw some pictures of cities in the advanced and in the developing world, you could easily know which is which by looking at the quality of its sidewalks.

GH — Why are sidewalks important?

EP — Because sidewalks show respect for human dignity. I mean, in developing countries, citizens with cars tend to think they are of a higher status and that they can carve out parking bays and take space out of sidewalks. Moreover, if we talk about transport policy, the concept of transport policy to an advanced city's secretary of transport immediately translates into how to reduce car use. In developing-country cities or underdeveloped-country cities, transport policy translates exactly into the opposite—how to facilitate car use, how to solve traffic jams.

Something that must be understood is that mobility and traffic jams are two different issues. Mobility is solved with public transport, great bus systems, subways, whatever, but this will not solve traffic jams. You can have a subway under every street, and you would still have traffic jams. The only way to solve traffic jams is to restrict car use, and the most obvious way of restricting car use is restricting parking. If you want to have a city without traffic jams, you will have to restrict parking. In some advanced cities, even parking in private spaces is restricted. In Central London for more than 40 years, new buildings have not been able to build parking so that people will have to use public transport, even high-income people. This is something that is not yet very well understood in most developing-country cities.

There are two reasons why car use should be reduced. One is for quality of life. Clearly, a city that is very friendly to cars is not very friendly to people. I mean, very wide roads, narrow sidewalks are not very pleasant to be around. Beyond quality of life, which is relatively subjective, there is also a mathematical issue. It's not possible to solve mobility in a large city just by making bigger roads and using cars.

Here's an example: Let's imagine in a city there was an earthquake or a war and there was only enough fuel to move 5 percent of the city's vehicles. To whom would you give this scarce fuel? If you gave it to private cars, the city would die because, clearly, a few people would move, but then the city could not function. People could not go to work. You could not move merchandise. The city would die. The rational thing most cities would do is give this very scarce fuel not to a few private cars but to trucks and buses so the city would still work well. Otherwise it would be committing suicide.

Now I ask—let's imagine that what is scarce is not fuel but space—which is the rational way, the democratic way of distributing road space? To whom should we give this scarce road space? I think, clearly, we should restrict more and more the use of private cars and have ever better public transport. You can have great public transport if you just have buses and exclusive lanes. You could go everywhere in a city very quickly. When will people use public transport? Whenever people use public transport, it's not because they love public transport or the environment; it's because public transport is more convenient. Basically, it's faster. It's much faster, and you don't have the hassle of parking.

The cities we dream of for the future are cities with hundreds of kilometers of streets only for buses, bicycles, and pedestrians. Hundreds of kilometers of pedestrian and bicycle streets only, great sidewalks, lots of life in the streets, great parks, plazas, sports facilities, cultural centers for music, for libraries. Cities where people will have great fun.

When I was a student many years ago in Paris, I was very, very, very poor. I lived in a very dumpy little room. I did not even have a shower. I had to share the toilet with 20 other dumpy little rooms like that. But then I had Paris. I went out, and the Paris I had was very similar to the Paris those rich people had. I could go to beautiful museums, to sidewalks, to parks, to the public spaces by the river. That's what a great city can do—create a lot of happiness for everybody.

GH — I like this idea of how, in a lot of cities, temporary interventions—we shot a lot of the Ciclovía yesterday and other places too—give people a chance to see what it could be like but in a very temporary way. There's no commitment really.

EP — Ciclovía was the seed for everything that we did in Bogotá. It first was created in the seventies, and then when Antanas Mockus became mayor, he increased it from 30 kilometers to 70 or 80, and then we increased it to 110, 120.

GH — Can you explain to us what Ciclovía is?

EP — Ciclovía is, in Bogotá, every Sunday we close about 120 kilometers of main streets, and we get like a million or a million and half people every Sunday jogging and riding bicycles. This is fantastic. This is a ritual because, first of all, people like to do what is bad, and since you've been a child they've told you, "Don't go into the street. Don't go into the street." So it's always fun to do all of this when you are allowed to do what you were never allowed to do. Also, you can see the city like you have never seen it before. You see the architecture, the trees. Because when you are in a car in a traffic jam, you can never see anything, with the noise, the exhaust.

It's a ritual; it's a ceremony where human beings reconquer the city for a few hours every week. It's a big battle because many upper-income people want to get rid of the Ciclovía and to have just all the space for cars. At one point in Congress, they approved a law to reduce it two hours, and we organized a huge movement, and everybody was against this reduction of the Ciclovía by two hours. On the contrary, we started doing a Christmas-night Ciclovía. Near Christmas, we do the same thing at night between six and midnight, and we get like three, four million people out. It's amazing.

Also, we have another ritual that is very interesting. When I was mayor, we asked the people to vote on a referendum, and we had two questions. One was whether they wanted to completely ban cars during peak hours every day beginning in the year 2015, so 15 years later. The other question was whether they wanted to have a car-free day the first Thursday of every February. There were some businessmen that made a huge campaign against us, not to vote no because they knew they were going to lose by far, but for people not to vote at all because that way we would not be able to reach the 33.3 percent of potential voters that was necessary to make it legally binding.

We narrowly missed getting the total ban of cars during peak hours every day, but we got the one car-free day approved. Every first Thursday of every February this eight-million-inhabitant city has no cars, only taxis, buses, and trucks, because the idea is not that the city gets paralyzed but to learn to live in a different way. Most people have much shorter travel times that day, less pollution, less noise, and the city works fine: 99.9 percent of the people go to their regular activities. They walk; they ride a bicycle; they take the bus. It's possible. It's a fantastic ritual. As it was approved through a referendum, it cannot be turned back, not by the president, not by Congress. The only way to do away with this would be to have another referendum.

[The next day, Enrique picks us up in a pickup truck loaded with bicycles and drives us to the outskirts of the city. Ben Wolf, our cinematographer for this trip, hopped into the back of a pedicab, and we all bicycled for about an hour.]

GH — Tell us about where we're riding now?

EP — Okay, here we are on part of the Porvenir Promenade. This is a 24-kilometer pedestrian and bicycle-only street, which I think is a revolution in the way urban life works. I think we should have hundreds of kilometers of pedestrian and bicycle-only roads in cities. This shows great respect for human dignity; extremely efficient mobility. In all these areas with lots of traffic jams, it's much faster using the Porvenir Promenade by bicycle than taking a car or a bus, and it's actually linked to bicycle parking in the TransMilenio stations. There are also bicycle taxis such as that one over there, pedicabs, which actually are sort of feeders to the TransMilenio system. It's a human-powered feeder. This kind of high-quality infrastructure for bicycles is important because before we had bicycle ways, low-income people were ashamed of using bicycles, because it was like being extremely poor. Now, a high-quality protected bicycle way shows that a citizen on a $30 bicycle is equally important to one in a $30,000 dollar car. Again, this is democracy at work.

When we first came here, this was completely flooded with sewage water, no sewage system, no services of any kind, no schools, nothing. Now we have fantastic infrastructure. We don't have pavement for cars yet, only a few roads have been paved for buses to come in, but there are parks; there are schools. For every house, they were able to get property titles.

Here, in the middle of this very low-income neighborhood, we have a high-quality community center, a child nursery for three hundred children, a very high-quality school, and even an indoor swimming pool. It's even better infrastructure than in the richest areas of the city. And here is something interesting: you can see how the pedestrians and bicycles have pavement, and the cars are in the mud. So it's a priority for the pedestrians and the bicycles, and then later sometime we will pay for the cars. But first the pedestrians, so this completely shows respect for human dignity, for everybody, not just those who have cars who normally think they are the important ones in developing-country cities.

—

Grady Gammage, Jr. (GG)/

December 2, 2010
Phoenix

Grady Gammage is a land use, zoning, and real estate attorney based in Phoenix, Arizona. He also has represented cities with regard to economic development issues and development agreements. Grady is a Senior Fellow at Arizona State University's Morrison Institute.

—

Gary Hustwit — I guess that we'll start with the easy stuff. How did you get involved in this?

> **Grady Gammage** — I'm sort of a frustrated architect. I grew up on a university campus in a city and watched buildings getting built and was always kind of fascinated by that. I thought of being an architect, but in the days when I was going to school, you had to draw, and I couldn't draw. I'm a talker. So I became a lawyer, but I sought out urban issues. What I mostly do is I'm kind of in between the political decision-making process about real estate and projects and development approvals and architects and developers who have a vision of what they want to do. I explain what they're trying to accomplish to a political body that gets to approve it. It's fun. It's been a good niche. Out of that, out of working on individual projects, I got started thinking about cities and about Phoenix in particular. In 2000 I ended up writing a book about why Phoenix is the way it is.

GH — Got it. Could you give us a summation your argument in the book?

> **GG** — Okay. I wrote this book to try to explain Phoenix to people. I did it largely because I was going to all these zoning hearings and battles, which are very public controversies here. They're on TV. They're on cable channels. There are lots of people who've moved here from somewhere else that are pissed off about government. They thought they were getting away from government, and then they got here. They discovered that development is getting near them, and they really want government to stop it from getting near them because they like things the way they are. So I felt a sort of missionary need to explain how Phoenix got to be the way it is.
>
> I still think the best book about cities is probably Jane Jacobs' *The Death and Life of Great American Cities*, which we tend to remember as this ode to Greenwich Village. The real contribution of it is making you realize that cities are the way they are because of millions of incremental decisions by

the people who live there about how they want to work, how they want to live, how they want to spend their time. Those incremental decisions that individuals make are made in the context of a particular technology, a particular government climate, and a particular geography. It's the coincidence of those influencing factors on the individual decisions people are making that make cities look the way they do.

Here's why Phoenix looks the way it does. Phoenix looks the way it does because it became a big city in the postwar environment of the latter half of the 20th century when the automobile was the dominant mode of transportation. Phoenix is built on a grid. It's an old farming town. You can drive anywhere you want. You can get from any place to any place else. That made a downtown less important. It distributed both the population and the places of work all over the place.

At the same time as there's that force of the automobile to disperse population, there are forces to concentrate population. One of those again is a transportation force, which was air travel. Phoenix was never a big railroad town. In the railroad era, you could have lots of medium and small cities. In the air-travel era, you have fewer, bigger cities because they're concentrated around airports. Phoenix was a winner in that. Tucson was a loser. Tucson didn't grow as much because it was too close to Phoenix, and Phoenix seized the air travel. In Phoenix, you have lots of public land that's hard to develop, and you have a water constraint. You have to be hooked up to water pipes to live here.

The result of those factors and the single-family detached-home building emphasis that happened post–World War II is that we have a relatively uniform density. From downtown to the edge, everybody lives in a single-family detached home on a quarter-acre lot. That's an oversimplification, but it's close. It's not that Phoenix is a remarkably low-density city. It's a remarkably uniform-density city. That makes it different than older cities that arose in an era when you had to be able to walk to get places—we don't walk here much; we get in our car and we drive—and when you didn't have air travel pushing everything together at the same time that the car was pushing everything out.

GH — I wonder if you could describe the process. A developer comes to you and says, "Here's the plans." Walk us through a typical scenario and all the sort of pitfalls that occur in that process.

GG — Let me talk about Phoenix and that process for just a minute. There is a perception people have when they drive around Phoenix that, "This place is awful. This is all unplanned." That isn't true at all. Phoenix is intensively planned. This is what we planned for. We may not like it now that we've got it; it may seem unduly bland and homogeneous. That's in part the result of planning. You reach conclusions about how uses should be separated. We don't have very many mixed-use places. We have single-family homes here at one density and single-family homes at another place at a slightly different density. We don't want the two to mix because that would result in too much friction between people who've paid $200,000 and people who've paid $500,000, and they really need to live in their own little enclaves.

In any event, the way the process operates in the capitalistic, pluralistic, Western democracy that is Phoenix is somebody gets ahold of a piece of property, usually ties it up subject to getting zoning approval. Lots of times the property already has zoning, but they want to change it for higher density or a greater range of use or something. This can be anything from a small site where somebody wants to build a multistory office building or an apartment complex to a thousands-of-acres tract where they want to build an entire master-plan community. Increasingly, the development of Phoenix has gone into these big tracts that people have managed to buy out.

So a developer has an idea of what he wants to do. Some developers are very intensely interested in the art form of development. They have a vision that they want to translate. Some developers are just interested in the bottom line. They have a spreadsheet and a yield they want to produce. So there's a whole range in there. Based on what they think the market wants, what they'll be able to sell quickly, their needs to capture enough revenue to repay the cost of the land and then the infrastructure going in on the land, they'll come up with a general scheme of what they want to do. They will then hire a land-use planner and a zoning lawyer. The land-use planner draws the drawings. The zoning lawyer tells them, "Yeah, this is going to be really hard to get approved. We're not going to be able to get that. You need to massage it a little bit. Put a park over here, and I can sell it in this area." The zoning lawyer tends to know the politics of the local approving body, which is usually a city council.

Then you file a case. There's a city planning staff that looks at your case and makes a professional judgment as to whether or not it satisfies their vision of the community and fits into the general plan. All cities have these general plans that show what they'd like to see happen in different areas, but that's all pretty malleable frankly. So the planning staff makes a recommendation. Then it goes to the Planning Commission, which is a citywide body appointed by the city council. At that point, you have to post big signs on the property saying that you're going get it rezoned for a new project.

Now the neighbors start to come out of the woodwork. Typically in Phoenix, there will be significant neighborhood opposition to anything, anywhere, at any time because we're a very populist place. It's a very middle-class town. Everybody has a say. We'll listen to everybody at great lengths. The system is set up to give them an opportunity to be heard. Immediately adjacent neighbors get special protest rights. They can trip a super majority at the city council. Any zoning case can be taken to referendum by a petition circulated that gets enough signatures. It gets put on a general election ballot. So it's kind of this free-for-all that happens, and as I said earlier, the zoning hearings are mostly on cable TV.

So you go to the Planning Commission, and the lawyer usually stands up, presents the case. The opposition, if there is any, and often there is, gets up. They present their case. The staff makes their recommendation, and the Planning Commission takes a vote. That vote is only a recommendation to the city council. Now it goes to the city council. There are American states that make many of their land-use and zoning decisions in a different model that's called a quasi-judicial model where there's a board or a hearing officer that is acting more like a judge, which is to say they're trying to find the right answer. They're trying to apply rules of evidence. They're trying to keep out extraneous information. They're trying to make a principled decision. We don't do that here. This is a legislative issue, so it's a free-for-all. You can lobby the city council. You can talk to them outside of the meetings. The neighbors can lobby the city council. You can raise money for city council candidates from either side. They vote just like a legislature votes. The zoning cases are all considered to be legislative in character.

So you have the hearing in front of the city council. You usually lobby them beforehand. You kind of know where the votes are. They vote on the case. Then you start the long process of doing the really detailed design of where the pipes go, where the sewers are, how big the streets are and getting it to the stage where you can start to deliver product. It usually takes six to nine months to get through that whole system.

GH — Do you think that the way Phoenix does it—like you're saying, the free-for-all kind of lobbying—do you think that's a good thing? Do you think it encourages abuses?

GG — There are pluses and minuses. Phoenix is not an overtly corrupt system at all. I have never even had a councilman say, "Slip me a little money, and I'll get you your zoning." Thirty years of this, I've never had that kind of a discussion with anyone. But corruption is a word that has broader meaning. The fact that we make these decisions in a political context is itself somewhat corruptive as an influence. It's just the way a state legislature is or the way Congress is. If there are lots of people in opposition to your case, even if it's a really good idea, you're going to have a very hard time getting it approved because those people are voters, and polititicians don't want to run over voters. On the other hand, if you are a developer who is well known to the city council, who is well regarded, who has raised money for all of them, who has gone to cocktail parties with all of them, you're going to get treated better than a guy they've never heard of. Those things are all true. Those are sort of inevitable corollaries of the fact that it's a political process.

I actually have written in the past that I would change the system here somewhat. I think it isn't corruption that concerns me as much as it is the absence of a vision for the city. The way we do it tends to lead to very ad hoc decisions. Here's a tract of land; I want to develop it. The issue is really, can I buy off the immediately adjacent neighbors into not causing too much trouble? That's the process. Shut up the immediate neighbors by giving them something, trees, buffers, walls, landscape, whatever it is, and you'll probably get approved. That's resulted in the city we have now, which is a city that frankly doesn't have a lot of distinction or character in many ways. It's kind of a bland, homogenized, suburban, postwar palette of beige stucco and red tile. I had a friend who grew up here who's now an architecture school dean in another part of the country. When he comes back here, he says, "Taco Bell ate my town. It devoured the fabric of Phoenix." It is what we have. I would like something with more distinction and more character and maybe some more points of punctuation in the urban fabric where there are higher-density nodes of more urban stuff.

To do that, you need a kind of an overriding vision, but it's hard to implement that when you have an ad hoc decision-making process. So I think we would be better served by making the community's general plan—which is this big, sweeping, sort of aspirational document about the city—the legislative decision that gets voted on by the city council. Then most zoning decisions would be treated as implementations of that in more of the quasi-judicial model. I've talked about that for 10 years around here, and I can't get anyone to agree with me. I'm like a lone voice, but I think that would make more sense.

GH — Yeah, it's not about how this project over here is going to really relate to this project over here or to the city at large.

GG — Yeah. I mean, think about New York for a minute. Is New York the way it is because it had that strong vision, or is New York the way it is because of the Jane Jacobs analysis I described a minute ago? It developed at a time when density was important. The elevator made it possible to build big buildings. Everybody had to commute in to the same place to work because you had to be able to bump into people and talk to them and have meetings with them. It's at an enormously important shipping channel. Is that what made New York New York, or was there some vision? It's bits and pieces of each. Central Park is part of a vision that made New York something special I think.

GH — When it comes to development, just in general and specifically in the Phoenix area, it seems like another one of the causes of sprawl is it's easier to get a blank slate outside the city.

GG — Yeah, when you put this enormous emphasis on what the citizens near a project think, the best thing you can do is build a project where no one lives near it. It's like a tautology. Go to the edge because there's nobody there, and they're not going to protest. Then the next person comes along, and they're like, "We have to go further out than you are so that your people don't protest." It is much easier to develop on the edge. The fact that we don't have an ocean that stops us on any given side, that we can keep moving farther and farther out as long as we keep extending the water pipes farther and farther out, does create an incentive for that.

I think there's a second factor, though, that's at work. This is, for better or worse, probably even gonna be more important in the next wave of development when it comes back, which is that, if you are an individual deciding how you want to live, and you're going to invest money in buying something, for many people it is an easier, simpler, and safer decision to buy a detached, single-family home. You don't have to have a co-op board that you deal with or the condominium association. You don't have to worry about the fact that your neighbor is unduly noisy because you're plenty of distance away from him.

In this last development wave, there was a perception that Phoenix was going to start becoming more dense, and we were going to build lots of condominiums. That didn't work out real well. You can go right across the street and film an empty 30-story tower that never got finished partly because, in a decision about whether to buy a $300,000 condo unit versus a $300,000 single-family home, the risks are less in the single-family home. For a developer to build condo units, you've got to build like a hundred of them at a time. If you're doing single-family homes, you can build like two at a time or one at a time. If the market's there, you can change your product. You can scale up. You can scale down. It's much easier to do that. So there are all kinds of economic reasons, I think, that also drive development to the edge in Phoenix, because it's a safer bet. It's just a safer bet.

Let me say one other thing about sprawl. There's a perception, if you listen to NPR, that sprawl is always bad and Phoenix is a poster child for bad sprawl, and sprawl is evil and undermines America. James Howard Kunstler is the sort of ultimate antisprawl diatribe guy who believes that it is undermining the patriotic character of America. One of his lines is, "No American ever fought and died for a Burger King." Phoenix is not, I think, a poster child for the kind of sprawl that gets decried by Kunstler or Richard Moe with the National Trust for Historic Preservation. The main negative of sprawl as it used as a pejorative term, to me, is the redistribution of a city that grew up under a different era. If you look at a place like Cleveland or Philadelphia or Detroit, what happened was they were classic industrial, hub-and-spoke cities where everybody commuted to the downtown. Then the influence of the automobile and the single-family, detached home was to redistribute that population. So it hollows out the core. It spreads everybody out over a larger area of land. The second major indictment people make of sprawl is that it eats up the bucolic rural villages of Vermont by overrunning them with subdivisions, that that would be a better lifestyle to preserve.

Phoenix isn't about any of that. Phoenix isn't a redistributing place. Phoenix gets denser every year. Phoenix and Las Vegas are two of the only American cities that become more dense every single year. It's not a city where we're taking a high-density population and redistributing it at a low density. We're building at the same density we've always lived at. Many of the developments on the edge of Phoenix are more dense than the way people live in Arcadia or areas closer to Phoenix. Nor are we overrunning rural, pastoral landscapes. Now, we are eating up desert, and the desert is really beautiful and really important. We've tried to learn a better way to develop in the desert, but it's been hard to do.

I don't think this is a poster child for sprawl. This is a poster child for an automobile-oriented, postwar urban fabric. This is what you get. If you take this urban fabric and you slap it up next to Philadelphia, then you create sprawl.

GH — So in general, you're not buying that sprawl is always bad, and density is always good?

GG — No, here's the deal. Let's be honest. I live on a three-quarter-acre lot. I like my backyard, and I like my swimming pool. I think living in a condo would be cute and interesting, and I'd like to do it about two months out of the year, but I like the way I live, so there you are. That's what it's really about at the end of the day.

GH — Can you do a little population-growth overview of Phoenix?

GG — One of the things I often explain to people about Western cities is a compare and contrast with Phoenix and Denver. At the turn of the 20th century, in about 1900, Denver, I think, had about 100,000 people. Phoenix had 5,000 people. At 1950, at the halfway mark, Phoenix and Denver were about the same size; they both had about 500,000 people. These are city-limits statistics on the two cities, not metro area. At the year 2000 or the late nineties, Denver had 550,000 people. It had basically stabilized. The metro area had grown around it. Phoenix at that point had 950,000 people. On a city-limits basis, Phoenix is more than twice as big as Denver today. That's why it's the fifth largest city, because its limits are so huge. Phoenix really exploded from about 1955 to the end of the century.

GH — Including both the city limits and metro area, how big is it?

GG — The population of the metro area is right under 3.5 million today. For a metro area, I think we're 12th largest in the country or something. City-limits Phoenix is now bigger than Philadelphia.

GH — Can Phoenix continue to sustain that rate of growth?

GG — I think the real question about the growth is about the nature of the economy here. This place is kind of a giant pyramid scheme that was built on the concept of importing people from the Midwest to live here because there's sunshine. The economy of Phoenix is based on sunshine and cheap land and enough water. That's worked because we could deliver houses that were a bargain, because people wanted to retire here into a single-family lifestyle and play golf. The fact that there were lots of people wanting to move here meant it was a good place to bring some industry. It's been sunshine and cheap land that are the basis of the economy. I don't know if that's going to keep working as effectively as it did in the last generation.

Phoenix is not as much of a retirement town as is commonly perceived. Our median age is actually below the national average because lots of people with lots of children move here and we have a fairly high birth rate. The retirement mecca aspect of Phoenix has been part of what has sold it and created an image. That was predicated on the retirement of people who had pensions. We don't have those anymore for the most part. It was predicated on people who wanted to retire to play golf. All the statistical surveying that's done says that demand is on the wane, that golf is not as popular anymore. There's also a lot of evidence that people don't want to retire as far away from home. They don't want to move across the country as much. So that may be changing.

We also have succeeded with industries like electronic chip manufacturing. That's largely gone; that's gone offshore. Then a big industry in

Phoenix after that was call centers. Call centers are largely gone; that's gone offshore. Phoenix has always been the last stop before industries move out of the US altogether because we've had cheap wages, we don't have labor unions by and large that are particularly influential, and we have a low-cost lifestyle. So we're almost like a third-world country or an emerging democracy or something. As the planet gets more global, that's going to become more and more difficult. Phoenix has not been a knowledge-based economy. It hasn't been the mecca of Richard Florida's creative class. Could it be? I don't know. There are lots of people sitting around trying to figure out, how do we get people who want to live in San Francisco to live in Phoenix instead? It's a tough sell.

Somehow we have to face that issue, or I think what will happen is our growth will flatten, and we may begin a slow, trickling decline. I don't think we will suffer any kind of catastrophic erosion of people here because we don't have a dominant industry. It's not like how automobile manufacturing killed Detroit. What's going to kill Phoenix? The absence of home building may kill it. That's a different sort of an industry. That's not a primary industry.

GH — What do you think is in the future for American cities?

GG — There are a bunch of interesting issues about what will happen to American cities in the future. When I wrote the book on Phoenix, I was enamored of the impact of the Internet age on cities. I tended to think it would have a dramatic effect, that just as a city like Phoenix became possible when the transportation modes changed, when the Internet became a dominant mode of communication, it would result in a lot more dispersion of employment opportunity. Therefore, people would not feel as much need to congregate in office spaces together as they had previously because we wouldn't need as much face-to-face interaction. I've changed my mind. I think that was wrong. All those of us who work from home or from different offices have learned, no, we really still like to interact with people. It is interesting, though, if you go to any Starbucks in any city in America, how many people you will see on a laptop working. That's like their office. They could do it at their apartment. They don't. They do it at Starbucks because you like to be around other people.

I think it does have an impact on cities. One of the things that has happened in Phoenix is that it has shaved the rush hour. We're not going to have to build as many big roads as we used to for rush hour because people can avoid rush hour by working from home until the traffic clears. Then you can get on the freeway. That is very noticeable in my law office. Everybody used to come in at eight in the morning. You never know when they're coming in now. If the traffic's bad, they just stay home and work from home. You can do that easily enough. They still come in, though.

I also thought after 9/11 that we might see an impact where we would no longer build buildings so tall and so vulnerable, and that we might see more lower-rise development. But I don't think that has really happened either.

Cities are increasingly going to be driven not by necessity—the necessity of transportation, the necessity of communication, the necessity of bringing bulk of products for delivery—but by choice. People like cities. People like living together. They like it in all kinds of different ways. The range of choice that people are going to be afforded is going to become ever greater, I think. In a place like Phoenix, many people are interested in living at somewhat higher densities and in somewhat more urban contexts. A lot of people in Phoenix are frustrated by the absence of a place to just go and hang out. Mill Avenue, which is near my office here, is such a place, but it's one of the few places like that in this metro area. All of that, I think, will result in more variety in both housing product and in urban form.

I do think that retail is probably going to pretty dramatically change. A lot of fungible retail that happens in big box stores in a place like Phoenix, Best Buys and such, I think that's going to go onto the Internet. If you're buying a Sony TV, it's a Sony TV. You may need to go look at it somewhere, but you know you want a 40-inch TV; it comes with a good warranty; you don't need to try it out. You don't even take it out of the box when you go to the store. Why not just have it delivered? In Phoenix, we have all these shopping centers. I'm not sure what's going to happen to all those. There is not going to be as much demand for physical retail presence as we have in a place like Phoenix, for all that fungible retail. The retail that you like to do, that you do because it's a way of communing with other people, because it's fun—you can try stuff on and talk to people about it or whatever—I think that will still be something that animates urban places, but I think it's going to change its character.

I think we're still going to build high-rise buildings. People like the views. They like seeing them. They like having those punctuation marks to the urban fabric. I think places like university campuses will continue to be places of importance where people want to go because it's an interesting thing to do. People care about the aesthetics and the quality of the environment they inhabit. They care about that in a natural context, but they also care about it in a man-made context. The greater freedom that will be afforded by the range of choices that people have in the future, I hope, will result in even more creative and interesting and unusual architecture and design. That's going to attract people to places and distinguish places. That's going to be increasingly important, because it's going to be a choice as to whether or not you go to those places. You're not going to have to go there.

GH — I wonder if, from an urban planning or an urban design standpoint, you could just give me sort of a checklist of the kind of questions or challenges that any city faces. What are the things that people in urban design have got to deal with? What's the range?

GG — If you're an urban designer today in the United States, the number one issue is parking. Where's the parking? How much parking do you need? How do you design the parking? Does the parking surround the building thereby separating it from the street? Is the parking hidden under the building? Is the parking in structures? Is the parking in flat parking lots? It's a sad commentary, but I cannot tell you the number of meetings I have been in over the years about a development proposal where I came to the sobering realization that it's driven by parking, that it's all about parking. There are a few places where it's not true: Manhattan, downtown San Francisco, downtown Chicago. Actually, in Chicago, parking is more important than it is in the other two in many ways. The average development thing, it's all about parking. How do we get the cars in? How do we get the cars out? Where do they stay while they're there? They're bigger than people are, and they're harder to accommodate. It's unfortunate because, from an urban design standpoint, what it does is it separates everything. In Phoenix, a parking lot is the worst place you want to be because, when it's 110 outdoors, the parking lot is 130. It's just the most awful environment imaginable, but it's inescapable.

So I think the number one issue that drives urban design is transportation—how do people and cars get in and out of places? If you're going to try to shift away from the car as we did here with our first effort at light-rail, it's very expensive, and you really have to figure it out and think about where it goes. The other issues, the infrastructure issues, the sewers and the water, the electric, the capacity of these systems to accommodate growth are all driving factors in that.

Then there are the aesthetic judgments that we tend to relegate to city councils in America. Where do we want tall buildings? Where do we not want tall buildings? How do we feel about tall buildings near houses? Those kinds of issues. How do we feel about small housing lots near big housing lots? Do we want to separate everything, or do we want to pull everything together? Those are the kind of big waves that run through urban design. Zoning is all about separating uses because it was about the impact of the industrialization of America. Factories suddenly getting built near people's houses didn't work out real well. We needed to, in advance, separate things. We probably got carried away with it and separated things way too much. So now the tendency is to try to reintegrate those kinds of things. You have mixes of uses, the infrastructure issues. Good urban design has to think about the market. You can't just design stuff that looks great but nobody wants. I think understanding how people decide what kinds of houses they want on the inside is very important, and how those houses look on the outside.

GH — It's funny, talking about cars and parking. We were just in Bogotá. Enrique Peñalosa is the ex-mayor there. He said, "I look at the constitutions of most countries, and I don't see the right to park written anywhere. Why do we as a government care about what you do with your car? Your car is your private property."

GG — Right. It's interesting, we debate this around here all the time. We, by and large, generally have very high parking requirements because we think government should be in the middle of that. Downtown Phoenix got rid of the parking requirements years ago. The problem we've got here is the market. There is a market expectation that parking will be free and abundant everywhere all the time. So I built this building 10 years ago. I have one parking space for every thousand square feet. That is one fourth to one fifth of what most office buildings in Phoenix have. It is a challenge to get tenants to come here. I knew it when I did it.

I knew this was a risk. I was trying to do an urban thing. I thought there would come a time when I would be able to reclaim that parking that's underneath the building for more usable space. I would say I lose 75 percent of the tenants who look at this place because there isn't enough parking on site. There's parking across the street. You have to pay because we're on the edge of a university campus. You pay for parking. Even in the building, you pay for parking. They don't want to do that. Everywhere in Phoenix, parking is abundant and free, and they think it should be at your front door at all times.

GH — Anything else you'd like to talk about, that you think people watching a movie about cities should hear?

GG — This is interesting in light of your movie about industrial design products. People understand, I think, when they go to buy a product that the design of the product is part of their choice. People buy a Braun coffee maker because it looks cool. People buy an LG cellular phone because it's nicely designed. This is a lot of the success of Apple computers. People are increasingly driven by the aesthetic of products when they consume them. I think that's going to continue to be an increasing piece of consumer choice. I wish they would think more carefully about that as they consume the products of a city.

I talk to people all the time who basically buy a house not because they want to live in it but because they want to resell it later on. So they believe that they must buy the blandest, most average house they can because it maximizes its resale potential. Houses are for consumption. They are for living in. Buy something you think is neat. Buy something that's cool. Buy something that's distinctive. Don't buy the most average thing you can because, when you do that, you drive the aesthetic of an entire place. That's the thing I would really like a movie about urban design to convey to people, is that they get to drive urban design just like they get to drive product design. It's just a little more remote in terms of how your choice influences what a city looks like.

—

Rahul Mehrotra (RM)/
January 8, 2011
Mumbai

Rahul Mehrotra is a practicing architect, urban designer, and educator. His firm, RMA Architects, was founded in 1990 in Mumbai and has designed and executed projects for clients that include government and non-governmental agencies, corporate as well as private individuals and institutions. Rahul is Professor of Urban Design and Planning and Chair of the Department of Urban Planning and Design at the Harvard Graduate School of Design. He's been active is many urban design projects in Mumbai.

Gary Hustwit — To start off, can you talk about the informal development in Mumbai and the reasons for it, the massive migration to the cities?

Rahul Mehrotra — Of course, the obvious reason for informal housing is the massive shift in demography that has sort of happened so quickly that it hasn't allowed the government to respond or react in terms of housing or creating a condition for appropriate housing. I think, on another level, the informal city that you see in Mumbai is also a reflection of the failure of government to create the appropriate context, and of course, it didn't have the capacity. There are many reasons why this didn't happen. But what is informal is normally assumed to be something that's outside the formal system, that has in some ways fended for itself and made a place to exist in a sense.

But I think in the planning discourse even the idea of the binary of the formal and the informal is not very useful. It sets us up in a binary, and where do you go from there? So then you grapple either with informal housing, or you grapple with formal housing. I think there's a space in between. I mean, I think there's space here for hybrid conditions. I think in an urban landscape like Mumbai, which is so unique, I think you've got to look at the planning problem quite differently. I think that is really the challenge. I don't know what the solution for this is, but I know that there is a challenge awaiting planners in that space.

I prefer using the word kinetic to describe Mumbai, because the binary of the formal and the informal is not useful. For design, I think you've got to create a third space, and for me, the kinetic is a great way to explain the city. It's a city that's ever transforming, and the kinetic, the temporal landscape is a large component of the city, a landscape that makes the city elastic in a sense. It's not only the poor that use it, and that's why it's useful to make these new categories that break away from the binary because the kinetic is also an attitude, an approach that the rich employ. In Mumbai, for example, in the maidans, the recreational grounds, there are these opulent weddings that take place. These are set up in the morning, and at midnight, they disappear. The cricketers take over the next morning. These are examples of how the city can actually expand its boundaries. It becomes an elastic condition.

I think, in Mumbai, to look for grand visions to steer the direction of planning is a mistake. I think Mumbai is about grand adjustment, and how do you strategize planning to engage with this sort of adjustment? It's efficient because the resources it deploys are minimal, but how it leverages those resources in the way a public space is used for four functions in the 24-hour cycle of the day is absolutely incredible. It requires creativity. It's ingenious. It's very local. It responds to the culture, and it's efficient. It's sustainable, and I think that's interesting.

GH — Everywhere I go in the city I see commercial residential development, like in the mill lands, and one of the first things I think is, "Who is going to be living in all these buildings?" I know it's not the poor farmers coming from the country.

RM — I think what has characterized planning in Mumbai or the growth of the city of Mumbai in last two or three decades is that it's an incredible example of completely laissez-faire growth. The decisions have been myopic. I think this stems from the fact that our political condition has been like that too. You've had five chief ministers running the city in the last eight years. These guys are accountable to a rural constituency. They're not even accountable to the people of Mumbai. I think the financial potential of Mumbai benefits rural constituencies in Maharashtra, and the residue of that is what's left in the city, which is this kind of destructive landscape of buildings that are sort of scattered over the urban landscape. I think what you're seeing emerging in the South Mumbai urban landscape is emblematic of laissez-faire development and emblematic of myopic decision-making, which stems from the fact that our politicians aren't accountable to the citizens.

I think the shift has to occur in the governance structure politically for the city to be cared for. I think what's interesting also is that till the sixties we had a patriarchal kind of elite who were concerned and invested in the city, and they had a voice, and they had a planning mechanism that actually responded to that. There was a vision. The decisions weren't always myopic. The politics were more stable. But since the nineties, since our liberalization economy in which the market is beginning to determine stuff, the government has been absolving its responsibility in terms of decision-making. I think the decade of the nineties and the first decade of the 21st century has been a gray zone where no one's really been responsible for the city, but yet it's prime real estate, and the opportune ones have managed to fleece it, to milk it, and it's become a site of real estate. It's no longer a city that is about people inhabiting it and what their aspirations are. I think this has been a difficult decade for the city, and I think it shows in the way the landscape has evolved.

GH — It seems like part of the problem is there are these poorer areas that weren't worth anything in the sixties, and the city has grown around these areas, and now suddenly commercial developers are moving in.

RM — Correct. I think when I say myopic, I mean that there's no broader visioning authority here. For example, the textile mill lands in Mumbai were given to textile entrepreneurs and industrialists for a particular purpose, which was to produce textiles. In our policy now, when there's a land conversion, why does that happen automatically? Maybe this land should come back to the city, or it should be given to other industry. Just the fact that this public land can be converted, without any discussion, into real estate for profit was a real mistake. I think it's really a pity, and I really do hold the community of architects and urban designers and planners responsible for not speaking up early enough about this question, for not being able to calibrate what the impact of this would be spatially.

The problems in planning in Mumbai are twofold. One is that you don't have the capacity to plan. For example, the Mumbai Metropolitan Region Development Authority, which is the visioning authority for the region, may have one or two planners; I'm not even sure they do. But they push files. They don't plan. They don't vision. And the Municipal Corporation, I think, doesn't even have a planner on their payroll. So there are no planners in the municipality of a city of 12 or 15 million people imagining what the spatial implications of policies, of what politicians decide, what bureaucrats decide, will be.

Then I think what makes that even worse is that there are really abstract instruments that are deployed for planning decision-making and formal imaginings of the city, instruments like FAR, which is the floor area ratio. That is how much you can build on a property. These are abstract because, when people are making those decisions, they don't know what the implication will be in terms of built form and where that will land. In Mumbai, you see 40-story buildings in the most bizarre locations because of FAR and transfer of development rights, and all these sort of abstract instruments have been deployed without calibrating what the spatial impacts will be.

GH — From an aesthetic standpoint, I wonder what kinds of changes in the urban design of the city could turn it back into a city for people instead of a city for real estate?

RM — Well, I think planning has a big role to play, and advocacy planning. More citizens and professionals have to become advocates for the city to create the critical feedback loops between a bureaucracy that is blind, often, to people and people who don't know how to express themselves. How does one create these feedback loops within the governance process? I think planning and advocacy planning have a big role to play here. There's not enough of that. Mumbai can boast a really pretty powerful and robust civil society, but there's not enough of it. That is one large problem.

The other thing that we have to deal with to make Mumbai more humane would be to accept the kind of pluralism that exists in the built environment. It's interesting that in India politicians use the metaphor of Shanghai and Dubai as the preferred images that they'd like to create for the city. There is a complete detachment there from ideology, because we are a democracy; those are autocracies. You can't remake the entire city in one image, so we're sort of on a treadmill trying to remake Mumbai in one image, and it's an impossibility. This is a highly pluralistic landscape with differences in economic groups, ethnic and cultural groups. I mean, the aspirations vary. I think planning has to come up with new imaginings of how this coexistence, this pluralism, these adjacencies can be resolved in spatial terms.

I don't think there is enough thinking in that direction, and I go back to this kind of idea of the binary of the formal and the informal. It's not productive because you lock yourself into two cities that are separated because one is formal and one is informal, but in reality they're synergistically linked. What are the physical manifestations of that condition? I think we're looking at the wrong metaphors, the wrong solutions, to respond to our own problem.

GH — Another thing about Mumbai: where are the big, open public green spaces? It seems like the few times that I've found parks maybe they've been jammed against a highway with car horns honking and everything else, and then there's a little park or one of those ovals.

RM — The maidans. Yeah. I think public space takes on a whole different form in a city like Mumbai. If you had to epitomize its pattern, it's about incremental growth. It's about lots of small moves. I think the last large kind of urban design gesture that was made in Mumbai was the promenade on Marine Drive, but everything else is sort of incremental. Now, from a social resolution perspective, that has great advantages. It's like many pixels on a screen. The more pixels, the greater the resolution. So when you walk on the streets of Mumbai, the bodies are very close to each other. There is a lot of social resolution because people have to coexist and, as a result, there's no space for big gestures.

I think the most robust cities in the world are cities that can actually balance big moves, large-scale gestures, with small moves, small-scale gestures. Sometimes you have cities that are only about big moves. I think Padang and Shanghai and Dubai are just about that. It's about screaming at a decibel level so the world can hear you. There are no small moves there that makes those places humane. Whereas in Mumbai, it's the reverse, where a million small moves makes it a very humane place. It's safe. You walk around; there is great amount of social resolution of the street. There's coexistence. There's dependency and affinity and all of the good humane qualities, but as a physical plan, it's a complete disaster, because there is no respite; there are no large parks; there are no clear gestures in the city. Space does not act as a point of release in your everyday experience.

GH — In the informal areas, you need massive plumbing and massive water infrastructure built. It seems like there are two ways to go. One, in some places like Dharavi, the government has probably wanted to relocate everyone or pack them into one section of it and then plot out the rest of it for development. Two, they could just put wiring, infrastructure, everything, in the area as it is with the residents as they are, which probably, from a money standpoint, is difficult.

RM — With Dharavi specifically, I don't believe the problems of Dharavi will be solved within Dharavi. It's a jigsaw puzzle that's packed in tight. There's no leeway. You need to move one component of this puzzle out and relocate it so that you have the space to maneuver. When I say the problems with Dharavi can't be solved in Dharavi, I mean that we also need to engage with larger evolutionary gestures, which means we've got to review the metropolitan region. We've got to look at industrial land and postindustrial landscapes in Mumbai where land is not being used efficiently, where it will be misused if we can't envision it within a kind of broader frame for the city. I mean the docklands in Mumbai, for example. There's 1,800 acres of land. Not even 200 acres are being used with any efficiency. It's a central government piece of land. It's not benefiting the city in any way.

I think if one could recycle that area so that you could have affordable housing that would take some pressure off Dharavi, then Dharavi could be redeveloped. Most people could stay in situ; some would be relocated. When you try to look at the problem within contained areas, these are highly complex problems because the wiggle room is very little. Unless planning in Mumbai can begin to engage much more squarely, much more forcefully, much more creatively with the larger metropolitan area and imagine the urban mechanism as an integrated, holistic system where both man-made and natural systems can be put into some kind of synergy, I think it's a disaster.

GH — Let's talk a little bit about the skywalks, the walkways. What was the impetus for them? Because, from an outsider viewpoint, especially at Bandra, it looks like they're elevated so that people can walk from the station without going down into the slum area.

RM — The politicians and city authority in Mumbai have, in the last 5 or 10 years, suddenly discovered what my friend Arjun Appadurai calls the new "weapons of mass construction," which is infrastructure. There are two sides to this. I do believe one side of investing so much in infrastructure is just the corruption related to it, so we're centralizing corruption. I think that's the cynical side of this equation. The other is that infrastructure can fix the problems. If you have to become a global city, you have to remake the city in one image. Infrastructure is what would do it, so you build these flyovers and skywalks.

I think unfortunately the intention here is to disconnect the city rather than connect the city. The city clearly is these two cities that coexist in the same space. One is what's called the informal city, the other the formal city, and that's why, again, these binaries are just not useful, because they begin to create a kind of antagonistic set of relationships. Infrastructure is being deployed in Mumbai, in a way, to disconnect these two cities. Now, historically, in the decades of the sixties and seventies, in spite of these big demographic shifts, the kind of synergy between the formal and informal was incredible. There's a dependency and affinity, but also a sense of rejection, and this sort of tension is what keeps it in balance. But I think they're connected, and they can't be detached. I think the moves right now are, through infrastructure, to detach and disconnect them.

The skywalks they've deployed in Mumbai are probably the most ridiculous kind of design solution that has been attempted, because, I mean, there is a huge irony here because the columns of these skywalks are so large, so they occupy the sidewalk below. Then what they create above is a skywalk which is the width of sidewalk that's on the ground. It's like just elevating the sidewalk. It's at a large cost. What it's doing is creating a disconnect between these two cities, so people from what is imagined as the formal city, from the Bandra Kurla commercial center, can go to the railway station avoiding the slum completely, which otherwise they'd have to navigate. This is a dangerous disconnect because I think it begins to have implications in the way social resolution breaks down. In Mumbai, because there is this incredible sense of coexistence on account of the densities, the large problems of the kind of disparities that occur actually get resolved in many other ways. It's slow, but separating them and not letting them collide is avoiding the problem.

GH — The reasons are probably pretty obvious in terms of why Indians are moving here from other parts of the country: opportunity. The whole thing that I think is interesting is the acceleration, that accelerated growth of cities, and this is global.

RM — This is global, yeah. I mean, in-migration to Mumbai has changed a great deal. I think it peaked in the eighties and nineties, and now I think the internal growth rate of the city is beginning to become larger than the in-migration. Of course, that's also because the city has achieved critical mass in terms of the population size. There are many reasons for that. I think through the sixties and seventies and perhaps eighties, it was distress migration. People from the rural areas were coming because they had no choices in the rural areas and also for the bright lights of the city. Now I think the internal growth in the city is larger. People come for new kinds of opportunities which don't exist where they come from. Also, as infrastructure in the country improves, people's mobility improves. They can come more easily in and out of the city, so people now, actually even the poor, divide their time between two locations. That brings some of that income and economic activity back into the rural areas, which is interesting.

You know, I think what's interesting in a city like Mumbai is it's an incredible city for the very poor, and it's an incredible city for the very rich. But for the very poor, it's way, way beyond what they can imagine in the rural conditions where they were totally marginalized or bonded labor— extreme forms of deprivation, in a sense. For the rich, it's incredible because it provides a whole range of services at very little cost. There's a kind of luxury that comes with it. The rich can afford to escape the city when the onslaught on their senses goes beyond the point that they can accept and survive.

The city is deadly and terrible for a very large middle class, which forms the bulk of the city. When I say middle class, I think a lot of people living in the slums are middle class. They are part of the formal economy. They can actually leverage resources. It's just that the limited supply of housing knocks them out of that market. The middle class in Mumbai is very large; I think 60 percent to 70 percent of the population would be that middle class. The middle class looks for a predictable city, a city where there are health services; there's good mobility; there are schools for their children and decent housing. That's what the politicians are playing on. The metaphors of Shanghai and Singapore are actually about more than being invested in the symbolism of the buildings and architecture. The real message there is that we can produce a predictable city, a city where basic services can be delivered. I think the use of those metaphors is actually linked to this issue.

GH — Just speaking globally, could we talk about the changes in the design of large cities over the past several decades or even before that and then the coming challenges? I think it's interesting to see how it's suddenly changed so much in the past 50 years, whereas you had 1,000 years before this to just get to cities that even had a million people maybe, and now there's this acceleration.

RM — I think what's interesting is that, till the sixties and the seventies, people celebrated world cities. It was a term that was popularized by people like Peter Hall, and world cities were cities that disproportionately governed the resources of the world, and they became powerful cities. They were cities whose meaning and raison d'être was sort of based on resources and managing resources and being able to modulate the flow of resources. Then you had the global city idea popularized by Saskia Sassen and others where cities were defined by how much of global capital flowed through them or that they controlled.

You simultaneously, and much more now, have kind of a definition that revolves around the notion of megacity, which comes from the World Bank, IMF, because this is about giving out loans and financial assistance, but based on population size. The way megacities were defined was the number of people that lived there. For me, that's a really interesting definition because it's the first time that you begin to start making demography and people the center of a definition. I think the challenge for urbanists, for politicians, for people involved in cities in the future will be, how do you manage demography? I think the physical plan of the city per se will not be able to determine the success of a city. Architecture will not be the only spectacle of the city. It can't. How you intersect architecture with mobility, with creating a humane environment through design, is going to be the critical challenge moving into the future.

What's also incredible is that I think we're like lemmings because, with climate change and oceans rising, the cities that are growing are all the coastal cities. We all seem to be flooding to the coastal cities like lemmings, and so I think the impact of climate change in cities in the future is going to be huge. It's going to be massive because the largest urban population is going to live in coastal cities. But as you have the effects of climate change in the hinterland of countries in terms of drought, in terms of fluctuations of climate and flooding and all of that, these cities, which are already large magnets, are going to become even larger magnets. That's why we're like lemmings, because we're going to be forced into jumping off the cliff because we want to gravitate to large cities, which are going to be affected then by the ocean. I think so. I mean, I think there's a massive crisis at hand, and perhaps one of the questions for the future, again for urbanists and their imagination, would be, how do you create sustainable forms of decentralization? Because decentralization in the form that it's taken through suburbia is completely unsustainable, and what does that mean?

I think in the Indian situation, for example, the big urban time bomb that we're sitting on is the 392 cities that are about a hundred thousand people today that are expected to be anywhere between five hundred thousand and a million people in the next 20 years. So potentially 400 million people of the 1.2 billion people in India in the next 20 years are going to be living in the 392 settlements that we don't even know the names of. What's mind-boggling is that those are the places where you could actually intervene. You could make a difference, but those are not on our radar, and what's on our radar is Mumbai. Everyone comes to Mumbai to look at Mumbai. Everybody goes to Calcutta. Everybody goes to Delhi. But this is not where the future urban landscape of India is going.

GH — I'm just wondering, what cities do you love around the world? What are some of your favorites cities and why?
    RM — Oh, that's always a difficult question.

GH — You lived in Michigan for a while, where were you? Lansing?
    RM — No, in Ann Arbor. It's not even in a city. Detroit was a city. I worked in Detroit for three years. I always said that you could solve both the problems of Detroit and Mumbai in one fell swoop if you just moved about five million people from Mumbai to Detroit.

GH — I'm sure Ford would love that. What are other cities you love?
    RM — I mean, you enjoy different cities for different reasons. I went recently to Mexico City. The energy and the scale and the fact that it was one of the world's largest cities but was largely low-rise but high density was really mind-boggling. Getting that kind of energy in a low-rise city was really quite refreshing because one enjoys that sense of energy in Manhattan, which is a high-rise city. The combination of those experiences is fantastic.

I think one of the most beautiful cities is San Francisco for many reasons besides the fact that when you throw a grid over topography like that you get stunning moments. I think what's powerful about San Francisco for me is twofold. One is that it's managed to organize itself in the landscape that it sits on in a very beautiful way in the way it's colonized land across the bay and its relationship to the topography. But more importantly what I like very much about that city is that there is a kind of pluralism of form there. You have a downtown that has high-rise. You have low-rise. It all works really well in those different adjacencies.

For me, Mumbai is interesting for that reason. Mumbai grew incrementally. It grew because of a number of landfills were done over a century, and every time a new landfill was done, that generation expressed its aspirations through a different kind of architecture on that piece of land. You have a whole range of architectural styles here, from the neo-Gothic, to art deco, to the International Style and all of that. I think the way it all sits, with kind of soft thresholds, is very beautiful.

What Mumbai can really teach the world in terms of urban planning is precisely how this kind of additive, incremental growth can create a very rich urban fabric, which sometimes doesn't occur in many new cities or cities that are growing very rapidly where both finance and power are deployed in a very singular fashion. Within that kind of autocracy, you get a very unidimensional city. I think Dubai and Shanghai and Singapore, in many ways, are now aware of this, and of course, all of them are trying to correct it. But I think Mumbai is diametrically opposite there. Architecture is not the primary spectacle, and the landscape is one of incredible pluralism, richness, and humanity as a result of that.

GH — Do think that most average citizens are aware of the design principles of their city?

RM — In Mumbai, I don't think people are so aware of design, and they don't even discuss it. Living in Mumbai is living for the day. If you get up in the morning, and you have your water, and the electricity is being sort of stable, and you're ready to go work, you're happy. You move on. You go on to the next day. The intensity of the city, its pulse, its flux, is just about adjusting yourself to the landscape that you live in. I think, among citizens, normally there's no discussion about design. I'm sure people have aspirations of where they want to get to, but I don't think they have the time or the energy to deal with it.

I think that's why the responsibility really squarely lies on professionals who are equipped to do this to become more powerful voices in the city; to create a critical mass of awareness, of perceptions; to make the critical connections to bureaucracies and to the politicians. Really, I think Mumbai desperately needs a critical mass of advocacy. It's a solvable problem. The problem has to be picked up differently. It's a unique condition. It's not about replicating solutions from elsewhere, about learning from elsewhere, but, I think, finding solutions that are very unique.

GH — What's the thing that really annoys you about your profession?

RM — I think there's too much emphasis on what I call the static city, which is the city that is made by architecture, the hardware of the city, which becomes, often, the overbearing spectacle of the city. There has to be a shift, in the discussion of urban design, to habitation, to how people use cities, and to the temporal landscape of the transformations that can occur in a city over time in space. I really believe that in the future, architecture is not going to be the only instrument by which you will make great cities, get people excited about cities, or make cities that are humane.

GH — Then what is?

> **RM** — Well, I think creating a balance in the urban system, which is where mobility and all of that come in. I think the opportunity for the city of the future, the aspiration that we should have as a profession for the city of the future, is for it to be one where there is a balance. I think the city can be thought of from inside out, and architecture can be kind of a logical expression of what happens. How does one make a balance between the different domains, so to speak, that can stacked up to make a city? And the domains that I refer to go all the way from mobility, lifestyle, water, food, energy, to built form. How can built form become one of seven or eight domains that we sort of put on equal footing? Unfortunately, in a lot of the cities, where capital is finding itself landing in the desert, in Abu Dhabi or in Dubai, the domain of built form becomes the primary one, and the city is set up as the spectacle of architecture without any attention to the other domains that make for a sustainable city.

GH — Do you think architecture as a practice is getting more attuned to its place in the city and not just thinking about the individual building?

> **RM** — Well, I mean, unfortunately in the decade of the nineties and the first decade of the 21st century when capital was wreaking havoc around the world, architecture became more and more autonomous, because it had the power of autonomy, and capital by nature is impatient. When it lands, it wants to be realized. It doesn't want to relate to anything around it, and I think that's what accelerated, also, the deployment of architects from around the globe to build in other parts, because they followed capital, capital that trusted them. I think the last two decades have been a complete crisis for architecture and especially the relation-ship between architecture and city making.

GH — But do you think that's changing within the practice?

> **RM** — Of course. Now everyone has become suspicious of capital, and no one trusts the impatience of capital. I think and I hope in architecture schools and planning schools the gears shift to making more humane environments, to looking at problems where we can deploy our skills actually to affect the lives of larger parts of our demographics. I think architecture and planning have to apply themselves to finding solutions for the urban poor in cities, for example. They have to apply their minds to solving problems of how you create appropriate synergies between natural systems and built forms of cities, how you get away from the idea that architecture is autonomous from the context that it sits in. I don't think we can afford that luxury any longer. I'm glad capital is evaporating because it's allowing room for new forms of innovation.

GH — Are there other areas of the city that you think, from an urban design perspective, would be important things for us to look at?

> **RM** — You should look at where I'm going to be working with my students, which is between Nariman Point the commercial district. There's a fishing village there, and that's easy to go into. They're very friendly, and you actually go through it, and you see fish drying, and you come to the edge of the water, and you suddenly see the high-rise buildings surrounding you. I think that's a good spot because it also epitomizes,

in a sense, the kind of nature of the city, of pluralism, of very disparate kinds of urban forms that are in close adjacency. It's a huge design challenge, so you can either have the power to remake it all in one image and make one master plan that makes it look like a Padang, or you can accept these differences and say, "How do you actually organize them in space?"

It's a whole different conception of urban design and urban planning, and like I said, it's not then about a grand vision which is cohesive, uni-dimensional, but it's about a grand adjustment where with some grand gestures you actually adjust to what the pieces are that exist there. In a democracy that's really necessary. Has democracy produced beautiful cities? Democracy produces cities which are about multiple negotiations. I mean, I think that's what Indian cities can teach the world. The multiple negotiations in democracy result in a landscape of pluralism. For a design, that's a completely different challenge. Unfortunately, in urbanism and as we urbanize, the models of successful cities are all cities that are not democratic cities, that are cities that come out of political landscapes of autocracy. This is an incredible contradiction, and it's sometimes really confusing because we look up to all the cities which are made by autocrats, which are not made by democratic systems.

GH — Yeah. Well, New York City—that's probably a city we look up to.

RM — But I'm saying today, with the new ones like Masdar or Dubai or Shanghai, every architect is like a carpetbagger showing up there. What happens is also the debate, the theory that gets constructed for urban design, uses these models, which are not applicable in a democracy. I mean, I think this is a much larger global discussion within the community of architecture and urban design: what is a city of democracy, and what is the urban design that emanates from a city or a landscape of democracy?

—

Sheela Patel (SP)/ January 10, 2011 Mumbai

Sheela Patel is the founding director of the Society for the Promotion of Area Resource Centers (SPARC), which she founded in Mumbai in 1984 as an advocacy group for the pavement dwellers of the city.

—

Gary Hustwit — I guess for starters, can you just give us a little bit of an overview of SPARC and what you do?

Sheela Patel — Okay. We're an organization of professionals whose main business is to produce places and spaces within slums for poor people, especially the women, to meet and to use that as their space to think through how they want to look at their lives, how they want to look at their relationships with the rest of the city. It's like creating a resource space for them, which is their own, through which they can begin to first develop a consensus on what they think they need and then to build the confidence and capacity to negotiate and have a dialogue with others.

GH — For the poor in Mumbai, it seems like there are different situations. There are the pavement dwellers, people that are also just encroaching in different places and building informal structures, and then the more established slums like Dharavi. Do you think you could give us a little bit of an overview of those different situations for someone that doesn't really know, for a global audience?

SP — So the first, most amazing situation here in this city is that almost 60 percent of people who live in this city live in slums. The word slums covers everything that falls below the development norms in terms of infrastructure and housing design norms and stuff like that. The other amazing situation in this city is that even 70 percent of people who live in formal structures live in one-room tenements. It actually reflects the huge housing and development crisis that this city faces, which also has among the highest amount of international real estate investment coming into the city. What that's doing is, it's produced a huge construction boom for the top 10 percent and then increasing crisis for everybody else.

One of the ways in which we segment this slum population is, first of all, by understanding how, historically, some people get entitlements and some don't. You have what are called regularized slums or recognized slums and those that are not recognized. The recognition is part of the politics of voting because now slum dwellers represent important voting blocks. One of the demands that people always have is security. When a particular cohort of settlements develops some legitimacy through how long they've been there and how much they impact the constituency, the political process provides them legitimacy of varying natures. In some cases, it's the right to be there. In some cases, you can get water. In some cases, you can construct a brick-and-mortar house. These are very subtle differences. If you look at the slums in the city, you'll see that there are different levels: absolutely soft, little, tent-like things, or you'll have really strong, good structures that are in slum-like locations, but once you go inside, you can't see that it's a slum. You have this whole range. That's from the point of view of construction differences.

The second thing would be, you'll have 5 percent of people who, if you walk on the road, you'll see that they just have a bundle of things around them. They don't have any structure. That structure only comes up at night. Those are people who are testing out whether they can stay there or whether they'll be evicted, and they have to do lots of informal negotiations to stay there. Our work is full of amazing histories of people, of who they had to negotiate with to stay where and what did they have to do.

Then you have these pavement colonies, which are people who live on sidewalks in shacks that come up like lean-tos against a wall. Most of these are in the Island City, and a majority of them are in the areas around the docks because, right from the 1920s and '30s when migrants came, these textile machines came from England, and they came in those boxes. The machine was removed, and the box became a home, and they line the area. You have this tradition in the city where everybody finds some work to feed yourself, but you don't have any home. You just go find a home, and you subsidize your job because you earn so little that you can't actually afford the transport costs. Your wage is a living wage to feed yourself, but it doesn't cover all the other costs that you have for living in the city. Next time you look at a pavement house, you'll see that the dimensions somehow came from those boxes sort of stacked up.

If you look at lands on which encroachment occurs, you have lands that belong to the municipality, so the pavement would be a municipal encroachment. Then you have different state government authorities that have land, which are all managed by what is called the Collector of the city. He's a person who's part of the revenue department, and he manages all these lands. Then there are lands that are owned by private parties. Then the fourth section is lands that belong to the central government. For instance, people who encroach along the railway line; people who are around the airport; people who are on Defense, Navy, or other kinds of lands—they are all what are called Central Government Lands. If you look at the hierarchy of these things, people who were on private land actually were the first to get protected because it was clear that they were paying rents to the private landowners. Then the state government ceded some of its land to produce this informal tenure of regulated slums. Even today, of the people who live on the pavement, people who live on Central Government Land are the most vulnerable because it's very evident that they will not get any security of tenure where they are today. Those are the sort of differences.

GH — Okay. I'm wondering if you could just talk about the challenges that people living in the slums face, like the personal challenges, sanitation, and all of these things. A lot of people don't really have any idea.

SP — The first real challenge, like I told you, is to negotiate the right to be there. Everybody thinks that people just come, and they squat, and they live there free; it's like freebies. Poor people pay 3 to 10 times the amount that you and I pay in cost terms. For instance, most of them have to buy water. They have to buy water, either from somebody who already has a tap and who uses this like an income-generating activity, or it's water that's stolen from the city, and there's somebody sitting on it and selling it. Same thing with electricity. The issue of sanitation is terrible. What constitutes a local definition of adequate water and sanitation is interesting. The local definition for sanitation in Mumbai is, if there is one toilet for 50 people—that is, 10 families have one toilet seat—it means they have adequate sanitation. Even by those standards, the city requires almost 30,000 seats. It's assumed that, if that provision is there in that neighborhood, that there's adequate sanitation. By all standards, this is very deficient, and the same goes for water. These are difficult things.

The other major problem is that—you've been to Dharavi. You have a situation in which an informal settlement gets ignored for a very long time, and because there's no space for growth, it gets denser and denser and denser. Then, as it has happened in this case, the city grows over it, and then the development comes in, and they say, "We want roads. We want a place to put the pipeline. We want to do this. We want to do development." The only way in which development comes in is you have to evict half the people to get the development in. People cling to their location. In a city, location is everything. So there's a war between that, and what is good for them conceptually but came too late.

The other terrible situation is that anybody who wants an individual solution to get out of a slum will have a lot of problems because the volume of houses produced for middle- and low-income housing just doesn't exist. Over a period of the last 30 to 35 years, you have a group of 20 percent of people who live in slums who, if you look at their financial situation, could actually pay installments for a modest home, but they don't make that choice because that home is 35 to 50 kilometers away, which means they'd lose their livelihoods. So they're like nonchoices.

GH — I'm really fascinated by the skywalks now. Tell me about the skywalks and what you think about them?

SP — Okay. The city's going through a huge transformation in terms of transport. You have a monorail coming in. You have new local trains. There are new stations coming up. There are new connectivities. The local train that we have, which has been like the life of this city, is now being extended to the metropolitan region, which means that people can actually afford to live further away. While all this was being discussed, it became very clear that there are some parts of the city where the roads just can't expand any more and there's no place for people to walk and for the road traffic to go.

We have had, in the past, some places where there were either bridges over the roads or ways to get to the train station through these things, which now they call the skywalk. The idea was that the Metropolitan Authority would look at these places where the skywalks would come in, and as people who represent the interest of the poor, we were saying, "It should also be a place where people should get hawking licenses." You have people who are commuting, and then you create space on the side for people to sell their wares to the commuters. That means that you take not only the people who walk but also the people who sell their wares, because this is another big crisis in the city, that the formal planning process just doesn't want to acknowledge that such a large percentage of people in the city earn their livelihood through vending.

We have an amazing vending law nationally that says cities should encourage this, but we have a High Court that wants all the hawkers to be removed because you have citizens groups who say it affects the people who are walking on the street, but it's the very same people who then buy from them. What is happening is, this crowding is producing conflict where there should actually be collaboration. A lot of people are trying to actually look at ways by which you can produce design that allows this coexistence, and we were trying to see if this could be done on these skywalks. As soon as the first skywalk came and this idea came, the middle-class citizens groups just slammed this, and they said no. They went to the High Court, and they said, "There should be no vending on the skywalks." From that point, our interest in the skywalks went up.

I think what has happened is that, as is the problem with everything that the government does, it doesn't explore how to produce a consensus in a locality. There are many parts of the city where there are skywalks which are not used, or where there is a need for a skywalk and there's no skywalk there. There are places where the skywalk should come and would be helpful to some people, but there are citizens groups who say, "This affects our privacy." It reflects, in many symbolic ways, the crisis of any infrastructure development, which reflects back to some of our fundamental beliefs that, before you make any change, you should try and look at how you can convince everybody that what you're doing is good for them. We've developed a culture in our city right now where the only way to survive is to go after your interest. You don't look at the fact that all cities require different classes of people who have to cohabit, that they are interdependent, and that the energy and the life of the city also comes out of informality.

GH — On the Bandra skywalk, literally you're walking above the slum. You're walking above the problems. We spent the afternoon yesterday with a group of families that had started farming on the railway land down there, just with informal tracts. We went down, talked to them, asked them why they came to the city and what they were doing there, which was really interesting. Apparently, they were renting the land. They were the paying the railroad for the farmland. But now the railroad stopped renting it.

SP — The history of that is very interesting. Fifty feet from the running track is what the railway likes to keep open. The idea is that, if a train collapses, there's space on both sides. What they did was, they would lease that land for farming, and over a period of time, the estate department of the railway and the person who was renting there subdivided the plots and started renting them out.

GH — Now all that land is going to be completely developed?

SP — Yeah. People are trying very hard to protect it. [Loud noise outside.] Yeah, that's also a signature of this city. They say that everybody in this city is slightly deaf because everybody's shouting at each other. It's the first time in our city—the last five years—that people are measuring noise pollution, and everything that's good has a bad side. One of the signatures of public life in the city is that public space is used for multicultural activities. We have a Ganesh Festival, and we have Navratri, and we have all these festivals that take over the street. Now because of the new sound pollution rules, everything has to close down by 10 p.m.

What this has done is that it has produced a crisis for the poor because they can only take over public space. They can't hire private spaces. We have a thing called Navratri and Dussehra where for 10 days young women and men dance together. It's almost like a mating ritual in an anthropological way. They take over streets, and they dance there, and you can do that only till 10 p.m. The better-off people then rent private places, and they'll dance there, and so as long as there's no sound emanating from there nobody knows what's happening, but then poor people will lose their cultural right to do that. You need a special dispensation for something to be carried on after 10:30 p.m.

GH — That's crazy! Maybe we could talk about the development issues a little bit more. We've been spending a lot of time in the Bandra Kurla complex. Who's moving into all these high-rises?

SP — That is also part of India's crisis, you know? It's like, all the international companies, why are they coming to India? Even if 15 percent of the 1 billion population can afford something, it's a huge number. In Mumbai, which has 12 million people, even if 10 percent of the people can invest, it's a large number. What is happening today in the real estate situation is that the larger the apartment you build, the higher the pricing you can charge. What you have in the city is the situation where a lot of people are investing in this as their second and third home, as an investment rather than as a place to stay. It's a strange situation. Then you have a lot of what we call nonresident Indians, people who live in the North who now, as they get older, want to live in two different places. It's like having a villa in France. You've got a house in the city. You rent it out for the time you don't want to be here, and then as you get older, you come here for the winters. All our cities in India suddenly swell in the winter months with the diaspora coming in when the weather is good here and it's terrible in the North. All these things are affecting our lives in different ways.

GH — Going briefly back to the skywalk thing, I just remembered that it was $300 million USD for the skywalk project, and I couldn't help thinking what $300 million could have done at the street level near those railroad stations like the Bandra station.

SP — You know, just to give you a parallel thing, I was talking to you about the local railway upgrading that was done. The cost of upgrading the public transport and the cost of the flyovers to improve the north-south and east-west roads for the cars cost the same amount. For the public transport, the government went to the World Bank, and it took 13 years to transact this project, and the government of Maharashtra paid the same amount at the same time for the 52 or 55 flyovers, which means that only 5 to 10 percent of people own cars in the city and you are ready to spend that in 2 years, but 65 percent of all trips in the city are done by public transport, and it took you 14 years to do that. Those are the kinds of choices that are producing all these aberrations. You're not dealing with the fundamental issues, and you're not looking at transformative things that can improve the quality of life of the bottom 30 percent because it requires care. It requires care; it requires negotiation; it requires ways to appease different political processes. Putting up skywalks is easier. You just put it on top. Whatever is quick construction, you do it.

GH — What are the things that you love about Mumbai?

SP — This is my city. I love it. If you look at international cities, a lot of people compare New York to Mumbai, meaning that you can be a very rich person with a fancy car, and the minute you step out of the car, you're just another city dweller. There's still that kind of attitude, that once you're on the street, it doesn't matter where you live; your dress isn't important; you are from the city. The city has an amazing secular and cosmopolitan heart, which is being battered at the moment. We have regional parties and we have a lot of political processes that want to claim the city for the sons of the soil, and many of us are saying, "Well, these parties haven't done anything for the sons of the soil, even when they were in power, so what are we talking about?" It's an angst-ridden constituency.

The other interesting thing which is happening, which is not related directly to Mumbai but I think will soon have an implication for it, is that we have a state called Bihar, which is one of the least governed states. Uttar Pradesh (UP) and Bihar are the two states from which there's been a huge out-migration, so it fans across the whole country. In Mumbai, every second or third migrant is from UP or Bihar, and they've been maligned. They've become the whipping boys or whipping families for all our local politicians. Our local politicians will say, "Oh, we don't want to build toilets in slums. It will encourage people to come," as if people come to shit.

What they've all done is that they've produced this multicultural environment in the city. In a strange way, the slums have also produced amazing security because day and night there are people on the street. There are many women's groups who've done surveys of different cities, and as you go from north to south, it gets safer for women. If you are on a public bus here in Mumbai, and you are standing next to me, and you even brush me like this accidentally, and I look at you, and I say, "What are you doing?" you have to leave the bus. You could get beaten up.

Women have that sense of confidence that if they scream for help—or if it's in the middle of the night, and I'm on the road, and I'm in a car, and I have a puncture, I don't have to call the automobile association. I can pay some money, and somebody will come and change my wheel. There's that energy in this city.

What's happening now is that there are many cities which are saying that migrants from Bihar are not returning from their holidays because now they're getting jobs in their own state. It's going to be interesting to see what happens when northern states hopefully get better governed, because right now a lot of migration occurs because of that inequality. What we have in our country is huge numbers of people who are landless. As agriculture gets more efficient and mechanized, there's surplus labor there, and the only thing people can do is come into the city and do menial jobs, and then they evolve and develop skills and stuff like that. We're going to see, even for the next 20 to 30 years, huge movements of people, and there's a lot to learn from this city because it's been dealing with these populations for a hundred years, but we are not learning from that.

Our politicians and bureaucrats, many times when I go to meet them, they say, "You shouldn't be working to provide security. You should be helping us send them back to the village." As though I can pick you up and put you back there. We say people are voting with their feet because the city's not just a place to work; it's aspirational. Your children have a better future. They have a better job. They can lose their caste and other identities which are restrictive. You come into a city; you develop a cosmopolitan identity. In your village, by the clothes that you wear and where you stay, you are stamped as being low caste or being untouchable.

Another example I'll give is, you know the time when you had this Hurricane Katrina? At the same time we had terrible floods here in Mumbai. And if you look at footage of what you saw in the media on Katrina and what you saw in Mumbai, there are two or three major differences. In Katrina, you saw very poor, helpless people who were stuck there because they couldn't run away. In Mumbai, rich, poor, everybody was stuck, and the people who looked after them were people from the slums. You were stuck in your car, which was flooded, and you had people from the neighboring slums coming with food and tea and rescuing your car, and those moments bring everybody together. In the last 10 years, we've had many bombings and all those kinds of things, and the whole city rises to support that process of dealing with that, which is not to say we don't have aberrations. We also have riots. But the city always comes up and tries to collaborate and make up. People who face the problems are always given some initial support before the state comes in, and that's the culture of the city.

GH — That's really powerful. I don't know where to go from there. You were talking about sanitation in the slums. Maybe talk more about that?
SP — There are different statistics about how many toilets are needed, okay? We'll always have different people spewing different statistics,

but if you just take Dharavi, in 1989, when the communities had done their first surveys, the ratio of people to a toilet seat was nine hundred people to a toilet seat, and today it's come down to six hundred.

The federation and SPARC are the main people who construct toilets in the city and then get communities to manage them. Finding a location within a dense slum to build a toilet is Herculean. The issue is not the construction of the toilet but finding a space to build the toilet and to deal with the infrastructure, because the other amazing, big piece of development trivia is that in the 1950s, when the major sewer and water lines were set in the city, all the slums were shown on the map as empty. You have a sewer system in the city which is not accessible to the poor, so when you build toilets, they don't have access to the sewer, so they have to have what are called safety tanks. The specification is that you build a safety tank on the basis of how many people shit there, but because the ratios are so terrible, a tank which should take a year to fill fills up in three weeks. The other postconstruction crisis is that the toilets become unmaintainable because of the amount of water they need. The postconstruction maintenance that poor people can't do themselves is so high that, within two to three years of constructing the toilet, it becomes dysfunctional.

Here again, like with the skywalk issue, instead of investing in these really basic things, the government will just keep rebuilding the toilets wherever there is space. They don't create a far-thinking policy to give incentives to people to create that space.

GH — Can you talk about the economic impact of the slums? I think the Western idea of a slum, or the one like Dharavi, is that it's a bunch of people squatting, freeloading.

SP — I think one of the real problems with the North's interpretation of the South is based on, first of all, how people look at welfare in general. What welfare has done in the North is it's somehow produced large groups of people who have not worked for many generations. When people from the North think of slums and they come here, they think of drunken people lazily lying down and everybody looking like they're in despair and beggars and stuff like that. In all our slums and in all our data, we see that two or three times the number of people per household need to work to earn a minimum wage. Everybody's working, and they're doing an amazing range of things.

All the recyclables in Mumbai come to Dharavi. They get aggregated, separated, and they are sent off to different factories. If the plastic and the paper that is collected doesn't go out of Dharavi on a regular basis, if it stops for three days, factories in different parts of the country stop working, you know? It's not just local. It has connections with global markets; it has connections with other cities; and it has connections with the locality.

Dharavi produces jobs for almost 65 to 70 percent of residents. Just imagine: five hundred thousand people who walk to work in the middle of the city. You have all of Mumbai's waste, even paper clips and pins and plastic. Now when you walk on the road, you see these scavengers with sacks, and they come and they collect everything. They sit on the pavement, and they sort things out. A professor from one of the universities in southern California came and talked to us about whether people in Dharavi needed a machine to separate plastic that was original from plastic that had already been recycled once or twice. I took him to see these people who'd bite the plastic and they'd tell you whether it's been recycled once or twice.

GH — But even beyond recycling, there's so much other business happening in Dharavi.

SP — Yeah, but what I'm saying is that there's that; there's this whole recycling thing. Then there's a huge food business. Dosas are lentil pancakes, and idlis are these steamed dumpling kind of things. Whether you go to a five-star restaurant or you go to this little man on the street who sells it for the workers, they are all made in vats the size of this room in Dharavi. Similarly, we have all kinds of other foods, fried stuff and roasted chickpeas. You just name all the savory stuff and it's all made here. An interesting story about that is that we took a very senior reporter from the *Times of India* to look at this food industry, and he wrote an amazing article. Subsequently, on reading this article—we have all these prestigious social clubs in the city—one of our captains of industry sent a letter to his club saying, "I hope we are not getting anything from Dharavi." As if he could find out.

GH — Could you talk about the way the city ultimately gets planned?

SP — When you look at the skyline of the city, you'll see you have 3-floor and 4-floor buildings, which are walk-up apartments, which was the style of construction up to the sixties. Then you had buildings that went up to 8 floors, which was in the seventies and eighties. Now things are going crazy, and people are competing with each other to build 25 and 30 floors, and now somebody's building a 60-floor residential building. Right now the city is doing its next 20-year plan. When the people who are doing the planning come to talk to me, I'm almost indifferent to it. They say, "Oh, we want citizens' involvement, and we want to make this plan people friendly," and nobody in the city believes that because what we really see is that the construction industry and the real estate developers on the one hand and the slum dwellers on the other are actually carving out the design of the city.

The poor people are doing it because the plan has no space for them. Nobody thinks that, if you're going to create an industrial space here and you get cheap labor, then they're going to come and work there, so if they come and work there, they should have a place near there to stay. There should be spaces designed for that. You've been to the Bandra Kurla Complex. For every man who works there, there are secondary, tertiary, and blah, blah, blah numbers of people looking after them. Every person who comes to work there has a car, has a driver who's sitting there all day. There's no place where these people can eat, so of course, the informal sector's going to come there and provide them food and whatever they want. Then you get shocked and say, "Oh, my pristine environment is getting messed up." That's how the poor invade spaces, and they actually create infrastructure and services which are needed, which should be planned.

What the real estate people are doing is they are getting a lot of money from the international hedge funds, who now have less ways to make investments in the North, so they're looking at cities in the South where they can make quick bucks. If you look at interviews of some of the captains of our real estate industry, they'll tell you that they have land banks. They have a person in every government department who's like a fixer who negotiates the deals, and they have a group of people who create these processes and transform rules and regulations and everything to produce housing or to capture public space. The result is that construction is happening in places where there should be open spaces. Land which should come back to the city for parks or residential areas for the poor or for schools or hospitals is all going for these new things that we have, which are called malls.

If you go to all these malls, nobody's shopping there, but they're all there. We had an article about two years ago, saying lots of poor people would come to malls because they were going to go on the escalators and everything. There was this big debate, "Should we allow poor people to come in?" Then the counterpoint was, "You'd better let them in because you have glass walls." This is the kind of strange thing that's happening. The government will provide space for a McDonald's, and at the McDonald's, you see in the ads you have patties that are made with potatoes. The local version of it is called *vada pav*, which is fried potato in batter which is stuck between the local bread with a nice spicy chutney. The vendor who provides this will be kicked out of his location, but McDonald's will get a space. Or if it's in a residential place, it will be turned into a commercial place. We have space for all these things, but we don't have space for the humble, local thing.

—

Sir Norman Foster (NF)/ March 22, 2011 New York

Sir Norman Foster is one of the world's most recognized architects. Over the past four decades his company, Foster + Partners, has been responsible for a wide range of work, from urban masterplans, public infrastructure, airports, civic and cultural buildings, offices and workplaces to private houses and product design. In 1999 he was awarded the Pritzker Prize, architecture's highest honor.

—

Gary Hustwit — Do you have a general philosophy about cities and what makes them work?

Norman Foster — In a way, it's obvious, but to state the obvious, architecture is important; the design of individual buildings is important, but the infrastructure which binds those buildings together, that's even more important. In sustainability terms, the total of the individual buildings and the infrastructure of movement accounts for about 70 percent of the energy consumed in an industrialized society. But for any of us who moves across a city, any city, the experience of those public spaces, squares, streets. transport—that determines how we feel about that day, that city, that place. So the importance of the infrastructure can't be overestimated.

New York is extraordinary in terms of its sustainability because it is so pedestrian friendly and has this public transport, but I remember, when we last talked about this, that you felt the loss of that personal mobility that you would experience in another kind of city. I think that's a real challenge—how you combine that freedom of mobility with a city which is a good urban experience and is sustainable, and I think that we'll see changing patterns in mobility. Those industries concerned with movement that traditionally make cars obviously are going to be continuing in that mobility business. Will the car be the same? Will it be something that you will own, or will you see a transition to the pattern which we're starting to see in cities where you don't own the bicycle, but you have access to it? Is that more freedom in the sense that you're not encumbered with the ownership? You don't have that responsibility. You don't have to pay for it. Or do you have a loss of a personal possession and identification? I think these are major issues. I mean, I remember Buckminster Fuller many years ago talking very eloquently on this issue of ownership. He was extending it, of course, to the home as well as those vehicles that would transport us between places.

GH — It's interesting. Once you give people the choice to own a car and encourage it, it's what drives or has driven the economy in a lot of countries for many years. When you start taking those choices away, that's when people start saying, "This is my right. I have a right to a car."

NF — Yes, and I think it is a key issue, and perhaps the challenge is, can you offer an alternative which gives all those benefits, attributes, in another form which is perhaps even more appealing and is sustainable in the long term?

GH — Do you remember the first time, maybe when you were a child or when you were in school, that you realized that cities were designed, when you first got exposed to the planning and the thinking of the design of cities?

NF — I can remember, as a child, growing up in a part of the city of Manchester, which was industrial and hard and urban and quite dense, and I can remember the proximity of shops, of cinemas and everything really being within walking distance. I can remember the first time going to a school where I would have to walk, take a bus, walk, and I became aware of the bigger picture. I can remember when I was older, about 16, leaving school, working in Manchester Town Hall, and making excursions in the lunch hour to discover buildings and architecture and being fascinated by that and perhaps unconsciously, at that point, discovering architecture myself, which kindled an interest, which led me to a public library to discover people like Frank Lloyd Wright and Le Corbusier. I think the city has always been a very strong influence even if I, at that point in my life, wasn't able to articulate that, to be able to talk about it, identify it. But that process was happening.

GH — Can you talk about the Corbusian ideals or philosophies in terms of design of cities in that time?

NF — I think that the kind of radical theories about cities and the city of the future have a somewhat curious history. In a cyclical sense, I think you could start to chart it historically from when the city became the great magnet. That is still the case in so many parts of the world. In those emerging economies, you can see it despite all the deprivation and the problems of the city in terms of poverty, sanitation, and so on. It still is an incredible magnet because it offers a wealth that the rural economies don't offer.

It offers much more, though. It offers emancipation from restrictive practices, taboos, discrimination. In a way, it's associated with freedom, and there's also a very powerful relationship between the consumption of energy in a society and political freedom. You can start to see patterns in rural India, for example, where the access to energy and power liberates the young women from carrying water over vast distances. Suddenly it's pumped and it's available, and these woman are free to be educated. Then the next pattern is, they have television, and they suddenly see what is happening in the cities and how the city offers all those other qualities that I've mentioned. Suddenly, there's a dissatisfaction that increases the movement to the city.

Then, as you have more wealth, more mobility, you can chart those points in time where there's been a flight from the cities that have become, in a way, synonymous with noise, congestion, pollution. You have that movement away into suburbia and the rationalization of suburbia by architects like Frank Lloyd Wright with Broadacre—a lot of parallels, at the time, with the thinking of Buckminster Fuller: the autonomous house that would be air delivered in remote locations where you didn't need roads, and you'd have your own zoom-mobile; the Dymaxion car would be the Harrier jet of the future. Frank Lloyd Wright and Le Corbusier and the *Ville Radieuse* with its towers, the elimination of Paris at a stroke, the Paris that we know and love, in the same way that, for the sake of the car, you almost had the destruction of Manhattan under Robert Moses.

But I think the enduring patterns and perhaps the big transformations of the city happen through technology, the technology that would take away the stinking mountains of horse manure, the horses, the sanitation problems, the smells. I think there was a eureka moment when the city became potentially cleaner, less polluting. I think that we might start to see, in terms of transportation, a softer, more gentle, cleaner form that reduces the congestion and so on—the equivalent today, if you like, of the open sewers of that past.

GH — Le Corbusier or Frank Lloyd Wright: have you felt the influence of their thinking in your work or in your consciousness?

NF — In a way, as architects, designers, artists, sculptors, painters, I think we all owe debts to those who've gone before and who've done work of quality, even if it's not named architects or artists but in the anonymous world, the people who carved Eskimo figurines or extraordinary bronzes or anonymous architecture—the cathedrals, the great barns, architecture without architects, as Bernard Rudofsky said, an individual who recognized that and created, in the sixties, this exhibition at the Museum of Modern Art here in New York. I think we're all influenced, but that doesn't mean to say that we mindlessly copy. I think it's a much more philosophical route.

I think that sometimes individuals move out of a profession and become very skilled at another profession which is not related to their core activity. Olmsted, who designed Central Park and was responsible for some extraordinary civic initiatives, moved out from another profession, journalism, and became an extraordinary expert in urban planning. I don't think, frankly, that Wright or Corbusier were successful in that transition. I don't think their visions of the city of the future are really that relevant. Maybe the lessons of that are very important.

But I think the vision of wiping away the urbanity, of life as being a series of tall towers in a verdant park, the versions that have been realized of that—maybe the failure was as much because they were done on the cheap; they were seen as a form of cheap political expediency, of delivering *x* dwellings. That's not to say that architects at that time, with others, didn't jump on that bandwagon.

What is interesting is that, with its various transformations, the traditional form of the city is proving to be very enduring over time, and in a way, New York, like many other cities, is testimony to that. London, for example, is a lower-rise city, but nonetheless high density low-rise with an abundance of green spaces, and it's quite interesting that the most dense spaces in London, like in many cities, are the most sought after. They're the most desirable. They don't have the individual garden; they have public parks. They're quite dense by comparison with a lot of the poorer parts of the city. I think it is choice. How do you offer choice in a sustainable future?

GH — I guess that's the point of this film.

NF — Yes. How do you maximize the use of space? How do you make more efficient, more human, more comfortable the experience of mobility? You'd think that space up there in the sky was free and unlimited as opposed to down here on the ground, but it's quite interesting that in a very short span of time the space up there has had to be rationed, rationalized, and the movement controlled. In other words, all those airliners that are passing in the sky are going on invisible highways. The individual pilots and crews are not in charge. That space is regulated. The speed is determined. There's an authority, a central authority, which is governing that and governing that now on a global basis.

An interesting question is, in terms of the optimization of space on the ground, the highways, will we see the same pattern? Google, for example, is very advanced in terms of its work on the robotic element of the car. Cars today have all that equipment on board. It's not been connected up, but you have the navigation system; you have the electronic controls. It's but a short step to go onto autopilot. Could you imagine the idea that you would be moved effortlessly along the highway? Suburbia would then be optimized to a far greater extent. Perhaps you could start to inject investment into the present suburbia, which is unsustainable as a pattern, but maybe you could transform that. Could you imagine reading your newspaper or checking your computer whilst the car transports you effortlessly and safely because it maintains a minimum distance? You're spared a lot of the upheavals of horrific accidents, traffic jams, delays. You could perhaps see the technology which we take for granted in the sky and that degree of regulation offering you a safer, more interesting, more sustainable experience. Of course, you might then come off onto a country lane, and you're back in driving mode, and you have then the freedom of movement, give or take some regulatory control.

GH — I'm interested in this idea of the regulated versus the unregulated, the formal versus the informal in the sense of the design of the city.

NF — That's the essence of the city, isn't it? That is the thing that attracts us to the city. It is the chance encounter; it's the unexpected. It's the planned—the things that we know—and the things that pop up unexpectedly and give that spontaneity, that variety. So it's always that balance between the riot of anarchy and the dead hand of authority. It's how you get that balance. It's how you get the safety, the security, the knowledge that you'll be able to start here, end up there, and go back there, but that something unexpected will happen along the way, that you'll make a discovery. That, in a way, is the magic of cities, that you're always discovering, that change is taking place, and in that sense, the only constant is change, but—and it's a big but—you need that degree of regulation.

It is almost like democracy itself. It's counterintuitive. I mean, very topical at the moment in terms of some of the upheavals that are happening in emerging societies, but how do you transition overnight into a democratic system, something that is always showing strains and stresses from time to time? But those societies have evolved over a long time, and the city is an expression of that in many ways in microcosm. It's quite interesting: in the some of the societies which are now being torn by inner strife and tensions and ambitions and repressions and so on, it is the public spaces which become the symbols, and in some cases even the statuary, the element in the heart which becomes so symbolic that it has to be torn down. Public space in some cities has its roots in the military. The boulevards of Paris, Haussmann—again, the military imperative, which in turn gives the humanity and the tree-lined avenues and the great vistas and terminations. So many of the things that make our lives, the miracles of medicine and so on, have been born out of horrific warfare, so there's always this dark and light side.

GH — How does that come into your planning? We were talking to someone in Mumbai, and you know, there are massive business complexes going up, and they were saying, "Every businessman who's going to be in there is going to have a driver who's going to be waiting around doing nothing during the day." So of course, informal vendors and a whole industry will spring up for them, and a lot of the times, that's not designed for, but it's the reality of a city like Mumbai. How does the inevitability of informal development, informal activity, come into the thinking in terms of design?

NF — It's an interesting point. We just finally surfaced on the West Kowloon cultural development, a competition that was first run in 2001, which we won, then in 2006, which we won, and finally this major competition in which we've been selected for the master plan. This is a major extension of Hong Kong as a city. Essentially what we've done is show how the city can grow and—by respecting the density and embedding the 17 cultural institutions which have been proposed, from opera houses to major museums of contemporary art, places for Chinese opera, cinemas, schools of music, performance spaces—shown how these can be a part of the urban fabric.

You learn from the DNA of Hong Kong, which is quite special to that city, because what happens is you get a vertical layering, so you get the richness of the public activities at the base and the incredible signage. We've analyzed that DNA and shown how it can be retranslated with literally the freedom to create the whole ad hoc eruption of signage, which occupies a particular proportion of the visual field. In other words, you walk down a street, and they've identified a number of different kinds of streets, but there's the big wide street and there's very narrow pedestrian streets; you'll feel the view. There's a certain amount of sky you'll see, a certain amount of signs.

If we create the zones for that, then we believe that we can create the framework which will allow all those chance activities, signage, to prosper, to create, to bubble, and to bring all those chance, unplanned encounters within the minimum framework. At the same time, this part of the city, this extension, will be with an awareness of the realities of transport as it is today, not transport as it was—horse drawn—at the time that these cities were designed. Therefore, there is a lower zone which siphons off the service traffic, the emergency services, although taxis and so on can still bring a degree of life to the pedestrian zone. It's not just a dead pedestrian zone. That then creates the opportunity for a big green park and, because it's a waterside site, up to two kilometers of edge trails and routes, bringing something that Hong Kong doesn't have at the moment: the great park with the indigenous species.

In a way, that shows a sensitivity and awareness of all those chance elements, which you cannot plan for, but on the other hand, if you're making a planned extension, you have to plan the infrastructure; you have to plan the section; and you have to plan, literally, the plan. So you continue the grid that you know works, and you modify that so that it works for the things which, at the moment, don't work. Because nobody wants to put their life on the block when they cross the road or worry about the child who strays into the path of a heavy bus, polluting fumes, and so on. If you can modify that, if you can address the things that don't work well but build on the things that you know work well, that, I think, is interesting as a designer to confront.

GH — I'd like to talk about China. If you had to describe Chinese urban-ism to someone who wasn't in the field, how would you?
NF — In terms of urbanism in China, I think it's very difficult to generalize. China is so vast, has so many different regions, places, cities. There are megacities with names that you and I will not be familiar with. They're not household names like Beijing and Shanghai, but it'll be difficult to think of two more different cities than Beijing and Shanghai. But when you think these are only two of so many conurbations, of so many millions, then it's difficult to generalize.

Obviously, one thing that you can say about China is that a process of urbanization, which is boiling and bubbling, is happening so fast. That process—which might have taken a hundred, two hundred years in the places that we take for granted here in North America, in Europe— is happening at 10 times the speed, so it's an overnight phenomenon. It's become the world's biggest market for cars. It's overtaking other industrialized societies in terms of its consumption of energy and man-ufacturing capability.

Is it going to learn the lessons from those older economies where you're seeing the deliberate embrace and proliferation of the bicycle? This is occurring at a point in China where the bicycle is disappearing and is seen as a symbol of obsolescence, deprivation, poverty, whereas the car is seen as a symbol of affluence, emancipation. Is China going to be able to learn from the most progressive examples? Is it going to learn from the mistakes of the car-borne societies? Is it going to go to Detroit and see what happens when the pinnacle of the automobile industry, with all its pride and might not so long ago, is now being overtaken and consumed by nature? Is it going to be able to learn from those suburban examples in America where we're seeing information technology bring extraordinary affluence to areas like the Bay Area with its mix of academia and research facilities?

I think the signs are more optimistic than pessimistic in the sense that China is embracing solar, is the biggest manufacturer of solar panels, has embraced a green agenda, is consciously moving the polluting industries out of city centers. I think that we're seeing all these trends magnified. What will that eventual pattern be? We can hope that there will be enlightenment and progression in terms of the urban models. I think it's very much a mixed picture at the moment, very difficult to make that judgment. Perhaps there are individuals that you can talk to who have that perspective from which we can learn. At the moment, I'm more an observer.

I've been privileged to be able to be part of a venture like Beijing Airport, which, if I pull back and reflect on it, is highly sustainable in the sense that it is one building rather than a proliferation of many different terminals. In that sense, it's compact. It also is about an extraordinary sense of civic pride, the kind of ethic if you like or philosophy that prevailed in the West in a previous century or a century even removed, the 19th century, when the railway station became a great cultural statement in terms of space and light and presence and welcoming and, in the most positive sense, was significant in this expression of pride, and we see that in key building emerging in China. I think there are a lot of patterns which are coming together. The perspective of time, of course, and not too long ahead, will tell us.

GH — On the subject of sustainability, can you talk a little bit about the Masdar City project?

NF — Masdar City is a planned community in Abu Dhabi. At its heart is an academic institution totally devoted to the study of renewable energy. Interestingly, it's coming from a society which has its wealth being generated by fossil fuel, by oil. This is a planned community, a university already active, a hundred students engaged in a whole series of experimental projects, so the very urbanity, the very physicality, of this city is experimental and seeks to nurture innovation through this academic institute and spin-offs, to engage in experiments.

Just to give one example, it's using expertise from Iceland, which has been developed there because it's the only geothermal society on the planet, which taps the wealth of energy below the surface. So that expertise is coming to the desert, and they're using the technology of deep drilling developed for the oil industry to tap a thermal source deep below the surface, which can then be converted freely into cooling as a renewable energy. Or it's developing new kinds of solar farms.

It's layered in the way that I've described our Hong Kong project, so it has a zone below the pavement level. The sidewalk is elevated to encourage gentle breezes, because anybody who's flown an aircraft know's that you don't have to go very high above the ground to find air movement. The air is still at the ground level, but you only have to go slightly higher, and you have movement.

Of course, traditional buildings created wind towers, which would tap the movement of air, the breezes above the desert floor, and that would force air past water to give it evaporative cooling, so they would hang cloth, rags, steeped in water. So by a lot of devices before the age of energy—cheap air conditioning, cheap fuel, unlimited gasoline—before then, human beings in hostile climates like the desert had to use ingenuity. They had to really work with the intellect to create refreshing environments.

Now, what we've done at Masdar is to put all those lessons together in terms of the narrower streets, the shading, no big windows or large areas of glass unless they're facing onto shaded areas, courtyards, wind towers, evaporative cooling, water, greenery—putting it all together. We've demonstrated scientifically with our own testing that we've lowered the temperature significantly, so then the next step is, inside a building, to use the minimum amount of energy with very efficient refrigeration to make a place. You can't offer something which is sustainable if it's not as good as the environment in an unsustainable place, because the level of expectation is still the same.

What is interesting is that it is really working, but it is an experimental project, and that project started off live with everybody knowing it was an experimental project. Of course, what has come along since are economic crises on top of economic crises, so we've seen another part of the Emirates suffer. We've seen aid being diverted from one economy to another economy. That's had a knock-on effect, and so this project now has to justify itself like any other project. It's recycling its own waste, but it doesn't have subsidies of the form that help other projects. It continues to expand. It will probably, as a result of the economic realities of the day, be phased over a longer period of time. It's a changed environment, but the reality is that it has students. The lights are blazing. I mean, a research institution is seven days a week/24, a highly conditioned environment, research laboratories, and it's alive and well and thriving on solar.

A lot of lessons have been learned. The original proposition was that everything would happen on site. But when you come down to the realities and discover that the water below that site is more saline than the water a few kilometers away, it obviously makes much more sense to purify the water a few kilometers away, which takes less energy, and then move that water to the site, in the same way that solar panels on the roof are still an element of Masdar, but the learning curve is such that you realize that there are difficulties in a desert environment very, very different from this environment here. It is more efficient to be able to use a newer generation of solar arrays, side based, than it is to put them on roofs, especially when you get into some of these newer technologies where you may have water pulsing through tubes at four hundred degrees centigrade because these experiments have developed the potential to focus mirrors and to provide an extraordinary level of heating. You don't really want that sitting on a rooftop.

You're also into issues of how utility companies work, because traditionally the utility company absorbs the cost of burying the pipes in a road and creates huge zones for that, and in a way, it's an investment ahead of the profitability of them being able to exert tariffs. But if you have the newer technologies, then the utility companies have not been prepared for that. They're not part of that. Of course, part of the bigger picture, how you really reduce energy and start to get communities not only consuming zero energy but actually harvesting energy, is turning the waste to energy. That transforms our whole attitude toward waste. Instead of waste being something that we take away and bury out of sight, out of mind, the idea that we transform that waste—that we burn it, we select it, and we generate energy through the waste—that is a whole new attitude. And of course, all the established patterns of the way that these things are handled need to be totally reexamined. In the end, it comes down to political enlightenment. That is a big step.

GH — How do you translate that to an existing city? Everybody likes to talk about sustainability, and I think that maybe they just think it means getting a hybrid car.

NF — Yes, it's a kind of green wallpaper.

GH — Yeah. So I'm thinking, in terms of the average city, half a million people somewhere, what are the kind of things you can do?

NF — Well, I think some cities are by their very nature more sustainable, so if you compare Copenhagen with the Detroit that we've been talking about, one is a car-borne city and, in that sense, a relatively new phenomenon. Cities in their traditional sense have been with us for five millennia. The automobile has been with us, you know, the blink of an eye. If you compare a city like Copenhagen, which has roughly the same populace and climate as Detroit, one is twice the density of the other and consumes one tenth of the energy of the other. One is blooming. The other is in decline. Detroit, in a way, is a kind of hero city for me because I love the automobile; I love the artifact; I love the history of the automobile, the innovation, the ingenuity. I'm sure that a city like that will, over time, reinvent itself. But that is, in a way, illustrative of the fact that some cities are, by their very nature, their model, if you like, better placed than others. I think that it does draw our attention; it does highlight; it does raise question marks over the car-borne city, and it does put quite a few ticks in the box of the traditional city with its reliance on the pedestrian friendly and so on.

Then you obviously have to go further. How do you retrofit those cities in such a way that they become more attractive, more pleasurable, less polluting, more sustainable? If you're shifting the focus to those emerging economies, which are creating new cities on greenfield sites, what model are they going to adopt? And if you have those cities which are established and doing well, and this is one great example here, New York, how do those evolve to be even better and more sustainable?

Then, the big question—how do those vast areas which have been born on the dream of everlasting cheap energy, which is a mirage which has evaporated—where we're seeing foreclosure; we're seeing lack of job opportunities because it doesn't have the layers; it doesn't have the range of opportunities the city offers, but nonetheless it is a reality—how do you transform that in such a way that it becomes more affluent, more friendly? And we've touched on all those issues. We've talked about the way in which, with maybe a degree of regulatory control over mobility, the way in which the mobility industry, the car industry, might change and adapt; the way in which, in those communities, which are essentially monoculture, maybe you can inject new usage. You can bring industries, new industries, maybe education, into them so they're not just vast, anonymous residential tracts.

These patterns will evolve over time. There's no crystal ball. You can have the futurologists who will say, "We'll paint this scenario. We'll paint that scenario." But there's as many scenarios as there are prophets.

GH — That was the next thing I was going to ask: over the next two hundred, three hundred years, how do you see cities evolving?

NF — A plurality. I think that one size is not going to fit all. If we look at the extraordinary increase in performance and miniaturization so that we all have one version of this [smart phone] in our pocket, it's the Bucky Fuller mantra of "doing more with less." If that is capable of informing the whole generation of energy and mobility, then if it's as friendly as some of these devices and has the transforming effect that we now take for granted of that digital revolution, if that revolution can take place in terms of mobility and energy generation—it's a bit like the Kennedy thing of the man on the moon that was born out of extreme hostility at that time, and threat, but it was a commitment. If you look at the beneficial spin-off from that space race, from NASA, that's been extraordinary in terms of a lot of the things that we take for granted in terms of life enhancing, lifesaving.

One's hope is that through the very hostile pressures of what we're seeing now in terms of the horrific cascade of events in Japan—the whole literally burning nuclear issue of that past generation of nuclear energy hard on the heels of the great natural disasters, the tsunami, the earthquake—and the shrinking carbon fuels, notwithstanding the new generation of natural gas and the fact that the carbon cycle is being typified by less carbon and more and more hydrogen, maybe out of these extreme pressures, the positive aspects of human nature will respond—the quest for innovation, for inquiry, the ever-changing cycle of, again, to quote Bucky, "doing more with less." I think the optimistic hope is that that will permeate those worlds of cities, energy, mobility and lead to something which is more exciting, more desirable, and humanistic. That's more or less it, isn't it really?

GH — These smart-cities initiatives as put forth mostly by companies that are in that technology, like IBM, Philips—I would say that kind of has to happen for this kind of energy efficiency.

NF — Yes. Masdar brings together a lot of that smart technology, a lot of these bigger patterns. It's a high performer, and you can measure that. It's not really the scale of a city; it's like a city in microcosm. It's an enclave within a larger, very highly energy-consuming society. I think it's significant that as an experiment, it's being born out of that region.

At the risk of repeating myself, you have to ask why there aren't more experiments of that kind, why they're not being funded by governments or by, as it were, coalitions of very enlightened and progressive industries. Because the technologies which have transformed cities in the past, what is the equivalent now of those new technologies? In other words, what we take for granted as being really very basic—the sanitation, the arteries, the networks of roads, which have transformed cities in the past—what, in 50 years' time when we look back, will we see as the equivalent of that? It won't just be the information highways, but it will be a combination of newer technologies which are about energy generation, about mobility, about creating an environment which is an improvement on the environment that we take for granted but is sustainable. The only alternative is a complete breakdown because we can't get it together, because we can't respond to that, and life as we know it will crumble, erode, and like that pattern in Detroit, will go back to nature, and that will be a terminal end.

As an architect, if you're not an optimist, you're not going to be able to survive professionally, so you have a belief in the future. And I'm aware of technology in terms of its evil manifestations, whether that's an atomic bomb, whether it's the horrors of warfare, but it's always worth remembering that all the things that make our lives less threatening, the technology of medicine and so on, so much of that has been born out of the darker side of our history.

—

Candy Chang (CC)/ March 30, 2011 New Orleans

Taiwanese-American artist Candy Chang creates interactive public art installations that challenge the perception of public space to help us make sense of our communities and ourselves. Her project *Before I Die* has been recreated in over 70 countries, including Iraq, China, Haiti, Brazil, Ukraine, Kazakhstan, and South Africa. In 2011 she cofounded Neighborland, an online/public installation tool for civic collaboration. I spoke with Candy in front of the first *Before I Die* wall, in the Faubourg Marigny neighborhood of New Orleans.

Gary Hustwit — So can you tell me about how you first got started with this *Before I Die* project?

Candy Chang — First off, I just wanted to make a nicer space for my neighborhood. That's it. There's a lot of beautiful architecture here. There's also some blight. I bike by this house all the time. I live a few blocks away. It's been sitting here collecting dust and graffiti for years. It's actually a really sad story. So I contacted the property owner to get permission to do something to it, and that's when I found out it's this single mother who felt really passionately about New Orleans and wanted to invest in it after Katrina. She bought this house, and she wanted to repair it. Then the contractor stole her money. She's been struggling since. It was a good lesson for me; I think it's really easy to demonize all the blighted-property owners as one collective entity of assholes who don't care about the neighborhood. Then I learned this, and I thought, well, every house has a story.

I thought, how can we make these neglected spaces constructive ones for the neighborhood? I feel very passionately about redefining the ways we use public space to share information that is important to our neighborhoods and to our personal well-being. This question—what do you want to do before you die; what do you want to spend your life doing?—it's a question that has really changed me in the last year. I feel like everybody should pause and think about it, so I did this.

GH — What's been the reaction to it? Even while you were doing it, what's been the reaction?

CC — I've been blown away. It's been great to figure out a way that people can stop and remember what's important to them in life and then to share and learn the hopes and aspirations of the people around them. I think it's a really enlightening way to learn about your neighbors. When I did this, it was this really awesome neighborhood project. A lot of people helped out along the way. When people asked about it, they were really into it. I thought it was interesting because the process was a little tough, to think, how do you change these spaces? Just changing a house like this that's been collecting dust and graffiti for years was actually pretty tough. I was surprised. I thought it was interesting that it wasn't the city that was the blockade. They were really supportive. Different entities of the city were really supportive. It was actually a few residents of this area who tried to stall it and stop it.

GH — Why would they?

CC — I think they were afraid that it was going to incite lewd comments. I said, "I will monitor it every day. I live a few blocks away." I think that's a really interesting issue. I understand their concerns. Right now the knee jerk reaction is, all informal messages in public space are bad. That's the default right now. There's no space for residents to share information in public. But you see what people are trying to do. You see it on lamp posts. In cities around the world, people are trying to post fliers to each other about community meetings and this and that. A lot of that stuff is actually really important to the neighborhood, but right now it's all grouped together as bad and illegal. All informal messages, all fliers, are bad and illegal. I don't think that's true. I think, as designers and planners, we need to see what people are trying to do and say, "Should we actually figure out what are people trying to do here, and should we help them do that?"

It's interesting because, if you look around, if you look at our public spaces and you look at our messages in public space, you might think that all we care about are sexy beers and fruity shampoos and the latest Hollywood movies, right? You think, does that really reflect what's important to us? In a built environment where citizens' fliers are illegal yet businesses can shout about their products on an increasing number of public surfaces, I think we need to consider whether our public spaces can be better designed so that they're not necessarily going to the highest bidder, but instead they're reflecting what's really important to our neighborhoods and to our personal well-being.

GH — That's a great point, because there isn't that space that's just, not only available, but that encourages people to want to post messages.

CC — Right, and I think that designers need to help validate that. If given the opportunity, would we have more to say to each other than, "Have you seen my cat?" Which is, right now, what people are trying to do. In dire need, I'll post this flier out in public space. There are so many things that, living in the same neighborhood, we could share with each other that would actually help us understand what's going on. Share local information. Right now it seems kind of funny that it's easier to reach out to the entire world than it is to reach out to your neighborhood.

That's another issue too: where to invest your time and energy. Who knows what a neighborhood needs, what a place needs, more than the residents, the people who live and work there? We're the ones who know exactly where the public transportation stops should go, what businesses we need locally, what things need fixing. I think we need better tools to share that information and make real changes happen. That's just it. Where do you put your energy? It's interesting: in New Orleans, people talk about planning fatigue. After Katrina, lots of people went to lots of community meetings and put lots of stickers on lots of maps. Oftentimes, they didn't really see any noticeable change. A lot of that energy they gave didn't really translate into anything happening. I think a lot of times people question, where do I put my energy? Which meetings are the ones where something is actually going to happen? We really need to think more about that.

The fact is, there are a lot of amazing people trying to get a lot of great things done: planting trees, trying to push for bike lanes, trying to change a dilapidated area into a greenway. I think the issue right now is, they need more manpower. When I go to these community meetings, they're always saying, "We need more volunteers. We know what we want. We're trying to push for this initiative, but we need more help. We need more manpower." How do you get those people with the latent energy in the neighborhood connected to each other? How do you easily connect the person who wants fresh produce with the food co-op that's been in the long-but-promising making for years to try to take that idea off the ground? How do you connect those people together? How do you connect the person who wants more trees in the neighborhood to the local initiative that's trying to plant trees? How do you connect the person who wants less blight to the three steps it takes to report it? How do you connect the person who wants to start a coffee shop with the local process of how to start a business? How do you connect the person who wants public transportation with the policy that you can vote on right now that would help make that happen?

There are these certain actions going on. There are people who are trying to get things done, and they need help. They need to find other people, and they need to spread their good word. That's what I'm trying to do with Neighborland in the future. Our time and energy is precious. We only have so much to give. What's the best way to give it to something that's really going to make a difference and do the thing that we want to get done?

GH — I think it's interesting too. Oh, this girl's taking photos.

CC — Yeah, it's great. Every time that I'm over here there are people who stop, and I hear heartbreaking stories about everyone's hopes and dreams. It's great. My friend's son was just in town, and this was his favorite thing. He calls it the wall of dreams. He said, "Before I die, I want to meet Mr. Whiskers," which was like his inner self, his power animal. He said, "I want to eat him." That's just the deepest thing ever. I don't even know how to respond to that. Actually, the kids are really fast with it. "Before I die, I want to eat all the candy and sushi in the world." "Before I die, I want to own a monkey." That was another kid. It's really awesome to see the range of responses. I love it. I'm blown away.

There are quite a few misspellings here right now. I like that they want to inspire a nation, but it's spelled "nathan." I like this: "Before I die, I want to tell my mother I love her." Tear. "Fall in love again." I love, "Before I die, I want to read the full constitution." That's awesome. You do that. "Before I die, I want to make it into hip-hop." That's good. "Do a cartwheel." That's great.

GH — People like posing in front of it.

CC — Yeah. Honestly, I didn't know what to expect. I am so surprised it's here every day. I'm very grateful it's here. You never know if it's going to get tagged over. I have no expectations. I know it's in public space. I know it's going to be temporary. At some point, someone's going to kill it. There are people who are trying to kill it in their own little way and steal the chalk holders every day, but while it's here, it's been pretty amazing. I'm blown away by the responses. From really funny to really heartbreaking. Really poetic.

GH — Like you were talking about earlier, even though there are city council meetings and people put a lot of energy into them, there's this whole segment of the population that isn't ever going to go to those. Having some way for them to engage and have input, even if it's anonymous, is so important.

CC — It's funny, because right now, when you talk about what the community wants, usually we just make it sound like the community wants this. Actually, oftentimes it's the five loudest people, the five people who can make it to the community meeting, who have the time to make it every week for three hours. There are a lot of people who don't have that time. Most of us don't, right? It's really interesting. William "Holly" Whyte said something great. He said, "Participation is a means, not an end. When treated like an end, it can be even more repressive than the authoritarianism it's trying to replace. At least with the authoritarian, we knew what he wanted. He wanted our sweat. Well, the new man wants your soul." I think that's just it. We only have so much time and energy to give. Where do you put that energy? How do you find the people? How do you self-organize to get things done and not waste your time?

GH — It seems like people think everything's online now and we should be able to connect with everyone online. I think people just assume, "Oh yeah, everybody's got web access. Everybody can get online." There's a huge section of the population that doesn't even have that as an option. This is way more democratic.

CC — Where better to help improve our public spaces than in public space, right? If we're talking about blighted houses or vacant storefronts, the people who live there, they know the things that they need, if it's a local grocery or community garden, butcher shop, art supply store, dancing school. All these ideas, that have been really interesting, have come out of the *I Wish This Was* project. Where better to provide that input than on the very space that we're talking about, the very space that we're trying to improve?

How do you improve the ways we can share information in public space? This actually reaches a much larger audience or a different audience than you'd find if you just used an online tool. That's what's been really great about the sticker project. I know a lot of those responses never would have existed if it was just an online forum. So how do you use different public spaces? The Internet is also a public space in itself. I feel like the Internet has really progressed a lot over the years and become this public forum. I think our physical public spaces could progress as well. I think we feel like we accomplished a lot just by having sidewalks. There was a certain time, a certain era, when that wasn't necessarily a given. It was all about cars, and communities had to fight hard to make a place for pedestrians and bicycles. Now I think we need to think about the next steps past that.

GH — Can we talk about the *I Wish This Was* stickers? How did the project start, and what were the steps that went into it?

CC — There'd been a thought that had been simmering for a while for me, which was, what if I could shape the businesses in my neighborhood? When I used to live in Chinatown in New York and I'd see a new store about to open—there's such a quick turnaround in New York—I'd think, "Oh, I hope it's a bookstore. I hope it's a bookstore." Then I'd be like, "Oh, another hair salon." That's the way it goes right now. When I was in Helsinki, we were working in this big office park, and we all wished there was a bar nearby. I thought, "If only some burgeoning bar owner knew there was a strong enough customer base here, they would gladly open nearby." Then in New Orleans, living here now, I was surprised there are so many vacant storefronts around when there are also so many people. Everyone's back in this neighborhood. There are so many people who want and need certain things. There's still not a local grocery store, which is a long and interesting story. I thought, "Well, what if residents had better tools to shape the future businesses in their neighborhood and beyond?" I thought, "Well, there are a lot of vacant storefronts. Where better to ask for specific input than on the storefronts themselves?"

I made these stickers that say, "I Wish This Was" with a space underneath. I put grids of blank stickers on neglected buildings around the city, with a little Sharpie pen to make it as easy as possible for people who are walking by to write what they wish was there. I put boxes of free stickers in businesses around the city. I've been blown away by the range of responses. People want certain businesses, like a butcher shop, a nursery, a dancing school, a taco stand, an art supply store. Then people want better infrastructure, like sidewalks repaired, and roads properly paved, and bike racks installed. It's been really interesting to see how people have been responding to each other's stickers. You'll see stickers that say, "I wish this was a grocery too," or "Three votes for a community bookstore," or "I second this," "I third that." In response to "a bakery," someone else wrote, "Well, if you can find the financing, I will do the baking." I think that's great. It leads to the bigger question—what if residents had better tools to shape the development of their neighborhoods, to shape the future business, to shape the spaces in between those businesses too? That's what I've been developing now, building upon that with Neighborland.

GH — I remember the first time I came and talked to somebody about it, they were like, "Oh yeah, I thought that was the city doing it. I thought that was a city government thing or an ad campaign or something."

CC — That's funny. To me, it's like a love child of urban planning and street art. It's a great lo-fi, low-tech, no-tech experiment in public space. I'm all for that. I'm all for being scrappy and trying things out and learning and quickly developing things from there.

GH — What are the future plans? Did you start selling the stickers online?

CC — Yeah. There's been an amazing response from people all over. I think that's what's interesting: it's a universal issue. I've gotten people writing, "There are a lot of vacant storefronts in my city too." I've made the stickers available online, and I'm getting lots of requests for translated versions too: Spanish, Portuguese, Chinese, Finnish. It's been pretty amazing, so I've been trying to figure out a way to expand it.

GH — Do you want to talk about what are the stickers are made of?

CC — Oh yeah. It was important to me that they were made out of vinyl so that they are very sticky but they can be removed in one piece, so future business owners can easily remove them without damaging property, without leaving a mark.

GH — It would be great to see somebody actually make something in one of the storefronts from the sticker suggestions. "Okay, I bought this building, and everybody seems to want a bakery. Let's open a bakery."

CC — That's what we're trying to do with *Neighborland*. We're trying to combine some sort of component in public space, like the stickers, with texting as well. What do you want to see here? Then there will be a website, an online tool, a mobile tool, that will just say, "I want blank in my neighborhood." You can see what other people want and say, "Me too." Then two people want a grocery store. Fifty people want a grocery store. A hundred people want it. Then you can share the information about what's going on around that topic and hopefully know what steps to then take to make that happen. There's only so much you can do on a sticker.

GH — But it's important. It's that first step in engaging someone that might not be the person that's going to go the board meeting. I think I was saying before, that idea of envisioning something different is such a key in design thinking. It's so cool when members of the public get engaged in it.

CC — Yeah, it's interesting. We've been talking to lots of residents and community groups as we're developing this tool and trying to unroll it in New Orleans now. We got a great grant to develop it in New Orleans, so I'm excited to walk it out in the next few weeks.

GH — I also think change is threatening to people, even a simple change like this, let alone changing their neighborhood. People have this concept of, I moved into this neighborhood because I liked it as it was, and I don't want things to change.

CC — Yeah. It's even interesting that I struggled so hard to get this done. I wanted to do it above board, the *Before I Die* wall. I did get permission from the property owner, from the neighbors on the block—they're the ones who have to look at it every day—from the neighborhood association's blight committee, from the historic district's landmark commission, from the arts council, from the City Planning Commission. I went through the proper channels, and I'm glad that I did, just to say, "Okay, it can be done." It was a little challenging. That's when I wondered, is there a way we can change the process so it's easier to turn a neglected space like this into something nicer? That's all I want to do. It was a little difficult.

It's interesting, because I think, in trying to get the support of community groups to do things like this, I realized it's really not in their interest to support anything that's different, that's risky, where there are unknowns. This is it. Whenever I'm trying to propose different ways to share information, certain people have been wary of it because they're afraid it will incite lewd comments, that it's going to start a graffiti war. How do you change that perception? I think it's too bad that the fear of graffiti trumps the desire for more constructive community input. I had no idea what was going to happen. I thought, maybe it's going to be this many penis doodles to this many thoughtful responses. As you can see, the responses have been incredible. I think it's worth a few penis doodles if that means that many more people are going to be able to share information, thoughtful information, productive information, with each other.

I hope, actually, that you don't use that.

GH — [Laughs.] You said "penis doodles" so quickly that for a second I was like, "What did you say?" Penisdoodles, like one word.
    CC — I can't talk anymore!

GH — I think we're good.
—

Grover Mouton (GM)/ March 31, 2011 New Orleans

Grover Mouton is an architect and the Director of the Tulane Regional Urban Design Center in New Orleans. The TRUDC conducts community outreach design initiatives for cities throughout the Gulf Region, and Mouton's students have also collaborated on international initiatives, including a new town design for Longpao, China.

I'd originally approached Grover about a project he and his students were working on with the city of Biloxi, Mississippi, as part of the effort to reconstruct Biloxi's waterfront in the wake of Hurricane Katrina. Unfortunately the timing didn't work out and we weren't able to follow that project to it's conclusion.

I spoke with Grover at the TRUDC offices at Tulane.
—

Gary Hustwit — You mentioned Buckminster Fuller before we started, how did he influence you?
Grover Mouton — I've met him.

GH — Really?
GM — Yeah. My cousin built three of the geodesic domes in Lafayette and lived in them. They were very good friends, very close. Nice guy. Fuller used to come to Lafayette.

GH — Really?
GM — Yeah, they were really good friends. Quite an amazing guy. My cousin had a beautiful house with a big alley of trees. He was an architect who was slightly mad but sweet. He had a big party, and he got on a horse and just rode around the house. Buckminster Fuller was there, wearing a cape. They got on famously, as you can imagine.

GH — Geodesic cape.
GM — That's all true.

GH — Tell us about the Urban Design Center.
GM — I direct this urban design center, which I established almost 18 years ago with a grant from an architect that I'd been working with named Arthur Davis. He did the Superdome, did a lot of other things. Basically what we've done is we've based the urban design center on the work of the Mayors' Institute on City Design. I created the southern district of that because prior to our engagement it was only large cities, and I felt that mayors really are a regionally based group, and so we create the north, south, and west block, and we

controlled the south for many, many years and just had an institute last year where mayors came in.

We also, through the American Planning Association, have done a great deal of work in China, almost all on the Yangtze River and in the delta. We did 50 acres in downtown Shanghai with a big development group, and we did a lot of work in Nanjing, which is older than Beijing by five dynasties before the Ming dynasty that was founded there. We did their big historic site, and that's where our present site is, and two additional new towns down the river.

I guess the most successful project, because it's being built right now, is in Changxing, which is a scenic highway, which I thought would be a good idea, to have a scenic highway on Lake Tai, which is very polluted, That's where Wuxi is, and that's what's talked about in all the newspapers for polluting. We were right across from it, and I said, "Why don't you have a scenic highway?" Because they can afford it, and we have all the areas along the highway that we can interpret. We did the drawings, and it was all done here at Tulane with very young people; the guy who laid it out was 21. He's at the GSD right now, and he was doing his portfolio and he looked on Google Earth, and they are building it. They didn't even tell us. They're building the entire highway for, I don't know, a billion RMB, because that's China. It's fun.

It's extremely dynamic. I remember when they called me. They said, "You have to go to Changxing." I said, "For what?" They said, "Oh, because you're going to present this concept." I said, "Okay." So I went. The big deal, and it's really a wonderful deal, was that the only reason we could do this highway was I could build a road on the consolidated cities, because when China develops they consolidate many of the villages, and I had a meeting with Nick Jenisch, the project director here, and I said, "Do you have a consolidated village plan?" He said, "Yes." I said, "Great." He shouldn't have ever told me that. I said, "Copy it." So we copied. When we were able to do the large road, they said, "How is it possible that you understand so much about the consolidated villages?" And I said, "It's very simple. You can just look at the map," which is not true.

In one of my projects—we've been working there 12 years—what happened was that I said, "Look, our budget is so big. Let's hire the best scholar in China, period. Let's hire him, bring him in." This was in Nanjing. So we hired her. She came from Yale, she was British, but she'd never been in Nanjing. She was in Jinjiang, and I said, "Well, listen, if our number one consultant is in Jinjiang, there must be something there really fabulous, so let's go." We go, and it's a wonderful old city. It's where the poets went, blah, blah, blah. I had the opportunity to have dinner with the secretary of the party for the whole precinct, and I said, "You know what? You're building a high speed rail from Shanghai to Beijing right through Jinjiang. Twenty million people will be one hour from one of your most beautiful cities. You need to put some serious guidelines on that and build a new town and a big expansion." He said, "Great." So I did this little drawing over dinner.

We visited the site later, and I said, "What are they doing?" They said, "They are building your road." I said, "They are building our road? We haven't designed anything!" They had taken this tiny, little sketch and started building the first road. That's how fast they work in China. Roads are very easy for them to build because there are so many workers. Roads and landscaping are the easiest things in the world for the Chinese to do.

The other funny story is, when we were working in Nanjing, we had a beautiful Ming Dynasty wall, which was the city wall. It's the last city wall, almost, in China because Beijing tore theirs down. Our site was very historic, I mean, Qing Dynasty housing, which the Chinese think is not old because it's 18th century. It's not Ming. They weren't that wild about it. So here is this Ming Dynasty wall, and here are all these individual buildings all over the wall. I said, "That's an amazing wall. Why are those buildings all over the wall?" They didn't say anything. When I came back to the site, they were all gone. They were just gone. That's how China is. You have to be really careful when you are making these recommendations. But that was 12 years ago.

GH — Now it would be even more like that probably.

GM — It's different, but it's very much the same. I think they're saying the correct things. They want to do the correct urban design. They want to do the correct planning. They're not doing these large-scale blocks, which is what everything in China was, huge blocks. Sustainability is an enormous term, but to what degree they understand what it means to do sustainable development—not buildings, that's different, but a sustainable city . . . It's very different, because it means that the cost of doing certain projects is going to go up, and the GDP is going to go down, which is not good for a Chinese city.

Our new town is as sustainable as it can be for any kind of master-planning activity, but to what degree will it actually be carried out? That's the big question.

GH — Could you talk about New Urbanism?

GM — Okay. I would like to talk a little bit about New Urbanism. The positive thing about New Urbanism is that they have educated all the mayors for me. That's wonderful. I think it's great. The mayors have all read all of the New Urbanism doctrine, and they are listening, and so that, to me, is wonderful. I think some of the plans in New Urbanism can work. But the architecture of New Urbanism is extremely problematic, and I think everyone would agree on that. The principles of New Urbanism make all the sense in the world. The plans don't always work. The density is so high in a New Urbanist plan, it's unbelievable. It's a developer's dream. The destiny is just out of sight, and I think that is what has moved so much of this New Urbanist position forward.

In China, in Shanghai, we did a kind of New Urbanist plan, but the buildings were as Shanghainese as possible. They scream success and financial value. I mean, they scream financial value, which is not what the New Urbanist schemes scream, but that's what Shanghai's all about.

GH — But what about the architecture? How do you characterize the architecture of New Urbanism?

GM — I think the character of New Urbanist architecture is like, it's going back to the original, like the French Quarter. That's the model. Right here in New Orleans, that's what the model is. That's fine for historic preservation. I live in the French Quarter. It's great, but I don't think you reconstitute a whole context of historic base in some othr city where there was no historic base, just because it worked here. Based on what? And this New England new town model, for me, that is the end. When they start all that, I'm totally gone on that one. I went to school in New England, and those cities are nice, but they're cold as can be, physically and visually. I think they're horrible. I don't want to be anywhere near them. But that's being very, very southern. If that's the base, they can have it all up there.

GH — Let's talk about the Lower Ninth.

GM — One of the things which is like taboo to a certain degree with many people is the Lower Ninth Ward. One would never say anything bad about the Lower Ninth Ward. The Lower Ninth Ward is the last ward before you hit St. Bernard, and most of the people that live in St. Bernard grew up in the Lower Ninth Ward. It was a tragic horror that happened there, and the photographs will show you. The problem with the rebuilding of the Lower Ninth Ward is there was no plan. It's like a bunch of architects from the West Coast doing all these buildings—no plan, no landscape plan—so I bring people there, and they can't believe it. I'm thrilled they are doing it because the notoriety for the city has been fantastic, and the movie star lives a block away from me . . . whatever his name is . . .

GH — Brad Pitt?

GM — Brad Pitt. My wife saw Brad Pitt this morning with five bodyguards. Isn't that wonderful? That's great. But it's not a place. It is not a place. It's something where architects had a lot of fun at a great expense. Those houses are very, very expensive. But the attempt and what Mr. Pitt and his foundation are doing is wonderful. It's a terrible neighborhood, but Central City is a terrible neighborhood. There are many terrible neighborhoods, and I think most people who go down there don't understand it at all.

It's supposed to be involved so heavily in the value of the environment, but even though they're LEED Platinum houses, they're $600,000 plus because there were maybe 15 consultants, and they changed their minds 15 times, so the bill goes up 15 times. I know because I know the construction person. It still has value because the notoriety is huge, and the publicity on it is enormous. Everyone wants to go to the Lower Ninth Ward. They get there, and they go, "Oh gosh, what is this?" It looks like you're in California somewhere, by the beach in Malibu. That's what it looks like to me. It looks like my best friend's mother's beach house, who's worth millions of dollars—the mother, not the house, because the houses are horrifying out there in my opinion. There is value, but there is no urban design value. There is no planning, and now I think they are admitting it, and they are perhaps going to do a plan, but to do something like that without a plan, without a landscape plan, without a landscape architect is against every simple rule. Just because the architects are so divinely wonderful isn't going to make a place wonderful. That's something I think a lot of people believe but very few people will go so far as to actually say it.

I have one little, funny story about it, though. Want me to say it? I don't think I'll get in trouble.

GH — Okay.

    GM — When they first started, they decided to put up these pink tents in the shapes of the buildings, so there was this wonderful patron of the arts, a very grand woman of New Orleans who's really knowledgeable and has an amazing collection of everything, houses included. I said, "I'm going to take you and show you the Lower Ninth Ward. There's an installation of pink houses. I think you'll get a kick out of it." I drive her out there, and she turns to me, and she says, "Schiaparelli pink." That's all she said, which I think summed it up.

GH — I don't even know what that means.

    GM — Schiaparelli pink is a certain pink that only the most beautiful dresses were made of, and no one would know Schiaparelli unless it was this woman, who has endless Schiaparelli dresses. The point being, it's high fashion. It's real high fashion. I'm going to get annihilated for saying that.

GH — I'm interested in how cities are shaped in the sense that it seems like it's this series of incremental decisions over time. When you say "urban design" to someone, they don't understand that everything is designed—the sidewalk width, or no sidewalk, et cetera. If someone asks you what urban design is, how do you describe it?

    GM — When someone asks me what urban design is—which they don't ask near as much as they used to, but they do ask because there isn't a great deal of urban design in the Deep South, which is one of the reasons I wanted to do this center—I say, "Look, it's simple. It's not designing buildings. It's designing districts. Can you think of a district? Do you understand the French Quarter is a historic district? All that it takes to make that district work is urban design. And think, there are other districts. Think of those other districts that you've worked in, and think of the pieces that make up a district and isolate a district. Urban design is basically isolating districts within the city if you are dealing with an existing city," which makes it very easy for the nonprofessional to understand what you're trying to do.

There's much more complicated agendas in terms of infrastructure, the systems, and the morphologies and so forth, but the simpler it's kept, the better and easier it's understood. Usually you say, "You know, architecture deals with buildings and sheltering people. They have to keep people hot, cold, and sheltered. Urban design is dealing with all of the issues that go into making a complex setting in what is defined as a district." I think that's the key, and that's the way that we design the cities in China, as multiple districts, and then you take each district and break it down into what it needs to be.

GH — Great.

    GM — That's kind of simplified.

GH — Yeah, but that's good. Another general question—what makes a good city? Obviously all cities are different, but there are some things that are universal. A lot of people say it's the people, or it's the culture.

    GM — I think what makes a wonderful city is the sort of dynamic feeling or the subliminal power or expression that the city has that a good designer picks up on immediately. I'm not wild about Beijing. Beijing is the company town. I'm not wild about Washington DC. It's the company town. I'm not wild about San Francisco, because we live in New Orleans, so San Francisco to us looks like, I don't know, what's the big deal about this place? Each person is going to have a different set of experiences that they bring. I went to San Francisco once, I was supposed to spend a week with some very powerful, grand people. I lasted two days. I said, "I'm out of here." It's freezing. I couldn't deal with any of it. I don't see what anybody sees in that place. But I think New York is fantastic. It's so powerful in everything it's done. I think Shanghai is completely out of sight. Kuala Lumpur is weird. You get to the point where you have weird cities, and you have very powerful cities.

    Boston is another city . . . I always say the only reason you go to Boston is to change planes to go to Paris. Tennessee Williams told me this; I'll never forget this. I said, "Tennessee, I'm going to school in Boston." This is when I lived in Rome, and Tennessee said, "Oh, you're going to hate it." I said, "Why?" He said, "Because everything works." I said, "Oh." And he's right. When you're in a city where everything works, it's not going to be a lot of fun. Look at New Orleans. It's a dysfunctional city, basically. The plan is somewhat dysfunctional. The politicians are somewhat dysfunctional. The people focus on things that have almost nothing to do with reality. So it's a fantastic city. Tennessee said that. You go to Boston, and you have this upper-middle-class, eastern-based, English, Anglo base, which to the Caribbean or the Frenchman is like, what are we doing here? Boston has some great things to it, but I would never want to spend much time there.

    I think what makes a great city are things that are almost out of your control, and then you enhance them. It's a big gamble because it's not a rational process, and you have to be really good at what you're doing. You have to be like Tennessee Williams. Look at what Tennessee wrote about. He wrote about everyday life, but in those days, it seemed out of sight. When you read *Suddenly, Last Summer*, you go, "Oh my God." Well, that was perfectly normal to him. Do you see what I'm saying? You have to try to understand that. In China and Asia, there are a lot of dysfunctional characters and characteristics that things can be based on, and you really can create. I don't think the Chinese understand what civil rights are. They never had it, so they are not going to understand it, nor will they want it to some degree.

GH — What about Los Angeles?

    GM — I love Los Angeles. I would live in Los Angeles in a minute. Los Angeles, to me, is wonderful. Of course, I have wonderful friends there who do amazing things. It's so American. It's so completely American, and it has nothing to do with anything. I loved it the minute I went there, but that's my sensibility. I'm sure a lot of people go there, and they go, "Oh my God, this is so horrific. You're in an automobile all the time." The thing people don't read about Los Angeles is people work really hard in Los Angeles. They go to bed really early. It's not a big party town like New York. Nobody goes to bed in New York. It's true. For most people, he biggest problem in LA when you're visiting is not getting a DUI. But I think it's America's power center like New York.

GH — Any other cities you want to comment on?

GM — I think it's interesting. We're around so many powerful Chinese leaders, and you ask them where they have been. None of them have been to Europe. They are not interested in Europe. Europe, to them, is dead. Of course, they are looking at Africa. They are looking for materials, raw materials. Now, there are beautiful quaint places. Like Kyoto is out of sight, but do you want to live in Kyoto? I don't, but I would say it's one of the most beautiful places I've ever been.

I like baroque. I like Rome. I think Rome is a great city. I don't like Florence. To me, it happened too early. It's what I always tell everybody. It's way too early. It's very important but much too early. It's very difficult to say to a student, and I don't think you'd want to say that because you'd never want to influence them away from the great Renaissance movement, but the baroque movement—I mean, look at England. They have hardly any baroque architecture. Blenheim Palace and a few other things. There's not a great deal of it. I think it all depends on what you want in a city, which makes it important to you. I like a lot of people running around doing all kinds of things. I don't want this formularized attempt at anything when I'm in a city. That's why Shanghai is so wonderful to me. Now, my partners hate it. They hate Shanghai. They love Beijing. They won't go to Shanghai for anything. They are there five minutes, and then they are out of there, because they like the company town. They like the power of Beijing. It's very, very power based. All the leadership is there. Every decision about China is made there.

GH — Do you like the Chinese people?

GM — Do I like them? I love Chinese people. I think they are wonderful. I think they are so much fun to be with. The Chinese people are like people from Southwest Louisiana. They love to eat. They eat all the time. They drink like fish. They work very hard, and they have a wonderful lifestyle, and they are on the move.

GH — How do you see them maintaining the pace of growth and, with this struggle for resources, the rate of development there?

GM — I call it the new China because it's a new China, and the way the new China has adapted and readapted so quickly and fast to such change and been rather successful, I think, points in the direction that they are going to be able to bridge that problem. The government is going through a slight change right now in that there will be a new premier, and the base is slightly different, and the appointment is different. They readapt very, very fast and much faster than the West.

I think that's a proven, understood statement. They are going to have problems with raw materials. Look at what happened in Japan. The number of nuclear plants online in China right now is huge. But I think that the leadership is strong enough to understand the limitations and will cull and cut back at the right time. They've done it before. I mean, an example of how they change is that most of the people we work with were in the Cultural Revolution and were in prison because they were intellectuals and designers and so forth, all of them, and so when I first went there, I said, "What do you think of the Cultural Revolution?" They said, "It was great." And they were in prison. You're like, whoa, but then you think, and you say, "Why?" And they say, "Well, we couldn't have what we have right now unless we had the Cultural Revolution."

It's a mindset that is so beyond me or anyone, but it's a reality for them. I don't understand that reality at all. I don't think we're programmed for it, but they are. The young people, it's a different story. This is the median age group. They adapt. They adapt and readapt and adapt. Look at SARS. Look how they adapted to that. They shut the whole country down. We were there. They didn't tell us what it was. They came on the plane in white suits, and we're like, "What's this all about?" I was like, "Gosh, this is fun. Oh my God, we're in this horrible, terrible thing." It's an attitude that you either take or you see five people coming on in white suits and have a nervous breakdown. They say they are taking everybody's temperature and yanking people off of planes, and I'm like, "Well, we're in China. I've got my shots. I don't have a fever." How they went through that is something. No one will know. They're not going to tell you. I don't think anyone knows what really happened. Beijing was totally shut down, because there was no communication physically with anyone, and it's the way they operate. They'll do that with the next problem they have.

GH — The last parting shot: If you were watching this film, what would you want to see?

GM — I would like to see someone who is really seriously versed in city design speak very carefully about the value of city design. That's very difficult, one, to find them and, two, to get them to speak. That's a very tough one.

GH — What would they say?

GM — I don't know. That's why I would like to see them. I have my own attitude, I already know that.

GH — But what do you really want to hear somebody say?

GM — What I would like to hear them say is that the design of the city is paramount, that the steward of the city is the public official, and that the designer plays a role but is not the maker of cities. That's what I would like because that's what I believe. I don't think designers really make the cities. They can design buildings. You get those great buildings like in Beijing, and you get other great buildings, but those designers are not designing the city. The cities are being put together by the politicians, and they need to understand that they are the stewards of the city. That's what needs to be understood. Some people do understand that, but not nearly enough.

What's interesting in China is that they're very interested in Western design. They don't have to have all these Western designers over there at all, and I think they are interested because China is like America at the turn of the century. There's enormous amounts of land and enormous amounts of opportunity, and we did things fairly well at the turn of the century—Chicago, Philadelphia, there are these wonderful examples. I think, subconsciously, that's what they understand. And I do think it's the power. I think America is a very powerful country, and they respect power, so they are willing to deal with the power-base designers. That's what I think, and I would like to hear that kind of statement made.
—

Michael Sorkin (MS)/ May 10, 2011 New York

Michael Sorkin is the principal of Michael Sorkin Studio, a New York City–based design firm devoted to practical and theoretical projects with a special interest in cities and green architecture. He is also the architecture critic at *The Nation* and is the author of numerous books on architecture and cities.

—

Gary Hustwit — Who shapes our cities? What are the different forces that historically have played a role?

Michael Sorkin — The genius and the difficulty of cities is that they are so composite, that they are hybrid, that the actors who shape them are innumerable and shifting. Nowadays one might say that private capital is one of the great movers in the pursuit of urban form, but also some other things are obviously important as well.

Government plays its role, greater or lesser. We're coming out of an era in which we have been educated to suspect government, so much of the constructive role that government plays is made more difficult by a reflexive opposition to any government intervention. This is unfortunate since governance in a representative democracy is the mode in which the collective operates in the city, and government needs to be empowered. We have big things to do in terms of converting cities to become more sustainable, more equitable, more beautiful, and government obviously has to play a leading role.

Clearly there are cultural forces, technological forces. We exist in the context of the technologies that are available to us. On the other hand, we need to demand technologies that produce the kinds of cities we want. We need to imagine transportation technologies that produce good cities, walkable cities, compact cities, cities in which everything is accessible. We need to demand the kind of technologies that will produce sustainable cities. This doesn't mean necessarily the most exotic, visionary technologies, but we need to insist that appropriate technologies are laid into our cities. We also need to demand new cities. The era in which cities can simply grow ad infinitum must end. These are not practical places. They are not sustainable places. They are not human places. We need the images, the possibilities, the sensibilities that will produce new cites of a radically more efficient kind. This is the project of a lifetime and certainly something I'm engaged in.

When you talk about the forces that shape the city, it's also important to observe that, in the course of history, different forces are differently empowered. We need to reverse course a little bit, and I should not say a little bit—we need to reverse course radically and empower citizens to shape their own environments. This doesn't mean that every citizen becomes an architect or a planner, but it means that citizens have to have the power to influence decisions, and citizens have to have a sufficient repertoire of images and possibilities and strategies so that they can, in a learned and active way, suggest what they want. They need the means to fulfill their own desires. This sometimes means that those desires are enlarged. We are, in this studio, great propagandists not simply for bigger roles for citizens but for the idea that there are many kinds of cities, many possibilities that people should be empowered to engage and to choose.

Cities and their form will always be the terrain of struggle as different interests contest for power, for position, and for influence in the shaping of the city, but to the degree that we can engage everybody in the city with the making of the city, then I think, by definition, we produce a better city, a good city.

GH — Let's talk about China. Can you give me an overview of Chinese urbanism at the moment?

MS — We are doing a fair amount of work in China, which is a perplexing and fascinating place to work. It's urbanizing at a massive rate as hundreds of thousands of people are coming in from the countryside and living in cities. On the good side, they are talking the talk about new and sustainable cities, and in fact, we are working on projects for the design of new cities. On the down side, there's still a little too much influence of modernist paradigms. Unfortunately, they are a little bit overly in thrall of the automobile as a transportation modality. But they are also building hundreds of miles of rail and laying in subways. They are thinking seriously about sustainable infrastructure.

China is obviously in an interesting position. This moment at which they have an authoritarian government and cheap labor supply means they can do really big things. On the other hand, one would not argue for the benisons of authoritarian governance in terms of the cultivation of democracy and citizen power in shaping cities. There's a little too much kitsch. There's a little too much reproduction of models that we have been through and rejected. One finds oneself in the curious problem of acting a little colonial in terms of advising them not to make the mistakes we've made. I guess every country is entitled to make its mistakes, but they are in a position to leap over a whole series of failed strategies in terms of urban form and urban infrastructure and really conjure new kinds of cities. We hope we can make a contribution to this and in the bargain begin to help them grow a culture of participation in city making.

GH — It seems like China is looking to the West for models but also for talent. It's mostly a lot of Western firms going over there and doing these things. Do you feel like there is some sort of a unified vision, or is it a lot of, "Let's get this group to do this city; let's get these guys to do this one"? Is it a hodgepodge feeling, or do you think there is some sort of overall vision?

MS — Things are proceeding at a truly phenomenal clip in China. What they risk is not a hodgepodge or too great a variety of solutions but too uniform a group of solutions. Because of the pace of the development, because of the moment in which we sit, because of the nature of the distribution of talent and experience, the cities in China are far too uniform at this point. What needs to happen over there is the cultivation of local talent and a real research into the armature that will allow them to create meaningful difference from city to city. There are regional cultural differences. There are obviously enormous differences in geography and climate and biology. There are also burgeoning differences in sensibility.

China has trained a remarkable cadre of architects and designers, and they won't need us very soon. We'll be dispensable. On the other hand, architectural culture is very globalized. Certainly, the idea that people from outside can be the source for the cultivation and creation of meaningful artistic differences as well as other kinds of structural differences in the planning of a city, that's odd, but at this point, it's we who need them. Speaking from my own perspective, there's no place else on earth where you are approached by a client who says, "Will you design a city of half a million people? We intend to build this in the next 10 years." For me as an urbanist, this is incredibly exciting. I believe that the destiny of the planet is very much tied to the creation of new cities, and this is a country that, for better or worse, is trying to put this imperative into practice.

GH — It seems like there's also been a lot of large-scale demolition of older forms there.

MS — That's right. One of the real disasters in China is the wholesale demolition of the historic urban texture. China has an incredible amount to teach us urbanists by way of good city form not only in specific architectural morphology but in the traditional urban textures of China, which are very tractable, very elegant, very meaningful in terms of good urbanism. Unfortunately, this notion of modernism or modernity being implicated in the complete destruction of the past is something very sad, very tragic that's going on over there. Fortunately, some people are rising up, and this is a way in which Chinese citizens are actually organizing a kind of legitimate field of approach to the government, in terms of retaining aspects of the historical fabric. It may be too little too late in lots of instances, and of course, a city of 10 or 20 million people with a small urban core by definition is overwhelming that core unless it learns its lessons for application in the larger city.

GH — Are there things that other cites can learn from the rapid urbanization of Chinese cities?

MS — I think we all have to learn the fact that it is possible to rapidly urbanize in a relatively controlled way. We neglect the larger form of the cities too much by deferring to the wisdom of the marketplace. China is a little more organized. They have a somewhat more problematized relationship to the market, although it's becoming a little too dominant. As I say, they have a very problematic relationship to a limited set of models for urbanization. On the other hand, here we are in New York City in which we fall all over ourselves to extend a subway line one stop, and in city after city in China, they are laying in entirely new subway systems, dramatic improvements in public transportation infrastructure. This is balanced with the fact that, when I first started going to China, it was very much a culture predicated on circulation by bicycle. In city after city in China, the bicycle has been wiped out and replaced by the car, so it's a question of one step forward, one step backward. They need to be a little more visionary, a little more succinct and sensitive in the nature of their vision, and to seek a more appropriate balance between the new and the traditional.

GH — It's interesting, the concept of negotiation. There you've taken away all the road blocks of negotiation. Here, to make that one subway stop, how much had to be negotiated? Maybe you could talk about just the idea of negotiation in cities.

MS — Obviously urban construction is always a negotiation between interests. We have gone a little too far in our country, in this city, in empowering big interests at the expense of small and more individual interests. We've also created a system in which neighborhoods and citizens gain their power by negation, not by proposition, so we need to redress that balance. One of the reasons things are so hard fought in New York is that's the only strategy open to people for participating in the process. The city and developers propose, and we oppose. This is a formula for stasis in many instances, although it does often produce a better result. Still, we need to differently empower citizens in localities to participate in the process by giving them the means to make plans, to articulate concrete suggestions rather than simply enter the game at the end of the day in an oppositional role.

GH — I wonder if we can touch on sustainability again. What makes a sustainable city?

MS — A sustainable city is obviously one that, in its form and workings, is respectful of the planet, that does not consume resources beyond what is an equitable distribution. Our project here is to try to push the limits of the fantasy of what is truly sustainable, and we are looking very much at the idea of the self-sufficient city. This interests me for political reasons as a tool for empowering cities to face up national governments as well as a whole series of multinational formations. Also, if we are going to take a strict inventory, if we really do the accountancy of what cities consume and what demands they place on the planet, then this is the way to measure it. This is the way to genuinely take responsibility for a city's performance and behavior in a planetary context. We need to be responsible for producing what we consume, and relegating this to a system of trading of carbon credits or relying on the low-wage labor of somebody in the developing world ultimately is not good enough.

If we believe in equity and equality and if we conceive of this as plan-etary, we in the West are dramatic overconsumers. We have enjoyed far more than our share for centuries. This is no longer possible, both in a political sense and also in the sense of modeling sustainability at the planetary scale. The calculation that one always hears is that, if the whole planet at its current population were to consume at the rate at which the United States and Western Europe do, the surface area of two additional planets would be required in order to feed and house and provide water and air for everybody. This does not seem to be a good solution in the short term. We need to radically adjust our patterns of consumption and the efficiency with which we consume resources and to think equitably about the fate of the earth. We're all in this together. I believe that cities, which are the most efficient way of deploying resources and the most energy-efficient pattern of civilization we've come up with yet, are absolutely key to the solution of this problem.

GH — When you talk about this with people who live in the suburbs, a lot of times they may argue, "This is America. I can live wherever I damn want to, and this is how and where I want to live."

MS — Sure. We don't want to interfere with people's freedom funda-mentally, but we need to be responsible for the costs. Suburbs are disproportionately expensive to the planet. We know that the ecologi-cal footprint of the typical suburbanite is three times that of the typical urbanite, and historically in America, we have dramatically subsidized the suburbs in a variety of ways: cheap FHA financing, accelerated depreciation on commercial projects, vast subsidies for highway infra-structure. Infrastructure in general is far more costly in the suburbs because of the lower densities. To provide a sewer line in the suburbs, you have to run many more miles of pipe per capita than you would in the city. If people want to live in the suburbs, then I think it is important, particularly in this age of fiscal wisdom and austerity, that the true costs of that differential lifestyle be paid. Suburban living is not going to be the refuge for cheap housing. Suburban living must represent the true costs of enabling it. I think that if we believe in the wisdom of market, once the true costs of this difference in lifestyle become part of the equation, then I think the culture will shift.

GH — Good point. That's what I was gonna say. How do you push people toward it? It seems like it's always, "They want us to all move into the cities and give up our land." It's almost become a political rallying cry.

MS — Fine. Let people live in the suburbs, but I don't wish to subsidize them, and I don't think that the planet should subsidize them either.

GH — This is kind of a wild card question: if you go to the theater to see this movie, what's something else that you just wish that somebody up there would say that you just don't hear talked about enough, or some-thing that most average citizens don't know about the design of their cities and should know?

MS — I think that in the context of where the planet is going now, the point that really needs to be reinforced is that cities are an intrinsically sustainable form of civilization and habitation. If we are going to solve the planetary environmental crisis—and I think people around the world are more and more attuned to the fact that it genuinely is a crisis—then the production of cities and the reinforcement of the best qualities of existing cities is something that has to be number one on the planetary agenda. If there was one point I would reinforce, it is exactly that cities are not simply the answer to pleasant lifestyles and democratic politics, but in terms of saving the planet from hyper-consumption, overpopulation, and the ravages of bad decisions about technology, good cities, properly conceived, well designed, are the answer.

—

Amanda Burden (AB)/ May 12, 2011 New York

Amanda Burden is a Principal at Bloomberg Associates, a consulting service founded by former New York City mayor Michael Bloomberg as a philanthropic venture to help city governments improve the quality of life of their citizens. She was the director of the New York City Department of City Planning and Chair of the City Planning Commission under Mayor Bloomberg from 2002 to 2013, and has a long history of involvement with urban design.

—

Gary Hustwit — I guess let's start with the easy stuff. What exactly does a planning commission do?

> **Amanda Burden** — Just to begin, the commission is a body of 13 people that don't make policy. They just vote on things. The real question is, what does the planning agency do? What does the Department of City Planning do?

GH — Okay.

> **AB** — The planning department for the city of New York is responsible for shaping its neighborhoods, its waterfront, its industrial lands, and its business districts and really shaping the form of the city and where it's going to grow, where it's going to develop, how it looks. What is important to me, right now, is how it feels.

GH — Can you maybe talk about some of the different forces and people and players involved that you mediate, I guess, in planning?

> **AB** — Let me talk a little bit about what the department's responsible for. The Department of City Planning has the function not only of shaping the city but determining its demographics and its population. In 2002, when Mayor Bloomberg was elected, the department completed a very important study on the city's population and projected population. Our demographic division, the Population Division, projected that New York City would grow by one million people by 2030, and that has shaped our policy ever since that time because we know that we're a city that has to grow. We welcome that growth. We're a dynamic city, a city that attracts immigrants, and growing is fantastic for a city. There are many cities that are not growing. We want to capitalize on that. Our challenge has been not only how to grow but where to grow in a city that's actually built out to its edges.
>
> The zoning in the city had not been looked at since 1961. That's almost 50 years. In 2002, we strate-

gically said, "How are we going to grow, and where are we going to grow?" The mayor said, very specifically, "We're a city of five boroughs, and I want economic opportunity in all five boroughs of the city." We're in Manhattan, Queens, Brooklyn, Staten Island, and the Bronx. Some of the boroughs really hadn't seen any focus at all. We looked at one of our greatest assets, which is our incredible mass transit system, and we said, "We can grow. We can grow strategically in the areas of the city that have good mass transit hubs." These areas hadn't seen any economic growth or investment for a really long time but had great opportunity. Again, spreading jobs, opportunity, housing: this is our strategy for accommodating growth around mass transit hubs. It wasn't called transit-oriented development. It was really Mike Bloomberg's strategy to grow the city.

We looked at areas like Jamaica, Queens, where the airport is. We looked at the hub in the Bronx connected to 125th Street. We looked at Downtown Brooklyn, which is just one subway stop away from Lower Manhattan, and we looked at Long Island City, which is one subway stop away from Midtown Manhattan. All of these places had great transit infrastructure and had been neglected for years. We said, "This is our way to create mixed-use business districts in all the boroughs and accommodate our growing population."

The strategy was an important strategy, but zoning could not do that all alone. In fact, zoning is a very crude tool. When I came on board for this job, I knew, because I'd sat on the Planning Commission, that zoning doesn't produce anything that you would want to look at, or live in, or really have much to do with it. My very first meeting, when we looked at Downtown Brooklyn, for instance, where we could accommodate a lot of growth, I knew that this wasn't going to work with just zoning. I said, "Draw what you think it should look like." That was the beginning of integrating urban design with zoning.

Not since the Lindsay administration in the sixties has urban design been thought of as a key part of city government and planning. Basically, that was the reinstitution of the Urban Design Group. I'll tell you why it's so important. The way we used to try to grow the city or change development plans is that we'd present the community with a drawing, a plan drawing, which said, "All right. You are going to get C64." Of course, they would say no. It's too frightening. They couldn't understand it. In fact, city planners couldn't understand it. Why is this important? Because if our plans aren't adopted by the communities and the city council, the elected officials that represent them, nothing happens to it. It doesn't get adopted. Nothing happens. And that's basically why the zoning hadn't changed in 50 years. We hadn't grown; we hadn't changed. Our boroughs were stagnant.

Design was a very important tool not only for explaining to ourselves what we're going to do but so we could have a composition of buildings, so that the plans would actually show a transitioning down to lower-density neighborhoods. We could present three-dimensional urban design master plans to community members, and to elected officials and to even other agencies who participated in this very complicated rezoning. We could then fine-tune, but we could also develop systems where communities could actively engage in the planning process, comment both in an informed way, an intelligent way, and a really effective way on these plans, which they knew. They know their communities better than we do. They got very, very engaged in this process and said, "Really? You know, Schermerhorn Street can't handle that much, but it could handle this much. I think, go a little bit more up on Livingston, but then it's got to drop down." Then we could refine and fine-tune our plans. The community felt that they're very much a part of the planning process.

These plans got adopted into law so that a development can proceed, and we have really changed how the planning process operates. These plans are now adopted. One hundred and ten large-scale rezonings have been adopted in exactly this manner. Design plays a very important role not only in shaping the city but getting these plans adopted and engaging a broad scale of the public in the process.

GH — I wonder if you could even break down the different stakeholders involved in any community redevelopment project a bit further?

AB — In order to make any of our projects possible, and they're broad scaled and ambitious, we have to win over the real estate community, property owners, community residents, businesses, elected officials, the other agencies in the city, including transportation, housing, economic development, environmental protection. Often, we have to go to the state and win over their regulators on the city waterfront, et cetera. This is a long, complicated process, and each one of these large rezoning plans takes from two to five years. You have to be very focused, have a clear vision and a clear strategy with a laser focus and huge amount of attention on getting it done.

Constantly, elected officials have to be very aware of what they're confronting in their communities. They really have to get into their heads and understand their challenges and then understand how they have to respond to their communities so that they can defend a change because, understand, the city has to grow, but change is very difficult. People are afraid of it because they haven't had a good experience with change. Change has usually brought something that's not only unfamiliar but out of context as well.

One of the key lessons or key tasks that I set for my planners is they must walk the streets over and over and over again before they even begin to draw any of those plans. The community has to feel that you understand the DNA of that neighborhood and what will really accommodate the needs for growth and affordable housing but that reflects what is strongest about that neighborhood. What's right in Astoria is completely wrong in Bayside. Every neighborhood has its own distinct character. There are almost two hundred neighborhoods in the city, and if we don't walk and walk and walk and draw—urban designers draw—

so that we understand what makes that particular neighborhood unique, what its DNA is, we are not getting anything passed. It also means that we haven't done our homework, so that's the first thing. It's to walk and walk and walk, then draw and understand, how much could this handle, and very importantly, does this neighborhood have a good mass transit system? Can it grow? That's the first thing.

Then, how much should it grow? Where should it grow? This is really on a street-by-street, block-by-block basis. We go lot by lot, one block at a time because you might walk in Jamaica, Queens, on a very broad boulevard, Hillside Avenue. That has a subway. This is a great place to grow; the subway runs right along it. You say, "Okay, we can have 12-story buildings here." Then you move one block to your right, and you'll see there's single-family homes. I remember, we had a large rezoning plan for Jamaica, and I walked Hillside Avenue. This looked great. This looked great. I was walking it one winter evening, with the borough president of Queens, and I just hadn't walked down a side street. On that side street, there were single-family homes. So we really had to develop a special kind of zoning. We wrote it out to have 12 stories on the avenue, but then there will be a transition piece that will transition down to the single-family homes, and that makes all the difference. So when you go to communities and say, "Here's our plans," if you know that that avenue is right next to a single-family home district, they know that you really understand their community, and then finally you can establish a sense of trust. If you do one rezoning like that, others will build on that. You still have to do the same methodology of it being fine-grained, to have really bold plans with a fine-grained urban design framework.

GH — Great. So what is urban design? What's the most basic description you can give of it?

  AB — Nobody agrees about what urban design is. I'll tell you what I think urban design is. Urban design is a juxtaposition of architecture and landscape architecture. It's integration of these two disciplines, which really encompasses city form. It's city making, but it brings a composition of buildings down to the street and the fine-grained texture of urban form at that level. So urban design is really the language of the city. When you walk down a street, everything you see has been designed: where that street wall meets the street, how wide the sidewalk is, where the tree pit is set, where a manhole is placed, how the manhole is designed, where the curb is set, how high it is, the width of the street, the height of the buildings, where they're set back. Each one of these things has been thought about and designed. Urban design is the key to city making.

GH — Do you think average citizens realize that everything is designed?

  AB — They might. I don't think it's common understanding how many components an actual making of a streetscape entails: the width of the sidewalk, the spacing of street trees, the number of storefronts, where the street line hits the sidewalk, how far it goes up before it's set back. Do the buildings actually line up? All of these things go into what makes a street feel comfortable and active.

Jan Gehl is the one who taught me the best lesson of all, which is you have to design a city by designing a street, but really at people scale. People scale not only means our height and how much we see, our cone of vision, but most importantly, and I'd never thought of this, how fast we move. If we walk at so many miles an hour or feet an hour or feet a minute, you have to have interest at exactly that pace. We know you can't have blank walls, but it means you have more than one store per block. We have just so many tools. We can't actually design architecture, we can't design the storefront, but at least we can set up these basic parameters that give you the best possibility that this will be a great street. That's what we try to do.

GH — How do you see the citizens' role in the process? I'm interested in educating citizens so at least they're part of the discourse.

AB — That's my personal passion. I have several personal passions. One is the streetscape and how it feels and public open space and how that engages a city. The second is—one of the most important things to me—engaging people who are going to feel this change, who are going to live in this neighborhood, who are going to really feel that this makes their lives better. We have changed the way the planning process functions, and I feel so passionately about this. I personally love to understand what makes a difference to people living in each neighborhood.

Zoning is a really complicated instrument, so one of the things I'm most proud of is we created the Zoning Handbook. I'll show it to you. It demystifies zoning; it has cartoons photographs, and it has all the elements. You can actually look in your neighborhood at what your zoning designation is. You can say, "I really don't want R2A. I want R3X. That looks like what I want, and that's a neighborhood that's in my hopes and dreams because that will actually give me a little more room. It could be a wider front yard, more of a backyard, more light and air between me and my neighbor." Or, "I really want a small apartment building, and oh, I see that. That's R5B." And, "I want to come to City Planning and get them to help me get R5B for my neighborhood."

Engaging the public can be very stormy. Any change, well, everybody says no. It's my responsibility, as Director of Planning for the city, to make sure we address the long-term goals of the city. At the same time, we have to keep the key defining elements of a particular neighborhood. I just have to balance the citywide goals with the neighborhood's concerns. Often, people don't want any change, but then, if you talk to them more, yes, they do want more affordability. They want the ability to invest. They want more stores that look like the stores that are familiar to them. They want more walkable streets. They want sidewalk cafés. They want these things, so by engaging with the planning agency, they can actually get these things. While we achieve citywide goals, we also address their local concerns.

Engaging the public is something that I really like to do, and then the accomplishment of all of us when we finally get that zoning adopted, then when we see these changes get built, it's really a magnificent change. When you look at Coney Island, when you look at

Bedford-Stuyvesant, when you look at Forest Hills, each one of these neighborhoods had a totally different objective. Now people see the results and it's really satisfying.

GH — Maybe we could talk a little bit about your process. Obviously, the department has a huge role. I imagine sometimes your job is kind of reigning in some of the commercial development, and other times it's probably encouraging it. Can you just talk about how that happens?

AB — First of all, it's a mindset. What is New York? It's a global city. It's a competitive city, and we have to compete on the global stage. That means that we have to be open to change, that we have to be an aspirational city where you can come and invest and bring entrepreneurs, and that the city is tolerant, it's changing, and it's attractive to investment. That's a mindset. The skyline should be changing. We should be open to something new like changing our relationship with the waterfront, which is very important now. Getting private development interested in the city has to be a positive thing. We want investment. We want the city to change. Yes, it's good for the economy, and it's good for taxes. It's good for jobs, and it's good for housing. We have to be a dynamic city. That's really important, so that's the mindset.

Then the challenge is, how do you get really good development? That's not so easy. We have to raise the bar, and we can't require great architecture, but I certainly can talk about it, that urban design and innovative architecture is a way for us to compete on the global scale. Innovative architecture can be contagious also.

You can look at one of my favorite projects, which is the High Line. The High Line is a great example, I've said, of using an old piece of urban infrastructure to create one of the most unusual parks in the world. This is a magnet not only for tourists but for private development. Architects, when they see something as magical as the High Line, are so interested in having their buildings be associated with such an incredible structure that it's attracted architects from around the world who are clamoring to build there. Not only have we instigated private development, but architects, through clients or maybe on their own accord, have tried to do their best work right around the High Line. This has been sort of a convergence of everything we like to see: private investment triggered by a public investment and then great architecture, which is a part of a growing innovative city. If we can create the environment for change like that, entrepreneurs will come to the city and say, "I want to be here because it has a great quality of life. It's changing, and it's open, and it's aspirational."

The High Line is one of my favorite projects, if not my favorite project. I went up on the line before I had this job. It was slated for demolition, and when I went out on it, I physically fell in love with this space. I had never seen anything like it. It becomes, through opportunistic planting, a garden in the sky. You could walk on it for a mile and a half and never come in contact with a car. If you love New York, it made you fall in love with New York all over again because you saw it from a special vantage point, an area just above the city, just enough to feel removed, but you could see people down below. I said, "This cannot come down." They said, "Well, everybody feels it's a blighting influence," and I said, "No, no, no, this can become the defining feature of a whole new neighborhood."

The zoning there was for auto repair. It had the gallery district, which is great, but the zoning was just for industrial use. But I didn't have any power. I actually sat as a member of the Planning Commission but had, really, no power. When Mike Bloomberg appointed me to be his commissioner, at the same time, another colleague of mine who is a city councilman, who was also a passionate advocate for keeping the High Line up and having this be one of the great parks ever, was appointed to be city council speaker. I said, "Yes, yes, we can now do this," and it was a priority for both of us. We were passionate about saving the High Line and helping Friends of the High Line, who had this vision to make this into one of the most defining features of New York City, which the mayor embraced, but only through incredible advocacy, ingenuity, and focus could we actually pull this off. Zoning was just one piece of it. I only played a role in the zoning and being obsessive. I knew if I didn't think about the High Line every single day, it was going to come down. That was my mindset.

Let me tell you why we needed to do something about the zoning. The High Line was on this elevated rail line and ran a mile and a half through three different neighborhoods. It was owned by the federal government. The federal government would not transfer it to the city. It would do so for one dollar, but only if all the property owners around it signed on. As you know, it was slated for demolition, and property owners hated the structure. But only when you go out and talk to people can you find out what the problem is. The problem was that there were 38 property owners who own land under and adjacent to the High Line who said, "We have no value for our property. We can't develop it." I said, "Oh, we can use an old zoning tool called transfer of development rights by creating a special district." So we created a special district just all around where the High Line is. We mapped out all the buildings and the heights that they could be developed to. As you know, it runs between 10th and 11th Avenue, so we reduced height on both of these avenues, unless you bought development rights from those property owners.

So the property owners were thrilled. Immediately, they had value. They got bids on their properties almost right away from the owners of property on the avenues, and they all signed on. The federal government transferred the High Line, and the rest was history.

GH — I wonder if we can talk a little bit about the idea of density and the pros and cons of density, and this is not just about New York but about any city. Are there benefits of denser cities versus sprawling suburbs?

AB — Well, anybody who understands sustainability has to believe in density, but anybody who loves cities has to also believe in density because a city is about density, diversity, openness, tolerance. That comes with the confluence of people living very close together where you have this spontaneous combustion of ideas and rubbing shoulders with people you wouldn't normally rub shoulders with and engaging in ideas, and with everything that happens with entrepreneurs, whether it's in the arts, or it's business, or it's in science. It's what happens in an agglomeration economy. But how you execute density means everything, I think, to a successful city.

The skyline is important, but how you design a skyline in different parts of the city is also important. The Manhattan skyline is completely different from the Brooklyn or Queens skyline. But more important than anything is how it engages the street. I don't think a lot of cities really care about that, and it's maybe because New York is a walking city, and we have to, by the way, be a walking city if we're going to be a sustainable city. We've been focusing not only on street life but, now, on cheap mobility and encouraging people to use their cars less and get out of their cars, making our subways better, providing alternatives for biking, for walking. We now have almost three hundred miles of bike lanes. We're going to start a bike share program. We have car share. A walkable city is essential to our sustainability. If we're going to have the kind of density that comes with 9.1 million people, we have to have alternatives to cars. We cannot have cars because of congestion. We cannot have them for cleaner air. We cannot have them for cleaner water. We cannot have them for a healthier lifestyle for New Yorkers, so making the city a walkable city is absolutely essential. The challenge is, how do we densify in place and have livability? And we do that through these things: by having alternatives to the automobile; walkable cities, which are walkable, bikeable; mixed-use cities, which focus on things like sidewalk cafés, street trees, public open spaces.

That's my personal passion, these small public open spaces that I was taught by Holly Whyte to study, these small parks like Paley Park, Columbus Circle, Bryant Park, which is larger, but these are public spaces that are designed. I recrafted all the requirements for these public spaces to make sure that they're inviting and well used. In these spaces, design detail makes all the difference. Holly Whyte's principles: movable chairs, and the spaces can't be elevated any more than such beyond the curbline. Having both sun and shade. That you should see seating before you enter a park so you know that it's inviting. There should be multiple kinds of seating. Many different reasons for people to come into a space. We used all these principles at Battery Park City Esplanade. If you're going to densify a city, these public spaces, even though they can be small, can make a huge difference to a city.

GH — Maybe we can talk a little bit about William Holly Whyte. I often think that this film has something in common with *The Social Life of Small Urban Spaces*, the book and film he made in 1980.
    AB — Of course. I was there when he made it. I worked for him.

GH — We do a lot of that same type of filming, kind of looking at behavior in public spaces. But I'd love if you'd just introduce Holly Whyte.
    AB — Well, I met Holly Whyte almost by chance in 1976 the day I'd received my degree in environmental science and ethology, which is animal behavior, and I actually didn't know what I was going to be doing at that time. I ran into a friend of mine that day on the street, and he

said, "What are you doing?" and I said, "I don't know what I'm going to do." He said, "What can you do?" and I said, "Well, I can take quantitative analysis of behavior," thinking that would be meaningless to him, and he said, "Come with me now." I walked with him to his office and met somebody who changed my life, and I get even emotional about it, because I met Holly Whyte.

He was an urbanologist who studied streets and urban public spaces. He said to me that day—as he talked to me out in the streets, he walked with me and he showed me—he said, "You can measure the health of a city by the vibrancy of its streets and public open spaces. Just look." And he showed me how people were using the street and standing in the middle of the street and who was using the ledges on Seagram's Plaza and how they kind of moved with the sun. Some people sat up higher, and some people sat lower, and they were watching the women on the street, and they were having a great time, and he said, "This is the city. This is what makes a city really great." I decided then that I actually could commit my life to public service by making great public open spaces in the city that I loved. It changed everything.

GH — Can you talk about his philosophies in terms of the shaping of those public spaces? You touched on it a little before, but lay it out.

AB — Everything for Holly about public spaces and why they worked had to do with them being accessible. They had to be inviting. You had to want to use them. The greatest tool was movable chairs. He loved to film this, how people, when they sit in a chair that's movable, they just move it just so much, so it's kind of their chair, and it's their place. But movable chairs also let you socialize. They let you be by yourself. They let you be part of the city or away from the city. His feeling about public space in the city was that, if you live this kind of a dense life in your smaller apartment, you need this space for contemplation, for recreation, for socialization, to be part of this city that is so vibrant. You can participate in it if you use the streets and if the streets are welcoming and vibrant, so he had these rules: No blank walls. Activity along the street fronts. Don't have sunken plazas. Don't have raised plazas. He would film Grace Plaza, which has about six steps, and he said you could have five, but six is just too much.

You have to be invited into a space. You know, Bryant Park used to be the biggest drug den in the world. You had so much drug activity there, and it was because you couldn't see into it, and when you were in it, you couldn't see out of it. Perfect for drug dealing, terrible for public space. So Holly's solution—he's the one who advised the redesign of Bryant Park—was to lower the outer edges so that you could see into and out of the park. Have the steps invite you in. Of course it changed, and it became one of the great public places in the whole city.

It's so important to have these spaces in the city because we are very diverse and demographically mixed. We have every race, age, culture, economic strata, and these public spaces are very important for the city to mix naturally. I'm a huge, passionate advocate for that, and I actually created an award as a legacy for Holly, an award for great urban public spaces, and it's a national award. It's for spaces that actually transform a city and transform how people feel about a city, transform how people use the space and also are a catalyst for private investment. Last year, Campus Martius in Detroit won the award, and I have just been traveling to look at the second recipient of the award. I have seen, throughout the country, how these central public spaces can be a transformative development in a city that feels it hasn't gotten anything done, and now it has got something done. That it brings together a diverse group of people, that it gives a sense of hope and aspiration, and that—not unimportantly—that private investment feels a sense of confidence, as they did in Detroit of all places, that the city has a future. Public space is a real key to transformation and can transform, not only neighborhoods, but can transform a whole city. I really believe that.

GH — Can we talk a little bit about Detroit as well?
AB — Sure. Have you been?

GH — Yeah, and we're going to do some filming there in a couple weeks.
AB — Detroit is one of the great American cities, and I think anybody who loves cities has to love Detroit. You know, it stands for America, the car. It has iconic architecture. New Yorkers, I think, are very emotional about Detroit. We want Detroit to succeed. We're very lucky in New York because we have a very diversified economy, and we try to keep it diversified on purpose, but we're a magnet for immigrants, and immigrants create a diversified economy. Detroit was based on a single economy, and it did very well for many years on that economy, but the world is flat, and competition came very quickly, and for whatever reason, they weren't able to be agile enough to keep people in that city for many, many reasons.

Now they have a challenge to, as Mayor Bing calls it, rightsize the city, and how they do that is just an enormous challenge. All of us, we empathize with that challenge, because I don't know how they're going to do it. They have strengths: they have a river, and they have a lot of architectural bones, they have a city center, and as I said, they built this new park, Campus Martius, which has become a center of activity. But it's a vast, spread-out city. It's not a dense city except around the center, and for all the workers in the automobile industry, they built an immense amount of homes very, very quickly. They have an affordable housing stock, so I think a lot of people will stay there, but how they're going to reconcile a very, very much less dense population with what their city services were meant to serve is a struggle.

GH — When we were in Mumbai—I think we were there just a week after you were down there—Rahul Mehrotra said, "We've got plenty of people here in Mumbai. We could just send five million Indians to Detroit, and it would totally change things."
AB — Mumbai is one of the most exciting cities I have ever been in because on any stretch of sidewalk, like 15 feet by 15 feet, there are 15 people who are doing something completely different. Everybody has a plan, and they're totally optimistic, and they're going to make it. Maybe somebody's having a little ceremonial service, and another person is

selling something interesting, and another person's going through his spreadsheet, and everything is going on in every inch of Mumbai, but it's a very optimistic city. I think it is an aspirational city, even though it has its own challenges.

GH — I wonder if you can talk this concept of invitation, like if you want more bike use, then you invite it by creating more bike lanes; if you want less cars, well, then you take lanes away. It seems counterintuitive to say, "Oh, you want less traffic? We'll take away lanes." People say, "Wait, that doesn't make sense. We need more car lanes, and that would decrease traffic." But it's actually the other way around, which is, I think, really interesting.

AB — You have to have a clear vision, and you have to be very courageous. In New York, you have to maintain mobility, but you have to have alternatives to the car. Bike lanes are a tremendous option for New York City, and you have to establish a complete network before it works. Before the network is completely built out, it's challenging. We have had two challenges: one, to lay out the full network, and then, inducing appropriate behavior of bicyclists. Bicyclists in the past, with an un-built-out network, had used bicycles for getting their heart rate up, and they like to bike really fast for delivering pizzas really fast, and we haven't had a social life of controlled bicyclists as they do in Copenhagen. There, there are so many people on bicycles, they have their own traffic lights for the bicycles, everybody behaves, and the cars and bicyclists are very compatible. We're in that transition period, and the Department of Transportation has just started a program called Don't Be a Jerk, which started, actually, yesterday, to induce better biking behavior from bicyclists. Because many people understand how important the bike lanes are to the city as the network is built out, but they are extremely angry at bicyclists who think they own the road and aren't sharing with cars or with pedestrians. People are very annoyed, so I think that better biking behavior is going to make a big difference.

One is building the network out. Two is better biking behavior and having bikes available to all New Yorkers. Now, we've found at City Planning, and we have a biking division here as well, that one of the biggest impediments to biking was that bikes were stolen, and why were they stolen? Because there was no safe place to put your bike, whether at home or at work. We have passed legislation to require secure bicycle parking in new buildings, because sometimes it's hard to retrofit all buildings. Over time, you will see every single building having a substantial amount of secure indoor bike parking, and that will make a big difference in incentivizing people to bike.

GH — In the past year and a half, I've bicycled more since the new lanes have been here, and I think the pedestrians are the ones who need better behavior, because I do as I'm supposed to as a bicyclist, but so many pedestrians are just absentmindedly walking out into the lane. Nobody looks. I mean, I've hit several people.

AB — Well, my first day in Copenhagen, of course I stepped right out into the sidewalk, and Jan grabbed me. He said, "You have to look." It's a culture change, and as this is built out and people get used to more bicyclists, pedestrians will not step off the curb into the bike lane. But this is actually a change, a huge change in culture, but it makes our city a world-class city, and many of the things we're doing have to do with, how do we compete on a global stage? How do we become a world-class city? How do we become the most sustainable city? How do we become the greenest city? And bicycling has to do with that. Design has to do with that. Architecture has to do with that. Making a green infrastructure for the city has to do with that. Clean air, clean water, attracting entrepreneurs through innovation, has to do with that. All of this ties together in becoming not only a global city but the greatest global city, and we have a lot of competition.

GH — Are there other things that you want to talk about, the takeaways, I guess, for people in the way they think about the design of the city?

AB — I think now more than ever, people are attracted to cities as magnets because cities are the places where your hopes and dreams can be fulfilled. Cities are multidimensional. New York City is part dense, skyscraper city, but it's also a city that is changing, and it's a city that is being transformed by reengaging with its waterfront. Historically in New York City, people arrived in the city at the water, and then they moved inland. We have the longest waterfront of any city in the entire world actually, the longest and most diverse. Over the past nine years, we've built parks all along the waterfronts of the five boroughs of the city. We built these parks, and people are now at the water's edge, and they are anxious to get on the water and into the water. This is a way to show that the city can change and transform itself into something else.

We actually look at our water as our sixth borough. We feel that it just changes the perception and the identity of the city. Why is this important? It's because every city should show that it's in motion, that it's in change, that, in fact, if you come to the city, you can find anything you want. You can find a single-family house. You can be in the tallest skyscraper in the world. You can start your own business. You can walk along the street and sit down at the sidewalk café and watch people go by that you never imagined you would see. You can turn a corner and see a building that has the most incredibly crazy design, and that's part of being in the city. Or you can be in a little park all by yourself or with your Kindle and just have that quiet time. A city is all those things, and it's also where you can earn a living and reach that dream that you never had.

GH — Excellent. Do you want to talk about how everything you see in the city has been designed?

AB — Okay. So urban design is really the language of the city. When you walk down a street, everything you see has been designed: where that street wall meets the street, how wide the sidewalk is, where the tree pit is set, where a manhole is placed, how the manhole is designed, where the curb is set, how high it is, the width of the street, the height of the buildings, where they're set back. Each one of these things has been thought about and designed. Urban design is the key to city making.

GH — Oh, we didn't talk about Jane Jacobs and Roberts Moses.

AB — Okay. Our plans have been very ambitious on a very grand scale, really redrawing the entire land-use blueprint of the city, because we have to grow by over a million people. Our plans, therefore, have been as ambitious as those of Robert Moses, but we really judge ourselves by Jane Jacobs's standards. How we grow in place while keeping what makes New York so unique is really our challenge.

As you know, Robert Moses was the master builder, and he planned by aerial planning. He planned by looking at the city from above, and how you could connect the city by major highways without any regard to what was happening at grade. His highway building destroyed entire neighborhoods for decades and decades. They're barely recovering now. He drove the Cross Bronx Expressway through the Bronx, and it is barely recovering now. The Gowanus Expressway. He cut off our entire island of Manhattan from the waterfront by building highways down the edges. His impact was profound, and his insensitivity was legendary, to the texture of the city.

His downfall came at the same time as the rise of Jane Jacobs, who really was the champion of the small-scale texture of a neighborhood and the essence of a city being the vibrancy of its neighborhoods and, as she called it, the ballet of the streets. The safety of a neighborhood, with eyes on the street, as she said. The security and value of knowing the members of a community and how you build a city with an active streetscape. That vibrancy is what is so special about so many of New York City's neighborhoods. Our challenge is to grow the city at a broad and very ambitious scale for a million people, growing in the right places, but to keep the diversity of New York City's neighborhoods, and that's how we judge every project. We judge ourselves by Jane Jacobs's standards and whether it feels vibrant, interesting, complex, and inviting.

—

Bruce Katz

(BK)/ May 13, 2011 Washington

Bruce Katz is a vice president at the Brookings Institution and founding director of the Brookings Metropolitan Policy Program. Katz served as Chief of Staff to Henry Cisneros, U.S. Secretary of Housing and Urban Development, from 1993 to 1996, and was a senior advisor to HUD Secretary Shaun Donovan during the Obama administration.
—

Gary Hustwit — Can you talk about the forces that shape our cities and how economic shifts and activity and redevelopment have always been a factor in how cities evolve?

Bruce Katz — Cities are always the physical manifestation of the big forces at play, in nations and across the world. They could be economic forces, the rise of nations like China, India, and Brazil. They can be social forces, migration of people within countries, across borders. The premier trend, in the United States and across the world, is urbanization, is the growth of cities, is the evolution of cities. If you care about any issue—economic growth and prosperity, environmental sanity, social inclusion—you need to care about cities. This is where the action is.

At different times in history, different things matter. Three centuries ago, or even further back, cities were located along rivers, on lakes. They were the centers of commerce, and that's what was required then. In this century, particularly post–World War II, particularly in the United States, highways, a different kind of infrastructure, was needed around the growth of cities in their metropolitan areas. In this century, it's broadband, it's wireless, it's information technology, as the core infrastructure within which cities function.

Cities are where things get concentrated. Cities are where assets agglomerate, where two plus two equals five, because of the mash up of smart people, talented workers, big firms, small firms, research institutions, intermediaries that provide skills to workers. That's what cities are: they're sort of magical places where people and firms and institutions come together and create new things. They constantly evolve and iterate. They're not stagnant. They're highly dynamic. What's wrong with that? They're not totally perfect.

GH — Can you discuss the roles that are involved in any kind of shaping of the city?

BK — The development of cities is affected by many different forces: Business, and different kinds of business, need certain kinds of cities, certain kinds of land at different times in history. As you think about the industrial revolution, we went to vertical factories, then horizontal factories, and to some extent we're going back to vertical. People have different preferences at different ages of their life—with children, without children, as they age. Government makes a big difference as to how they plan cities, whether they plan cities, what they invest in. Do you invest in sprawl, or do you invest in density? That's the big issue within the United States, particularly in the 20th century and this century.

Many forces affect the development of cities, and cities obviously share many similarities, but there also incredible distinctions, and that's really interesting from a competitiveness perspective. At the end of the day, cities are competing for people, they're competing for investment, they're competing for firms, and so how they developed, whether they're livable, whether they're sustainable, whether they're economically focused, whether they're easy places to do business in, will affect their prosperity, now and over time.

GH — Maybe we can kind of contextualize that within present day, US terms, those same kind of ideas.

    BK — The United States is an urban and metropolitan nation. Eighty-three percent of our population lives in cities and their metropolitan areas. Ninety percent of our gross domestic product comes from these places, and when you think about the assets that really drive national economies—innovation, human capital, infrastructure, quality places—it's almost all within our cities and metropolitan areas.

The US still thinks of itself as a nation of small towns. Our zeitgeist is somewhat early 20th century, when the reality is we're a powerful metropolitan nation, and we're powerful because we have these cities and metropolitan areas that are driving the national economy, participating in global commerce, attracting and retaining talent from all over the world. The US needs to understand, if we're going to prosper in this century, who we are and why we are so successful and what assets we have to build on. We need to think, frankly, going back to our founding, more like Alexander Hamilton and less like Thomas Jefferson. Thomas Jefferson represented the sort of rural, agrarian perspective of American evolution. Hamilton was more about, let's produce, let's compete, let's innovate, let's attract to our shores talented workers from all over the world. We need a 21st-century perspective about our nation that starts with our metropolitan engines as the vehicle for broader prosperity.

GH — How would you fit in Detroit and the Rust Belt cities into this?

    BK — We built in the 20th century, and frankly even going back into the late 19th century, some very powerful cities and metropolitan areas in the industrial heartland, in New England and the Midwest and portions of the South. We think about these places, like Detroit and Pittsburgh and Milwaukee and smaller places like Toledo and Dayton, as really iconic industrial cities. As the United States began to shift away from production to consumption and to a postindustrial economy, these places began to have dramatic issues, complicated by racial and ethnic segregation.

My view about this century is the United States needs a different kind of growth model post-recession. We need to think about an economy, and then build one, that is driven by exports and more integration with the global economy, powered by low carbon—we have to be the vanguard of the clean energy revolution—and fueled by innovation. Not just ideas that we generate but the production and deployment of what we invent. If we can get back to a vision of United States as a productive and sustainable economy, I think, actually, many of these older industrial places that didn't prosper in our postindustrial period of the late 20th century can prosper again in this century. But we need to connect a different kind of macro vision to the metro places that can actually drive that vision. If we don't have that macro vision, and if we don't understand the incredible assets and legacies of these older industrial places, I think the US as a whole will not prosper in this century.

GH — How do you fix a city that's gone through that kind of decline?

BK — Detroit was once two million people in a metropolitan area that really was the center of industrial production, not just in United States but in the world. The city has shrunk back to about seven hundred thousand people. It's a city of 138 square miles. You could fit Boston and San Francisco and Atlanta inside the boundaries of the city of Detroit. It's that big. So when you have seven hundred thousand people as opposed to two million people, you have to shrink back. You've got to scale back to your neighborhoods and your areas where there's concentration, where there is this livability and urbanity: clearly the downtown, clearly the Woodward Corridor, clearly the area where Henry Ford Medical Center and Wayne State and many of the civic institutions are located, and then many neighborhoods that still have good bones, good infrastructure that we can build on again.

But it's not just about the arrangement of people and transit and homes. It's about what these people do. I think Detroit's decline was a reflection of the United States moving away from its industrial base to this postindustrial future. We need to embrace manufacturing, production, innovation, exports to the rising countries like Brazil, India, and China as the future of our economy. If we do that, if we spend less time worrying about consumption, home building, and retail and more about how the United States again becomes the productive, innovative engine of the world, I think places like Detroit, and the people living in Detroit, can prosper again. So it's both what happens locally—smart planning, so that you can concentrate and agglomerate the people, the assets you have—but it's also a smart national vision that then gets delivered through your cities and metropolitan areas. It's both. It's the macro and the metro.

GH — Can you talk about those other global cities that US cities are competing with. Where did all the economic activity shift to?

BK — What we've seen in the last several decades is the rise of countries like China, India, and Brazil and billions of people around the world entering the economic mainstream. The rise of these countries is the rise of their cities. When countries compete, it's because they're urbanizing and they're industrializing, whether it's China, with Shanghai and Beijing and Shenzhen and then dozens of other cities with millions of people, or whether it's India, but not just Delhi and Mumbai, but Bangalore and many other cities of large, medium, and small size. Urbanization is essentially the key trend as economies evolved to a more mature status.

What we need to understand in the United States is that the US needs to serve this global demand. As cities urbanize, as they begin to create a middle class, that creates demand for many different kinds of goods and services. The US needs to understand that that's how we need to orient our economy, to serve that rising demand in addition to serving the demand coming out of our own country of 310 million today, 400 million by, let's say, 2045.

The US has been, in some respects, a very diverse country but a very insular country. We don't get out much, all right? Only 28 percent of Americans have a passport. We need to understand that our future prosperity is aligned with the urbanization of China, India, and Brazil. Both at the macro scale and at the city scale, we need to create these relationships and linkages between our cities and their cities, between our firms and their cities, so that we can ensure prosperity for our country going forward. Urbanization is the key trend in this century. It's not just the rise of countries in the abstract. Our country, China, India, Brazil, Germany, the United Kingdom—they're powerful economies because they're urban economies.

GH — It's interesting, the kind of massive urbanization and big population shifts—it's funny because we're not seeing that in United States, so I think a lot of people just don't understand.
> BK — Well, we are seeing at the metro scale.

GH — Sure, but not on the level of a Mumbai.
> BK — You know, we're a more disaggregated country. We're not England, which looks to one city, or France. I mean, we have many cities, and therefore none of them are of huge size. The United States is a metropolitan nation. Our top hundred metros are two thirds of our population and three quarters of our GDP. Every one of these metros has over five hundred thousand in population. The big ones, obviously, like New York, Chicago, and LA, are at 18 million and 12 million and 9 million. So that's when you're at the scale like some of the Chinese cities and the Indian cities.

But we are a very diffuse country, a varied country with many different cities and metropolitan areas, each of which has a very distinct kind of economy. I think one of the most interesting things, as our nation comes out of this recession and the sluggish recovery, is to understand that, for places to succeed in the 21st century, they need to build on their special assets and attributes and advantages. They need to strengthen their strengths.

When you think about the economy that preceded the recession, which was a consumption-driven economy, a debt-driven economy, you know, a Walmart is a Walmart is a Walmart. You go to suburban Phoenix, or you go to suburban Pittsburgh, it all looks the same. If you ask, what does Phoenix export in the world versus what Pittsburgh exports; what's the distinctive low-carbon, clean-energy play of Pittsburgh versus Phoenix; what are the innovative aspects of a Phoenix versus Pittsburgh?— they're very different from each other. I think what the United States needs to learn in this century is to build on those distinctive assets.

We need a national government—it'd be nice to have one—that can set the platform for smart, sustainable growth, price carbon and invest in transformative infrastructure, all these wonderful things—have a sane immigration policy—that other countries do. But while we're waiting for that, I think every city and metropolitan area in this country can spend time understanding who they are, and then strengthen what makes them distinctive in this global economy, and then no one can out-compete the United States. We have incredible assets and a zeitgeist of entrepreneurialism and integration and assimilation that makes us the most distinctive society in the world and therefore, perhaps, the most preeminent economy for this century.

I think the architectural community and more broadly the design community, the city planning community, has an incredible role to play because they help cities find their special voice, their distinctive brand that distinguishes them from other places. Again, I mean, for me, what makes cities special is how different they are from each other. It's not like going to a suburban mall outside of Philadelphia versus outside of a Phoenix or outside of Denver versus outside of Detroit. There's a sameness to that. I think you lose sense of where you are. When you're in a downtown with a distinctive kind of architecture, some historic, some modern, with a distinctive kind of waterfront, with a distinctive kind of physical landscape, both within the city and the broader metropolitan area, you have a sense of place; you have a sense of belonging.

Frankly, in a world where we're all completely wired and connected, we're all overly caffeinated, where we all can basically go anywhere within a relatively short period of time, there's something special about this distinctiveness. What I always say to cities is, understand yourself first and foremost, and if you're going to embrace the architectural community, do it in such a way that reflects your specialness.

GH — Do you think the global elite architects are doing this?

BK — Well, I think the global elite architects, their most powerful contribution is the notion that cities matter and that iconic architecture can help brand the city and provide a platform for global recognition and a platform for city prosperity. They have contributed dramatically to cities being at the center of economic conversations, social conversations, environmental conversations. Many of the global architects have embraced the need to respond to climate change as part of their ethics and as part of their profession.

GH — Can you talk a little bit about social housing? It would be great if you can give us a little bit of historical perspective.

BK — The birth of social housing in the United States really goes back to the New Deal. Our public housing program was started in the 1930s, 1937 to be exact. The history of social housing in the United States is a complicated one. For many decades starting in the 1930s, but particularly in the 1960s and '70s, we built a certain kind of social housing. Frankly, in many places, they were warehouses for the poor. They embraced a certain kind of modernist architecture. They were isolated from the broader community. We covered over streets so that we could have campuses of social housing. These places over time, frankly, became cancers in many of their cities. They became the locus of much of the distress that cities and their older suburban communities were facing— poverty, crime, schools that didn't function.

For the past two decades in the United States, we have begun to turn to a different model of social housing: economically integrated housing, mixed-use housing, housing that becomes part of the fabric of neighborhoods and cities, housing that provides a platform for people not just to live in a particular place but to move up the ladder of opportunity with skills training and access to jobs.

In the nineties and in the last decade, we actually had to tear down a tenth of our public housing because it didn't work anymore. It didn't work for people, it didn't work for neighborhoods, and it didn't work for cities. There's a different vision of social housing that is now unleashed in the United States that it still playing itself out. Frankly, at a time of fiscal austerity, the biggest question is, how can we do more of this with less funding? Probably the same issues that many other countries, particularly in Europe, will face in the coming decade. But the vision— economically integrated housing and housing that works for people, neighborhood, and city—is the right vision.

GH — Do you want to talk about HOPE VI? It would be great just to single out a few of those projects that you think are particularly done well.

BK — In the late '80s and early 1990s, there was a recognition that there was a group of public housing projects in the United States, housing over a hundred thousand families, that had cease to work for people: Cabrini-Green in Chicago, Robert Taylor Homes in Chicago, Richard Allen Homes in Philadelphia. This was the cancer in many of our urban neighborhoods. And so in the early 1990s, what the Congress did, and then particularly during the Clinton administration under the leadership of Henry Cisneros, is put forward a different vision—let's tear down the housing that doesn't work, particularly those high-rises, those isolated high-rises that had become the platform for negativity, and let's transition to a different kind of housing—smaller scale, more economically integrated, more connected to the fabric of neighborhoods.

If you go across the United States now, you will see a lot less of the public housing that we all have in our collective consciousness, particularly these high-rises like the State Street Corridor in Chicago. What you'll see now is affordable housing that is well designed, that actually is serving people better. And a mix of people: very low-income folks, low-income workers, moderate-income workers, and even some middle-class families, because much of this housing is actually located not that far from downtown areas that have also come back as the United States has begun to balance its growth.

Probably one of the most signature interventions of the national government over the past several decades, about, probably, 8 to 10 billion in total investments, is a complete remake of public housing. It's probably one of the most successful interventions. We all talk about the failure of government. Here's where government recognized it had created a problem by the way in which it had built its social housing, and then started self-correcting over the course of the last 15 years.

GH — And are there specific ones you want to talk about?

BK — So if we went to the north side of St. Louis 20 years ago, 30 years ago, what you would see is a collection of very large public housing projects that were basically undermining the ability of that neighborhood, the ability of the city, and the ability of the people living there to succeed.

We tore down the Pruitt-Igoe houses in the 1970s. We all remember that iconic image. But starting in the early 1990s, we began to tear down a series of these other high-rises. What we created in place were places like Murphy Park: smaller scale, mixed income, literally 20 minutes from the downtown, with a public school that is the most technologically wired in the state of Missouri. It's a place that can now attract a mix of people, a mix of families, and the firms that will follow, retail, groceries, dry cleaners, and other firms that can employ people living in the community. So we went from a disaster zone that, frankly, was the outcome of the way in which we had built these communities. What we had basically built were warehouses, not communities, not housing.

We've transferred over to something very different. What any American would see going to the north side of St. Louis now is a neighborhood, not housing project, a neighborhood, a community, a place that works, for children, for families, for the elderly. That's a vision, and frankly in the last 20 years, we had to destroy in order to create. It's been tough, contentious, complicated, and not successful everywhere, but Murphy Park is an example of what we can do as a country and what we can do as communities.

The idea for HOPE VI came from Richard Baron. Richard Baron is a developer, grew up in Detroit, lives in St. Louis, who has a big vision for the future of Detroit, which is to daylight the streams coming out of the Detroit River to create a 21st-century park and production area for the city of Detroit. Detroit reflects the possibilities of the United States in this century.

We tend to think about some of our cities as reflecting the failures, but if we think creatively, if we think as entrepreneurs, if we go back to the sort of American gene, the American DNA, and we think about, what could these places be in a 21st-century economy—you can see Canada from Detroit, right? You can get up, look out the downtown, and you can see Windsor. In the 21st-century economy, the proximity to our largest trading partner is an incredible asset. There is no reason why in 15, 25, 35 years we shouldn't be looking at a very different Detroit and a very different southeast Michigan.

But we have to change our mental state of what, first, the American economy should look like. It should be more production oriented, export oriented, innovation fueled. We shouldn't be innovating in financial derivatives. We should be innovating in how to crack the code on low carbon and climate change, and we should be doing that in places like southeast Michigan, given the legacy of production and innovation and science and engineering. That's what we should be doing. And then we should be exporting our most innovative goods and services to the world so that these places can grow in more sustainable ways.

We need to get back to a sense of optimism and possibility for our country, and frankly that starts with our cities. Because that's where it comes together. We can have all of these ideas about how a country evolves and what our role in the world is. At the end of the day, it happens in real places, in real communities, like Detroit, like Pittsburgh, like Milwaukee, or some of the newer parts of the country that have been built over the last 50 years. Each one of them has the ability to prosper in a very different and disruptive century if it recognizes what it's good at and strengthens its strengths.

GH — If you had to define what urban design is, how would you do that?
BK — I think urban design needs to ultimately serve what makes cities succeed. Cities are mash-ups. Cities are places where lots of different people and lots of different institutions—economic, civic, educational—come together and create something more than the sum of the parts, right? So urban design has to allow for that. It has to allow for proximity, for multiple modes of transportation, not just the auto, but mass transit and biking and walking. It has to respect the fact that rivers and lakes, places that we turned our back on during the industrial era, are now places that need to be the heart of our metropolitan areas because they again have that distinctive look. They enable so many different generations and people across different races, and classes, and ethnicities to come together in a community. So urban design needs to fundamentally serve what is special about "cityness," a great phrase that Saskia Sassen has used.

They can't be overly prescriptive. A design that works in one part of the country (the United States—we're so varied; we're so distinctive) might not work in a different part of the country. I'm more for experimentation, variation, distinctiveness, as opposed to the one cookie cutter that gets played out, whether it's design, or architecture, or some broader neighborhood planning, in place after place after place. I think that violates the whole notion of what make cities special. What I like about this country and traveling around the rest of the world is what's different about different places. I mean, that to me is that special asset that cities bring. They all uniformly serve a certain kind of function and role, but their physical manifestation is different because of different culture, different historic legacy, the time in which they were built, and the genius of their own innovators.

GH — It's interesting when you talk about using the cookie-cutter solution. Especially in cities in places like China, when they're building cities from scratch for a million people every other week, are they taking the right lessons from what we've done, or are they just saying, this is what the West's model is, car based or whatever, and just repeating the things we've seen here?

BK — I think the possibilities of city building in this century are enormous because there is such disruptive change underway with the acceleration of technology and the progress of technology. We can build cities now that are fundamentally integrated, that have the ability to reduce our use of energy, water, electricity. The promise of this century is that we can build cities that align with a very different environmental and technological moment. We're in a moment of technological acceleration, where technology embedded in cities enables us to experience cities in very efficient and dynamic ways. If you go to Tokyo today, with your cell phone you can basically get on the train, buy a cup of coffee, go to a commercial facility in the station, and buy certain goods, buy certain services, right? Technology enables an incredible level of integration and efficiency for people and for places. What cities also have to respond to, which technology enables us to do, is climate. I mean, cities should be the vehicles for dealing with climate. City building in this century should be completely different than city building in the 20th century—fossil fuel driven, car dependent, all the things that we now understand undermine our ability to have a sustainable planet and, frankly, over time, a prosperous economy.

As China builds its cities, as India builds its cities, they can't just take the recipe from 20th-century America and apply it to 21st-century China or 21st-century India. That would be horrendous for them. It would be horrendous, frankly, for all of us. Technology, environmental sensitivity, a sense of what's different about this century, have to animate and drive their urbanization. And for us back here in the United States, or for many of the European cities and metropolitan areas, we're going to have to retrofit our cities for a different century. We're going to have to take account and deploy these technological possibilities so that our cities are lowering carbon, at the same time being more prosperous, at the same time working for more people.

It's a different kind of urbanism in the 21st century: still being explored, still evolving, not quite there yet, very messy, very contentious in place after place, very complicated. Because you're dealing with all the different elements of cities. You're dealing with transport. You're dealing with housing. You're dealing with production and manufacturing. You're dealing with logistics. You're dealing with the way in which millions of people interact every day, on streets, in the Twittersphere, right? Very different, but we're evolving it, and I think there is an energy around cities in this century. There's an optimism about cities in this century.

There's a sense we're creating something that's truly global, and we're creating networks of people, not experts, but people at all strata of society who are involved in the building of something special and distinctive. I'm city obsessed. I mean, I've always been city obsessed. I grew up in New York, so who would not be? This is the century for city lovers. This is the century where we get to build and retrofit places that work for people, that work for the economy, that work for the environment and work for nations. This is where it happens.

GH — Let's talk about federal government policy and how it relates to cities and city building. What are the things in place, or what are the things that the federal government should do?

BK — My views of national governments, federal governments, is that what they principally need to do is set the platform for smart and sustainable growth in cities and metropolitan areas. That means something different in this century than in the past century. Price carbon, absolutely. Invest in advanced research and development, particularly around clean energy, but also around health. Invest in transformative infrastructure. That might be rail or transit. It might be EV infrastructure—electric vehicle infrastructure—or transmission lines. It might be the retooling of manufacturing for a different century of production. It might be smart cities: technology embedded within urbanization.

National governments can build a platform for smart investments from the public realm that really have to be aggregated at the national scale and then what I would call smart rules of the road: smart trade, smart immigration. Have open societies, inclusive societies, smart patenting. That's what you want your federal government or national government to do. You set that platform, and cities will take off; metropolitan areas will take off. The genius of cities is this collection of innovators and the agglomeration and concentration of talent at all scales to create special and distinctive places. We don't need national governments to muddle around. We don't need national governments to micromanage. We need them to set a platform and a foundation for urban and metropolitan innovation.

GH — Could you discuss mayors and their role?

BK — I think the genius of the American system is that we have elected officials at the local scale and at the metropolitan scale who have power. They can tax at the local scale. They can make land use and zoning decisions. They obviously have to deliver critical services, either directly or indirectly, like schools, education, public safety.

The city level, and the metropolitan level as well, is where things actually happen. National governments pass laws. State governments pass laws. Mayors do stuff. As Michael Nutter, the mayor of Philadelphia, says, they're the get-stuff-done party. They prize place over party, collaboration over conflict. You don't see a lot of these ideological disputes or partisan disputes that permeate the national character of politics in the United States play out the local scale because, at the local scale, people are focused on doing things and making their place better.

Whether it's Rendell in Philadelphia, succeeded ultimately by Michael Nutter; Daley in Chicago, now succeeded by Rahm Emanuel; or a whole host of mayors—Antonio Villaraigosa in LA, Gavin Newsom when he was mayor of San Francisco, Michael Bloomberg in New York, Cory Booker in Newark—these are the people with a pulse in the United States in the political class. They want to get on the ground and create something that has legacy, that is sustainable over time. They don't think in two year cycles. They think in 50 and 100 year cycles, because they know that the future is very much a product of the past, right? When you think about where this country goes or where another country goes, it is a legacy of the smart interventions we made or that prior generations made.

I think that, frankly, as we think about the United States moving forward in this century, the energy, the entrepreneurial dynamism, comes up from the bottom. Led in many places by elected officials, mayors, who can really be the orchestra leaders, doing what they're supposed to be doing, but also then pulling together these magical networks of universities and business and philanthropy and labor and the environmental activists and community and creating something that is, not just distinctive for the moment, but lasting over time.

And that's where the energy is in the United States. That is our genius. Our genius is a federal republic where so much can happen at the "lower levels" of government and society. We're not waiting for the regulations. We're not waiting for a Washington bureaucrat, you know, to give us permission. This is not a "may I" society. This is a "get it done" kind of country, and that very much happens at the city level and at the metropolitan level.

GH — I like that idea that, when you look at a city, you're not just looking at whatever you actually see; you're looking at hundreds of years of incremental decisions and creativity and successes and failures, all this stuff that goes into a very banal looking cityscape.

BK — Cities very much, particularly physically, inherit the past. They inherit what was good about the past: buildings that were built with iconic architecture, particularly when you think of the earlier part of the 20th century—the Carnegie Libraries, the city halls, the seats of government. They inherit the waterfronts and whether they're accessible; the downtowns and whether they have density, and livability, and connectivity; the transit systems, whether they're bus or rail.

The challenge for city leaders is what of the past you burnish and leverage off of, and what do you need to rethink? Because particularly after World War II, the United States began to move from "cityness," the special distinctive assets of urban places, and a lot of the low-density thinking that has permeated the US in our suburbs began to infiltrate city thinking: "We better look more like suburban density if we really want to succeed and prosper."

I think cities are going back to basics now. Where they have this historic, iconic architecture or these legacy transit systems, they're building on them in a 21st-century way. When they've made stupid mistakes in the past century, freeways that frankly we should never have built in the first place that block access to the waterfront, or high-rise public housing that needs to be torn down, they're doing that.

The bottom line about cities is they're sort of like people. You have to constantly evolve. You have to mature. You have to change with different times, understand what's special and needs to be preserved and conserved, and then what really needs a level of rethink and radical intervention. City leadership needs, in many ways, both conservative people, who really want to keep what's working, and radicals, who want to shake things up. It's that special mix, I think, that makes cities the distinctive engines of nations.

—

Jon Bird (JB)/ April 27, 2011 Brighton

The Tidy Street Project in Brighton, England, interested me for several reasons. It's a unique way to engage a community in a conversation about sustainability, but it's also a public art project. I thought it encompassed a few ideas we wanted to explore in *Urbanized*, so one of the project's coordinators, Jon Bird, walked us through it.

—

Gary Hustwit — Can you talk about some of the goals of the projects you're doing here?

> **Jon Bird** — We're interested in using technology to make people more aware of patterns of behavior so, potentially, they can change them. In this project, we were interested in making people more aware of their electricity usage.

GH — So where are we? What street this is?

> **JB** — We're in Tidy Street, which is a short street, a residential street near the center of Brighton. It's an old street. The houses were built in the 1840s, and there are about 50 houses here.

GH — Why did you choose it?

> **JB** — We chose to do the project on this street for a number of reasons. One was that we already knew a family who lived here who were quite interested in joining in the project. Also, they are quite active in the community, so we thought that they could help us champion the project to get other people involved. The second thing is, we were interested in doing a public display, so we wanted other people to be able to see it. This is near the city center, so lots of people walk down this street. We thought that would raise some awareness as well in a larger community.

GH — Do you want to break it down: what people did, how they recorded it, and the demographics?

> **JB** — Although we were interested in using technology to make people more aware of their electricity usage, we actually went for a very low-tech method of recording electricity usage. Rather than using smart sensors, each day we got the participants to go down to their electricity meter, write down the reading, and then they went to our website and put that number in. On the website, they would get some feedback graphs which would show how their electricity usage had changed day to day. It also showed how the average of all the participants had changed day to day. It also showed them how they compared to the

Brighton average. That was one type of feedback, the web feedback. We decided to do a public display as well. The reason for that was, they have a street party here every year where they close off the road. That was where I mainly got the participants. I came down and told them about the project, and all the people signed up. One of the things they were very keen on having was an artwork, a public artwork, as part of the project. They had done another public art project about five years ago and really enjoyed it. They liked the sense of community it gave them, so we said we'd do that. We decided that we would turn the street, essentially, into a big graph. This was in collaboration with Snub, a street artist here in Brighton.

On the street, we showed how the average usage of the participants compares to the Brighton average. It's five hundred feet long, and we recorded for three weeks. Each day, we painted a new entry on the graph showing how they compare. If you're looking down the street, you can see how their electricity usage changed over time.

GH — What were some of the reactions or experiences of the participants? Talk about their before-and-after thoughts.

JB — One of the pieces of technology we gave them was an appliance meter. That was really important for them, because once they got an idea of how their overall electricity was changing, they then wanted to identify which particular appliances were using more electricity. They were quite surprised by some things. For example, most of them were surprised by how much an electric kettle would use. There were simple things like that: they got insight into how much appliances used and then how they could start saving money. They realized, as well, that lots of appliances that they left on standby still used electricity. They started switching things off at night—really simple. Also just turning off lights if they weren't in a room. I don't think they had to change their behavior in a massive way to have quite a significant reduction in their electricity usage.

The public display had a big effect on the participants too. They told us it really made them feel like a community. Often they had to explain the display to people walking past. They explained it to their families and their friends, but also to just passersby. It made them feel quite proud that they were involved.

GH — Could you talk some more about the community aspect?

JB — Yeah. One of the most important insights from this project is that, although technology can be useful in raising awareness, it's not sufficient. One of the participants told us that his electricity supply company had given him a small meter, but very quickly he just ignored it. It's the social engagement, making them feel like a community, which really affected them in this project and led to this reduction.

GH — Do you think this made them think more about, not only their energy use, but the electricity use of the other people on the street and even, kind of as an extension of that, the city's electricity use?

JB — One of the interesting things we wanted to find out in this project is, which comparisons are the most effective for changing people's behavior or increasing their awareness? On the website, obviously they could compare their own usage over time, and they could compare their usage to their neighbors'. We also showed them how they compared to the city average. After that, we had data which showed them how they compare to regions in the UK and other countries. In the future, I think we could get the data for other cities as well. It's an open question, though, which comparisons are most effective. Our approach was just to provide lots of comparisons and let them find the one that was most useful for them.

GH — Would you say the project has been a success?

JB — Over three weeks, yes. All of them report that they have an increased awareness of their electricity usage and have got a better idea about which appliances in the house use electricity. It's also been a success in that we've been approached by lots of different organizations who want to do something similar. They want to use our software to let people manually record their electricity usage, and they're also interested in how they can use public art displays to engage communities. We'll hopefully be doing this project with more streets in Brighton.

We've also been asked if we would take this approach to Abu Dhabi, which would be an interesting challenge because they use more natural resources per capita than any other place in the world. We have to think about things like, what would be an appropriate public display for Abu Dhabi? The basic idea of this approach can be applied to all sorts of different communities, but the key thing is to actually go into the community, and it's important to engage them and get them participating and to find out what's significant for them. I don't think you can just go and impose a solution on them. It's very important to go through this participation process, and that takes time. You have to find champions for the project in the communities. You have to find out what form of public art they would like and find out what motivates them.

GH — A lot of people talk about sustainability, and it seems like a big concept, but really it's about this type of small-scale effort. What's so great about the project is it's so DIY; it's not a big-budget kind of thing, but yet it's very effective.

JB — Yes. The main lesson we can learn about sustainability from this project is that, although it starts with individuals, a really important factor in people's behavior is their community. People are influenced by what other people are doing around them. So if you can engage them as a community, they seem to be more motivated and more likely to change their behavior. It's important not to impose that change on them. What you want to do is find a way of engaging them and motivating them.

This public art plays that function. If we had just done the web-based feedback, I don't think it would have been as effective. The people have all mentioned that. If you ask them, "Did the public art influence you? Did it change your behavior?" they often say, "Not really, but it was really important for the project. We either wouldn't have done the project if not for the artwork, or we wouldn't have been as motivated if it hadn't been for the artwork."

A key theme of this project was that we didn't impose a solution top down, but the project came out of the participation of this community, and finding a solution that they wanted and that suited them. If we wanted to expand this project and apply it to other streets and communities, one of the implications is that you have to spend a lot of time working with that community. You might like to think that we could have this top-down approach, a cookie-cutter approach, one solution that will fit all communities. I'm actually quite skeptical of that. If we want to change behavior, we've got to realize that people are different, and they're individuals.

GH — Right, and everybody uses electricity differently, even home to home. How do you make it bigger than the individuals, bigger and more collective?

JB — In this street, some of the participants were single people, pensioners. Some lived in a shared house. Some were families. Some of them work at home, so they have more computers on. So people are different in the way they use electricity, but they're also different in what motivates them. If we're going to encourage people to change, we can't force change on them, because that will not be sustainable. Behavioral change has got to come from the person themselves. That's why it's really important to get them engaged in the project and for them to find value in it. Forcing change won't lead to long-lasting change.

Over the first three weeks of the project, the average electricity usage of the participants came down by 15 percent, which is great, but we have to be a bit tentative about that result. The worry is, they won't sustain it. That's why we've got a second phase for a further six months, and most of the participants are continuing to participate. We're also going to be recording the gas usage in the same way as well. They're going to read their gas meter and put it into the website. It's promising, and we're hoping that that change will be sustained.

—

Oscar Niemeyer (ON)/ May 21, 2011 Rio de Janeiro

In 2009 I was invited to screen *Objectified* in Rio de Janeiro, Brazil. At that point, I knew that I was going to make *Urbanized*, so when I was traveling for screenings I also brought a camera along to get footage of the different cities I was visiting. I knew that I wanted to include Brasília in the film and tried to meet with Oscar Niemeyer while I was in Rio, but he was in poor health when I was there. I did manage to make it to Brasília on that trip and shot the footage that was included in *Urbanized*.

Two years later, when I interviewed Sir Norman Foster in New York for the film, he mentioned that he was going to Rio a few months later to meet Niemeyer, whose health had since improved. Foster invited me to come along and film the conversation, which was to be moderated by curator and editor Hans Ulrich Obrist. The footage of Niemeyer in *Urbanized* was filmed in the context of that conversation. We're including an excerpt of that conversation here.

Niemeyer passed away in December 2012 a few days shy of his 105th birthday.
—

Hans Ulrich Obrist — There were so many reasons for this conversation, but one of them is that both Oscar and Norman have invented cities. Obviously there is the example of Brasília, and then Norman invented Masdar, an ecological city for the 21st century.

> **Oscar Niemeyer** — Brasília was developed by Lúcio Costa, a very competent Brazilian architect. I was in charge of the architecture. When people come to talk to me, usually architects, I generally emphasize the social aspect of it. I think that architecture is important, but life is more important.

Norman Foster — I find myself repeating the idea that the infrastructure, the public spaces, the connections, the urbanity, are perhaps more important than the individual buildings, and those are the social spaces. Those are the public spaces, the squares, the routes, the parks. That is perhaps what binds the buildings together. I think that, in a way, what I enjoy about Oscar Niemeyer's work is that even the individual building is very much about the public promenade, the public dimension, in a way that is almost like the city in miniature, which is about public spaces.

HUO — The last time we had an interview together, Niemeyer told me that Brasília was not only a utopia but also a necessity. Norman said a similar thing when we did an interview about Masdar. Masdar was a necessity. So I think it would be nice if you could tell us a little about that, Norman.

NF — Well, Masdar tries to learn from traditional spaces in the desert and the way in which traditional buildings use shading. It creates quite narrow streets and is very pedestrian friendly. All of this is conducive to a sustainable future. Masdar tries to give priority and importance to the pedestrian, putting the car below the pedestrian. It tries to learn from traditional buildings in the past that used shade—shaded streets, shaded openings—and it was also about youth because the first part of Masdar is a university. So it's about young people finding ways to create renewable sources of energy. It's about the future.

It would be very interesting to know in what way Brasília would be different if Oscar were to do it again today. I know that he was more involved with the architecture than the planning, but it would be interesting to see what approach he would take today.

ON — I respect Brasília very much, but everyone has different ideas about certain things. I thought about changing the center of the city a bit to give the capital a more monumental image, but they decided not to carry out that idea, so the Brasília that you studied is a simple, rational city that underlines architecture. What do you think about the urbanism of Brasília?

NF — I'm seeing it on Sunday, and I am greatly looking forward to going there. I love everything that I've seen of the architecture. I find it inspirational, and I can't wait to see it in reality. It's probably difficult to give an opinion about the city until I see it myself. I think creating a city as a completely new entity is always an interesting challenge.

HUO — Most cities grow organically over centuries. Instant cities like Brasília and now Masdar are very rare.

NF — Yes, although I suspect that Brasília has grown organically out from the heart.

ON — People like Brasília. It is rational, and it maintains a somewhat urban aspect. I think Brasília has a very good side. Lúcio was a very talented architect, and he put his heart and will into the project. Once it was finished, it became a city of a certain importance. I remember that it was made in a hurry, from one day to the next. He presented the project in 15 days.

NF — What impresses me from the images that I have seen is the way that the architecture is able to create so many different identities. I think it is quite extraordinary that, in a way, the vocabulary of the architecture is able to create religious buildings, or a building about law. I find that an extraordinary achievement.

ON — We did what we could, each with our own ideas. Brasília adapted itself to the location. Brazilians like Brasília: it is a place to stop, to rest. I think Brasília is fantastic. The forest, the hills. This is a very nice country, isn't it?

HUO — The last time I was here a couple of years ago, Oscar also told me about another city, an instant city he had planned for Angola and which I think was four times bigger than Brasília.

> **ON** — The city of Brasília is welcoming. It's full of vegetation, a bit like Brazil, which is full of things, full of charm. However, I always point out that Brasília is not my work but Lúcio's.

NF — I have this image of these very generous spaces and the way in which the urban spaces then find public spaces within the buildings in a similar way to colonnades, but that I'll wait to see. The more I think about the work of individual buildings, the more I realize the importance of the public spaces that they create, just as cities create them as well.

But I think what makes Oscar's buildings so special is precisely the public spaces, and that's true of both his early and later works. Walking the ramps of the Niterói Contemporary Art Museum today was a great experience. Before you even get into the building, there's that wonderful ceremony. The ramps are almost like a dance in space, enabling you to see the building from different viewpoints before you actually enter it. And that I find magic, absolutely magic.

> **ON** — That was my goal. I think that architecture is about invention. We can obtain the intended result from a project, but to invent something is very different. Architecture should not only be about designing a building that works well. It can also be beautiful; it can be different; it can be surprising, can't it? In fact, surprise is the main element of a work of art.

NF — It works wonderfully.

> **ON** — The curves and the ramps offer beautiful solutions. Did you go to the Alvorada Palace? There you will see the columns in which I inverted the regular form. They develop into a curve that creates distance in respect to the balcony. It's an example of how we can play with architecture without compromising good function. The palace has no sills, just a set of curves and columns.

NF — I am greatly looking forward to it.

HUO — We have spoken about many different projects, but we haven't spoken about the current moment, now. I am very curious about what you, Oscar, have been working on today or in the last couple of days. Could you tell us a little bit about what you have been drawing and thinking lately?

> **ON** — I have a lot of work: buildings, sets of buildings. I have just finished the Oscar Niemeyer International Cultural Centre in Spain. People really liked the project: two buildings in a huge square where it was easy to maintain the relationship between the filled and the empty spaces, as well as the relationship between the two buildings.
>
> I am also working on a very interesting project in Germany. I've been commissioned to make a "modern house," which will not be built to live in but to attract attention to what a residence can be nowadays. I find it interesting because it's a project that will influence the minds of

the visitors. Norman, we have a publication for you that covers my work over the last 10 years.

NF — Incredible! How wonderful! I thought we were going to be shown the drawings. It's wonderful. I look forward to studying it.

HUO — And which is the most recent of all these new projects?

ON — It is a work on religion, a book about all of the churches and chapels that I have built throughout my career. I was amazed to see how many churches I have worked on, 23 of them!

Now I am working on a vast, beautiful cathedral in Belo Horizonte. I am an atheist, but the challenge of a cathedral is so beautiful, so rich, that it allows you to use many ideas.

NF — And it's wonderful that you're going back to the place of your first commission, which was also a church.

ON — Yes, that's true. I had to build a chapel, a little church. When we were going to start the design, I decided we would plan it without a pencil, just in my imagination. So I pictured a really big cross with the architecture of the church coming out from the arms of the cross. It's beautiful and simple: religion is marked by the cross, and the church emerges from it. We spent more time imagining the project than actually building it. Whenever I start a project, I already have an idea for it. We can imagine everything in our minds, even the interiors of a building.

NF — It is beautiful because the cross becomes the architecture! It is interesting that a very small chapel and the vast cathedral are both also about the public space, which leads you to the interior.

ON — The idea is very simple; it is just based on the cross.

NF — They are both very urban projects. Quite interesting.

ON — When I started working on the cathedral for Brasília, I thought I would make it round; then I stretched the columns and that was it! The problems with light and other things came later in the project, but the initial idea was to make more generous spaces, larger ones that become higher with the ceiling, so I could vary the architecture . . . We tend to want spans. When you go to Brasília, you will see the 180-meter-high Brasília Digital TV tower, made of concrete, which fits the city well.

In the Palace of Alvorada, instead of doing vertical columns, I did curved ones. They look nice. André Malraux was here, and he said that the curves were "the most beautiful columns since the Greek ones." Have you been to Greece, to the Parthenon? It has huge columns.

HUO — Do you have any unrealized dreams? Are there any projects you would like to work on?

ON — I would like to build a stadium, a completely different kind of stadium. I thought of doing one with a 200-meter-high dome, from which the stands would emerge. It is an interesting subject. I would also like to create a mosque. Work is what makes architecture pleasurable, but sometimes it's hard. I spend so much time thinking—thinking about the project, about the problems of it, about the conditions for edification. Architecture is fascinating. The works that I have seen of Foster are beautiful. We are always learning!

NF — It's a wonderful passion to share. We are very fortunate.
—

Eduardo Paes (EP)/ May 21, 2011 Rio de Janeiro

Eduardo Paes became the mayor of Rio de Janeiro in 2008. During his term, he has created programs such as Porto Maravilha (revitalization of the port area), Morar Carioca (urbanization of all the favelas), UPP Social (development of social programs in pacified favelas), the Rio Operations Centre (a high-tech nerve center that monitors all municipal logistics), and the establishment of the BRT system (four express corridors for articulated buses that will connect the whole city).

—

Gary Hustwit — How would you describe the urban of design of Rio de Janeiro?

Eduardo Paes — Rio is pretty different from most other cities because we've got a great natural asset here, which is nature. You've got the biggest urban forest right in the middle of the city, and great mountains, so it's always something that you need to deal with. How do you connect the design, what the architects and designers do to the city, to this beautiful view? This is the great advantage of this city. It's an asset, but at the same time, architects, or bad architects, can be mean to the city. I think that the biggest challenge for the city of Rio is, how do you build, how do you design while connecting with this natural shape of the city?

Rio has a great history. It's the only case of an empire, the Portuguese empire, where the emperor, escaping from Napoleon, came to his colony. So if you go to the beginning of the 19th century, you've got some great architecture from this period, from the period of the emperor living in the city. Then you go to the mid-20th century, and you've got the modern architects or the ones that were developing Brazil. This is a good phase for Rio with good examples of Rio architecture. You can also see terrible examples, where the design and the architecture almost fight with the beautiful landscape of the city.

GH — In terms the mayor's role in the urban design process, would you say it's a big one? Making decisions that shape the physical shape of the city and also the cultural character?

EP — In the case of Rio, the city has a weird history. It's a city that has been, at least in the 20th century and the beginning of the 21st century, kind of escaping from itself. If you look at the development of Rio, it starts from downtown, this neighborhood around here; goes to Copacabana, then it gets bad;

goes to Ipanema, then it gets bad; goes to Leblon, then it gets bad. The city of Rio has been growing to the west and always leaving the consolidated part of the city behind. What we're trying to do now is move back, not only because the cost is high to go to new neighborhoods, to go to new spaces, but because you've got great spaces that can be redeveloped.

The example of what I would like for my city is what we are doing in the port area. You've got a big, big area right in downtown Rio. It was completely abandoned. We're reshaping this area. We want this to be a big example of what we want to see. We want to rediscover areas of the city that we completely abandoned by going to new areas. Let's rediscover the areas we have.

GH — That brings up the idea of this heritage and conservation. It's a balance between conserving the old things in the city and the old buildings in the city and the old places and also leaving room for growth and for commercial rehabilitation. Can you talk a little bit about trying to keep that balance?

EP — I mean, like every city, you cannot miss the characteristics or the great architecture that you have. Once again, I will use this example of the downtown area, of this poor area. If you go there, you're going to see a place where the slaves would arrive in Brazil, where the slaves would arrive in the city of Rio, and there's great architecture there.

I think for a long time we stayed with this idea of conserving the old style of the city. There was kind of a conservative vision that said, okay, we should keep this area free of new buildings, of new architecture, and so this was not good for the city because things were kept as they were, but they were completely abandoned. So you got a bunch of conserved beauties, but they weren't being used. What we try to do now is, the city can have a mix. The difference for Rio is that it's a balance between the old architecture that goes with the nature of the city—I mean, you have to look at the skyline of the mountains—and how you can bring new construction, new architecture, new design to some areas of the city that are completely old.

That's why we decided in the port area to build a pier, which is a great pier. We needed something different there, so that's where you mix the old things and the modern things without being aggressive. I don't know if you're going to be able to show an image of the Museum of Tomorrow that Calatrava did, the project, but it's fantastic because it doesn't fight with the old architecture. It doesn't fight with the skyline of the mountains. It doesn't fight with the beautiful monastery that we have close by. So this is the kind of thing that we want to do now.

GH — Is there a bridge in the port area that's going to be demolished?

EP — Yeah, yeah. I mean, in Brazil, from the mid-20th century until the military dictatorship, there were some crazy things done. I would say it's the dictatorship of the car. Every time you start to build new roads, this is tough in Rio because of the mountains. The worst crime that has ever been done to the city was cutting the shoreline right in downtown, in Guanabara Bay, which has a beautiful view. From one side, you see Sugarloaf. From the other side, you see the skyline of the mountains, the interior of the state of Rio. Then you come and see the normal, horrible viaduct, so we're going to tear that down, build a tunnel in a certain area, and make the cars go underground. So this is something that is going to completely reopen things.

Most parts of Rio are very open to the sea, but when you go to the most beautiful area, which is downtown, it's degraded. It's the most beautiful area. Then you have this viaduct that is almost an obstacle between the city and the ocean.

GH — It seems like a lot of cities have the same issue. Seattle's doing the same thing.

EP — I mean, a great example is Barcelona. In spite of the fact that they don't have a viaduct there, they had train lines. And there's the example of Boston. There's a bunch of good examples all over the world where they are tearing down these viaducts.

I think it's a big change that has to do with what I said before. When you move further from downtown, when you make your city bigger, you will always need more cars. When you need more cars, when you go further, you need these crazy things like viaducts and big tunnels and big roads.

When we decide to reinvest and rediscover some consolidated areas of the city, we're telling people, you are going to live close to where you work. This mix of places to work and places to live, it's the right thing to do. So that's the only way we can tear down viaducts, and people can walk. People can use the bike lanes. Rio is not as easy as Copenhagen, as Amsterdam. It's kind of hot here, so it's not easy to go to work during the summertime by bike, but if you get people closer, then that's going to be a great change in the city.

GH — Yeah, because I imagine density is a kind of a unique thing here. There's only so dense you can get with the hills. I don't know how many more people you can have in Botafogo, for instance. But there's that argument of density versus sprawl and spreading out. Could you talk a little bit about urban design and disaster risk prevention and about how those factors are affecting Rio's design, or the kinds of things that you or any mayor has to think about when it comes to preparing for environmental risks?

EP — When you talk about natural disasters in Rio, you talk about rain. We have tropical rains every summer, and Rio, with all the hills it has, has a history of great disasters, great floods, and people dying. When you live in a country like Brazil, when you live in a city like Rio with so many social differences—the law says you cannot build on the hills; you cannot build on the mountains, but then there's the necessity of the poor people. So they build, and there's this characteristic of the urbanization of Rio, which is the slums, the favelas. This is something very interesting about

Rio because you have the really poor people living in some of the most valuable areas of the city. I mean, some of the favelas of Rio have the best view of the city. Right in front of Copacabana beach, if you go to some of the favelas, you can see the best view of the city.

So Rio has a challenge, which is, we are not moving the slums from where they are, so how can they be safe there, and what kind of things can you build there that are not very aggressive so they don't fight with the view of the mountains, of the hills? It's something that we always try to protect, the nature, the hills. Not only because of beauty but because of the possibility of natural disasters, and at the same time, it's always a challenge: how to keep these people there, how to urbanize these favelas, how to get urbanization that does not fight with the mountains. That's the characteristic of our city. We're not going to change that. We're not going to get rid of the poor people in these central areas. We used to see the favelas as a big problem. I mean, they are a problem, but they are there. They are a reality of the city. So how can you get this mix of people, which I think is always good for a city, poor and rich people, getting together?

There's something else about Rio that I'd like to say here. No city in the world has a more democratic space than Rio. When you talk about the beach, if you go to Ipanema, if you go to Copacabana, what you see is the richest lady lying right next to the poorest lady from the slum, and probably most of the time, the poorest lady has a much more beautiful view than the richest lady. This mix is good. That's what makes Rio very open. That's what makes Rio very friendly. That's what makes Rio very relaxing. It's not a formal city, and I think it's much because of this mix.

GH — Can you talk a little bit about technology? I know that Rio's been doing things with IBM. Can you talk about the technological tools that you can use? How would you apply those to a city like this, how can they help, and what are the issues that you look at with them?

EP — That's a big priority for us. We just built an operations center for the city. You can use technology not only for preventing disaster. We're building up, with IBM, a forecast system so that we can see the floods coming and get the city ready for disaster. We're using technology not just for security, which is the usually case in most of the cities in the world. What we're trying to do here is say, how can we take care of the people using technology?

With this operations center that we built, we can get all the departments of the city together, at least those that deal with the everyday life of the people. With the information you can get, with the changes you can make in the traffic, in the sewage system, you can really change the everyday life of the city. I don't know if you went to our operations center, but it's fantastic. You've got all the departments of the city there. We've got a big screen, bigger than NASA's. That's what I like. If NASA's gets bigger, I'll make my operations crew's screen bigger too.

The other thing is, how can we connect to people? There's obviously the issue of democracy or representative democracy, which is the best system developed until now, so we're going to stick with that. We're going to still be a democracy, a democratic country, a democratic city. But most of the people don't feel that they are represented by even the mayor or a local city council member. So we got a system from IBM that can help address that. It's a system that IBM uses inside its company that we're going to use too. We can go to a certain neighborhood, and people will have the opportunity for like a week to use this system, this software that IBM developed, which they call Jam, and people will be able to tell the mayor what's important for that specific neighborhood.

We also copied New York's 311 system, that allows people to call in and report issues in their neighborhood. Here we have something that's called 1746. So you've got many tools that allow you to have direct contact between the public servants and the people of the city. We try to use lots of technology now.

GH — Let's talk about urban design and crime and violence. Are there ways to change the actual, physical design of the city or the favelas to have an impact on violence reduction?

EP — I mean, completely. When you put good lights on the streets, you completely change the security of the place. The big problem that we face is that there aren't big roads inside the favelas. There are always narrow streets, and obviously that's bad for security. When we talk about favelas, when we talk about urbanizing favelas, the first thing we try to do is at least open one big road. At least open big spaces for squares where people can meet because the favelas in Rio don't have open spaces. When you don't have open spaces, you don't have people on the streets. When you don't have people on the streets, when you have narrow streets, there's much more crime. All the projects we're doing to urbanize favelas try to deal with this issue.

Then there's the urbanized area of the city, the consolidated area of the city, where all the time we try to build things to take care of the security issue. And that's open spaces. That's the question of how you deal with nature, not having nature build up dark spaces. We're against surrounding squares with fences. In Rio, we think they're supposed to be open all the time, 24 hours a day. These are the kind of things we try to deal with.

GH — You've got the World Cup in 2014; you've got the Olympics in 2016. This is obviously unique to Rio, but for any city, how do large events like this impact it?

EP — It's a great opportunity. When you talk about the World Cup, when you talk about the Olympics, even the word "Olympic" means something that is hard to achieve. So when you are an Olympic city, when you have the Olympics coming to your city, it's the time to do the things that are hard to achieve. It's the time when you can dream, and that can change a lot.

I remember some advice that I got from Pasqual Maragall, the former mayor of Barcelona. I think Rio has a lot of similarities with Barcelona. He told me, "Eduardo, there are two kinds of Olympic Games. There's the kind of Olympic Games that uses the city, and then there's the city that uses the Olympic Games." Barcelona did that, and that's what Rio's going to do. We're trying to use the Olympic Games to make big changes here. You can convince people that things that are hard to do are possible, because you've got to schedule; it's got to be ready by that certain date. So you can make big physical changes in your city. We can completely change the transportation system in Rio. I mean, these days we've got like 15 percent of the people using mass transport. By 2016, we're going to have 50 percent of the people using mass transport.

Another thing is that you can change the culture of the people concerning their city. Rio, for the residents, the Cariocas, is like their wife or their mother-in-law. They can say bad things about them, but they never let other people say bad things about them. So the relation of the Cariocas with the city is interesting because everybody's so proud of Rio, everybody's so in love with Rio, but we don't take very good care of the city.

So the Olympics also means an opportunity to change the culture of the people in how they deal with the city. I mean, it's crazy how much garbage the Cariocas put on the streets. It's almost 40 percent of our garbage costs. Not collecting garbage from people's houses, but collecting garbage in streets. So these are things that we can try to work on. It's a great opportunity to change the way we deal with the city, with the infrastructure of the city, and the Olympic Games are going to be used to make those changes.

GH — But when the games are done, how will those infrastructure changes continue to affect the city?

EP — The interesting thing about the IOC, the International Olympic Committee, is that when they decide to go to a certain place, they are always worried about legacy. We're building almost a hundred kilometers of Bus Rapid Transit here. It's not a subway. It's using buses. It's a smarter way to do it. It started in Brazil, in Curitiba. Nobody who comes to the Olympic Games, not the athletes, not even the media, are going to use our BRTs. But because we put on the legacy plan of the city that we were going to build BRTs, they are going to be built. So the Olympic Games has a lot to do with legacy. What can be left for your city for the next day after the Games end?

I'm going to give two examples here, cities that I think are similar to Rio, and I hope I'm not going to be offensive to anyone, but look at Athens, and look at Barcelona. I mean, Athens, they did lots of great construction. It's a fantastic city, but it's still the same. The Olympic Games didn't change the way we see Athens or the everyday life of the Greek people that live in Athens. When you go to Athens, you still go to the Acropolis, see the Parthenon, and then you get a ship and go to the islands.

But look at Barcelona. In Barcelona, what they did was so intelligent and so smart that they changed the urbanization of the city, the way the city deals with itself, the way people deal with the city, and the image of the city. So this is our opportunity. It's how we see the games from a legacy point of view for the city.

GH — Could you tell us a little more about your operations center?

EP — We're learning every day there. We inaugurated it on the 31st of December last year, so it's been running for five months, and we learn every day. You've got all the technology, but you've got to change the culture of the people. How can you make them work together? How do you use all the tools you have available there? Say there's a traffic problem in an area; you've got a tow truck close by. How do you connect that guy and make him get there faster? It's very interesting.

GH — What are the different operations that happen in the center?

EP — It ranges from traffic lights to the sanitation department of the city to what we call civil defense here, which is taking care of disasters if they happen. There's social assistance. There's the subway. There's the trains. There's the power company. There's the gas company. You've got all that on a big screen, and using those tools, you can make a big difference. You've got the school system. You've got the health system, all the hospitals. You can connect straight to someone in a hospital.

Let me give you an example: If you see in the power grid that there is a lack of energy in a certain area of the city, you can see where the schools are there, and call the director of the school and say, "Okay, you're going to be without power for five hours. Make preparations." The nice thing about it, the beauty of it, is that it works 24 hours, seven days a week. Because I know that mayors, what we suffer from most is when it's the middle of the night and something happens. What are you going to do? So you've got to have someone empowered by you to make the decision there. You've got to have the opportunity for someone to reach you so you can make the right decision. So with this operations center, if they cannot reach the mayor, the COO there has complete power. He can do whatever he wants. He's the boss at that time, and he has everything available for him to make the decision there, and that is a big, big difference.

GH — Can we talk a little more about that balance of informal development, the favelas, of people just kind of taking their own initiative, versus the formal development and how the city plans for it or responds to it?

EP — That's a characteristic of Rio that we cannot say is a good characteristic. You cannot let people do whatever they want in the city. What we're trying to do now is say, okay, we have a reality. We need to deal with it and try to formalize the favelas. Get some rules. I mean, they cannot be as strict rules as they are on the asphalt down here, but we've got rules. You've got to put public services there. When I say public services, I'm not only talking about education, health, and social assistance. I'm talking about having the law there, and I'm not talking only about police work. I'm talking about, okay, if you have a law that the height of a house can only be two floors, and the guy there starts to build a third one, you've got to be tough with him.

What we've been trying to do is make the favelas more formal and, at the same time, make the law in Rio, the urban law, more of a reality. Because sometimes the rules are so strict that you're almost telling people, "Be informal." Because we don't want you to do this, we don't want you to do that, and people do it. So when you're in the more developed parts of the city, you can be less strict. When you go the slums, you need to be a little bit more strict.

GH — Do you want to talk about other cities that you enjoy going to? Do you have favorite cities?

EP — I like messy cities. Let me try to explain that. [Laughing.] Let me try to explain. I like cities; it's obvious. Because what cities are is a fantastic mix of people. There are beautiful places. I don't want to be offensive again, but just last week I was in Switzerland—beautiful. If you go to Lausanne, Geneva, Zürich, they're so perfect, but I would never live there. When you go to a place like Paris, when you go to a place like London, when you go to a place like New York, what you see is this mix of people. And that's what I mean when I say I like the mess of a city. It's like there's a certain lack of rules sometimes, which is necessary for people to interact.

Rio is special that way. The meeting points in Rio are the streets. Because of this culture of going to the beach, because of this beautiful nature that we have, people are always outside. So I like cities where people are outside, where people get together, where you have this mix of poor and rich, of all kinds of natural beauty. I like cities like that. That's why I like my city.

GH — [Laughs.] That's good.

EP — I'm against all public order in Rio. I need to do it, but I'm against it.

GH — Really?

EP — Just kidding. But it's interesting. There's a place called Baxio Gávea. It's a bunch of bars, very informal. People that live there, they want to shoot those people drinking beer on the streets. And there are some restaurants, and the guys put the tables on the sidewalk, and the law doesn't allow that. I mean, I'm the mayor, I need to follow the law, but if it was a matter of my opinion, I'd say just put the tables there. The other day, city workers went there and took one of the tables away while this guy was sitting having a beer. So he sat down on the sidewalk, and put his beer there and kept drinking. I would've done the same as that guy. We need to understand that we need to have people on the streets in cities. If people are inside, indoors, the city's not a livable place.

So, obviously, you need to respect rules. I mean, you've got the problems of people wanting to sleep and other people are drinking and making a mess, but there's a line there. You cannot go too far in either direction. You need to respect that because these are the characteristics of cities. People need to be on the streets.

GH — Yeah, Jan Gehl, the Danish architect, has said you can gauge the success of a city by the amount of time people spend outside and in the downtown area. It's about inviting people to do that.

EP — There are these two artists who come from São Paulo. They are living in Rio now, and the other day I met them, and I said, "Do you like Rio? I mean, do you enjoy it?" One of them said, "Yes, I like it, but the culture is so different." I said, "Why?" And she said, "Because, you know, the Cariocas always say, 'Okay, see you.' They pass by. They never invite you to their homes." And I said, "Because we don't go home here. We are all in the streets, so we're going to meet in the streets."

If you go to Leblon, Ipanema, if you go to the suburbs, there's this great culture. If you go to the suburbs of Rio, the neighborhoods where the houses are, you know where people talk? They put their chairs on the sidewalks. The gossip goes on there. That's what makes Rio Rio.
—

Noah Chasin (NC)/ May 30, 2011 New York

Noah Chasin teaches the history and theory of urban design at Columbia University's Graduate School of Architecture, Planning, and Preservation.

—

Gary Hustwit — First, could you talk about all the players involved in urban design?

Noah Chasin — The thing about urban design is, unlike a solitary enterprise of an artist sitting in her or his studio, what you really have is a multidisciplinary group of people coming together, working on the same project but coming from very different perspectives, having different agendas and different roles. You've got the designer or the group of designers. You have the developer or the group of developers. You have the state and federal and city agencies. You have the public, which is a major component. You have landmarks commissions or other historically minded groups. They all come together trying to find what is at stake in the project and to work against and with each other in order to bring it to fruition.

You begin with the site. Then you bring the people in. The preliminary design is proposed. Then you move forward and start to engage the different players and the different actors. It really is a dramatis personae. This is not an isolated enterprise. It is something that is always dynamic. It is always a struggle for agency, and this is something that is very unique about urban design as opposed to any other creative enterprise.

GH — And what are the forces that shape cities? Even outside of design, I'm thinking about things like war and natural disasters. Some cities are planned and designed and well thought out. Others are completely out of our control.

NC — It's very different to talk about a city that is what I like to call a palimpsest, layers of different historical accretions over time, which may have just started as a small settlement and has grown into a megalopolis. Other times you have fully planned cities that have sprung up from a tabula rasa and began from the sketch or design of a single individual or group of individuals. Then when you talk about war, when you talk about natural disasters, those are things that can never be really fully anticipated. Although, I think increasingly we can anticipate some things given what we have experienced and drawing upon the history and the knowledge we have of what happens to cities in natural and man-made disasters, you know, if you think about World War II, if you think about New Orleans or the Philippines. It's all of these different factors that one has to take into account. It's definitely something that I think a lot of urban designers are starting to take much more seriously. Sort of the prophylactic approach.

GH — [Laughing.] The prophylactic approach?
    NC — Well, that's the correct usage of that term.

GH — I think most people will think . . .
    NC — Well, it does mean that. I use that in class all the time, and people don't usually crack up, although I always figure that they're going to.

GH — Could you give us a sort of 100 AD to the late 1800s CliffsNotes-style history lesson on cities?
    NC — Historically, cities, as I have said, have come into being for many different reasons. I think you could say that most cities began with some sort of a concatenation of individuals living in a particular place. Whether they were living there for protective reasons; whether they were living there because of a shared set of cultural beliefs; whether they were living there as a result of staving off a natural enemy, whether it be animals or weather, typically you find people sort of grouping together, and gradually that builds outward.

If you think about some of the earliest cities, even going back to Roman times, first century AD, you find cities on the tops of hills with walls around them. Those walls are there obviously for protection, as is the hill, you know, this advantage that one has being at the top of a hill in terms of surveillance, in terms of protection. The walled city is circumscribed. It only has a certain amount of space, so you start to deal with issues of density. That's when you start to have the spread of cities or the movement of people to different areas.

As you move forward in time, you find that cities grow up around very specific logistical issues, for example, on a port or at the foot of a mountain, somewhere that is advantageous specifically for trade. It's almost always an economic question. It's close to a trade route. It's close to a port. It's close to a place for distribution, import and export. The idea of the city as an entity is something that is never just born out of the mind of a designer. It's always tied to specific needs of that particular area, drawing upon natural resources, using the topography to be, usually, as protected as possible in some of the ways that I mentioned earlier and then also to be as advantageous as possible in terms of an increasingly global flow of capital, as we see much more now in the 21st century.

GH — Can you talk about the various movements in urban planning like City Beautiful?
    NC — Sure. By the mid-1800s, industrialization had been a reality for a couple of decades already in the major cities of Western Europe. The congestion, the insalubrity, the unlivability of those cities made it such that there needed to be some sort of solution. What ends up happening

in Paris, which is the famous example of modernization, is that Baron Haussmann under Napoleon III comes in and radically demolishes the city, eliminating all its medieval streets, its slums, its areas that don't really function in a modern way, and rebuilds the city with the concentric arrondissement articulation that we have now and the common street facade, the roof line, the roundabouts, and other iconic elements of Paris. That sets the tone for the kind of modernization that can start to happen and does begin to happen throughout Europe.

In the United States, we were also having an industrial revolution of some sort. It wasn't quite as acutely felt within the cities as it was in Europe. America was struggling with something else, which is it didn't have a really strong architectural legacy going back further than a hundred years at that point and, in fact, was struggling with the precise problem of having a kind of eclecticism that made it very difficult to understand what an American style would be. There was, of course, no real vernacular style because we hadn't been here that long—Americans, that is. There wasn't any sort of inherited style. You had the English. You had the Germans. You had Eastern Europeans. There were all these different cultures that were moving here en masse during the later 19th century. They were bringing with them different vernacular styles, but you still had within the schools of architecture, as you did in Europe, the academic style, which is neoclassicism. Everything is based on the Greek and Roman archetype. That was seen as very good for civic building but not necessarily good for a more pedestrian type of building. In the late 19th century, this eclecticism was really starting to weigh on the minds of people who were thinking large scale about America's cities.

Daniel Burnham, who was a very important architect and city planner, as they were called at the time, an innovator and somebody who was extremely well respected in Chicago, started to advocate for a neoclassical approach to the city. In 1893, with the World's Columbian Exposition that was held in Chicago, these gigantic grounds that were built for this exposition were done in a thoroughly neoclassical style, eliminating any kind of eclecticism, eliminating any sort of variance that would be at odds with a strict neoclassical orthodoxy. It was a wildly successful exhibition to many people, except for a lot of forward-thinking architects, Louis Sullivan included, who had actually participated in the show but who believed that this exposition set American architecture back several centuries as a result of its reactionary response to, for example, the skyscraper style, which was introducing a new, American vernacular into the architectural landscape of cities.

City Beautiful was a movement that came out of the 1893 World's Columbian Exposition and was started by Daniel Burnham to try to bring the axial, symmetrical grand boulevards and large civic arenas of classical architecture into American cities. That was already present at the World's Columbian Exposition. Some of the other people involved in this were Fredrick Law Olmsted, who is the designer of Central Park among many other parks. The success of the World's Columbian Exposition gave strength to the City Beautiful movement.

GH — Can give some other examples of buildings or squares that are specifically based on City Beautiful?

    NC — I can give you some examples of plans that were based on it. The first real plan to benefit from this or to be an example of the City Beautiful movement was the Mall in Washington, DC, which came together as a result of Burnham and a group of others, who decided to level out the mall to make it into a grand civic space in our nation's capital directly in front of the major civic buildings and to organize that space in such a way as to make it a place for gathering, presumably for public discourse but also for just public life in general. Rather than having a city that was decentralized, to give it a visible and functional center. You see the same thing in other cities: There's the Civic Center in Philadelphia. There's the Civic Center in San Francisco. There's the Civic Center in Cleveland. These are all different areas that were direct results of the City Beautiful movement—these grand plazas usually with civic buildings on the periphery, large lawns in the center, and they are typically places for gatherings of various sorts, whether it's concerts or debates or other forms of political activity.

GH — Or drug dealing.

    NC — Drug dealing sometimes. The thing is that they are radically public. They are articulated as a vast, grand, symmetrical public space. Actually, the notion of antisocial behavior is kind of prohibited by the very plan itself. That's the whole point of the City Beautiful—that if you maintain the rigorous orthogonal, geometric, axial, symmetrical logic of classical architecture and classical planning, then people will become just the same way. In other words, they will also be falling into line and acting in a way that's becoming of this monumental, grand, beautiful space. That was the idea. This is a prevailing idea in urban design, that people are influenced by their spaces and that, if you create a space that has sort of a grandeur, that celebrates itself as a special place, people walking into that space will feel something of the genius loci, the specificity of the space, and will act accordingly.

GH — Do you think that ever really works?

    NC — No. I think it's quite the opposite. This is the same problem that the modern movement, which I am sure we will talk about a little later, got into, which is that it presumed that a space can have a universal effect on a group of people, not taking into account something that exists at the very heart of human interactivity, which is antagonism and disagreement and debate. I don't mean that in a bad way. I mean in a good way. You can't have orderliness and disagreement perfectly meshed within each other. There has to be the possibility of transgression. That's why very often these civic spaces turn into the sorts of spaces that are a little bit dodgy.

Garden city was the next real movement in the sort of urban configurations. Ebenezer Howard, in the late 19th century, came up with the idea of the garden city, which was a self-contained economic entity, a new typology for a city that was in proximity to a larger city but was fully and entirely enclosed unto itself. It had industry. It had agriculture. It had its own administrative functions. Through a very complicated shareholder relationship with a group of so-called responsible citizens, it was an economically self-sustaining venture in which the people bought into the garden city shareholders' association, and thus it didn't have to rely upon taxes from elsewhere or pay taxes to a larger city.

The garden city proved to be incredibly durable and was in fact incredibly influential on the modernist movement. In the late twenties, when CIAM, the International Congresses of Modern Architecture, got together to really foreground the notion of a modernist architecture as the appropriate response to the increasing modernization of everyday life, it was an attempt to try to do away with the tyranny of classicism, with this enduring sense that orthogonality and axial symmetry was the only way to functionally construct a proper city. It was through the four functions that CIAM came up with, which were living, working, recreation, and transportation—which were already articulated by Ebenezer Howard in the late 19th century—that the functional aspect of the city was conceived. All of the modernist projects that you see coming out of the twenties and into the early thirties are based upon these four functions that were codified in a document called the Athens Charter in 1933.

When you think about the typical modernist city, you see that the plan is literally striated out into these different bands separated by greenbelts. All of the different functions are separated out. The different forms of transportation, automobile traffic, air traffic as they imagined it to be part of the city experience, and pedestrian traffic were all separated out, so you didn't have to worry about walking around and getting hit by a car. The greenbelts provided areas for recreation and also just contemplation. They were set up as buffers between, let's say, the administrative realm and the domestic realm. Industry was at the periphery just as it was with the garden city movement. You have this kind of fully formed idea that is not based upon the axiality of classical planning but, rather, is something that is meant to be fully functional.

The way that Le Corbusier would have thought about it is, just as he called a house a machine for living in, this city would be a machine also for living in, but for a much larger group of people. In effect, the city was meant to be as economical and as functional as an automobile or a steamship or an airplane, where there are no extraneous parts, where all of the different functions are completely separated out, and where everything works independently but also all together as a perfectly functioning whole.

GH — Could you talk about Brasília? How did the ideas of Le Corbusier and the modernist movement lead into that?

NC — Le Corbusier was the most influential of the modernist city planners and architects. His idea of the modern city was first articulated in the *Ville Contemporaine*, then later fully articulated in the radiant city, the *Ville Radieuse* from 1930. Those were projects that really took these four functions from the Athens Charter and brought them to bear on an ideal city. The *Ville Contemporaine* and the *Ville Radieuse* were both sort of idealized notions of a city that could be built somewhere, perhaps anywhere. These two plans—both of which, by the way, were very heavily influenced by the garden city—became the benchmark of modernist city planning. You see any number of iterations of this up through the thirties, at which point all architecture and all urban design more or less stopped during the war, to be commenced after the war.

Then very quickly, in 1947 when the partition of the Indian subcontinent happens, Nehru decides to build a new capital city once Lahore has been partitioned off and given to Pakistan. (That was the capital of the region.) This is where we see it starting to happen on a grand, international scale. Eventually Corbusier is given the opportunity to build his radiant city in the city of Chandigarh, which is a new capital city. It was deliberately chosen for its central location, although it's not actually really centrally located in India, but it was meant to be a symbolic capital that was no longer tied to the colonialist past of India. A new city, a tabula rasa, and Corbusier is finally getting his opportunity to build this, and this is one of his great achievements in urban design.

One of his disciples, Lúcio Costa, is given, about a decade later, the opportunity to do a similar thing in Brazil—because of a newly elected governor, the desire to move the capital away from the coast lands where the traditional seat of power had been, also issues of colonialism—to create a new capital city. The city of Brasília was designed by Lúcio Costa and eventually with the collaboration of his former student Oscar Niemeyer. Brasília is a city that, like Chandigarh, was built in a sort of tabula rasa situation in a completely new area with no restrictions whatsoever, as if it was an alien city that had just landed somewhere in the middle of a field.

GH — Was that the peak of the modernist ideal?
NC — Yeah, Brasília in many ways represented the first time that the possibility of a modernist urban design could actually be realized. The *Ville Radieuse* plan was always something that was very idealized. It saw its first full articulation in Brasília. That was commissioned in 1955. It represents the first fully modernized city built from the ground up.

Urban design as a discreet discipline has actually only existed since 1956. In 1956, the Harvard School of Design had an interdisciplinary panel symposium on this question of urban design, which stated that the notion of planning, as it had been called before, or city planning or urban planning, all of which are very different things from urban design, needed to be rethought and put under the label of urban design. Josep Lluís Sert, a Spanish architect then working in New York who was the former president of CIAM, had stated that it was the interdisciplinarity—they invited real estate developers; they invited sociologists; they invited architects, landscape designers, all sorts of different disciplines to this conference—that meant that urban design cannot be done by architects alone. It needs to be a separate discipline.

The proceedings of that conference were then published in *Progressive Architecture* in 1956. That was the first time that the term "urban design" was used, as discreet from town planning or urban planning or architecture. I mean, it was always practiced by architects before that, or landscape designers, but it was never thought of as a separate discipline. This is now why we have, in architecture schools, architecture, urban planning, and urban design, and they are completely separate disciplines. It's important to know.

GH — Can you talk about cars, the impact of cars on the design of cities?

NC — The 1950s is when the automobile starts to have a real impact on cities, especially American cities, and largely a detrimental effect. Not only do you have increased means of access to the city, the tunnels and bridges bringing more cars into the cities creating congestion and noise and other insalubrious conditions, but also radically changing how cities are designed. You have suburban sprawl, which comes as a result of the sense of entitlement and self-determination that Americans feel with regard to how they live. They want to live in a solitary home. They want to have an individual car that allows them to drive exactly the way they want to, from their home, to their office, to their place of recreation, and back again. Suburban sprawl is increasingly becoming a global issue, especially in developing countries.

GH — Speaking of suburbs, can you talk more about their develpoment?

NC — What is very curious about suburbs is that, from the beginning of recorded time, there has been this vacillation between the desirability of living in the periphery of the city and then living in the center. This goes back and forth throughout time. I would say that probably in the 1950s is really when the major suburban sprawl starts happening in the United States, but it's even going back—if you think of Brooklyn Heights as one of the first suburbs ever—even back into the 1850s. But with the rise of suburbia in the 1950s, you have a whole new typology of living, these bedroom communities that exist outside the city that are facilitated by an increasing amount of automobile ownership and the ease with which people can get in and out of the city as a result of bridges and tunnels being built to facilitate that kind of access for people that live in the periphery.

The concern that arises is that the result of increasing suburbanization is the loss of the heart of the city. This is something that was a preoccupation of many of the architects in the so-called avant-garde, who really railed against this suburbanization and worried about the loss of the civic center, of the public sphere that existed only in an urban context.

Jane Jacobs—who is a community advocate who really believes in living in the city but having a mixed-use, vibrant neighborhood feel within the city—is somebody who really resists both the sort of monumentalization of the city that we talked about earlier with the City Beautiful movement and also the suburban sprawl, feeling that one can have the kind of neighborhood feeling in the city while still having all of the enticements of the city. One of the big missed opportunities in her mind is that the city is not well organized in such a way as to create a mixed-use environment, that there's large swathes of the city, for example, Wall Street, where there are people there from seven until three, and then nothing goes on at night. For her, to be able to spread the activities of the city out over the entire city, rather than having parcels which are more residential or more business oriented, would be a way of creating these kinds of neighborhoods and these kinds of experiences that people are fleeing the city to try to find, when in fact, if there were just a certain set of negotiations that took place within the city, they could find that sort of experience within the context of the city itself.

GH — Could you talk about Detroit and the different responses to the Detroit scenario?

NC — Yeah. Detroit, which maybe more so than any other American city is identified with industry, has become such an anti-industrial city now that we have to look at it through a completely different lens. I would almost use the term self-organized urbanism to describe what is going on there, which is something that is happening globally, but in the sense that there is a kind of possibility, a sort of DIY aesthetic that does in fact exist in the city that is allowing for a lot of individual initiatives to happen that, because of various ordinances and legal issues, in any other city would be impossible. Not to say exactly that it is the Wild West frontier, but it's certainly a city that is open to an interpretive impulse that I think a lot of other cities don't have right now.

You see that in the urban agricultural movement not only with community gardens but also these large-scale commercial gardens. You see it with the repurposing of, for example, small churches whose congregations have abandoned them. They are turning them into community centers. There are all sorts of different retrofitting practices not only on an urban scale but also on an architectural microscale that are happening in the city, that are happening as a result of the fact that the city itself physically is too large for its population.

This issue of shrinking is something that is in fact a problem with a lot of major cities. We've seen huge decreases in the populations in many major cities across the world and then gigantic growth in other cities. But regarding the question of rightsizing the city, of creating a community that is the proper size for the city, and the question of sustainability, which is one of the things that lies at the heart of this whole question of shrinking cities—cities are not going to be able to maintain themselves at certain sizes as a result of issues of sustainability. The notion of sustainable growth or sustainable development is a very heavily criticized one. There is no such thing. People such as Herman Daly argue sustainable growth is a kind of mythopoeic idea that says, as long as we are cognizant and aware and responsible, then things will continue to grow; no. In fact, there needs to be a qualitative growth as opposed to a quantitative one. The shrinking-cities phenomenon is one of the ones that really needs to be addressed through this kind of logic. Sustainability, from an economic, from an environmental, and from a social perspective, is something that needs to be taken into account when a city such as Detroit tries to rebuild itself.

GH — One a personal level, which cities do you like, and which cities do you dislike?

NC — It would be easy to say that I love New York City because I live here and because it's a city that I know better than any other city. In terms of cities that I dislike in particular just in terms of the experience of them, I always sort of feel like, when you arrive in a city, you get a great feeling about it, or you get a slightly queasy feeling about it, an almost alienated feeling about it. One of the cities that I have been to probably five times and yet have not ever been able to reconcile myself to is Athens, a city that in so many ways is thought of as the epitome of democracy and great culture. It actually doesn't have a great planning tradition. In fact, Athens is a chaotic city. It's a dirty city. It's not a very attractive city. If you go to the Acropolis, you see that it's surrounded by congested urban detritus. It's a very alienating city to me.

GH — And other cities? What are some cities that you like that you travel to? What are some of your favorite cities to go to and why?

NC — I really love—I only spent two weeks there—Istanbul, which is a really fascinating city, largely because of the profoundly multicultural nature of it. New York is multicultural in one sense, but you don't have a thoroughly Islamic culture living cheek by jowl with a thoroughly secular society as you do in Istanbul. The mix of the sort of modern and the ancient, the incredible complexity of the city not only in terms of its social fabric but also in terms of its terrain, the river running through it, the Asian side versus the European side—it's an extremely complicated and difficult but incredibly rewarding city to be in.

GH — Are there other ones that you hate?

NC — Of course, easily my least favorite city in the United States is Washington, DC. Unlike many capital cities, it's sort of the low point of one's experience in traveling to a country, in particular with all of the racial tension that exists there and this complete seeming obliviousness to that; the design of the city, which seems so utterly sterile and yet, once you move outside of the civic areas, is just completely chaotic; the real socioeconomic strata that are more purposefully put in place than I have seen in any other city, certainly in the United States.

GH — What else?

NC — Another city that I really love is Moscow. Moscow, like Istanbul, although not nearly as multicultural, is a city that I have been to only in post-Soviet times, but it's so ruthless and so edgy and so kind of terrifying in a certain way just because of its massiveness. You've got the ring of Stalinist skyscrapers on the periphery and then just this maddening rush of extraordinarily attractive, wealthy people mixed with the general mass of people all spinning around in this city center. Then you go down into the subway, and I think infrastructure is something that always is very telling about a city. As probably a lot of people know, the Moscow subway system is the only thing that ever worked under the Soviet system. It is fantastic. It runs to the second. Every single station is dedicated to a different historical figure or a different theme. They're beautifully designed. They are efficient and clean and comprehensive throughout the city and very, very easy to negotiate even if you can't read Cyrillic.

GH — Talk about the future of the city and the city form and the sustainability of the city. What are some of your thoughts about that?

NC — I definitely believe that cities are going to have to be more autonomous and less heteronomous—in other words, less top-down planning and more bottom-up planning. I think a lot of the principles of self-organized or ad hoc urbanism are going to come to the fore and be incorporated in a much more deliberate way, in other words, encouraged as opposed to just happening. Places like Lagos, where it just sort of happens out of necessity, are one thing. But the idea behind self-organized cities is a really powerful one that I don't think has been fully embraced yet by the urban design community in the sense that the paradox of giving form to a city that is in fact a very organic, multivalent object with many different citizens doing many different things seems very difficult to reconcile.

The idea of a self-organized city is one where the inhabitants, all of whom have very specific needs and requirements and desires, are taken into account by the designer or the group of designers such that the form of the city accurately reflects that which the citizens themselves are requiring and/or desiring. It's almost a sort of a feedback loop whereby the designers are soliciting advice from the inhabitants, who then create, through the mind of the designer, the kind of city that will best and most effectively meet their needs.

GH — I think a lot of times it feels like people either like a space or they don't, but the design of it is probably something that they don't specifically think about.

NC — Yeah, it's a shame that people don't spend more time ruminating on their urban environment. One of the things that will help to make future cities more effective and more responsive to individuals' needs is if people really think about what it means to walk through a city and what it means to experience a specific spot in the city, realizing that everybody experiences a city in a very different way. The great thing about spaces is that there is no universal monolithic way of experiencing a space, especially an urban space. One person may be looking down at the ground. One person may be looking straight forward. One person may be looking up. In each case, they are going to have a very different spatial awareness and spatial experience of the city.

Being aware of your environment (and I mean that in a very literal sense, sort of an empirical sense) looking around, noticing whether a boulevard is a wide one or whether a street is a very narrow one, recognizing what it means to be caught in the midst of a bunch of high-rises versus being out in a space that is much less densely occupied by buildings and people— these sorts of things, just the sensory response to being in a space is something that a lot of people don't really stop to think about. Especially in an urban context, which tends to have an accelerated cycle of existence, people don't really stop to think about things. If more people could spend some time thinking about what could be improved in a city or, how would my life be more enjoyable if the city could configure itself in such a way as to facilitate this or that?—that's something that I think is a lost opportunity.

I do think that over the past 10 years architecture and urban design have come more to the forefront. There are more people blogging about it. There are more people reading about it in the newspapers, seeing it on the Internet, and thinking about it and having discussions about it. I just would like to see that proliferate. For me, that will only feed into what I really believe to be the future of urban design, which is this kind of reciprocal relationship between the inhabitant and the designer. Unless there is that reciprocity, that give and take, that discussion and dialogue, people will get cities that are designed without an awareness of the cultural, historical, even economic nuances that exist within the city. It is very important. As cities become more ethnically diverse, there are going to be even more needs that need to be met by the city. Every ethnic group has different cultural needs, different religious needs, different social needs. Taking into account the increased ethnic diversity that we're finding in cities is going to mean that cities are going to have to be retrofitted to accommodate these new types of populations.

GH — Is there anything else you can think of that you would want to see discussed in the film?

NC — The only other thing that I would say is that I don't think people have given enough thought to the sustainability of cities and that in fact living in an urban environment has a lot of beneficial effects with regard to sustainability, which people don't necessarily realize. They think that cities are the most profligate users of fossil fuels. In fact, it's often quite the opposite, that it's a much more economical way of living and a much more sustainable way of living. I would like to see more studies done that show the feasibility of sustainable design practice on an urban scale.

—

Mark Covington (MC)/
June 3, 2011
Detroit

Mark Covington is a lifelong resident of Detroit and the founder of the Georgia Street Community Gardens. Mark was out of work and began cleaning up empty lots near his grandmother's house, only intending to get rid of the litter and garbage. But as he cleared away the corner, he became inspired to turn it into a community garden to help revitalize his troubled neighborhood.

There's been no shortage of media coverage on the challenges facing Detroit, but I was interested in the idea that one person can still make a difference in their city, no matter how modest the project.

—

Gary Hustwit — You grew up in this neighborhood?
Mark Covington — Yeah, I grew up right down the street. Actually, I grew up all around here.

GH — What are your memories of this area when you were a kid?
MC — I remember being known by everybody and knowing everybody. There's hardly any house around here that I, or my brothers, didn't go in. We could go and get something to eat if we were hungry. If you did something wrong, you got a spanking and you got sent home to daddy or mama or your grandmother. It was like a village. Everything we needed was right here. Discipline, fun, food. It was all right here. The lots that we're sitting on now, these lots have been vacant probably anywhere from 15 to 20 years, probably a little longer. The first lot was a bakery, a Polish-Italian bakery, and it was torn down right before I graduated high school. I've been out of high school coming up on 21 years. [Laughs.] Then there was a yard and a house and then a four-family flat used to be right here. In the late '80s, early 1990s, I remember the houses that used to be in an orchard, the store that used to be on the corner there, a house that used to be behind us, the houses that used to line where those new houses are built. I remember all that. It used to be full. It wasn't empty.

GH — And now it's—
MC — Now we've got a bunch of vacant lots in our neighborhood. It's not always a bad thing if you think about it. [Laughs.] Some of us like open space. If we had help from the city to keep the lots cut, it would look more like green space instead of overgrown weeds and trees.

GH — Maybe tell us about the start of the community garden project.

MC — We started our community garden project—April 8 was actually the first day we came out, in 2008. We started cleaning it out. But the planning started at the end of February of 2008, beginning of March, when I came outside and saw a bunch of garbage and stuff on the curbs and in the lots. There actually wasn't any grass out here. The people who built the houses in the next lot over, they actually used these lots as a staging area for the soil or dirt and their equipment. There wasn't any grass out here, and I wanted to clean them up after seeing all the garbage. That's something I never saw in the neighborhood when I was growing up, and I wanted to do something about it. Being out here cleaning up, we were able to talk to neighbors. People were coming up to see what we were doing, why we were doing it, and then you kind of get into those political conversations, and conversations about what's going on in the neighborhood. We found out that a lot of people didn't have lights and gas, or they were struggling to pay for electricity and gas and water. They were choosing food over medicine or medicine over food, and we decided we needed to make the project a little bigger.

GH — So you had the idea to make it a garden, to actually plant things?

MC — Well, at first we thought we'd just put in a couple of rows of vegetables to keep people from dumping in it; not necessarily to feed people. It was like planting a flower or something so that people would think it looks nice and pretty and they wouldn't want to dump on it. But finding out about those situations with some of the people in the neighborhood, it kind of turned into being about healthy food choices, cheap food, because we were giving it away for free, and then it just started snowballing from there.

GH — What were you doing before this?

MC — I was an environmental service technician.

GH — Did you get laid off, or did you quit your job?

MC — No, I got fired. I guess I talked too much about safety, which is what they taught me. I guess I was an advocate for safety, and they tried to find a way to get rid of me.

GH — That was with the city?

MC — No, it was a private company. Whenever they asked me to go out of town, I went, because I wanted to go make some money. I did everything from cleaning poop off of Kmart and Walmart signs to cleaning oil spills in Cincinnati, Ohio.

GH — But you'd never thought about being a gardener or a landscape architect?

MC — No. Gardener, community activist, none of that. [Laughs.] It didn't even cross my mind. I've always had a big heart, and I've always kept up our property, but I didn't think I'd be an advocate for community redevelopment. But it happened.

GH — I guess it seems like, if you're not gonna do it—

MC — Well, it's kind of scary to think, if I hadn't done it, what it would look like now. It's kind of scary.

GH — Before there were probably markets around, and like you said, everything you needed was right here in the neighborhood.

MC — Well, when I was younger, we had Chatham, which was the big grocery chain in the seventies and early eighties, and then it turned into a Farmer Jack, and now it's Farmer John. We don't really have any national chains in the city or the neighborhood. On Harper Avenue, which technically was considered our commercial strip, we had car dealerships, clothing stores, theaters, bars, lounges, restaurants, everything you can imagine. You didn't have to leave the neighborhood. You had everything here. But people just picked up and moved away.

GH — And now it's mostly fast food restaurants?

MC — Yeah, Coney Island hot dogs, Kentucky Fried Chicken. We've got Captain Jay's now, which is not a bad restaurant. They definitely have some good chicken. We have pizza. We've got one burger place down the street, but it's like McDonald's and Burger King. It just runs the gamut. Everything is not real close, but it's fairly easy to get to, but it's not healthy.

GH — Since you've started this project, what's been the reaction from the community?

MC — It's been good. We don't get a lot of help from the neighborhood, but they respect it. They don't tear it up. They come to our events. I'd say that's enough support. I'll take that. Nobody's robbing us or stealing the stuff we're trying to put down. They come out and enjoy it. Every once in a while, you'll see people out here sitting around in the shade, especially in the park across the street.

GH — And when there's food to pick, when the vegetables are ready?

MC — Oh, when it's time to harvest, they're here. [Laughs.] Twenty-four hours, seven days a week. Usually the only thing that we have left over is tomatoes, because we plant a lot of tomato plants. I guess a lot of people don't like ripe tomatoes in our neighborhood. They want fried green tomatoes, so they pick the tomatoes when they're green, but once they start ripening, we have a little bit left over. But everything else, from collard greens to broccoli to beans, there's nothing left in the garden.

GH — What other things do you grow?

MC — Okra, hot peppers like cayenne and jalapeño. We used to have banana peppers, but this year we didn't put banana peppers in. We have carrots, broccoli, cabbage, kale, some lettuce, some beans, corn—Hey, Mister! That's one of the elders—tomatoes, basil, fennel. We've got lemon balm, lemon thyme, oregano. I know there's some more stuff that I'm missing.

GH — You have animals too?

MC — Yeah. Actually, it started when I got into composting. I kept hearing people talk about chicken manure and how it helps with the nitrogen and stuff, and I said, "Wow, I can keep some chickens. I don't see what's so bad about keeping a couple of chickens." Then it turned into a couple more chickens. Then we started working with kids too, so every year we had to come up with something that was gonna pique their interest. The first year it was the garden itself. The second year it was chickens. Then last year it was a goat. The goat came about like: somebody asked if we wanted a goat. I was like, "Is it healthy and friendly?" They said, "Yeah," so I said, "Yeah, I want it." I built a pen for him. Actually, still to this day—it's kind of a carry-over from last year—there's still excitement around the goat. We also have two ducks.

GH — Can you talk about the events that you're doing?

MC — Yeah. We're getting ready to plan our street fair, which will be our second annual street fair. We have entertainment and food. It's like a big picnic, and hopefully it will get a little bit bigger every year. Last year it rained on us, but we still had a lot of fun. We have giveaways of school supplies and backpacks every year for the kids. Last year we did 100 giveaways.

GH — How are you getting funding to keep operating?

MC — Strictly donations. We've got one person that donates—well, technically the community center is all her; she did it financially. But we get donations from around the world really, twenty dollars here, a hundred dollars there. We had one grant that we got for four thousand dollars that we didn't even ask for. Somebody saw us on the Internet who was on a board, or a friend of theirs is on a board of some foundation in New Mexico, and they sent us an unrestricted grant saying the only thing they wanted was a report on how we're progressing, which is our blog and our website. Everything else has been donations.

GH — What's the city's response been? What have they done?

MC — Nothing, really. [Laughs.] Lately I guess we're kind of getting recognized as a community organization, so I guess that's something. I understand the city's broke, but there are certain things; like if we clean up a vacant lot, I don't see why it should be trouble for the city to come and pick up the stuff that we collect out of the vacant lot. But as far as the permit process goes with the community center, they've been very helpful. I have no complaints. Well, one: they gave us an unofficial inspection once, and they didn't tell us that we needed to widen the length and the rise of some stairs, so we ended up having to pay an extra $3,000 after we did the framing in the building. But I guess there had to be something. It couldn't just go perfectly. Other than that, we haven't had any problems with the city. I can't say that they're against what we're doing because I know that's not the case. I think that whatever they can do that's reasonable, they'll do now.

GH — Do you think things are starting to get better for the city?

MC — I think they are. I think the administration is on the right track, in a way. It's still kind of scary not knowing what's gonna happen as far as the Detroit Works Project, whether this neighborhood is even gonna exist 10 years, 20 years from now. I don't want to go anywhere, but my fear is the neighborhood won't exist.

I think it's going in the right direction. We've gotta do something. If the mayor's willing to be the one to do it, let him do it. I know that negates what I just said, but there's a lot of organizations and people in the city and neighborhoods that are trying to do something, and I think that he should look at those as examples and see how he can help that be a part of the Detroit Works Project.

GH — But do you think most of the change and the effort is being put out by citizens, not necessarily the city?
MC — Yeah, it's definitely by the citizens. Look at this. People come here and they look and they say, "It looks like a community here." And it's nothing other than the city letting us do it, because we don't own the lots; the city owns them. But other than them letting us do it—that's really the only thing the city has done. It's our blood, sweat, and tears that's done it, us trying to find funding so we can get wood to boost some raised beds or getting flowers donated or buying flowers to plant, using our gasoline and our equipment to keep the lawn cut.

I think that they're going in the right direction because they're asking for input, but I think they need to get out and ride around and see what's going on, because if they came here and saw what was going on, I don't think they would want to close this down. I think they would want to build upon it. I don't want to see the whole city turned into a farm. I would love to see some of the vacant lots become new houses, apartment buildings, or whatever. I envision a recreation center somewhere in the neighborhood where the kids can go and play basketball all year round. I'd like to see the commercial strip redone on Harper Avenue. I'm hoping that we can get to the point where we're a catalyst for that type of development, but I think they need to come and see what we're doing, and maybe they can help move people here. This is not happening all over the city, but there's a lot of parts of the city where stuff like this is happening.

GH — Stuff like the garden program?
MC — Yeah, there's a lot of community gardens going on, maybe not on this big of a scale, but all of us want to do something like this.

GH — It's funny: you were saying earlier that you don't like bugs.
MC — [Laughs.] I like seeing worms. I don't have a problem with picking up worms and stuff, but spiders, I don't know if they bite or not. I'm six-two, 330 pounds, talking about some bugs. [Laughs.]

GH — You were saying before, you don't know if you want to kill them now because they might be—
MC — Pollinators, especially bees. I don't swat at bees or wasps anymore. I see a bee hive or a wasp hive, I'm not thinking, "Get rid of the wasp hive." Leave it alone. Let's walk away. I actually want to keep bees too. I'm going to a beekeeping class tomorrow.

GH — Really?
MC — Yeah. I don't know how I'm gonna do it, though, because I think that's one fight I'll probably have with the neighbors, finding somewhere

to keep the bees. I can't keep them in the backyard because we have too many family events. I can't put them in the orchard because it's too much shade. I'll figure out something.

GH — How long has your family been here?

MC — My grandmother bought the house we're in in 1969. My dad had seven kids: five boys and two girls. My mother only had four.

GH — Is everybody still in the neighborhood, or have most of the families moved away?

MC — My baby sister is at Kentucky State University. My baby brother lives with my stepmother on the west side. I've got another brother that lives in Oak Park, and then my sister and I are here on Georgia, and I've got another brother around the corner and another brother that's like five minutes away.

GH — What's the plan for looking at other lots and maybe expanding the garden?

MC — Well, I tell people that a big part of it is a beautification project for the neighborhood. I'm not gonna put anything in here that's gonna look bad. Some of the lots, like the lot behind us and the lot across the street, I want to turn into flower gardens. A lot of people use this lot as a walk-through, so I want to do a wood-chip path and continue the path all the way across the alley into the next street, but I want to plant some flowers and stuff so it'll look nice when people walk through plus it'll help pollinators come. I want to see butterflies, hummingbirds. I know we've got some birdhouses around. Maybe I need to get a couple of bat houses so we can get rid of mosquitoes. Mosquitoes are not pollinators. That I do know.

GH — What's been the hardest thing about the project?

MC — Not enough time. I can complain all day long about not getting enough help, but for some miraculous reason, it gets done. We get certain groups that come out and help us, and we get a lot accomplished, but it's time. Maybe if I can get two or three hours added onto a day, I can do it faster.

GH — Are there any funny stories about things that've happened during the past couple years of doing this?

MC — Well, we try to plant a variety. Now we've got about 18 varieties in the garden, but a couple of years ago there was an older man here. The collard greens were gone, people had picked all the collards, and he was picking the leaves off the broccoli, and I said, "You know that's broccoli, right?" And he said, "Tasted like collards last week." There's a lot of funny stories. Matter of fact, the guy who just walked past, his brother's 22 or 23 years old now. The first time he saw me picking carrots out of the garden, he didn't even know that carrots came out of the ground. He said, "Are those carrots?" I was like, "Yeah." "I didn't know carrots came out of the ground." I was like, "Where'd you think they came from?" "Out of the bag!" [Laughs.] I was like, "Are you kidding me? You didn't watch Bugs Bunny?" There's a lot of those stories.

GH — So this is an educational project and a food project!

MC — Oh yeah. You should have seen when we grew potatoes. The Georgia Street II garden was a kind of an overflow garden. Even now, I wake up in the morning, and I go out to the front porch, and there will be flats of flowers or vegetables sitting on the porch that people have donated. This particular year, and we had gotten some potatoes. So we were down there in the garden with some of the kids, and we were taking a broad fork and pulling up the potatoes, and they were like, "What are those?" I said, "Potatoes." They were like, "Like french fries?" I said, "No, potatoes make french fries." They was like, "They come out of the ground? Ugh!" [Laughs.] We get that all the time. There's always something that we have out here that's totally new to people. We've even had some older people that didn't know okra grew the way it grows.

GH — Sounds like we're all so disconnected from what we eat.

MC — Yeah, or that garlic bulbs are in the ground under the dirt. It's like, "Oh, is this the garlic?" He's picking off the seedpod that's on top. "Is this the garlic?" "No, that's the seed." "Where's the garlic?" "There it is, underground." It's like, wow. They had no idea that sunflower seeds came out of the sunflower. It's like, oh my goodness.

GH — Do the kids also like just running around?

MC — Oh yeah. When we have our movie nights and stuff out here, they're all over the place. Another funny story is the hot peppers. We had some habanero peppers growing, and you know, habanero peppers are very, very hot. They're very small, but they are hot. They were testing each other to see who could eat them and not scream the loudest or the fastest. So they would take a bit and start counting to see how long it would take for them to have a reaction. I don't touch the stuff anyway. I did one time and I thought I was gonna throw up. I'm not into spicy foods.

GH — Then why are you growing them?

MC — Because people like them. Some stuff I grow because I like it, but if somebody asks for something, I try to grow it for them. Like corn. The garden down the street that we did, half of the lot was corn, but you really don't get a lot of corn because of the birds and the squirrels. So this year I said, "I'll do corn here, corn down the street, and see what happens."

There's this one lady; she's an evangelist. She comes by every year. She wants mustard greens and turnip greens, and it's like, that's something that I need to find another spot for or extra space for, because every time we plant it—we've got two beds over there now, but once they get to the point where they can be picked, they go real fast. So she'll come back around, and she's like, "Where's the mustard greens?" I'm like, "They took them all. They're all gone. You gotta come. They're here all night." She gave me her card one time. "Call me when they're ready." I'm like, "Come on now." Every year she donates three or four dollars for seeds for mustards and turnips, but she hardly ever gets any.

GH — So how many gardens are we talking about here, can you give me a list of the different projects?

MC — Right now that are done already? We have the main community garden, which is Georgia Street Community Garden, which is these four lots here. Then across the street, there's two vacant lots where we did an orchard. I think there's 11 trees over there now, fruit trees: pears, peaches, plums, apples, cherries. That's across the street. Then across the street from that is our community center. We actually got that building, technically, for a dollar plus back taxes and water bill.

In the beginning, we had planned on opening the store back up as a store with no liquor sales, no cigarettes, but as we started redeveloping it and rehabbing it, we found out we needed the space for movie nights, at night, you know, when mosquitoes are out. We need to go in there if it rains. So we turned that into our multipurpose room, and the house part of it is going to be our offices and a computer lab and a library. We're working with a couple of places that are trying to get us Internet access throughout the neighborhood. I don't know if you saw the guys that rode the bikes by a minute ago. They're called the East Side Bike Riders. They were the catalyst for us getting that, which hopefully we'll know for sure by the end of this month. The plan is we'll be the Internet hub, and then we'll have Wi-Fi antennas all across the neighborhood where everybody can get Internet access. It's supposed to be set up to where we can charge if we want to or give it for free if we want to. But that's on the fast track, I'm hoping we can get that done in the next couple of months.

Then next to that, we have our greenhouse park that was donated to us by a trance music group called Above and Beyond. They came out in September of last year and wanted to do a video of transforming a vacant lot into something that the community can use. They had somebody design the park, and I liked it, and so that was done in a day from nine to—I think it was like five o'clock when we were done.

Down the street, we have Covington Farms, which is the garden right next to our house. Last year it was supposed to be an experimental market/family garden, but I don't really have a lot of time to stay home. Then down the street from that, we have two more community gardens: Holcomb Street Community Garden and Georgia Street II. Georgia Street II was technically an overflow garden because we kept getting so many plants and stuff donated.

So far, that's it. My overall vision is, like I said, to have a rec center in the neighborhood; to do some type of housing redevelopment; whether it's single family homes or multifamily homes, in the neighborhood; and the commercial strip. We want to try to get some type of businesses to come back into the neighborhood and provide jobs.

GH — I'm interested in people's role in making this. It seems to me like a lot of times people just expect somebody, the city government or somebody else, to do it. Then certain people want to get involved and literally get their hands dirty and do something. What are your thoughts on, I don't know, that guy living in that house over there? What should everybody be doing?

MC — I definitely don't expect everybody to do this, to do what I do, but—I'm trying to say this nicely—you need to get off your butt and take care of your own. If you take care of your own, everything else will fall into place. It doesn't matter if you're renting or you own a house. If you've got a busted blind in the window, you need to take it out and change it. If your porch needs painting, you should paint it. It doesn't matter if you're renting or not. If your grass needs cutting, cut it. Plant some flowers or something. Do something to make it look nice. We say, "One house, one block, one neighborhood at a time." Literally that's what you need to do. You can have a sense of community by doing your little section. You don't have to do the whole block. You don't have to do the whole neighborhood. You don't have to do the whole city. Just take care of yours.

But the thing about it is, once you start taking care of yours, you're gonna want to do something else. It spreads. You take care of yours; you plant some flowers; you make it look nice; it makes your neighbor think, "Oh, I need to cut my grass." The neighbors start cutting their grass. Then it just keeps going from there. That's how you change things one house, one block, one neighborhood at a time. But it's like, get off your butt. Quit sitting and waiting on somebody to do something for you. Quit waiting on checks and food stamps and do something. And if anyone wants to come and talk to me about that statement, then let them come on and talk to me.

GH — How are you able to do what you do?

    MC — I am blessed to have a mother and a grandmother who support me. Really a family, my brothers and my sisters, even though they don't get out here and dig in the dirt, I can't say I've missed a meal not working. I don't have a full-time job, but I'm blessed to have a mother and a grandmother that support what I'm doing and what I'm trying to do.

GH — What do you think makes a good city?

    MC — Good people. It doesn't matter if you have two thousand, three thousand, four thousand, ten thousand police officers. It's the people who still commit the crimes. If you had good people, those crimes wouldn't happen. Even though it's a small few, it's still that small few that make it worse for everybody else. It's the people.

GH — Can we talk numbers in terms of how many crops you're generating? It looks modest, but I don't get the sense that it is.

    MC — No, it's not modest. It's hard to say, because this year I'm supposed to weigh it; I haven't been. It doesn't look like I'm lazy, but there's certain things that I'll pick out and I'll be lazy about, and that's like trying to keep track of how many people come through the garden, how many people sign in at our events. I don't worry about that stuff. It's just another layer of work that I don't need.

We have 31 raised beds for vegetables and edible flowers. That's over here. Then there's 2 beds over here with strawberries in them. Then we've got all the raspberries and blackberries over here. That's not including the 5 beds we have down at the Holcomb Street Garden.

Then the 24 varieties of vegetables that we have in our home garden. [Laughs.] It's impossible.

GH — How many people roughly do you think you feed during the year?

MC — That's hard to say too. I'll get a phone call at like one or two o'clock in the morning saying there's people in the garden with flashlights. picking, so I don't know.

GH — You're okay with that?

MC — Yeah, I don't have no problem with it. My thing is, just don't tear it up. We had a couple of times where people pulled a whole cabbage out of the ground instead of cutting the cabbage and letting cabbage sprouts grow so people can eat a little bit more, but some people just don't know. Other than that, as long as they don't tear it up, they can come out here; I don't care what time. As long as they ain't asking me to pick it for them, I'm cool with it. We get some people that will say thank you, and then you've got some people that don't say nothing. I've run into some people that think the city pays for this stuff. I had some people think that I get paid to do this.

GH — Would that be okay? Would you want to get paid?

MC — If I could get paid to do this, I'd be in heaven. This is what I want to do. I feel like this is my calling. I would do this in a minute. I wake up at five thirty, six o'clock in the morning, and it's like, "Dang, I gotta hurry up and get out there." When I was working a job, I'm was going to bed at night thinking, "Dang, I gotta get up at five thirty, six o'clock in the morning," and it's not like that. Now it's like, "Dang, it's eleven thirty. I gotta go to bed. Aww. I can't wait till six o'clock. I'm gonna water first thing in the morning, and then I'm gonna do this." I try to plan out what I'm gonna do that day. It's kind of exciting.

—

VPUU Project/ June, 2011 Cape Town

The VPUU Project in the Cape Town township of Khayelitsha interested our team due to its simple yet powerful concept, that you could reduce violence in an urban area simply through better design. The methodology of the VPUU team was inspiring. They spent years in the community researching the issues before proposing an intervention, and have continued to involve residents in every phase of the project. I believe much of the project's success is due to this long term strategy, and not simply looking for a quick fix.

We spoke with four of the project's participants: Alastair Graham, one of the project coordinators for the City of Cape Town; Kathryn Ewing, Urban Designer and Architect at SUN Development; landscape architect Tarna Klitzner, and architect Jacqueline James.
—

Jacqueline James (JJ)/ Architect, Jonker Barnes Architects

Gary Hustwit — For starters, can you give me a little bit of an overview of the VPUU project?

Jacqueline James — Okay. VPUU is Violence Prevention through Urban Upgrading. A feasibility study that was done in Khayelitsha in about 2002 identified four specific areas to focus on, and they're generally connected to transport interchanges. The first one we started working on was a pedestrian walkway that extended from the Khayelitsha railway station, which is one of five railway stations in Khayelitsha, through pretty undefined land, across the suburb of Harare, and toward the informal settlement. There were a lot of crime hot spots within the area, so the project looks at those problems and creates interventions. And it might not just be buildings. It could be occupying space, but it could also be something as simple as lighting or paving. But we work with the community to establish what the issues are and then what the suitable intervention should be.

GH — Could you talk a little bit about the conditions in Khayelitsha before this, like five years ago?

JJ — Khayelitsha was a settlement that was developed in the eighties, supposedly for the working people, but there was no planning that was put in place. It was quite fragmented development, and there was a lot of open space and detention ponds for rainwater flooding that were interspersed between the developments, so there was no integration, no connectivity. That's basically what we've been looking at in the VPUU project—trying to integrate what is there and make the spaces safer.

GH — So the crime rate was really quite high before?

    JJ — There were hot spots of crime, specifically along this pedestrian route that we've been working on. There's not much informal settlement within the suburb of Harare, but Khayelitsha consists of both formal and informal. So yes. There was a crime survey that was done right in the very beginning and a lot of interaction with the local community so they could say what their fears were and also their perceptions of crime.

GH — I think it's interesting just talking to people there. There's maybe a sense of suspicion about the idea of a government-sponsored initiative, or indifference to it.

    JJ — I guess that's come from a lot of promises being made in the past and then not fulfilled, so the community does treat us quite suspiciously: "Yes, we've heard this before, but what are you really going to do about it?" There's a lot of work that we as professionals need to do in developing their trust. I'm working very closely with the residents.

GH — Can you talk about the concept of the active boxes, what they are and what the purpose is?

    JJ — The idea of the active box, specifically along the pedestrian walkway in Harare, was to provide a vertical element that one could see as one was walking along the pedestrian route, and they also are meant to be places of safety. They're designed in such a way that there's a flexibility of use, but in each case, there's some point of activity on the ground floor, be it trading or meeting. There's always a space for a caretaker who manages the facility and also provides safety, so if, for instance, you are walking along the pedestrian route and you feel unsafe for whatever reason, you can always see where the next active box is, and you know that you can go there, and it'll be safe. We've used red for their exteriors, so they're very clearly visible during the day, and then they're down-lit at nighttime, so they are these light points. They're light boxes at nighttime.

GH — Can you explain the position of them, the spacing?

    JJ — Places were identified where there were crime hot spots, but also, just from an urban planning point of view, they were kind of knuckle areas, meeting points, that sort of thing.

GH — I'm assuming the one at the station was the first.

    JJ — No, actually the one at Precinct 3 was the first along the pedestrian walkway, but there's one on the cycle route at Harare Peace Park; that was actually the first one we did. It was an existing single-story building that was underused within an informal play area. We put an additional floor on it and created the verticality and the circulation space, so that really became the first one. But the first new building that we did was the Precinct 3 Active Box with the open park as an integrated development.

GH — Are there other things, I guess from an architectural standpoint, about the active-box design that you want to talk about?

JJ — Yeah. We were trying to keep buildings simple, simple to construct, because we're using quite a lot of local subcontractors, local laborers, and then also searching for products and methods of building that would be robust and stand the test of time. We chose to use a metal cladding because it is robust, and it's vibrant; it can be seen. And then we were also looking at products that are environmentally friendly and building methods that are as environmentally friendly as possible, and we're constantly researching, seeing what works, so each new building we do, we take on board what we've learned and try and improve that. Sometimes it's just simple things like solar heating or measuring the water in the systems, that sort of thing, water management.

GH — Can you talk about the live-work spaces?

JJ — We were wanting to get back to the traditional form of working downstairs and living upstairs. It's been done all over the world for a couple of centuries now, but we've kind of lost that habit, and people are having to travel great distances to get to work, especially from Khayelitsha, and there are a lot of entrepreneurs in Khayelitsha. We did a survey of who was doing what and what kind of space they required. That's how the concept developed, and it also has to do with activating spaces during the day and at nighttime. For instance, in Harare Square, people will be trading on the ground floor; they're eyes on the street, eyes on the space, so there's that natural surveillance and the activity, and then in the evening they're living there, so the activity is a 24-hour thing. Also, of course, people aren't spending all of their money on transport; they don't have to worry about child care because children can stay at home and things like that.

GH — And what sort of businesses can go into them?

JJ — That's been quite interesting. There's been a learning curve because at the beginning we thought there'd be more workshop spaces for small welders—not noisy things, but the welders, the carpenters, the upholsters, that sort of thing—but it's mostly been people who want offices there, so we're having to adapt the plans to suit. But we designed them in a flexible way so that they could grow either as a family grew or as the business grew. We're just adapting as we go.

GH — With the active boxes, since now they're constructed, what are your thoughts when you go back and see them being used?

JJ — It is great to see how they are being used, especially in the case of the Precinct 3 Active Box. It's been used for quite significant events, such as the handing over of the bid book for Cape Town's Design Capital bid for 2014. And it's also nice to go to the active boxes at Precinct 1 at the station to see the trading happening and to see products being displayed. It adds this new layer to a building and personalizes it. We're also learning along the way, seeing how people use the spaces, seeing how we could design them in the future, seeing how to make them better. Lots of lessons to learn. For instance, at the station, we just put roller-shutter doors in thinking that it was going to be a more informal-formal kind of trading, but actually people want to close up their spaces, so there's a need for a door closure, something glass perhaps, and then the roller-shutter doors. You learn along the way. We also learned that maybe we could improve the lighting that washes the building, so we're looking at LEDs for that. It's a big learning curve. It's a massive learning curve.

GH — Obviously, it's participatory design in a lot of ways.

JJ — Absolutely. Especially with the Station Active Box. There was a group of informal traders that were trading there, and they organized into a committee, so they were great to work with. We worked with them closely along the way, making models and showing them how it was going to work and trying to understand how they operated. That was very, very useful.

GH — It seems like the kind of top-down approach to many social architecture projects or government interventions is maybe a big cause of some of the failures.

JJ — Oh, absolutely. In a lot of the VPUU projects, you've probably noticed that none of them are fenced in. People can walk right up to the buildings, and there's virtually no vandalism that's taking place. We're working closely with the community right from the beginning, understanding their needs, and taking them through the design process and the management of the facilities afterwards and the maintenance. They've really taken ownership, and there's a pride. In some cases, the general workers or the caretakers were formerly working on the sites as the community liaison officers, and then they've applied for the general worker jobs, so they're staying with the project, which is fantastic.

GH — Yeah, because a lot of times people think of a project as, "Oh, there's a start date; then the completion date. Okay, we're done."

JJ — Yeah, and that's the great thing about VPUU. It's not just about constructing a building. It's about working with a community right from the beginning, starting with urban concept plans, and then moving on to precinct plans and working with surveys, working with the community, getting a real understanding, and then a building is part of the end product, but it's not the only end product. It goes beyond that: the maintenance, the management. And it's a magnificent community to work with. They've been absolutely great. Developing friendships and partnerships and seeing how local contractors and leaders have been developing—it's brilliant. It's just really enriching.

GH — It's also interesting because it kind of speaks to the role of urban design in people's lives. Maybe lots of people aren't really aware of how the design of a space or a city or the interrelationship of buildings really affects their daily lives.

JJ — It certainly does, and it's hard to design against crime. I think it's quite easy to take the theories that we learn while we study and try and overlay those, and it doesn't always work. You really need to work with the community, and it isn't sufficient just to say, "Well, we'll have a community participation meeting to show them what we're going to do." You actually need to work with them right from the very beginning. The proof is in the pudding, I guess.

GH — How did you get involved with the project?

> **JJ** — How did I get involved? Actually, it was kind of interesting, because I was just working on a part-time contract on something else completely, and I'd heard about the project and was really interested, and they asked me to come on board, and, yeah, I've been working on it for five and a half years and running it from this office.

GH — For people in this community or even more broadly, what do you think is the awareness of the urban design around them?

> **JJ** — I think they're aware of the fact that the spaces are accessible, and they're aware that the spaces are safer than they were. Those are the things that impact people's lives, so whether you call it urban design or safety or their perception of safety, I think it is having an impact, and I think you can also see the impact it's having in that the spaces aren't vandalized. They're well looked after.

GH — They're taking ownership, taking pride.

> **JJ** — Definitely taking pride and ownership. The participatory process that's so key to the VPUU project is vital to any development.

GH — Are there any other good stories about the process, anything that sticks out?

> **JJ** — There's quite a few things. It's prompted me to go and learn how to speak Xhosa, and that's great, and when you work with a community and you speak their language, it's an amazing difference. What I find really rewarding is that, for instance, for the Precinct 3 Active Box, the mosaic panel on one of the walls and the security screens were made by local welders. We came with a building, but now it has the personalized layer of the local people and their craft, and it makes it a much richer building.

GH — I love the mosaics on the library as well.

> **JJ** — Brilliant, fantastic, and in fact, those mosaic artists did some work for the World Cup stadium at the bus station. It tells a story.

GH — That's good. In terms of the lighting-placement stuff, were you very involved with that?

> **JJ** — That was Tarna Klitzner.

GH — Actually, we're going right to talk to her now.

> **JJ** — She'll tell you a lot about the mosaic ladies because she instigated the whole process. There were workshops held beforehand on memory and cultural issues and things like that to establish the story, but she'll tell you all of that.
>
> —

Tarna Klitzner (TK)/ Landscape Architect, VPUU Project

Gary Hustwit — So tell me what you find most interesting about this project.

Tarna Klitzner — This project, the VPUU project, is particularly interesting for a number of reasons. I think the landscape architecture is interesting, and I'll explain why, but it's also because Khayelitsha was completely designed. In the early eighties, when the government at the time conceived of Khayelitsha, they re-formed the sand dunes that were there. They didn't take any cognizance of the natural systems on the site at all.

This space, the urban park, it's part of a bigger system, which is the storm-water system that is structured through Khayelitsha. It is really an example of the problems that occur everywhere along the storm-water system, which is that houses back onto it, and there's been no frontage onto it historically—that is, before any development was done around it, all the new developments. It's a storm-water overflow area. Sometimes it's really soggy and wet, and you can't cross it so easily. Also, because of its position embedded in the environment, there are shortcuts across it for people.

Historically, the way urban design has happened in South Africa is along what are seen as major routes. That's where all the infrastructure happens, the pedestrian routes and upgrading. Here, the different tack the VPUU took was they actually spoke with the community. Right at the beginning when they spoke with the community, they said they wanted safe pedestrian routes and safe places to walk. For us, once we heard that, it was very exciting that that's the way they'd approach the project, which meant the decision as to where the routes went wasn't the normative position for the routes, which is along the main roads and more around transport and buses, but more where people are actually walking, which were those desire lines that cut their way through the settlement, which was both the formal settlement and an informal settlement. It consists of both sets of fabric. That, for us, was very interesting—that this route was actually determined by the community.

Then what's also very lacking in the area is places for children to play and recreational space. That was another aspect that was worked into the urban design concept, that this would also be a place of play because it's fairly embedded, so it's fairly safe in one way, because there isn't traffic on the sides, so you don't have to worry about children to that degree, but also because people are moving through it. It could constantly be observed. Those were the criteria.

We also had to make sure that we still kept the park as a detention basin so it could contain a one-in-a-hundred flood when the rains do occur. That was great because that gave us the opportunity to change the levels in the space, which isn't an opportunity you always have. Especially when you're working on public spaces, the budgets are quite constrained. Here it was great because we could use that natural fall in the land and use it for an advantage. We made steps as seats, and they also define those play spaces so people don't walk across them. Having a lawn area—like that one space is grass—is quite unnatural in this environment because, when children play on it, it's no longer a lawn area; it very quickly becomes a dry patch, and nothing has a chance to grow. Because it is recessed, people don't naturally walk across it, so that preserves it in a sense. We also made the one space much smaller than the other space so that the bigger children tend to play on the larger space, and the smaller space attracts the smaller children. It was those sorts of design ideas that informed it.

As a landscape architect, the question is, how much do you need to actually design? We really believed that it needs to be a space that's negotiated with the community. Whatever their needs might be in terms of the space, those have been included. But apart from that, there was also the sense that they needed to be participating in a very active way, in a way, making and designing as well. So how much does the landscape architect actually design? Because the team is huge. It's not just me. The team, as you know, is quite an extensive group, so I'm just a tiny part of it.

The sense was that the kinds of things that we felt we would have an input and a say on were the positioning and the location of the fields and ensuring that you still have this clear route through, then some of the other elements that have been included as well. There is this notion of defining the boundary, which is the little stone wall you see that is built and clad with calcrete. Putting this little wall around the edge of the property of the public space defined public and private. When we started working on the site at the beginning, we thought the site was a certain size. When we went back, informal development had encroached on what we perceived as the site. Because VPUU have got such a good process in place, talking to the community and with them, those people moved. They happily moved, and it was no issue. Then the boundary was determined, and the wall is now in place. What's also part of the wall is it's not solid everywhere. It's got openings in it. The idea is to encourage people to move from the space into their dwellings and, in that way, encourage front doors and windows onto the square, and you start getting that public frontage.

Also, when we worked, there were some existing hedges, and we worked very carefully to retain them so we didn't damage anything. Now they've grown quite big, and they're very beautiful in the square. They help define the edge of the square.

GH — Can we talk a little bit about the lighting?

TK — Okay. The idea with the lighting is, it's a very tight grid. It's a 10-square-meter grid of the lower-level, what we call pedestrian-scale lights that are about four and a half meters high. The idea is that you have really good lighting in the space because what makes spaces unsafe in Khayelitsha or anywhere at night is when there is not good lighting and when the surface isn't smooth and easy to walk on. You can easily trip, or someone can easily hide somewhere. The idea of the lighting is there's this cover, the 10-meter grid, and then there are the high masts. The high masts are quite wonderful. At night, when they go on, the children just appear from the fields out of nowhere. They just arrive, and they start playing in the space. That was the idea of the high masts, that it would be a place that children could play in until late at night. They do. When the high masts come on, it's about nine o'clock at night. There are always children in the space, which is really quite amazing and great, just to see that it is being used. That is the idea. Light at night makes the space safer.

The tree planting, you'll see, is fairly limited in the space, because there was the fear of people hiding. There's a perception that people hide behind trees, and it's easy for them to hide. The main routes are kept quite clear, but we do have some copses of trees, so the idea is that if you want to go and sit under the shade of the tree and you feel secure enough to do that, you can, but it's not where you want to walk. Your walking routes are quite clear.

GH — I like the whole idea of linking the different sites.

TK — We're just about to start on that project. Actually, we went on site yesterday with a contractor to start that project. It's called "the links" because it's linking these different urban squares, the one which is more the recreational square, which is this square, and the other, which is Harare Square, then all the way up to the informal settlement.

That project's just started. The materials are exactly the same. We're using the same materials. There will be some seating spaces along the edge, but the principle of defining the difference between public and private is what we're really working with. We'll have this low wall that meanders through, and it'll be very well lit. That is about to start as well.

GH — Especially in a situation like Khayelitsha but also just in general, how important do you think the design of public space is to the life of the people in that city and the sense of community?

TK — Cape Town is very different in its different areas, and the role of the public space is very different. I live in Sea Point, and the role of the promenade—I don't know if you've been down through the promenade yet, but it's actually unbelievable. The promenade serves the whole city, depending on what festivals are happening in the city. You will find on Ramadan it's full. People come from all over the city, and they use that space in a very positive way. It has a very different use, a space like that that is right next to the sea.

In Khayelitsha, this particular space is different from Harare Square, which you've seen as well, which is more an urban business square, and the taxis are there. It's got a completely different role. There are traders. It's very much about the trading and the commerce, whereas this square is very much a community space. Even though people move through it, it's about recreation. It has got quite active recreation as well, but also passive recreation. It's that ability, as a person, to be able to sit somewhere and watch others walk by. If you're lonely, there was no place to go. If you want to meet your friends in Harare, there are very few places to go. It's that notion of just that release of a city, especially in a dense environment where—I know that the houses seem like they're not dense in the vertical dimension, but in a lot of those especially informal settlements, it's very, very dense in terms of the way people are living cheek to jowl. There isn't much relief in those spaces, so this enables that. It enables a positive space where you can meet and relax away from home. It has a very positive role to play.

It's interesting because I meet people along the way. I do stick out when I go to Khayelitsha, so if they see me in other environments, they often recognize that they've seen me in Harare, and then they'll say, "We love that space. We like going to that space." That's quite amazing. It actually has made a difference. Consciously, it's made a difference to people.

GH — Yeah, I was going to say, what has the people's reaction to the project been?

TK — You must have heard some of the comments. You heard "Princess 3"? I don't know if you've heard that one. It's called Princess 3 by some people, the square. It was Precinct 3 to all of us because it was the third precinct along the route, so we just called it Precinct 3. Then somewhere along the line one of the community members nicknamed it Princess 3, so that's what it's called. People called the active box Helen Zille's House. I mustn't mention that one because it's political, but she was the mayor at the time. People, they responded in different ways. But what was the question?

GH — Why do they call it Princess 3?

TK — They call the square Princess 3 I think just because it was the notion that it had been beautified. It was a space that had been beautified unlike other spaces adjacent that had just been left. What's interesting for me is, this space—nobody wanted to own the space. It was just a neglected space that really nobody was interested in. Now, since all this upgrading, it's actually caused contention in the sense that people see it as theirs. It's quite positive. You never think of making something contentious as positive, but you start to realize, now it has value, and that's wonderful, the fact that it now has value. From their point of view, it actually is a space that people now have pride in, and they want to be part of it.

The artwork that's in the space, the mosaics, we think, went a long way to also giving people a stamp of ownership. In the local community, everyone who was interested nominated their name and then took part in a training workshop to do the mosaics and then also a symbols workshop to generate symbols for the space with an artist, Lovell Friedman. She worked with their symbols, and they made their own mosaics. It's wonderful.

Quite a few of those members who trained there, they worked around the stadium. Some of the mosaics that happened there with the bus system, they did some of those as well. That was very nice, to see them move from one area to another and take the skill and work somewhere else. The same group of those people, the ones who proved to be very competent at it, she's using them in all sorts of projects now. They're working on quite a few projects, so that's nice.

I think that's also advantageous, to see that the project has enabled quite a few people to be skilled in these little businesses. We need cages around the trees because the goats eat the trees. I don't know if you've ever seen what goats do. One pushes the tree down for the other one to eat the top of it, so we have to put the cages around the trees, so we used recycled materials. Some local guys made the tree cages. They also have some welding skills, so they did some metal work for us. Since then, they've made burglar bars for different projects in the area, and they've been involved in all sorts of things. So that's also very nice, to see how that has worked through. The idea of the project was also that transference of skills and then to enable people to carry on working afterwards. It's not just a one-off project. And it has done that in all sorts of ways.

GH — It seems like traditionally with an intervention like this it would be like, "Okay, here's the completion date, then we're gone. Good luck."

TK — For me, I've worked on quite a few projects where the ideas were wonderful, and supposedly there'd be participation, but there was no carry through. I think the big difference also is the maintenance. You can't do a project and then just leave it. The weeds come up, things break, and if you don't fix it immediately, then things continue to break. A big part of this project is the ongoing maintenance. As part of VPUU, they have trained local community members to be part of that maintenance. I'm sure they've explained all that part of it, how they actually sustain the project.

GH — If you had to identify a concept or a methodology here that other areas of the world or other cities could use, what would it be?

TK — Whenever I speak about it, I'm always asked that. Apart from the fact, obviously, that working with community is really important, Khayelitsha is very specific because it's got a very good community organizational system in place. So working with a community, and I think firstly the community needs to set up its own systems so that you have something you can work with which works from the top all the way down, right down to street committees. You need that system in place whether or not it's part of the project, so that you're not just working with the people who have the loudest voice, but you actually are working with people on the ground and the real concerns are coming through.

I think, apart from that, it's the team. It's understanding that it's not just about one designer or just about what is seen as the main group of designers. It's a huge team, and it's very varied. I think that's the difference on this project, the fact that economists are talking to designers are talking to social workers. Everyone is talking about the project from their different points of view, so they inform one another. Often, you don't have those conversations. You don't have the opportunity to have those conversations. I think that has really made a difference for us.

—

Kathryn Ewing (KE)/ Project Manager, VPUU Project, City of Capetown

Gary Hustwit — So do you want to talk about Khayelitsha and what it was like before or just kind of give us an introduction to this area or this settlement?

Kathryn Ewing — Khayelitsha is an interesting township, as it is called in South African terms. The biggest problem with the township when it was built was that it's so far removed from the city, so we are actually sitting a good 25 kilometers outside of the center of the city. It was built in what's called the Cape Flats, the dunes systems. We are dealing with a very harsh climate here, but we've got about six hundred thousand people living in Khayelitsha, which is an immense amount of people per square meters of area. It's the most densely populated settlement area in Cape Town. For me, what is so exciting about Khayelitsha, though, is that the social structures are very strong. Because of its background and everything that happened here, the dynamics are very interesting to start working with, because you've got this strong social structure that is in place, although that comes with its challenges in itself as well.

In terms of where we focus, we focus on what are known as the safe node areas, and safe node areas, this one that we're in at the moment being Harare and the others being both in the formal and the informal areas of Khayelitsha. We're looking at an informal settlement of roughly about six thousand households. We're looking at four people per household, so 24,000 people for the informal settlement, which is like the size of a small town in itself. In the formal areas, you're getting a different sort of density but sort of the same number of people per area in square meter terms.

GH — Could you talk about what the living conditions were like in Khayelitsha that led up to the VPUU project?

KE — What is quite interesting about Khayelitsha is there are very dominant storm-water systems that were designed by engineering standards sort of in a system where there are big open spaces. Now, we are actually sitting at the moment in Harare Park. This was an open part of the storm-water system. Very desolate and unsafe. Very unsafe. So the idea was to transform the very unsafe areas that form part of the storm-water system into something that is more positive and something that has more of an identity within these spaces, because large, vast tracks of open, underutilized land, they just become crime hot spots.

GH — So this area wasn't lit or anything?

KE — No. Because it was a sort of the leftover space, it was seen as a dumping ground for all sorts of things. This is just one of the nodes along the route, but the key is it's a location that works for us with our safety principles for urban design, which entail surveillance, movement routes, aesthetics—which is kind of a key one, especially in areas where people relate to what's happening in buildings and public spaces. In that sense, it was a dumping ground that was then transformed into something else, but it's just one node along the links of a much bigger system, and I think that that is what is important to try and realize. What we've been trying to do is connect things not only spatially but also socially as well.

GH — On the idea of movement routes, the route here that we're seeing that's now lit, was that more of an informal or formal route before, or what was it?

KE — It's certainly guided by existing conditions, that people were walking through here, but I wouldn't say that they were particularly safe. You would be walking through sort of underutilized rubbish land in a sense. I mean, I wouldn't walk through here previously, and now it's become a real hub for people to walk through here. Crime is still a problem, but I think by creating more active surveillance and positive threshold conditions on the edges, so getting people involved in your open spaces, it allows your movement routes to become more than just where people are moving through.

For me, it forms a key connection from the railway station all the way up to the main Harare Square, which is the developing node, and then also up over into the informal settlement, which is just over the hill. It's not only about connecting your local areas. It's actually integrating many different communities. Although the movement route is quite simple in terms of putting it in, it's very complex in terms of what it's doing from a spatial sense and a social sense.

GH — Okay, even talking about active surveillance: when people think surveillance, they think, you know, CCTV cameras. Could talk a little bit about that, the idea that it's really just about people, the eyes on the streets?

KE — Yeah. What one can see in the spatial conditions just as you go down the path is that there are low walls, but you can still look over them. It's trying to get people on the other side of the wall to play a more active role in what's going on. What has been interesting about the park here is how people have changed their front doors. They were previously on the other side, and now people relate more to the movement route, and that creates more positivity along there. It also serves up economic opportunities. Having more people around automatically gives more of a community spirit and takes away the sense of people hanging around for no good. In terms of the safety principles for a safe neighborhood, active surveillance can only be vital.

I mean, the thought of actually putting in CCTV cameras—the budget is extreme, but not only that: you've got to have somebody who's con-stantly managing it and maintaining it, and it takes it away from that real community sense. Whereas if we deal with it in the community, you get people taking identity from it and belonging and ownership and interest in what goes on. I mean, if you've got kids playing down here at ten at night, you kind of want to look over and see that they are all okay. I think that that, in terms of active surveillance, is crucial from those perspectives.

GH — I'm imagining we would not be seeing what we're seeing here happening five years ago.

KE — No. No, we've got a couple of photographs from five years ago that show just this sort of expanse of land, and it's changed hugely in the last three years. It's become a real thoroughfare.

GH — Can you talk about the active box? Just describe to us what that is.

KE — Along the whole linkage in this route, the idea was every five hundred meters you would have a lookout point or a lookout tower. I like to see it more in the urban principle of what it means in a context rather than looking at more of the architecture of what the active box does. But the active boxes, they act as landmarks, so you can always refer to them en route, and the idea was that they were vertical, so you have an elevation, and that they became beacons of light at nighttime. They're also occupied 24/7, so there's always a caretaker and somebody always involved. They form little points where you can also have economic activity and also a coming together of communities, but I think the main thing for me is the highlighting of the landmark and the safety of knowing that every five hundred meters someone is just looking over you and making sure that you carry on your journey in a safe manner.

GH — Maybe talk about engaging the residents in the process?

KE — The nice thing I feel that the VPUU project does is that it involves communities in such a way that you actually end up learning more about design than you do without the community. Design is often taught in a way that you do not look beyond what it is that you design, what you think is right. Communities actually drive you in a different process that you are guided by, designing things that you never thought you would.

In terms of how the VPUU process works, it sets up committees. The committees that are set up are crucial for forming decision-making processes. Also, their input is very valuable. So forming project committees becomes a crucial point in understanding priorities, setting up local strategies, trying to make decisions that involve many interest bases. It's normally 50 percent political interest and 50 percent people from faith-based organizations or local NGOs or small dance groups or something like that. You're getting a range of people who are involved in making those decisions, and it's those people who become your main design informants and guide you through the process of design. So it's not just a product. It actually becomes a process.

Once those committees are formed, it's not to say you're disassociated from the rest of the community. You're still getting buy-in from the rest of the community through baseline surveys and household surveys that are a constant, particularly the household surveys. But the committees drive certain aspects of how one then can take it through to once you've implemented projects. What does it mean after you've implemented the project? Because that's another part of the design. You normally never actually ever think beyond what happens when one builds a building or puts down a public park, that it needs to have a life of its own, and the communities are crucial for taking on the operation and maintenance after that, but only if they've been through the process. If they don't have a sense of belonging and ownership over the project, then it's very difficult to get people involved in feeling like they're part of the space.

GH — Were there instances, just in the VPUU project here, when there was something that you hadn't really thought of or realized, and then community input completely changed the way you thought about it?

KE — I'm going to refer to the informal areas here, because of course you've got very little infrastructure, so you're guided very much by what is existing, the urban systems that are already set up. What was crucial about the work we were doing here is that we were trying to develop safe walkways on a similar principle of movement routes, but what actually happened is that we worked with a group of people who were involved in education from the community who talked about the idea of spaces where people gather and come together and meet. This started forming into how we actually started working on early childhood development public space areas. That was crucial for informing the broader urban design principles of how we worked, our safe walkways, which were originally just a walkway that one walked on but then became completely something else, a series of spaces which were a platform for many things, but mainly geared around education. That was driven predominantly by the community.

GH — Maybe you can just do a little bit of a catalog of the different interventions: the lighting, the active boxes, the square.

KE — I always go through it as I would walk through from the railway station. If I'm getting off a train, where do I come from? Where do I first arrive? You first arrive at what is known as Precinct 1, but it's also something that needs a name from the community. Precinct 1 is about your trading. It's an economic space. It's right there by your train station. It's always busy with people moving quite fast through there and also some people stopping to chat. The Precinct 1 Active Box forms your first port of call when you arrive.

Then there is an upgrade link that is currently happening, but it's not on the ground yet, but that walkway links you through to the Harare Urban Park. That forms the next node, so to say, along the route from the train station. It's well lit. The lighting has also been done at a much closer spacing than normal standards to give you a sense of not only human scale but also to provide a lot more light. So illumination, really lighting it up. There are children playing in the space late at night, which is fantastic. There are still concerns and problems with such spaces because we're still vulnerable in many other sectors, but I think that what it forms is a vibrant, dynamic urban park.

Then one walks up the hill, and you arrive at Harare Square. You've got the civic nature of the library there and the live-work units that are very new thinking in terms of housing and how you can get that going in many other parts of the world. It's sort of second nature. We have to get away from just the delivery of the housing to actually delivering something that's more engaging in an urban environment. The new business hub that is going up there as well, it creates a very different nature to the more sporting and recreational space of Harare Urban Park.

Once you arrive at the top of Harare Square, you actually then can turn around and look back down where you've come from, and the active boxes can guide you through where you've come. We're actually quite lucky in this project in having that sense of walking through and being able to turn around and reflect on the space. The views up at Harare Square, they're quite beautiful, and they show us how we can appreciate our city. You know, you see down to Kwamfundo School. And just to have a little bit of green in these environments is very valuable and precious, like a little green jewel. To keep those maintained is a lot of work, but actually the impact that it has on you is immense. Even with the little green space down here in the urban park, you can get that sense that it's refreshing and it's nice to have.

Once one leaves Harare Square, then you meander your way through the more residential streets to come up onto the main road system at the back, and then you can move through Monwabisi Park, which is in the informal settlement, and you get a very different sense there of moving between the formal and the informal and how that merges. We've only just started to implement in the informal areas, so only once we can actually start connecting all these pieces of the pie will you be able to then get a whole connectivity between the formal and the informal.

GH — Have you got a sense of what the community's thoughts are on the results of the spatial changes?

KE — I haven't directly engaged with people, but I think I come and sit here quite a lot to see how people are using the space and just observe. We spend a lot of time trying to understand how people do use space, because often we're designing when they don't use it. For me, by observing and listening, one can learn a lot. I know there's a lot of positive reaction to what the project has created and a lot of people wanting the project to move into their areas, so that can only come from what the communities themselves are saying.

GH — I was going to ask too, what can other cities around the world and other places take from the lessons that you've learned here?

KE — We use a very simple step-by-step methodology. Although it's simple, it's very complex, if that makes any sense. First of all, you're forming your committees, and you're forming strong relationships and partnerships between different people. You're then taking it into your safe node areas, so there's how one sets up a safe node area working very closely with your urban design principles of surveillance and threshold conditions, giving identity to areas. And then how do you bring these all together in sort of an integration of uses and assembly points?

It's quite clear in terms of how the urban design principles can work very easily in different environments. Crucial to those is understanding your context. I think that's what we put a lot of time into, and I think that's where a lot of projects fail. It's listening to people. It's talking to people. It's watching. It's walking around, observing, filming, photographing all the time to try and monitor what's happening. Then I think it's the implementation phase that's actually the easier part in terms of the process. But it's always working the whole time along with the community so they're part of the process and then going through right down to what happens afterwards: managing it, maintaining it, having an operation plan so that it doesn't just end, so that the project continues, because that is also the downfall of a lot of projects, that they come to a standstill. In other words, there is never an end, and I like that about what it is and how communities change as well. I think it can be change *with* the communities or setting up structures that you can adapt to go along with the change.

I think, in terms of if one wanted to replicate it, it's quite an easy task to take, but it's knowing that you're part of the process, so you're not going to end up with just a product.

GH — That's a really good point. A lot of the time that is the attitude: there's the issue, and here's the solution, bam, and then, okay, on to the next thing.

KE — Yeah, we'll disappear. I mean, how does one work with community in terms of spatial design? It's a very difficult task. We've been trying to come up with ways of how you can work a process through with people who have a very basic understanding of how you read a plan or how you read a map, trying to create games and tools that you can use with community but that can continue all the way through, and then hopefully people can learn through the process as well.

I mean, if you're working with children, one learns a lot, and how they then transfer that sort of information through to their parents is interesting as well. We're trying in informal areas to focus on childhood development, but it's just in its initial stages, but I think we've already learned a lot, as I was saying previously, about how one can change your design or mold it.

GH — That's good. Anything else you want to say?

KE — I don't know. The project is very exciting. It's an amazing project to work on because there's always something around the corner that you never expected, and I think you learn, and I think if you're learning along with the process, you can only be enhancing the environment itself. You feel humbled at times because it's the unexpected, and what you almost want or what you think is right is sometimes not right at all. I think that is a wonderful way of working with communities—not necessarily the solution, but it's one way to make better environments for people who want to actually be involved in those areas.

GH — It's interesting, doing that through design and the idea of the role of design and design thinking in these processes that people in the community or the users might not be really aware of.

KE — What I also find interesting is we have the different work streams, and we work very closely with the social crime prevention. Not only the community are teaching you how to design but also the social conditions, like how do we allow platforms for people to come and have a public speech about rape or HIV? Do you create an open platform, or do you create a closed platform? It automatically starts giving you design steps to start working your way around this.

A lot of that has also come, for me, from the informal area where I've been working, because there's so little there. Even the smallest of interventions has a big impact, and how do we engage that? We just put a container facility down in Monwabisi Park, and it's been a wonderful sort of process, because we've had difficulties in getting the container up and running to operational standards, but there's a group of people, and we call them facility guardians, and they've taken ownership over the facility. They are the community, and they have decided to look after the facility as part of our process of social crime prevention and the neighborhood watch process, which is all about volunteers. It's been really nice to see how people feel like they're part of the process, and we haven't even finished the facility yet. They put in a bed, and they have coffee and tea going all the time and stuff, so it's actually quite nice when you go there. It's quite dynamic. It's not how we envisaged it to happen. "Always expect the unexpected" is one of my mottoes.

—

Alastair Graham (AG)/ Project Manager, VPUU Project, City of Capetown

Gary Hustwit — For starters, can you tell us about Khayelitsha and the history of the area, how and why it was created?

Alastair Graham — Sure. Khayelitsha is a dormitory residential suburb which was established during the apartheid era. It was specifically developed as a dormitory residential area with no economic base, no real industry, economy, nothing like that. People lived here, and they were required to travel out of the area to gain access to jobs. It was a place which was not integrated with the city at all. It's about 28 years old currently, and it's probably in the region of six hundred thousand people living here. There's different figures, but I think six hundred thousand is probably more or less correct.

GH — How big of an area are we talking about?
AG — I would say more or less 50 square kilometers.

GH — Can you talk about the conditions leading up to the project, what were the challenges involved?
AG — Khayelitsha was characterized by very high levels of violent crime, very poor socioeconomic conditions, very poor levels of service to individuals within households. If you looked at Khayelitsha about four years ago when we last did an overall survey of the township, 65 percent of the population of Khayelitsha were living in shacks. Those informal

settlements are characterized by a lack of access to basic services, very poor health conditions, and very, very high crime rates.

The VPUU program focuses on geographic focus areas or safe node areas. We look at areas with a population of between 50,000 and 100,000 people. Our objectives are to improve the quality of life, to improve the socioeconomic situation, and to improve safety and security. Our other objectives are to address social, economic, cultural, and spatial exclusion which happened as a result of apartheid. Those are our main objectives.

GH — It seems with any urban design project, the politics are so complex just to get very basic things done.

AG — Yeah. Politically within South Africa, the government is playing a kind of numbers game, especially with the delivery of houses. It's about meeting a certain number within a certain period of time. Issues of quality of design, they fall by the wayside. Generally it's the single-dwelling residential format. One house, one plot, which has been promoted through the housing subsidy system of the government. For us, that's very problematic.

Generally what's happened is that these dormitory residential suburbs were established. The apartheid legislation fell away. We still sit with the impact which apartheid had on human settlements. It hasn't changed. Apartheid laws could still be in place, and it probably wouldn't look much different. What we're doing within this program and also within the informal settlement program is to focus on the collective good or the shared good or, in physical terms, the public environment, so basic services and things which people share within the public environment. We don't focus on the delivery of housing, so it's not individual good which we're looking at. What you'll see here outside, within Harare, is a pedestrian route that stretches from Monwabisi Park informal settlement all the way through to Khayelitsha Central Business District. Along that, different investments are made. It's a strategic focus within this community. I'll explain a little bit later on how that kind of decision of intervention was arrived at.

GH — Could you talk about the community role both in the design of the interventions and the also the ongoing involvement?

AG — Generally, our methodology, what it looks at is, as a first step, forming a partnership with the community at all the levels within the community. We have a coordinator of community consultation; he does a really brilliant job. Then within each safe node area we have a community facilitator from Khayelitsha who's deployed to those communities. They manage the relationship between the program and the community, and they represent the community. They ensure on a daily basis that we're engaging with the appropriate structures and promoting this issue of partnership. You could say, instead of empowerment, we look at negotiated solutions.

So the first step is the partnership with the community. The next thing we'd look at within that process is a baseline survey to establish with the community what the conditions are within the area. What we've done initially within the VPUU program is to look at two aspects. We'd like to find out what the community's understanding of crime is and how crime manifests itself, especially in terms of how it impacts on their lives. Then we'd look at an assessment of the local economy. We'd do a business survey to gather that data.

With respect to the crime mapping and the understanding of how the community understands crime, we would do something which we call rapid urban appraisal. We would engage with the community within the different sectors: sports, arts, culture, law enforcement agencies, civic organizations, other community representatives, schools, church groups. With each group, we would look at mapping crime on a large aerial photograph. We'd bring the maps together, and it would start to give a picture of how crime actually manifests itself within the physical environment. Why is a particular space, like this one, a crime hot spot? What are the issues? There's lack of passive surveillance. The properties aren't facing the detention pond. This is a detention pond behind us. All the other houses face the road on the other side, so there's no passive surveillance behind the homes. It's not a positive space. It's been designed to flood three times a year, and that's all it does, but it's a place where dead bodies are getting dumped and where rapes and murders are happening. One of the worst crime hot spots in Cape Town or probably in the whole of South Africa was the particular space we're sitting in now.

So that crime mapping would start to identify these crime hot spots. The business survey, the way we started it when we started the program was to go door to door and to go to every single property within the area, pick out all the businesses, and then go through a process of training community members to administer a questionnaire to the businesses identified to unpack what it is they're doing, how they get their product in, who's protecting their stuff when they leave, how many people do they employ? We start to understand the local economy. What are the potential opportunities? What are the things which they've missed out on, which perhaps could be introduced through this program to stimulate local business? Where would they like to do business if they had a choice?

One of the things which emerged within this business survey was that there's no business-owned property. In terms of the zoning scheme and the planning for the area, people are doing business illegally out of their own residential properties or wherever they can get a piece of land. So the zoned property for business doesn't exist. When we asked them, "Where would you like to do business?" it was often where the worst crime hot spots are. What does that tell us? That tells us that the criminal elements and the criminal activities occupied the space with economic potential. That becomes one of the first clues. If we can work with the community and invest especially within those places where there's a crime problem but there's also economic potential, we can start to help the community to positively occupy dangerous space. That becomes one of the fundamental issues.

Typically what government in South Africa has done is they have a menu of things which they do normally, and they've done them historically, and they continue to do them. It's not often meeting the needs of the community. It's missing the target. Then the community doesn't take ownership of it, and it becomes vandalized. City government doesn't maintain it, and it becomes a crime hot spot. So those are the alternatives. You have a public environment which is not serving its function for the community. It's actually a dangerous space where you don't let your kids go after dark or early in the morning because they become the victims of crime.

GH — Obviously, we see the success in terms of kids playing here, and this is a very active public space. Could you give us a statistical idea of how it's impacting crime in Khayelitsha as a whole?

AG — We measure the crime levels by working with the police, and we run a household survey, which picks up on indicators which have been agreed upon with the community with respect to success and failure and the extent to which people feel safe. The murder rate has come down by approximately 40 percent in the area since VPUU started. That 40 percent basically accounts for the murders which happen within the public environment. The other two thirds or 60 percent is what happens behind closed doors. You could argue that the investment within the public environment has, to a large extent, resolved the violent crime.

It's not just the physical investments. It's also the programs and the investment in people. Our social development coordinator, our social crime prevention coordinator, they'll also talk to you about the neighborhood patrols which we run, the promotion of volunteerism within the community, et cetera. But the crime levels have dropped dramatically within the public environment. Much longer-term interventions are required to start addressing crime which is happening behind closed doors like domestic violence.

GH — What are the next phases of the project? Is it moving more into the informal settlement?

AG — There's a mixture. We've worked typically within formal areas. I've mentioned dormitory residential suburbs, and this is a Black African township. This is how it originally established itself. It's got a particular crime pattern to it and a particular dynamic to the community. We've now moved into more informal settlements. I think Kathryn might have mentioned that we've got five pilot informal settlement improvement areas of which three are in Khayelitsha. There's one down south and another one in Philippi. Collectively, in that group of settlements, there's about 25,000 households living in shacks. I don't know if you've seen the shacks yet or not, they're made out of mostly roof sheeting and pieces of wood and black plastic. Generally that's what they're made out of, and people are living on the ground. That project has started fairly recently. It started about a year ago. We did all of the agreements, and we worked out a project plan that's up and running at the moment.

We're currently finishing off Phase 2 of the VPUU program within Khayelitsha. What we're entering into now from the 1st of July onwards is Phase 3, where we look at spreading the program into Manenberg and Hanover Park. Those are two suburbs within the more central area of this depressed part of the city, so a little bit north of here. They're areas which are characterized by gangsterism, something which you might be more familiar with from America. It's a kind of Chicago. Every street or city block has a gang in it. These gangs are linked to the prisons. The retail drug trade is a big issue within the area. There's a lot of fighting between gangs over territory. The gang activity has found its way into the schools. There's a lot of violent crime. In the last couple of months, I think there have been about 10 killings there from shootings between these gangs.

Within Manenberg and Hanover Park, a significant drug is methamphetamine, which you probably know in the States. Here it's called tik. I think about 25 percent of school kids are using tik within Manenberg and Hanover Park. It becomes a real problem when they're trying to maintain their habits and to get money to buy the drugs. They steal from their own families. There's violence within families. People lose their ability to judge whether they're doing something right or wrong. They end up actually hurting family members and members of the community to get their next fix.

GH — Can there be an urban design solution to that?
    AG — You know, what we can say is that the real crime hot spots within the community are the places where the retail drug trade's happening. That's one thing. Obviously there needs to be programs around rehabilitation, drug treatment, alcoholism treatment. That's something which we're looking at as well. Then the programs around dealing with victims and perpetrators, reinforcing the schools.

    If we look at the schools on the Cape Flats—when we say the Cape Flats, that's the area of poverty of the city. It's historically been called the Cape Flats. Within Mitchell's Plain and Khayelitsha, there's about 110 schools, of which two thirds are primary schools, one third high schools. All of the schools, all that they're offering kids is classroom activity. The kids go into the classroom, they receive their lessons, and that's it. There's no sport. There's no cultural activities. When I went to school, I could choose from a whole menu of different activities which I could become involved in. That doesn't exist within the poorest communities within Cape Town. Those kids are out on the street. They're a very vulnerable group from one or three in the afternoon. Generally, both of their parents are working or trying to earn some kind of a living. It becomes a recruiting ground for the gangs as well and a recruiting ground to get people addicted to maintain the actual drug retail trade. So it's not necessarily only urban design, it's about investment in the children, investment in the schools, the social programs.

GH — Maybe we can talk about the involvement of FIFA and the role of sports in this.
    AG — Sure. There's a pedestrian route which runs up and down from the informal settlements to Khayelitsha CBD. There's also a cycle route which runs across the space laterally, which was developed by the city

about eight years ago. It wasn't designed very well. It also became a place which was occupied by violent crime. When we were looking at the options with the community on how to deal with this space, there were two important corners. One was this one, which is now occupied with this active box building to anchor this edge of the square, and on the other corner we didn't have anything.

What happened was that the Khayelitsha Development Forum had approached FIFA. We didn't know anything about it. It was at the time when the planning for the 2010 World Cup was happening. They had heard that FIFA was going to develop 20 sports centers for 2010 across Africa of which five were coming to South Africa. What they felt was, as it was I think the 25th anniversary, at the time, of Khayelitsha, they would like to mark that with the establishment of the first center. I got called in together with Michael Krause by the Khayelitsha Development Forum to assist them in identifying a site. We immediately thought, the perfect place for this thing is here, and the scale of that project was a kind of scale which fitted quite well within this environment. Unfortunately, the Khayelitsha Development Forum had identified much higher order sites, entry points to Khayelitsha where a project of this size might have been lost. We went through the process of thinning down the list of sites chosen until we arrived at this one.

The basic philosophy behind this project is that it's attracting kids to sport. There's a small Astroturf soccer field with kickboards on the side. It's 20 meters by 40 meters, and it's got proper goals with nets and everything. The kids are attracted to the sport, and they're getting access to health and life skills, education and counseling, especially for abused children. So it's a facility which starts to provide those other tools which kids need apart from the education they're receiving in schools.

It's an extremely well-used facility. It's accommodating both girls and boys equally. It's teaching them how to deal with conflict. They do role-plays. You'll probably be able to go film some of it later because the activities are happening now during school holidays. It was something which kind of landed in our lap. Fortunately we had the ability to incorporate something like that. We've had flexibility, and we make our own decisions within the team on how we do the development with the community. I think it worked out well for everybody. We invested some of the funds to construct that center. FIFA invested others. We've got a service provider called Grassroot Soccer. Grassroot Soccer is running the center initially for a period of five years. They have an agreement with our sport and recreation department on the offerings each year, of how the center runs.

GH — I can only imagine, for a kid in the community suddenly to have this really cool world-class field, it must be the greatest thing in the world.

AG — It is. For the children, that's absolutely fantastic. They're using that facility every single day. The Astroturf, I think, is of a quality that will last for 10 years. What it's shown in terms of mainstreaming for the city is that there are other options apart from grass fields, which the city typically provides, full-sized, grass soccer fields, which require watering and maintenance. This is a very low-maintenance option, and it can accommodate way more activity on it. The city's now starting to roll out similar facilities within other communities. It was a relatively small project but with an extremely high impact within the community and within the city.

I forgot to mention, the approach and the process of designing and deciding on the sites and coming up with the management plan and all of the agreements which were put in place for that facility, FIFA's now using those as best practice. They're going to be using them in Brazil for the 2014 soccer World Cup. So a lot of what was learned here—and this was the first one developed in the world—is now going to be replicated as FIFA moves on.

GH — If there's a takeaway, I guess, from the lessons that you've learned in the VPUU project, how would you sum it up?

AG — I would say that I think the biggest thing is the partnership with the community. I haven't gone into much detail around that, but it's a thing which happens at many levels. It's happening every day of the week, that partnership with the community.

I think the second thing is we've been fortunate enough to develop and integrate a plan for the entire community and to have sufficient control that we can implement it over a defined period of time. That's a really big thing because our departments within government are operating within silos. They generally operate separately on an ad hoc basis. So to be able to leverage that control of how things get implemented has been a big success factor. Without that, I don't think this would have happened.

—

Edgar Pieterse (EP)/ June 27, 2011 Cape Town

Edgar Pieterse is an urban scholar, writer and creative agent whose interests include the theory and practice of policy discourses and interventions to make African cities more just, open and accessible. He holds the South African Research Chair in Urban Policy at the University of Cape Town and is director of the African Centre for Cities. He is the author of numerous books and the co-editor of the ongoing *The African Cities Reader* series.

What initially drew me to Edgar was his expertise on African cities, but I quickly learned that his ideas on urbanism are truly global.

—

Gary Hustwit — Okay, I guess for starters, just maybe tell us a little bit about the ACC?

Edgar Pieterse — Sure. The African Centre for Cities is university based. It's three years old now. We set it up in 2008, and really it was a response to the university recognizing that the urban question in Africa is massive, and it's totally under-researched and under-studied. More importantly, most of the urban challenges require different disciplines to come together to provide their particular perspective on an issue. The question was, how do you create an interdisciplinary forum across the university that can draw in the strengths of different disciplines and different faculties? In that sense, the ACC is a massive experiment because, of course, universities are designed to produce specialists in particular disciplines, and as with all experiments, we're learning a lot. It's good fun, but we're making a lot of mistakes, and we have to figure this out basically as we go.

One of the interesting issues that has emerged is that, if you're going to deal with the scale and the rapidity of change in African cities, you're going to need similar centers across the continent in various universities, and we've gone looking, and they don't exist. This is really peculiar—a continent with seven hundred million people, about three hundred or four hundred million of whom are urbanized, and there is no dedicated research capability in the universities to deal with the consequences of rapid urbanization.

What we do is applied research. We look at very specific urban challenges, and we bring different knowledge to bear on those problems and try and see whether, through the interaction between practitioners, scholars, and activists, we can generate new understandings and possibly solutions to some of the questions.

Over and above that, we're also redesigning curricula so that the professionals that emerge out of universities can be more equipped and more realistic about what the realities are that they're going to enter and have the right set of sensibilities to not have a professional arrogance or have an academic distance that doesn't allow them to get involved in the grit of what is emerging in these cities. Because you need that capability to see the solutions, if you will, with other people.

The third thing that we do is to not lose sight of the almost pure academic exercise, so some of our work is more theoretical. We think that you cannot divorce good policy work or good applied research from the bigger philosophical, theoretical questions: What's an African city? What makes it unique? How do we understand African urbanism at this particular time in history, and how can those philosophical ideas help us to think more effectively about what constitutes a viable response to the challenges?

GH — Would you say that rapid urbanization is the biggest issue for African cities?
EP — Yes, of course, because Africa, along with Asia, its urban transition is just taking off. In all other parts of the world, it's pretty much completed, so you see there urbanization rates of between 70 to 80 percent. Your challenge is more how to deal with people who are in the cities, whereas in Africa and Asia, the issue is that you've got all this growth happening over the next 20 to 30 years, basically a doubling of the urban population. At the same time, we haven't really dealt with the people that are already there, and so it's a combination of dealing with widespread poverty manifested most explicitly in Africa in pervasive slums and all of the living conditions attendant to that. In addition to that, you've now got to think about dealing with the doubling of that population. What makes it particularly difficult in Africa is that the United Nation is telling us that almost all of those people that will urbanizing will also be poor. It's not as if you're getting a massive influx of skills and capital and resources, but you're rather getting a massive influx of people that need a lot of support to be able to find a foothold in the city and to have a viable livelihood.

How to deal with that combination of things is a unique problem, the scale of it, and to compound things, the states in most African countries are still in denial about this. It's not as if they're putting in place the measures or the resources or the preparatory steps to really come to terms with this transition and to respond effectively. A good example of that is if you look at the discourse that comes from the African Union or from the NEPAD program, which is an African development agenda. All of it is about the second green revolution. It's about this vision of how Africa's role in the global economy over the next 20 to 30 years is to become the food basket of the world. Now, of course, that's laudable at one level, but if your vision about the future of the continent is essentially still agricultural and rural, you are fundamentally missing what is really going on. This is, in a way, almost the biggest challenge we're confronting—to raise the understanding and the awareness amongst people who control the resources that inform our developmental structure, to raise awareness amongst them about just what is actually going on and what the scale of the urban question is and how urgent it is to have a concerted response.

GH — A lot of the projects we've looked at around the world are very laudable, really interesting projects, but I don't think the majority of governmental responses are that effective.

EP — Absolutely. Two things: One is, it's very easy to get incredibly pessimistic and talk about just the prospects looking forward, because if you just look at the numbers and the trend lines, it's profoundly depressing. I mean, you just want to slit your wrists basically. This is not a healthy area of research and engagement, but that's it. At the same time, what we know from history is that you really need a small group of innovators, a small group of people that can demonstrate how to do things differently. Once that gets mainstreamed, change happens really quickly. There's some tipping point that happens, and then all of a sudden it becomes absolutely normal and the right thing to do things in a particular way.

The people who, in a way, pioneer those ideas, if they took the pessimistic view, if they were just clinical and followed the scientific trends and evidence, they'd never innovate. You need a sense of sort of dogged optimism and a sense of passion that the problem is solvable at one level and that, in fact, more than that, there is something about the confluence of obstacles that makes this an incredibly challenging and interesting design problematic. I mean design, both in the very broad sense of the term and also as a set of almost philosophical, theoretical ideas to think about what is going on, and what are the underlying drivers and dynamics here that we need a language for still. There are people who are finding contradictions in this really difficult situation and finding gaps and ways in to innovate and to do some really interesting things.

I think the challenge we have at the moment is, how do you connect these points of innovation and the really interesting platforms? Because typically it's not an individual. Typically it's an interesting lateral network of people in the city or in a neighborhood that is able to cross traditional boundaries and that can almost have an outlaw mentality. They find each other, and they find ways of knitting together their various agendas to begin to push back against the mainstream inertia, if you will, on dealing with the urban challenges. I think that at one level, almost within a city, you want these people to find each other, to work well; you want to create the platforms to make that possible, to give them some room to maneuver. Then over and above that, you need to network these people across cities and across territories.

GH — Some of the things you just said sort of apply to the VPUU. Can you give us a Khayelitsha 101, just to give us some background on it?

EP — Sure, I will do that and also look a little bit into the bigger South Africa story. South Africa is interesting. It's almost a parable, right? One of the fundamental challenges confronted by cities everywhere, whether they're wealthy or poor, is this intensifying problem of what one could call dual cities: the city for the wealthy, the globally connected, the mobile middle class, and the city for the people who are marginalized from those opportunities, who can't access them because they're not part of the knowledge economy. They don't have the education; they don't have the training; they don't have the papers. These very stark social divides, which are growing, are manifesting spatially increasingly, so the middle class are often opting out of universal state delivery systems in these cities, and they're privatizing, basically, access to services, security, gardening, whatever the case may be. Because they want to live in this incredibly pristine and isolated set of conditions that allow them, if you will, to be a city within a city, but the net consequence of that is of course that the state doesn't have the resources or the capacity to deal with the people who are off the grid or are marginalized.

This sort of crude dynamic—in a way, really the ultimate paradigm of it was the apartheid city. That's exactly what the South African government used to do of course: the white population, which was a small minority, 10 percent of the population, got to live in urban environments in suburban conditions that were equivalent to a Scandinavian country or Canada or something, if not a higher per capita living standard, and that was on the back of excluding 80, 90 percent of the population from these opportunities. Because cities concretize inequalities and exclusions in the built fabric, it means that you sit with 40-, 50-, 60-, 100-year legacies, because roads are roads, and roads are going to last you 60 to a 100 years. Townships are built. They're there.

Khayelitsha is a very interesting story because it's one of the youngest townships in South Africa. It was built in the 1980s, so it's really recent, and it offered the latest example of the then local authority trying to concentrate a growing African black population in the city at the periphery of the city. It was a response to a growing informalization, to slums, to a whole bunch of really difficult urban problems, but moreover, it also represented a perfect security solution because you could isolate a potentially rebellious community. You design the road infrastructure so that military tanks and so forth could get into two or three access points, and they could shut down the area; they could cut it off from the rest of the city. More importantly, you could also design it in a way that people were sort of told, or they understood, they were not citizens of the city. They were meant to just be in dormitory settlements where they could literally sleep, get on a train to get to work in the day, and go back to that, but they weren't expected to live a full urban life, have access to culture, to art, to spiritual opportunities, to sport, et cetera, et cetera. That's how Khayelitsha grew up, but of course, as with all authoritarian conceits, it didn't work. It couldn't contain the messiness of real life.

Also, it became where new urban dwellers settled in the city. Land was the cheapest; you could access some space to put up your shack; and because it was large—it's probably close to half a million people there now—it was easy to evade surveillance by the state. That meant that by 2010 or the last five years or so, in the mid-2000s, Khayelitsha was really sort of the darkest example of what I call the new apartheid legacy that we have. You have people still marginalized, excluded along apartheid lines. They're physically trapped, and that then becomes a trap for all kinds of other disadvantages—you're far from work opportunities, et cetera—and within that, what happens is that, obviously, it's a perfect pressure-cooker environment for all the worse social ills to breed in. In Khayelitsha, particularly social violence, crimes against person, crimes against business, and so on, were basically off the charts, and it's very clear that that has got clear, spatial, social drivers underneath it.

GH — Could you talk about jobs and the economic issues in cities here?

EP — Sure. Again, I think South Africa is quite an extreme example. In South Africa, the official rate of unemployment is 30 percent of the labor force, and that excludes people who've stopped looking for work. If you add them in, you get up to 35 percent. If you look at those between the ages of 16 and 24, you go up to 55 percent unemployment. It is by any sort of description a massive, massive social crisis. Because these young unemployed people are also concentrated, especially within these townships and informal settlements, it's a recipe for all kinds of challenges. As you know, South Africa has the highest HIV prevalence, so of course, the prevalence will be double in that cohort what it is for the rest of the population.

Where do you begin? What do you do? How do you start, right? Because South Africa is completely integrated into the global economy, what that has meant is that deindustrialization has pretty much set in and is the norm in the formal economy. Young people who haven't completed high school and don't have some form of additional training have basically no prospect of any kind of formal employment. That's the bottom line. If you then consider that more than 50 percent of children in South Africa in the school system will drop out halfway through high school, you can imagine the scale of it. If you further consider that of the black kids who finish high school, only 5 percent will have the right subjects and marks to enter university. And of that 5 percent, only 20 percent have math so they can do engineering or something like that. Basically it's an utter disaster. It's not going to go away anytime soon because of course education reform and changes take generations. What do you do? Where do you start?

One of the things we have to learn from and think about is what India is doing in its rural areas through its Employment Guarantee Scheme. Essentially, what India is doing in rural India is to guarantee every household a hundred days of paid work a year, and they organize various institutions to manage this process at the village level. It's been one of the most successful antipoverty programs in the world and linked also to some of the things Brazil has done to deal with both unemployment and poverty. But even in those countries, you're not talking about unemployment above 10 percent. You know, you're talking about a very different magnitude of issues.

What we have to think about for our cities is basically to create what I would call new categories of work. We've got to look at ecological services as a public good. One of the interesting paradoxes of the apartheid legacy is that you get very generous spaces, right? The poor also live in basically suburbs or suburban landscapes, so you've got massive parks; you've got massive pavements; you've got all these open spaces that need maintenance. The river systems are pretty badly degraded, and we've got a massive alien vegetation problem in our cities, which undermines agricultural productivity and also the prospects of urban agriculture. There is no reason why one can't have large-scale public works types of programs that do ecological service restoration work. The important thing about that is that I think that there's something spiritually really profound about getting young people to reengage nature, right? I think if one can combine these programs with kind of educational programs as well about how we rethink our relationship with ecology, it could really be profound, and so there's no reason why you can't extend that pedagogy into all primary and high school learning environments.

That's one set of issues. The other is, because of the massive prevalence of HIV and other diseases like tuberculosis and so forth, we've got an imperative to do what we call home-based care, because obviously you can't absorb these people into hospitals and clinics. We literally need an army of people who can visit households, make sure people are taking their antiretrovirals, that their diets are suitable for what they're taking, and so on. And again, if you add this up, you're talking about tens of thousands of jobs, home-based care jobs. If we sort of draw a circle around something called the care economy and we create intermediary institutions to structure these things, to organize them well, to support them, that can be an incredibly powerful platform to rebuild social cohesion and to rebuild a sense of purpose. Like ecological work, I think social care work can be incredibly restorative for people who've sort of fallen through the cracks.

Then there are the very conventional public works things. If you drive around in our townships, you'll see that in our primary and high schools there are very generous playgrounds, but they can't be maintained. The proportion between the building and, if you will, the recreational areas is completely out of whack. Again, it's a legacy from the past. There is no reason why we can't, again, create these sort of work groups of people that can specifically do maintenance of these spaces, do gardening within them, and so forth and so forth.

You can go through a whole range of things where it is relatively easy to imagine and to design a series of public-good jobs that obviously won't be paid a formal wage or necessarily the minimum wage, but what it can do is provide a bridge out of this condition of extreme marginalization and no prospect of work into something that benefits society at large and makes the city work. Because at the moment the city doesn't work for most people, and it's because its network of open space, its network of social space, is completely degraded and not maintained.

The final point to make about that is that, if you do these things well, there is also no reason why it can't be a mechanism to get the middle class and, if you will, the privileged in our cities to provide support and to engage through a kind of social media platform. These are ways that you can begin to create social connects. There are hundreds of lawyers and accountants and teachers and whatever who want to do something. They want to be engaged in the city, but they don't know how. They don't have the mechanisms. If you have these kinds of programs, they will need accountants. They will need technical support to make them work well. But all you really need is the emotional connect with the middle class.

In our case, the biggest issue is that the middle classes don't go to the townships. They never set foot there. They don't run into informal settlement. They have no conception of what it looks like or the people who live there, and in a way, sort of finding ways to cross that social distance would, I think, be one of the key things that would generate jobs, because these are people that can see business opportunities. They can support entrepreneurial effort if they're there and they provide the support, and we've got all the resources in our society, but somehow we're not able to activate these opportunities to deal with the jobless problem.

GH — Something that I've seen with slums like Dharavi for instance is almost kind of romanticization of informal settlements, maybe because there is this variety to them.

EP — Yes. So you're asking about whether there is a romanticization of informality. I mean, it's an interesting challenge. Well, so the first thing I'd say is yes. At one level, because of the negative stereotypes and the disregard that some decision-makers have for, if you will, what's going on in informal settlements, there's an important kind of ideological work that needs to be done to convince them or to persuade them that these are not just spaces of poverty and abjectness and vice and so forth. In fact, there's logics at work here, and for people to keep life and limb together in those contexts implies incredible ingenuity and capacity and so on. Of course, those arguments are valid, and they're important, and they need to be made, and you need a degree of that sort of statement to draw people in and to get people to take the settlement seriously. That's one step in an awareness-raising process, but it is important that one doesn't get sucked into the *Slumdog Millionaire* kind of idea that there's fundamentally a golden thread, and there's a rainbow at the end of every slum and so on.

Really, to live there is hell, right? You are very likely to be raped at some point in your life. You're very likely to suffer extreme vulnerability. You're very likely to often go without food. You're going to pay 20, 30, 40, 50 times what middle class households pay to get a liter of water, and you can't give your children what they want and need in life, and you can't in any way gloss over or romanticize that as a daily reality that you've got to negotiate and navigate. I think it is equally important to also be confronted by and learn from just how harsh and painful and violent everyday life is in those contexts, in very large slums like in Kibera or in India where, for example, you've got to suffer the daily indignity of defecating in the open. I mean, just that point alone sort of makes the point.

The struggle is, how does one recognize and validate the ingenuity involved in negotiating life in the slum but at the same time be honest about the profound social injustice implied with people living like that? Because, if you don't recognize people's capacity for invention and creation within these settings, you're never going to take participatory design seriously, right? You're always going to have a benign top-down response. If you also don't recognize that people live in pretty inhumane conditions, you won't recognize that there's certain basics that governments just need to get on. They need to provide water and sanitation, and they must provide energy. You can't have years and years and years of participatory process to just do certain things which you need to do which are just a question of equity in the city. One has got to, in a way, keep both things in mind all the time. It's really important, and in that context, romanticization is not much of a help, but at the same time, we have to recognize we need to tell certain stories that can grab people's imaginations. Sometimes that means you overromanticize.

I mean, the thing about *Slumdog Millionaire* is in fact that, for whatever my glib sort of criticism was of it earlier, it was able to put this question of slum living and its pervasiveness in the minds, in the imaginations of probably billions, or I don't know, but hundreds of millions of people, which, you know, a book that I write or whatever will never achieve ever. It's not to kind of knock the power of narrative, I suppose, and representation, but of course, in and of itself, it can be deeply problematic.

GH — I like the idea of the narrative of a city and how that's kind of formed and reinforced and changes and also how design is part of that. We could talk for a while just about that.

EP — There is something very interesting—I mean, because we work with chemical engineers through to people in the arts, it's fascinating, and so I sort of sit in the middle of these things, and everything is interesting to me. This is exactly the thing—the engineers have a linear rationality, and arts people have a narrative rationality, and it is about, how can you fuse those two very different ways of thinking about things and coming at problems into something different? So for the engineers, documentary and novels are things I use as the teaching tool to sort of confront them with just how much in life technology can't solve, right? Just to understand that you need humility to be a good designer. Just to make that point that there are multiple rationalities at work always, and your technology will be embedded in these multiple rationalities, and you'll be a good designer if it can respond in some ways to that or at least have an awareness of that. That's exactly this point about narrative: it captures a different way of thinking about things and being in the world.

GH — Yeah, it's interesting as it applies to cities, to how people are really living. There's always this idea of the city; I guess a lot of the causes of this kind of rapid urbanization are just about very day-to-day things like jobs, money, food, education, but there is also that dream of what the city is.

EP — I mean, it's interesting because in the last five years or so there's been a shift in the general awareness or consciousness about this urban question, and I suppose it's this hype around being 50 percent urban as a species or whatever. It has in a way induced again this yearning for a utopia, the idea that there is a kind of a design solution that can deal with the environmental question—cities being the main contributor to CO_2 emissions and that they're fundamentally sort of the cause of environmental unsustainability.

There's this need for figuring out a new way of being, a new way of living, in terms of the basics of family life and career and jobs and mobile jobs and all of this stuff, the prospect of being able to work in an urban environment that's not necessarily a large city, right? It's been interesting for me at least, as a kind of nontechnical person, to just see, at the level of these eco-cities like Masdar or Dongtan or whatever, the massive reinvestment in this very old idea that there is somewhere waiting out there a perfect form and shape of the city that can solve all our problems, and also this idea that somehow you can get rid of the messiness of urban life. In a way, what makes cities interesting is that they're messy and unpredictable and chaotic and crazy, and they throw up the unexpected, which is what fuels us. It's an interesting thing. Also, some of the designers around Masdar, these things, I mean, it's fine. If they want to do R&D for the world, no problem, and if they want to use oil money for it, even less of a problem, but the point is how the superstar architects latch on to these things, because I think they do think that somehow they can leave a utopian legacy, and I'm just tickled by that. It's curious. It's interesting.

GH — It comes back to kind of that Corbusian, modernist ideal, the separation of functions.

EP — Well, it's seldom mixed income, but it has to be mixed use. Yes, obviously I come across this a lot, and my thing always is, "Okay, so in that mixed use, show me the income spectrum, and then we'll talk. If you can crack that in a mixed-use environment, fine, we can talk, but don't sort of get all excited about mixed use."

GH — Because normally it's not mixed income.

EP — Yeah, exactly. Basically it's just creating really pristine and very comfortable, very self-satisfying environments for us, for the cappuccino-drinking middle class elite. I want to walk between the movie house and the library and whatever, but the reason it can exist is because it excludes people who can't afford that lifestyle. That's the bloody point. If you can design that, which I totally agree with as a principle, but in a way that is equitable and democratic and can give access to everybody, then we can talk; then I'm interested. But if you're doing more of the same garden cities crap, I mean, anybody can do that.

GH — Can we talk a little bit about public space and the role of public space? This is universal to cities everywhere. In the film, there's a lot of talk about democracy in public space.

EP — Look, my take on the public space thing is very pragmatic. Yes, it has all of these important political and other resonances, but I think they're completely overstated, okay? I think of that in very pragmatic terms because in most slums of the world and in most poor areas the domestic living environment is so overcrowded and so cramped that you have to live your life, if you will, on the street to have a viable life, economically, socially, and in other ways. Within those contexts, in a way, the premium space within poor settlements in particular is the public spaces, but these have to be public spaces that can do multiple things. They've got to facilitate access to livelihood, to trading opportunities, et cetera, et cetera. They've got to facilitate access to the very romantic sort of European notion of the public space as the space for the ambler, for chance encounters, et cetera. I think they should do those things as well, but also they've got to really respond to things like spiritual needs.

So a big challenge in cities of the Global South is where you congregate for spiritual activity. People use, of course, every nook and cranny, but this is something that is really fundamental to how people keep themselves together, if you will, in very harsh environments, and if one can recognize and validate that and facilitate it through appropriate design of public space, that's an important thing.

My personal view is that the most important investment in these environments is investment that can animate and activate cultural life, so of course, within that I'll include public space, but I think that there is something more profound. There's something about how we remake the fundamental process of education through the arts. I think that if we can figure out how to get our children particularly, even before primary school, but in the primary school years to have access to structured opportunities of becoming proficient in a range of the arts as a way of locating themselves in the world and building critical faculty, the investment we make into, if you will, basic education as society will have much, much greater returns.

For me, it's the key if public space can be thought of as being the premium, premium space in poor neighborhoods, the most important multifunctional space and something that requires the most urgent attention. But of course, because of all of those uses it has to have, it has to be done in a way that allows people to design it themselves because they're going to maintain it. They've got to use it. I think that there's been generally a kind of homogenization of a set of design principles for public spaces in these areas, and I'm deeply skeptical and weary of those things because I think that they just preclude a really organic process from emerging.

So that's my spiel on it. As I've said, these are very pragmatic things. In Cape Town, for example, we've put a ton of money into the public spaces for the elites. We've pedestrianized the downtown. Jan Gehl was here, and he told us which streets we should do. We're ticking all the boxes on how you revitalize and make your downtown walkable and all the cool stuff you should be doing as part of creating the scene for Richard Florida's creative class to feel happy and safe and comfortable and all inspired and creative in Cape Town. Of course, this is detracting from what is required in terms of what VPUU should be doing and others like that but on a much larger scale, right?

If your look proportionally, I'm pretty sure, and I haven't done the research, so I'm sort of speculating, but if you put the budget of downtown public space revitalization next to what VPUU got and what we're spending on public spaces in the townships in Cape Town—I'm sure you're talking about this, right?—the orders of magnitude and difference would be enormous. And I suspect this is going on pretty much everywhere. On the back of this creative class discourse with this focus on walkability and all of this stuff, there's just the kind of urban renewal focus that I think is really distorting the debate around how fundamental good public spaces are particularly in poor areas of cities.

GH — Yeah. I wasn't in Khayelitsha five years ago before it started, but I can only imagine, I mean, by just seeing now that it's been a big, big benefit. Even the idea they could have a little world-class football field is so great.

EP — Exactly. And symbolically that's so powerful because, if you're driving on any of our main arteries, you just see the kids playing on the edges, right? One thing that's particular about South African cities is that the most important social and sporting activity for ordinary kids is not prioritized. That's why that's so fantastic. For me, it's sport, it's culture that's key. By culture, I mean things like choral societies. In South Africa, we've got a very long tradition of choirs, and it's an incredible tradition. Something like that, which is really pervasive across class, across race, a cultural tradition which is just reinventing itself despite the influx of global culture—it's like, why are we not using that as a key social design intervention in the city? It's beyond me.

We've got this amazing facility in downtown, which is the old city hall. So the municipal government is no longer there, but it's still a public facility. It's got a big organ, and the acoustics are designed for classical music. When I was in government, we put forward this proposal to make it a hub for choral music, but across all genres, and really the one thing that every Capetonian community could relate to would be this space where they'd know they would go and listen to things. Then you use that copresence as a way of slowly building hybrids and so on. Of course, because of a simple fucking thing like maintenance contracts, we couldn't persuade the city to release the building for this, but anyway it's a long story.

GH — Can we talk about citizens' role in the design of their cities, both formally and informally? It seems there are different levels of A) awareness of the design and B) the sense that they do have an active role.

EP — Yeah, I mean, this is a very tricky thing. Again, I'm not of the school of thought that citizens have to participate in everything, and then you do it. I think that completely misses the point, and cities are very complex systems and very complex ecologies. They also represent the copresence of different temporalities, right? If you decide to put a road somewhere, you're making a commitment to urban form for a hundred years in a particular way. It makes no difference how much the adjoining communities participate. That road will have that function for that period of time.

One of the challenges about citizen participation is to really think through what the different moments and the different points for engagement are, and how do you create legitimacy for citizen voice? It's really important not just to aggregate participation at the individual household level in a local project, which is one moment, but also to recognize that you need citizens to be organized into social movements and other federated structures so that they can have an input about the billion-dollar investments that are going to last for 50 years and for 100 years. But it is inappropriate for an individual household to have that decision-making power, if you know what I mean. To just talk about citizen participation in the design of the city as an obvious and natural good, I think, is a bit too simplistic. We've got to think in more differentiated ways about what the different moments and points of intersection and engagement are in the design process.

When you think of citizen design, it is equally important to recognize, if you will, what is subterranean design and what is above-ground design. Of course, the subterranean designs are all these billion-dollar investments in terms of your energy system, your water system, your drainage system, and all of these things—your broadband footprint and so forth—which usually are the purview of a very small group of people with a lot of power who in a way design for the long, long term. That sets the parameters or the framework within which particular design decisions above ground happen for a neighborhood or for a household.

How to democratize the subterranean design is a critical question that is not on the agenda at the moment. Nobody is really talking about that. It is really vital because the subterranean design structures the energy efficiency and the carbon output of a city. If we're saying that a typical city in Europe or North America has to reduce its carbon footprint by 80 percent over the next 40 years, that means every decision made now about a network or about a metro or about a power station or about anything is fundamental to that outcome. Who represents the interest of the citizens in arbitrating that? We know that we can't trust the elected politician to fulfill their duty because they're usually captured by vested interests who are more interested in getting a return on the capital of that investment. That is a large area of your citizen engagement with design that is still unspoken and invisible.

In Cape Town at the moment, they're having a massive internal discussion in the planning department and with the engineers and so on about how Cape Town's growth of the next 15 to 20 to 30 years will be structured because what they have to decide is, in the north of the city, the furthest most point from Khayelitsha, all the bulk infrastructure is at max capacity, but all the middle-class development pressure is there. Their decision is not about, should they put bulk there or not? Do they want the middle class to go there or not? That's not the debate. The debate is, should it be on the coast, or should it be in a northern zone of the city that's basically outside of the nuclear zone from the power station and also, from a sea-level-rise point of view, not as vulnerable. That's the discussion, right? They're going to make a set of investments that is going to, in a way, lock the city into a particular form and shape for the next 100 years. Do you think there's any citizen engagement with that? Do you think people in Khayelitsha are even aware of this debate?

GH — Yeah, that's interesting, the idea that there is so much activity literally underground that people don't know about. You've even got to think, where the sanitation is going to be focused can have a huge impact on outlying areas or poor areas that don't have sanitation.

EP — Yeah, exactly. Of course, just stepping back at that scale, the big design debate at the moment is, how do you restructure the resource flows in cities so that you create a circular metabolism? So in other words, you have less of the output in terms of waste that just sort of pollutes the environment, pollutes the groundwater, pollutes the soil, and so on, but rather you structure your infrastructure and your buildings in a way that allows you to recycle everything. If you want to talk at a paradigmatic level, that's the big-paradigm debate at the moment: how do you achieve that? Of course, the Scandinavian cities are way ahead in solving this problem, and it helps if you have a $50,000-per-capita society. Then you can think about these things, and you can solve them, but that, again, sort of doesn't really get to, if you will, the immediate political economy of these kinds of questions of infrastructure.

GH — Is that what the future of the cities is really dependent on, more sustainability?

EP — Well, yes. Because of the ineffectiveness of the global institutions around an international governance arrangement to deal with climate change, even though those institutions are ineffective, from my reading at least, it's clear that for the private sector and particularly multinational corporations, the penny's dropped. They're redoing their business model basically. They're assuming a postcarbon economy, and they're doing long-term R&D to figure out how that's going to pan out and what that means, and that ironically is creating a pressure on governments to have more balls, to deal with the question, right? At the moment, you've got first-mover problems with the governments because all of the decisions they need to make basically will be politically unpopular in the short term. So none of them are willing to do sort of what they have to do, except, as I said, in the Scandinavian countries and to some extent Germany.

Outside of that, I mean, we're way behind where we need to be in terms of, obviously, the scale of the adaptation challenge. It seems obvious that we will miss all the targets, so temperature rise is clearly going to get to 4, 4.5 percent, and we're going to have disastrous consequences that will impact mainly on the most vulnerable and the poorest people.

But businesses are making the shift, and so I think we're sort of 20 years out from very, very profound changes, which will impact how cities are structured and organized. Some cities will be further ahead of the curve than others. Most cities will be way behind the curve. Essentially what I anticipate is going to happen is that a new set of business strategies will emerge amongst the global utilities where they will take some of these new technologies, the most sustainable technologies, and they will sell them to cities like Cape Town and so on. I think that the big business interests in the urban infrastructure space will figure out how to make money on the sustainability agenda in the next 10 to 15 years. I do foresee that the biggest drive for urban reorganization or restructuring or reform will be the sustainability imperative. Particularly, it's a kind of resource and energy efficiency imperative. It's not sustainability in the broadest sense of the term in which you would think of social sustainability and social inclusion and these kinds of questions. It's going to be a much narrower focus that will essentially respond to, how do we organize the suburban life of the middle class? I mean, that's basically what it's going to be.

GH — Could you talk about the idea of density in big cities?

EP — It's such a cultural issue. It is so profoundly sociocultural that it's very difficult to talk about it or think about it in a uniform way. Obviously, from a resource-efficiency point of view, density makes a lot of sense. It does provide quite an important thinking principle for redesigning mobility, redesigning the relationship between different functionalities in the city, but it would be a massive error to confuse a design idea or principle with real-life cities and real-life processes. I think what we will see is a movement toward greater densities in different manifestations but an incredible variety of how that is interpreted and manifested at an urban scale in different cultural contexts.

GH — It seems to me like sustainability or arguments around density ended up getting demonized by people who say, "Oh, don't tell us how to live. I want to live in the suburbs. That's my right."

EP — Look, I mean, I think that probably in the US context in particular and certainly in South Africa, where our urban form mirrors the American urban form, there will be great resistance from the middle classes who still live in suburbs to densification and all of what goes with it. But that resistance will simply be met with new taxation instruments in 10 to 15 years' time when the new urban management and urban infrastructure technologies require a more compact urban form. I can't envisage American cities somehow becoming European cities over the next 30 to 40 years. That's unforeseeable, but there will definitely be much greater movement toward compaction, and that will be achieved through taxation. I mean, that's going to be how municipalities are going to drive that agenda. Yeah, I think the resistance will be there, and it will be loud, and it will be aggressive, but I think that, for governance, they won't have a choice.

GH — That's the other hot-button issue, though: "Taxing, oh no."

EP — Yeah, that is true.

GH — It's interesting to see, obviously mostly in a very American context, how politicized it's becoming. It seems like it's only getting more so as these issues come more to the fore.

EP — But it will shift. I mean, I think as soon as the business models of the big utilities line up with this agenda—and as I said, I think that's sort of 10 to 15 years out—it will shift. I've got very little doubt about that. Often, as in the American case, you've got such incredible cultural, political sound and fury, and then something shifts, and then everybody just adapts, and they find something else that Sarah Palin says to be obsessed about. I mean, I think America is quite singular in that sense. I don't think that the kind of public discourse is structured in the same way. I think it's a very North American manifestation, but maybe I watch too much Jon Stewart.

GH — If you're going to watch a film about the design of cities, what's the one thing you would want somebody to say in that film?

EP — I'm assuming that the kind of broad outlines of Kyoto will be achieved by 2050 so that there will be a 60, 70 percent reduction in carbon from the 1990 levels. Working back from that, now that means for North America and Europe an 80 percent reduction. If you work back off that, what that means is, how everything is organized, from how you get about, what you consume, how things are packaged, how things are labeled, everything, it will be completely different in just 30 years' time, 40 years' time. That will happen predominantly in cities, that radical transformation. That's the one side.

On the other side, in Asia and Africa, you're going to have completely new cities that are going to spring up that are going to try and, particularly in Asia, capitalize on all new thinking about how we can reorganize cities. So you're going to have actual, real-life built environments that will function completely differently from everything we think and know about cities in just the next 30 years. We're on the cusp of this unbelievably dramatic set of forces coming together that will change things, and then we must remember, sort of at the bottom of that, that this is the only opportunity we'll have to deal with the social-justice question. The big temptation is to see this as a delicious technological R&D opportunity and to forget that it is actually the biggest political opportunity we have for social justice and economic justice. I want people to see that choice and to realize that the bulk of the hype is on this kind of techno- fix trajectory and that the voices that are trying to say, "No, no, no, it is a political question," are being silenced in the debate, or they're not particularly articulate, or they're not projected, or whatever. I don't know how the hell you do that in practice, but that would be the answer to your question.

GH — If you look at a city and the shape of a city, there are so many influences and facets that it's almost incomprehensible how a city ends being designed. Could you talk about that?

EP — I'll give you my take on that. Let me talk about what annoys me. It's quite interesting. I've been working on cities and local government questions for the last 20 to 25 years and mainly in the South African context, but in the last 10 years more on the broader African, Global South kind of axis. It's been very interesting to see that quite dramatic and recent growth and awareness about the importance of cities and urban questions and all of that and how people come at it with sort of . . . they've got the solution, right? They've got the answer. Like, why can't people see that this is a manageable problem?

I always use a quote by Italo Calvino, which I can't recite, but I could read it for you from a book. He describes cities as a rebus that conceals a desire that is undecipherable, and that's it. Cities, by definition, you can't get them. They're elusive. They elude any kind of comprehensive understanding. That's what makes them cities, because they represent such an intense confluence of people, of ideas, of agendas, of interests, and so forth that it is beyond any mechanism to contain that. The very energy of cities is that incomprehensible sort of confluence of things. That's what drives cities forward. Of course, that dynamic attracts a lot of very bright, very clever, very interesting, very driven people who think that they can contain that chaos and that they can offer the solution to it. Because there are so many of those types around, it just reinforces this unmanageable and illogical dynamic of cities.

I think that a big part of understanding what the design implications of cities are is, in a way, just folding yourself into that—I don't want to use "chaos" because that's the wrong word, but an intense indeterminacy. Just throwing yourself into it and allowing yourself to let go. It's kind of a Buddhist idea I suppose, which I know nothing about, but I suspect it's something along that line. Allowing yourself to just be sort of within that as a way of having the right disposition to think about, what are the opportunities for intervention? Where are the moments, and how do they connect to what other people are doing?

So I'm interested in that choreography, innovators or people who are thinking about this not to solve it but to think about how they can get hold of a piece of it and really work on it in an imaginative way and artic-ulate that with other people doing the same thing. That choreography, I think, can work with this inner chaotic sort of logic of cities in a really beautiful way, in a way that can throw up really profound artistic and phil-osophical registers for us, because for me fundamentally, as a species, first and foremost we need things that can power our imaginations, that can get our passions going, and that can give us a sense of meaning. That is not a brick. It is not a pipe. It is an idea. It is an imaginary. That's what I'm interested in: how do you engender this choreography for fan-tastic imaginaries to flourish? And cities offer that.
—

Rem Koolhaas (RK)/

August 2, 2011 Rotterdam

Rem Koolhaas has been called "The World's Most Controversial Architect," and was awarded the Pritzker Prize in 2000. He's also renowned as an urban thinker and provocateur. I spoke with Rem in the offices of his firm, OMA, in Rotterdam.

—

Gary Hustwit—Why is the design of so many cities so bad?

> **Rem Koolhaas** — Are you asking why is the design so bad, or are you asking why are so many cities so bad?

GH — I guess both.

> **RK** — I think that very few cities these days are really designed, and that may be partly the problem, the reason why they are so bad. But I would also say that currently we are not really quite capable of conceptualizing cities in a particularly exciting way. I think that currently, particularly since we have entrusted in the market economy so much power to decide how cities come out, I think there is a really fundamental problem, and that fundamental problem also calls into question the whole notion of designing, of course.

GH — Maybe this is one of the reasons that you started to do more work in China, but it seems like in most places the government role has been decreased, and it's just the market and for-profit developers who are dictating the design.

> **RK** — I think that's part of the issue. I think the issue is twofold. First, that, basically, the kind of client that now initiates urban development is no longer the public sector. It's more private sector. I also believe that our vocabulary is really very, very used up and finished, and there's been very little rethinking of what cities can be.

GH — Why would you reinvent? Why would you spend the time? It's so much easier just to do the same thing.

> **RK** — Yeah, but there is this incredible, counterproductive effort to create uniqueness on the basis of repetitive ingredients. I think that it's like a bento box. There's this and that, and basically the formula doesn't really work, I think. It's finished, basically. But, at the same time as it is finished, it is still kind of applied in overwhelming numbers.

GH — How do you change that?

> **RK** — I think, in the end, it has to be a political change, and I'm not only saying that as a crazy activist. I am optimistic given the fact that, at my age, I have experienced maybe two or three entirely different political systems, so I'm not pessimistic that this current situation will not come to an end or be modified drastically or really change. I think that if you saw what happened in America yesterday and what's happening in Europe, then it's clear that some phase is coming to an end.

GH — I wonder if this can be attributed to the fact that there are so many forces at play in the shaping of a city. There's no—

> **RK** — No overriding responsibility.

GH — Yeah, and maybe China is somewhat different.

> **RK** — Yeah, well . . . I'm kind of reluctant to really treat China as a model. I think, actually, what is happening there is an incredible production of cities at a really, truly astonishing scale. For that reason, there are both good and bad examples. Simply the scale itself, of course, creates a certain coherence and certain abilities that we seemingly have lost. The ability to mobilize the forces to regenerate cities that seems to simply have dissipated here, or disbanded. You have a feeling there was an army, it once was able to do things, but the army doesn't exist anymore.
>
> In China, I mean, of course we do different things. We look at cities, and we look at how the urban condition is changing, and we try to do cities, or we try to do urbanism, and doing urbanism is even more hit or miss than architecture. We have very little involvement at this point in actual operations where you could say we are trying to make a piece of city. We just won a big competition in Doha, and there we are developing next to an airport. That is the first really serious effort at urbanism since maybe the late eighties. That's almost a 30-year interval.

GH — What about just architecture projects in China?

> **RK** — Architecture projects in China . . . I actually don't see that much difference. Architecture is a very complex effort everywhere. It's very rare that all the forces that need to coincide to actually make a project proceed are happening at the same time. I would say it's as complex in China as it is in Italy. I don't think it's particularly easy anywhere. In China, we were extremely lucky. There was a small window through which projects of exceptional architecture and vision could enter. I think the Olympic stadium was an example, but I think that window is now—not so much closed, but it's become a much more normal situation. There's not this exceptional attention. I think the challenge now is as complex as in America to really get intelligent, good things to do.

GH — It seems interesting that, from what I've seen, it's really haphazard. There are a lot of Western companies and groups and even student groups involved. We interviewed some students in New Orleans who are designing a city for four hundred thousand people in China. I don't know what the strategy is for the Chinese government. Is it just to get everybody's ideas and try them all?

RK — There's some of that. I think that the Chinese government is, of course, very powerful, but China's so unimaginably big that it's like a continent in itself. There's an incredible diversity and, I would also say, a lot of initiatives that are more or less private, or at least centered on particular individuals. I don't think that there is a blanket policy.

GH — Do you see the "instant cities" as a good experiment, or are the Chinese doomed to make the same mistakes as Western cities?

RK — It's very difficult to say. The Chinese are basically struggling with the same issues. They are struggling with traffic, struggling with public space, struggling with density, struggling with how big a city should be. Should it be defined? Should it have history? Should it not have history? I think all the issues are essentially the same. What is, of course, different is so much of it happens in a single territory and at the same time.

GH — With the CCTV building, can you talk about your process in terms of how a building like that relates to the city around it? What were some of the considerations?

RK — There were a number of very crucial considerations. It was in a new business district. That meant, in the contemporary situation, that it would be one among a series of high-rise buildings, and so the first consideration was, how could you create place in a collection of high-rise towers? Because towers consume place, but very few towers manage to create a sense of publicness. That was the main consideration, and that really explains the shape as not something that is only taking away from the city but actually defining a larger-than-itself moment in the city. That is a key thing in the terms of urbanism.

GH — Looking at it now, do you have other thoughts about how the building has turned out?

RK — So the building is there now. Have you seen it?

GH — Not yet, I'm going soon. Actually, I have a friend who is a filmmaker in Beijing who, over the years, during the construction and even now, has been filming it, filming the building.

RK — I mean, some things you need to see in real life to see whether or not it works, but for me, one of the more interesting parts of it is that it's the kind of building that doesn't have a single identity, and your slightest movement in the city actually changes the building completely. Sometimes it's a circle, but sometimes it's a tower or a hammer. Sometimes it's a very forceful building. Sometimes it's a very weak or almost awkward building. This is, for me, the most, let's say, new dimension of it. It's a building that has an almost unlimited amount of different identities.

GH — That kind of changing identity, is that a characteristic that you value or that you seek? What are the qualities that are important to you in a building?

RK — I would say that every major building really demands its own ambitions and its own very specific scenario in terms of what you are trying to achieve with it. This quality of instability was a very important thing in China's context because everything is so emphatic, and everything is so there. It was really interesting to find a building that was escaping from that rigor and escaping from that monumentality in a way. But on the other hand, it's true that I am interested in things that can change their character. I don't know whether you know the building that we did for Prada, but it's a building that, if you turn, changes completely. It's definitely an interest in changeability. This was, at the scale of the city, a kind of first experiment.

GH — That's another thing I wanted to talk about: the wiping out of the old in China and the question of preservation versus building. Maybe we could talk about how your *Cronocaos* project is a response to that. In China, it seems like there isn't much in terms of preservation of the old.

RK — Of course, we are speaking of and criticizing China, having carried out our own destruction in the West, and so we basically have a degree of sophistication that perhaps the Chinese don't have, but we earned it the hard way, and we came to our senses when it was almost too late. In that sense, again, there is not a lot of fundamental difference.

I think what is very difficult about the whole issue of preservation is that each territory really has its own tradition of how physical and how permanent structures are. The vast majority of Asian vernacular is actually very flimsy. If you know Indonesian cities, the kampong is made out of bamboo, and I would say that the *hutongs*, the original texture of Beijing, are also very, very improvised. We've made some very serious efforts to really look at how you can preserve the substance of what you want to preserve. Sometimes you discover that the houses are half-built of corrugated iron and half-built of improvised brick or wood, et cetera. The difficulty is that you want to maintain a way of life rather than, in many cases, the physical infrastructure that maintained that way of life. In that sense, I would say that the whole of Asia has a very complex and difficult obligation to rethink what preservation means in its own way.

You know, there's this tradition where certain temples are rebuilt every twenty years. I think that's a particularly Asian way of conceptualizing permanence. It doesn't literally have to be the same thing, but we make the same efforts at a regular interval. It's almost like a ceremony. In the meantime, China itself has woken up to this whole issue of preservation of heritage, so there's already an enormous push to explore and exploit the heritage that they have.

GH — Do you think that push has gone too far, though, in Western cities?

RK — I mean, the point of *Cronocaos* was not to say it was going too far. It's also not the point to say nice contemporary architecture is frustrated because there's too much preservation. It is more to connect a number of dots that were not connected before and simply make a kind of investigation asking, what is the scale of preservation, and toward what kind of condition are we evolving unless we address this issue or unless we create greater intelligence about it? Particularly with the discovery that, if you add every regime of preservation up at the moment, you get 12 percent of the world. That was really a wake-up call. That's a significant discovery that no one else had made. It's really more a call to arms than saying it's gone too far or it's wrong.

GH — To discuss it. Bring it up for discourse.

RK — Yeah.

GH — What are the things that make you angry about architecture?

RK — What makes me angry about architecture? I'm an architect but also a writer. You could say that writing has been a form of anger management or a consistent effort to explore the conditions in which architecture has made me mad. I'm not saying that that in itself reduces the anger or reduces the pain, but it does create a kind of framework in which, at least, I understand why certain things are the way they are, even though they are painful or unsatisfying.

Anger is not really the right word. If you ask, "What frustrates you about architecture?" then I would say that there is an incredible amount of wasted effort in the profession, a huge amount of wasted effort. A fair amount of it is generated through the procedure of competitions, which is really a complete drain of intelligence. I don't know any other profession that would tolerate this. At the same time, people say, you are important, we invite your thinking, but we also announce that there is an 80 percent chance that we will throw away your thinking and make sure that it is completely wasted. I mean, that is basically an insane situation.

GH — True. I've started thinking more and more about the similarities between filmmaking and architecture. Do you think there are commonalities between the two?

RK — There are a number of commonalities. Both are complex because they require huge amounts of money. They're both about teamwork, obviously, and I personally think that you can look at filmmaking and it has a number of elements, such as narrative plot, montage, and jump cuts, and procedures that you could find an equivalent to in architecture very easily. Having been involved in movies in my early life, I think, really facilitated my sense of what architecture would be.

GH — Is it the idea of storytelling through architecture?

RK — Yeah, I think that narrative, particularly for our office, is really very crucial. It's not so much that we continually tell stories, but that we want to be disciplined about how each operation embodies a narrative, embodies an ambition, embodies intentions, and has an aim. I think that we use some of the conventions or laws or discipline of narrative to make sure that those are tight and work well.

There are also more and more direct similarities, in terms of the montage or the abrupt transition from one scene to another, which I would say is also perhaps particularly common in our work, and which is directly related to the experience of film.

GH — Do you think people, ordinary citizens, are aware of how designed the urban environment is?

RK — It's maybe difficult to speak about ordinary citizens. I mean, there is obviously an enormous amount of attention to design, and we all suffer from illogical or inept planning, and we all more or less consciously enjoy good planning or good environments, so I would say there is a high level of awareness, on the whole. I've never complained about it, and if you look at some of our buildings or operations that are generated or, let's say, incubated with the participation of large numbers of people, not clients, but public bodies, basically municipal audiences, then I would say, on the whole, it's always been a very productive dialogue. I've never felt that we necessarily knew more or knew better, and we were always able to establish a dialogue. That also has to do with this kind of discipline of narrative. You have to define your story.

GH — Yeah, but that idea of a public, participatory process—
RK — I think it can be fun and also productive, and I think if it's successful, it really anchors something in a community, which I think is ultimately the best guarantee that something survives and performs well. I'm not skeptical about it, actually.

GH — I think so many times it's like everybody talks about it, and what is actually being done is just lip service.
RK — Tokenism, yeah.

GH — Is that what you think?
RK — No, I don't want to be defensive, but I want to, in a way, defend the profession. I've tried to do this publicly, in a lecture in Harvard. I think that, in architecture circles, the ideas of ecology and the ideas of protecting the planet and considering the planet as a single entity and being completely aware of your responsibilities and potential within that context has been very, very well established. I think that we were talking—we, as architects—we were probably already talking about it in the twenties. Perhaps even in the 19th century there were people considering it.

I would say that we are the first to think about it. When I was a student in the sixties, Buckminster Fuller was an inevitable point of reference, and there is also a very important dimension of ecology there. We were always aware of it, but we could rarely find the people to pay for it. I think that now we are in a really paradoxical situation in that we have the people to pay for it but for the wrong reasons: as a brand, as a reason for branding more than for an authentic experience or authentic aims. I would say it's one of our most intimate concerns, which is, in a way, hijacked for more or less commercial reasons.

GH — It still almost always boils down to behavior, behavior of people.
RK — Other people and your own behavior.

GH — Yeah. You can build whatever you want to build, but if people aren't willing to live sustainably—
RK — Yeah, yeah, I know, and of course, it's all about consuming, and I think that, in the last 20 years, the sizes of houses have doubled or tripled or quadrupled, so right there it's hopeless.

GH — What do you think is the future of cities, or what kind of cities are we going to have 50 years from now?

RK — I find that extremely difficult to answer. Basically, if you go back 50 years, and if you look at the difference between a city now and in '61, it's almost zero. It's ironic that the city is a phenomenon that is receiving an enormous amount of attention, but in spite of our best efforts, I would say that it rarely receives the creativity or the kind of investment in thinking that it requires.

I'm sure that in 50 years traffic will be better. I'm sure that the car will no longer be petrol driven, et cetera, et cetera. I'm also expecting that there will be a smoother and less onerous form of infrastructure, because with infrastructure the problem is it's either completely absent or incredibly heavy-handed, and there's nothing in between. I think that that is one very crucial thing that needs to be invented, a kind of light infrastructure.

I think that the countryside has, in large parts of the world, disappeared, except that we haven't understood that. I think that a very important part of the near future is that people will become more aware of the interdependency of what is city and what is non-city. I hesitate to call it countryside. I think that there will be, also, a more systematic movement between the two.

What I think I'm seeing in cities like Dubai, but also in cities here and cities like London, is that larger and larger parts of the city are actually inhabited in theory but not in practice. There are a lot of people that buy for investment and that move a couple of times a year between two different places. I think that there's a kind of strange process: the most dense form that we know is actually thinning in terms of its use. This phenomenon, which we've called a thinning, in which all the physical manifestations are there, but somehow the life is kind of withdrawn from it, is going to be very crucial.

GH — How do you see your role in this, in the shaping of cities, and also your inspirations for it, your motives in a way?

RK — It's very difficult to talk about roles today because a role is no longer something that you can proclaim because we've become horribly dependent on demand. That is why I think that, in the time of Frank Lloyd Wright or Le Corbusier, there could be still a role. You could still consider yourself one of the important people who define the future of the city. I don't think you can have that kind of illusion anymore.

What we've been trying to do is inject, at strategic points, the kind of information or the interpretation or the description or the words or the concepts that at least alert you to what is going on and that give you also a way of discussing what is going on. It's a much more modest ambition, perhaps. That is how, partly by design and partly by default, we've had to adjust our goal, I would say. Then, of course, there will be moments where, as an extreme exception, we are in a position to actually make statements that might have a kind of exemplary effect.

GH — What do you think is the most pressing thing for us to talk about? What are the things that you want to hear people discussing now?

RK — I am still teaching at Harvard, but my biggest investment in Harvard was in the nineties, the mid-nineties, and basically what I really wanted to do then was create an awareness of how the city had changed, that it was no longer a designed object but more the uncertain outcome of an almost infinite number of forces that were operating at any one time. Perhaps the best expression of that was *Mutations*, and I wanted to address people's attention to China, so I wrote the book on China, and I was really wanting to alert the world that commercialism was going to be the driving force behind the projects and cities and that, without us paying any attention to it, there were a vast number of strategies, developments, and economies that were geared up for that transformation.

After that, the city became *the* subject to some extent, and everyone is now talking about of cities, because there's this famous statistic that more than 50 percent of mankind lives in cities. But that was, for me, the moment to start looking at what all these people left behind. We will live in cities, but what is the situation that is left behind? That's what I'm looking at now, and I see really, really drastic things going on in the former countryside.

On the one hand, there is incredible transformation of agriculture into an industrial process, incredible reuse of abandoned infrastructures, villages and their curious tourism. Or maybe tourism is not quite the word. Their curious double life. Enormous sections of Switzerland, for instance, are full two weeks a year, and the rest of the year they're completely empty. Completely empty to the point that they really need caretakers to manage that kind of emptiness and to manage the illusion that it's got to maintain that it's still Switzerland, and if you look carefully, you see that, actually, tractor drivers are recruited from Sri Lanka to maintain Switzerland. Maids are recruited from Thailand to enable people to inhabit the farms, and blah, blah, blah.

You also see how, for instance, the drive for sustainable energy is turning many farmers into energy farmers and therefore is creating accidents waiting to happen in very amateurish and systematic approaches to wind farms and solar collectors. Basically creating a mess. You also see how the word "eco" can completely denature vast territories. In Tuscany, for instance, there are now tourist organizations that buy spreads, fifteen by fifteen kilometers, that they want to maintain that then becomes tourist sites.

In my view, the country is evolving even faster than the city, so that's what I'm looking at now.

GH — Lagos was one of the cities that you gave a lot of attention to. *Lagos Wide & Far*, is that what that was called, that DVD?
    RK — Yeah.

GH — I liked that a lot. Have you been looking at African cities very much recently?
    RK — I'm constantly trying to work in African cities, and not commercially. We really became involved in Lagos at the moment it reached rock

bottom, and that was, in a way, the most interesting thing to see: what happens to a city when it reaches the point of no return? But actually, then, because the political situation became slightly better, it kind of really improved, and I would say, over the last ten years, it's been slowly but surely improving a lot.

I've tried to give some advice to the government. What is the sequence of solving problems? If you have two thousand problems, it becomes very difficult to know where to begin and what the interrelationship is between two things. That was a really fascinating commission to think about: what is the most important one, and then what is the next one? I'm trying to get that kind of work in Africa, but it's very, very difficult. We've tried to work in Libya, in preserving the desert, for instance. There are a lot of efforts we make that are almost unilateral. That, in a way, testifies to the fact that there is currently a huge absence in that area of clients that could conceptualize and commission that kind of thing.

GH — I asked you before about what makes you angry about architecture. Now I would like to ask the opposite. What makes you inspired and joyful about it? What inspires you about practicing it?

RK — What inspires me? I mean, a country like Italy is very interesting as a kind of metaphor for the current moment, because there are so many things that could drive you to despair, but there are also so incredibly many things that are completely wonderful and that basically show, without too much effort and in a quite natural and convincing way, how unbelievably beautiful the world can be. It's the one country where those two things are very, very close together, and that is very inspiring and remains very inspiring.

GH — Do you think that applies in other places?

RK — I guess so. Yeah, to some extent. So how many people will you interview for the film?

GH — Oh my gosh, probably 40 or 50 people. I mean, sometimes we look at one project. We were in Cape Town in one of the townships looking at this violence-prevention-through-urban-design project that they did there, and there are five architects, the landscape architect, and the people of the township who have contributed to the project. So one project could be a dozen people. But then, also, sometimes we might do a profile of one person. It's a lot. It's going to be messy, but I think cities are sort of messy.

RK — Was *Helvetica* more organized?

GH — I think *Helvetica* might have been easier to structure because it had a more focused topic. Cities are more complex in that there are so many more players involved.

RK — I thought it was such an incredible idea to make a film out of that. I'm really embarrassed I haven't see it.

GH — You should. There are a few Dutch designers in it. Wim Crouwel is in it, of course. It's interesting because you look at one small thing, one typeface. Then that leads to this whole world of visual communication and advertising and all these other things, how people are influenced by something as simple of a font, the shape of a font as you read it. I think most people don't think about those things. They think, "Are you kidding me, a film about a font? This is going to be really boring."

I was just a fan of graphic design and typography, and I wanted to see those people in a movie, people like Wim Crouwel or Massimo Vignelli, just see them talking about what they do. Then that kind of rolled over into *Objectified*, which was product design and industrial design, so Jony Ive and Dieter Rams and all the people who design the objects that we have around us. And now this is the third, final film.

    RK — So you see it, really, as kind of an escalation of scale?

GH — Kind of, but it wasn't intentional. I think, as I did more traveling for the films, I became more aware of cities.

    RK — What is your own take on them?

GH — I think there are a lot of problems in cities. I really don't know how things will play out in the future, but I always think that the idea of incremental design changes or creative solutions can somehow always improve things. At least I like to look at that impulse and the people that are doing those things. I think that's inspiring for me to see, and hopefully we'll spread those ideas more, or spread the kind of thinking that it's possible to change things.

I don't think most people think about changing something like their city. They might think about changing their street or their house, and they might realize that things are changing in their city, but getting involved in that is not part of the normal discourse. And people don't see what other cities are doing around the world.

    RK — Have you already filmed in China?

GH — We were going to try to go to Shenzhen when you were there last month, but we're about to do some filming in Beijing and Shanghai. But it's interesting, I don't think I really understand why I'm making the films until a few years after I finish them. Then I'll look back, and I'll have a better idea.

    RK — So you only know after you've finished it? Or some time close to the end?

GH — Yeah, maybe a year later or so. Then I can start to see more of the underlying reasons. It's more of an exploration for me, the travel and having these discussions. It's exploring the subject, and then the audience watching the film is getting to explore it as well. I'm not an expert, but I'm really curious, and I really want to know more.

    RK — Is it all interviews, or do you also show words and writing?

GH — It's pretty much all interviews. There might be some statistics or other information that we want to show. There's a lot of observational filming threaded through the conversations. And my voice is not in the film, there's no narration or anything like that. The film just kind of throws you from project to project or person to person or city to city or designer to designer. I like to have people who are watching the film make their own connections.

      RK — They don't have to be told.

GH — Yeah, I'd rather not lead them through it or hold their hand too much. That little bit of confusion is good, I feel, in a documentary. You think, "Why are we in Shenzhen, and what's this thing we're looking at?" Then you figure it out; you connect the dots. I think that's much more engaging. That's been my approach on these films.

—

Yung Ho Chang (YHC)/ August 11, 2011 Beijing

—

Yung Ho Chang is a Chinese-American architect, professor of architecture at MIT, and former Head of the Department of Architecture at MIT. He taught in the US for 15 years before returning to Beijing to establish China's first private architecture firm, Atelier FCJZ.

—

Gary Hustwit — How do you remember Beijing when you were a child versus now? How has the city changed?

Yung Ho Chang — Every day when I go through the city, I see a city I don't recognize a bit. It's a new Beijing, but I'm not sure if I like it very much, visually at least. Now I go through the town to come to work on the west side, in the northwest actually, and I live on the east side. I used to live in this area. I grew up in *hutongs*. When I was growing up, there were only two colors in a summer like this: one was the green of the trees; the other was the gray of all the architecture, the bricks. That's it. It was very different from any other city, including other Chinese cities, but also it was a city that offered a very unique quality of life. Once in a courtyard, you had a piece of sky. You had a courtyard, a garden, so you were in touch with the earth and heaven. I don't think a lot of cities offer that. Anyway, that was the Beijing I grew up with. It's still very much there. The memory is very vivid, but the new Beijing is something else.

GH — I want to talk about that more later, but first, do you think more of the older parts of Chinese cities should be preserved? What are your thoughts about preservation versus new development?

YHC — I think definitely there should be a much stronger effort to preserve the old city fabric. Not the individual buildings. We have already preserved a fair amount of important buildings, but a city without fabric is more like a museum or an exposition. It doesn't really offer you the experience of being in that city, although it offers you maybe some monuments. That's one thing.

Another thing: I think it was totally a mistake to see culture as being in the way of economic development. I think the more Beijing could save its fabric—although I think there's very little left already—the more, actually, it would help at least the tourist industry, and there would be a chance for Beijing to flourish. Unfortunately, I think 30 years ago or even before that, when the new development started, there was a lack of a vision, to say the least, as to how the culture of Beijing would be part of the development. So I never really appreciated the slogan "New Beijing." When we had the Olympics, it was like, "New Olympics—New Beijing." I think it would have been a lot more interesting if we said, "New Olympics—Old Beijing." Old Beijing, this nine-hundred-year-old city, could host a contemporary Olympics. That would be a lot more fascinating.

GH — Do you think that the old Beijing is lost then?

YHC — The fabric is very much lost, although Beijing as a population—the way we speak, the way we eat, the way we've always had a very active, artistic, intellectual life—that's very much here. So Beijing becomes, in a way—I was going to say an invisible city. It's visible, of course. But what you see does not really matter that much: all these skyscrapers and things, the shopping malls. If you go into the little tiny theaters to see the dramas and you see the independent productions of maybe some art events, exhibitions, then you meet people who really know the city. That's all still there.

Luckily, because I was born here and grew up here, I'm connected with a lot of these people. Beijing still feels like the old days in that way because my father, who was an architect, had friends in the arts and in music and so on. It's all there. Unfortunately, if you are here for a short period of time as an outsider, it's more like Kafka's castle. It's not so easy to get in, but once you get in, you see it all, and it's very interesting. That's why, after all, I still live here and work here. Shanghai would be a more comfortable city, more like the city I was describing. You can get more urban pleasure on a daily basis there, but Beijing is different. There's so much going on, but yet I think the urban spatial structure is actually very much ruined.

GH — You mentioned you grew up in a *hutong*, the old style neighborhoods of narrow streets and alleys. Does your childhood home still exist?

YHC — No, it's gone. I grew up in the Wangfujing area. It's a major shopping area. My parents and my brother and I, we would take walks after dinner in summertime around the Wangfujing area, not for shopping, just walking around without a purpose, sort of wandering. We used to do that, but now it's gone. Now we live in a comfortable, contemporary compound; there's a nice garden, but it's not the same. When we used to walk around, I remember, on the street, we'd meet people, friends and relatives, and then you'd stop and you'd greet them. That kind of feeling of living in a city is not here anymore.

GH — How would you describe the current state of urbanism in China, and how is it evolving?

YHC — My criticism is this: China has been, in the past 30 years, building abstract cities. Cities were conceived and designed to be part of the economic development, which is okay, but I think livability was really ignored until very recently. It's not convenient, it's not comfortable, and there's very little choice of different ways of living. So people would come to the city to get a job or to start their own career one way or another, but yet they live in a less than basic situation, meaning that they would have a problem doing the everyday shopping; sending kids to school would be a challenge. Community work itself is still very much a problem in Beijing, let alone sustainability. In the end, I don't believe sustainability is something we do for the earth, but rather, we do it for ourselves. If we didn't burn as much energy, then we would have less pollution today, and we would live in a better world. We'd see more clear sky and so on. Although in Beijing the cultural roots are so strong that it's flourishing right now, in general I do believe in the past 30 years we paid a very dear price to achieve the economic miracle, if you wish, really on the environmental front, on the cultural front, and the city fabric is also a cultural loss.

Beijing was designed. The whole city, in a way, was only one building, because it's totally designed and planned out. Although it wasn't built at one time, there was a very clear structure for the city to grow in. There are a couple of places you can see it. There's a coal hill behind the Forbidden City. Jingshan now it's called. It used to be called Meishan because it was a pile of coal for the Forbidden City to burn in the winter. I remember going up there. You saw, because it was all pitched roofs, it was like an ocean of gray-tile roofs with trees popping up. It just went on and on, and it was really spectacular. I saw that in the seventies from a Beijing hotel on the top of, at that time, the newer and taller park. It was a real experience seeing Beijing that way. Now that's gone.

I don't know. I hope the country is getting even richer and now we can rebuild that Beijing. It's pretty small compared with the overall new Beijing. I have a feeling we would have the money, but whether we have the will to do it, we'll see.

GH — If we go to Jingshan Park today, we won't see this?

YHC — You won't. Well, you'll see a bit, but you'll see all kinds of high-rises popping out. I had a very interesting conversation with a planner who worked for the city all her life. At that time—this is probably 10 years ago—she was already retired, and she was very open about her observations. She also said she went up to the coal hill, and she looked around. She thought, like I did, "Beijing is getting really ugly." Then she looked more carefully at the different parts. She realized everything was done more or less according to the vision her team had. Really, it wasn't by accident Beijing became the way it is now. It was really kind of the wrong vision to start with.

This is something a little more technical: it doesn't matter where in Beijing; if you get a piece of land, you are only allowed to build on 30 percent of the land. There's no density. Then you have to have 30 percent greenery, and you have to have 30 percent hard pavement and so on. So the buildings have small footprints, and they usually are much higher than, of course, what we had before. It makes a city of objects. These objects are not related in any way. So it becomes a collection of these object buildings, not quite in a park because in the end you have only 30 percent greenery, but yet there's no street wall; there's no street front and so on and so on. Then you see kind of a chaotic city. But before, if you can imagine, all the buildings were made of this one set of forms. You know, I'm talking about the old Beijing with courtyards and *hutongs*. They oriented it in a very consistent way. It literally made this continuous fabric, and the quality of living there was higher than what we have now.

For me, the biggest problem of the recent development—first of all, it is not culture. Culture is a very important issue, and if we destroyed a lot of these cultural relics and fabrics but living in the city for the people was better, maybe I'd say, "The hell with the culture here. We really have a better life, and you can still go to the museum or maybe a movie theater to see a good documentary and learn bit of old Beijing." But I think we paid a high prices for a city that doesn't work that well.

As an architect, because I think about this and we work on projects related to these issues, I think actually to some extent we can fix it. When a road is too wide, there's still a way to bring it down to a narrower, more human scale, and so we can rebuild. I was feeling a bit ambitious when I said rebuild the whole of the old Beijing, but we can rebuild parts of it. We can still think about what Paris has: a modern city next to the old Paris. We can still do a bit of that. We can take a few of the high-rises out in the center of the city. That's all possible. I hope that one of these days maybe the times will change and I'm still here to take part.

GH — There are so many so-called instant cities built in China or being built in China. Do these present an opportunity to redefine how a city can be designed, or are they duplicating Western cities?

YHC — Well, I don't think they're duplicating Western cities, but I have to say, most of these cities are cities without quality. Although partially it has to do, again, with what the authorities and the planners saw and still probably see as the right forms for cities. There's quite a bit of aesthetic judgment involved, in my mind. Really, they are all pretty much anticity.

There are two things you see in all of the new cities. One is megablocks. They are usually 400 by 400 meters and up. I'm being very conservative, 400 by 400 would be the smallest. In New York City, it's 60 by 120 meters. You can imagine the smallest if it's 400 by 400. Then the roads—because I don't want to call them streets; they are not streets; they are roads—they would start from 30 meters wide and go up to 100, 120 sometimes, with beautiful landscapes in the middle. But that's, again, not an urban street. It's a road decorated with landscape. It still doesn't make a city.

Those mistakes, they didn't have to happen, even if you built a city fast. I'm struggling to tell people that's not the only kind city we have to do. What's interesting about architecture is this: if you tell people ideas, people often are very suspicious, even if you tell them something really kind of obvious, but yet, if it were already there, a lot of people would support it. They would love it. They would embrace it. Outside of Shanghai—it's not built yet, but it's on the way—we're doing 40 by 40 meter blocks. It's tiny, but it's outside of Shanghai. It could be actually a copy of an American office park. But with the kind of competition today, our clients and also the city planning bureau already knew—we started like three years ago—that megablocks and super roads may look nice, but they doesn't make a livable place. For the clients, of course, they like to think of it as a different way to attract companies and people.

Let me just say one important thing. We started that project by asking one question. The first question I asked the clients was, where do the people who will be working in these buildings go for lunch? I know Steven Holl, a New York architect, asks that question too. From there, we started a very different conversation, and then they appreciated our approach. They think, in the end, making money is about the quality of life. If you don't get that, what does money do for you? We also started to say, "Okay, there are choices for lunch. Could they meet friends from other companies in the same town?" We got a lot of support. We like to show there is at least an alternative way of making cities. Our city is going to be built pretty fast too. I think that, since we're still right in the middle of a pretty fast urbanization, cities will be built kind of fast, but I really hope that collectively we can correct some of the mistakes made in the past 30 years.

GH — Do you think there are misconceptions in terms of how people in the West view Chinese cities?

YHC — Yes, but it's hard to summarize it. I think there's several misunderstandings. One is that a lot of people think there's no master plan for our cities, especially cities like Shenzhen. I don't blame them. If you go there and you see the reality, you would think that way. But in fact, in Beijing, in all these cities, there is a master plan, and it's pretty rigorously followed, and it's updated every so often, I think for Beijing at least every five years. Although there is corruption, and the Chinese have a belief in flexibility, so there are a lot of exceptions. Even with that, I'd say the cities are built according to some ideas, but because the result is the way it is, people from elsewhere think there is no central planning.

The second thing is the opposite. I think it was probably inspired by Rem Koolhaas's observations. He was one of the first people who pointed out there's perhaps a different way of thinking about the city in China. He suggested to his Western colleagues: "Take a look. Don't hang on only to that set of values we have in Europe." He did that in the States when he wrote the book on New York City and talked about how it's different than the European cities. He didn't write a book about Houston, and now of course we all understand that that would have made maybe an even stronger argument. The whole city of Houston is very suburban, so it doesn't make sense to use the criteria for a European city to compare it with Houston. These are different cities. Rem made that point, and then a lot of people followed and started to discuss Chinese cities in that way, saying how different the new Chinese city is. It's true, but don't forget, humans are pretty much alike. If Beijing is not convenient for you, for someone from the States, it's not convenient for a local person either. There are very basic things a city has to do, and I don't think having the open-mindedness of embracing a new Chinese city should give a person the liberty to overlook all these issues.

GH — How has the increase in automobile use in China affected the design of cities?

YHC — The number of cars in Beijing—God, I think maybe it's around six million, but that's a very rough number. I don't know if that is overall or just the private cars. It means a city that was first conceived for some carriages now has to deal with that number of cars; and now with the wrong idea of having these wide roads, not a density of smaller roads, but rather fewer big roads; and also with the lack of development of public transit. They're doing quite a bit now, but for years there was a lack of development of really efficient public transportation. Also there's the notion of having the automobile industry as one of the pillars of the economy. And now we have a huge issue in cities, especially in Beijing, because the private car ownership here is the highest in China. Of course, the wide roads are for cars not for people, not for people to walk on the street, not for people to bike on the street, but just for cars.

People in the new middle class here, they've never owned a car in their lives. A lot of people are buying a car, in a way, for the heck of it. You know, "I never had one. I want to have one. Even if it's too hard to drive during the weekdays, I'll use it on the weekend." I had cars in the US. I have a car here today, so I understand that, but the problem is that, the way the city has been developing, it doesn't give people choices about whether you need to drive or not. In New York City, you could drive, right? But you also could take the subway. You can take a bus and so on. It's getting a bit better now, but we still have this problem. When we're talking about transportation and circulation of a city, we're talking about a network. It's got to have a certain kind of density so that you don't have to ever walk very far to a subway station and so on. Somehow that net is not very well woven, so a lot of people have to drive, and that really is a problem.

Now the Chinese economy is booming regardless, but I think this kind of city that we have is going to hurt it, and the cars are going to hurt it. Eventually people will say, "It's just easier to get into the subway," and they'll want to drop the car, but now cars are a big problem also for pollution. The coal situation in the winter is getting better because we burn more natural gas for central heating rather than coal, but of course now the car emissions are a big issue. I hope the government knows how much damage the cars are really doing to our cities.

GH — You mentioned sustainability before. What are your thoughts about sustainability in Chinese cities?

YHC — I'm actually working on something. It's not a commissioned work. Nobody asked me to do it, but I live here; I work here; I get an idea or two once a while, so now I have this kind of a laundry list of things Beijing could do to be more sustainable. I want to say first, when I'm thinking about sustainability, I'm also thinking about livability. Make the city more convenient and more comfortable. For instance, I was talking about streets. Now the streets are very wide, and these wide streets, they can become big parking lots in a way, but there is no way for them to be good shopping streets, let alone urban spaces. If we could redesign the streets in Beijing, for instance divide the wide streets into two, one a pedestrian commercial street, the other wide enough for cars, the street life would be better, and meanwhile, it would encourage people to walk. So sustainability is not only about using technology, it's about inviting people to live in a different way. With a nice shopping street, why should people go into a mall? We all enjoy a bit of sunshine and even rain now and then.

That's kind of an idea we're using. We're finishing up a commercial area near Tiananmen, and instead of a covered shopping mall, we're doing an open-air thing, which means we're basically building a whole series of courtyards, bigger than the residential ones, but it's the same idea. But also, it's more fun because we intentionally designed a way to connect these courtyards, a little bit like a labyrinth, and as you go through them, you'll discover nice places to eat and shop. Then people won't complain about the heat in the summer or the coldness in the winter because you're offering them something different.

That is the way I'm thinking. I'm using these two examples to show how it could be achieved without spending major bucks on some new technology. Although, technology is evolving so fast. I do believe, in this part of the world, we could've used more wind energy. Right? We're so close to the Gobi Desert and so there's a lot of wind, and we can harvest that. We have a decent amount of sun, so solar is another one. We should have a much more comprehensive plan that would bring some really low-tech and high-tech strategies together. The city would be a lot better. I think that it's not good enough just to bring the GDP up. There are a lot of things we care about. I think quality of life is going to be the next thing for urbanization in China.

GH — How would you describe most private development companies in China? Are they a positive influence in the urban design of major cities, or are they negative?

YHC — It depends. I think it's quite mixed. A lot of these private companies are more adventurous; they're willing to try things that are a bit different. However, for me, there's still too much thinking—creative thinking, by the way—about marketing. As an architect, I don't believe there is enough creative thinking in the actual product, the design of which is critical. In general, I think that it's very good that today we have the state-owned development companies and then we also have these private developers. I wish that these private developers' influence could be more on the product front.

I know a couple of them are actually really interesting people. They are thinking of crazy ideas. There is one guy who is planning I think a one-cubic-kilometer city. He is totally serious about it. He thinks about a city, you know, one thousand meters wide and one thousand meters deep and one thousand kilometers in height and very dense. I have seen some images. It's still a little premature probably as a product, but I can't help appreciate that effort. If it happens, even if it doesn't work that well, I would applaud his effort and, of course, the architect's effort. China can't offer each family a suburban house. We have 1.4 or 1.5 billion people, and we don't really have the land. It's just not possible. So there have got to be different ways to build cities to live differently. That idea is totally crazy. Who knows? We need some more crazy ideas.

A lot of my clients are private developers. They are quite open-minded. It has to do with this great transformation of the economy and the culture that is happening right now in China. They are not as sure, perhaps, as a Western developer of how the housing will be, or the market will be, so they are willing to take a little more risk.

GH — Are there other issues facing Chinese cities in the future?
YHC — I think there are three: it's livability, sustainability, and affordability. The first two we already discussed. The city has to be livable. It's no longer enough to be a place you would start your career and have a job, but it has to be a city where you'd bring up your family. A city is where you enjoy life. I think we're going in that direction, although for me, we need a lot clearer vision to really understand how urban people live and then how we would be able to organize the city differently now than in the past 30 years.

For instance, urban people stay up at night, work, play, and so on, so a 24-hour convenience store would be a very important thing. America might have actually invented it, but it didn't really take off that much there. But if you go to Tokyo, every two hundred meters there is a 7-Eleven, which is American. So you can always get something to eat and even send a parcel out, even get your visa now or something, your passport. That level of convenience and the livability of a city, we can see it has already started in Shanghai, and that is the direction, but there are many aspects, including transportation and so on.

Sustainability we talked about a little bit. I think there are some major issues there. It's hard to tackle in an existing city, but when we build new cities, then we can really do better. What's the right density? What's the right scale? How to mix different programs. How to mix transportation. There are a lot of ways to do that. It's not that we don't have the technique or know-how; rather, maybe we don't really understand the city well enough to do them.

The third one is also very a big issue. Big cities like Beijing and Shanghai are decent; it's not the best. An upper-middle class kind of apartment would easily be over a million US dollars in Beijing and Shanghai today. What does that mean? If you compare that with the income of the middle class, not a lot of people can buy that. It means that we are building a lot, and in past years, we were selling and buying a lot, but after all, that's an activity of only a few people. The apartments are sitting there empty because these rich whoevers were buying a whole row of the same apartments in a high-rise. Well-known people would do that. He doesn't want to put the money in the bank, so he would do that. You know, maybe he could rent them out, but more likely he'll just let them sit there. As an investment, of course.

That's going to be a big problem. People who need a place to stay wouldn't be able to afford one, and now, you know, the new law that started last year says you can't buy apartments like this. The people who have the money can't buy a whole lot of them. For me, that's really not a bad idea. And then what do we do? The market part I don't know, but I think we need to do more intelligent design and planning so that we can have products that aren't as expensive so more people can afford them. Then there are going to be people still living in the city and enjoying the city. Otherwise, we are going to have ghost towns. We already do, not in Beijing and Shanghai, but outside of them, very strange places like all those cities in Mongolia. There are a lot of developments, a lot of houses sitting there sold but without a soul in them. This is not right.

GH — Yeah, that makes sense. Okay, last question: what other world cities do you like and why?

YHC — I really like big cities. For me, going to a big city is about adventure and discovery. A city has to have some mystery. Usually I'm very busy with my work, so I don't really get to do a lot of research or preparation before I go, which is kind of okay. If you go to Tokyo, there are famous streets. You go to Ginza; you go to Omotesandō and so on. Yet you can just wander into some small neighborhoods and parks, and then you find something unexpected. You know, a bowl of good noodles. Who knows? That's the pleasure of a city.

A city that doesn't really have a density of things is not very interesting. Because I also love nature. In the US, if a city doesn't offer that kind of density of humanity, I would go to Yosemite. So I never really could clearly understand, or I understand it perhaps, but I could never appreciate the suburban city. I lived in Houston. When you're driving in the city, every block looks the same, although probably there are a lot of a mysteries in there too. Then last year I was in Rio, and again there is a bit of chaos. You see that in the juxtaposition of architecture from different times and nature and the artificial. It is a fun city, even without the beach. You go to the beach; it's fine, but there are other beaches that are just as nice. But when you really explore Rio, it's very fun.

I guess if I can kind of sum up my idea of a city, I think a city is an interesting jungle for me. I like to go for adventure in the city.
—

Ellen Dunham-Jones (EDJ)/ August 17, 2011 Atlanta

Ellen Dunham-Jones teaches architecture at the Georgia Institute of Technology, is an award-winning architect and a board member of the Congress for the New Urbanism. She is the co-author, with June Williamson, of the book *Retrofitting Suburbia: Urban Design Solutions for Redesigning Suburbs.*

—

Gary Hustwit — This is going to be really basic, but could you talk about what urban design is? Just give me a cocktail-party definition.

Ellen Dunham-Jones — Okay. I think urban design is the arrangement of the buildings and the spaces that, on the one hand, create those plazas and the public spaces in between buildings. Then you aggregate them, and you get a neighborhood. Then you aggregate a couple of neighborhoods, and you begin to get a city.

Some urban designers work more at the scale of the design of the sidewalk, the street lamp, the bench, the storefront. Others are really working at the scale of, how do we arrange a lot of different buildings and uses? What is it we want next to each other? How many coffee shops does it make sense to have?—which we've sometimes begun to question. It's the arrangement in the neighborhoods. Then other urban designers are really working at the scale of an entire metropolis. What's the watershed, and how do we have to think about the systems of green that are threading through our cities and how those meet up with our systems of transportation, our systems of where we live?

People come at urban design usually either from an architecture background or from a city planning background. The reality is you really need quite a bit of both and some engineering and landscape architecture certainly as well. You need to know the regulations, the policies, the planning side. You also need to be able to draw and to envision what a place is going to be like when you start to throw all these systems together and arrange the pieces.

GH — Can you talk about the different roles, the different people involved in that?

EDJ — Generally, our cities are shaped by the combination of the public sector and the private sector. You have individuals who are looking for places to live and places to work, whether they're companies or households. Private developers are generally the ones who are hiring the architects to design a particular set of uses on a particular piece of property, but they're being guided by policies, whether it's the zoning regulations or street design guidelines, that have been produced by either the local planning municipality or the public works officials who have all sorts of regulations to make sure that the fire trucks can get through the streets, and the street cleaners.

There are a lot of different people involved in shaping our cities. There's the local county public health official who has to make sure that we're building healthy communities. They're actually charged with and used to have a much larger role in really protecting health and safety. The engineers are making sure that we can get around and that we get enough water and power. You've got all sorts of systems that have to be plugged in together. Then there's still just the individual retailers, the individual people who are going to lease the buildings and give them the street life and yet also the privacy, and there are the parks.

There are a lot of different components, but generally the urban designer is the person who's producing the master plan vision. They're aware of all of the needs and they're bringing everybody together to talk about what the particular needs in that particular place and climate are, and then they try to draw it all up and say, "Now, is this going to work?" Then they get a lot of feedback because it doesn't always work the first time.

GH — I'm always fascinated by the fact that a lot of urban design seems to be reacting to something like a population shift or an economic downturn, and then the other side is this broad vision. Maybe those things are, I don't know, at odds or maybe working together.

EDJ — At different times in history and certainly in different places, you get different levels of control. When the Wild West was settled, if you could get on a horse fast enough to get out and just stake your claim, there weren't a whole lot of rules and regulations about what you could build, and in the US, home rule is still very, very important. Private property rights are very strong. In some places, people can develop more or less whatever they want. Once a city begins to get established, then you start seeing controls coming in.

The whole notion of actually trying to make sure that you didn't have industry right next to residences and recognizing that that really was a public health problem meant that by early in the 20th century we began to see zoning laws in almost every city across the country. It took an act of Congress to give municipalities the power to actually say to private property owners, "Sure, that's your property, but you don't have the right to put a noxious factory right there because there's people living right next door." We began to start controlling our cities in many, many more ways. Still, you go around the country; every municipality has its own unique zoning laws. Every part of the world has different kinds of controls and incentives that result in very different kinds of places.

GH — Okay. A very general question, but if you were asked what makes a good city, what are some of the kind of things you need to have?

EDJ — I love cities, and not everyone does, but I really love cities. What I love is to be able to walk to a variety of places very easily and be constantly entertained along the way. It might be that I'm passing beautiful parks, and I'm getting a bit of an escape from the city, the hustle and bustle. It might just be people watching, all the diversity of loads of different kinds of people. I might be entertained by seeing a variety of architectures, passing some historical building right next to something brand new that I've never seen before.

To me, cities help you feel like you're part of something much larger than just yourself, that you're part of this continuum of history, this diversity of people, but that you also all have something of a shared stake. I love to occupy the public streets or parks, the public realm that we hold in common. There's a feeling of being part of this much larger agenda, and I love the energy that I get. It can be a big, bustling city, or it can be a very small town, but if it's still a small town where the buildings are facing each other, where people are interacting and know each other, I think you get that same sort of energy and sense of common interest, but still people can chart their own paths.

GH — Can you maybe talk a little bit about the role of public space in cities, carrying on from what you were saying?

EDJ — One of my favorite authors who's talked about public space is Hannah Arendt, who was a philosopher in the forties and up through well into the sixties. She really idealized the ancient Greeks. She, I think, has been as eloquent as anyone. She claims that what the ancient Greeks taught us was that the city is the polis—politics is the polis; it's the same word for the ancient city—and we need it to learn to live together well. That's from Aristotle. The city is where you learn that.

Hannah Arendt also distinguishes between what she calls social space and public space. Public space is the space of endurance. It's the cultural continuity of a city, things that we will memorialize and that endure in the culture. Whereas she describes the social as things that are cyclical and constantly necessary for life but that really belong in the private realm, so food, having children, clothing. Shopping is part of the social realm. It's a necessity. To the ancient Greeks, everything private was deprived of the glory of the public realm. Nowadays we tend to sort of invert that. We tend to think the private is often higher or better, but she pointed out that for the Greeks, I mean, women and slaves were deprived the public realm. It was not a utopian society for everybody by any stretch, and she was well aware of that.

This notion of public space as truly the space of democracy, I think, is a really amazing concept. I think Hannah Arendt would be quite disappointed at the degree to which shopping today really serves as our primary public space. That's not the same as democracy. That's speaking to just pretty mundane, cyclical, absolutely necessary, and perfectly delightful parts of our lives. There is still something quite important about the real role of public space to link us to those larger common agendas.

GH — Let's talk about the mid-20th century in terms of changes in urban design and strategy and the modernist philosophies of urban planning. Can you talk about what it was like and then what changed, and maybe talk about the growth of the cities, population shifts?

EDJ — The postwar period is quite a fascinating period because it was a time of enormous change. The veterans all returned back from the war. In the US, there was a whole series of policies to really try to encourage and enable vets to be able to buy mortgages and to suddenly pursue the American dream, which is a phrase that was actually coined in the thirties. It's really after the war that suddenly automobile ownership becomes much more prevalent. We began a pattern of development that was absolutely based on suburbanization. The American dream was certainly perceived to be home ownership and one's own little piece of dirt. Those early houses in the early sort of Levittowns, they were only 800-square-foot houses for a family of four. That was absolutely considered a tremendous step up from what, at the time, was perceived as overcrowding in the cities. Getting out into the suburbs with a car was very much the dream.

Economically, every new house meant that people also had to buy a refrigerator and a TV. I mean, it just fueled the postwar economy. Throughout the US, our industries were booming. Land development was rampant, and we essentially emptied out an awful lot of our cities with the population heading out to the suburbs. It was perceived as a very modern lifestyle, a very healthy lifestyle with lower density, more access to greenery.

Again, those were fairly small lots and fairly small houses in the fifties, but you jump up to today—the average house size is closer to about 2,200 square feet, and that's more often for a family of only about 2.6 people, not that family of 4. Then it comes with two, if not even three cars now. The basic process of suburbanization has been continuing, but we've been getting larger and larger lots, more and more cars, and at distances now that require us to drive much further. Suddenly, now that scenario is not quite as healthy as it was perceived to be at one time.

The Centers for Disease Control and various researchers have been finding correlations between suburban sprawl and human sprawl. Obesity rates have gone up in relation to sedentary lifestyles of people who have to commute very long distances and then live in neighborhoods that don't have sidewalks. We're seeing the obesity rates leading to heart disease, diabetes and seeing a tremendous rise in car crashes especially, the leading cause of death for our children. Yet we still tend to think of suburbia as this healthy, modern choice, even though we're increasingly recognizing that there are some very negative consequences to the pattern now that it's gotten as extreme as it has—certainly the problems with health, problems with dependence on foreign oil, problems with polluting and greenhouse gas emissions, impacts on climate change. In general, in the US, urban dwellers have about one third the carbon footprint of suburban dwellers, because of all the driving but also because detached buildings have that many more surfaces to leak energy out of.

There's more and more awareness and desire for some alternatives. I think a lot of folks are also beginning to realize that the suburbs aren't as affordable as they were when it was a little 800-square-foot house built in the late forties. Now the savings associated with drive-till-you-qualify affordable housing—the assumption being you're going to get the cheaper house with more land further and further out—the savings associated with that house are completely eaten up by the additional cost of transportation. None of us know quite how high gas prices are going to go, but we know they're not ever going to be really cheap again. There will be alternative fuels, but are they going to be cheap? The suburban lifestyle has been a very beloved lifestyle for generations now, but there are a lot of reasons that a lot of folks are beginning to rethink it.

GH — Can we talk about social housing in the mid-century or of course earlier, the projects and the assumptions that led to that development and then, I guess, the reaction against those principles?

EDJ — It's fascinating how the desire to create a healthy environment led urban design and planning enormously throughout the 20th century. In the fifties or postwar, there was a sense that the older tenement housing in urban-core inner cities was designed with very poor ventilation. It did tend to be quite overcrowded. The desire for more light and air in particular tended to foster arguments that said, "We've got to clear these slums. An urban renewal. We're going to just wipe out all of these small little tenement buildings, and we're going to now build big buildings, tall, with lots of light and air, and set them into green parks."

The ideal was this notion of towers in the parks, which really was an idea from the twenties, but we didn't get to start building it until the postwar: either the rebuilding of bombed out parts of Europe, or it was also the strategy for a lot of public housing in the US. It was assumed to be sort of healthy. You wanted lots of space between the buildings, lots of air, lots of light. The consequences were that the buildings tended to be isolated from the rest of their neighborhoods. The parks more often became parking lots. They weren't great parks. They really weren't maintained. Children who now went out into the parks weren't being supervised by their parents, who were up in the tall buildings. You got a lot of social dysfunction problems. While the idea initially was that public housing was designed for workers, it increasingly became concentrations of people who were not working, and you had children growing up not knowing anyone who went to work so then repeating that same cycle.

We've seen a real reinvention of public housing that in some ways has actually gone back to the old urban design patterns of, we need to reintegrate the housing into the city, try to give the children growing up in public housing more of an opportunity to be integrated into the everyday life of the city and to know people who go to work so that they can begin to learn that lifestyle for themselves. We've been rebuilding on the same sites. We've been tearing down a lot of that fifties and sixties barracks housing, tower housing, and replacing it with mixed-income projects, restoring the street grids that used to be there, and essentially matching the architecture to whatever the surrounding context is so that instead of them being "the projects," which was always isolated and somewhat stigmatized, now it's much more continuous and much more integrated, kind of rich, poor, everybody, being much more integrated together.

GH — This is where we can maybe talk about Jane Jacobs, because a lot of her initial writing was a reaction to the social housing projects in New York, and it brings in the mixed-use ideas. Can you introduce her?

EDJ — Jane Jacobs was a journalist; she was not trained as a professional architect or planner or anything. In the early sixties, she began writing based on her experiences of what was happening in New York City. She lived in Greenwich Village, which was mostly a neighborhood of four- to five-story walk-up townhouses and apartment blocks, very walkable, always had a little bar on the corner, the kind of neighborhood where you would know your local butcher.

At the same time, the transportation engineers were trying to put through some major highways cutting right across the city, connecting up all the new bridges and tunnels. They'd already demolished some good chunks of the city to put in high-rises. There was a plan for some more highway construction that would have knocked down most of her neighborhood. She began to write about what she thought the planners really weren't seeing and understanding. They were looking at problems from the sort of 30,000-foot height, and she was really looking at it from the perspective of someone living there on the street.

Jane Jacobs was really the first voice who came in and argued for the value of places where the buildings are close to the street because then they make the street a safer, more comfortable place for pedestrians, that it's not just about the cars. She argued for the need for how the old neighborhoods had a mix of uses. You had people living there, working there, you had shops. It was all very convenient and didn't rely on the car. You could walk to everything.

The new model was an idea of separating out the functions. It was a model of the city that said, we'll put all the residences over here, then the government functions and the government center over here. Shopping will all be at a big shopping center or a mall over here, with big highways to connect us and get us everywhere. In the fifties, gas was incredibly cheap. Cars were fun. There were a lot of people that really thought that was a great, modern, progressive way to live.

Most of us are really glad that Jane Jacobs spoke out for the need to still hang on to that older style of neighborhood. She was really the first to say, these aren't slums. These aren't overcrowded, miserable, poor places. There's an incredibly rich social structure here that actually works incredibly well. She talked about the importance of having eyes on the street, of people who know each other. Not everybody knows each other; strangers are more than welcome to walk through and be comfortable, but enough people know each other that, if somebody's kid throws a rock through a window, someone else is going to see it and tell their mother. She talked about the value of neighborhoods and the value of having cheap space. If everything is new and modern, inherently it's a little bit expensive. There's no space for the nonprofits, the low-profits, the music teacher. There's only room for the spaces of consumption, the places that are going to sell us things.

In the city's drive to modernize, she was a voice of saying, we should be keeping much of this and valuing it and learning from it. Her book *The Death and Life of Great American Cities* is such a tremendous textbook of lessons, and very common sense experience-based lessons, on what it takes to make and build a really great neighborhood.

GH — That idea of designing things to be very orderly and rational has come up a lot in my other films too. It must be part of the same impulse.

EDJ — Absolutely. I think modernist city or urban planning is very similar to modern graphic design or modern industrial design. It's sort of minimalist, very ordered, very rational: separate everything out. On the one hand, of course it makes a certain logic to say, "You don't want cars and pedestrians in the same place. It's not safe." There's a logic to separating things out, but as we've certainly come to experience, if you design the city so that every single trip has to be made by a car, suddenly you're not zipping around anymore. You're stuck in enormous traffic jams. You have incredible congestion. Our street system is all about separating everything out, and things only connect to the big arterial roads that get crowded. We don't tend to have the grid street connections that the older cities had where, oh, if that street is crowded, well, I've got an alternative route I can easily take. We've really been rediscovering that some of those older patterns worked pretty well. That's a lot of what the Congress for the New Urbanism has been about.

GH — I guess we can talk about New Urbanism? Could you give just the background and history of the movement?

EDJ — Yeah. In the early eighties, as we began to recognize more and more of these problems, suburbia was increasingly being called sprawl, and it had really gotten so congested. As we saw more and more of those problems, different folks began exploring different alternatives.

On the West Coast, you had Californians like Peter Calthorpe really interested and concerned about how destructive sprawl was to the environment. His interest was in transit-oriented development as a much more environmentally sensible way to operate once you're moving out of the cities. He was working on that in the eighties. Then on the East Coast in Florida, you had Andrés Duany and Liz Plater-Zyberk. Their principal focus was the social disconnect of people in suburbs. As house lots got larger, people didn't really know their neighbors, and they lost the sense of community in many, many suburbs. You see whole suburbs where you see the garage door more than you see a front door. Nobody really interacts. They seem to be houses for cars. So they were beginning to try to build communities that really allowed and facilitated more social interaction, had more public spaces, more of a mix of uses. It was almost quasi—social engineering. It's not requiring people to be social, but it's at least facilitating that.

Judy Corbett with the Local Government Commission in California brought the East and West Coast together, and they recognized that, even though they were interested in different things, they had a common enemy, which were the regulations that at this point absolutely perpetuated the system of sprawl. They started this group called the Congress for the New Urbanism. It's been meeting for almost 20 years now. It's a forum that gets together to share strategies. Early on it was about how to get around the regulations that didn't allow mixed-use, connected street grids, or a variety of income price points all in the same community and the incorporation of transit. Folks were getting together and sharing their strategies, showing projects they had done with each other. Increasingly now, the congress has been working on changing those regulations and making much more sustainable development patterns legal and spreading the word about the tools of how to do this and how to rediscover some of the principles behind making much more walkable places with a mix of uses, a mix of incomes.

GH — Can you give a short description of the principles and philosophy of New Urbanism?

EDJ — New Urbanism has a charter with 26 principles. What it basically comes down to is walkable, compact, connected communities. If you can make a place that's walkable, that's fairly dense—it's going to have a range of densities—and then complete—it's got a mix of uses, mix of incomes, and all of that—and is connected, hopefully by transit, multiple modes, whether it's bikes, walking, transit and car, then that's the kind of thing that New Urbanism is really focused on.

We refer to the urban-to-rural transect as a way of always thinking about where you are on the transect within a larger region and the fact that it's all interconnected. Whether you're building in the city, in the suburbs, in the countryside, it's all one big system in terms of our water, our air, our transport. If you're primarily interested in affordable housing or you're primarily interested in environmental preservation, what's really important is to recognize how those two actually impact each other. If we're trying to just stop growth, we're going to increase prices and decrease the amount of affordable housing. CNU has been a great forum for bringing together the multiple perspectives and recognizing we can't solve any one problem unless we are working on all of them. You can't solve any one in just one place. You really have to work on these in terms of the whole metro.

GH — You hear all these criticisms from certain groups: "They want us to move back, they want to shove us into the city. We have the right to be out here in the suburbs."

EDJ — Again, the transect is really about trying to accommodate, from urban to rural, as many choices as possible. I think the reality is our regulations for the last 50 years have really only allowed us to build suburban projects. Yes, there's suburban apartments, and then there's suburban single-family homes, but that was pretty much the only two choices. What the New Urbanists have been doing is, in general, I think we've been creating more urban places because that's the choice that hasn't been available. But the idea is always to have a range of choices and also to try to level the playing field so that the folks who make a more urban choice aren't subsidizing the folks who are making a more suburban or rural choice. Everyone's got to kind of pay their way, but it's certainly not about eliminating the idea that you provide people with options.

GH — So we talked about the creation of suburbs, and I'd like to talk about the idea now of the retrofitting of suburbs, but first, could you define sprawl for me?

EDJ — Defining sprawl is a little bit like defining pornography: You know it when you see it. It's a parlor game amongst academics. There is no consensus on any one, single definition of sprawl.

The suburbs from the 1920s tended to be fairly close in to the core of the city; they were leafy, and they had fairly large lots with fairly large houses. Most of those 1920s suburbs are still highly valued places with very individual, different houses. Then we start to see more and more of the mass builders, which starts with William Levitt building Levittown in New York in late 1940s, but it's certainly increased to the point now where we have these massive developments by large-home builders where every house is the cookie cutter, looking exactly the same. Then you have to multiply that by having all of the chain store retail where every single store, every big box, looks exactly the same. When you see the pattern, suddenly it doesn't matter whether you're in Phoenix or in Atlanta. Basically you're getting the exact same development pattern, just with a few more palm trees or cacti to give you a little local flavor. Then you start seeing all the traffic problems and the pollution problems. That's when people really start saying, "This is now sprawl. This is not just suburbia. This has actually become something that doesn't hold value."

What has become so interesting, I think, is a lot of properties that are only 30 years old, 20, in some cases even less, but a lot of those suburban properties now start to hit about 30 years old, and we see dramatic reductions in their value. It's as if we've been building a disposable society. It's an enormous change for us. Earlier generations of buildings, not all of them stick around or last, but we had a culture of building that was more enduring. A lot of what we've been building for the last 50 years is reaching the end of its building life-span, and it's providing us with now some opportunities to really rethink, what kind of city do we want? What kind of buildings, therefore, do we want to replace these failing properties with?

GH — Do you want to talk about the shrinking city phenomenon?

EDJ — Yeah. Cities are extremely dynamic organisms. Throughout the history of the world, we've watched civilizations that bloomed and then collapsed. Similarly, we see now amongst our cities and our suburbs, some of them are growing and are still booming, and more and more people want to live there, and others are shrinking. In many cases, it's certainly a change in the economy of the industrial Rust Belt, a lot of the northern parts of the country. Detroit, Flint, Cleveland, are cities that have been losing population quite dramatically. At the same time, we're seeing a lot of our southern and western cities, certainly DC, Atlanta, many in California, have been rising in population. Not just the metro areas but the cities themselves have become increasingly valued.

We see quite a mixed bag of different things happening in the country right now. There are places where we're seeing the cities emptying out, but the suburbs are still growing. We're seeing places where the cities are emptying out, and now the suburbs are becoming farmland. We're seeing places where the cities actually are doing pretty well, but now the edges are full of foreclosures, the zombie subdivisions; it's the suburbs that are really what are shrinking and cutting back. Then we still have some places where we're still seeing more and more suburbs being built. There are different dynamics happening, operating in very different ways throughout the country.

Overall, I think the recession has clearly brought development to a halt in most places. DC is a bit of an exception, but most of the country has seen things come to a halt. The loss of credit to get mortgages, loss of credit in general, is going to very much alter some of those patterns, and I don't think the sprawl building is going to be coming back anywhere near to the same level that it was at. I think we're going to see a tremendous return as people try to infill properties back closer in because it is a more affordable way to live. The *land* is not as affordable, so it's tricky as people are trying to figure out the best ways to do that.

GH — What about the concept of retrofitting?

EDJ — So a lot of what is happening now is this interest in looking at these underperforming properties and figuring out what to do with them. We've got an enormous number of empty big-box stores, dead and dying malls. We've got aging office parks, commercial strip corridors that have seen their better days, and aging garden apartment complexes and plenty of subdivisions that are continuing to lose value. What my coauthor, June Williamson, and I have been doing for the last several years is just trying to catalog and document cases where those properties have been retrofitted into more sustainable places in one way or another.

We tend to describe that according to three basic strategies. First is simply reinhabiting them with more community-serving uses. There's loads of really creative examples that people have come up with, whether it's turning a big-box store into a library, a school, a church.

We've also seen examples of redevelopment certainly in those places where the economics makes sense, a lot of the first rank suburbs. So the second strategy is redevelopment, which is where you're really talking about urbanizing and densifying a lot of suburban properties. It's quite surprising how many, in particular, dead malls now have been redeveloped into downtowns with walkable public streets, retail at the ground floor, residential and office above, providing their towns with a town center, a downtown that that suburb never had before. The mall served to some degree as a de facto downtown. Now they have even more of a mix of uses and, I think, a more sustainable downtown.

The third strategy is regreening, because densification certainly is not going to work everywhere. The reality is, we built a lot of our suburbs in places that we probably never should have. Before the Clean Water Act, it was very common to drain the wetlands to put in commercial development in particular. Now if some of those commercial properties are aging, it makes a lot of sense sometimes to go ahead and reconstruct the wetlands, daylight the creeks that have been culverted in under the parking lots, and reintroduce farming to increase local food production. We're finding a really wide range of things that folks are doing with some of these underperforming properties.

GH — How have the demographics changed in suburbs?

EDJ — We all think of suburbia as family focused. The reality is that's not actually who lives there anymore. Two thirds of suburban households in the US do not have kids in them. That number is expected to continue to rise for at least another 15 years. The baby boomers, who were the babies that suburbia was initially built for after the war, they're still there, but they're not having babies anymore. They're hitting retirement age, starting to hit retirement age. Then behind them, you have Generation X, but they're a small generation. They're having babies, but there aren't enough Gen Xers to fill all the existing single-family homes that the baby boomers will vacate. Coming up behind Gen X is Gen Y, the Millennials. They're a huge generation, even bigger than the baby boomers. Most of them have not yet really started having kids. We expect them to probably delay childbirth till fairly late for a variety of reasons. What you have is a lot of retiring empty nesters and then a lot of young professionals out in suburbia. Suburban job growth has outpaced city growth by a factor of about six.

When you ask these groups what is it that they're really looking for— many of them are living in single-family homes. The retirees, many of them are looking to downsize, but they want to age in place. They want to stay in their community, but they don't want to still take care of the big house. They want to be active. They want to volunteer with organizations. They want to be very engaged in lots of activities. There are some demographers who call them the yeepies, Youthful Energetic Elderly People into Everything. The yeepies, as they retire, they're in the suburbs, but they're looking for a more urban lifestyle in their same community.

At the same time, you've got Gen Y. Actually, 77 percent of Gen Y says they want to live in an urban core. This generation, they grew up in the suburbs, 75 percent of them, but they grew up watching TV shows like *Friends* and *Seinfeld*. What they're really aspiring to is a much more urban lifestyle. Since their jobs are, frankly, more likely to be out in the suburbs, they're going to end up living in the suburbs, but they're still looking for a more urban lifestyle.

GH — I'm interested in the role of commercial developers. What drives them, and how has that changed the landscape of cities?

EDJ — Land, as a commodity, we tend to treat it with our regulations as if it's all the same. But in fact, every parcel is obviously unique. You can't replace it. We treat it as if this is a free market where it all just has equal value. The role of a developer is to go in and look and perceive where he sees an advantage. Where does he see a real opportunity? *This* land is much more valuable. Developers have found ways to look for what it is that it's got. What can I build there and why? As soon as a new road is built or a new highway, that suddenly now opens up the land near it for development. It's now accessible given that transportation link. What's been happening with retrofits is every time a new mass transit station is extended out into the suburbs, wow. Suddenly now that triggers a lot of redevelopment of the land. The developers are really the guys who are finding and looking for those opportunities and then looking to see: "Okay, am I going to be allowed to put as much building on it as I need to be able to cover the cost of buying the land and bringing in the utilities and actually providing the project so I can still walk away with some profit?"

It's interesting. In the US, developers in the early 20th century were seen as heroes. They built these wonderful places that we could go and live in. They were seen as people who had helped their community, were very invested in their community. Since development has become much more global, now we've got these large-production builders who are operating in multiple cities. They're not really based in that community; they're just looking for potential profitable land. They've built these enormous new developments, and the reputation of developers has certainly suffered as a result and deservedly so.

We're also starting to see, I think, some developers who really are genuinely interested in being town builders, in returning to that role. They may have made a fortune on some kind of an online business or something. Now they want to do something tangible and leave a legacy that they can be proud of and that they will live in. That's been an enormous change.

GH — Totally off topic: do you have any thoughts on China and the rate of urbanization there?

EDJ — The thing that concerns me most about China and its development patterns is a statement that I read recently from one of their leading economists of the state, who said that China right now spends approximately 35 percent of gross domestic product on consumption, but they aspire to become a more mature economy like the US and spend 70 percent on consumption. I question whether that's the right goal to aspire to in the first place. The second part of this economist's statement was, "Therefore, we plan to build one hundred new shopping malls in the next two years in China."

My concern is, even if your goal is you want to increase consumption and shopping, there are other alternatives to a Western-style shopping mall. A lot of Chinese shopping malls are very much embedded in their cities. They're multistory, but they still tend to be single use. Many of them are extremely empty. There are some failed, dead malls already in China, in much of Southeast Asia. They've been building retail so quickly and getting themselves to this very high-end market so fast that it's actually accelerated the decline. There are 10-year-old malls that are already beginning to fail. It saddens me to see so many of the same processes repeating themselves in what I think is a very unsustainable manner. It prompts all sorts of speculation on my part.

I think there's tremendous opportunities given that China is urbanizing, and they're doing wonderful things in terms of transit and really building incredible transit systems. I hope that they will also rethink some of our retail models so that they can design places that will be more retrofitable in the future and not just require the same kind of demolition and restarting that is exactly what we've been going through.

GH — It seems like a global phenomenon. It's not just in retail but also obviously in car use. It ends up being aspirational. So it seems like more cities are just building more massive flyovers and cutting the cities up with highways.

EDJ — Yeah, it's strange. The UN has considered suburban sprawl a Northern Hemisphere problem of the developed economies and not a problem for developing countries. A lot of the World Bank policies are really just to invest in highways and to invest in these very auto-oriented, truck-oriented urban development patterns.

I think it's really a shame. There's so much opportunity to actually build on the existing, much more sustainable urban development patterns. Yes, there are going to be megacities, and the megacities require tremendous infrastructure and very serious attention to that. There are ways to do it that are much more walkable and more sustainable and transit oriented than a lot of what we've seen. The UN made a big deal about the fact that global population hit seven billion in 2010 and declared that we are now in the era of the city. The images that tend to go with that are images of Hong Kong and extreme high-rise urbanization, whereas the reality is that our land consumption has continued to exceed population growth. We've been growing in population but at lower and lower densities. I would argue that the megacity has more often actually been a megasuburb. There are certainly examples like Hong Kong, but what we're seeing in a lot of places is density without much urbanization. It's still the single uses, dense single uses but that don't add up to those synergistic places which help you live a much more sustainable lifestyle.

GH — Is this also a situation where large cities that are near each other are all starting to connect via their suburbs, turning them into these megazones or something?

EDJ — One of the big academic questions right now and certainly for future generations is, what's the real difference between unhealthy sprawl and a healthy, polynucleated city or metro area? Because certainly the suburbs are increasingly becoming nodes in their own right and cities in their own right. The old model of the city at the core with rings of cascading density hasn't been true for the last 30 years certainly, 30 or 40, but that model is still how we tend to think of things. The suburbs are growing now as these nodes, so we're seeing much more networked, polycentric systems. I think when you have a lot of existing sprawl, having that polycentric system overlaid on top of it now reduces the overall trip lengths, so you do get a healthier system. We really don't yet know quite what the tipping points are, quite at what point it's less sustainable and where it gets more sustainable.

GH — What do you think the citizens' role is in the design of a city?

EDJ — That's a great question. Urban planners absolutely value the role of citizen input into the design of cities. In the fifties, there was a sense that the planners knew more than the uneducated masses, and it makes sense that we will tell everyone what should be happening. In reaction to that attitude, which has been completely discredited, now there's tremendous attention to all the different ways we can try to engage the public and educate the public somewhat along the way so that the people can be making really informed decisions. Absolutely, there's a tremendous interest in that, in getting the public involved.

The difficulty is that you're never going to get everybody to really be involved, and it can come down to a bit of mob rule. Who speaks the loudest? Who has the time to actually come to the city meetings, and who are the folks who don't? Their voices are not heard. It's a very imperfect system, but certainly it's now commonplace to have design charettes where you do involve the public, give them an opportunity to vote on and see the processes. I think that the real challenge is trying to figure out how to try to get citizens to project ahead enough. Most people, when you ask them, "Do you like where you live?" they say, "Yes, I like where I live." It doesn't mean it's perfect, but they like it. Most people are pretty resistant to any kind of change around where they live because they like it already.

Most people feel that if they're serving on a local neighborhood planning board, volunteering their time—and bless them for doing so—their job is to protect the neighborhood and, whatever it was that made it attractive to them when they first moved in, to keep those same qualities in place. The real challenge, especially in the suburbs, is for people to recognize that, well, if what was attractive to you 40 years ago was this was a great neighborhood to raise kids in, but 75 to 85 percent of new households through 2025 will not have kids in them, you might not be protecting your neighborhood. You might be sinking your neighborhood by not allowing the neighborhood to grow and evolve for that changing demographic. I think the challenge often is for citizens to be both given more information but also given a chance to really imagine, what's the future of my neighborhood? How might it change in a really positive way so it'll be just as relevant to my kids as it was to me but relevant in very different ways?

It's interesting. In the US we tend to view our cities as very dynamic places now. Seeing building cranes is a sign of a healthy downtown. But we tend to view our suburbs as sacrosanct. They should remain forever frozen in whatever form they were first built in. If you go to community meetings in general in suburban places, more so than in urban places, you can find people who feel they have a right to expect it not to change. I think it's time to let the suburbs grow up. We have these incredible demographic changes and a market that is looking for some other choices. We have this environmental knowledge now that the pattern that we put in place is quite destructive. We really have an obligation to try to fix those problems. And we have a lot of aging, underperforming properties that are providing us with an opportunity to do exactly that.

GH — It seems like when ordinary citizens do get involved, it's only when the cranes start appearing and the bulldozers go to work, even though there were probably public input sessions and hearings on these projects for years and years before.

> **EDJ** — Nothing brings a community together like a crisis or a change. I'm quite an optimist on that. I tend to view change as an opportunity. Clearly, for a lot of people, change makes them very anxious. They're worried about it, especially when their home is their primary savings and investment. People have every right certainly to be nervous about things. Frankly, the fact that people don't trust that the changes are going to be good changes speaks to a lot of the failures of my profession in the past. I don't blame them for being suspicious.
>
> I think citizens absolutely should be as involved as they can. I love seeing some of the really creative things that people have been coming up with. There's a town in Texas where, for two days as an art project, they did what they called *Build a Better Block*. Just one city block. The two sides of it were totally vacant and pretty decrepit looking. For two days, they brought in trees and little plastic planters. They set up sidewalk displays just on milk crates, and they brought in some streetlights that were just on wheels. They occupied the storefronts. It so transformed the place, so transformed the vision, that now the whole community has absolutely rallied around it. It's the community which is now demanding, "We've got to find developers." They're demanding to their planning agencies, "We want to make this really happen. We've got to revitalize this place because now we can see what it actually could be."

GH — Yeah, it's that idea of being able to envision and experience a different scenario than what's actually there. I've found that's a trait of good designers, actually, that "what if?" impulse. That's something that can really be used to engage the public. Okay, over to you: what are the things you'd want to hear discussed if you're sitting in a movie theater watching a film about urban design?

> **EDJ** — Oh boy. I think part of what's so fascinating about cities and their suburbs and their larger regions is the wide variety of lifestyle choices that they afford. I have my preferences of where I want to live. I certainly would never tell anybody mine is the right choice and everyone else has made the wrong choice. At the same time, I do think, especially with the environmental crisis and issues of climate change, that we do as a society have to begin to decide whether some of these choices come with additional cost, whether, okay, if people want to choose what is a particularly high-carbon lifestyle, in some way or another they'll be taxed that much more on it so that the choices become a little more linked to larger societal goals and, frankly, necessities. I think we need to have a lot of choices, but we also need to be aware of how those choices have different impacts. I think for people to recognize that within their own city there's this wealth of choices is an incredibly positive and powerful thing.
>
> I hope that you make a movie that a lot of kids will want to go see as they try to imagine their future, and what kind of neighborhood they're going to live in. One of the exercises I gave to my students last semester was I said, "You have to write up the program for the neighborhood you want

to live in 10 years from now. What do you want in that neighborhood? What don't you want in that neighborhood?" They had to be quite realistic about saying, "If I want lots and lots of open space, but I also want transit access every 10 minutes, no, that doesn't fly." There are rules that they had to work with as far as how frequently there would be transit and what kind of densities there could be.

I think there are some really basic understandings about the trade-offs that are required between the amount of open space and density, how much time one is willing to spend commuting versus the distance that one is willing to live from things versus the size of one's private property. Is one willing to make the trade-off that, "I want to be right in the thick of it, and I'm willing to not have a yard because I've got a fantastic public park right near me"? Since I'm so immersed in this world, I'm often surprised at people who have a knee-jerk reaction about assuming the lifestyle that they want, and they never even explore all that incredible range of choices.

Most of us live our lives having very different kinds of needs at different times of our lives. One of the big challenges that we're facing in this country is the aging of the baby boomers who might have started off in that little Levittown eight-hundred-square-foot house. As their families grew and they became more affluent, they got bigger and bigger houses further and further out. That big house that had all that privacy and was great for raising the kids—now as they're older, suddenly that privacy can become isolating and lonely. The neighborhood that didn't have any cut-through traffic and seemed, again, great while you were raising the kids now means you can't walk and get anywhere.

At different times in our lives, we need quite different things. Cities are complex animals, and so are we.

—

Special thanks

Jessica Edwards, Hazel Hustwit, the Hustwit family, the Edwards family, the Holcomb family, Joe Luxton, Michael C. Place, Nicola Place, everyone at Build, Katie Herman, Mariam Aldhahi, Anne Quito, Alice Twemlow, Luke Geissbühler, Brian Betancourt, Versions Publishing, Laurence Oliver, Radovan Scasascia, Lucy Raven, Alex Abramovich, Ivorypress, Chris Young, and all our Kickstarter backers who helped make this book possible.

More thanks

Alberto Algaba, Stefanie Andersen, Apple, Yazid Azahari, Billy Bacon, Seth Bannon, Emil Beckman, biki berry, Joe Beshenkovsky, Susan L. Booker, Ph.D., Alexander Borisenko, Jeff Bowden, Al Briggs, John Bruesewitz, Jordan Buetow, Brad Buschette, Daniel Callan, Matthew Carter, John Caulkins, Zhenghao Chen, Larry Cheng, Gary Cohen, Coudal Partners, James Coxon, Wil Cruz, Michael Culyba, Hillman Curtis, Nicholas Danaher, Mike Day, François Joseph de Kermadec, Jutta Degener, Design Indaba, Rasmus Due, Ellen Dunham-Jones, Sparky Ellis, El Ten Eleven, Niels Epting, Douglas Ewald, Ex Lovers, Experimental Jetset, Leonardo Eyer, Tomas Liberg Foshaugen, Kevin Fritz, Full Frame, Rob Gill, Mohammed Yasin Hakim, Tony Han, John S. Hansen, Charles Brian Harmon, Ruth Ann Harnisch, Rayhan S. Hasan, Mike Heighway, John Hergenroeder, Andrew Hoerner, Hot Docs, Brigid Hughes, Kristopher Hunt, Grant Hutchinson, IDEO, Thomas Isaacson, Adrian Jean CGD, Jeff, Tim Jetis, Scott Fitzgerald Johnson, alxndr jones, Andres Lopez Josenge, Brian Jouan, Jesse Kaczmarek, Kaleemux, Gareth Kay, Ben Kempas, Margaret Kessler, Kneadle, Simon Korzun, Betsy Kenny Lack, Jason Lancaster, Ray Larry, Desmond T H Lim, Christina Raye Lim, Molly Lindley, Rich Lo, Sandy Macdonald, Steve MacLaughlin, John Manoogian II, Jonathan Marlow, Paul Masatani, Charlie McBrearty, Sean McBride, Colin McCluskie, Jonny McConnell, Dustin Mierau, Mikeboon, Debbie Millman, Tana Mitchell, Dylan Moore, Ciprian Morar, Manu Moreale, Noreen Morioka, Michelle Mortimer, David Moulton, Yuka Ototsu Nakamura, Adam Newbold, Damien Newman, Donny Nguyen, Albert Nguyen, Nicolas-Loïc, Liz and Ken Nielsen, Sami Johannes Niemelä, Peter Nowell, Robert Occhialini Jr., Seyi Ogunyemi, Christopher J Pace, Robert Padbury, Joshua Peek, Giancarlo Pellegrino, Karen Tanizaka Pellegrino, Pentagram, Carlos Miguel S. Pineda, post utility, Thom Powers, Adam Proehl, Pamela Puchalski, Stuart W. Purdy, Ahmad S. Ragab, John S. Reha, Martin Rendel, Hal Riley, Genaro Solis Rivero, Mark Robillard, Helio Rosas, Jaron Rubenstein, Rich Saguirre, Paul Sahre, Sumio Sakai, Jorren Schauwaert, Alexander Schoner, Constantin Schuler, Jane Shibata, Sergey Sidorov, Shelby Siegel, Erik Spiekermann, Ivy Simon, Mitch L. Smith, Carter Smith, Luis Sosa, Jason Speck, Andy Spencer, staen, Nancy Stetson, Eric Stevens, Kapil Suri, SxSW, Alex Teschmacher, Thomas, TIFF, Jakob Trollbäck, Chuck Tso, University of Huddersfield, Mario Van der Meulen, Hans verschooten, Matthias Wagner, Christopher Wallace, Vincent Wanga, Craig Ward, Todd Zaki Warfel, Adam Webb, Matthew Weingarden, Ross Wendell, Adam Wickert, Cam Wilde, Ivan Wilson, Jr., Ben Wolf, and James Kyoon Yun.

And you.